Lecture Notes in Computer Science 10422

Advanced Research in Computing and Software Science
Subline of Lecture Notes in Computer Science

More information about this series at http://www.springer.com/series/7408

Francesco Ranzato (Ed.)

Static Analysis

24th International Symposium, SAS 2017
New York, NY, USA, August 30 – September 1, 2017
Proceedings

Springer

Editor
Francesco Ranzato
Dipartimento di Matematica
University of Padova
Padua
Italy

ISSN 0302-9743 ISSN 1611-3349 (electronic)
Lecture Notes in Computer Science
ISBN 978-3-319-66705-8 ISBN 978-3-319-66706-5 (eBook)
DOI 10.1007/978-3-319-66706-5

Library of Congress Control Number: 2017951308

LNCS Sublibrary: SL2 – Programming and Software Engineering

Printed on acid-free paper

This Springer imprint is published by Springer Nature
The registered company is Springer International Publishing AG
The registered company address is: Gewerbestrasse 11, 6330 Cham, Switzerland

Preface

Static Analysis is recognized as a fundamental tool for program verification, bug detection, compiler optimization, program understanding, and software maintenance. The series of Static Analysis Symposia has served as the primary venue for the presentation of theoretical, practical, and applicational advances in the area. Previous symposia were held in Edinburgh, Saint-Malo, Munich, Seattle, Deauville, Venice, Perpignan, Los Angeles, Valencia, Kongens Lyngby, Seoul, London, Verona, San Diego, Madrid, Paris, Santa Barbara, Pisa, Aachen, Glasgow, and Namur. This volume contains the papers presented at SAS 2017, the 24th International Static Analysis Symposium. The conference was held on August 30th - September 1st, 2017 at New York University, New York City, NY, USA.

The conference received 64 initial abstracts that materialized into 50 full submissions, each of which was reviewed by at least three Program Committee members. The Program Committee accepted 22 papers, which appear in this volume. As in previous years, authors of SAS submissions had the chance to submit a virtual machine image with artifacts presented in the paper. In accordance with this, 16 submissions came with an artifact. Artifacts were used as an additional source of information during the evaluation of the submissions.

The Program Committee also invited three outstanding researchers to present invited talks: Alex Aiken (Stanford University, USA), Francesco Logozzo (Facebook, Seattle, USA), and Peter Müller (ETH Zurich, Switzerland). Additionally, the program included two invited tutorials given by leading researchers: Josh Berdine (Facebook, London, UK), Roberto Giacobazzi (IMDEA, Spain and University of Verona, Italy). We warmly thank them for accepting the invitations.

SAS 2017 featured three associated workshops. The 7th Workshop on Numerical and Symbolic Abstract Domains (NSAD 2017), the 8th Workshop on Static Analysis and Systems Biology (SASB 2017), and the 8th Workshop on Tools for Automatic Program Analysis (TAPAS 2017) were held before SAS, on August 29th, 2017.

Many people and institutions contributed to the success of SAS 2017. We would like to thank the members of the Program Committee, who worked hard at carefully reviewing papers, holding insightful discussions during the on-line Program Committee meeting, and making final selections of accepted papers and invited speakers. We would also like to thank the additional referees enlisted by Program Committee members. The work of the Program Committee and the editorial process were greatly facilitated by the EasyChair conference management system. We are grateful to Springer for publishing these proceedings. A warm word of thanks goes to Patrick Cousot for leading the local organization of the conference at New York University. Finally, we would like to thank our sponsors: Amazon, the Courant Institute of Mathematical Sciences of New York University, the Dipartimento di Matematica "Tullio Levi-Civita" of the University of Padova, Facebook, and Springer.

July 2017 Francesco Ranzato

Organization

Program Committee

Elvira Albert	Complutense University of Madrid, Spain
Jade Alglave	University College London, UK
Josh Berdine	Facebook, UK
Aleksandar Chakarov	University of Colorado, Boulder, CO, USA
Liqian Chen	National University of Defense Technology, China
Maria Christakis	University of Kent, UK
Pierre Ganty	IMDEA Software Institute, Spain
Alberto Griggio	FBK-IRST, Italy
Arie Gurfinkel	University of Waterloo, ON, Canada
Thomas Jensen	Inria, France
Laura Kovacs	Vienna University of Technology, Austria
Ana Milanova	Rensselaer Polytechnic Institute, NY, USA
Anders Moller	Aarhus University, Denmark
Kedar Namjoshi	Bell Labs, NJ, USA
Andreas Podelski	University of Freiburg, Germany
Francesco Ranzato	University of Padova, Italy
Xavier Rival	Inria/ENS Paris, France
Ilya Sergey	University College London, UK
Fausto Spoto	University of Verona, Italy
Harald Søndergaard	The University of Melbourne, Australia
Caterina Urban	ETH Zürich, Switzerland
David Van Horn	University of Maryland, MD, USA
Arnaud J. Venet	Facebook, USA
Eran Yahav	Technion, Israel

Additional Reviewers

Besson, Frederic
Correas Fernández, Jesús
Dietsch, Daniel
Dohrau, Jérôme
Fedyukovich, Grigory
Ferrara, Pietro
Frehse, Goran
Gange, Graeme
Gleiss, Bernhard
Gordillo, Pablo
Greitschus, Marius
Irfan, Ahmed
Jaroschek, Maximilian
Kafle, Bishoksan
Karpenkov, Egor
Khalimov, Ayrat
Krishna, Siddharth
Li, Huisong
Martin-Martin, Enrique
Navas, Jorge A.
Popeea, Corneliu
Rebola Pardo, Adrian
Robillard, Simon
Román-Díez, Guillermo
Sankaranarayanan, Sriram
Schachte, Peter
Schilling, Christian
Schrammel, Peter
Steinhöfel, Dominic

Abstracts of Invited Talks

Proving Program Equality: Recent Progress and New Applications

Alex Aiken

Stanford University, Stanford CA 94305

Abstract. How can we automatically prove two programs are equal? And why would we want to? This talk summarizes progress over the last several years on fully automatic techniques for proving equality of non-trivial programs. The general approach is to use a combination of static and dynamic analysis, and in particular to guess the crux of the proof of equivalence from observations of the states of program executions. We then use standard static verification techniques to check that the hypothesized equivalence in fact holds. We first motivate the technique in a simpler setting, a guess-and-check algorithm for finding loop invariants, and then show how that approach can be extended to a guess-and-check algorithm for program equivalence.

We will present a number of applications, many of which are related to proving the correctness of compiled programs. One well-known application for equality checking is to confirm that the unoptimized and optimized versions of a particular function produced by a compiler are in fact equal. But because our method accepts any two programs as input and makes no assumptions at all about how those programs were produced, we can also compare the output of different compilers and apply our approach when the infrastructure for techniques such as translation validation does not or cannot exist.

This talk is based on work published in [1–4].

References

1. Churchill, B., Sharma, R., Bastien, J.-F., Aiken, A.: Sound loop superoptimization for google native client. In: Proceedings of the Conference on Architectural Support for Programming Languages and Operating Systems, pp. 313–326, April 2017
2. Sharma, R., Aiken, A.: From invariant checking to invariant inference using randomized search. In: Proceedings of the International Conference on Computer Aided Verification, pp. 88–105, July 2014
3. Sharma, R., Schkufza, E., Churchill, B., Aiken, A.: Data-driven equivalence checking. In: Proceedings of the International Conference on Object-Oriented Programming, Systems, Languages, and Applications, pp. 391–406, October 2013
4. Sharma, R., Schkufza, E., Churchill, B., Aiken, A.: Conditionally correct superoptimization. In: Proceedings of the International Conference on Object-Oriented Programming, Systems, Languages, and Applications, pp. 147–162, October 2015

From Bug Bounty to Static Analysis

Francesco Logozzo

Facebook Inc., Seattle, WA, USA
logozzo@fb.com

In bug bounty programs, individuals get recognition and compensation for reporting bugs, in particular security vulnerabilities. Facebook, Google, Microsoft, Uber and many other companies have implemented bug bounty programs. Once a bug is reported, security engineers should find all the existing instances of the bug and make sure that they are removed from the code base. They are also in charge to make sure the bug is not reintroduced in the future. This process is long, tedious, and inherently non-scalable.

Static analysis can help solving this problem. Given a generic and scalable abstract interpreter, one can refine or add a new abstract domain to capture the reported bug, and all the other instances if any. In general this process requires some iterations with the security engineers, often to add some security-specific knowledge to the analysis. The new analysis is used to find all the existing instances in the existing codebase. In some cases it can also patch the code automatically [1]. The refined analysis is automatically run on all the code changes submitted for review, capturing accidental re-introductions of the bug before it lands on master. The main take aways are that:

(i) Focusing the static analysis on vulnerabilities reported via bug bounty means having a data- and evidence-based static analyses which focuses on problems that matter in practice.
(ii) Having a close collaboration between security engineers and static analysis experts is beneficial for both. Security engineers have a powerful tool that dramatically improves their job. Static analysis experts get a very high quality feedback for the development of the tool.

Reference

1. Logozzo, F., Ball, T.: Modular and verified automatic program repair. In: Proceedings of the OOPSLA 2012, pp. 133–146. ACM (2012)

Reasoning with Permissions in Viper

Peter Müller

Department of Computer Science, ETH Zurich, Switzerland
peter.mueller@inf.ethz.ch

Many recent verification techniques use the notion of permissions to verify programs that access resources such as memory. In particular, there are dozens or even hundreds of separation logics and related formalisms that use permissions to reason about side effects, various forms of concurrency, memory management, I/O behavior, and liveness properties. This plethora of logics provides a foundation to tackle a wide variety of complex verification problems. However, each of these logics requires its own techniques and tools to infer and check program properties, which is a major impediment for practical applications.

This talk introduces the Viper infrastructure[1], which provides an intermediate language as well as verification backends based on symbolic execution, verification condition generation, and abstract interpretation, respectively. The intermediate language can encode a wide range of verification problems and permission logics. The backends infer and check program properties; since they operate on the intermediate language, they can be re-used across source languages and verification logics, which reduces the effort of building verification tools dramatically. We will give an overview of the Viper language, illustrate how to encode some advanced verification problems, and give an overview of the available tool support.

1 http://viper.ethz.ch.

Contents

Probabilistic Horn Clause Verification

Aws Albarghouthi(✉)

University of Wisconsin–Madison, Madison, USA
aws@cs.wisc.edu

Abstract. Constrained Horn clauses have proven to be a natural intermediate language for logically characterizing program semantics and reasoning about program behavior. In this paper, we present *probabilistically constrained Horn clauses* (PCHC), which incorporate *probabilistic variables* inside otherwise traditional constrained Horn clauses. PCHC enable reasoning about probabilistic programs by encoding them as Horn clauses. Encoding probabilistic program semantics as PCHC allows us to seamlessly handle procedure calls and recursion, as well as angelic and demonic forms of nondeterminism. We formalize PCHC semantics and present a verification algorithm that can prove probabilistic safety properties of programs. We present an implementation and evaluation of our approach on a number of probabilistic programs and properties.

1 Introduction

Constrained Horn Clauses have emerged as a natural logical formalism for stating a wide spectrum of program verification and synthesis problems and solving them automatically with generic Horn clause solvers [5]. For instance, given a sequential program P and a safety property φ, we can construct a set of *recursive* Horn clauses whose solution is a *safe inductive invariant* that entails correctness of P with respect to φ. A key advantage in this two-tiered methodology is the clear dichotomy between the syntactic object, the program P, and its semantic interpretation, encoded logically as a set of Horn clauses. Thus, the generic Horn clause solver is completely unaware of the programming language of P. Indeed, as Grebenshchikov et al. [25] have shown, a simple Horn clause solver can be the target of a range of program models and correctness properties—including concurrent programs and liveness properties over infinite domains.

To handle richer programs and properties, such as termination and temporal properties, researchers have enriched traditional Horn clauses with additional features, such as quantifier alternation [4,6]. In this paper, we present an extension of constrained Horn clauses to the probabilistic setting, in which variables draw their values from probability distributions. Doing so, we enable reasoning about safety properties of *probabilistic programs*: standard programs with probabilistic assignments. Probabilistic programs are used in a plethora of applications, e.g., modeling biological systems [28,29], cognitive processes [23], cyber-physical systems [42], programs running on approximate hardware [7,41], and randomized algorithms like privacy-preserving ones [16], amongst many others.

F. Ranzato (Ed.): SAS 2017, LNCS 10422, pp. 1–22, 2017.
DOI: 10.1007/978-3-319-66706-5_1

Thus, by extending Horn clauses and their solvers to the probabilistic setting, we expand their applicability to many new domains.

We define the semantics of probabilistic Horn clauses as a probability distribution over the set of *ground derivations*. There are two key high-level advantages to reasoning about probabilistic programs in terms of probabilistic Horn clauses. The first advantage of our formulation is that it enables us to define Horn clauses over any first-order theory with an appropriate probability measure. In the simplest case, we can have propositional Horn clauses, where variables draw their values from Bernoulli distributions. In more advanced cases, for example, we can have real arithmetic formulas where variables are drawn from, e.g., Gaussian or Laplacian distributions. This provides a flexible means for encoding program semantics with appropriate first-order theories, as is standard in many hardware and software verification tools. The second advantage we gain from Horn clauses is that we can naturally encode loops, procedures, and recursion. Thus, our Horn clauses can encode probabilistic programs with recursion, a combination that is rarely addressed in the literature. Further, we extend our probabilistic semantics with *angelic* and *demonic non-determinism*. This allows us to reason about variables that receive non-deterministic values, for example, in programs with calls to unknown libraries. Angelic and demonic non-determinism allow us to compute best- and worst-case probabilities for an event.

The probabilistic safety properties (*queries*) we would like to prove about our Horn clauses are of the form, e.g., $\mathbb{P}[Q(x) \rightarrow x > 0] > 0.9$, which specifies that the probability of deriving a positive value in the relation Q (which might encode, say, the return values of the program) is more than 0.9. To prove probabilistic properties, we present a verification algorithm that, like its non-probabilistic counterparts [24,25,27,37], iteratively unrolls recursive Horn clauses to generate an under-approximating set of Horn clauses that encodes a *subset of the total set of possible derivations*. To compute the probability of an event in the under-approximation, we demonstrate how to encode the problem as a *weighted model counting problem* over formulas in a first-order theory [11,12]. *The algorithm iteratively considers deeper and deeper unrollings—maintaining a lower and an upper bound on the probability of interest—until it is able to prove or disprove the property of interest.*

From a problem formulation perspective, our approach can be seen as an extension of Chistikov et al.'s probabilistic inference through model counting [12] to recursive sets of constraints. From an algorithmic perspective, one can view our approach as an extension of Sankaranarayanan et al.'s algorithm [42] to programs with recursion and non-determinism.

Contributions. To summarize, this paper makes the following contributions:

- We present *probabilistically constrained Horn clauses* (PCHC) and define their semantics as a probability distribution over of the set of derivation sequences. Our formulation allows us to encode probabilistic safety verification problems over probabilistic programs that contain procedures and recursion.
- We extend the semantics of PCHC to encode angelic and demonic forms of non-determinism, following the semantics used by Chistikov et al. [12]. In the case

where all variables angelically draw their values and there is no probabilistic choice, PCHC are equivalent to CHC.
- We present a verification algorithm for proving or disproving probabilistic reachability properties. Our algorithm iteratively considers larger and larger under-approximations of the Horn clauses and reduces the verification problem to weighted model counting.
- We present an implementation and evaluation of our approach on a number of probabilistic programs and properties. Our results demonstrate the utility of our approach at handling probabilistic programs with rich features such as non-determinism and recursion.

2 Overview

We illustrate our technique (Fig. 1) on two simple examples.

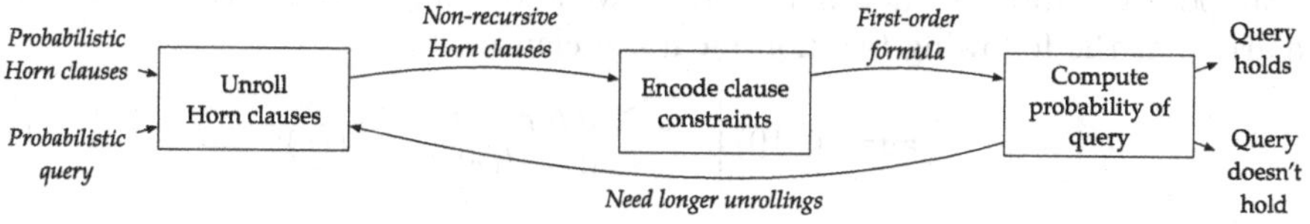

Fig. 1. Overview of proposed approach

Recursive program. Consider the illustrative program in Fig. 2(a). This is a recursive function that samples a real value for x from a Gaussian distribution (with mean 0 and standard deviation 10). If the value of x is negative, it recursively calls itself; otherwise, it returns x. The program *almost always* terminates—i.e., terminates with probability 1—and always returns a positive value.

Figure 2(b) shows a recursive Horn-like encoding of the program as a predicate f. There are two things to note here: First, we allow disjunctions in the body of the clause (the left hand side of the implication $\rightarrow$).[1] Second, on the left hand side of the bar ($|$) we list probabilistic variables and their corresponding probability distributions. In this case, we have $x \sim \mathbf{gauss}(0, 10)$, indicating the value of the real-valued variable x is drawn from a normal distribution. Observe how our clause has both probabilistic variables (x) and traditional ones (y and r). In the absence of probabilistic variables, the semantics are exactly those of constrained Horn clauses.

Suppose we want to prove that the program returns a value greater than 5 with probability greater than 0.3. This is a *probabilistic safety property*, which

[1] While in the non-probabilistic setting we can represent the function by two clauses (one representing the base case and one the recursive call), we need to combine the two clauses in the probabilistic setting. See Sect. 6 for a detailed explanation.

```
fun f():
  x ~ gauss(0,10)
  if (x >= 0) ret x
  ret f()
```

(a)

$$x \sim \mathsf{gauss}(0,10) \left| \begin{array}{l} x \geqslant 0 \wedge r = x \\ \vee\, x < 0 \wedge f(y) \wedge r = y \end{array} \right. \longrightarrow f(r)$$

(b)

Fig. 2. Example probabilistic program and its Horn clause encoding

we encode as a query of the form $\mathbb{P}[f(r) \to r > 5] > 0.3$. To prove that this query holds, we proceed as illustrated in Fig. 1.

Unrolling Horn clauses. We begin by unrolling the recursive Horn clause into a set of non-recursive clauses. This is analogous to fixing the depth of the stack in the program. The process is standard top-down unrolling, beginning with the predicate that appears in the query—this is similar to what is implemented in constrained Horn solvers [24,37].

Suppose we unroll to depth 1, that is, we allow only a single recursive call. We arrive at the following two non-recursive clauses:

$$C_1 : \quad x \sim \mathsf{gauss}(0,10) \left| \begin{array}{l} x \geqslant 0 \wedge r = x \\ \vee\, x < 0 \wedge f'(r) \end{array} \right. \longrightarrow f(r) \tag{1}$$

$$C_2 : \quad x' \sim \mathsf{gauss}(0,10) \left| \begin{array}{l} x' \geqslant 0 \wedge r' = x' \\ \vee\, x' < 0 \wedge \mathit{false} \end{array} \right. \longrightarrow f'(r') \tag{2}$$

Observe how the body of C_1 refers to $f'(r)$ and C_2 defines the predicate f'. The second clause, effectively, encodes a fresh clone of the function f. Observe also the *false* in the body of C_2; this indicates that no more recursive calls can be made.

Encoding Horn clauses. Unrolling Horn clauses is effectively producing an *underapproximation* of a program's executions. Thus, if we compute the probability that the non-recursive clauses satisfy $f(r) \to r > 5$, we get a *lower bound* on the actual probability. Similarly, by computing the probability of the negation of the event, i.e., $f(r) \to r \leqslant 5$, we can derive an *upper bound* on the actual probability. (We formalize this in Sect. 4.) For illustration, we show how to compute a lower bound on the probability that the query holds by encoding non-recursive clauses as a *model counting* problem.

Our encoding is analogous to that used by constrained Horn solvers. The result is as follows, where φ_i encodes clause C_i:

$$\varphi_1 \equiv (x \geqslant 0 \wedge r = x) \vee (x < 0 \wedge b) \qquad\qquad \varphi_2 \equiv b \Rightarrow (x' \geqslant 0 \wedge r' = x')$$

Note the introduction of the Boolean variable b, which indicates whether the recursive call is taken or not.

Probability computation. Now, to compute the probability that $r > 5$, we construct the formula:

$$\varphi \equiv \exists b, r, r'. \varphi_1 \wedge \varphi_2 \wedge r = r' \wedge r > 5$$

The free variables of φ are only x and x'—i.e., the probabilistic variables. The constraint $r = r'$ connects the values of the two clauses. We can now compute the probability that this formula is satisfied, assuming x and x' get their assignments by drawing from the Gaussian distribution $\mathtt{gauss}(0, 10)$. Depending on the first-order theory we are working with, this form of *weighted* model counting requires different techniques. Since we are operating over reals, this is an integration problem. We refer the reader to Sect. 6 where we survey different model counting techniques.

Eliminating the quantifier from φ, we get $x \geqslant 5 \vee (x < 0 \wedge x' \geqslant 5)$. The probability of satisfying φ is thus ~0.46.[2] Note that this is a lower bound on the actual probability of returning a value that is greater than 5. By looking at longer unrollings of the Horn clauses, we arrive closer and closer to the actual probability. For our purposes, however, we have managed to prove that the query holds with a probability greater than 0.3.

```
fun q()
  flag = nondet()
  x ~ gauss(0,10)
  if (flag) x = x + 5
  else x = x - 5
  ret x
```

(a)

$$x \sim \mathtt{gauss}(0,10) \left| \begin{array}{l} \mathit{flag} \wedge r = x + 5 \\ \vee\ \neg \mathit{flag} \wedge r = x - 5 \end{array} \right. \longrightarrow q(r)$$

(b)

Fig. 3. Simple non-deterministic example and its Horn clause encoding

Forms of non-determinism. In the program discussed above, the only form of non-determinism in a program's execution was probabilistic choice. In many scenarios, we also want to reason about non-deterministic events for which we cannot assign a probability. We illustrate this with the example shown in Fig. 2. The variable `x` gets its value drawn from `gauss`(0,10). Then, depending on the value of the Boolean variable `flag`, which is chosen nondeterministically, `x` gets incremented or decremented by 5.

Our approach allows two different treatments of nondeterminism: *angelic* and *demonic*. In the angelic case, the intuition is as follows: an execution satisfies the property if there *exists* a set of values for nondeterministic variables that makes the execution satisfy the property. Our semantics follow those of Chistikov et al. [12]; effectively, we can think of non-determinism as being able to observe all probabilistic choices made in an execution, and then make its decision.

In our example, the probability $\mathbb{P}[q(r) \rightarrow r > 0]$ is ~0.69, assuming `flag` is chosen angelically—i.e., `flag` always takes us through the desired path, the one

[2] $\mathbb{P}[\varphi] = \mathbb{P}[x \geqslant 5] + \mathbb{P}[x < 0] * \mathbb{P}[x' \geqslant 5]$. Since $x, x' \sim \mathtt{gauss}(0, 10)$, we have $\mathbb{P}[x \geqslant 5] \approx 0.308$ and $\mathbb{P}[x < 0] = 0.5$.

that increments `x` by 5. Alternatively, we can treat `flag` as a demonic variable: an execution satisfies the property if *all* values of nondeterministic variables satisfy the property. In our example, the only executions that satisfy $q(r) \rightarrow r > 0$ are the ones where `x` draws a value that is greater than 5. This is because `flag` will demonically steer execution to the `else` branch of the conditional. Thus, in the demonic setting, the probability of the query is ~0.31.

Operationally, angelic variables are handled by existentially quantifying them in the encoding of unrolled Horn clauses; demonic variables, on the other hand, are universally quantified.

3 Possibilistic and Probabilistic Horn Clauses

We begin by defining required background on non-probabilistic Horn-like problems, and define their semantics in terms of derivations. This paves the way for presenting our extension to the probabilistic setting, described in Sect. 3.3.

3.1 Preliminaries

Formulas. We assume formulas are over a fixed interpreted first-order theory $\mathcal{T}$, e.g., linear integer arithmetic. We assume we have a set $\mathcal{R}$ of uninterpreted predicate symbols. We use φ to denote a formula in the theory $\mathcal{T}$. Given a formula φ, we use $vars(\varphi)$ to denote the set of free variables in φ. We say that a formula is *interpreted* if it does not contain applications of predicates in $\mathcal{R}$.

CHC. A *constrained Horn clause* (CHC) C is of the form

$$\varphi_C \rightarrow P_{n+1}(\boldsymbol{x}_{n+1})$$

where $\{P_1(\boldsymbol{x}_1), \ldots, P_n(\boldsymbol{x}_n)\}_{n \geqslant 0}$ is the set of all uninterpreted predicate applications that appear in the formula φ_C; all $P_i(\boldsymbol{x}_i)$ appear positively in φ_C (i.e., under an even number of negations); and $\boldsymbol{x}_i$ denotes a vector of variable arguments to predicate P_i. We will use $P_i(\boldsymbol{x}_i) \in \varphi_C$ to denote that $P_i(\boldsymbol{x}_i)$ appears in φ_C. All free variables in a CHC are implicitly universally quantified. The left hand side of the implication ($\rightarrow$) is called the *body* of C, while the right hand side is its *head*. Given a clause C, we will use H_C to denote its head $P_{n+1}(\boldsymbol{x}_{n+1})$.

Ground instance. Given a CHC C and a substitution σ, which maps every variable in C to a constant, we use σC to denote the *ground instance* of C where each variable is replaced by its respective substitution in σ, that is, $\sigma\varphi_C \rightarrow \sigma H_C$.

Example 1. Consider the clause

$$C : x + y > 0 \rightarrow f(x)$$

and the substitution $\sigma = [x \mapsto 1, y \mapsto 2]$. The ground instance σC is

$$1 + 2 > 0 \rightarrow f(1)$$

■

3.2 Possibilistic Horn-Clause Problems

CHC problems. A CHC problem $\mathcal{H}$ is a tuple $(\mathcal{C}, \mathcal{Q})$, where $\mathcal{C}$ is a set of clauses $\{C_1, \ldots, C_n\}$, and the *query* $\mathcal{Q}$ is of the form $Q(\boldsymbol{x}) \rightarrow \varphi$, where $Q \in \mathcal{R}$, $vars(\varphi) \subseteq \boldsymbol{x}$, and there are no uninterpreted predicates in φ. We assume that Q does not appear in the body of any $C \in \mathcal{C}$. Throughout the paper, we shall always use Q to denote the predicate symbol appearing in the query.

Semantics. Intuitively, a CHC problem's semantics are defined by the *least solution* (interpretation) of the predicates in $\mathcal{R}$ that satisfies all clauses $\mathcal{C}$. We say that a query $\mathcal{Q}$ *holds iff* in the least solution of $\mathcal{H}$, all elements of Q satisfy φ, i.e., that $\forall \boldsymbol{x}.\, Q(\boldsymbol{x}) \rightarrow \varphi$. In program terms, φ is the set of *safe states*.

Derivation sequences. We shall define least solutions in terms of *derivation sequences*. Given a problem $\mathcal{H} = (\mathcal{C}, \mathcal{Q})$, a derivation sequence d is a finite sequence of ground instances of clauses in $\mathcal{C}$:

$$\sigma_1 C_{i_1}, \sigma_2 C_{i_2}, \ldots, \sigma_n C_{i_n}$$

where:

1. For all $j \in [1, n]$, each ground predicate in the body of $\sigma_j C_{i_j}$ should appear as the head of a $\sigma_k C_{i_k}$, for some $k < j$; otherwise, it is replaced by *false*.
2. For all $j \in [1, n]$, $\sigma_j \varphi_{C_{i_j}}$ is satisfiable.

For a derivation sequence d, we shall use $\boldsymbol{c}_d$ to denote the vector of constants in the head of ground instance $\sigma_n C_{i_n}$.

It follows that a query $Q(\boldsymbol{x}) \rightarrow \varphi$ holds *iff* for every derivation sequence d that ends with Q as the head of the last ground instance, we have $\sigma\varphi$ is satisfiable, where $\sigma = [\boldsymbol{x} \mapsto \boldsymbol{c}_d]$. For conciseness, we use $d \models \varphi$ to denote that d derives a value that satisfies φ.

Example 2. Consider the two clauses

$$C_1 : x > 0 \vee g(x) \rightarrow f(x)$$
$$C_2 : f(x) \wedge y = x + 1 \rightarrow f(y)$$

Consider the two substitutions $\sigma_1 = [x \mapsto 1]$ and $\sigma_2 = [x \mapsto 1, y \mapsto 2]$. The sequence $d = \sigma_1 C_1, \sigma_2 C_2$ is a derivation sequence. ■

n-derivations. To pave the way for our probabilistic semantics, we shall redefine what it means for a query to hold in terms of *n-derivations*: the set of derivations of length $\leqslant n$. We define all such derivations by first *unrolling* the set of clauses $\mathcal{C}$ to a new non-recursive set $\mathcal{C}_n$. This is shown in Algorithm 1.

The algorithm unrolls the set of clauses $\mathcal{C}$ in a top-down fashion, beginning with the predicate appearing in the query $\mathcal{Q}$. In UNROLL, we use $\mathcal{C}(P_i^k)$ to denote the set of all clauses in $\mathcal{C}$ whose head is an application of P_i. We use the superscript k to denote *primed* values of a predicate symbol; primes are used to ensure

Require: $n > 0$

function UNROLL$((\mathcal{C}, \mathcal{Q}), n)$
  $\mathit{rels} \leftarrow \{Q\}$ $//\mathcal{Q} = Q(\boldsymbol{x}) \rightarrow \varphi$
  $\mathcal{C}_n \leftarrow \emptyset$
  for i from 1 to n **do**
    $\mathit{cls} \leftarrow \{\mathit{fresh}(C, P_i^k) \mid C \in \mathcal{C}(P_i^k), P_i^k \in \mathit{rels}\}$
    $\mathcal{C}_n \leftarrow \mathcal{C}_n \cup \{\mathit{cls}\}$
    $\mathit{rels} \leftarrow \{P_i^k \mid P_i^k \in \varphi_C, C \in \mathit{cls}\}$
  return $\mathcal{C}_n$

Algorithm 1: Unrolling a set of Horn clauses

that the resulting unrolling is not recursive. The function $\mathit{fresh}(C, P_i^k)$ takes a clause $C \in \mathcal{C}$ and returns a new clause where the predicate in the head of C is replaced with P_i^k, and all occurrences of predicate symbols in the body are given fresh (unused) superscripts.

We assume that all clauses in $\mathcal{C}_n$ have mutually disjoint sets of variables. We also assume that $\mathcal{C}_n \subseteq \mathcal{C}_{n+1}$, for all $n \geqslant 1$—that is, UNROLL always picks canonical names for variables and predicates. We use $\boldsymbol{x}_\infty$ to be the vector of all variables appearing in all clauses in the (potentially infinite) set $\mathcal{C}_\infty = \bigcup_{n=1}^{\infty} \mathcal{C}_n$. Variables in $\boldsymbol{x}_\infty$ are ordered canonically, e.g., in order of generation in UNROLL.

Example 3. Recall the Horn clause problem in Fig. 2 from Sect. 2. The problem was unrolled for $n = 2$, resulting in the two clauses C_1 and C_2, shown in Formulas 1 and 2. ■

Queries and n-derivations. Given a (potentially infinite) set of clauses $\mathcal{C}' \subseteq \mathcal{C}_\infty$, we shall use $\sigma\mathcal{C}'$, where σ maps each variable in $\boldsymbol{x}_\infty$ to a constant, to denote the set of all derivation sequences that (i) are formed from ground instances in $\{\sigma C \mid C \in \mathcal{C}'\}$ and (ii) end in a clause with $Q(\boldsymbol{c})$ in the head.

The following theorem formalizes what it means for a query to hold in terms of ∞-derivations.

Theorem 1. *A query* $\mathcal{Q} = Q(\boldsymbol{x}) \rightarrow \varphi$ *holds* iff $\{\sigma \mid d \in \sigma\mathcal{C}_\infty$ *and* $d \not\models \varphi\} = \emptyset$.

The idea is that a query holds *iff* there does not exist a substitution σ that results in a derivation d that falsifies the formula φ.

3.3 Probabilistic Horn-Clause Problems

Now that we have defined traditional Horn clause problems and their semantics, we are ready to define *probabilistically constrained Horn clauses* (PCHC).

PCHC problems. A PCHC problem $\mathcal{H}^p$ is a tuple of the form $(\mathcal{C}^p, \mathcal{Q}^p)$ (for clarity, we drop the superscript p below):

- Each clause $C \in \mathcal{C}$ is defined as in CHC: $\varphi_C \rightarrow H_C$. However, the set of unbound variables that appear in C are divided into two disjoint vectors:

$\boldsymbol{x}_C^p$ and $\boldsymbol{x}_C^a$. We call $\boldsymbol{x}_C^p$ the set of *probabilistic variables*, whose values are drawn from a *joint probability distribution* $\mathcal{D}_C$. The variables $\boldsymbol{x}_C^a$ are *angelic variables.*
- The probabilistic query $\mathcal{Q}$ is a pair of the form $(Q(\boldsymbol{x}) \to \varphi, \theta)$, where $\theta \in [0,1)$. We would like to prove that the probability of deriving an element of Q that satisfies φ is greater than θ.

Semantics of PCHC In CHC problems, the semantics are such that an element is either derived or not; here, an element is derived with a probability. The following semantics of PCHC problems are inspired by Kozen's seminal work on the semantics of probabilistic programs [31].

Using the UNROLL procedure in Algorithm 1, we analogously unroll clauses $\mathcal{C}$ into sets $\mathcal{C}_1 \subseteq \mathcal{C}_2 \subseteq \ldots$. The set of variables $\boldsymbol{x}_\infty$ appearing in $\mathcal{C}_\infty = \bigcup_{n=1}^{\infty} \mathcal{C}_n$ is broken into two disjoint vectors $\boldsymbol{x}_\infty^p$ and $\boldsymbol{x}_\infty^a$, where $\boldsymbol{x}_\infty^p$ denotes all *probabilistic variables*, and $\boldsymbol{x}_\infty^a$ denotes all *angelic variables.* We treat the variables $\boldsymbol{x}_\infty^p$ as random variables distributed according to their respective distributions in $\{\mathcal{D}_C\}$. We shall assume existence of a *probability space* $(\Omega, \mathcal{F}, \mathbb{P})$ where *outcomes* Ω are valuations of $\boldsymbol{x}_\infty^p$, defined through substitutions σ^p; *events* $\mathcal{F}$ are sets of substitutions; and $\mathbb{P}$ is a probability measure over sets of substitutions. We assume existence of events $\Sigma_n^\phi \in \mathcal{F}$ defined as

$$\Sigma_n^\phi = \{\sigma^p \mid \exists \sigma^a, d \text{ s.t. } d \in \sigma^a(\sigma^p \mathcal{C}_n) \text{ and } d \models \phi\},$$

for $n \in [1, \infty]$ and interpreted formula ϕ with free variables in $\boldsymbol{x}$ (the variables in the query $\mathcal{Q}$). That is, Σ_n^ϕ is the set of all substitutions to probabilistic variables that yield derivations of length $\leqslant n$ and satisfy ϕ. Observe the substitution σ^a: this is used to pick values for the angelic variables $\boldsymbol{x}_n^a$. We note that when n is ∞, the definition of Σ_∞^ϕ is as defined above, using the set $\mathcal{C}_\infty$.

The following theorem states two key properties of Σ_n^ϕ that we exploit later.

Theorem 2. *(a) For all $n \in [1, \infty)$, $\Sigma_n^\phi \subseteq \Sigma_{n+1}^\phi$. (b) $\Sigma_\infty^\phi = \bigcup_{n=1}^{\infty} \Sigma_n^\phi$.*

Proof. (a) Suppose that $\Sigma_n^\varphi \not\subseteq \Sigma_{n+1}^\varphi$. Then, there must be an assignment $\sigma_p \in \Sigma_n^\varphi$ such that $\sigma_p \notin \Sigma_{n+1}^\varphi$. By construction, we know that there exists a sequence of unique clauses $C_1, \ldots, C_k \in \mathcal{C}_n$, and a substitution σ_a to $\boldsymbol{x}_a$ such that derivation $d = \sigma_p \sigma_a C_1, \ldots, \sigma_p \sigma_a C_k$, clause C_k is of the form ... $\to Q(\boldsymbol{x})$, and $d \models \varphi$. By monotonicity of UNROLL, we know that $\mathcal{C}_n \subseteq \mathcal{C}_{n+1}$. So, we know that $d \in \sigma_p \sigma_a \mathcal{C}_{n+1}$ and therefore $\sigma_p \in \Sigma_{n+1}^\varphi$.

(b) The $\Leftarrow$ direction is similar to the above proof, since $\mathcal{C}_n \subseteq \mathcal{C}_\infty$. The $\Rightarrow$ direction: Take any $\sigma_p \in \Sigma_\infty^\varphi$, then there is a σ_p' that is σ_p with a substitution for all $\boldsymbol{x}_\infty^a$ such that there is a derivation $d = \sigma_p' C_1, \ldots, \sigma_p' C_k$ such that $d \models \varphi$. By monotonicity of UNROLL, we know that $\{C_1, \ldots, C_k\} \in \mathcal{C}_l$, for some $l \in [1, \infty)$. Therefore, $d \in \sigma_p' \mathcal{C}_l$ and $\sigma_p \in \Sigma_l^\varphi$. ■

Example 4. Recall the function f and its associated PCHC problem in Fig. 1. In Sect. 2, we considered an unrolling with $n = 2$. The set $\Sigma_2^{r>5}$ is the following set of substitutions to $\boldsymbol{x}_\infty^p = (x, x', x'', \ldots)$—in our unrolling in Sect. 2, we only have x and x'; variables $x'', \ldots$ appear in longer unrollings:

$$\Sigma_2^{r>5} = \{[x \mapsto c, x' \mapsto c', x'' \mapsto c'', \ldots] \mid c \geqslant 5 \vee (c < 0 \wedge c' \geqslant 5)\}$$

Note that only x and x' are constrained in the substitutions, since they are the only ones that appear in unrollings of length 2. We computed that $\mathbb{P}[\Sigma_2^{r>5}]$ is ~0.46, as the values of c and c' are drawn from $\mathtt{gauss}(0, 10)$. ■

The following definition formalizes what it means for a query to hold.

Definition 1. *A query* $\mathcal{Q} = (Q(\boldsymbol{x}) \rightarrow \varphi, \theta)$ *holds* iff $\mathbb{P}\left[\Sigma_\infty^\varphi\right] > \theta$.

The intuition is as follows: take the set of all substitutions σ^p that can derive an element that satisfies φ (for some σ^a), and compute the probability of picking a substitution in that set.

We assume that $\mathbb{P}\left[\Sigma_\infty^{true}\right] = 1$. In other words, *almost all* substitutions of the probabilistic variables result in a derivation. This is analogous to the *almost-sure termination* property of probabilistic programs, which stipulates that a program terminates with probability 1.

4 Probabilistic Horn Clause Verification

Overview. The high-level idea underlying our algorithm is as follows. Ideally, we would like to compute the probability of picking a substitution σ^p that results in a derivation $d \models \varphi$, for some assignment σ^a of the angelic variables. However, σ^p is over an infinite set of variables. To make the problem manageable, we begin by considering substitutions that result in derivations $|d| \leqslant n$, for some fixed n. By doing so, we compute a *lower bound* on the probability, since we consider a *subset* of all possible derivations. By iteratively increasing the value n—i.e., look at longer and longer derivations—we converge to the actual probability of the event of interest.

Since for all $n \in [1, \infty)$, $\Sigma_n^\varphi \subseteq \Sigma_{n+1}^\varphi$, we have the fact that $\mathbb{P}[\Sigma_n^\varphi] \leqslant \mathbb{P}[\Sigma_{n+1}^\varphi]$. Our algorithm iteratively increases n, computing the probability $\mathbb{P}[\Sigma_n^\varphi]$ at each step, until it can prove that $\mathbb{P}[\Sigma_n^\varphi] > \theta$. Additionally, as we will see, the algorithm can disprove such properties, i.e., prove that $\mathbb{P}[\Sigma_n^\varphi] \leqslant \theta$, by maintaining an upper bound on $\mathbb{P}[\Sigma_n^\varphi]$.

Encoding derivations. The primary step in making the algorithm practical is to characterize the set Σ_n^φ and figure out how to compute the probability of picking an element in that set. We make the observation that the set Σ_n^φ can be characterized as the set of models of an interpreted formula Ψ_n^φ in the first-order theory $\mathcal{T}$. Then, the probability becomes that of picking a satisfying assignment of Ψ_n^φ. This is a *model counting* problem, where models additionally have a probability of occurrence. In what follows, we present an encoding of Ψ_n^φ. In Sect. 6, we discuss different mechanisms for model counting.

function $\text{ENC}(\mathcal{C}_n, \mathcal{Q})$
  return $\exists \boldsymbol{b}, \boldsymbol{x}_n^a . \varphi \wedge \text{ENC}_C(Q(\boldsymbol{x}))$

function $\text{ENC}_C(P(\boldsymbol{x}))$
  $D \leftarrow \emptyset$
  for all $\varphi_C \rightarrow P(\boldsymbol{x}') \in \mathcal{C}_n$ **do**
    map each $P_i(\boldsymbol{x}_i) \in \varphi_C$ to fresh Bool variable b_i
    $\phi \leftarrow \varphi_C[b_i/P_i(\boldsymbol{x}_i)] \wedge \bigwedge_{P_i(\boldsymbol{x}_i) \in \varphi_C} b_i \Rightarrow \text{ENC}_C(P_i(\boldsymbol{x}_i))$
    $D \leftarrow D \cup \{\phi \wedge \boldsymbol{x} = \boldsymbol{x}'\}$
  return $\bigvee D$

Algorithm 2: Encoding of a set of clauses (input $\mathcal{C}_n$ is accessible by ENC_C)

Our encoding algorithm is presented in Algorithm 2, as the primary function ENC, which is similar to other encodings of Horn clauses, e.g., [37]. Given a set of clauses $\mathcal{C}_n$ and a query $\mathcal{Q} = (Q(\boldsymbol{x}) \rightarrow \varphi, \theta)$, ENC encodes the clauses in a top-down recursive fashion, starting with the predicate $Q(\boldsymbol{x})$. In each recursive call to $\text{ENC}_C(P(\boldsymbol{x}))$, it encodes all clauses where $P(\boldsymbol{x})$ is the head of the clause. Uninterpreted predicates $P_i(\boldsymbol{x}_i)$ in the body of a clause are replaced with fresh Boolean variables, which indicate whether a predicate is set to true or false in a derivation. Finally, all angelic variables $\boldsymbol{x}_n^a$ and freshly introduced Boolean variables $\boldsymbol{b}$ are existentially quantified, leaving us with a formula where the only variables are the probabilistic ones. (Recall the encoding in Sect. 2 for a concrete example.)

For a fixed n, we shall treat the set of models of Ψ_n^φ as a set of substitutions to $\boldsymbol{x}_n^p$. The following theorem states that the set of models of Ψ_n^φ is the same as the set of substitutions in Σ_n^φ.

Theorem 3. *For all $n \geqslant 1$, $\Psi_n^\varphi = \Sigma_n^\varphi$. (We assume that variables that are not in Ψ_n^φ but in $\boldsymbol{x}_\infty^p$ can take any value in models of Ψ_n^φ.)*

Iterative probability approximation algorithm. Algorithm 3 shows our overall algorithm. For now, ignore the gray lines 9 and 10. As discussed above, it iteratively increases the value of n attempting to prove that the query holds.

The algorithm VERIFY (without lines 9–10) is sound, that is, only returns correct solutions. VERIFY is also complete, relative to existence of an oracle for computing $\mathbb{P}[\Psi_n^\varphi]$ and assuming $\mathbb{P}[\Sigma_\infty^\varphi] > \theta$.

Theorem 4. VERIFY *is sound. If $\mathbb{P}[\Sigma_\infty^\varphi] > \theta$, then* VERIFY *terminates.*

Proof. Soundness follows from Theorem 3. Suppose that the query holds, then we know, from Theorem 2, that $\lim_{n\to\infty} \mathbb{P}[\Sigma_n^\varphi] > \theta$ and $\forall i \in \mathbb{N}. \mathbb{P}[\Sigma_i^\varphi] \subseteq \mathbb{P}[\Sigma_{i+1}^\varphi]$. By definition of limit, we know that there exists an n such that $\mathbb{P}[\Sigma_n^\varphi] > \theta$. ■

Disproving queries with upper bounds. The algorithm so far is only able to prove that a query holds—it cannot prove that a query does not hold, because it

1: **function** VERIFY $(\mathcal{C}, \mathcal{Q})$
2:     **for** $n \in [1, \infty)$ **do**
3:         $\mathcal{C}_n \leftarrow$ UNROLL$(\mathcal{C}, n)$
4:         $\Psi_n^\varphi \leftarrow$ ENC$(\mathcal{C}_n, \mathcal{Q})$
5:         ▷ *prove that the query holds*
6:         **if** $\mathbb{P}[\Psi_n^\varphi] > \theta$ **then**
7:             **return** $\mathcal{Q}$ holds
8:         ▷ *prove that the query does not hold*
9:         **if** $1 - \mathbb{P}[\Psi_n^{\neg\varphi}] \leqslant \theta$ **then**
10:             **return** $\mathcal{Q}$ does not hold

Algorithm 3: Verification algorithm

only computes lower bounds on the probability. Now consider the entire VERIFY algorithm, i.e., including lines 9 and 10, which also computes upper bounds. We now provide a sufficient condition for making the algorithm complete in both directions—proving and disproving that a query holds.

The restriction is as follows: for any query $(Q(\boldsymbol{x}) \rightarrow \varphi, \theta)$,

$$\Sigma_\infty^\varphi \cap \Sigma_\infty^{\neg\varphi} = \emptyset$$

Effectively, this ensures that derivations are completely dictated by the probabilistic variables; in program terms, this is (roughly) like ensuring that the only source of non-determinism in a program is probabilistic choice. Now, we can compute an *upper bound* for $\mathbb{P}[\Sigma_\infty^\varphi]$ by simply computing the value of $1 - \mathbb{P}[\Sigma_n^{\neg\varphi}]$, for any $n \in [1, \infty)$. Thus, if $1 - \mathbb{P}[\Psi_n^{\neg\varphi}] \leqslant \theta$, we know that the query does not hold. If we perform this check at every iteration of VERIFY, we ensure that the algorithm terminates if $\mathbb{P}[\Sigma_\infty^\varphi] < \theta$. Notice that if $\mathbb{P}[\Sigma_\infty^\varphi] = \theta$, the upper bound might come asymptotically close to θ but never get to it.

Theorem 5. VERIFY *is sound. If* $\mathbb{P}[\Sigma_\infty^\varphi] \neq \theta$, *then* VERIFY *terminates.*

Proof. By definition, $\mathbb{P}[\Sigma_\infty^\varphi] + \mathbb{P}[\Sigma_\infty^{\neg\varphi}] = 1$. Therefore, $\mathbb{P}[\Sigma_\infty^\varphi] = 1 - \mathbb{P}[\Sigma_\infty^{\neg\varphi}]$. Since $\mathbb{P}[\Sigma_n^{\neg\varphi}] \leqslant \mathbb{P}[\Sigma_\infty^{\neg\varphi}]$, for any $n \in [1, \infty)$, we know that $\mathbb{P}[\Sigma_\infty^\varphi] \leqslant 1 - \mathbb{P}[\Sigma_n^{\neg\varphi}]$, thus ensuring soundness. Termination follows from the fact that $\lim_{n\rightarrow\infty} \mathbb{P}[\Psi_n^{\neg\varphi}] \geqslant 1 - \theta$, assuming $\mathbb{P}[\Sigma_\infty^\varphi] < \theta$. ■

5 Angels and Demons

We now discuss extensions of PCHC problems with *demonic non-determinism.*

Analogous to angelic variables, we add a set of demonic variables $\boldsymbol{x}_C^d$ for every clause C. That is, now, every clause C has free variables divided amongst three disjoint sets: $\boldsymbol{x}_C^p$, $\boldsymbol{x}_C^a$, and $\boldsymbol{x}_C^d$. We now redefine Σ_n^φ as follows:

$$\Sigma_n^\varphi = \{\sigma^p \mid \forall\sigma^d.\, \exists\sigma^a, d.\, d \in \sigma^d(\sigma^a(\sigma^p\mathcal{C}_n)) \text{ and } d \models \varphi\}$$

In other words, we can only add σ^p to the set if *every* assignment to demonic variables leads to a derivation of an element in φ.

Notice that the alternation of quantifiers indicates that demonic non-determinism is resolved first, followed by angelic non-determinism. We can also consider arbitrary quantifier alternations, by dividing demonic and angelic variables into sets of variables that get resolved in a certain order. For our purposes, we will restrict our attention to cases where demonic non-determinism is resolved first. Informally, demonic variables can maliciously pick substitutions σ^d such that there is no σ^a that results in a derivation. If we flipped the quantifiers to $\exists\sigma^a. \forall\sigma^d$, then, effectively, the angelic variables get to divine a substitution for σ^a such that no matter what substitution σ^d the demonic variables are possessed with, a derivation $d \models \varphi$ exists.

Implementing non-determinism. In the demonic case, we can construct the formula Ψ_n^φ just as in Algorithm 2, but we quantify out the demonic variables: we use $\forall \boldsymbol{x}_n^d. \Psi_n^\varphi$. The intuition behind the choice of quantifier directly follows from the definition of Σ_n^φ above.

In presence of demonic non-determinism, VERIFY loses its termination guarantee in Theorem 4.

6 Algorithmic Details

In this section, we discuss some of the subtleties of PCHC problems. We then discuss instantiations of our approach with various model counting techniques.

6.1 Decomposition and Non-determinism

We now discuss key design decisions in encoding and verification.

Decomposition. Consider the following Horn clause C, where $\texttt{unif}(0, 10)$ is the uniform distribution over reals between 0 and 10.

$$x \sim \texttt{unif}(0, 10) \mid x \leqslant 1 \vee x \geqslant 8 \rightarrow f(x)$$

Suppose we decompose the clause C into two clauses, C_1 and C_2, by splitting the disjunction:

$$x_1 \sim \texttt{unif}(0, 10) \mid x_1 \leqslant 1 \rightarrow f(x_1)$$
$$x_2 \sim \texttt{unif}(0, 10) \mid x_2 \geqslant 8 \rightarrow f(x_2)$$

In the non-probabilistic setting, this transformation would result in a semantically equivalent set of clauses. In our setting, however, we get a semantically different set of clauses. This is because we duplicate the probabilistic variables, resulting in two *independent* variables, x_1 and x_2. Suppose we want to compute the probability that $f(x) \rightarrow$ *true*. In the first case, the answer is 0.3. In the second case, the answer is 0.28.[3]

---

[3] Since $\mathbb{P}[x_1 \leqslant 1 \vee x_2 \geqslant 8] = 1 - \mathbb{P}[x_1 > 1 \wedge x_2 < 8] = 1 - 0.9 * 0.8 = 0.28$.

Remark 1. We could alternatively just assume that x_1 and x_2 are the same variable in C_1 and C_2. This view drastically complicates the semantics: we now have variable sharing between clauses, and the semantics of unrollings need to take that into account. Given that we also have recursion, we have to reason about which instances of clauses in the unrolling are sharing variables and which are not (for instance, in Sect. 2, when we unrolled the recursive clause, we constructed a new copy with an independent variable x'). To simplify the semantics of PCHC, we opted to enrich the formulas that can appear in Horn clauses, rather than encode and manage probabilistic variable independence explicitly.

Non-determinism. We now discuss a related issue. One might wonder: why not compute the probability for each subset of the clauses separately and sum the answers? In program terms, we can view this as computing the probability of individual program paths separately, e.g., as in Sankaranarayanan et al.'s algorithm [42].

Unfortunately, in our setting, non-determinism does not allow us to decompose the problem. Consider the following example:

$$x \sim \texttt{unif}(0,10) \mid (b \wedge (x \geqslant 2 \iff r)) \vee (\neg b \wedge (x \leqslant 4 \iff r)) \rightarrow f(r)$$

where b and r are angelic Boolean variables. This encodes the following program:

```
   x ~ unif(0,10)
   b = nondet()
π1 if (b) ret x >= 2
π2 else ret x >= 4
```

Suppose we have the query $f(r) \rightarrow r = \mathit{true}$. The probability that the query holds is $8/10$, because angelic nondeterminism always leads us through the then branch of the conditional. Consider the approach where we compute the probability for one disjunct at a time—i.e., one program path at a time. The following clause defines path π_1, which takes the then branch of the conditional. The clause satisfies the query with a probability of $8/10$:

$$x \sim \texttt{unif}(0,10) \mid (b \wedge (x \geqslant 2 \iff r)) \rightarrow f(r)$$

The following clause, encoding π_2, satisfies the query with probability $6/10$:

$$x \sim \texttt{unif}(0,10) \mid (\neg b \wedge (x \geqslant 4 \iff r)) \rightarrow f(r)$$

Adding the two probabilities results in 14/10. Approaches that divide the program into paths and sum up the results assume that different paths are mutually exclusive—i.e., the program is deterministic. In non-deterministic programs, the events of taking different paths are *not* mutually exclusive, therefore, we cannot simply add the probability of the two events. Our approach considers both paths simultaneously through encoding, resolving the non-determinism and discovering that the probability of the query is $8/10$.

6.2 Model Counting Modulo Probability Spaces

Overview. In Sect. 4, we assumed existence of an oracle that, given a formula Ψ_n^φ, can compute the probability that it is satisfied, assuming the values of variables $\boldsymbol{x}_n^p$ are drawn from some probability distribution. Suppose, for instance, that Ψ_n^φ is a propositional formula and that there is a joint probability distribution $p(\boldsymbol{x}_n^p)$. Then, we define

$$\mathbb{P}[\Psi_n^\varphi] = \sum_{\boldsymbol{c} \in \{0,1\}^n} \mathbb{1}([\boldsymbol{x}_n^p \mapsto \boldsymbol{c}]\Psi_n^\varphi)\ p(\boldsymbol{c})$$

where the *indicator function* $\mathbb{1}(\phi)$ is 1 if ϕ is *true* and 0 otherwise.

Suppose, alternatively, that Ψ_n^p is a formula over real linear arithmetic and there is a joint probability density function $p(\boldsymbol{x}_n^p)$. Then, we define

$$\mathbb{P}[\Psi_n^\varphi] = \int \mathbb{1}(\Psi_n^\varphi)\ p(\boldsymbol{x}_n^p)\ d\boldsymbol{x}_n^p$$

That is, we integrate over region $\Psi_n^\varphi \subseteq \mathbb{R}^n$, weighted by the probability density.

The above problems are hard, for instance, in the propositional setting, the counting problem is #P-complete. Nonetheless, there are efficient approaches for various first-order theories; we survey prominent techniques below. Our algorithm, of course, is agnostic to the technique used for computing probabilities.

Approximate guarantees. Approximate techniques come in two flavors: (*i*) statistical approaches that utilize *concentration inequalities*, and (*ii*) PTIME randomized approximation schemes (PRAS) with access to an NP oracle (e.g., a SAT solver) [43]. Both approaches provide (ϵ, δ) guarantees, where they produce a result that is within a multiplicative or additive error of ϵ from the exact result, with a probability $1 - \delta$ of being correct. Recently, there has been progress in practical PRAS algorithms [2,9,12], due to developments in SAT and SMT solvers.

Hard guarantees. Other approaches attempt to produce *exact* answers. For instance, recent work has utilized *cone decomposition* [3,14] to integrate polynomial probability density functions over linear real arithmetic formulas. Other work considered over- and under-approximating linear real and integer arithmetic formulas as a set of cubes to produce upper and lower bounds on the probability [42].

7 Implementation and Evaluation

Implementation. We have implemented a prototype of our technique that (*i*) takes programs in a simple Python-like language with procedure calls, probabilistic assignments and non-deterministic ones; (*ii*) converts the program and a query of interest to a PCHC problem; and (*iii*) verifies the query. All programs are encoded in linear real arithmetic.

Recall that we need to compute $\mathbb{P}[\Psi_n^\varphi]$ at every iteration of VERIFY, and that Ψ_n^φ is quantified. To do so, we apply a simple Monte-Carlo-based sampling approach that proves $\mathbb{P}[\Psi_n^\varphi] > \theta$ with a 0.99 confidence—using *Hoeffding's concentration inequality*. Specifically, the approach draws an assignment for the probabilistic variables, substitutes the assignment in the formula Ψ_n^φ, and checks whether the result is SAT. Given that the formula is quantified, this is an expensive process. If the formula is existentially quantified, then evaluating a sample is NP-complete. One could also eliminate the quantifier, and then each sample evaluation is just a simplification of the formula. We have, however, found that quantifier elimination degrades performance in this case, and it is better to evaluate each sample with a call the SMT solver. On the other hand, for universally quantified formulas, we have found that it is very important to perform quantifier elimination first, as iteratively calling the SMT solver to evaluate samples on universally quantified formulas is infeasible. As such, we only perform quantifier elimination in the presence of demonic nondeterminism—which requires universal quantifiers. We use Redlog [1] for quantifier elimination.

Remark 2. We opted for an approximate approach to model counting because our formulas are over quantified LRA and non-trivial distributions, like Gaussians, that established exact volume computation tools are unable to handle. For example, LattE [14]—which is used in a number of tools [3,22]—can only integrate a piecewise polynomial function over a polyhedron.

Benchmarks. We collected a set of benchmarks that is meant to exercise the various features of our approach. Table 1 shows the list of benchmarks along with a description of each. The family of benchmarks `simple*` are variants of the illustrative example in Fig. 1, where we enrich it with angelic and demonic forms of nondeterminism with which it decides the distribution to draw the value of `x` from. We then consider the classic McCarthy91, `mc91`, recursive function, where we impose a distribution on the possible inputs and compute the probability that the return value is greater than 91. We consider an *approximate* version of `mc91`, where the *adder* may flip the least significant bit from 0 to 1 with a small probability. `mc91-equiv` computes the probability that the approximate version `mc91-approx` returns the same result as the exact version `mc91`. The family of benchmarks `chat-*` are random-walk programs taken from Chatterjee et al. [10] (who are interested in termination). The programs contain demonic and angelic nondeterminism (in case of `chat-fig2`, both). The query we check is about the probability that the random walk ends in a certain region on the grid.

Evaluation and discussion. Table 1 shows the results of running our algorithm with a 10 min timeout per benchmark ('–' indicates timeout). For each benchmark, we pick three values for θ that gradually increase the difficulty of the verification process by forcing VERIFY to perform more iterations. Most benchmarks complete within 90 s.

We found two primary sources of difficulty: The first difficulty is dealing with universal quantifiers. Consider, for instance, `simp-dem` with $\theta = 0.3$. Here, VERIFY needs to unroll the recursion up to depth 5, resulting in a difficult formula

Table 1. Experimental results: Iters is the number of iterations; θ is the query threshold; Time (s) is the total running time; and QETime is quantifier elimination time.

Benchmark	Iters	θ	Time	QETime	Description
simple	1	0.4	6.3	0.0	Example from Fig. 2
	2	0.6	12.6	0.0	
	4	0.8	25.4	0.0	
simp-ang	1	0.4	6.6	0.0	Example from Fig. 2 with angelic determinism for the choice of `x`'s distribution
	2	0.6	13.5	0.0	
	3	0.8	20.4	0.0	
simp-dem	4	0.1	45.5	20.9	Example from Fig. 2 with demonic determinism for the choice of `x`'s distribution
	4	0.2	45.4	20.9	
	5	0.3	530.2	505.9	
mc91	2	0.2	6.7	0.0	McCarthy91 function with a distribution on possible inputs
	2	0.3	6.6	0.0	
	–	0.4	–	–	
mc91-approx	2	0.4	6.8	0.0	McCarthy91 function with an approximate adder
	3	0.5	14.0	0.0	
	6	0.6	51.4	0.0	
mc91-equiv	3	0.7	15.2	0.0	Prob. of equivalence between an approx. and exact `mc91`—using self-composition
	4	0.8	25.9	0.0	
	–	0.9	–	–	
chat-fig2	3	0.2	7.3	1.0	From Chatterjee et al. [10]: random walk with demonic and angelic nondeterminism
	3	0.3	7.3	1.0	
	–	0.4	–	–	
chat-rw1	6	0.1	38.2	0.0	From Chatterjee et al. [10]: 1-dimensional random walk
	8	0.2	57.8	0.0	
	11	0.3	90.9	0.0	
chat-rw2-dem	3	0.1	14.7	2.3	From Chatterjee et al. [10]: 2-dimensional random walk with demonic non-determinism
	3	0.2	14.6	2.3	
	–	0.3	–	–	

for quantifier elimination, as shown by the time taken for quantifier elimination. Similarly, `chat-fig2` and `chat-rw2-dem` (both of which contain demonic nondeterminism) timeout at larger values of θ while waiting for quantifier elimination to complete. In the future, we plan on investigating efficient underapproximations of quantifier elimination [26] that result in good-enough lower bounds for probabilities. The second source of difficulty is the exponential explosion in the size of the unrolling—and therefore the encoding—which occurs in problems like `mc91`. In the non-probabilistic case, recent work [33] has dealt with this problem by merging procedure calls on different execution paths to limit the explosion. It would be interesting to investigate such technique in the probabilistic setting.

To the best of our knowledge, there are no automated verification/analysis tools that can handle the range of features demonstrated in our benchmark suite. In the next section, we survey existing works and describe the differences.

8 Related Work and Discussion

Probabilistic program analysis. There is a plethora of work on analyzing probabilistic programs. Abstraction-based techniques employ abstract domains to compute approximations of probability distributions [13,38,39]. By unrolling program executions, our approach does not lose precision due to abstraction. The closest approach to ours is that of Sankaranyanan et al. [42] where computing the probability of an event is reduced to summing probabilities of event occurrences on individual paths. First, our intermediate language of Horn clauses allows natural handling of recursive calls; additionally, we handle nondeterminism, which, as discussed in Sect. 6, is handled unsoundly in the path-based technique. Similarly, Sampson et al. [41] perform path-based unrolling, but do not provide whole-program guarantees.

Other techniques for program analysis include axiomatic and exact ones. Exact techniques, like PSI [21], involve finding a closed-form for the return values of a given program, using rewrite rules and symbolic execution. To our knowledge, none of the existing exact techniques can handle nondeterminism and/or recursive procedures. Axiomatic techniques synthesize expectation invariants from which a post-condition of interest may be deduced [8,30,36]. Compared to our approach, these techniques do not handle procedures, are not guaranteed to prove properties of the form in this paper, and are restricted in terms of variable types and distributions used. Axiomatic approaches, however, excel at characterizing the probability of an event in terms of inputs. It would be very interesting to study expectation invariants in the context of PCHC. Note that our semantics of non-determinism are slightly different from those used by McIver and Morgan [36]; we discuss this more below when describing Luckow et al.'s work [35].

Probabilistic and statistical model checking. Compared to probabilistic model checking, our approach allows encoding semantics of arbitrary recursive programs, as long they fit in an appropriate first-order theory. Probabilistic model checkers like PRISM [32] are often restricted to reasoning about finite-state Markov chains. Statistical model checking [34] applies statistical testing to prove properties with high confidence. We applied statistical testing in our evaluation to compute probabilities with high confidence, where our testing was over quantified formulas encoding Horn-clause unrollings.

Model counting. Like other recent techniques, our approach reduces probabilistic analysis to a form of model counting. Chistikov et al. [12] apply a similar technique to encode single-procedure programs and use approximate model counting with an NP oracle. Our approach can be viewed as a generalization of Chistikov et al.'s formulation to programs with procedures and recursive calls.

A number of other analysis techniques for probabilistic programs employ model counting [19,22,35]. The closest work to ours in that space is that of Luckow et al. [35]. There, the program also involves non-determinism in the form of a sequence of Boolean variables (a schedule) and the goal is to find an assignment that maximizes/minimizes probability of an event. There are two key differences with our work: First, we do not only admit Boolean non-deterministic variables, but we can also handle, e.g., real-valued non-determinism. Second, our non-determinism semantics are slightly different: We follow Chistikov et al. [12], where non-determinism follows probabilistic choice. In the future, we plan to investigate the alternate form of non-determinism used by Luckow et al. [35], where non-deterministic variables are resolved first. In such case, the weighted model counting problem turns into E-MAJSAT (which is in NP^{PP}), where the goal is to find a satisfying assignment to the non-deterministic variables that maximizes the weighted model count of the formula.

Probabilistic Horn clauses. In artificial intelligence and databases, Horn clauses have been extended to the probabilistic setting, e.g., [15,20]. The semantics and usage are quite different from our setting. Probabilities are usually associated at the level of the clause—e.g., a rule applies with a 0.75 probability. Our approach incorporates probabilistic variables with the clauses themselves and is over infinite domains, e.g., reals.

Probabilistic recursive models. There have been a number of proposals for probabilistic models that involve recursion. For instance, probabilistic pushdown [17] automata and recursive Bayesian networks [40]. In probabilistic pushdown automata, and equivalently recursive Markov chains [18,44], variable domains are finite and probabilities are applied only on transitions. Our approach allows for infinite domains and probabilistic choice allows encoding probabilistic control-flow transitions in a program as well as probabilistic assignments.

Horn clause solving. As discussed throughout the paper, our algorithmic contribution adapts existing Horn clause solving algorithms to the probabilistic setting. Specifically, most existing algorithms, e.g., HSF [24,25] and Duality [37], employ an tree unrolling of Horn clauses, but are concerned with finding inductive invariants as opposed to probability bounds.

9 Conclusion

We introduced probabilistically constrained Horn clauses (PCHC), and presented an algorithm for proving/disproving probabilistic queries. Our semantics incorporated a form of angelic/demonic non-determinism, where, effectively, angelic/demonic variables can look into the future. This is, for instance, different from the semantics used by McIver and Morgan [36]. In the future, we plan to handle such semantics by extending techniques like Luckow et al. [35] to our Horn-clause setting. Another interesting avenue for future work is to incorporate some form of loop summarization, so that we can reduce probabilistic inference over infinitely many derivations to a fixed set, therefore avoiding iterative unrolling.

References

1. Redlog. http://www.redlog.eu/
2. Belle, V., Van den Broeck, G., Passerini, A.: Hashing-based approximate probabilistic inference in hybrid domains. In: Proceedings of the 31st Conference on Uncertainty in Artificial Intelligence (UAI) (2015)
3. Belle, V., Passerini, A., den Broeck, G.V.: Probabilistic inference in hybrid domains by weighted model integration. In: Proceedings of the Twenty-Fourth International Joint Conference on Artificial Intelligence, IJCAI 2015, Buenos Aires, Argentina, 25–31 July 2015, pp. 2770–2776 (2015). http://ijcai.org/Abstract/15/392
4. Beyene, T.A., Popeea, C., Rybalchenko, A.: Solving existentially quantified horn clauses. In: Sharygina, N., Veith, H. (eds.) CAV 2013. LNCS, vol. 8044, pp. 869–882. Springer, Heidelberg (2013). doi:10.1007/978-3-642-39799-8_61
5. Bjørner, N., Gurfinkel, A., McMillan, K., Rybalchenko, A.: Horn clause solvers for program verification. In: Beklemishev, L.D., Blass, A., Dershowitz, N., Finkbeiner, B., Schulte, W. (eds.) Fields of Logic and Computation II. LNCS, vol. 9300, pp. 24–51. Springer, Cham (2015). doi:10.1007/978-3-319-23534-9_2
6. Bjørner, N., McMillan, K., Rybalchenko, A.: On solving universally quantified horn clauses. In: Logozzo, F., Fähndrich, M. (eds.) SAS 2013. LNCS, vol. 7935, pp. 105–125. Springer, Heidelberg (2013). doi:10.1007/978-3-642-38856-9_8
7. Carbin, M., Kim, D., Misailovic, S., Rinard, M.C.: Verified integrity properties for safe approximate program transformations. In: Proceedings of the ACM SIGPLAN 2013 Workshop on Partial Evaluation and Program Manipulation, pp. 63–66. ACM (2013)
8. Chakarov, A., Sankaranarayanan, S.: Probabilistic program analysis with martingales. In: Sharygina, N., Veith, H. (eds.) CAV 2013. LNCS, vol. 8044, pp. 511–526. Springer, Heidelberg (2013). doi:10.1007/978-3-642-39799-8_34
9. Chakraborty, S., Fremont, D., Meel, K., Seshia, S., Vardi, M.: Distribution-aware sampling and weighted model counting for SAT (2014)
10. Chatterjee, K., Fu, H., Novotný, P., Hasheminezhad, R.: Algorithmic analysis of qualitative and quantitative termination problems for affine probabilistic programs. ACM SIGPLAN Not. **51**(1), 327–342 (2016)
11. Chavira, M., Darwiche, A.: On probabilistic inference by weighted model counting. Artif. Intell. **172**(6–7), 772–799 (2008)
12. Chistikov, D., Dimitrova, R., Majumdar, R.: Approximate counting in SMT and value estimation for probabilistic programs. In: 21st International Conference on Tools and Algorithms for the Construction and Analysis of Systems, TACAS 2015, Held as Part of the European Joint Conferences on Theory and Practice of Software, ETAPS 2015, London, UK, 11–18 April 2015. Proceedings, pp. 320–334 (2015). doi:10.1007/978-3-662-46681-0_26
13. Cousot, P., Monerau, M.: Probabilistic abstract interpretation. In: Seidl, H. (ed.) ESOP 2012. LNCS, vol. 7211, pp. 169–193. Springer, Heidelberg (2012). doi:10.1007/978-3-642-28869-2_9

14. De Loera, J., Dutra, B., Koeppe, M., Moreinis, S., Pinto, G., Wu, J.: Software for exact integration of polynomials over polyhedra. ACM Commun. Comput. Algebra **45**(3/4), 169–172 (2012)
15. Raedt, L., Kersting, K.: Probabilistic inductive logic programming. In: Raedt, L., Frasconi, P., Kersting, K., Muggleton, S. (eds.) Probabilistic Inductive Logic Programming. LNCS, vol. 4911, pp. 1–27. Springer, Heidelberg (2008). doi:10.1007/978-3-540-78652-8_1
16. Dwork, C.: Differential Privacy. In: Bugliesi, M., Preneel, B., Sassone, V., Wegener, I. (eds.) ICALP 2006. LNCS, vol. 4052, pp. 1–12. Springer, Heidelberg (2006). doi:10.1007/11787006_1
17. Esparza, J., Kucera, A., Mayr, R.: Model checking probabilistic pushdown automata. In: Proceedings of the 19th Annual IEEE Symposium on Logic in Computer Science, 2004, pp. 12–21. IEEE (2004)
18. Etessami, K., Yannakakis, M.: Recursive markov chains, stochastic grammars, and monotone systems of nonlinear equations. In: Diekert, V., Durand, B. (eds.) STACS 2005. LNCS, vol. 3404, pp. 340–352. Springer, Heidelberg (2005). doi:10.1007/978-3-540-31856-9_28
19. Filieri, A., Păsăreanu, C.S., Visser, W.: Reliability analysis in symbolic pathfinder. In: Proceedings of the 2013 International Conference on Software Engineering, pp. 622–631. IEEE Press (2013)
20. Fuhr, N.: Probabilistic datalog—a logic for powerful retrieval methods. In: Proceedings of the 18th Annual International ACM SIGIR Conference on Research and Development in Information Retrieval, pp. 282–290. ACM (1995)
21. Gehr, T., Misailovic, S., Vechev, M.: PSI: exact symbolic inference for probabilistic programs. In: Chaudhuri, S., Farzan, A. (eds.) CAV 2016. LNCS, vol. 9779, pp. 62–83. Springer, Cham (2016). doi:10.1007/978-3-319-41528-4_4
22. Geldenhuys, J., Dwyer, M.B., Visser, W.: Probabilistic symbolic execution. In: Proceedings of the 2012 International Symposium on Software Testing and Analysis, pp. 166–176. ACM (2012)
23. Goodman, N.D.: The principles and practice of probabilistic programming. ACM SIGPLAN Not. **48**(1), 399–402 (2013)
24. Grebenshchikov, S., Gupta, A., Lopes, N.P., Popeea, C., Rybalchenko, A.: HSF(C): a software verifier based on horn clauses. In: Flanagan, C., König, B. (eds.) TACAS 2012. LNCS, vol. 7214, pp. 549–551. Springer, Heidelberg (2012). doi:10.1007/978-3-642-28756-5_46
25. Grebenshchikov, S., Lopes, N.P., Popeea, C., Rybalchenko, A.: Synthesizing software verifiers from proof rules. ACM SIGPLAN Not. **47**(6), 405–416 (2012)
26. Gulwani, S., McCloskey, B., Tiwari, A.: Lifting abstract interpreters to quantified logical domains. ACM SIGPLAN Not. **43**, 235–246 (2008). ACM
27. Gurfinkel, A., Kahsai, T., Komuravelli, A., Navas, J.A.: The SeaHorn verification framework. In: Kroening, D., Păsăreanu, C.S. (eds.) CAV 2015. LNCS, vol. 9206, pp. 343–361. Springer, Cham (2015). doi:10.1007/978-3-319-21690-4_20
28. Heath, J., Kwiatkowska, M., Norman, G., Parker, D., Tymchyshyn, O.: Probabilistic model checking of complex biological pathways. Theoret. Comput. Sci. **391**(3), 239–257 (2008)
29. Jha, S.K., Clarke, E.M., Langmead, C.J., Legay, A., Platzer, A., Zuliani, P.: A bayesian approach to model checking biological systems. In: Degano, P., Gorrieri, R. (eds.) CMSB 2009. LNCS, vol. 5688, pp. 218–234. Springer, Heidelberg (2009). doi:10.1007/978-3-642-03845-7_15

30. Katoen, J.-P., McIver, A.K., Meinicke, L.A., Morgan, C.C.: Linear-invariant generation for probabilistic programs. In: Cousot, R., Martel, M. (eds.) SAS 2010. LNCS, vol. 6337, pp. 390–406. Springer, Heidelberg (2010). doi:10.1007/978-3-642-15769-1_24
31. Kozen, D.: Semantics of probabilistic programs. J. Comput. Syst. Sci. **22**(3), 328–350 (1981)
32. Kwiatkowska, M., Norman, G., Parker, D.: PRISM 4.0: verification of probabilistic real-time systems. In: Gopalakrishnan, G., Qadeer, S. (eds.) CAV 2011. LNCS, vol. 6806, pp. 585–591. Springer, Heidelberg (2011). doi:10.1007/978-3-642-22110-1_47
33. Lal, A., Qadeer, S.: Dag inlining: a decision procedure for reachability-modulo-theories in hierarchical programs. ACM SIGPLAN Not. **50**, 280–290 (2015). ACM
34. Legay, A., Delahaye, B., Bensalem, S.: Statistical model checking: an overview. In: Barringer, H., et al. (eds.) RV 2010. LNCS, vol. 6418, pp. 122–135. Springer, Heidelberg (2010). doi:10.1007/978-3-642-16612-9_11
35. Luckow, K., Păsăreanu, C.S., Dwyer, M.B., Filieri, A., Visser, W.: Exact and approximate probabilistic symbolic execution for nondeterministic programs. In: Proceedings of the 29th ACM/IEEE International Conference on Automated Software Engineering, pp. 575–586. ACM (2014)
36. McIver, A., Morgan, C.C.: Abstraction. Refinement and Proof for Probabilistic Systems. Springer, New York (2006)
37. McMillan, K.L., Rybalchenko, A.: Solving constrained horn clauses using interpolation. Technical report MSR-TR-2013-6 (2013)
38. Monniaux, D.: Abstract interpretation of probabilistic semantics. In: Palsberg, J. (ed.) SAS 2000. LNCS, vol. 1824, pp. 322–339. Springer, Heidelberg (2000). doi:10.1007/978-3-540-45099-3_17
39. Monniaux, D.: An abstract monte-carlo method for the analysis of probabilistic programs. ACM SIGPLAN Not. **36**, 93–101 (2001). ACM
40. Pfeffer, A., Koller, D.: Semantics and inference for recursive probability models. In: AAAI/IAAI, pp. 538–544 (2000)
41. Sampson, A., Panchekha, P., Mytkowicz, T., McKinley, K.S., Grossman, D., Ceze, L.: Expressing and verifying probabilistic assertions. ACM SIGPLAN Not. **49**(6), 112–122 (2014)
42. Sankaranarayanan, S., Chakarov, A., Gulwani, S.: Static analysis for probabilistic programs: inferring whole program properties from finitely many paths. In: ACM SIGPLAN Conference on Programming Language Design and Implementation, PLDI 2013, Seattle, WA, USA, 16–19 June 2013, pp. 447–458 (2013). doi:10.1145/2462156.2462179
43. Stockmeyer, L.: On approximation algorithms for #p. SIAM J. Comput. **14**(4), 849–861 (1985)
44. Wojtczak, D., Etessami, K.: **PReMo**: an analyzer for **P**robabilistic **Re**cursive **Mo**dels. In: Grumberg, O., Huth, M. (eds.) TACAS 2007. LNCS, vol. 4424, pp. 66–71. Springer, Heidelberg (2007). doi:10.1007/978-3-540-71209-1_7

Combining Forward and Backward Abstract Interpretation of Horn Clauses

Alexey Bakhirkin[1,2(✉)] and David Monniaux[1,2]

[1] Univ. Grenoble Alpes, VERIMAG, 38000 Grenoble, France
{alexey.bakhirkin,david.monniaux}@univ-grenoble-alpes.fr
[2] CNRS, VERIMAG, 38000 Grenoble, France

Abstract. Alternation of forward and backward analyses is a standard technique in abstract interpretation of *programs*, which is in particular useful when we wish to prove unreachability of some undesired program states. The current state-of-the-art technique for combining forward (bottom-up, in logic programming terms) and backward (top-down) abstract interpretation of *Horn clauses* is query-answer transformation. It transforms a system of Horn clauses, such that standard forward analysis can propagate constraints both forward, and backward from a goal. Query-answer transformation is effective, but has issues that we wish to address. For that, we introduce a new backward collecting semantics, which is suitable for alternating forward and backward abstract interpretation of Horn clauses. We show how the alternation can be used to prove unreachability of the goal and how every subsequent run of an analysis yields a refined model of the system. Experimentally, we observe that combining forward and backward analyses is important for analysing systems that encode questions about reachability in C programs. In particular, the combination that follows our new semantics improves the precision of our own abstract interpreter, including when compared to a forward analysis of a query-answer-transformed system.

1 Introduction

In the past years, there has been much interest in using Horn clauses for program analysis, i.e., to encode the program semantics and the analysis questions as a system of Horn clauses and then use a dedicated Horn clause solver to find a model of the system or show its unsatisfiability (see e.g., [11]). In particular, collecting semantics of programs and reachability questions can be encoded as *constrained Horn clauses*, or *CHCs*.

With this approach, Horn clauses become a common language that allows different tools to exchange program models, analysis questions and analysis results. For example, as part of this work, we implemented a polyhedra-based abstract

This work was partially supported by the European Research Council under the European Union's Seventh Framework Programme (FP/2007-2013)/ERC Grant Agreement nr. 306595 "STATOR".

F. Ranzato (Ed.): SAS 2017, LNCS 10422, pp. 23–45, 2017.
DOI: 10.1007/978-3-319-66706-5_2

interpreter for CHCs. We use an existing tool SeaHorn [22] to convert questions about reachability in C programs into systems of CHCs, and this way we can use our abstract interpreter to analyse numeric C programs without having to ourselves implement the semantics of C. Additionally, Horn clauses allow to build complicated abstract models of programs, as opposed to implementing the abstraction mostly as part of the abstract domain. For example, D. Monniaux and L. Gonnord propose [36] a way to abstract programs that use arrays into array-free Horn clauses, and we are not aware of a domain that implements their abstraction.

On the other hand, this approach makes it more important to implement different precision-related techniques and heuristics in the analyser, since we have little control over how the problem description is formulated, when it is produced by an external procedure. One technique that is important for disproving reachability using abstract interpretation is the combination of forward and backward analyses. The idea is to alternate forward and backward analyses, and build an over-approximation of the set of states that are both reachable from the program entry and can reach an undesired state (Patrick and Radhia Cousot give a good explanation of the technique [18, section 4]).

Patrick and Radhia Cousot also propose to use a combination of forward and backward analyses a for logic programs [17]. Their combination is based on the intersection of forward (bottom-up, in logic programming terms[1]) and backward (top-down) collecting semantics, which, as we observe in Sect. 3, is too over-approximate for our purposes. The current state-of-the-art technique for combining forward and backward analyses of Horn clauses is query-answer transformation [28]. The idea is to transform a system of Horn clauses, such that standard forward analysis can propagate constraints both forward from the facts, and backward from a goal. Query-answer transformation is effective, e.g., B. Kafle and J.P. Gallagher report [28] that it increases the number of benchmark programs that can be proven safe both by their abstract interpreter and by a pre-existing CEGAR-based analyser. Still, query-answer transformation has some issues, which we outline (together with its advantages) in Sect. 2.3 and revisit in Sect. 3.2.

To address the issues of the existing techniques, we introduce a new backward collecting semantics of CHCs, which offers more precision when combining forward and backward abstract interpretation. We show how the analysis based on the new semantics can be used to prove unreachability of a goal and how every subsequent run of the analysis yields a refined model of the system. In particular, if the goal is proven to be unreachable, our analysis can produce a model of the system that is disjoint from the goal, which allows to check the results of the analysis and to communicate them to other tools. These are the

---

[1] In this paper, we use the terms *bottom-up* and *top-down* in the meanings that they bear in logic programming and thus they correspond to *forward* and *backward* analysis respectively. In program analysis, *bottom-up* may mean *from callees to callers* or *from children to parents in the AST*, but this is *not* the meaning that we intend in this paper.

main contributions of this paper. To evaluate our approach, we take programs from the categories "loops", and "recursive" of the Competition on Software Verification SV-COMP [2]. We use the existing tool SeaHorn to translate these programs to systems of Horn clauses. We observe that the alternation of forward and backward analyses following our new semantics improves the precision of our own abstract interpreter (i.e., it allows to prove safety of more safe programs) including when compared to forward analysis of a query-answer-transformed system.

2 Background

We say that a *term* is a variable, a constant, or an application of an *interpreted* function to a vector of terms. To denote vectors of terms, we use bold letters. Thus, $\mathbf{t}$ denotes a vector of terms; $\varphi[\mathbf{x}]$ (assuming elements of $\mathbf{x}$ are distinct) denotes a formula φ, where the set of free variables is the set of elements of $\mathbf{x}$; and $\varphi[\mathbf{x}/\mathbf{t}]$ denotes a formula that is obtained from φ by simultaneously replacing (substituting) every occurrence of $x_i \in \mathbf{x}$ with the corresponding element $t_i \in \mathbf{t}$.

CHCs. A constrained Horn clause (CHC) is a first order formula of the form

$$\forall X. \big(p_1(\mathbf{t_1}) \land p_2(\mathbf{t_2}) \land \cdots \land p_n(\mathbf{t_n}) \land \varphi \Rightarrow p_{n+1}(\mathbf{t_{n+1}}) \big)$$

where p_i are uninterpreted predicate symbols, $\mathbf{t}_i$ are vectors of terms; φ is a quantifier-free formula in some background theory and does not contain uninterpreted predicates or uninterpreted functions; and X includes all free variables of the formula under the quantifier. Following standard notation in the literature, we write a Horn clause as

$$p_{n+1}(\mathbf{t_{n+1}}) \leftarrow \varphi, p_1(\mathbf{t_1}), p_2(\mathbf{t_2}), \cdots, p_n(\mathbf{t_n})$$

that is, with free variables being *implicitly* universally quantified. We use a capital letter to denote an *application* of a predicate to *some* vector of terms (while for predicate symbols, we use lowercase letters). Thus, when the terms in predicate applications are not important, we can write the above clause as

$$P_{n+1} \leftarrow \varphi, P_1, P_2, \cdots, P_n$$

The predicate application P_{n+1} is called the *head* of the clause, and the conjunction $\varphi, P_1, P_2, \cdots, P_n$ is called the *body*. A CHC always has a predicate application as its head. *But*, we assume that there exists a distinguished 0-ary predicate $\mathfrak{f}$ that denotes falsity and is only allowed to appear in the head of a clause. A clause that has $\mathfrak{f}$ as its head is called an *integrity constraint*. For example, an assertion $\psi \leftarrow \varphi, P$ can be written as the integrity constraint: $\mathfrak{f} \leftarrow (\varphi \land \neg\psi), P$.

A *system* is a set of CHCs that is interpreted as their conjunction.

Models of CHCs. We say that an *atom* is a formula of the form $p(c_1, \cdots, c_n)$, where p is an n-ary predicate symbol and c_i are constants. We denote the set of all atoms by $\mathbb{A}$.

An *interpretation* is a set of *atoms* $M \subseteq \mathbb{A}$. One can say that an interpretation gives *truth assignment* to atoms: an atom is interpreted as *true* if it belongs to the interpretation and as *false* otherwise. This way, an interpretation also provides a truth assignment to every formula, by induction on the formula structure.

For a system of CHCs, a *model* (or *solution*) is an interpretation that makes every clause in the system *true* (note that all variables in a system of Horn clauses are universally quantified, and thus the model does not include variable valuations). We call a model $M \subseteq \mathbb{A}$ *safe* when $\mathfrak{f} \notin M$ (many authors prefer to call an interpretation M a model only when it does not include $\mathfrak{f}$, but we prefer to have both notions). A system of CHCs always has the *minimal* model w.r.t. subset ordering (see, e.g., [26, section 4]). If a system has no clauses of the form $P \leftarrow \varphi$, its least model is $\varnothing$. We call a system of CHCs safe iff it has a safe model. In particular, for a safe system, its least model is safe, and thus, for a safe system, there exists the smallest safe model. For every system of CHCs, the set of atoms $\mathbb{A}$ is the greatest (unsafe) model, but a safe system in general may not have the greatest safe model.

Fixed Point Characterization of the Least Model. A system of CHCs $\mathbb{H}$ induces the *direct consequence relation* $\mathbb{T}_{\mathbb{H}} \subseteq \mathcal{P}(\mathbb{A}) \times \mathbb{A}$, which is constructed as follows. A tuple $(\{p_1(\mathbf{c_1}), \cdots, p_n(\mathbf{c_n})\}, p_{n+1}(\mathbf{c_{n+1}})) \in \mathbb{T}_{\mathbb{H}}$ iff the system $\mathbb{H}$ contains a clause $p_{n+1}(\mathbf{t_{n+1}}) \leftarrow \varphi, p_1(\mathbf{t_1}), \cdots, p_n(\mathbf{t_n})$, such that $\varphi \wedge \bigwedge_{i=1}^{n+1} \mathbf{c_i} = \mathbf{t_i}$ is satisfiable.[2] In particular, every clause of the form $p(\mathbf{t}) \leftarrow \varphi$ induces a set of *initial transitions* (or *initial consecutions*) of the form $(\varnothing, p(\mathbf{c}))$, where $\varphi \wedge (\mathbf{c} = \mathbf{t})$ is satisfiable. Direct consequence relation can be seen as a variant of a direct consequence function discussed by J. Jaffar and M.J. Maher [26, section 4].

Note that $\mathbb{T}_{\mathbb{H}}$ is unlike an ordinary transition relation and relates a *set* of atoms with a single atom that is their direct consequence. To work with such a relation, we can adapt the standard in program analysis definition of post-condition as follows:

$$\mathrm{post}(\mathbb{T}_{\mathbb{H}}, X) = \{a' \mid \exists A \subseteq X.\, (A, a') \in \mathbb{T}_{\mathbb{H}}\}$$

Then, the least model of $\mathbb{H}$ can be characterised as the least fixed point:

$$\mathrm{lfp}_{\subseteq} \lambda X.\, \mathrm{post}(\mathbb{T}_{\mathbb{H}}, X) \tag{1}$$

As standard in abstract interpretation, we call the fixed point (1) the forward (bottom-up, in logic programming terms) collecting semantics of $\mathbb{H}$. In general, every pre-fixpoint of the consequence operator, i.e., every set M, s.t. $\mathrm{post}(\mathbb{T}_{\mathbb{H}}, M) \subseteq M$ is a model of $\mathbb{H}$.

Analysis Questions. Given a system of CHCs $\mathbb{H}$, the analysis question may be stated in a number of ways. Often we want to know whether the system is safe, i.e., whether the least model of $\mathbb{H}$ contains $\mathfrak{f}$. More generally, we may be

[2] There may be a slight abuse of notation here. When writing down the set as $\{p_1(\mathbf{c_1}), \cdots, p_n(\mathbf{c_n})\}$, we do *not* assume that all p_i or all $\mathbf{c_i}$ are distinct and that the set has exactly n elements.

given a set of goal atoms $A_g \subseteq \mathbb{A}$. Then, the analysis question will be whether the goal is unreachable, i.e. whether the goal and the least model are disjoint. In this case, we start by computing a (reasonably small) model M of $\mathbb{H}$. If $M \cap A_g = \varnothing$, we conclude that the goal is unreachable. Otherwise, we either report an inconclusive result (since the computed M will in general not be the smallest model), or attempt to compute a refined model $M' \subset M$.

Alternatively, we may want to produce a model of $\mathbb{H}$ that gives us some non-trivial information about the object described by $\mathbb{H}$. In this case, we usually want to produce some reasonably small model, which is what abstract interpretation tries to do. The goal may or may not be given. For example, we may be only interested in some part of the object (say, a subset of procedures in a program), which is described by a subset of predicates Π. Then, the goal will be the corresponding set of atoms $A_g = \{p(\mathbf{c}) \mid p \in \Pi\}$.

2.1 Abstract Interpretation of CHCs

Abstract interpretation [15] provides us a way to *compute an over-approximation* of the least model, following the fixed point characterization. To do so, we introduce the *abstract domain* $\mathbb{D}$ with the least element $\bot$, greatest element $\top$, partial order $\sqsubseteq$ and join $\sqcup$. Every element of the abstract domain $d \in \mathbb{D}$ represents the set of atoms $\gamma(d) \subseteq \mathbb{A}$. Then, we introduce the abstract consequence operator $\text{post}^\sharp$ which over-approximates the concrete operator post, i.e., for every $d \in \mathbb{D}$, $\gamma(\text{post}^\sharp(H, d)) \supseteq \text{post}(\mathbb{T}_\mathbb{H}, \gamma(d))$. If we are able to find such element $d_m \in \mathbb{D}$ that $\text{post}^\sharp(H, d_m) \sqsubseteq d_m$ then $\gamma(d_m)$ is a pre-fixpoint of the direct consequence operator and thus a model of $\mathbb{H}$ (not necessarily the smallest one). At this point, it does not matter how we compute d_m. It may be a limit of a Kleene-like iteration sequence (as in our implementation) or it may be produced by policy iteration [20,31], etc.

One can expect that an element $d \in \mathbb{D}$ is partitioned by predicate, in the same way as in program analysis, domain elements are partitioned by program location. In the simple case, every element $d \in \mathbb{D}$ will have a logical representation in some theory and one can think that it maps every predicate p_i to a quantifier-free formula $\delta_i[\mathbf{x_i}]$, where $\mathbf{x_i}$ correspond to the arguments of p_i. For example, when using a polyhedral domain, d will map every predicate to a conjunction of linear constraints. For simplicity of syntactic manipulations, we can assume that $\mathbf{x_i}$ are distinct vectors of distinct variables, i.e., a given variable appears only in one vector $\mathbf{x_i}$ and only once.

From this, we can derive a recipe for Kleene-like iteration. Let $d \in \mathbb{D}$ be the current fixpoint candidate that maps every predicate p_i to a formula $\delta_i[\mathbf{x_i}]$. We try to find a clause $p_{n+1}(\mathbf{t_{n+1}}) \leftarrow \varphi, p_1(\mathbf{t_1}), \cdots, p_n(\mathbf{t_n})$ (where $n \geq 0$), such that the following formula is satisfiable:

$$\varphi \wedge \delta_1[\mathbf{x_1}/\mathbf{t_1}] \wedge \cdots \wedge \delta_n[\mathbf{x_n}/\mathbf{t_n}] \wedge \neg\delta_{n+1}[\mathbf{x_{n+1}}/\mathbf{t_{n+1}}] \qquad (2)$$

If it is, we find a *set* of models of (2), and if some model assigns the vector of constants $\mathbf{c_{n+1}}$ to the variables $\mathbf{x_{n+1}}$, we join the atom $p_{n+1}(\mathbf{c_{n+1}})$ to d.

In a polyhedral analysis, we usually want to find in every step a *convex* set models of (2). Assuming the formula is in negation normal form, there is a naïve way to generalize a single model to a convex set of models by recursively traversing the formula and collecting atomic propositions satisfied by the model (descending into all sub-formulas for a conjunction and into one sub-formula for a disjunction). In general though, this corresponds to a problem of finding a model of a Boolean formula that is in some sense optimal (see, e.g., the work of J. Marques-Silva et al. [34]). When the set of CHCs is produced from a program by means of large block encoding [10] (e.g., SeaHorn does this by default), then φ is disjunctive and represents some set of paths through the original program. Finding a convex set of models of (2) corresponds to finding a path through the original program, along which we need to propagate the post-condition. In program analysis, a similar technique is called *path focusing* [23,35].

Checking the Model. Given an element $d \in \mathbb{D}$, we can check whether it represents a model by taking its abstract consequence. If $\text{post}^\sharp(\mathbb{H}, d) \sqsubseteq d$ then $\gamma(d)$ is a pre-fixpoint of the direct consequence operator and thus is a model of $\mathbb{H}$. When d can be represented in a logical form and maps every predicate p_i to a formula $\delta_i[\mathbf{x_i}]$ in some theory, we can check whether it represents a model (i.e., that for every clause, the formula (2) is unsatisfiable) using an SMT solver. Being able to check the obtained models provides a building block for making a *verifiable* static analyser.

2.2 Program Analysis and CHCs

Different flavours of Horn clauses can be used to encode in logic form different program analysis questions. In particular, CHCs can be used to encode invariant generation and reachability problems. In such an encoding, uninterpreted predicates typically denote sets of reachable memory states at different program locations, clauses of the form $P_{n+1} \leftarrow \varphi, P_1, P_2, \cdots, P_n$ encode the semantics of transitions between the locations, clauses of the form $P \leftarrow \varphi$ encode the initial states, and the integrity constraints (of the form $\mathfrak{f} \leftarrow \varphi, P$) encode the assertions. In this paper, we limit ourselves to invariant generation and reachability, but other program analysis questions (including verification of temporal properties [9]) can be encoded using other flavours of Horn clauses. For more information, an interested reader can refer to a recent survey [11].

Example 1 - Parallel Increment. Consider a program in Fig. 1. It starts by setting two variables, x and y, to zero and then increments both of them in a loop a non-deterministic number of times. An analyser is supposed to prove that after the loop finishes, x and y have equal values. This program also has an unreachable condition $x < 0$ upon which only x is incremented, which will be useful in the next example. The program in Fig. 1 can be encoded into CHCs as shown in Fig. 2, where the predicate p denotes the set of reachable states at the head of the loop, and its arguments denote the variables x and y respectively. From the point of view of abstract interpretation, such a system of CHCs represents a program's collecting semantics. For simple programs, as the one in Fig. 1,

```
x = y = 0;
while (*) {
  if (x ≥ 0) {
    x += 1; y += 1;
  } else {
    x += 1;
  }
}
assert(x == y);
```

Fig. 1. A program that increments x and y in parallel.

$$
\begin{aligned}
&p(x, y) \leftarrow x = 0 \wedge y = 0\\
&p(x + 1, y + 1) \leftarrow x \geq 0, p(x, y)\\
&p(x + 1, y) \leftarrow x < 0, p(x, y)\\
&\mathfrak{f} \leftarrow x \neq y, p(x, y)
\end{aligned}
$$

Fig. 2. Horn clause encoding of the program in Fig. 1.

a model of the system of CHCs directly represents an inductive invariant of the program. For the more complicated programs (e.g., programs with procedures) this may no longer be true, but in any case, if we find a safe (not containing $\mathfrak{f}$) model of the system of CHCs, we can usually conclude that the program cannot reach an assertion violation. A model that we find with abstract interpretation will assign to every predicate an element of some abstract domain; for a numeric program this may be a convex polyhedron (or a small number of polyhedra) in a space where every dimension corresponds to a predicate argument. Thus, for us to be able to prove safety of a program, the system of CHCs has to have a safe model of the given form.

Horn clause encoding of programs without procedures is typically straightforward and results in a system, where every clause has at most one predicate application in the body; such clauses are often called *linear*. Encoding of programs with procedures is also possible, but there are multiple ways of doing it. We now give an example of a program with a procedure.

```
void inc_xy() {
  if (x ≥ 0) {
    x += 1; y += 1;
  } else {
    x += 1;
  }
}
...
x = y = 0;
while (*)
  inc_xy();
assert(x == y);
```

Fig. 3. A program that increments x and y in parallel using a procedure.

$$
\begin{aligned}
&p(x, y) \leftarrow x = 0 \wedge y = 0\\
&p(x', y') \leftarrow f(x, y, x', y'), p(x, y)\\
&\mathfrak{f} \leftarrow x \neq y, p(x, y)\\
&f(x, y, x + 1, y + 1) \leftarrow x \geq 0, f_c(x, y)\\
&f(x, y, x + 1, y) \leftarrow x < 0, f_c(x, y)\\
&f_c(x, y) \leftarrow \mathit{true}
\end{aligned}
$$

Fig. 4. A possible Horn clause encoding of the program in Fig. 3.

Example 2 - Parallel Increment Using a Procedure. Consider a program in Fig. 3. Similarly to Example 1, it starts by setting two variables, x and y, to zero and then increments both of them in a loop, but this time by calling an auxiliary procedure. Again the procedure has an unreachable condition $x < 0$ upon which it only increments x. If we encode this program into CHCs directly (without inlining of `inc_xy`), we may arrive at a system as in Fig. 4. This roughly corresponds to how the tool SeaHorn encodes procedures that do not contain assertions. As before, the predicate p denotes the reachable states at the loop head. A new predicate f denotes the *input-output relation* of the procedure `inc_xy`. If $f(x_1, y_1, x_2, y_2)$ holds, this means that if at the entry of `inc_xy` $x = x_1$ and $y = y_1$ then at the exit of `inc_xy`, it *may* be the case that $x = x_2$ and $y = y_2$. In general, every predicate that corresponds to a location inside a procedure, will have two sets of arguments: one set will correspond to the state at the entry of the procedure (as the first two arguments of f) and the other, to the corresponding state at the given location (as the last two arguments of f). Note that another new predicate, f_c, is purely auxiliary and does *not* denote the reachable states at the at the initial location of `inc_xy`. To solve the system in Fig. 4, we need to approximate the full transition relation of `inc_xy`, which includes approximating the outputs for the inputs, with which the procedure is never called. If we analyse this program in a polyhedral domain, we will notice that the full input-output relation of `inc_xy` cannot be approximated in a useful way by a single convex polyhedron. But if we restrict the analysis to the reachable states, where $x \geq 0$ always holds, we will be able to infer that `inc_xy` increments both x and y, and this will allow to prove safety of the program.

One may argue that we should alter the way we encode procedures and constrain f_c to denote the set of reachable states at the entry of `inc_xy`. But when building an analysis tool, we should cater for different possible encodings.

2.3 Combination of Forward and Backward Program Analyses

Example 2 demonstrates the general problem of communicating analysis results between different program locations. In an inter-procedural analysis, often we do not want to explicitly build the full input-output relation of a procedure. For the inputs, with which a procedure may be called, we *do* want to find the corresponding outputs, but for the other inputs we may want to report that the output is unknown. This is because often, as in Example 2, the full input-output relation will not have a useful approximation as a domain element. At the same time, a useful approximation may exist when we consider only reachable inputs. Similar considerations hold for intra-procedural analysis. If we want to prove that an assertion violation is unreachable, we do not need to explicitly represent the full inductive invariant of a program. Instead, we want to approximate the set of states that are both reachable from the initial states and may reach an assertion violation. If this set turns out to be empty, we can conclude that an assertion violation is unreachable. This technique is standard for program analysis, and in Sect. 3, we adapt it to CHCs.

An alternative technique for Horn clauses is query-answer transformation [28]. Given the original system of CHCs $\mathbb{H}$, we build the transformed system $\mathbb{H}^{\mathrm{qa}}$. For every uninterpreted predicate p in $\mathbb{H}$ (including $\mathfrak{f}$), $\mathbb{H}^{\mathrm{qa}}$ contains a query predicate p^q and an answer predicate p^a. The clauses of $\mathbb{H}^{\mathrm{qa}}$ are constructed as follows.

- *Answer clauses.* For every clause $P_{n+1} \leftarrow \varphi, P_1, \cdots, P_n$ (where $n \geq 0$) in $\mathbb{H}$, the system $\mathbb{H}^{\mathrm{qa}}$ contains the clause $P^a_{n+1} \leftarrow \varphi, P^q_{n+1}, P^a_1, \cdots, P^a_n$.
- *Query clauses.* For every clause $P_{n+1} \leftarrow \varphi, P_1, \cdots, P_n$ (where $n \geq 0$) in $\mathbb{H}$, the system $\mathbb{H}^{\mathrm{qa}}$ contains the clauses:

$$\begin{aligned}
&P^q_1 \leftarrow \varphi, P^q_{n+1} \\
&P^q_2 \leftarrow \varphi, P^q_{n+1}, P^a_1 \\
&\cdots \\
&P^q_n \leftarrow \varphi, P^q_{n+1}, P^a_1, \cdots, P^a_{n-1}
\end{aligned}$$

- *Goal clause* $\mathfrak{f}^q \leftarrow$ *true*.

Then, forward (bottom-up) analysis of $\mathbb{H}^{\mathrm{qa}}$ corresponds to a combination of forward and backward (top-down) analyses of $\mathbb{H}$.

We experienced several issues with the query-answer transformation. For linear systems of CHCs, forward analysis of $\mathbb{H}^{\mathrm{qa}}$ corresponds to a single run of backward analysis of $\mathbb{H}$ followed by a single run of forward analysis. For non-linear systems, this gets more complicated, though, as there will be recursive dependencies between query and answer predicates, and the propagation of information will depend on the order, in which query clauses are created. We observed that is not enough, and for some systems the analysis needs to propagate the information forward and then backward multiple times. This usually happens when the abstract domain of the analysis cannot capture the relation between the program variables.

Example 3. In Fig. 5, we show a synthetic example of a program that needs more than one alternation of forward and backward analysis to be proven safe. Notice that this program is safe, as after entering the `if`-branch in line 4 we have that $x > 0$ and $x = ky$ for some $k \geq 0$, therefore y is also greater than 0, and this is not changed by adding x to y in lines 5–6. If we work in a polyhedral domain, we cannot capture the relation $\exists k \geq 0.\, x = ky$ and therefore should proceed with the safety proof in a different way, e.g., as follows. First, we run a forward analysis and establish that at lines 5–7, $x > 0$, since these lines are inside the `if`-branch. Then, we run a backward analysis starting with the set of states $y < 0$ at line 7, which corresponds to the assertion violation. Since the loop in lines 5–6 can only increase y, we establish that for y to be less than zero in line 7, it also has to be less than zero in lines 1–6. Finally, we run forward analysis again and establish that for the assertion violation to be reachable, x at line 4 has to be both greater than zero (so that we enter the *if*-branch), and less-or-equal to zero (because x starts being zero and in lines 2–3 we repeatedly add a negative number to it), which is not possible. While this particular example is synthetic, in our experiments we observe a small number of SV-COMP programs where a similar situation arises.

```
x = 0; y = *;
while(*)
  x += y;
if (x > 0) {
  while(*)
    y += x;
  assert(y ≥ 0);
}
```

Fig. 5. Program, where polyhedral analysis needs to propagate information forward and backward multiple times.

A more subtle (but more benign) issue is that when solving the query-answer-transformed system, we are actually not interested in the elements of the interpretation of p^a, which are outside of p^q, but this is not captured in $\mathbb{H}^{\mathrm{qa}}$ itself. Because of this, p^a may be over-approximated too much as a result of widening or join. Perhaps this is one of the reasons why B. Kafle and J.P. Gallagher propose [28] to perform abstract interpretation in two phases. First, they analyse the transformed system $\mathbb{H}^{\mathrm{qa}}$. Then, they strengthen the original system with the interpretations of *answer* predicates and run an analysis on the strengthened system.

To address these issues, we decided to adapt the standard (for program analysis) alternation of forward and backward analysis to CHCs. We return to the comparison of our approach to query-answer transformation in Sect. 3.2.

3 Combining Forward and Backward Analysis of CHCs

Patrick and Radhia Cousot proposed a backward (top-down) semantics for Horn clauses, which collects atoms that can appear in an SLD-resolution proof [17]. We take their definition as a starting point and define a new backward semantics and a new more precise combined forward-backward semantics. Then we show, how we can use our new semantics to disprove reachability of a goal and to refine a model w.r.t. the goal.

Backward Transformers and Collecting Semantics. First, let us introduce the pre-condition operation as follows. For a system $\mathbb{H}$,

$$\mathrm{pre}(\mathbb{T}_{\mathbb{H}}, A') = \{a \mid \exists A \subseteq \mathbb{A}.\, \exists a' \in A'.(A, a') \in \mathbb{T}_{\mathbb{H}} \wedge a \in A\}$$

Then, for a system $\mathbb{H}$ and a set of goal atoms A_g, the backward (top-down) semantics is characterized by the least fixed point:

$$\mathrm{lfp}_{\subseteq} \lambda X. A_g \cup \mathrm{pre}(\mathbb{T}_{\mathbb{H}}, X) \tag{3}$$

which corresponds to the semantics proposed by Patrick and Radhia Cousot. This definition of backward semantics has a drawback though. The intersection of forward semantics (1) and backward semantics (3) *over-approximates* the set of atoms that can be derived from initial clauses (of the form $P \leftarrow \varphi$) and can be used to derive the goal.

Example 4. Let us consider the following system of CHCs, where p is a unary predicate and $c_1, \cdots, c_5$ are constants

$$\begin{aligned} &p(c_1) \leftarrow \mathit{true} &\quad p(c_5) &\leftarrow p(c_3) \\ &p(c_2) \leftarrow p(c_1) &\quad p(c_5) &\leftarrow p(c_2), p(c_4) \\ &p(c_3) \leftarrow p(c_1) && \end{aligned} \tag{4}$$

The forward semantics (1) for this system is the set $\{p(c_1), p(c_2), p(c_3), p(c_5)\}$ (note that the atom $p(c_4)$ cannot be derived). Let us assume that the set of goals is $A_g = \{p(c_5)\}$. Then, the backward semantics (3) for this system is $\{p(c_1), p(c_2), p(c_3), p(c_4), p(c_5)\}$. The intersection of forward and backward semantics is $\{p(c_1), p(c_2), p(c_3), p(c_5)\}$, even though the atom $p(c_2)$ is not used when deriving the goal $\{p(c_5)\}$ (because we cannot derive $p(c_4)$). If we implement an abstract analysis based on the intersection of semantics (1) and (3), this will become an additional source of imprecision.

3.1 Forward and Backward Analyses Combined

We wish to define a combination of forward and backward semantics that does not introduce the over-approximation observed in Example 4. For that, we propose the *restricted pre-condition* operation that we define as follows. For a restricting set $R \subseteq \mathbb{A}$,

$$\mathrm{pre}|_R(\mathbb{T}_{\mathbb{H}}, A') = \{a \mid \exists A \subseteq R.\, \exists a' \in A'.\, (A, a') \in \mathbb{T}_{\mathbb{H}} \wedge a \in A\}$$

Now, we can define the combined forward-backward collecting semantics as follows:

$$\begin{aligned} &\mathrm{lfp}_{\subseteq} \lambda X.(A_g \cap M) \cup \mathrm{pre}|_M(\mathbb{T}_{\mathbb{H}}, X) \\ &\text{where } M = \mathrm{lfp}_{\subseteq} \lambda X.\,\mathrm{post}(\mathbb{T}_{\mathbb{H}}, X) \end{aligned} \tag{5}$$

One can show that this semantics denotes the set of atoms that can be derived from initial clauses (of the form $P \leftarrow \varphi$) and can be used to derive the goal (we defer an explanation until Sect. 5). For example, one can see that for the system (4) discussed in Example 4, computing this semantics produces the set $\{p(c_1), p(c_3), p(c_5)\}$, as expected.

Introducing a restricted pre-condition operation is common, when a combination of analyses cannot be captured by the meet operation in the domain. For example, assume that we want to analyse the instruction $z := x + y$ in an interval domain. Assume also that the *pre*-condition is restricted by $x \geq 3$ (e.g., obtained by forward analysis) and the *post*-condition is $z \in [0, 2]$. In this case, *unrestricted* backwards analysis yields no new results. But if we modify the pre-condition operation to take account of the previously obtained pre-condition ($x \geq 3$ in this case), we can derive the new constraint $y \leq -1$.

It may however be unusual to see a restricted pre-condition in concrete collecting semantics. To explain it, in Sect. 5, we introduce tree semantics of CHCs and show how concrete collecting semantics is itself an abstraction of tree semantics. In particular, the intersection of forward and backward tree semantics abstracts to (5).

Abstract Transformers. As standard in abstract interpretation, we introduce over-approximate versions of forward and backward transformers, resp. $\mathrm{post}^\sharp$ and $\mathrm{pre}^\sharp$, s.t. for $d, r \in \mathbb{D}$,

$$\gamma(\mathrm{post}^\sharp(\mathbb{H}, d)) \supseteq \mathrm{post}(\mathbb{T}_{\mathbb{H}}, \gamma(d)) \qquad \gamma(\mathrm{pre}^\sharp|_r(\mathbb{H}, d)) \supseteq \mathrm{pre}|_{\gamma(r)}(\mathbb{T}_{\mathbb{H}}, \gamma(d))$$

Abstract Iteration Sequence. In concrete world, the combination of forward and backward analyses is characterized by a pair of fixed points in (5). In particular, we have the following property:

Proposition 1. *If we let* $M = \mathrm{lfp}_{\subseteq} \lambda X.\, \mathrm{post}(\mathbb{T}_{\mathbb{H}}, X)$ *and* $M' = \mathrm{lfp}_{\subseteq} \lambda X.(A_g \cap M) \cup \mathrm{pre}|_M(\mathbb{T}_{\mathbb{H}}, X)$ *then* $\mathrm{lfp}_{\subseteq} \lambda X.(\mathrm{post}(\mathbb{T}_{\mathbb{H}}, X) \cap M') = M'$.

That is, concrete forward and backward analyses need not be iterated. We give the proof of this a bit later. In the abstract world, this is not the case, as has already been noted for program analysis [18]. In general, given the abstract goal $g \in \mathbb{D}$, the combination of abstract forward and backward analyses produces the sequence:

$$\begin{aligned}
&b_0,\, d_1,\, b_1,\, d_2,\, b_2,\, \cdots,\ \text{where} \\
&b_0 = \top,\ \text{and for } i \geq 1, \\
&\mathrm{post}^\sharp(\mathbb{H}, d_i) \sqcap b_{i-1} \sqsubseteq d_i \\
&g \sqcap d_i \sqsubseteq b_i \\
&\mathrm{pre}^\sharp|_{d_i}(\mathbb{H}, b_i) \sqsubseteq b_i
\end{aligned} \tag{6}$$

In principle, this iterations sequence may be infinitely descending, and to ensure termination of an analysis, we have to limit how many elements of the sequence are computed. In our experiments though, the sequence usually stabilizes after the first few elements.

Propositions 2 and 3 respectively show how we can refine the initial model w.r.t. the goal and how we can use the iteration sequence to disprove reachability of the goal.

Proposition 2. *For every* $k \geq 1$, *the set* $\gamma(d_k) \cup \bigcup_{i=1}^{k-1} \left(\gamma(d_i) \setminus \gamma(b_i)\right)$ *is a model of* $\mathbb{H}$.

We present the proof in Appendix A.

Observe that for some abstract domains (e.g., common numeric domains: intervals, octagons, polyhedra), the meet operation is usually exact, i.e. for $d_1, d_2 \in \mathbb{D}$, $\gamma(d_1 \sqcap d_2) = \gamma(d_1) \cap \gamma(d_2)$. Also, for such domains we can expect that for $r, d \in D$, $\mathrm{pre}^\sharp|_r(\mathbb{H}, d) \sqsubseteq r$. In this case, the forward-backward iteration sequence is descending: $b_0 \sqsupseteq d_1 \sqsupseteq b_1 \sqsupseteq d_2 \sqsupseteq \cdots$, and computing every subsequent element d_i provides a tighter model of $\mathbb{H}$ (assuming d_i is distinct from d_{i-1}). This comes at a cost, though, since the refined model will not in general be expressible in the abstract domain of the analysis. For example, in a polyhedral analysis, when d_i and b_i are maps from predicates to convex polyhedra, expressing the model given by Proposition 2, requires finite sets of convex polyhedra. If we wish to check if such an object M is indeed a model of $\mathbb{H}$, we will need to check that M *geometrically covers* its post-condition. This can be done using a polyhedra library that supports powerset domains and geometric coverage (e.g., Parma Polyhedra Library [7]) or with an SMT-solver.

Now, the proof of Proposition 1 becomes straightforward.

Proof (of Proposition 1). Let $M'' = \mathrm{lfp}_{\subseteq}\lambda X.(\mathrm{post}(\mathbb{T}_{\mathbb{H}}, X) \cap M')$, i.e. $M'' \subseteq M'$ by definition. From Proposition 2, $(M \setminus M') \cup M'' \subseteq M$ is a model of $\mathbb{H}$. Since M is the smallest model, $(M \setminus M') \cup M'' = M$ and $M'' = M'$.

Proposition 3. *If there exists $k \geq 1$, s.t. $d_k = \bot$, then there exists a model M of $\mathbb{H}$, s.t. $M \cap \gamma(g) = \varnothing$ (i.e., the goal is unreachable).*

Proof. If $d_k = \bot$ then $\gamma(d_k) = \varnothing$, and from Proposition 2, $M = \bigcup_{i=1}^{k-1} \big(\gamma(d_i) \setminus \gamma(b_i)\big)$ is a model of $\mathbb{H}$. From (6), it follows that for every i, $\gamma(g) \cap \gamma(d_i) \subseteq \gamma(b_i)$, that is $(\gamma(d_i) \setminus \gamma(b_i)) \cap \gamma(g) = \varnothing$. This means that $M \cap \gamma(g) = \varnothing$.

Thus, when there exists k s.t. $d_k = \bot$, we obtain a *constructive* proof of unreachability of the goal that can later be checked.

Result of the Analysis. Propositions 2 and 3 provide a way to give additional information to the user of the analysis, apart from the verdict (*safe* or *potentially unsafe*). Suppose, we compute the iteration sequence (6) up to the element d_k and then stop (whether because $d_k = \bot$, or the sequence stabilized, or we reached a timeout, etc.). The object d_k in itself may not be interesting: it is not a model of $\mathbb{H}$, it is not a proof or a refutation of reachability of the goal. If the user wishes to check the results of the analysis, we may give them the whole iteration sequence up to d_k. Then, the user will need to confirm that the sequence indeed satisfies the conditions of (6). Alternatively, we may give the user the refined model of $\mathbb{H}$, i.e. some representation of $M = \gamma(d_k) \cup \bigcup_{i=1}^{k-1} \big(\gamma(d_i) \setminus \gamma(b_i)\big)$. This will allow the user to not only check the model, but also, e.g., produce program invariants that can be used by another verification tool (e.g., Frama-C [3], KeY [5], etc.). Representation of M may require an abstract domain that is more expressive than the domain of the analysis, but may be more compact than the whole iteration sequence. Alternatively, if d_i and b_i can be represented in logical form in some theory, so can M.

Which Analysis Runs First. In the iteration sequence (6), forward and backward analyses alternate, but which analysis runs first is actually not fixed. We may start with forward analysis and compute d_1 as normal, or we may take $d_1 = \top$ and start the computation with backward analysis. A notable option is to do the first run of backward analysis in a more coarse abstract domain and switch to a more precise domain in subsequent runs. For example, the initial run of backward analysis may only identify the predicates that can potentially be used to derive the goal:

$$\begin{aligned}
&\mathrm{lfp}_{\subseteq}\lambda X.\Pi_g \cup \mathrm{pre}(T_\Pi, X), \text{ where} \\
&\Pi_g = \{p \mid p(\mathbf{c}) \in A_g\} \\
&T_\Pi = \big\{(\Pi, p') \mid \exists (A, a') \in \mathbb{T}_{\mathbb{H}}.\, \Pi = \{p \mid p(\mathbf{c}) \in A\} \wedge a' = p'(\mathbf{c}')\big\}
\end{aligned} \tag{7}$$

Then, we can take $d_1 = \top$, b_1 to be some abstraction of (7), and starting from d_2, run the analysis with a more precise domain. In program analysis, restricting attention to program locations that have a path to (i.e., are backward-reachable from) some goal location, is a known technique. For example, K. Apinis, H. Seidl, and V. Voidani describe a sophisticated version of it [6].

3.2 Revisiting the Query-Answer Transformation

In principle, the iteration sequence (6) can be emulated by an iterated simple query-answer transformation. Let $\mathbb{H}$ be the original system of CHCs. Let the element b_k of the iteration sequence (6) map every predicate p_i to a formula β_k^i. In particular, b_0 will map every p_i to *true*. Then, d_{k+1} can be found as a model of the system $\mathbb{H}_{k+1}^d$. To construct, $\mathbb{H}_{k+1}^d$, for every CHC $P_{n+1} \leftarrow \varphi, P_1, \cdots, P_n$ (for $n \geq 0$) in the original system $\mathbb{H}$, we add to $\mathbb{H}_{k+1}^d$ the clause $P_{n+1} \leftarrow \varphi \wedge \beta_k^{n+1}, P_1, \cdots, P_n$. Now let the element d_k map every P_i to a formula δ_k^i. Then, b_k can be found as a model of the system $\mathbb{H}_k^b$ that is constructed as follows. For every CHC in the original system $\mathbb{H}$: $P_{n+1} \leftarrow \varphi, P_1, \cdots, P_n$, we add to $\mathbb{H}_k^b$ the clauses $P_1 \leftarrow \varphi \wedge \bigwedge_{i=1}^n \delta_k^i, P_{n+1}$ through $P_n \leftarrow \varphi \wedge \bigwedge_{i=1}^n \delta_k^i, P_{n+1}$. Also, we add to $\mathbb{H}_k^b$ the goal clause $\mathfrak{f} \leftarrow \mathfrak{f}_k$. If we compute the elements of the iteration sequence up to d_k, then the function that maps every p_i to $\delta_k^i \vee \bigvee_{j=1}^{k-1} (\delta_j^i \wedge \neg \beta_j^i)$ represents a model of the original system $\mathbb{H}$. In particular, when $d_1 = \top$, and $k = 2$, this produces a model, where every p_i maps to $\beta_1^i \Rightarrow \delta_2^i$.

Thus, one has a choice, whether to take a fixpoint-based approach, as we did, or a transformation-based approach. From the theoretical point of view, one will still have to prove that the iterated transformation allows to prove unreachability of the goal and to build a refined model, i.e., some analog of Propositions 2 and 3. As one can see in Appendix A, this is not trivial for the steps beyond the second. From the practical point of view, we believe that our approach allows to more easily implement some useful minor features. For example, the iteration sequence (6) naturally constrains b_i to be below d_i and d_i to be below b_{i-1}, which in some cases makes widening and join less aggressive. It should be possible though to achieve a similar effect for the query-answer transformation at the expense of introducing additional predicates and clauses.

On the other hand, an advantage of query-answer transformation is that it can be used as a preprocessing step for the analyses that are not based on abstract interpretation. For example, B. Kafle and J.P. Gallagher report [28] that it can improve the precision of a CEGAR-based analyser.

4 Implementation and Experiments

We implemented our approach in a prototype abstract interpreter. It can analyse numeric C programs that were converted to a system of CHCs with the tool SeaHorn [22] (the input format is currently a technical limitation, and we wish to remove it in the future). The implementation is written in OCaml and available online [4]. A notable feature of SeaHorn is that it introduces Boolean variables and predicate arguments even for programs without Boolean variables. To represent sets of valuations of numeric and Boolean variables, we use Bddapron [27].

We implement Kleene-like iteration as outlined in Sect. 2.1, which is similar to path focusing [23,35]. Iteration order and choice of widening points are based on F. Bourdoncle's [13,14] recursive strategy (except that we implement it using a worklist with priorities). As an SMT solver, we use Z3 [12]. For comparison, in addition to the forward-backward iteration sequence (6), we implemented an analysis based on query-answer transformation.

To evaluate our implementation, we took C programs from the categories *loops* and *recursive* of the Competition on Software Verification SV-COMP [2]. SeaHorn operates on LLVM bytecode produced by Clang [1], and the resulting system of CHCs depends a lot on Clang optimization settings. For example, constant folding may remove whole computation paths when they do not depend on non-deterministic inputs. Or, Clang may replace recursion with a loop, which will make SeaHorn produce a linear system of CHCs instead of a non-linear one. In our experiments, we compiled the input programs with two optimization levels: `-O3` (SeaHorn's default) and `-O0`. As a result, we get a total of 310 systems of Horn clauses, out of which 158 are declared safe by SV-COMP. Since we cannot prove unsafety, our evaluation focuses on safe systems. Out of 158 safe systems, our tool can work with 123. Other systems use features that are not yet supported in our tool (division, non-numeric theories, etc.). Out of 158 safe systems, 74 are non-linear.

First, we evaluate the effect of combined forward-backward analysis. The results are presented in Table 1. We compare three approaches. The first is the one we propose in this paper, i.e., based on the forward-backward iteration sequence (6). We compute the elements of (6) up to d_5. If we decrease the limit from d_5 to d_3, we can prove safety of 2 less programs; increasing the limit to d_7 gives no effect. The second one a 2-step analysis based on query-answer transformation [28]. First, it runs forward analysis on a query-answer transformed system, then injects the interpretations of answer predicates in the original system and runs forward analysis again. We implemented this analysis ourselves, and thus we are *not* directly comparing our implementation to the tool Rahft [30], where this analysis was first implemented. Finally, we also run a simple forward analysis. In Table 1, we report the number of programs that we *proved safe* with every approach. One can see that our approach has a small advantage over both query-answer transformation and simple forward analysis. Interestingly, B. Kafle and J.P. Gallagher report [28] a *much* greater difference when moving from simple forward analysis to query-answer transformation. This can be attributed to three factors. First, their set of benchmarks is different, although it includes many programs from the same SV-COMP categories. Second, their benchmarks are, to our knowledge, not pre-processed by Clang. Third, as B. Kafle and J.P. Gallagher themselves report, some issues solved by adding backward analysis can as well be solved by path focusing, which our tool implements.

For reference, we also compare our tool to the solver that is integrated with SeaHorn (to our knowledge, it is based on the tool SPACER. [32,33]). We present the results in Table 2. SeaHorn can prove safety of more programs, which is expected since our tool is in an early stage of development.

Table 1. Comparison of abstract interpretation strategies.

		Proven safe		
Safe	Supported	This paper	QA	Fwd
158	123	87	82	76

Table 2. Comparison to SeaHorn's builtin solver (with 1 min timeout).

	This paper	SeaHorn
Proven safe	87/123 (70%)	133/158 (84%)

5 Tree Semantics of CHCs

In this section, we briefly introduce tree semantics of CHCs. Trees are not convenient objects to work with, and studying tree semantics is not the main purpose of this paper. Thus, our description will not be fully rigorous. Rather, our goal is to give the reader an intuition of why we construct collecting semantics (especially, backward and combined semantics) in the way we do, which is perhaps best explained when collecting semantics is viewed as an abstraction of tree semantics.

For the purpose of this section, a *tree* is either a leaf node containing an atom, or an interior node that contains an atom and also has a non-zero number of child subtrees.

$$\text{Tree} ::= \mathit{leaf}(a) \mid \mathit{tree}(a \leftarrow t_1, \cdots, t_n)$$

where $a \in \mathbb{A}$ and every t_i is a tree. The *root atom* of a tree is naturally defined as

$$\mathit{root}(\mathit{leaf}(a)) = a \qquad \mathit{root}(\mathit{tree}(a \leftarrow t_1, \cdots, t_n)) = a$$

The set of *leaves* of a tree is defined as

$$\mathit{leaves}(\mathit{leaf}(a)) = \{a\} \qquad \mathit{leaves}(\mathit{tree}(a \leftarrow t_1, \cdots, t_n)) = \bigcup_{i=1}^{n} \mathit{leaves}(t_i)$$

The tree semantics of a system of CHCs $\mathbb{H}$ is a set of trees, where the parent-child relation is defined by the direct consequence relation $\mathbb{T}_\mathbb{H}$. To get more formal, let us first define the post-condition operation on trees as follows:

$$\begin{aligned} \text{post}^t(\mathbb{H}, X) = &\{\mathit{tree}(a' \leftarrow t_1, \cdots, t_n) \mid t_1, \cdots, t_n \in X \\ &\wedge \exists (A, a') \in \mathbb{T}_\mathbb{H}.\, |A| = n \wedge A = \{\mathit{root}(t_1), \cdots, \mathit{root}(t_n)\}\} \cup \\ &\{\mathit{leaf}(a) \mid (\varnothing, a) \in \mathbb{T}_\mathbb{H}\} \end{aligned}$$

Intuitively, the operation performs two distinct actions: (i) it produces a trivial tree $\mathit{leaf}(a)$ for every initial transition $(\varnothing, a)$; and (ii) for every non-initial transition (A, a'), it creates every possible tree $\mathit{tree}(a' \leftarrow t_1, \cdots, t_n)$, where t_i are elements of X, and their roots correspond to distinct elements of A. Then, we can define the *forward tree semantics* of $\mathbb{H}$ as the least fixed point:

$$\text{lfp}_\subseteq \lambda X.\, \text{post}^t(\mathbb{H}, X)$$

Intuitively, this is the set of trees, where leaves are initial atoms, and parent-child relation is defined by the direct consequence relation. One can say that this is the set of derivation trees induced $\mathbb{H}$. A notable property of forward tree semantics is that it is *subtree-closed*, i.e., with every tree, it also contains all of its subtrees.

Let us now define the *set-of-atoms* abstraction of a set of trees. First, let us define an auxiliary predicate that tells whether an atom is a node of a tree.

$$\begin{aligned} &\mathit{isnode}(a, \mathit{leaf}(a')) = (a = a') \\ &\mathit{isnode}(a, \mathit{tree}(a' \leftarrow t_1, \cdots, t_n)) = (a = a') \vee \bigvee_{i=1}^{n} \mathit{isnode}(a, t_i) \end{aligned}$$

Then, for a set of trees T, its set-of-atoms abstraction is

$$\alpha^t(T) = \{a \mid \exists t \in T.\, \mathit{isnode}(a, t)\}$$

In particular, when T is subtree-closed, one can show that

$$\alpha^t(T) = \{\mathit{root}(t) \mid t \in T\} \tag{8}$$

Let us observe that the set-of-atoms abstraction of the forward tree semantics is exactly the forward collecting semantics:

Proposition 4. $\alpha^t(\text{lfp}_{\subseteq}\lambda X.\,\text{post}^t(\mathbb{H}, X)) = \text{lfp}_{\subseteq}\lambda X.\,\text{post}(\mathbb{T}_{\mathbb{H}}, X)$

Proof (sketch). This is an instance of *exact fixed point abstraction* [16, theorem 7.1.0.4], and to prove the proposition, we need to show that

$$\alpha^t(\text{post}^t(\mathbb{H}, T)) = \text{post}(\mathbb{T}_{\mathbb{H}}, \alpha^t(T)) \tag{9}$$

This is not true for an arbitrary T, but can be shown as true when T is subtree-closed, as it follows from (8). The post^t operation preserves subtree-closure, thus Proposition 4 can be seen as a fixed point in the lattice of subtree-closed sets, where (9) holds and thus exact fixed point abstraction holds as well.

Let us now define the *backward tree semantics*. For a set of trees T, let $\text{pre}^t(\mathbb{H}, T)$ be the set of trees that are produced from trees in T by replacing a single leaf containing $a' \in \mathbb{A}$ with a subtree $\mathit{tree}(a' \leftarrow a_1, \cdots, a_n)$, s.t. $a_1, \cdots, a_n$ are distinct, and $(a', \{a_1, \cdots, a_n\}) \in \mathbb{T}_{\mathbb{H}}$. Also let $T_g = \{\mathit{leaf}(a) \mid a \in A_g\}$. Then, the backward tree semantics of $\mathbb{H}$ is the least fixed point

$$\text{lfp}_{\subseteq}\lambda X.T_g \cup \text{pre}^t(\mathbb{H}, X)$$

Intuitively, this is the set of trees where the root is in A_g, and parent-child relation is defined by the direct consequence relation.

Let us define a *pre-tree* of a tree t to be an object that is a tree and that is produced by selecting a number (possibly, zero) of non-root interior nodes and replacing every such interior node $\mathit{tree}(a \leftarrow t_1, \cdots, t_n)$ with the leaf $\mathit{leaf}(a)$.

A notable property of backward tree semantics is that it is *pre-tree-closed*, i.e., with every tree, it also contains all of its pre-trees. One can show that when T is pre-tree closed,

$$\alpha^t(T) = \bigcup\{\mathit{leaves}(t) \mid t \in T\}$$

Similarly to the forward case, the set-of-atoms abstraction of the backward tree semantics is exactly the backward collecting semantics.

Proposition 5. $\alpha^t(\mathrm{lfp}_{\subseteq}\lambda X.T_g \cup \mathrm{pre}^t(\mathbb{H}, X)) = \mathrm{lfp}_{\subseteq}\lambda X.A_g \cup \mathrm{pre}(\mathbb{T}_{\mathbb{H}}, X)$

Proof (sketch). The proof idea is similar to that of Proposition 4. We need to show that $\alpha^t(T_g \cup \mathrm{pre}^t(\mathbb{H}, T)) = A_g \cup \mathrm{pre}(\mathbb{T}_{\mathbb{H}}, \alpha^t(T))$ which does hold when T is pre-tree-closed; and pre-tree-closure is preserved by the transformer $\lambda X.T_g \cup \mathrm{pre}^t(\mathbb{H}, X)$.

Now, let us consider the intersection of the forward and backward tree semantics: $\big(\mathrm{lfp}_{\subseteq}\lambda X.\,\mathrm{post}^t(\mathbb{H}, X)\big) \cap \big(\mathrm{lfp}_{\subseteq}\lambda X.T_g \cup \mathrm{pre}^t(\mathbb{H}, X)\big)$. This is the set of trees that have initial atoms as leaves and a goal atom as root. We can now observe that the combined forward-backward semantics (5) is exactly the set-of-atoms abstraction of this object.

Proposition 6.
$$\begin{aligned}&\alpha^t\Big(\big(\mathrm{lfp}_{\subseteq}\lambda X.\,\mathrm{post}^t(\mathbb{H}, X)\big) \cap \big(\mathrm{lfp}_{\subseteq}\lambda X.T_g \cup \mathrm{pre}^t(\mathbb{H}, X)\big)\Big)\\ &= \mathrm{lfp}_{\subseteq}\lambda X.(A_g \cap M) \cup \mathrm{pre}|_M(\mathbb{T}_{\mathbb{H}}, X)\\ &\quad \textit{where } M = \mathrm{lfp}_{\subseteq}\lambda X.\,\mathrm{post}(\mathbb{T}_{\mathbb{H}}, X)\end{aligned}$$

To see intuitively why this is true, let $t \in \big(\mathrm{lfp}_{\subseteq}\lambda X.\,\mathrm{post}^t(\mathbb{H}, X)\big) \cap \big(\mathrm{lfp}_{\subseteq}\lambda X.T_g \cup \mathrm{pre}^t(\mathbb{H}, X)\big)$ and let us observe which atoms may appear in t at different depth. We know that $\mathit{root}(t) \in A_g \cap M$. At depth one, we will observe sub-trees that have initial atoms as leaves and can be combined to produce t. One can see that the set of atoms at depth one is $\mathrm{pre}|_M(\mathbb{T}_{\mathbb{H}}, A_g \cap M)$. Similarly, the set of atoms at depth two is $\mathrm{pre}|_M(\mathbb{T}_{\mathbb{H}}, \mathrm{pre}|_M(\mathbb{T}_{\mathbb{H}}, A_g \cap M))$. Continuing this way, we get that the set-of-atoms abstraction of the intersection of forward and backward tree semantics is $\mathrm{lfp}_{\subseteq}\lambda X.(A_g \cap M) \cup \mathrm{pre}|_M(\mathbb{T}_{\mathbb{H}}, X)$.

To summarise, the combined forward-backward semantics (5) is the set-of-atoms abstraction of the intersection of forward and backward tree semantics. Since set-of-trees intersection and set-of-states abstraction do not commute, we need to introduce the restricted pre-condition operation to define the combined semantics.

6 Related Work

Combining forward and backward analyses is standard when analysing programs. A good explanation of the technique is given by Patrick and Radhia Cousot [18, section 4]. They also propose to use it for the analysis of logic programs [17]. Their combination is an intersection of forward and backward collecting semantics.

F. Benoy and A. King were perhaps the first to apply abstract interpretation in a *polyhedral domain* to constraint logic programs [8]. J.P. Gallagher et al. in a series of works (see, e.g., [28,37]) apply it to specialized CLPs or CHCs. Previous sections discuss the differences between their approach and ours. Later work by B. Kafle, J.P. Gallagher, and J.F. Morales [29,30] introduces another analysis engine that is not based on abstract interpretation. M. Proietti, F. Fioravanti et al. propose a similar analysis [19] that iteratively specializes the initial system of CHCs by propagating constraints both forward and backward and by heuristically applying join and widening operators. This process is repeated until the analysis arrives at a system that can be trivially proven safe or a timeout is reached. Notably, this analysis avoids explicitly constructing the model of the original system.

Multiple researchers were advocating using Horn clauses for program verification, Including A. Rybalchenko [21], N. Bjørner, and others. A survey was recently made by N. Bjørner, A. Gurfinkel, K. McMillan, and A. Rybalchenko [11]. Tools that allow to solve problems stated as systems of Horn clauses include E-HSF [9], Eldarica [39], Z3 (with PDR [25] and SPACER [32,33] engines), and others. As our implementation is in early development, we do not make a detailed comparison to these tools.

Path focusing was described by D. Monniaux and L. Gonnord [35] and implemented by J. Henry, D. Monniaux, and M. Moy in a tool PAGAI [23]. This is an approach to abstract interpretation, where one uses an SMT solver to find a path through a program, along which to propagate the post-conditions.

7 Conclusion and Future Work

In this paper, we introduce a new backward collecting semantics, which is suitable for alternating forward and backward abstract interpretation of Horn clauses. We show how the alternation can be used to prove unreachability of the goal and how every subsequent run of an analysis yields a refined model of the system. Experimentally, we observe that combining forward and backward analyses is important for analysing systems that encode questions about reachability in C programs. In particular, the combination that follows our new semantics improves the precision of our own abstract interpreter, including when compared to a forward analysis of a query-answer-transformed system.

We see the following directions for future work. *First*, we wish to be able to infer models that are *disjunctive* in a meaningful way. Currently, as we use Bddapron, we produce models where a predicate maps to a disjunctive formula, but the disjunctions are defined by the Boolean arguments of the predicate, which are often unrelated to the interesting facts about numeric arguments. We wish to explore how partitioning approaches designed for program analysis [24,38] can be applied to the analysis of Horn clauses. *Second*, we note that currently, for the combination of forward and backward analyses to work, we need to explicitly specify the goal (`query`, in terms of SeaHorn language). It would be nice though, if we could use the benefits of the combined analysis (e.g., analysing the procedures only for reachable inputs) without having an explicit goal. For that, we will need to be able to distinguish, which of the clauses of the form $P \leftarrow \varphi$ denote the program entry (the `main()` function in C terms), and which correspond to the procedures (recall Figs. 3 and 4). So far, the only solution we see is that this information needs to be communicated to our analyser as part of the input. *Finally*, we observe that so far we evaluate our approach using CHCs that result from reachability questions in relatively simple C programs. These CHCs are also relatively simple and in particular contain at most two predicate applications in the bodies. We wish to evaluate our approach using more complicated CHCs, e.g., that result from cell morphing abstraction [36], but successfully analysing such systems requires to be able to produce disjunctive models.

A Proofs

Proposition 2. *For every $k \geq 1$, the set $\gamma(d_k) \cup \bigcup_{i=1}^{k-1} \big(\gamma(d_i) \setminus \gamma(b_i)\big)$ is a model of $\mathbb{H}$.*

Proof. For convenience, let us replace the direct consequence relation $\mathbb{T}_\mathbb{H}$ with two objects: the set of initial atoms $\mathbb{I}_\mathbb{H} = \{a' \mid (\varnothing, a') \in \mathbb{T}_\mathbb{H}\}$ and the set of consecutions $\mathbb{T}_{\vec{\mathbb{H}}} = \{(A, a') \in \mathbb{T}_\mathbb{H} \mid A \neq \varnothing\}$. Then, for every $R, X \subseteq \mathbb{A}$, $\text{post}(\mathbb{T}_\mathbb{H}, X) = \mathbb{I}_\mathbb{H} \cup \text{post}(\mathbb{T}_{\vec{\mathbb{H}}}, X)$ and $\text{pre}|_R(\mathbb{T}_\mathbb{H}, X) = \text{pre}|_R(\mathbb{T}_{\vec{\mathbb{H}}}, X)$.

Now let us consider the first three elements of the descending sequence, d_1, b_1, and d_2. For d_1 it holds that $\mathbb{I}_\mathbb{H} \cup \text{post}(\mathbb{T}_{\vec{\mathbb{H}}}, \gamma(d_1)) \subseteq \gamma(d_1)$. That is, $\gamma(d_1)$ is a model of $\mathbb{H}$ and the lemma statement holds for $k = 1$.

For b_1, it holds that $(\gamma(g) \cap \gamma(d_1)) \cup \text{pre}|_{\gamma(d_1)}(\mathbb{T}_{\vec{\mathbb{H}}}, \gamma(b_1)) \subseteq \gamma(b_1)$. This means that for every conseqution $(A, a') \in \mathbb{T}_{\vec{\mathbb{H}}}$, if $A \subseteq \gamma(d_1)$ and $A \cap (\gamma(d_1) \setminus \gamma(b_1)) \neq \varnothing$, then $a' \in (\gamma(d_1) \setminus \gamma(b_1))$.

Finally, for d_2 it holds that $(\mathbb{I}_\mathbb{H} \cup \text{post}(\mathbb{T}_{\vec{\mathbb{H}}}, \gamma(d_2))) \cap \gamma(b_1) \subseteq d_2$. First, this means that $\mathbb{I}_\mathbb{H} \subseteq (\gamma(d_1) \setminus \gamma(b_1)) \cup \gamma(d_2)$. Indeed, by definition of d_1, $\mathbb{I}_\mathbb{H} \subseteq \gamma(d_1)$ and by definition of d_2, $\mathbb{I}_\mathbb{H} \cap \gamma(b_1) \subseteq \gamma(d_2)$. Second, this means that $\text{post}(\mathbb{T}_{\vec{\mathbb{H}}}, (\gamma(d_1) \setminus \gamma(b_1)) \cup \gamma(d_2)) \subseteq (\gamma(d_1) \setminus \gamma(b_1)) \cup \gamma(d_2)$. Indeed, let is pick an arbitrary $(A, a') \in \mathbb{T}_{\vec{\mathbb{H}}}$, s.t. $A \subseteq (\gamma(d_1) \setminus \gamma(b_1)) \cup \gamma(d_2)$. There are two possible cases. If $A \subseteq \gamma(d_2)$ then by definition of d_2, either $a' \in \gamma(d_2)$, or $a' \in (\gamma(d_1) \setminus \gamma(b_1))$. If $A \not\subseteq \gamma(d_2)$ then $A \cap (\gamma(d_1) \setminus \gamma(b_1)) \neq \varnothing$, and $a' \in \gamma(d_1) \setminus \gamma(b_1)$. This proves the statement of the lemma for $k = 2$ and also provides the base case for the following inductive proof.

Now let $k > 2$, $L_k = \bigcup_{i=1}^{k-1} \big(\gamma(d_i) \setminus \gamma(b_i)\big)$, and $M_k = \gamma(d_k) \cup L_k$. Let the induction hypothesis be that: $\mathbb{I}_\mathbb{H} \subseteq M_k$, $\text{post}(\mathbb{T}_{\vec{\mathbb{H}}}, M_k) \subseteq M_k$ (i.e., M_k is a model of $\mathbb{H}$), and for every $(A, a') \in \mathbb{T}_{\vec{\mathbb{H}}}$, if $A \subseteq M_k$ and $A \cap L_k \neq \varnothing$, then $a' \in L_k$.

Then, let us consider the two subsequent elements: b_k and d_{k+1} and the two sets: $L_{k+1} = M_k \setminus \gamma(b_k)$ and $M_{k+1} = L_{k+1} \cup \gamma(d_{k+1})$.

For b_k it holds that $(\gamma(g) \cap \gamma(d_k)) \cup \text{pre}|_{\gamma(d_k)}(\mathbb{T}_{\vec{\mathbb{H}}}, \gamma(b_k)) \subseteq \gamma(b_k)$. That is, for every $(A, a') \in \mathbb{T}_{\vec{\mathbb{H}}}$, if $A \subseteq \gamma(d_k)$ and $A \cap (\gamma(d_k) \setminus \gamma(b_k)) \neq \varnothing$, then $a' \in (\gamma(d_k) \setminus \gamma(b_k))$.

For d_{k+1} it holds that $(\mathbb{I}_{\mathbb{H}} \cup \text{post}(\mathbb{T}_{\overrightarrow{\mathbb{H}}}, \gamma(d_{k+1}))) \cap \gamma(b_k) \subseteq \gamma(d_{k+1})$.

First, observe that $\mathbb{I}_{\mathbb{H}} \subseteq M_{k+1}$. Indeed, we know that $\mathbb{I}_{\mathbb{H}} \subseteq M_k$ and that $M_{k+1} = (M_k \setminus \gamma(b_k)) \cup \gamma(d_{k+1})$. By definition of d_{k+1}, $\mathbb{I}_{\mathbb{H}} \cap \gamma(b_k) \subseteq \gamma(d_{k+1})$. Thus, $\mathbb{I}_{\mathbb{H}} \subseteq M_{k+1}$.

Second, let us pick an arbitrary $(A, a') \in \mathbb{T}_{\overrightarrow{\mathbb{H}}}$, s.t. $A \subseteq M_{k+1}$. Since M_k is a model of H, we know that $a' \in M_k$. But then, there are three possible cases. (i) If $A \subseteq \gamma(d_{k+1})$, then either $a' \in \gamma(d_{k+1})$, or $a' \notin \gamma(b_k)$. That is, $a' \in (M_k \setminus \gamma(b_k)) \cup \gamma(d_{k+1}) = M_{k+1}$. (ii) If $A \subseteq \gamma(d_k)$ and $A \not\subseteq \gamma(d_{k+1})$, then $A \cap (\gamma(d_k) \setminus \gamma(b_k)) \neq \varnothing$, and $a' \in \gamma(d_k) \setminus \gamma(b_k) \subseteq M_{k+1}$. (iii) Finally, if $A \not\subseteq \gamma(d_k)$, then $A \cap L_k \neq \varnothing$, and from the hypothesis $a' \in L_k$. There are no other possible cases. This means that $\text{post}(\mathbb{T}_{\overrightarrow{\mathbb{H}}}, M_{k+1}) \subseteq M_{k+1}$ and thus M_{k+1} is a model of $\mathbb{H}$. Also, from (ii) and (iii) it follows that for $(A, a') \in \mathbb{T}_{\overrightarrow{\mathbb{H}}}$, if $A \subseteq M_{k+1}$ and $A \cap L_{k+1} \neq \varnothing$, then $a' \in L_{k+1}$.

References

1. Clang: a C language family frontend for LLVM. https://clang.llvm.org/. Accessed July 2017
2. Competition on software verification (SV-COMP). http://sv-comp.sosy-lab.org/. Accessed July 2017
3. Frama-C software analyzers. https://frama-c.com/. Accessed July 2017
4. A path focusing abstract interpreter for horn clauses. https://gitlab.com/abakhirkin/hcai. Accessed July 2017
5. Ahrendt, W., Beckert, B., Bubel, R., Hähnle, R., Schmitt, P.H., Ulbrich, M. (eds.): Deductive Software Verification - The KeY Book - From Theory to Practice. Programming and Software Engineering, vol. 10001. Springer, Heidelberg (2016). doi:10.1007/978-3-319-49812-6
6. Apinis, K., Seidl, H., Vojdani, V.: Side-effecting constraint systems: a swiss army knife for program analysis. In: Jhala, R., Igarashi, A. (eds.) APLAS 2012. LNCS, vol. 7705, pp. 157–172. Springer, Heidelberg (2012). doi:10.1007/978-3-642-35182-2_12
7. Bagnara, R., Hill, P.M., Zaffanella, E.: The parma polyhedra library: toward a complete set of numerical abstractions for the analysis and verification of hardware and software systems. Sci. Comput. Program. **72**(1–2), 3–21 (2008)
8. Benoy, F., King, A.: Inferring argument size relationships with CLP($\mathcal{R}$). In: Gallagher, J. (ed.) LOPSTR 1996. LNCS, vol. 1207, pp. 204–223. Springer, Heidelberg (1997). doi:10.1007/3-540-62718-9_12
9. Beyene, T.A., Popeea, C., Rybalchenko, A.: Solving existentially quantified horn clauses. In: Sharygina, N., Veith, H. (eds.) CAV 2013. LNCS, vol. 8044, pp. 869–882. Springer, Heidelberg (2013). doi:10.1007/978-3-642-39799-8_61
10. Beyer, D., Cimatti, A., Griggio, A., Keremoglu, M.E., Sebastiani, R.: Software model checking via large-block encoding. In: Proceedings of 9th International Conference on Formal Methods in Computer-Aided Design, FMCAD 2009, Austin, Texas, USA, pp. 25–32. IEEE, 15–18 November 2009
11. Bjørner, N., Gurfinkel, A., McMillan, K., Rybalchenko, A.: Horn clause solvers for program verification. In: Beklemishev, L.D., Blass, A., Dershowitz, N., Finkbeiner, B., Schulte, W. (eds.) Fields of Logic and Computation II. LNCS, vol. 9300, pp. 24–51. Springer, Cham (2015). doi:10.1007/978-3-319-23534-9_2

12. Bjørner, N., de Moura, L., Wintersteiger, C.: Z3. https://github.com/Z3Prover/z3. Accessed July 2017
13. Bourdoncle, F.: Sémantiques des langages impératifs d'ordre supérieur et interprétation abstraite. Ph.D. thesis, École polytechnique (1992)
14. Bourdoncle, F.: Efficient chaotic iteration strategies with widenings. In: Bjørner, D., Broy, M., Pottosin, I.V. (eds.) Formal Methods in Programming and Their Applications. LNCS, pp. 128–141. Springer, Heidelberg (1993). doi:10.1007/BFb0039704
15. Cousot, P., Cousot, R.: Abstract interpretation: A unified lattice model for static analysis of programs by construction or approximation of fixpoints. In: Graham, R.M., Harrison, M.A., Sethi, R. (eds.) Principles of Programming Languages (POPL), pp. 238–252. ACM (1977)
16. Cousot, P., Cousot, R.: Systematic design of program analysis frameworks. In: Aho, A.V., Zilles, S.N., Rosen, B.K. (eds.) Principles of Programming Languages (POPL), pp. 269–282. ACM Press (1979)
17. Cousot, P., Cousot, R.: Abstract interpretation and application to logic programs. J. Log. Program. **13**(2–3), 103–179 (1992)
18. Cousot, P., Cousot, R.: Refining model checking by abstract interpretation. Autom. Softw. Eng. **6**(1), 69–95 (1999)
19. De Angelis, E., Fioravanti, F., Pettorossi, A., Proietti, M.: Program verification via iterated specialization. Sci. Comput. Program. **95**, 149–175 (2014)
20. Gawlitza, T.M., Seidl, H.: Precise program analysis through strategy iteration and optimization. In: Nipkow, T., Grumberg, O., Hauptmann, B. (eds.) Software Safety and Security - Tools for Analysis and Verification, NATO Science for Peace and Security Series - D: Information and Communication Security, vol. 33, pp. 348–384. IOS Press (2012)
21. Grebenshchikov, S., Lopes, N.P., Popeea, C., Rybalchenko, A.: Synthesizing software verifiers from proof rules. In: Vitek, J., Lin, H., Tip, F. (eds.) Programming Language Design and Implementation (PLDI), pp. 405–416. ACM (2012)
22. Gurfinkel, A., Kahsai, T., Komuravelli, A., Navas, J.A.: The seahorn verification framework. In: Kroening, D., Păsăreanu, C.S. (eds.) CAV 2015. LNCS, vol. 9206, pp. 343–361. Springer, Cham (2015). doi:10.1007/978-3-319-21690-4_20
23. Henry, J., Monniaux, D., Moy, M.: PAGAI: a path sensitive static analyser. Electron. Notes Theor. Comput. Sci. **289**, 15–25 (2012)
24. Henry, J., Monniaux, D., Moy, M.: Succinct representations for abstract interpretation. In: Miné, A., Schmidt, D. (eds.) SAS 2012. LNCS, vol. 7460, pp. 283–299. Springer, Heidelberg (2012). doi:10.1007/978-3-642-33125-1_20
25. Hoder, K., Bjørner, N.: Generalized property directed reachability. In: Cimatti, A., Sebastiani, R. (eds.) SAT 2012. LNCS, vol. 7317, pp. 157–171. Springer, Heidelberg (2012). doi:10.1007/978-3-642-31612-8_13
26. Jaffar, J., Maher, M.J.: Constraint logic programming: a survey. J. Log. Program. **19**(20), 503–581 (1994)
27. Jeannet, B.: Bddapron. http://pop-art.inrialpes.fr/~bjeannet/bjeannet-forge/bddapron/. Accessed July 2017
28. Kafle, B., Gallagher, J.P.: Constraint specialisation in horn clause verification. In: Asai, K., Sagonas, K. (eds.) Partial Evaluation and Program Manipulation (PEPM), pp. 85–90. ACM (2015)
29. Kafle, B., Gallagher, J.P.: Tree automata-based refinement with application to horn clause verification. In: D'Souza, D., Lal, A., Larsen, K.G. (eds.) VMCAI 2015. LNCS, vol. 8931, pp. 209–226. Springer, Heidelberg (2015). doi:10.1007/978-3-662-46081-8_12

30. Kafle, B., Gallagher, J.P., Morales, J.F.: RAHFT: a tool for verifying horn clauses using abstract interpretation and finite tree automata. In: Chaudhuri, S., Farzan, A. (eds.) CAV 2016. LNCS, vol. 9779, pp. 261–268. Springer, Cham (2016). doi:10.1007/978-3-319-41528-4_14
31. Karpenkov, E.G., Monniaux, D., Wendler, P.: Program analysis with local policy iteration. In: Jobstmann, B., Leino, K.R.M. (eds.) VMCAI 2016. LNCS, vol. 9583, pp. 127–146. Springer, Heidelberg (2016). doi:10.1007/978-3-662-49122-5_6
32. Komuravelli, A., Gurfinkel, A., Chaki, S.: SMT-based model checking for recursive programs. In: Biere, A., Bloem, R. (eds.) CAV 2014. LNCS, vol. 8559, pp. 17–34. Springer, Cham (2014). doi:10.1007/978-3-319-08867-9_2
33. Komuravelli, A., Gurfinkel, A., Chaki, S., Clarke, E.M.: Automatic abstraction in SMT-based unbounded software model checking. In: Sharygina, N., Veith, H. (eds.) CAV 2013. LNCS, vol. 8044, pp. 846–862. Springer, Heidelberg (2013). doi:10.1007/978-3-642-39799-8_59
34. Marques-Silva, J., Janota, M., Belov, A.: Minimal sets over monotone predicates in boolean formulae. In: Sharygina, N., Veith, H. (eds.) CAV 2013. LNCS, vol. 8044, pp. 592–607. Springer, Heidelberg (2013). doi:10.1007/978-3-642-39799-8_39
35. Monniaux, D., Gonnord, L.: Using bounded model checking to focus fixpoint iterations. In: Yahav, E. (ed.) SAS 2011. LNCS, vol. 6887, pp. 369–385. Springer, Heidelberg (2011). doi:10.1007/978-3-642-23702-7_27
36. Monniaux, D., Gonnord, L.: Cell morphing: from array programs to array-free horn clauses. In: Rival, X. (ed.) SAS 2016. LNCS, vol. 9837, pp. 361–382. Springer, Heidelberg (2016). doi:10.1007/978-3-662-53413-7_18
37. Peralta, J.C., Gallagher, J.P.: Convex hull abstractions in specialization of CLP programs. In: Leuschel, M. (ed.) LOPSTR 2002. LNCS, vol. 2664, pp. 90–108. Springer, Heidelberg (2003). doi:10.1007/3-540-45013-0_8
38. Rival, X., Mauborgne, L.: The trace partitioning abstract domain. ACM Trans. Program. Lang. Syst. **29**(5), 26 (2007)
39. Rümmer, P., Hojjat, H., Kuncak, V.: Classifying and solving horn clauses for verification. In: Cohen, E., Rybalchenko, A. (eds.) VSTTE 2013. LNCS, vol. 8164, pp. 1–21. Springer, Heidelberg (2014). doi:10.1007/978-3-642-54108-7_1
40. Sharygina, N., Veith, H. (eds.): CAV 2013. LNCS, vol. 8044. Springer, Heidelberg (2013)

Abstract Semantic Diffing of Evolving Concurrent Programs

Ahmed Bouajjani[1], Constantin Enea[1(✉)], and Shuvendu K. Lahiri[2]

[1] IRIF, Univ. Paris Diderot, Paris, France
{abou,cenea}@irif.fr
[2] Microsoft Research, Redmond, USA
shuvendu@microsoft.com

Abstract. We present an approach for comparing two closely related concurrent programs, whose goal is to give feedback about interesting differences without relying on user-provided assertions. This approach compares two programs in terms of cross-thread interferences and data-flow, under a parametrized abstraction which can detect any difference in the limit. We introduce a partial order relation between these abstractions such that a program change that leads to a "smaller" abstraction is more likely to be regression-free from the perspective of concurrency. On the other hand, incomparable or bigger abstractions, which are an indication of introducing new, possibly undesired, behaviors, lead to succinct explanations of the semantic differences.

1 Introduction

The lifetime of a software module includes multiple changes that range from refactoring, addition of new features to bug or performance fixes. Such changes may introduce regressions which in general are hard to detect and may reveal themselves much later in the software's life-cycle. Dealing with this issue is particularly difficult in the context of concurrent programs, where the bugs are characterized by subtle interleaving patterns that tend to manifest in the field while passing an extensive testing phase.

Checking whether a change in a program is regression-free reduces to a standard, single-program, verification problem assuming a specification of the possible regressions is provided, for instance, using assertions. However, such specifications are rarely present in practice.

A different perspective, which avoids the need for specifications, would be to compare the two versions of a program (before and after the change) under a certain abstraction, which is precise enough to distinguish common specifications. Typical examples involve (bi)simulations, sets of reachable configurations[1], and

This work is supported in part by the European Research Council (ERC) under the European Union's Horizon 2020 research and innovation programme (grant agreement No. 678177).

[1] By configuration, we mean the tuple of thread-local states together with the state of the shared memory.

F. Ranzato (Ed.): SAS 2017, LNCS 10422, pp. 46–65, 2017.
DOI: 10.1007/978-3-319-66706-5_3

equality between input-output relations. Simulations define a partial order over the set of all programs (bisimulations define an equivalence relation), which in practice, relates very few programs across refactoring, bug-fixes, or adding new features. For instance, a transformation that is widely used in bug-fixing consists in reordering program statements within the same thread. For realistic programs, there exists no simulation relation between a program obtained by applying such a transformation and the initial version, or vice-versa. Therefore, using simulations as an indicator of regression-freeness, i.e., the new version is considered regression-free when it is simulated by the old version, would lead to too many false negatives. The same holds when comparing two programs with respect to their reachable sets of configurations. Comparing input-output relations is also not suitable in our context, because of the concurrency. Such relations are hard to compute and also, hard to use for checking regression-freeness, because of the non-determinism introduced by the thread scheduler.

In this paper we propose a new approach for comparing two closely related concurrent programs (subsequent versions of programs), which allows to relate more programs than simulations, for instance. The goal of this approach is to give feedback about interesting differences as opposed to noise from any change, without relying on user-provided assertions. From the perspective of concurrency, interesting differences concern, for instance, enabling new interferences from other threads (e.g., reading new values written by other threads), or new violations of atomicity (for some decomposition of the program in atomic blocks, which is implicit in the mind of the programmer).

The starting point of our approach is a program semantics based on traces [21], which are compact representations of sets of interleavings. A trace is a graph where nodes represent read and write actions, and edges represent the *program order*, which relates every two actions executed by the same thread, and *data-flow dependencies*, i.e., which action writes the value read by a read action, and in which order values are written to the memory. A trace represents all the interleavings which are consistent with the program order and the data-flow dependencies. The traces of two programs can be compared assuming a matching relation between variables and statements in the two programs, such that matching statements read and respectively, write the same set of variables (modulo the variable matching). Roughly, if this matching relation is an isomorphism between two traces of different programs, then the sets of configurations reachable in the interleavings represented by these two traces are the same (modulo the constants used in the statements).

We define a partial order relation between programs based on abstract representations of sets of traces. We use abstract representations instead of sets of (concrete) traces because ordering programs with respect to the latter has the same disadvantages as the use of simulation relations or sets of reachable configurations (see Sect. 2 for an example). For instance, bug fixes based on statement reordering or modifying the placement of the synchronization primitives lead straightaway to incomparable sets of traces – the set of actions or the program order are different.

As a first abstraction step, we consider "projected" traces, where roughly, the program order and all the synchronization statements are omitted[2]. This allows us to expose differences that concern only the data-flow in the program and not, for instance, the order in which different variables are assigned, or the synchronization mechanisms used to constrain the interference between threads. Replacing lock/unlock primitives with wait/nofity or semaphores induces no difference with respect to sets of projected traces provided that the set of possible schedules remains the same.

Then, we define abstractions of sets of projected traces, called *abstract traces*. Every abstract trace contains a graph structure describing the *union* of the projected traces it represents. The nodes of this graph correspond to program statements and the edges correspond to data-flow dependencies present in *some* projected trace. We restrict ourselves to loop-free programs which implies that these graphs are of bounded size. Handling loops will require some predefined equivalence relation between statements, a node in the graph representing an equivalence class with respect to this relation. Adding information about which sets of dependencies are present together in the same projected trace allows to refine a given abstract trace. Abstract traces are parametrized by an integer k which bounds the size of the sets of dependencies that are tracked (whether they occur in the same trace). We define a partial order between abstract traces which essentially corresponds to the fact that every set of dependencies in one abstract trace occurs in the other one as well. An abstract trace not being "smaller" than another one implies that the set of concrete traces corresponding to the first one is not included in the set of concrete traces corresponding to the second one (and thus reveals a difference in thread interference). However, on the opposite side, the "smaller than" relation does not imply trace set inclusion unless k is big enough (roughly, the square of the program size). Instead, it can be thought of as an *indicator* for not introducing undesired behaviors, whose precision increases as bigger values of k are considered.

This abstraction framework enables a *succinct* representation of the difference between two programs. For a fixed k, the size of the abstract trace is polynomial in the size of the input program while the size of a complete set of traces is in general of exponential size. Small values of k allow to explain the difference between two programs in terms of small sets of dependencies that occur in the same execution, instead of a complete trace or interleaving.

We show that the problem of deciding the difference with respect to abstract traces of a fixed rank k between two versions of a loop-free program[3] (before and after a program transformation) can be reduced to a set of assertion checking queries. This reduction holds for programs manipulating arbitrary, possibly unbounded, data. The assertion checking queries can be discharged using the existing verification technology. In the context of loop-free *boolean* programs, we

[2] Our framework is not bound to a specific set of program order constraints and statements to be preserved in the projected traces – they can be chosen arbitrarily.

[3] This reduction can be applied to arbitrary programs assuming a bounded unrolling of loops.

show that this problem has a lower asymptotic complexity than the problem of deciding the difference with respect to concrete sets of traces. More precisely, we prove that the first problem can be reduced to a polynomial number of assertion checking queries and that it is Δ_2^P-complete, while the second problem is Σ_2^P-complete. (We recall that Δ_2^P, resp., Σ_2^P, is the class of decision problems solvable by a polynomial time, resp., NP time, Turing machine augmented by an oracle for an NP-complete problem.) This complexity gap shows that the latter problem cannot be reduced to a polynomial number of assertion checking queries unless P = NP.

As a proof of concept, we have applied our framework to a benchmark used for the ConcurrencySwapper synthesis tool [5]. This benchmark consists of pairs of programs, before and after a bug fix, that model real concurrency bug fixes reported in the Linux kernel development archive (www.kernel.org). The reachability queries have been discharged using the LazyCseq tool [11,12] (with backend CBMC [8]). These experiments show that comparing abstract traces for small values of k, i.e., $k \in \{1, 2\}$, suffices to detect interesting semantic changes while ignoring the irrelevant ones. Moreover, the semantic changes are presented succinctly as a small set of data-flow dependencies between program statements, instead of a complex interleaving. This facilitates the task of spotting bugs by allowing the programmer to focus on small fragments of the program's behavior.

2 Motivating Examples

We provide several examples to illustrate the abstract semantic diffing framework proposed in this paper and its potential use in verifying concurrency bug fixes.

The program on the left of Fig. 1 is a typical concurrency bug found in device drivers [5], where the second thread may read an uninitialized value of `x` (initially, all variables are 0). Since the second thread runs only when `flag` is set to 1, fixing such a bug consists in permuting the two instructions in the first thread such that `x` is initialized before `flag` is set to 1. The modified version is listed on the right of Fig. 1. Note that the two versions (before and after the fix) have incomparable sets of reachable configurations: the configuration ($\texttt{flag} = 1, \texttt{x} = 0$) is reachable in the first program but not in the second, and ($\texttt{flag} = 0, \texttt{x} = 1$) is reachable in the second but not in the first one. This also implies that there exists no simulation relation from the fixed version to the buggy one, or vice-versa.

Our approach compares abstract representations of data-flow dependencies [21] in the two programs. These dependencies come in two forms:

- *read-from* dependencies from actions writing to a variable to actions reading that variable (specifying the write that a read receives its value from), and
- *store-order* dependencies which specify the order in which writes to the same variable are executed in the memory.

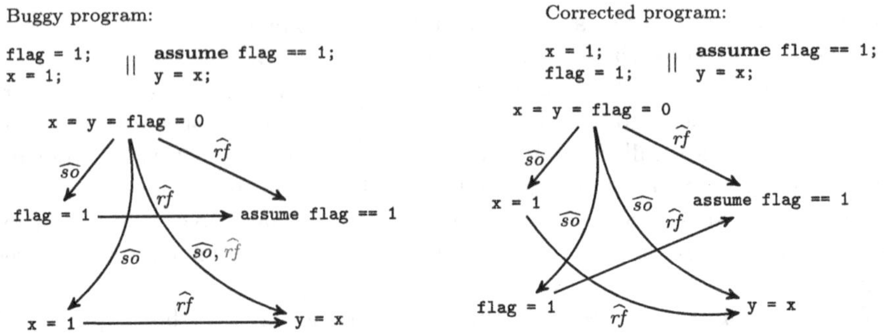

Fig. 1. The program on the left is considered buggy since there exists an execution where y takes an uninitialized value of x. The second program fixes this bug by permuting the statements in the first thread. The bottom part of the figure pictures their abstract traces of rank 1. Read-from, resp., store-order, dependencies are represented by edges labeled with $\widehat{rf}$, resp., $\widehat{so}$. The second program is a refinement of rank 1 of the first one, but the reverse is not true.

The bottom part of Fig. 1 pictures an abstract trace for each of the two programs where only individual dependencies are tracked (whether they occur in some trace), i.e., of rank 1. We can notice that the set of dependencies in the fixed version is a strict subset of the set of dependencies in the original (buggy) version. This fact suggests that the bug fix has removed some behaviors but introduced none. This is not a theoretical guarantee but its likelihood can be increased by considering abstract traces of bigger ranks. Moreover, the difference between the abstract trace of the buggy version and the one of the fixed version consists of one read-from dependency, from a fictitious write which assigns initial values to the variables, to the read of x in y = x. This dependency is a succinct description of all the interleavings containing the bug, which read an uninitialized value of x. The fact that this dependency doesn't occur anymore in the fixed version implies that the buggy behaviors have been removed.

In general, exposing the difference between the data-flow in two programs may require computing *sets* of data-flow dependencies occurring in the *same* execution of one program and not the other one, i.e., abstract traces of rank $k > 1$. Figure 2 lists two programs doing two parallel increments of a shared variable x, without synchronization on the left and protected by locks on the right. In this case, there exists no data-flow dependency admitted only by the first program or only by the second, i.e., the abstract traces of rank 1 are identical. However, there exists a *pair* of data-flow dependencies which occur in the same execution of the buggy program (that has no synchronization) and not in the corrected one (that uses locks): the two reads of x (from the assignments to temp1 and temp2) can both take their value from the initial state. Our framework allows to witness such differences for fixed values of the rank k.

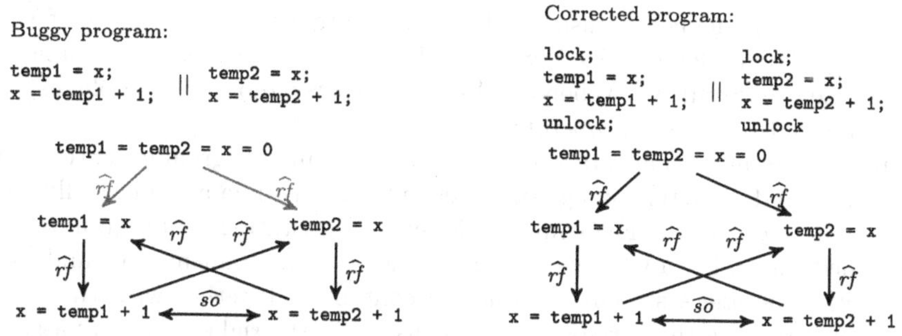

Fig. 2. Two programs doing two parallel increments of `x`. The bottom part of the figure pictures their abstract traces of rank 1. For readability, the $\widehat{so}$ dependencies starting from the assignment representing initial values are omitted. Considering abstract traces of rank 2, the pair of red $\widehat{rf}$ dependencies belongs to the abstract trace of the buggy program but not to that of the correct version. The second program is a refinement of rank 2 of the first one because it has less (pairs of) dependencies which occur in some execution. The reverse doesn't hold.

3 Multi-threaded Programs

We consider a simple multi-threaded programming model in which each thread executes a bounded sequence of steps corresponding to assignments, boolean tests, and synchronization primitives. The semantics of a program is defined as a set of traces [21], which are partially-ordered sets of read or write actions.

Let Vars be a set of variables. The grammar of Fig. 3 describes our language of multi-threaded programs. For generality, we leave the syntax of expressions e in assignments and **assume** statements unspecified. We allow expressions $e = *$ where $*$ is the (nullary) non-deterministic choice operator. Note that **if-then-else** conditionals can be modeled using **assume** statements and the non-deterministic choice. To simplify the exposition, we assume that the same variable doesn't appear in both the left and the right part of an assignment (e.g., we forbid assignments of the form x := $x + 1$). This simplifies the trace semantics given hereafter, and it could be removed assuming that the program is first rewritten to static single assignment form. Also, we consider a minimal set of synchronization statements, $\mathsf{lock}/\mathsf{unlock}$ over a unique lock object. However, our approach easily extends to any class of synchronization primitives. The set of variables in a statement s, resp., a program P, denoted by $\mathsf{Vars}(s)$,

$$s ::= x \texttt{ := } e \mid \textbf{assume } e \mid \mathsf{lock} \mid \mathsf{unlock} \mid s \texttt{ [] } s \mid s\texttt{; } s \mid$$
$$P ::= s \mid P \,||\, P$$

Fig. 3. The syntax of our language. Each program P is the parallel composition of a fixed number of threads – ; denotes the sequential composition and [] the non-deterministic choice between two control-flow paths. Also, $x \in \mathsf{Vars}$ and e is an expression over Vars.

resp., $\mathsf{Vars}(P)$, is defined as usual. The set of statements s over a set of variables $V \subseteq \mathsf{Vars}$ is denoted by $\mathsf{Stmts}(V)$. The set of statements of a program P is denoted by $\mathsf{Stmts}(P)$. When all the variables range over the booleans, the program is called a *boolean program*.

Program configurations are variable valuations, and program executions are defined as usual, as interleavings of statements (we assume a sequentially consistent semantics). In the following, we define representations of program executions called *traces*. For a variable x, $\mathbb{W}(x)$ is the set of assignments to x and $\mathbb{R}(x)$ is the set of `assume` e statements where e contains x together with the set of assignments reading the variable x (i.e., x occurs in the right part). We assume that $\mathsf{Stmts}(P)$ contains a fictitious statement init assigning initial values to all the program variables. We have that $\mathsf{init} \in \mathbb{W}(x)$ for every x. The synchronization primitives lock and unlock are interpreted as both a read and a write of a distinguished variable l. Thus, $\mathbb{W}(l) = \mathbb{R}(l) = \{\mathsf{lock}, \mathsf{unlock}\}$.

Essentially, a trace consists of three relations over the program statements, which represent the data and control dependencies from a program execution. The *store order so* represents the ordering of write accesses to each variable, and the *read-from relation rf* (from writes to reads) indicates the assignment that a read receives its value from. The *program order po* represents the ordering of events issued by the same thread. These relations represent a sequentially consistent execution when their union is consistent with the composition of *rf* and *so* (known also as the *conflict relation*).

Definition 1 (Trace). *A trace of program P is a tuple $t = (S, po, so, rf)$ where $S \subseteq \mathsf{Stmts}(P)$, $\mathsf{init} \in S$, and po, so, and rf are binary relations over S such that:*

1. *po relates statements included in the same thread,*
2. *so relates statements writing to the same variable, i.e., $so \subseteq \bigcup_x ((S \cap \mathbb{W}(x))^2$, and for each variable x, it defines a total order between the writes to x where init is ordered before all the other writes,*
3. *rf relates writes and reads to the same variable, i.e., $rf \subseteq \bigcup_x (S \cap \mathbb{W}(x)) \times (S \cap \mathbb{R}(x))$, and associates to every read of a variable x a write to x, i.e., the inverse of rf is a total function from $S \cap \mathbb{R}(x)$ to $S \cap \mathbb{W}(x)$, and*
4. *the union of po, so, rf, and $rf \circ so$, is acyclic.*

For a program P, let $\mathsf{Traces}(P)$ be its set of traces. Figure 4 lists two programs and their sets of traces.

4 Abstracting Traces

We are interested in comparing the set of behaviors of two programs according to *abstract* representations of traces. These representations are defined in two steps. We first define a projection operator that removes a given set of statements (defined by a set of variables), e.g., synchronization primitives, and the program order from all the traces of a given program[4]. Such a projection operator focuses

[4] Our framework can be extended such that the projection operator removes only a user-specified fragment of the program order.

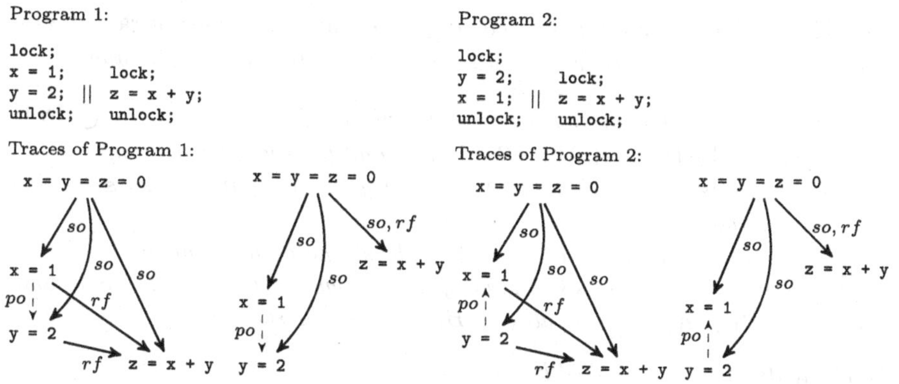

Fig. 4. Two programs over the same set of statements but with different program orders, and different sets of traces. For readability, we write x = y = z = 0 instead of init for the statement that assigns initial values to variables, and we omit lock/unlock statements.

on the differences in cross-thread data-flow interferences, and ignores details that are irrelevant for standard safety specifications (which are agnostic for instance to the state of the synchronization objects). Then, we define an abstract domain for representing sets of traces obtained through projection, which is based on a graph structure describing the union of all the traces in a given set.

For a program P, a set V of variables is called *closed* when P doesn't include a statement s that uses both a variable in V and a variable outside of V, i.e., $\mathsf{Vars}(s) \subseteq V$ or $\mathsf{Vars}(s) \cap V = \emptyset$ for each $s \in \mathsf{Stmts}(P)$. For example, in the case of the programs in Fig. 4, the set of variables $\{\mathtt{x}, \mathtt{y}, \mathtt{z}\}$ is closed, and $\{\mathtt{x}, \mathtt{y}\}$ is not closed because of the statement $\mathtt{z} := \mathtt{x} + \mathtt{y}$. For a closed set of variables V, a V*-trace* of P is a tuple $t = (\mathsf{Stmts}(V) \cap S, so, rf)$ obtained from a standard trace $t' = (S, po', so', rf')$ of P by preserving only the statements over the variables in V and removing the program order, i.e., $so = so' \cap (\mathsf{Stmts}(V) \cap S)^2$ and $rf = rf' \cap (\mathsf{Stmts}(V) \cap S)^2$. Since V is closed, the relations so and rf in t satisfy the properties (2) and (3) in Definition 1.

The set of all V-traces of a program P is denoted by $\mathsf{Traces}[V](P)$.

For example, the programs in Fig. 4 have the same set of V-traces where $V = \{\mathtt{x}, \mathtt{y}, \mathtt{z}\}$. This holds because V-traces don't contain the lock/unlock statements and the program order.

We define a parametrized abstraction for a set of V-traces that contains all the statements in those traces, the union of the store order, resp., read-from, relations, and for a parameter k, all the non-singleton sets of so or rf dependencies of size at most k that occur together in the same V-trace. As the parameter k increases, the abstraction is more precise. For two sets A and B, and $k \geq 2$, $\mathcal{P}_k(A, B)$ is the set of pairs (A', B') where $A' \subseteq A$, $B' \subseteq B$, and $2 \leq |A' \cup B'| \leq k$.

Definition 2 (Abstract trace). *For $k \geq 1$, an* abstract trace of rank k *is a tuple* $\widehat{t} = (S, \widehat{so}, \widehat{rf}, \widehat{sets})$ *where S is a set of statements with* init $\in S$ *and*

- $\widehat{so}$ *and* $\widehat{rf}$ *are two relations over statements in S such that* $\widehat{so} \subseteq \bigcup_x (S \cap \mathbb{W}(x))^2$, $\widehat{rf} \subseteq \bigcup_x (S \cap \mathbb{W}(x)) \times (S \cap \mathbb{R}(x))$, *and for every variable x,*
  - $\widehat{so}$ *contains* (s_1, s_2) *or* (s_2, s_1), *for every two assignments* $s_1, s_2 \in S \cap \mathbb{W}(x)$, *and*
  - *every read on x is related by* $\widehat{rf}$ *to at least one assignment to x*
- $\widehat{sets} = \emptyset$ *if* $k = 1$, *and* $\widehat{sets} \subseteq \mathcal{P}_k(\widehat{so}, \widehat{rf})$, *otherwise. When* $k \geq 2$, *we assume that* $A_1 \cup B_1 \not\subseteq A_2 \cup B_2$ *for all* $(A_1, B_1), (A_2, B_2) \in \widehat{sets}$.

The elements of $\widehat{sets}$ *are called k-clusters.*

The relations $\widehat{so}$ and $\widehat{rf}$ represent the union of the store order and read-from relations in a given set of V-traces, respectively. Therefore, $\widehat{so}$ is not necessarily a total order, and the inverse of $\widehat{rf}$ is not necessarily a total function, when considering statements that assign or read the same variable (i.e., they don't satisfy the properties (2) and (3) in Definition 1). Also, to avoid redundancy, we assume that the elements of $\widehat{sets}$ are incomparable. Figures 1 and 2 contain examples of abstract traces.

The *concretization* of an abstract trace $\widehat{t}$ of rank k, denoted by $\gamma(\widehat{t})$, is the set of traces formed of some dependencies in $\widehat{t}$ and which contain at least one set of dependencies in $\widehat{sets}$, if $k \geq 2$. Formally, $\gamma(\widehat{t})$ for an abstract trace $\widehat{t} = (S, \widehat{so}, \widehat{rf}, \widehat{sets})$ of rank k is the set of V-traces $t = (S', so, rf)$ where $S' \subseteq S$, $so \subseteq \widehat{so}$, $rf \subseteq \widehat{rf}$, and if $k \geq 2$, then $u|_1 \subseteq so$ and $u|_2 \subseteq rf$ for some $u \in \widehat{sets}$. We use $u|_i$ to denote the i-th component of the tuple u. Note that a trace in the concretization of $\widehat{t}$ may not necessarily use all the statements in $\widehat{t}$.

We define an order relation $\leq$ between abstract traces, which requires that they contain the same set of statements and the "smaller" trace contains less dependencies or sets of dependencies.

Definition 3 (Order relation). *For $k \geq 1$ and two abstract traces* $\widehat{t_1} = (S, \widehat{so_1}, \widehat{rf_1}, \widehat{sets_1})$ *and* $\widehat{t_2} = (S, \widehat{so_2}, \widehat{rf_2}, \widehat{sets_2})$ *of rank k,*

$$\widehat{t_1} \leq \widehat{t_2} \text{ iff } \widehat{so_1} \subseteq \widehat{so_2},\ \widehat{rf_1} \subseteq \widehat{rf_2},\text{ and } \widehat{sets_1} \subseteq \widehat{sets_2}.$$

Lemma 1. *The order relation $\leq$ defines a lattice over the set of abstract traces.*

5 Interference Refinement

We define a notion of refinement between two programs, called *interference refinement* (or refinement for short), which holds under the assumption that the two programs are structurally similar. Essentially, we assume that there exists a mapping between variables in the two programs, and a mapping between statements, such that every two related statements read and respectively, write the same set of variables (modulo the variable mapping). Then, interference refinement is defined as the inclusion of V-trace sets for some set of variables V (modulo the statement mapping). We then give an abstract notion of interference refinement that uses abstract traces instead of sets of V-traces.

Let P_1 and P_2 be two programs, and V_1 and V_2 closed sets of variables of P_1 and P_2, respectively. A pair (v, s) is called a *statement matching* when $v : V_1 \rightarrow V_2$ is a bijection and $s : \mathsf{Stmts}(P_1) \cap \mathsf{Stmts}(V_1) \rightarrow \mathsf{Stmts}(P_2) \cap \mathsf{Stmts}(V_2)$ is a bijection such that $s \in \mathbb{W}(x)$ iff $s(s) \in \mathbb{W}(v(x))$ and $s \in \mathbb{R}(x)$ iff $s(s) \in \mathbb{R}(v(x))$ for each $s \in \mathsf{Stmts}(P_1) \cap \mathsf{Stmts}(V_1)$ and $x \in V_1$. To simplify the exposition, in the rest of the paper, we consider statement matchings where v and s are the identity. Extending our notions to the general case is straightforward.

Let P_1 and P_2 be two programs, and V a set of variables which is closed for both P_1 and P_2.

Definition 4 (V-Refinement). *A program P_1 is a* V-interference refinement *(or V-refinement for short) of another program P_2 iff* $\mathsf{Traces}[V](P_1) \subseteq \mathsf{Traces}[V](P_2)$. *Also, P_1 and P_2 are* V-interference equivalent *(or V-equivalent for short) iff P_1 is a V-interference refinement of P_2 and vice-versa.*

We define an approximation of V-refinement, called *(V, k)-refinement*, that compares abstract traces of rank k instead of concrete sets of V-traces. More precisely, (V, k)-refinement compares abstract traces that *represent* the V-traces of a program in the following sense: the sets of dependencies in the abstract trace are not spurious, i.e., they do occur together in a concrete V-trace, and the abstract trace contains all the sets of dependencies up to size k that occur in the same V-trace. Forbidding spurious (sets of) dependencies guarantees that V-refinement doesn't hold when the approximated version doesn't hold, while completeness allows to prove that the approximated version does imply V-refinement for big enough values of k.

Definition 5. *An abstract trace $\widehat{t} = (S, \widehat{so}, \widehat{rf}, \widehat{sets})$ of rank k* represents *a program P for a closed set of variables V when*

- *for every two statements $s_1, s_2 \in S$, $(s_1, s_2) \in \widehat{so}$, resp., $(s_1, s_2) \in \widehat{rf}$, iff there exists a V-trace $t = (S', so, rf) \in \mathsf{Traces}[V](P)$ such that $(s_1, s_2) \in so$, resp., $(s_1, s_2) \in rf$, and*
- *if $k \geq 2$, then for each $u \in \mathcal{P}_k(\widehat{so}, \widehat{rf})$, $u \in \widehat{sets}$ iff there exists a V-trace $t = (S', so, rf) \in \mathsf{Traces}[V](P)$ such that $u \in \mathcal{P}_k(so, rf)$.*

For any abstract trace $\widehat{t}$ representing a program P for a closed set of variables V, we have that $\mathsf{Traces}[V](P) \subseteq \gamma(\widehat{t})$.

Definition 6 ((V, k)-Refinement/Equivalence). *A program P_1 is a* (V, k)-refinement *of another program P_2 iff there exist $\widehat{t_1}$ and $\widehat{t_2}$ two abstract traces of rank k representing P_1 and P_2 for the set of variables V, respectively, such that $\widehat{t_1} \leq \widehat{t_2}$. Also, P_1 and P_2 are* (V, k)-equivalent *iff P_1 is a (V, k)-refinement of P_2 and vice-versa.*

When V is understood from the context, we may use refinement of rank k instead of (V, k)-refinement.

Example 1. Distinguishing two programs with respect to the notion of (V, k)-equivalence may require arbitrarily-large values of k (these values are however polynomially bounded by the size of the programs). Indeed, we show that there exist two programs which are $(V, k-1)$-equivalent but not (V, k)-equivalent, for each $k \geq 2$.

Figure 5 lists two programs that make k parallel increments to a variable `x`, for an arbitrary $k \geq 2$. The increments are non-atomic in the first program, and protected by a semaphore `s` initialized with $k - 1$ permits in the second program (`acquire` acquires a permit from the semaphore, blocking until one is available, while `release` returns one permit to the semaphore)[5]. The first program admits all the executions of the second one and one more execution where all the k threads read the initial value of `x`. Therefore, the first program has a trace that contains the set of read-from dependencies from `init` to each assignment `temp1 = x`,...,`tempk = x` (the k read-from dependencies marked in red in Fig. 5). This is not true for the second program where the semaphore synchronization disallows such a trace.

Let us consider the closed set of variables $V = \{\texttt{x}, \texttt{temp1}, \ldots, \texttt{tempk}\}$. Every set of at most $k - 1$ *so* or *rf* dependencies occur together in the same V-trace of one program iff this holds for the other program as well. Therefore, the two programs are $(V, k-1)$-equivalent. However, the two programs are *not* (V, k)-equivalent, more precisely, the first program is not a (V, k)-refinement of the second one. The abstract trace representing the first program contains a k-cluster which is the set of read-from dependencies from `init` to each assignment `temp1 = x`,...,`tempk = x`. □

A direct consequence of the definitions is that V-refinement and (V, k)-refinement coincide for big enough values of k. The number of read-from and respectively, store-order dependencies, in a V-trace is bounded by $|\mathsf{Stmts}(P) \cap \mathsf{Stmts}(V)|^2$. Therefore, there exist at most $2^{2 \cdot |\mathsf{Stmts}(P) \cap \mathsf{Stmts}(V)|^2}$ V-traces, which implies that V-refinement and (V, k)-refinement coincide when k reaches this bound. Otherwise, we have only that V-refinement implies (V, k)-refinement.

Theorem 1. *For every $k \geq 1$, P_1 is a (V, k)-refinement of P_2 when P_1 is a V-refinement of P_2. Moreover, there exists $k \leq 2^{2 \cdot |\mathsf{Stmts}(P) \cap \mathsf{Stmts}(V)|^2}$ such that P_1 is a V-refinement of P_2 iff P_1 is a (V, k)-refinement of P_2.*

6 Checking Interference Refinement

We show that checking whether a program is *not* a (V, k)-refinement of another one, for some closed set of variables V and some $k \geq 1$, is polynomial time

[5] The simple syntax we considered in Sect. 3 doesn't include `acquire`/`release` actions, but they can be easily modeled using lock/unlock.

First program:

```
temp1 = x;         ||  temp2 = x;         ||...||  tempk = x;
x = temp1 + 1;         x = temp2 + 1;              x = tempk + 1;
```

Second program:

```
acquire(s);            acquire(s);                 acquire(s);
temp1 = x;         ||  temp2 = x;         ||...||  tempk = x;
x = temp1 + 1;         x = temp2 + 1;              x = tempk + 1;
release(s);            release(s);                 release(s);
```

Abstract traces:

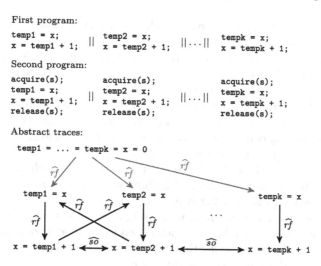

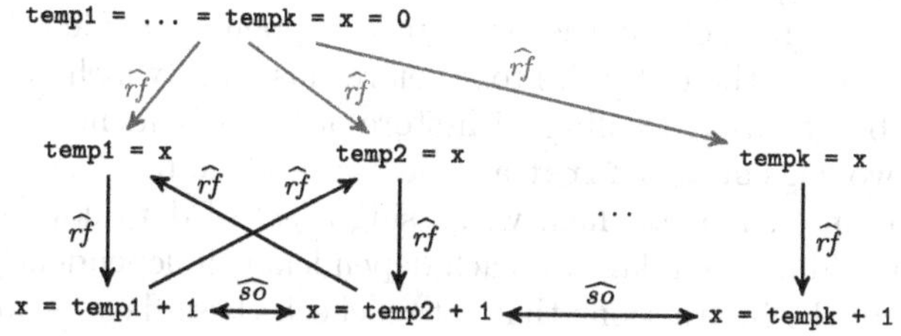

Fig. 5. Two programs doing k parallel increments of x. The two programs have the same abstract trace of rank 1 which is partially given in the bottom part of the figure; we omit some of the $\widehat{so}$ dependencies for readability. The abstract trace of rank k of the first program contains a k-cluster which is the set of read-from dependencies marked in red (they occur in the same trace) while this is not true for the second program.

reducible to assertion checking. This reduction holds for programs manipulating data coming from arbitrary, not necessarily bounded, domains. Instantiating this reduction to the case of boolean programs, we get that this problem is in Δ_2^P when k is fixed, and in Σ_2^P, otherwise. We show that these upper complexity bounds match the lower bounds. As a corollary, we get that deciding whether a program is *not* a V-refinement of another one is also Σ_2^P-complete.

The following intermediary result shows that checking whether a fixed set of data-flow dependencies occur together in some V-trace of a program P is reducible to assertion checking in an instrumentation of P. The instrumentation uses a set of boolean flags to witness the order between two assignments on the same variable, in the case of store order dependencies, or that an assignment on a variable x is the last such assignment before a statement reading the value of x, in the case of read-from dependencies. For instance, let us consider a fragment with three threads of the first program in Fig. 5.

```
                          temp2 = x;                  [
temp1 = x;                [                           temp3 = x;
[                         x = temp2 + 1;              if ( rf_saw_first &&
x = temp1 + 1;        ||  if ( rf_saw_first &&    ||       !rf_saw_write )
rf_saw_first = true;           !rf_saw_second )        rf_saw_second = true;
]                           rf_saw_write = true;      ]
                          ]                           x = temp3 + 1;
```

The read-from dependency from the write to x in the first thread to the read of x in the third thread can be witnessed using three boolean flags rf_saw_first, `rf_saw_write`, and `rf_saw_second`, which are initially false and which are updated atomically with the program's statements. The flag `rf_saw_second` is true for all executions whose trace contains this read-from dependency (and only for these executions)[6]. For readability, we use brackets instead of synchronization primitives to delimit atomic sections.

The flag `rf_saw_first` is set to true when the write in the first thread happens, `rf_saw_write` is set to true when any other write to `x`, i.e., the write to `x` in the second thread, happens after the one in the first thread, and `rf_saw_second` is set to true when the read of `x` in the last thread happens, provided that the write in the first thread was the last write to `x` before this read (which is equivalent to `rf_saw_write` being false). Dealing with store-order dependencies is simpler, it requires only two flags `so_saw_first` and `so_saw_second` to witness that a write happens before another one. Then, witnessing a *set* of data-flow dependencies can be done by adding such flags for each dependency, independently. Note that the placement of the instructions that set or check these flags is only based on syntax and their addition is easy to automate.

In formal terms, let

$$D_{rf} \subseteq \bigcup_x (\mathsf{Stmts}(V) \cap \mathbb{W}(x)) \times (\mathsf{Stmts}(V) \cap \mathbb{W}(x)) \text{ and}$$
$$D_{so} \subseteq \bigcup_x (\mathsf{Stmts}(V) \cap \mathbb{W}(x)) \times (\mathsf{Stmts}(V) \cap \mathbb{W}(x))$$

be two sets of read-from, resp., store-order dependencies, and let $D = D_{rf} \cup D_{so}$. For each $(s_1, s_2) \in D$, P is instrumented with two boolean variables `saw_first`$[s_1, s_2]$ and `saw_second`$[s_1, s_2]$ such that `saw_first`$[s_1, s_2]$ is atomically set to true when s_1 is executed, and `saw_second`$[s_1, s_2]$ is atomically set to true when s_2 is executed, provided that `saw_first`$[s_1, s_2]$ is already true. Additionally, when $(s_1, s_2) \in D_{rf}$, a variable `saw_write`$[s_1, s_2]$ is set to true whenever `saw_first`$[s_1, s_2]$ is true, `saw_second`$[s_1, s_2]$ is false, and a statement writing to the same variable as s_1 is executed. Also, `saw_second`$[s_1, s_2]$ is set to true when additionally, `saw_write`$[s_1, s_2]$ is false (this is to ensure that s_1 is the last write before s_2). The instrumented program is denoted by $P[D]$.

Lemma 2. *There exists a V-trace $t = (S, so, rf)$ of P such that $D_{rf} \subseteq rf$ and $D_{so} \subseteq so$ iff $P[D]$ reaches a program configuration where* `saw_second`$[s_1, s_2]$ *is* `true` *for all* $(s_1, s_2) \in D$.

For a fixed k, checking (V, k)-refinement needs to consider only fixed size sets of dependencies. Therefore, the following holds.

Theorem 2. *Let P_1 and P_2 be two programs. Checking whether P_1 is* not *a (V, k)-refinement of P_2 is polynomial time reducible to assertion checking.*

---

[6] Equivalently, the assignment `rf_saw_second = true` can be replaced by `assert false`. Then, this assertion fails whenever this read-from dependency occurs in some trace of the program.

Proof. The program P_1 is not a (V, k)-refinement of P_2 iff there exists a set of dependencies D (of size at most k) such that D occur together in some V-trace of P_1, but no V-trace of P_2. Since the number of possible sets D is polynomial in the size of P_1 and P_2, a polynomial reduction to assertion checking consists in enumerating all the possible instances of D and checking whether D occurs in the same V-trace of P_1 or P_2 using the result in Lemma 2. □

The algorithm proposed in the proof of Theorem 2 reduces the problem of checking non (V, k)-refinement, for a fixed k, to a polynomial set of assertion checking queries and leads the way to the reuse of the existing safety verification technology. This will be demonstrated in Sect. 7.

For boolean programs, assertion checking is NP-complete[7], so checking (V, k)-refinement for any k is in Σ_2^P. We show that it is also Σ_2^P-hard.

Theorem 3. *Let P_1 and P_2 be two boolean programs. Checking whether P_1 is not a (V, k)-refinement of P_2 is Σ_2^P-complete.*

Proof. A Σ_2^P algorithm for deciding non (V, k)-refinement starts by guessing a set of dependencies D (of size at most $2 \cdot |\mathsf{Stmts}(P) \cap \mathsf{Stmts}(V)|^2$), and then proceeds by checking that the dependencies in D occur in the same V-trace of P_1 (which by Lemma 2 can be decided in NP) and in none of the traces of P_2 (which again by Lemma 2 is in co-NP).

To prove Σ_2^P-hardness we show that deciding the satisfiability of an $\exists^*\forall^*$ boolean formula can be reduced to checking (V, k)-refinement for some k which depends on the number of existential variables in the boolean formula. Let $\exists \vec{x}\ \forall \vec{y}.\ \varphi$ be a boolean formula in prenex normal form (without free variables), where $\vec{x} = (x_1, \ldots, x_n)$ and $\vec{y}$ are vectors of boolean variables. Also, let P_1 and P_2 be the following programs:

Program P_1:

```
x_1 = 0 [] x_1 = 1;          assume done;
...                          t_1 = x_1;
x_n = 0 [] x_n = 1;     ||   ...
y⃗ = ★;                       t_n = x_n;
done = 1;                    b = a;
a = 1;                       assume ¬φ;
```

Program P_2:

```
x_1 = 0 [] x_1 = 1;          assume done;
...                          t_1 = x_1;
x_n = 0 [] x_n = 1;     ||   ...
y⃗ = ★;                       t_n = x_n;
done = 1;                    assume ¬φ;
a = 1;                       b = a;
```

We assume that all variables are 0 in the initial state. Let $D_{\vec{x}}$ be a set of read-from dependencies that includes either $(x_i = \mathtt{0},\ t_i = x_i)$ or $(x_i = \mathtt{1},\ t_i = x_i)$ for each $1 \leq i \leq n$. Then, let $D = D_{\vec{x}} \cup \{(\mathtt{a} = \mathtt{1}, \mathtt{b} = \mathtt{a})\}$ (the latter is also in rf).

Since the assignment `b = a` in P_1 is executed in every complete interleaving, there exists a trace of P_1 that contains all the read-from dependencies from D. This set of dependencies occurs in a trace of P_2 only if there exists some valuation for $\vec{y}$ such that φ is `false`. This implies that P_1 is not a $(V, n+1)$-refinement of P_2 where V is the set of all variables of P_1 iff $\exists \vec{x}\ \forall \vec{y}.\ \varphi$ is satisfiable. □

[7] Recall that we consider programs without looping constructs and procedure calls.

Following the same lines of Theorem 3, we can show that the problem of checking non (V, k)-refinement becomes Δ_2^P-complete when k is fixed. Essentially, the set of dependencies that need to be tracked are now of fixed size and they can be enumerated explicitly (as stated in Theorem 2).

Theorem 4. *Let P_1 and P_2 be two boolean programs. For a fixed but arbitrary $k \geq 1$, checking whether P_1 is* not *a (V, k)-refinement of P_2 is Δ_2^P-complete.*

Proof. The problem can be decided using a similar algorithm as in Theorem 3. Instead of non-deterministically guessing the set of dependencies D, we enumerate all such sets of dependencies of size k which are at most $O(|\mathsf{Stmts}(P) \cap \mathsf{Stmts}(V)|^{2 \cdot k})$ many.

To prove Δ_2^P-hardness we show that deciding the satisfiability of an $\exists^* \wedge \forall^*$ boolean formula can be reduced to checking $(V, 1)$-refinement. Let $\exists \vec{x}.\ \varphi_1 \wedge \forall \vec{y}.\ \varphi_2$ be a boolean formula (without free variables), where $\vec{x}$ and $\vec{y}$ are vectors of boolean variables. Also, let P_1 and P_2 be the following programs:

Program P_1:

```
x⃗ = ⋆;        ||  assume (done && φ1);
a = 1;        ||  b = a;
done = 1;
```

Program P_2:

```
y⃗ := ⋆;       ||  assume (done && ¬φ2);
a = 1;        ||  b = a;
done = 1;
```

We assume that all variables are 0 in the initial state. Let $V = \{\mathtt{a}, \mathtt{b}\}$ and $D = \{(\mathtt{a} = \mathtt{1}, \mathtt{b} = \mathtt{a})\}$ be a singleton set of read-from dependencies.

The assignment `b = a` in P_1 is executed if and only if there exists some valuation for $\vec{x}$ such that φ_1 holds, i.e., the formula $\exists \vec{x}.\ \varphi_1$ is satisfiable. Therefore, the dependency $(\mathtt{a} = \mathtt{1}, \mathtt{b} = \mathtt{a})$ occurs in a trace of P_1 iff $\exists \vec{x}.\ \varphi_1$ is satisfiable. By the definition of V, this is the only dependency possible in P_1, which may imply non $(V, 1)$-refinement. Furthermore, this dependency doesn't occur in a trace of P_2 if and only if the formula φ_2 holds for all valuations of $\vec{y}$, i.e., the formula $\forall \vec{y}.\ \varphi_2$ is satisfiable. Consequently, P_1 is not a $(V, 1)$-refinement of P_2 iff $\exists \vec{x}.\ \varphi_1 \wedge \forall \vec{y}.\ \varphi_2$ is satisfiable. □

7 Experimental Evaluation

To demonstrate the practical value of our approach, we argue that our notion of (V, k)-refinement:

- can be checked using the existing verification technology,
- witnesses for semantic differences (bug introduction) with small values of k,
- enables succinct representations for the semantic difference,
- is a relevant indicator of regression-freeness.

To argue these points, we consider a set of bug fixes produced by the ConcurrencySwapper synthesis tool [5] which model concurrency bug fixes for Linux device drivers reported at www.kernel.org[8]. We check whether the fixed version

[8] They are available at https://github.com/thorstent/ConcurrencySwapper.

Table 1. Experimental data for checking (V, k)-refinement. The size of the difference between the abstract trace of the original (buggy) and the fixed version, respectively, is the number of (sets of) dependencies occurring in one and not the other.

Name	#loc	#threads	k	# (sets of) possible dependencies	Size of the difference	Time
`r8169-1`	24	2	1/2/3	6/21/41	1/5/11	6.35 s/12.93 s/20.27 s
`r8169-2`	25	2	1/2/3	6/21/41	1/5/11	4.93 s/10.22 s/16.44 s
`r8169-3`	33	3	1/2/3	3/6/7	1/3/3	2.74 s/5.43 s/8.03 s
`i2c-hid`	27	2	1	27	2	45.65 s
`i2c-hid-noA`	27	2	1/2	27/237	0/4	42.34 s/24.3 m
`rtl8169`	256	7	1	94	3	37.27 m

is a (V, k)-refinement of the original one and vice-versa. We use this benchmark without modifications, except the use of the `pthread` library for managing threads (otherwise, the programs are written in C), and unfolding loops once.

We have added the annotation that reduces (V, k)-refinement checking to assertion checking (explained in Theorem 2) and used LazyCseq [11,12] (with backend CBMC [8]) for checking the assertions. LazyCseq is a bounded model checker that explores round-robin schedules up to a given bound on the number of rounds. We have used a bound of 4 for the number of rounds, which was enough to compute abstract traces that represent the considered programs (according to Definition 5). We have checked manually that these abstract traces are complete, i.e., that they contain all the sets of dependencies which occur in the same V-trace (up to the given bound). The fact that they don't contain spurious sets of dependencies is implied by the completeness of the bounded model checker. All the bug fixes except `i2c-hid` and `i2c-hid-noA` that consist in adding locks, are based on statement reordering[9]. This allowed us to consider closed sets of variables that consist of all variables except variables of type lock, and statement matchings (v, s) where v and s are the identity.

The results are reported in Table 1. Each line corresponds to a pair of programs, the version before and after a bug fix or a set of bug fixes implemented during the evolution of a Linux driver, r8169, i2c-hid, or rtl8169. We list the number of lines of code (loc) and the number of threads of the original version (before the bug fix). Checking refinement of rank 1 requires enumerating all pairs of statements accessing the same variable, at least one being a write, called *possible dependencies*, and verifying whether they occur in some execution of the original or the fixed version. To indicate the difficultly of the benchmark we give the number of such possible dependencies, or sets of possible dependencies of size at most k, when $k > 1$. Note that the number of possible dependencies is usually much smaller than the square of the number of statements. All measurements were made on a MacBook Pro 2.5 GHz Intel Core i7 machine.

[9] Studies of concurrency errors, e.g., [5,18], have reported that reordering statements for fixing bugs is very frequent (around 30% of the fixes are based on reorderings).

We consider several values of k for each example and in all cases we get that the fixed version is a refinement of rank k of the buggy version. Also, except for `i2c-hid-noA` with $k = 1$, the abstract trace of the correct version is *strictly* smaller than the one of the buggy version. The `i2c-hid` example contains some assertions that fail only in the buggy version. These assertions participate in read-from dependencies which allow to distinguish the buggy from the corrected version with abstract traces of rank 1. Removing these assertions requires abstract traces of rank 2 to distinguish the two versions. This fact is demonstrated in the `i2c-hid-noA` example which is exactly `i2c-hid` without those assertions.

These results indicate that comparing abstract traces of small ranks is enough to reveal interesting behaviors, in particular bugs (the abstract trace of the buggy version is always different from the one of the corrected version). Therefore, (V, k)-refinement for small values of k is a relevant indicator of regression-freeness. Note however that there is no theoretical connection between abstract trace difference and the presence of bugs. Moreover, (V, k)-refinement continues to hold when k is increased, as shown by the results in Table 1.

The difference between the abstract traces of the original and the fixed version, respectively, consists of few (sets of) dependencies. For the first three examples and $k = 1$, the difference consists of a single read-from dependency showing that a particular variable gets an uninitialized or undesired value (like in the example from Fig. 1). In the case of the fourth example when assertions are present, the difference between abstract traces of rank 1 consists of 2 read-from dependencies which correspond to two failing assertions. When assertions are removed, i.e., in the example `i2c-hid-noA`, the difference between the abstract traces of rank 2 consists of few pairs of dependencies similar to the example in Fig. 2. The buggy version of the example `rtl8169` contains 3 bugs that are repaired in the correct version. The difference between the abstract traces contains an explanation for each bug.

The running time increases with the number of threads and possible dependencies. However, since the presence of a set of dependencies (in some execution) reduces to an independently-checkable assertion, the verification process is easily parallelizable. Also, we didn't use assertion checking to exclude some dependencies that are obviously not feasible because of thread creation/join (i.e., reading from a write that belongs to a thread not yet created). As future work, we plan to investigate static analyses for filtering out such dependencies.

8 Related Work

The work on refinement checking [1] provides a general framework for comparing traces of two programs. However, in most instances one of the programs serves as a specification with very limited concurrency.

Joshi et al. [14] checks if a given concurrent program fails an assertion more often on an input compared to another concurrent program — the second program is usually limited to sequential interleavings only. Our approach does not require the presence of assertions to compare the two concurrent programs as it exploits the structural similarity between the two programs. The work closest to ours is the work on regression verification for multi-threaded programs [7]. This paper proposes a proof rule to prove that the input-output relations for two multithreaded programs are the same. This approach cannot distinguish between two transformations that introduce and respectively, remove a bug. In both cases, the proof rule will fail to establish equivalence w.r.t. the input-output relation.

Generalizations of good or bad program executions using partial orders have been previously used in the context of assertion checking or program synthesis [5,6,9]. The notion of trace robustness proposed in the context of weak memory models [3,4] compares a program running under a weak memory model with the same program running under Sequential Consistency (SC). The focus there is to check if a program admits behaviors which are not possible under SC while our goal is to compare two programs running under SC.

There has been interest in applying program analysis towards the problem of comparing two versions of a program, in the context of sequential programs. Jackson and Ladd [13] used the term *semantic diff* to compare two sequential programs in terms of the dependency between input and output variables. For most concurrency related transformations, such a metric is unlikely to yield any difference. There has been work on equivalence checking of sequential executions across program versions using uninterpreted function abstraction and program verifiers [10,15]. Verification Modulo Versions [16,17] compares two sequential programs w.r.t. a set of assertions. Differential symbolic execution [20] summarizes differences in summaries of two procedures, and Marinescu et al. [19] use symbolic execution for generating tests over program differences.

9 Conclusions

We have presented an approach for comparing two closely related concurrent programs whose goal is to give feedback about interesting differences, without relying on user-provided assertions. This approach is based on comparing abstract representations of the data-flow dependencies admitted by two subsequent versions of the same program. This comparison is reducible to assertion checking which enables the reuse of the existing verification technology.

As future work, we plan to investigate static analyses for discarding data-flow dependencies which are not interesting or not feasible. This can be also used to minimize the number of assertion checking queries when checking (V, k)-refinement. Moreover, we consider extending our theory to programs that contain loops where the main difficulty is that traces contain an unbounded number of copies of the same statement (when inside a loop). The idea would be define a new abstraction of traces that collapses together occurrences of the same statement from multiple iterations of a loop. On the practical side, we aim at a more thorough experimental evaluation of this approach in the context of other program transformations. On one side, we plan to consider more general program edits than reordering statements or modifying synchronization primitives which need to consider more general statement matchings than the identity. Also, we plan to investigate other classes of program transformations besides bug-fixing, such as refactoring, addition of new features or performance fixes. For instance, in the context of performance fixes, the new version of the program may allow more behaviors (interleavings). Our approach would produce a succinct representation of the new behaviors (in terms of small sets of dependencies), which may help in validating their correctness.

References

1. Abadi, M., Lamport, L.: The existence of refinement mappings. Theor. Comput. Sci. **82**(2), 253–284 (1991)
2. Biere, A., Bloem, R. (eds.): CAV 2014. LNCS, vol. 8559. Springer, Cham (2014)
3. Bouajjani, A., Derevenetc, E., Meyer, R.: Robustness against relaxed memory models. In: Hasselbring, W., Ehmke, N.C. (eds.) Software Engineering 2014, Kiel, Deutschland, GI. LNI, vol. 227, pp. 85–86 (2014)
4. Burckhardt, S., Musuvathi, M.: Effective program verification for relaxed memory models. CAV **2008**, 107–120 (2008)
5. Černý, P., Henzinger, T.A., Radhakrishna, A., Ryzhyk, L., Tarrach, T.: Efficient synthesis for concurrency by semantics-preserving transformations. In: Sharygina, N., Veith, H. (eds.) CAV 2013. LNCS, vol. 8044, pp. 951–967. Springer, Heidelberg (2013). doi:10.1007/978-3-642-39799-8_68
6. Černý, P., Henzinger, T.A., Radhakrishna, A., Ryzhyk, L., Tarrach, T.: Regression-free synthesis for concurrency. In: Biere and Bloem [3], pp. 568–584
7. Chaki, S., Gurfinkel, A., Strichman, O.: Regression verification for multi-threaded programs (with extensions to locks and dynamic thread creation). Formal Methods Syst. Des. **47**(3), 287–301 (2015)
8. Clarke, E., Kroening, D., Lerda, F.: A tool for checking ANSI-C programs. In: Jensen, K., Podelski, A. (eds.) TACAS 2004. LNCS, vol. 2988, pp. 168–176. Springer, Heidelberg (2004). doi:10.1007/978-3-540-24730-2_15
9. Farzan, A., Kincaid, Z., Podelski, A.: Inductive data flow graphs. In: Giacobazzi, R., Cousot, R. (eds.) The 40th Annual ACM SIGPLAN-SIGACT Symposium on Principles of Programming Languages, POPL 2013, Rome, Italy, 23–25 January 2013, pp. 129–142. ACM (2013)
10. Godlin, B., Strichman, O.: Inference rules for proving the equivalence of recursive procedures. Acta Inf. **45**(6), 403–439 (2008)
11. Inverso, O., Nguyen, T.L., Fischer, B., Torre, S.L., Parlato, G.: Lazy-CSeq: a context-bounded model checking tool for multi-threaded c-programs. In: Cohen, M.B., Grunske, L., Whalen, M. (eds.) 30th IEEE/ACM International Conference on Automated Software Engineering, ASE 2015, Lincoln, NE, USA, 9–13 November 2015, pp. 807–812. IEEE Computer Society (2015)
12. Inverso, O., Tomasco, E., Fischer, B., La Torre, S., Parlato, G.: Bounded model checking of multi-threaded C programs via lazy sequentialization. In: Biere and Bloem, pp. 585–602
13. Jackson, D., Ladd, D.A.: Semantic Diff: a tool for summarizing the effects of modifications. In: Proceedings of the International Conference on Software Maintenance, ICSM 1994, Victoria, BC, Canada, September 1994, pp. 243–252. IEEE Computer Society (1994)

14. Joshi, S., Lahiri, S.K., Lal, A.: Underspecified harnesses and interleaved bugs. In: Field, J., Hicks, M. (eds.) Proceedings of the 39th ACM SIGPLAN-SIGACT Symposium on Principles of Programming Languages, POPL 2012, Philadelphia, Pennsylvania, USA, 22–28 January 2012, pp. 19–30. ACM (2012)
15. Lahiri, S.K., Hawblitzel, C., Kawaguchi, M., Rebêlo, H.: SYMDIFF: a language-agnostic semantic diff tool for imperative programs. In: Proceedings of the 24th International Conference on Computer Aided Verification, CAV 2012 (2012)
16. Lahiri, S.K., McMillan, K.L., Sharma, R., Hawblitzel, C.: Differential assertion checking. In: Joint Meeting of the European Software Engineering Conference and the ACM SIGSOFT Symposium on the Foundations of Software Engineering, ESEC/FSE 2013, Saint Petersburg, Russian Federation, 18–26 August 2013, pp. 345–355. ACM (2013)
17. Logozzo, F., Lahiri, S.K., Fähndrich, M., Blackshear, S.: Verification modulo versions: towards usable verification. In: ACM SIGPLAN Conference on Programming Language Design and Implementation, PLDI 2014, Edinburgh, United Kingdom, 09–11 June 2014, p. 32. ACM (2014)
18. Lu, S., Park, S., Seo, E., Zhou, Y.: Learning from mistakes: a comprehensive study on real world concurrency bug characteristics. In: Eggers, S.J., Larus, J.R. (eds.) Proceedings of the 13th International Conference on Architectural Support for Programming Languages and Operating Systems, ASPLOS 2008, Seattle, WA, USA, 1–5 March 2008, pp. 329–339. ACM (2008)
19. Marinescu, P.D., Cadar, K.C.: high-coverage testing of software patches. In: Joint Meeting of the European Software Engineering Conference and the ACM SIGSOFT Symposium on the Foundations of Software Engineering, ESEC/FSE 2013, Saint Petersburg, Russian Federation, 18–26 August 2013, pp. 235–245. ACM (2013)
20. Person, S., Dwyer, M.B., Elbaum, S.G., Pasareanu, C.S.: Differential symbolic execution. In: Proceedings of the 16th ACM SIGSOFT International Symposium on Foundations of Software Engineering, 2008, Atlanta, Georgia, USA, 9–14 November 2008, pp. 226–237. ACM (2008)
21. Shasha, D., Snir, M.: Efficient and correct execution of parallel programs that share memory. ACM Trans. Program. Lang. Syst. **10**(2), 282–312 (1988)

Learning Shape Analysis

Marc Brockschmidt[1(✉)], Yuxin Chen[2], Pushmeet Kohli[4], Siddharth Krishna[3], and Daniel Tarlow[1]

[1] Microsoft Research, Cambridge, UK
mabrocks@microsoft.com
[2] ETH Zürich, Zürich, Switzerland
[3] New York University, New York, USA
[4] Microsoft Research, Redmond, USA

Abstract. We present a data-driven verification framework to automatically prove memory safety of heap-manipulating programs. Our core contribution is a novel statistical machine learning technique that maps observed program states to (possibly disjunctive) separation logic formulas describing the invariant shape of (possibly nested) data structures at relevant program locations. We then attempt to verify these predictions using a program verifier, where counterexamples to a predicted invariant are used as additional input to the shape predictor in a refinement loop. We have implemented our techniques in Locust, an extension of the GRASShopper verification tool. Locust is able to automatically prove memory safety of implementations of classical heap-manipulating programs such as insertionsort, quicksort and traversals of nested data structures.

1 Introduction

A number of recent projects have shown that it is possible to verify implementations of systems with complex functional specifications (e.g. CompCert [27], miTLS [6], seL4 [24], and IronFleet [19]). However, this requires highly skilled practitioners to manually annotate large programs with appropriate invariants. While there is little hope of automating the overall process, we believe that this annotation work could be largely automated.

A key problem in verification of heap-manipulating programs is the inference of formal data structure descriptions. Separation logic [33,36] has often been used in automatic reasoning about such programs, as its frame rule favors compositional reasoning and thus promises scalable verification tools. However, the resulting techniques have often traded precision and soundness for automation [12], required extensively annotated inputs [20,31,35], or focused on the restricted case of singly-linked lists (often without data) [3,5,7,9,13,17,18,29,34].

P. Kohli—Now at Google DeepMind.
D. Tarlow—Now at Google Brain.

F. Ranzato (Ed.): SAS 2017, LNCS 10422, pp. 66–87, 2017.
DOI: 10.1007/978-3-319-66706-5_4

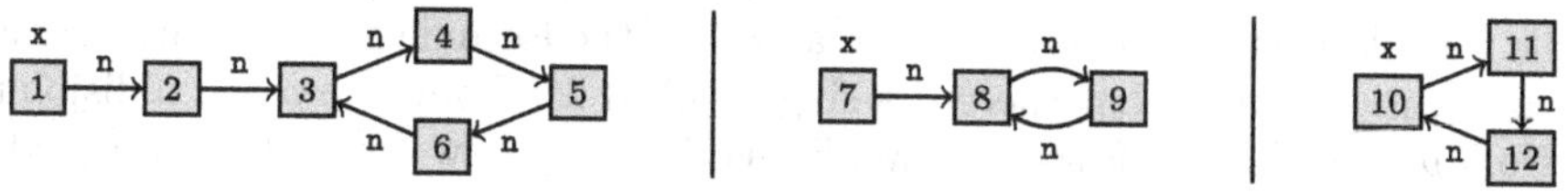

Fig. 1. Three heap graphs.

We follow earlier work and infer likely invariants from observed program runs [14–16,39–43]. At its core, finding a program invariant is searching for a general "concept" (in the form of a formula) that overapproximates all occurring program states. This is similar to many of the problems considered in statistical machine learning, and recent results have shown that program analysis questions can be treated as such problems [15,16,22,32,38–41]. With the exception of [32,38], these efforts have focused on numerical program invariants.

We show how to treat the prediction of formulas similarly to predicting natural language or program source code in Sect. 3. Concretely, we define a simple grammar for our abstract domain of separation logic formulas with (possibly nested) inductive predicates. Based on a set of observed states, a formula can then be predicted starting from the grammar's start symbol by sequentially choosing the most likely production step. As our grammar is fixed, each such step is a simple classification problem from machine learning: "Considering the program states and the formula produced so far, which is the most likely production step?" Our technique can handle arbitrary (pre-defined) inductive predicates and nesting of such predicates, and can also produce disjunctive formulas.

We show how to use this technique in a refinement loop with an off-the-shelf program verifier (GRASShopper [35]) to automatically prove memory safety of programs in Sect. 4. We experimentally evaluate our approach in Sect. 5. There, we show that our shape analysis performs well on automatically generated synthetic data sets similar to our training data. Furthermore, we show that Locust is able to fully automatically verify programs from a standard test suite that are beyond the capabilities of other tools. Finally, we evaluate our method on a selection of programs handling nested data structures, which are at the core of much low-level code such as device drivers [5].

2 Example

Our central goal is to predict a separation logic formula describing the data structures used at a given program location from a set of observed program states. A core requirement is that the predicted formula should generalize well, i.e., also describe different, but structurally similar program states. For this, we first convert program states into *heap graphs*, in which memory locations are nodes, pointers are edges and program variables are node labels (we drop all non-heap information). As examples, consider the three graphs in Fig. 1, representing program states with a program variable x. These three heap graphs can be described by the separation logic formula $\exists p.\Pi : \mathsf{ls}(\mathtt{x}, p, \ldots) * \mathsf{ls}(p, p, \ldots) * \mathsf{emp}$.

While we will discuss Π below, the remainder of the formula means that there is a heap location p such that there is a singly linked list from x to p and a disjoint list from p to itself. In this section, we discuss in detail how our method proceeds on the example graphs; the general method and technical details are discussed in the following sections.

Our method predicts this formula by constructing it iteratively, following its syntactic structure. We predict fromulas from a fragment of separation logic described by a grammar (cf. Fig. 4). The syntax tree for the predicted formula in this grammar is shown in Fig. 2. We generate formulas by starting with a singleton tree containing the grammar's start symbol and repeatedly expanding the leftmost leaf nonterminal in the syntax tree. At each step, the grammar allows only a few expansion rules, and we use a machine learning component to predict the next expansion step based on the partial syntax tree generated so far and the heap graphs provided as input. These predictions are made on features that represent general structural information about graph properties such as cyclicity, connections between labeled nodes, etc. This component is trained beforehand on a large amount of automatically generated, program-independent data (cf. Sect. 3.3). Thus, all of our predictions are based on learned patterns that were observed in the training data, and do not depend on hardcoded rules.

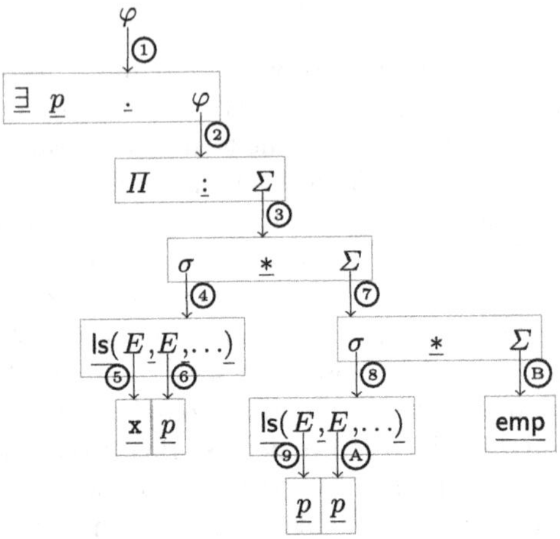

Fig. 2. Syntax tree of $\exists p.\Pi$: $\mathsf{ls}(\mathtt{x}, p, \ldots) * \mathsf{ls}(p, p, \ldots) * \mathsf{emp}$. Expansion of Π skipped, terminal symbols underlined, boxes indicate result of a single grammar production, circled indices indicate the order of productions.

Initially, the syntax tree contains only φ. In production step ①, the root nonterminal φ can be expanded to either $\exists\mathcal{V}.\varphi$ or $\Pi : \Sigma$. Intuitively, choosing the former allows us to introduce a label for a node that we believe we will need to reference later in the procedure. To decide which production to choose, we extract a feature vector for each heap node that contains information about the number of incoming and outgoing edges and distance to other nodes with labels. Based on these features, our method predicts that we should introduce an existential quantifier for a fresh variable name (in this case p), and computes that it is most likely to refer to node 3 in the leftmost graph (resp. 8 in the second and 10 in the third) in Fig. 1. We attach the label p to these nodes for the remainder of the procedure, and extend the syntax tree according to the production $\exists p.\varphi$.

Next, in step ②, we expand the newly obtained φ nonterminal using the same procedure, but with a feature vector modified by the newly introduced label.

This time, the production $\Pi : \Sigma$ is chosen. Π is a "pure" formula (i.e., not concerning heap shapes, but equalities between program variables and similar information), which we deterministically compute (cf. Sect. 3.3). We thus focus on Σ, the "spatial" formula describing heap shapes.

In step ③, the choice is between emp (implying that we believe that we are done describing the heap) and $\sigma * \Sigma$, which means that we predict that there are more heap regions to describe. We extract a feature vector summarizing structural knowledge about the heap graphs, (e.g., "are there nodes with in-degree i and out-degree j") and syntactic knowledge about the formula (e.g., "how many program variables have not been used yet in the formula"). Based on this, we predict that Σ should be expanded to $\sigma * \Sigma$, where σ is a "heaplet" that describes a single shape on the heap.

Now, in step ④, we choose whether the next heap region we describe is a list or a tree. We use similar features as for Σ to predict that σ should be expanded to $\mathsf{ls}(E, E, \ldots)$,[1] i.e., we predict that there is at least one list in the heap.

The E (expression) nonterminals declare where this list begins and ends, and can be expanded to either a variable or the special 0 value. To make choices in steps ⑤ and ⑥, we extract a separate feature vector for each program variable and 0, again combining knowledge from the heap graphs (e.g., "are there nodes with in-degree i and out-degree j reachable from v") and from the partially generated formula (e.g., "has v already been used in the formula", ...). From these features, we predict the most likely identifier to expand E with. Our predictor chooses x here, but could equally well return p. Next, we need to expand the second E nonterminal. Here, we additionally consider a "reachable from syntactic sibling" feature, which allows our system to correctly rule out x and instead choose p.

The process continues for the remaining nonterminals in the same manner, using a frame inference to compute the *footprint* of already generated predicates $\mathsf{p}(v_1, \ldots, v_n)$ (i.e., heap nodes described by p). For instance, for the leftmost graph of Fig. 1, after predicting $\mathsf{ls}(\mathtt{x}, p, \ldots)$ we compute its footprint as $\{1, 2\}$. We use this information by restricting heap graph feature extraction to nodes outside of the footprint of already generated predicates; this provides enough information for the system to make progress and not get "stuck" predicting the same things repeatedly. Eventually (step Ⓑ), we predict that Σ should be expanded into emp, indicating the empty heap.

3 Predicting Shape Invariants from Heaps

In Sect. 3.1, we first present a general technique to predict derivations in a grammar G from a set of objects H, given functions that compute features from H. We then show how to apply this to our setting in Sect. 3.2, using a grammar for separation logic as G and heap graphs as input objects, and discuss the features used. Practical aspects of extending this core technique to a useful shape analysis tool (e.g., how to generate training data) are discussed in Sect. 3.3.

[1] We will discuss the role of ... in Sect. 3.2.

3.1 General Syntax Tree Prediction

Let G be a context-free grammar, $\mathcal{S}$ the set of all (terminal and nonterminal) symbols of G, and $\mathcal{N}$ just the nonterminal symbols. We assume that every sentence generated by G has a unique syntax tree, which we represent as a tuple $\mathcal{T} = (\mathcal{A}, g(\cdot), ch(\cdot))$ where $\mathcal{A} = \{1, \ldots, A\}$ is the set of nodes for some $A \in \mathbb{N}$, $g : \mathcal{A} \to \mathcal{S}$ maps a node to a terminal or nonterminal symbol from the grammar, and $ch : \mathcal{A} \to \mathcal{A}^*$ maps a node to its direct children in the syntax tree. A partial syntax tree $\mathcal{T}_{<a}$ is a syntax tree $\mathcal{T}$ restricted to nodes $\{1, \ldots, a-1\}$, where the ordering on nodes comes from the order in which they are predicted.

We assume there is an underlying unknown distribution $p(\mathcal{T} \mid H)$. This matches the observation that in our setting, there is no unique "correct" formula describing a set of heap graphs. Instead, many formulas (from the trivial "true" to formulas without inductive predicates, concretely describing the full observed heap) are valid candidates. Our problem is to learn this distribution, so that we can predict a syntax tree $\mathcal{T}$ given a set of objects H. As the set of valid syntax trees is extremely large, simply learning a mapping from inputs to a previously enumerated set of syntax trees is impractical. Instead, we learn this distribution following a technique that predicts source code from natural language [2]. The key idea is that instead of considering the probability of the full tree, we decompose the problem into learning the probability distributions for productions in our grammar, conditional on the inputs and the partial syntax tree generated so far.

$$p(\mathcal{T} \mid H) \simeq \prod_{\{a \in \mathcal{A} \mid g(a) \in \mathcal{N}\}} p(ch(a) \mid H, \mathcal{T}_{<a})$$

This decomposition allows us to treat the problem as a sequential prediction task in which we predict the syntax tree in a depth-first left-to-right node order. A further simplification step to aid learning is to not operate directly on input objects and syntax trees, but instead to compute a feature vector encoding existing domain knowledge $\boldsymbol{f} = \phi_N(H, \mathcal{T}_{<a}) \in \mathbb{R}^{D_N}$ (where D_N is the number of features for N) that depends on the considered nonterminal N, the input objects H and the partial syntax tree $\mathcal{T}_{<a}$ generated so far.[2] The learned probability distribution is thus $p(\mathcal{T} \mid H) \simeq \prod_{\{a \in \mathcal{A} \mid g(a) \in \mathcal{N}\}} p(ch(a) \mid \phi_{g(a)}(H, \mathcal{T}_{<a}))$.

We use two different models for these per-nonterminal probability distributions, depending on the production rules for N in G. If N has a fixed number of production rules in G (for example, $\varphi \to \exists \mathcal{V}.\varphi \mid \Pi : \Sigma$) then we view this as a standard multiclass classification task, i.e., where a probability is assigned to each allowed production ("class") based on a feature vector. If N can be expanded to any terminal from a dynamic set (for example E, which stands for any variable in scope at this point), then we instead learn a function that assigns

[2] While we have experimented with avoiding this simplification to side-step the need for feature engineering by operating directly on input graphs [28], the resulting system was substantially harder to train and slightly less precise, as it had to learn domain knowledge from the training data.

a score to each production. We then obtain a probability distribution over the productions from these scores by a normalization procedure (see below). In both cases, we have a $\mathsf{Predictor}_N(\boldsymbol{f};\theta)$ function for each nonterminal N that assigns probabilities to each production allowed by G based on the input feature vector. θ denotes learnable parameters of this function. In practice, we use a neural network with one fully connected layer for the classification tasks and a two layer network for the ranking tasks, such that θ consists of the weights used in each layer.

The pseudocode for this procedure PlatypusCore is given in Algorithm 1, which is initially called with a syntax tree containing only the grammar's start symbol. Note that Algorithm 1 is entirely independent of the semantics of the generated syntax tree. All domain knowledge about the meaning of the generated syntax and how it is related to the input objects needs to be encapsulated in the construction of ϕ_N, which extracts features to be used by the generic machine learning components. We discuss our choices for ϕ_N below.

Algorithm 1. Pseudocode for PlatypusCore (extension of [2])

Input: Grammar G, input objects H, (partial) syntax tree $\mathcal{T} = (\mathcal{A}, g, ch)$, nonterminal node a to expand

$N \leftarrow g(a)$ {nonterminal symbol of a in $\mathcal{T}$}
$\boldsymbol{f} \leftarrow \phi_N(H, \mathcal{T}_{<a})$ {compute features (see Sect. 3.2)}
$P \leftarrow$ most likely production $N \rightarrow \mathcal{S}^*$ from G considering $\mathsf{Predictor}_N(\boldsymbol{f})$
$\mathcal{T} \leftarrow$ insert new nodes into $\mathcal{T}$ according to P
for all children $a' \in ch(a)$ labeled by nonterminal **do**
    $\mathcal{T} \leftarrow \mathsf{PlatypusCore}(G, H, \mathcal{T}, a')$
return $\mathcal{T}$

To train the overall system, we assume we are given a training set of $(\mathcal{T}, H)$ pairs drawn from the desired distribution (we discuss the details of this procedure for our setting in Sect. 3.3). To obtain training data for the individual $\mathsf{Predictor}_N$ functions, we follow our PlatypusCore procedure. For each syntax tree node a labeled with a nonterminal N, we extract the feature vector $\boldsymbol{f} = \phi_N(H, \mathcal{T}_{<a})$, but retrieve the chosen production rule P from the ground truth syntax tree $\mathcal{T}$ to generate a pair $(\boldsymbol{f}, P)$ which can be used to train the classifier or ranker for nonterminal N.

3.2 Predicting Separation Logic Formulas

To use the PlatypusCore algorithm for shape analysis, we need to specify the input objects H, the output grammar G, and the feature extraction function ϕ_N and predictor $\mathsf{Predictor}_N$ for each nonterminal.

Inputs. Our inputs are directed—possibly cyclic—graphs representing the heap of a program and the values of program variables. Intuitively, each graph node v

corresponds to an address in memory at which a sequence of pointers $v_0, \ldots, v_t$ is stored.[3] Edges reflect these pointer values, i.e., v has edges to $v_0, \ldots, v_t$ labeled with $0, \ldots, t$. The node 0 is special (corresponding to the `null` pointer in programs) and may not have outgoing edges. Furthermore, we use unique node labels to denote the values of program variables $\mathcal{PV}$ and auxiliary variables $\mathcal{V}$, which can be introduced by existential quantification.

Definition 1 (Heap Graphs). *Let $\mathcal{PV}$ be a set of program variables and $\mathcal{V}$ be a set of (disjunct) auxiliary variables. The set of* Heap Graphs $\mathcal{H}$ *is then defined as* $2^{\mathbb{N}} \times 2^{(\mathbb{N}\setminus\{0\})\times\mathbb{N}\times\mathbb{N}} \times (\mathcal{PV} \cup \mathcal{V} \to \mathbb{N})$.

Outputs. We consider a fragment of separation logic [33,36]. Our method allows the *separating conjunction* $*$, list-valued *points-to* expressions $v \mapsto [e_1, \ldots, e_n]$, existential quantification and higher-order inductive predicates [5], but no $-\!\!*$. As pure formulas, we only allow conjunctions of (dis)equalities, and use the constant 0 as the special null pointer. We will only discuss the singly-linked list predicate ls and the binary tree predicate tree in the following, though our method is applicable to generic inductive predicates. The following grammar describes our formulas, where nonterminals $\mathcal{V}$ and $\mathcal{PV}$ can be expanded to any terminal from the corresponding sets.

$$\begin{array}{lll}
\varphi ::= \exists \mathcal{V}.\varphi \mid \Pi : \Sigma & \Sigma ::= \mathsf{emp} \mid \sigma * \Sigma & \sigma ::= \mathsf{ls}(E, E, \lambda\mathcal{V}, \mathcal{V}, \mathcal{V}, \mathcal{V} \to \varphi) \\
\Pi ::= \mathit{true} \mid \pi \wedge \Pi & \pi ::= E = E \mid E \neq E & \quad \mid \mathsf{tree}(E, \lambda\mathcal{V}, \mathcal{V}, \mathcal{V}, \mathcal{V} \to \varphi) \\
E ::= 0 \mid \mathcal{V} \mid \mathcal{PV} & & \quad \mid \mathcal{V} \mapsto [E \ldots E] \mid \mathcal{PV} \mapsto [E \ldots E]
\end{array}$$

Semantics are defined as usual for separation logic, i.e., $h \models \sigma_1 * \sigma_2$ for some $h = (V, E, \mathcal{L}) \in \mathcal{H}$ if h can be partitioned into two subgraphs h_1, h_2 such that h_1 (resp. h_2) is a model of σ_1 (resp. σ_2) after substituting variables in σ_1 and σ_2 according to $\mathcal{L}$. The empty heap emp is true only on empty subgraphs, and $v \mapsto [e_1, \ldots, e_n]$ holds iff $V = \{v\}$ and for all $1 \leq i \leq n$, there is some edge (v, i, e_i). For detailed semantics, see [33,36]. The semantics of inductive predicates are the least fixpoint of their definitions, where nested formulas describe the shape of a nested data structure. For example, we define ls and tree as follows.

$$\begin{aligned}
\mathsf{ls}(x, y, \varphi) \equiv & (x = y) \vee (\exists v, n. x \mapsto [v, n] * \mathsf{ls}(n, y, \varphi) * \varphi(x, y, v, n)) \\
\mathsf{tree}(x, \varphi) \equiv & (\exists v, l, r. l \neq 0 \wedge r \neq 0 : x \mapsto [v, l, r] * \mathsf{tree}(l, \varphi) * \mathsf{tree}(r, \varphi) * \varphi(x, v, l, r)) \\
& \vee (\exists v, r. r \neq 0 : x \mapsto [v, 0, r] * \mathsf{tree}(r, \varphi) * \varphi(x, v, 0, r)) \\
& \vee (\exists v, l. l \neq 0 : x \mapsto [v, l, 0] * \mathsf{tree}(l, \varphi) * \varphi(x, v, l, 0)) \\
& \vee (\exists v. x \mapsto [v, 0, 0] * \varphi(x, v, 0, 0))
\end{aligned}$$

Note that our definition of ls implies that $\mathsf{ls}(x, x)$ holds both for empty list segments as well as cyclic lists, and $\mathsf{tree}(x)$ implies that $x \neq 0$. We use $\top \equiv \lambda v_1, v_2, v_3, v_4 \to \mathit{true} : \mathsf{emp}$ to denote "no further nested data structure". Thus, $\mathsf{ls}(x, y, \lambda f_1, f_2, e_1, e_2 \to \mathsf{tree}(e_1, \top))$ describes a list of binary trees from x to y.

[3] Here, we discard non-pointer values.

Example 2. A "pan-handle list" starting in i_2 is described by $\varphi(i_1, i_2, i_3, i_4) \equiv \exists p.\mathsf{ls}(i_2, p, \top) * \mathsf{ls}(p, p, \top)$, where an acyclic list segment leads to a cyclic list. Here, p is the existentially quantified node at which "handle" and "pan" are joined.

The formula $\psi(x) \equiv \mathsf{tree}(x, \varphi)$ describes a binary tree whose nodes in turn contain panhandle lists. An example of a heap satisfying the formula ψ is shown in Fig. 3. Blue nodes are elements of the tree data structure, having three outgoing edges labeled 0, 1, 2. Each of the green boxes in Fig. 3 corresponds to a *subheap* that is described by the subformula φ. In each of these subheaps, one node is labeled with p, which is not a program variable, but introduced through the existential quantifier in φ.

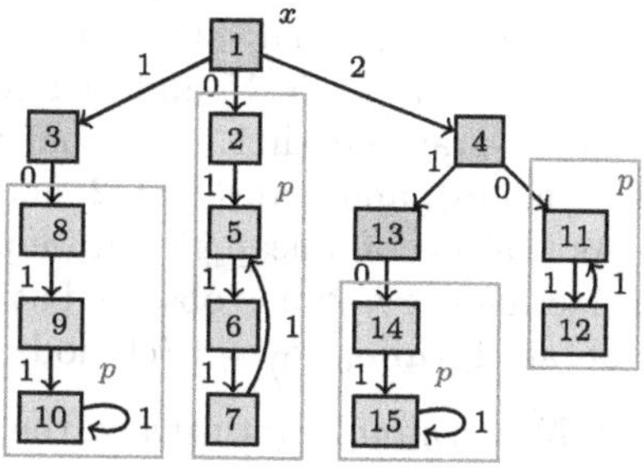

Fig. 3. Tree of panhandle lists.

We found that our procedure PlatypusCore was often unnecessarily imprecise when generating the pure subformula Π and $\mapsto$ atoms, which can simply be computed deterministically. Thus, we restrict our machine learning-based component to handle inductive predicates, and generate Π deterministically using a nullness and aliasing analysis (see Sect. 3.3). While this can lead to predicting $\mathsf{ls}(x, y)$ even if $x.\mathtt{next} = y$ in all observed states, our deterministic extension procedure then yields $x \neq y \wedge x.\mathtt{next} = y$. Our grammar thus simplifies to Fig. 4, where Π is now a terminal symbol.

$$\varphi := \exists \mathcal{V}.\varphi \mid \Pi : \Sigma \qquad \Sigma := \mathsf{emp} \mid \sigma * \Sigma$$
$$E := 0 \mid \mathcal{V} \mid \mathcal{PV} \qquad \sigma := \mathsf{ls}(E, E, \lambda\mathcal{V}, \mathcal{V}, \mathcal{V}, \mathcal{V} \to \varphi) \mid \mathsf{tree}(E, \lambda\mathcal{V}, \mathcal{V}, \mathcal{V}, \mathcal{V} \to \varphi)$$

Fig. 4. Grammar used by our Platypus procedure.

Predicting Flat Formulas. We will first discuss the definitions of ϕ_N for the case where the input is a single graph h with nodes V, and predict formulas from a restricted separation logic grammar without nesting.

For any syntax node a, we define $\mathcal{I}(\mathcal{T}_{<a})$ as the set of identifiers that are in scope at point a in the partial syntax tree. Similarly, $\mathcal{D}(\mathcal{T}_{<a}) \subseteq \mathcal{I}(\mathcal{T}_{<a})$ is the set of "defined" identifiers that occur as first argument of any predicate, following the intuition that $\mathsf{ls}(x, y)$ and $SLtree(x)$ define the data structure starting at x.

An important class of features is based on the notion of *n-grams* of heap graphs. A 1-gram simply describes the in-degree and out-degree of some node v, i.e., is a pair $(indeg(v), outdeg(v)) \in \mathbb{N}^2$. n-grams extend this idea to a sequence of n connected nodes in a heap graph, e.g., a 2-gram is a pair of the 1-grams for two nodes connected by an edge in h. Based on this, we also define a refined measure of depth. For a path $v_1 \dots v_t$ in the heap graph, we define its *1-gram depth* as the number of times the 1-gram changes, i.e., $|\{i \in \{1 \dots t-1\} \mid$

$indeg(v_i) \neq indeg(v_{i+1}) \vee outdeg(v_i) \neq outdeg(v_{i+1})\}|$. Then, $depth(v)$ is the minimal depth of paths leading from a node labeled by a variable in $\mathcal{PV} \cup \mathcal{V}$ to v. In our method, we extend 1-grams by this depth notion, i.e., represent each node by a $(indeg(v), outdeg(v), depth(v))$ triple. Intuitively, this information helps to discover the level of data structure nesting. As an example, consider Fig. 3 again. There, nodes 1, 10, 5, 15 and 11 have 1-gram depth 0, nodes 3, 4, 13, 6, 7 and 12 have 1-gram depth 1 (note that we haven't drawn the edges to 0 for some "tree" nodes), and nodes 8, 9, 2, and 14 have 1-gram depth 2.

As features of a heap graph, we use presence of n-grams in that graph, only considering the n-grams observed at training time. Thus for the graph in Fig. 3, we obtain $1gram_{(0,3,0)} = 1$ (cf. node 1), $1gram_{(1,3,1)} = 1$ (cf. node 3) and so on.

Σ, σ Nonterminals. Intuitively, the production choices for these nonterminals depend on the structure of the heap graph that has not been described by the partial syntax tree generated so far. As discussed above, we compute the footprint of (i.e., those heap nodes described by) already predicted predicates. We denote the set of nodes covered by predicates predicted up to syntax node a as $V_{<a}$.

Using this, we compute features for Σ, σ as the 1-grams and 2-grams from above restricted to the nodes $V \setminus V_{<a}$, i.e., those nodes that are not covered by the data structures described by the partial formula predicted so far. Their node degrees, contained in the 1-gram features, are indicators of the data structures present in the remaining heap. Additionally, we also include a feature reporting the number of identifiers not defined yet, i.e., $|\mathcal{I}(\mathcal{T}_{<a}) \setminus \mathcal{D}(\mathcal{T}_{<a})|$.

E Nonterminals. Here, we pick an expression as argument to a predicate. This decision depends on how well the part of the heap graph reachable from the expression matches the semantics of the surrounding predicate and possibly already predicted other arguments. The set of legal outputs differs at each syntax node a: When making a prediction for E at node a, the set of legal outputs is $\mathcal{I}(\mathcal{T}_{<a}) \cup \{0\}$; i.e., the set of all identifiers that are in scope at this point and 0, which varies for each prediction. Thus, we treat this as a ranking task and, unlike the earlier case where we had a single feature vector, we compute one feature vector $\boldsymbol{f}_{E,z}$ for each $z \in \mathcal{I}(\mathcal{T}_{<a}) \cup \{0\}$.

To this end, we compute 1-gram and 2-gram features as above for each expression z separately, restricted to those heap graph nodes reachable from the node labeled by z. We also extract boolean features signifying if z is part of a non-trivial strongly connected component of the heap graph, or has a path to a strongly connected component. Additionally, to relate z to already predicted arguments of the same predicate, we define the sequence of "enclosing defined identifiers" $e_1, \ldots, e_t \in \mathcal{I}(\mathcal{T}_{<a})$, i.e., identifiers appearing in predicates enclosing the currently considered node a. As an example, consider the partially predicted formula $\mathsf{ls}(x, E, \ldots)$, where we are interested in predicting the expression at E. Here, we have $e_1 = x$ (for nested data structures, $e_2, \ldots$ correspond to the identifiers chosen in the outer data structures). We use a boolean feature to denote reachability of (resp. from) each $e_1, \ldots, e_t$ from (resp. of) z.

Furthermore, we refine our notion of reachability. We say that v "reaches" v' if there is path $v = v_0, \ldots, v_t = v'$ in the heap graph. If furthermore no $v_1 \ldots v_{t-1}$ is labeled by another identifier, we say that v "directly reaches" v'. If all edges used on the path have the same label, then we say that v "simply reaches" v'. Finally, we also say that x "syntactically reaches" y if our partial syntax tree $\mathcal{T}_{<a}$ contains a predicate $\mathsf{p}(x, \ldots, y, \ldots)$.

Thus, for an identifier z labeling heap graph node v, we use these features:

- The frequency of 1- and 2-grams reachable from v.
- v is part (resp. reaches a node that is part) of a strongly connected component of the graph.
- v reaches (resp. reaches directly, simply, or syntactically) the enclosing identifier e_i for $i = 1 \ldots t$.
- v is reached (resp. reached directly, simply, or syntactically) by the enclosing identifier e_i for $i = 1 \ldots t$.

To implement $\mathsf{Predictor}_E$, we use a neural network NN (with learnable parameters θ^E) to compute scores $s_z = \mathrm{NN}(\boldsymbol{f}_{E,z}; \theta^E)$ for each identifier. We normalize these scores using the softmax function to get a probability distribution over identifiers (a common trick to reduce the influence of outliers). The probability of expanding E by z is thus $p(z) = \frac{\exp(s_z)}{\sum_{z' \in \mathcal{I}(\mathcal{T}_{<a}) \cup \{0\}} \exp(s_{z'})}$.

φ Nonterminals. Here, we need to decide whether to declare new identifiers via existential quantification, so that we can refer to nodes not labelled by program variables (e.g., for panhandle lists). Thus, we not only predict *that* we need a quantifier, but also by which graph node it should be instantiated. To use this information later on, we allow modifying the input H after a production step (between line 4 and 5 of $\mathsf{PlatypusCore}$). In this case, we add the newly introduced identifier as a label to the corresponding node.

We thus predict, independently for each node $v \in V$, the probability that it is referred to by a new existential variable. We proceed similar to the E case and compute a feature vector $\boldsymbol{f}_{\varphi,v}$ for each node $v \in V$. As features we again use standard graph properties, such as membership in a strongly connected component, existence of labels for a node, its in-degree and out-degree. Additionally, we also use features comparing these values to each nodes' direct neighbors, i.e., "has higher in-degree than average in-degree of neighbors".

To make a prediction, we use a neural network NN (with learnable parameters θ^φ) to compute a score $s_v = \mathrm{NN}(\boldsymbol{f}_{\varphi,v}; \theta^\varphi)$. Unlike the E case where we have to choose one option from many, here each v is an independent decision, and so we use the sigmoid function[4] $p(v) = \frac{\exp(s_v)}{1+\exp(s_v)}$ to get the probability that v is labelled by a new identifier. When choosing a production for φ, we thus compute probabilities for each v independently and return $\arg\max_v p(v)$ as the probability of declaring a fresh identifier. If more identifiers are required, they can be added in subsequent grammar expansion steps.

[4] Note that the softmax function used in the E case is the generalization of the sigmoid function to many values.

Predicting Nested Formulas. We now discuss the general case, in which we have several input heap graphs H, and data structures may in turn contain other data structures. This requires us to make predictions that are based on the information in all graphs, and sometimes on several subgraphs of each of the graphs. As an example, consider again the heap in Fig. 3, and imagine that we have successfully predicted the outer part of the corresponding formula, i.e., $\mathsf{tree}(x, \lambda i_1, i_2, i_3, i_4.\varphi)$, and are now trying to expand φ. This subformula needs to describe all the subheaps corresponding to the contents of the green boxes in Fig. 3. Again, we modify the input H to reflect the newly introduced identifiers. So for our example, we would replace H with one heap graph with labels $\{x \mapsto 1, i_1 \mapsto 3, i_2 \mapsto 8, i_3 \mapsto 0, i_4 \mapsto 0\}$ for the leftmost box, one with labels $\{x \mapsto 1, i_1 \mapsto 1, i_2 \mapsto 2, i_3 \mapsto 3, i_4 \mapsto 4\}$ for the second box, and so on.

Everything but φ Nonterminals. We use the same features from Sect. 3.2, but lift them to handle a set of heap graphs H. We compute feature vectors for each heap graph independently as before, and then *merge* them into a new single feature vector by computing features based on the maximum f_{max}, minimum f_{min}, and average value f_{avg} across all H for each feature f. We also use the same $\mathsf{Predictor}_N$ functions.

φ Nonterminals. This covers the case in which we predict that we need to insert an existential quantifier. In Fig. 3, this is the prediction of $\exists p$, where p corresponds to one node in each of the green boxes. We again lift the feature extraction as mentioned above, but as the number of nodes may differ between the different heap graphs, we cannot simply lift the $\mathsf{Predictor}_\varphi$ from above.

This problem is a basic form of the structured prediction problem [4]. Suppose there are R heap graphs. For each of the graphs, there is a set of nodes V_r which may require an existential quantifier to be described in our setting (in Fig. 3, these are the contents of the green boxes). Let y_v be a boolean denoting the event that a new identifier is introduced for node v. We train a neural network like in the single-heap case so that the probability of introducing an existentially quantified variable for node v is $p(y_v = 1) = \frac{\exp(s_v)}{1+\exp(s_v)}$, where s_v is the score output by the neural network.

We now need to compute the probability of introducing a new identifier (for all graphs) in terms of the scores s_v (which only take one graph into account). We first set the probabilities of illegal events (i.e., predicting that one graph requires an existential quantifier, but another one does not) to 0. Then, the probability of not declaring a variable is $\prod_{1 \le r \le R} \prod_{v \in V_r} (1 - p(y_v = 1)) = \prod_{1 \le r \le R} \frac{1}{Z_r}$, where $Z_r = \prod_{v \in V_r} (1 + \exp(s_v))$. The probability of the event y_v^r of selecting exactly node v from graph r is

$$p(y_v^r = 1) = \frac{\exp(s_v)}{1 + \exp(s_v)} \prod_{v' \in V_r, v' \neq v} \frac{1}{1 + \exp(s_{v'})} = \frac{\exp(s_v)}{Z_r}.$$

As the choice of node from each graph is independent given that we are declaring a new identifier, the probability of choosing the set of nodes $\{v_r\}_{1 \le r \le R}$ is the product $\prod_{1 \le r \le R} \frac{\exp(s_{v_r})}{Z_r}$. Noting that all legal joint configurations have the same denominator $\prod_r Z_r$, we can drop the denominator and compute the normalizing constant for the constrained space later. The total unnormalized probability of declaring a variable is the sum of the unnormalized probabilities of all ways to choose exactly one node from each graph r, which can be rewritten as $\prod_{1 \le r \le R} \sum_{v \in V_r} \exp(s_v)$. Normalising this, the probability of not introducing an existential quantifier is $\frac{1}{1+\prod_{1 \le r \le R} \sum_{v \in V_r} \exp(s_v)}$ while the probability of introducing an existential is $\frac{\prod_{1 \le r \le R} \sum_{v \in V_r} \exp(s_v)}{1+\prod_{1 \le r \le R} \sum_{v \in V_r} \exp(s_v)}$.

To make predictions for all graphs at the same time, we use the above to decide whether to introduce an existential quantifier. If not, we choose the $\Pi : \Sigma$ production. If we decide to use the $\exists \mathcal{V}.\varphi$ production, then we draw one node from each graph according to a softmax over the scores; i.e., the probability of choosing node v in graph r is $\frac{\exp(s_v)}{\sum_{v' \in V_r} \exp(s_{v'})}$.

3.3 Shape Analysis with Platypus

To obtain a shape analyzer, we have extended the procedure PlatypusCore to also produce disjunctive invariants and deterministically compute pure subformulas. Finally, whereas Algorithm 1 selects a production "greedily" in line 3 (i.e., it will always pick the most likely one), we have generalized this behavior to instead also sample productions using the probabilities obtained from the $\mathsf{Predictor}_N$ function. This allows to iteratively obtain more and more formulas from Platypus, recovering from cases where the system is uncertain about the correct formula.

Training the Analyzer. Training the logistic regressors and neural networks from above requires large amounts of training data, i.e., sets of heap graphs labeled with corresponding formulas. To obtain this data, we generate synthetic data by fixing a small set of program variables $\mathcal{PV}$ (typically of size 2 or 3) and enumerate semantically valid derivations of formulas in our grammar, similar in spirit to [23]. Then, we enumerate models for each formula by expanding inductive predicates until only $\mapsto$ atoms remain. From this we read off heap graphs by resolving the remaining ambiguous possible equalities between variables. The result is a set of pairs (φ, H) such that $h \models \varphi$ for every $h \in H$. We compute the unique syntax tree $\mathcal{T}_\varphi$ of each φ to get the desired training data pairs $(\mathcal{T}_\varphi, H)$.

Pure Subformulas. We use a deterministic procedure to expand the nonterminal Π describing the pure part of our formulas, using simple aliasing and nullness analyses. Namely, for all pairs of identifiers $x, y \in \mathcal{PV} \cup \{0\}$, we check if $x = y$ or $x \neq y$ holds in all input heap graphs. Similarly, for all fields f and $x \neq 0$, we consider the possible equalities $x.f = y$. Π is then set to the conjunction of all (dis)equalities that hold in all input graphs.

Handling Disjunctions. We found *disjunctive* separation logic formulas to be needed even for surprisingly simple examples, as in many cases, the initial or final iteration of a loop requires a different shape description from all other steps. In our setting, the problem of deciding how many and what disjuncts are needed can be treated as a clustering problem of heap graphs. In machine learning, the clustering problem is the task of grouping a set of samples in such a way as to group "similar" samples together. The notion of similarity depends on the target application and is normally defined through a distance measure. A widely used and effective clustering method is k-means clustering, where the aim is to find k cluster centers such that the sum of the distance of every point to the closest cluster center is minimized.

For our setting, we convert the input heap graphs into feature vectors capturing reachability between program variables and use the Euclidean distance between these feature vectors as a distance measure between graphs. Following our notion of different kinds of reachability from above, we define a function $r_h(u, v)$ ranging from 0 if there is no connection between the nodes labeled by u and to 1 if u and v are labels on the same node, with steps for different kinds of reachability. Using this function, we define $\boldsymbol{f}_h$ as the vector $\langle r_h(u, v)\rangle_{u,v \in \mathcal{PV}}$ for some fixed order on $\mathcal{PV}$. In our implementation, we run the clustering algorithm for $k \in 1..5$ and predict formulas for all generated clusterings.

4 Refining and Verifying Shape Invariants

We construct our fully automatic memory safety verifier Locust (pseudocode in Algorithm 2) by connecting our shape predictor from Sect. 3 with the program verifier GRASShopper. For this, we keep a list of *positive* $S^+(\ell)$ and *negative* state samples $S^-(\ell)$ for every program location ℓ at which program annotations for GRASShopper are required (i.e., loop invariants and pre/post-conditions for subprocedures). We first sample initial states (cf. Sect. 4.1) and use these to collect a first set of positive samples corresponding to valid program runs by simply executing the program. Then we obtain a set of candidate formulas from Platypus for each location and enter a refinement loop. If verification using these candidates fails, we get a counterexample state at some location ℓ, which we use to extend the sets $S^+(\ell)$ and $S^-(\ell)$. As it is possible that no correct set of program annotations can be found (due to an incorrect program or imprecisions in our procedure), we report failure when the same counterexample is reported for the second time (i.e., we have stopped making progress).

To simplify the procedure, we assume that Platypus always returns the most precise formula from our abstract domain holding for the given set of input heap graphs (†). While this assumption is not formally guaranteed, Platypus was trained to produce this behavior (by choosing training data according to this principle), and we have observed that it behaves like this in practice.

Algorithm 2. Pseudocode for Locust

```
Input: Program P and entry procedure p with precondition φ_p, locations L requiring
    program annotations
1: I ← sample initial states satisfying φ_p                                {see Sect. 4.1}
2: S⁺ ← execute P on I to map location ℓ ∈ L to set of observed states
3: while true do
4:     for all ℓ ∈ L do
5:         while true do
6:             φ'_ℓ ← obtain fresh formula sample from Platypus(S⁺(ℓ))
7:             if exists φ'_ℓ consistent with all S⁺(ℓ), S⁻(ℓ) then         {see Sect. 4.3}
8:                 φ_ℓ ← φ'_ℓ
9:                 break (continue on line 4)
10:    P' ← annotate P with inferred φ_ℓ
11:    if GRASShopper(P') returns counterexample s then
12:        if s is new counterexample then
13:            update S⁺, S⁻ to contain s for correct location              {see Sect. 4.2}
14:        else return FAIL
15:    else return SUCCESS
```

4.1 Initial State Sampling

We assume the existence of some set of preconditions describing the input to the main procedure of the program in separation logic.[5] To sample from these preconditions, we can add `assert false` to the beginning of the program. Then, every counterexample returned by GRASShopper is a model of the precondition. To get more samples, and to ensure different sizes of input lists, we add cardinality constraints to the precondition. For example, to force a list starting at `lst` to have length ≥ 3, we add `requires lst.next.next != null`. States at other locations are then obtained by executing the program from the initial sample.

While this strategy is complete relative to the fragment of separation logic supported by GRASShopper, it is slow even for simple preconditions. Thus, we have implemented a simple heuristic sampling algorithm for preconditions using only simple predicates. If we detect that a precondition is simple enough for our heuristic, we use it instead to generate sample states of varying sizes.

4.2 Handling Counterexamples

If the program is incorrect, or the current annotations are incorrect or insufficient to prove the program correct, then GRASShopper returns a counterexample at a location ℓ. Depending on the context of such a counterexample and its exact form, we treat it as a positive or negative program state sample as follows.

[5] Conceivably, these could be provided by users in a pre-formal language and translated to separation logic using an interactive elaboration procedure. Alternatively, given a test suite, Platypus could predict the initial precondition as well.

- Case 1: A candidate invariant does not hold on loop entry. The counterexample state is reachable, but is not covered by the candidate loop invariant, and thus, the counterexample can be added as a positive sample to $S^+(\ell)$.
- Case 2: A candidate loop invariant is not inductive. This is an implication counterexample [15,40], i.e., a state s that is a model of the candidate loop invariant and a state s' reached after evaluating the loop body on s. Based on our assumption (†), we conclude that s is likely to be a reachable state, and thus s' is. Hence, we treat s' as a positive sample and add it to $S^+(\ell)$.
- Case 3: A postcondition does not hold for a state s. Again, by (†), we conclude that s is a reachable state, and thus add the counterexample to $S^+(\ell)$.
- Case 4: Invalid heap access inside the loop. The counterexample state is consistent with the candidate loop invariant, but triggers an invalid heap access such as a `null` access. It is a negative sample and is added to $S^-(\ell)$.

4.3 Consistency Checking

For each prediction returned by the predictor, we check its consistency with the positive and negative samples obtained so far. This is needed because Platypus cannot provide correctness guarantees, and does not make use of negative samples. Thus we check each returned formula φ_ℓ for consistency with the observed samples, i.e., $\forall h \in S^+(\ell).h \models \varphi_\ell$ and $\forall h \in S^-(\ell).h \not\models \varphi_\ell$. As in our sampling strategy, we use the underlying program verifier for this. For this, we translate a state h into a formula φ_h that describes the sample h exactly, by introducing variables n_v for each node v and representing each edge (n, f, n') as $n.f \mapsto n'$. Then h is a model of φ_ℓ iff all models of φ_h also satisfy φ_ℓ. However, since by construction φ_h only has the model h, this is equivalent to checking if $\varphi_h \wedge \varphi_\ell$ has a model. This can be checked using a complete program verifier such as GRASShopper by using $\varphi_h \wedge \varphi_\ell$ as precondition of a procedure whose body is `assert false`.

5 Related Work and Experiments

We implemented the procedure PlatypusCore from Algorithm 1 as a stand-alone tool Platypus in F#, also containing the feature extraction routines and support for data generation. The core machine learning models (Predictor$_*$) are implemented in TensorFlow, using a small Python wrapper. Finally, we have extended GRASShopper [35] with the procedure from Sect. 4. The source code for Locust and Platypus is available at https://github.com/mmjb/grasshopper.

Limitations. As our method relies on a trained machine learning component, we cannot give any completeness guarantees. However, our integration with a program verifier checks that returned results are correct. This means that our performance depends on that of the underlying verifier, and in fact, time spent in GRASShopper dominates verification time. As our verification technique relies on observing a sample of occurring program states, it is sensitive to the choice of input samples (randomly sampled, taken from a test suite, or provided by a human) used in the sample collection phase. However, this is a limitation shared by other dynamic analysis systems, such as Daikon [14].

5.1 Related Work

Memory safety proofs have long been a focus of research, and we only discuss especially recent and close work here. (Bi)-abduction based shape analyses [10–12,25,26] have been used successfully in memory safety proofs, and can also be used to abduce needed preconditions or the required inductive predicates. In another recent line of work, forest automata have been used to verify heap-manipulating programs [1], but require hard-coded support for specific data structures.

In property-directed shape analysis [21], predicate abstraction over user-provided shape predicates ((sorted) list segments, ...) is combined with a variation of the IC3 property-directed reachability algorithm [8] to prove memory safety and data properties. This can be viewed as continuation of three-valued logic-based works (e.g. [37]), reducing the data type specification requirements. Similary, SplInter extends the Impact [30] safety prover with heap reasoning based on an interpolation technique for separation logic. Finally, we note that in prior work on shape analysis for nested data structures [5], abstractions of heap graphs using inductive predicates were found using manual heuristics and enumerative search routines. Core parts of our method could be adapted to replace these by directed, learned search.

A recent line of work is the use of machine learning techniques for inferring *numerical* invariants [15,16,22,39–41]. In these methods, a machine learning model such as a decision tree is trained on observed program states using standard optimization techniques, and the trained model is interpreted as program invariant. However, while the translation from separating hyperplanes or decision trees to standard invariant formats is straightforward for numerical data, no such correspondence exists in the domain of heap data. In our approach, a predictor is trained offline, independent of the considered programs, and at test (i.e., verification) time produces invariant candidates. Thus, our method cannot make use of negative examples obtained at test time, but does not require a close correspondence between the structure of the learned model and target invariants. Closest to this work is [32] which infers likely heap invariants from program *traces* (i.e., it infers shapes from usage patterns) using machine learning techniques.

5.2 Platypus Experiments

To evaluate Platypus itself, we have generated two large data sets following our procedure from Sect. 3.3. The first set contains all formulas we enumerate for three variables without using nested predicates (327 formulas in total), and the second set contains a random sample of 4% of the 36822 formulas we enumerate for two variables with one data structure nesting level (i.e., we used 1472 formulas

Table 1. Precision of Platypus on synthetic data

Dataset	Greedy	Precision @1	@5	@10
Trained on 3 var., no nesting data:				
3 var., no nesting	92.68%	86.88%	91.30%	96.43%
Trained on 2 var., nested data:				
3 var., no nesting	70.50%	69.37%	73.36%	78.40%
2 var., with nesting	24.11%	24.53%	33.42%	34.19%

in total). For each formula, we have generated 500 models (for the nested dataset, we subsampled this again, picking 100 of the generated states at random). We split both datasets into training, validation and test sets using a 3:1:1 split along the formulas (i.e., no formula appeared in both training and test sets).

For our evaluation, we run Platypus on groups of 5 states generated as models for the same formula at a time, producing 10 formula predictions for each group of states. Note that due to our formula-based split into training and test sets, both the tested states as well as the corresponding ground truth formula have not been seen by the system before. As checking logical equivalence between the formulas produced and the ground truth formula is expensive, we instead approximate this by canonicalizing variable names and the order of commutative elements in the formulas before comparing for exact (string) equality. We report accuracy of our "greedy" mode (i.e., the result obtained by always picking the most likely production) as well as top K accuracy (i.e., how often the correct formula was in the K most probable formulas from the set of 10 sampled formulas) for $K \in \{1, 5, 10\}$, and display the results in Table 1.

Furthermore, we evaluate the accuracy of the per-nonterminal predictors, using a model trained on the two variable with nesting dataset and tested on the three variable no nesting dataset. Table 2 reports how often the production rule predicted with highest probability (i.e., the one chosen in our "greedy" syntax tree sampling strategy), using features extracted under the assumption that all prior nodes of the syntax tree were predicted correctly, is indeed correct.

Table 2. Precision per nonterminal.

Nonterminal	Accuracy
φ	73.03%
Σ	99.86%
σ	99.70%
E	87.66%

Analysis. We observe that on data structures without nesting, Platypus performs very well, and that it generalizes reasonably well from one dataset to another. Most notably, we found that generalizing to a larger number of program variables posed no problem at all. Most wrong predictions are due to wrongly predicting the need for existential quantifiers, or wrongly identifying the heap graph nodes corresponding to these.

While performance on nested data structures is less encouraging, a detailed analysis yielded that most mistakes occurred on formulas that are unlikely to appear in practice (such as $\mathsf{tree}(x, \lambda t, l, d, r \rightarrow \mathsf{ls}(d, l, \top))$, where each tree element has a data field containing a list to its left child). In experiments involving more realistic data structures (cf. below), we observed no such problems.

5.3 Locust Experiments

To validate that we can infer formulas for algorithms used in practice, we have evaluated Locust on a number of standard example programs. For this, we consider all example programs processing singly-linked lists with integer data distributed with GRASShopper. These include standard algorithms such as list traversal, filtering and concatenation, as well as more complex algorithms such as quicksort, mergesort and insertionsort. Furthermore, we considered four simple traversal routines of nested list/tree data structures. We again use our model trained on the two variable with nesting dataset and compare Locust as a memory safety prover to S2/HIP [25,26], Predator [13] and Forester [1]. The full set of results is displayed in Table 3, where a ✓ indicates that a tool was successful, and ✗ that it failed (either explicit failure or timeout after 300 s). For Platypus, we also note the number of disjuncts in generated invariants, and for Locust the number of iterations in the counterexample-refinement loop.

Table 3. Results of memory safety provers on GRASShopper benchmarks.

Example	Platypus	Locust	S2/HIP	Forester	Predator
`concat`	✓ (1 disj.)	✓ (1 it.)	✓	✗	✓
`copy`	✓ (1 disj.)	✓ (1 it.)	✗	✓	✓
`dispose`	✓ (1 disj.)	✓ (1 it.)	✗	✓	✓
`double_all`	✓ (1 disj.)	✓ (1 it.)	✗	✓	✓
`filter`	✓ (2 disj.)	✓ (1 it.)	✗	✓	✓
`insert`	✓ (1 disj.)	✓ (1 it.)	✗	✓	✓
`insertion_sort`	✓ (2 disj.)	✓ (1 it.)	✗	✓	✓
`merge_sort`	✓ (3 disj.)	✓ (4 it.)	✗	✗	✗
`pairwise_sum`	✓ (1 disj.)	✓ (1 it.)	✗	✓	✓
`quicksort`	✓ (1 disj.)	✓ (1 it.)	✗	✗	✗
`remove`	✓ (2 disj.)	✓ (1 it.)	✗	✓	✓
`reverse`	✓ (2 disj.)	✓ (1 it.)	✗	✓	✓
`strand_sort`	✓ (3 disj.)	✓ (5 it.)	✗	✓	✓
`traverse`	✓ (1 disj.)	✓ (1 it.)	✓	✓	✓
`ls_ls_trav`	✓ (1 disj.)	✓ (1 it.)	✗	✗	✗
`ls_ls_trav_rec`	✓ (1 disj.)	✓ (1 it.)	✗	✗	✗
`tr_ls_trav`	✓ (1 disj.)	✓ (1 it.)	✗	✗	✗
`ls_tr_trav`	✓ (1 disj.)	✓ (1 it.)	✗	✗	✗

Analysis. Our results indicate that generalization from synthetic data used to train Platypus to programs works well. For example, whereas our training data was restricted to two program variables, the most complex program example, `strand_sort`, required an invariant involving six variables. In most cases, our strategy of sampling initial program states is sufficient, but the `merge_sort` and `strand_sort` examples show that additional counterexamples are indeed useful to generalize predictions. Finally, as Locust is not optimized for time (e.g., each Platypus invocation starts a .Net VM and initializes a Python interpreter) we do not report detailed runtimes. However, the core shape analysis (factoring out these startup times) took around a second for these benchmark programs.

6 Conclusion and Future Work

We have presented a new technique for data-driven shape analysis using machine learning techniques, which can be combined with an off-the-shelf program verifier to automatically prove memory safety of heap-manipulating programs. All of our contributions have been implemented in our tool Locust, whose experimental evaluation shows that it is able to automatically prove memory safety of programs that other state-of-the-art tools fail on.

Future Work. We plan to extend this work in three aspects. Firstly, we aim to extend Locust to support the introduction of existential quantifiers that Platypus allows. Secondly, one aspect of Platypus that still requires manual and skilled work is feature extraction, which can make extending the tool to handle new inductive separation logic predicates precisely hard. We would like to automate the extraction of relevant features for each production rule, and have already made steps in this direction. We recently introduced Gated Graph Sequence Neural Networks [28] — a technique that leverages deep-learning techniques to make the predictions directly on graph-structured inputs instead of feature vectors. We plan to integrate this into our framework. Initial tests have shown promising results, but some of the features supported by Platypus (most significantly, disjunctive formula predictions) are not yet available in this new method. Finally, we are interested in integrating our method with interactive program verification assistants, to support verification engineers in their daily work.

Acknowledgements. We thank Martin Hruška and Quang Loc Le for help with running their tools S2/HIP, Forester, and Predator for the experiments. We also thank Thomas Wies for valuable feedback on drafts of this paper.

References

1. Abdulla, P.A., Holík, L., Jonsson, B., Lengál, O., Trinh, C.Q., Vojnar, T.: Verification of heap manipulating programs with ordered data by extended forest automata. Acta Inf. **53**(4), 357–385 (2016)
2. Allamanis, M., Tarlow, D., Gordon, A.D., Wei, Y.: Bimodal modelling of source code and natural language. In: ICML 2015, pp. 2123–2132 (2015)

3. Alur, R., Cerný, P.: Streaming transducers for algorithmic verification of single-pass list-processing programs. In: POPL 2011, pp. 599–610 (2011)
4. Bakir, G.H., Hofmann, T., Schölkopf, B., Smola, A.J., Taskar, B., Vishwanathan, S.V.N.: Predicting Structured Data. MIT Press (2007)
5. Berdine, J., Calcagno, C., Cook, B., Distefano, D., O'Hearn, P.W., Wies, T., Yang, H.: Shape analysis for composite data structures. In: Damm, W., Hermanns, H. (eds.) CAV 2007. LNCS, vol. 4590, pp. 178–192. Springer, Heidelberg (2007). doi:10.1007/978-3-540-73368-3_22
6. Bhargavan, K., Fournet, C., Kohlweiss, M., Pironti, A., Strub, P.: Implementing TLS with verified cryptographic security. In: SP 2013, pp. 445–459 (2013)
7. Bouajjani, A., Drăgoi, C., Enea, C., Sighireanu, M.: Abstract domains for automated reasoning about list-manipulating programs with infinite data. In: Kuncak, V., Rybalchenko, A. (eds.) VMCAI 2012. LNCS, vol. 7148, pp. 1–22. Springer, Heidelberg (2012). doi:10.1007/978-3-642-27940-9_1
8. Bradley, A.R.: SAT-based model checking without unrolling. In: Jhala, R., Schmidt, D. (eds.) VMCAI 2011. LNCS, vol. 6538, pp. 70–87. Springer, Heidelberg (2011). doi:10.1007/978-3-642-18275-4_7
9. Brotherston, J., Distefano, D., Petersen, R.L.: Automated cyclic entailment proofs in separation logic. In: Bjørner, N., Sofronie-Stokkermans, V. (eds.) CADE 2011. LNCS (LNAI), vol. 6803, pp. 131–146. Springer, Heidelberg (2011). doi:10.1007/978-3-642-22438-6_12
10. Brotherston, J., Gorogiannis, N.: Cyclic abduction of inductively defined safety and termination preconditions. In: Müller-Olm, M., Seidl, H. (eds.) SAS 2014. LNCS, vol. 8723, pp. 68–84. Springer, Cham (2014). doi:10.1007/978-3-319-10936-7_5
11. Brotherston, J., Gorogiannis, N., Petersen, R.L.: A generic cyclic theorem prover. In: Jhala, R., Igarashi, A. (eds.) APLAS 2012. LNCS, vol. 7705, pp. 350–367. Springer, Heidelberg (2012). doi:10.1007/978-3-642-35182-2_25
12. Calcagno, C., Distefano, D., O'Hearn, P.W., Yang, H.: Compositional shape analysis by means of bi-abduction. J. ACM **58**(6), 26 (2011)
13. Dudka, K., Peringer, P., Vojnar, T.: Predator: a practical tool for checking manipulation of dynamic data structures using separation logic. In: Gopalakrishnan, G., Qadeer, S. (eds.) CAV 2011. LNCS, vol. 6806, pp. 372–378. Springer, Heidelberg (2011). doi:10.1007/978-3-642-22110-1_29
14. Ernst, M.D., Perkins, J.H., Guo, P.J., McCamant, S., Pacheco, C., Tschantz, M.S., Xiao, C.: The Daikon system for dynamic detection of likely invariants. Sci. Comput. Program. **69**(1–3), 35–45 (2007)
15. Garg, P., Löding, C., Madhusudan, P., Neider, D.: ICE: a robust framework for learning invariants. In: Biere, A., Bloem, R. (eds.) CAV 2014. LNCS, vol. 8559, pp. 69–87. Springer, Cham (2014). doi:10.1007/978-3-319-08867-9_5
16. Garg, P., Neider, D., Madhusudan, P., Roth, D.: Learning invariants using decision trees and implication counterexamples. In: POPL 2016, pp. 499–512 (2016)
17. Gotsman, A., Berdine, J., Cook, B.: Interprocedural shape analysis with separated heap abstractions. In: Yi, K. (ed.) SAS 2006. LNCS, vol. 4134, pp. 240–260. Springer, Heidelberg (2006). doi:10.1007/11823230_16
18. Haase, C., Ishtiaq, S., Ouaknine, J., Parkinson, M.J.: SeLoger: a tool for graph-based reasoning in separation logic. In: Sharygina, N., Veith, H. (eds.) CAV 2013. LNCS, vol. 8044, pp. 790–795. Springer, Heidelberg (2013). doi:10.1007/978-3-642-39799-8_55
19. Hawblitzel, C., Howell, J., Kapritsos, M., Lorch, J.R., Parno, B., Roberts, M.L., Setty, S.T.V., Zill, B.: IronFleet: proving practical distributed systems correct. In: SOSP 2015, pp. 1–17 (2015)

20. Itzhaky, S., Banerjee, A., Immerman, N., Nanevski, A., Sagiv, M.: Effectively-propositional reasoning about reachability in linked data structures. In: Sharygina, N., Veith, H. (eds.) CAV 2013. LNCS, vol. 8044, pp. 756–772. Springer, Heidelberg (2013). doi:10.1007/978-3-642-39799-8_53
21. Itzhaky, S., Bjørner, N., Reps, T., Sagiv, M., Thakur, A.: Property-directed shape analysis. In: Biere, A., Bloem, R. (eds.) CAV 2014. LNCS, vol. 8559, pp. 35–51. Springer, Cham (2014). doi:10.1007/978-3-319-08867-9_3
22. Jung, Y., Kong, S., David, C., Wang, B., Yi, K.: Automatically inferring loop invariants via algorithmic learning. MSCS **25**(4), 892–915 (2015)
23. Kennedy, A.J., Vytiniotis, D.: Every bit counts: the binary representation of typed data and programs. JFP **22**(4–5), 529–573 (2012)
24. Klein, G., Andronick, J., Elphinstone, K., Murray, T.C., Sewell, T., Kolanski, R., Heiser, G.: Comprehensive formal verification of an OS microkernel. TOCS **32**(1), 2 (2014)
25. Le, Q.L., Gherghina, C., Qin, S., Chin, W.-N.: Shape analysis via second-order bi-abduction. In: Biere, A., Bloem, R. (eds.) CAV 2014. LNCS, vol. 8559, pp. 52–68. Springer, Cham (2014). doi:10.1007/978-3-319-08867-9_4
26. Le, Q.L., Sun, J., Chin, W.-N.: Satisfiability modulo heap-based programs. In: Chaudhuri, S., Farzan, A. (eds.) CAV 2016. LNCS, vol. 9779, pp. 382–404. Springer, Cham (2016). doi:10.1007/978-3-319-41528-4_21
27. Leroy, X.: Formal verification of a realistic compiler. CACM **52**(7), 107–115 (2009)
28. Li, Y., Tarlow, D., Brockschmidt, M., Zemel, R.: Gated graph sequence neural networks. In: ICLR 2016 (2016)
29. Magill, S., Tsai, M., Lee, P., Tsay, Y.: Automatic numeric abstractions for heap-manipulating programs. In: POPL 2010, pp. 211–222 (2010)
30. McMillan, K.L.: Lazy abstraction with Interpolants. In: Ball, T., Jones, R.B. (eds.) CAV 2006. LNCS, vol. 4144, pp. 123–136. Springer, Heidelberg (2006). doi:10.1007/11817963_14
31. Moy, Y., Marché, C.: Modular inference of subprogram contracts for safety checking. J. Symb. Comput. **45**(11), 1184–1211 (2010)
32. Mühlberg, J.T., White, D.H., Dodds, M., Lüttgen, G., Piessens, F.: Learning assertions to verify linked-list programs. In: Calinescu, R., Rumpe, B. (eds.) SEFM 2015. LNCS, vol. 9276, pp. 37–52. Springer, Cham (2015). doi:10.1007/978-3-319-22969-0_3
33. O'Hearn, P., Reynolds, J., Yang, H.: Local reasoning about programs that alter data structures. In: Fribourg, L. (ed.) CSL 2001. LNCS, vol. 2142, pp. 1–19. Springer, Heidelberg (2001). doi:10.1007/3-540-44802-0_1
34. Navarro Pérez, J.A., Rybalchenko, A.: Separation logic modulo theories. In: Shan, C. (ed.) APLAS 2013. LNCS, vol. 8301, pp. 90–106. Springer, Cham (2013). doi:10.1007/978-3-319-03542-0_7
35. Piskac, R., Wies, T., Zufferey, D.: GRASShopper. In: Ábrahám, E., Havelund, K. (eds.) TACAS 2014. LNCS, vol. 8413, pp. 124–139. Springer, Heidelberg (2014). doi:10.1007/978-3-642-54862-8_9
36. Reynolds, J.C.: Separation logic: a logic for shared mutable data structures. In: LICS 2002, pp. 55–74 (2002)
37. Sagiv, S., Reps, T.W., Wilhelm, R.: Parametric shape analysis via 3-valued logic. TOPLAS **24**(3), 217–298 (2002)
38. Sharma, R., Aiken, A.: From invariant checking to invariant inference using randomized search. In: Biere, A., Bloem, R. (eds.) CAV 2014. LNCS, vol. 8559, pp. 88–105. Springer, Cham (2014). doi:10.1007/978-3-319-08867-9_6

39. Sharma, R., Gupta, S., Hariharan, B., Aiken, A., Liang, P., Nori, A.V.: A data driven approach for algebraic loop invariants. In: Felleisen, M., Gardner, P. (eds.) ESOP 2013. LNCS, vol. 7792, pp. 574–592. Springer, Heidelberg (2013). doi:10.1007/978-3-642-37036-6_31
40. Sharma, R., Gupta, S., Hariharan, B., Aiken, A., Nori, A.V.: Verification as learning geometric concepts. In: Logozzo, F., Fähndrich, M. (eds.) SAS 2013. LNCS, vol. 7935, pp. 388–411. Springer, Heidelberg (2013). doi:10.1007/978-3-642-38856-9_21
41. Sharma, R., Nori, A.V., Aiken, A.: Interpolants as classifiers. In: Madhusudan, P., Seshia, S.A. (eds.) CAV 2012. LNCS, vol. 7358, pp. 71–87. Springer, Heidelberg (2012). doi:10.1007/978-3-642-31424-7_11
42. Yorsh, G., Ball, T., Sagiv, M.: Testing, abstraction, theorem proving: better together! In: ISSTA 2006, pp. 145–156 (2006)
43. Zhu, H., Petri, G., Jagannathan, S.: Automatically learning shape specifications. In: PLDI 2016 (2016)

Securing the SSA Transform

Chaoqiang Deng[1] and Kedar S. Namjoshi[2(✉)]

[1] New York University, New York City, USA
deng@cs.nyu.edu
[2] Bell Laboratories, Nokia, Murray Hill, USA
kedar.namjoshi@nokia-bell-labs.com

Abstract. Modern optimizing compilers use the single static assignment (SSA) format for programs, as it simplifies program analysis and transformation. A source program is converted to an equivalent SSA form before it is optimized. The conversion may, however, create a less secure program if fresh SSA variables inadvertently leak sensitive values that are masked in the original program. This work defines a mechanism to restore a program to its original security level after it has been converted to SSA form and modified further by a series of optimizing transformations. The final program is converted out of SSA form by grouping variables together in a manner that blocks any new leak introduced by the initial SSA conversion. The grouping relies on taint and leakage information about the original program, which is propagated through the optimizing transformations using refinement proofs.

1 Introduction

A compiler carries out a transformation of a high level, abstract program to low level executable code. Ensuring that compilation preserves program semantics is, therefore, a critical question. It has received much attention, both from the point of view of detecting errors in existing compilers (cf. [11,20] and related work) and from the viewpoint of formally guaranteeing correct compilation (cf. [12,15] and related work). In today's world, it is important to also guarantee that compilation does not weaken security properties. For example, compiler transformations should not inadvertently introduce new pathways that leak sensitive data. It is this issue that is considered in this paper.

Correctness and security turn out to be distinct issues. A well-known illustration is the dead-store elimination optimization, which removes a store instruction from a program if the value stored is never used. This has an unfortunate consequence that removal of stores may introduce an information leak. A simple example is the program shown on the left in Fig. 1. It reads a password into a variable x, checks it for validity, and subsequently clears the secret from x by setting it to 0. As the value 0 stored to x is never used, this store is removed (silently) by the dead-store optimization. That leaves the password on the stack or in a register longer than was originally intended, making it possible for an attack elsewhere in the program to obtain the password. The optimization is

F. Ranzato (Ed.): SAS 2017, LNCS 10422, pp. 88–105, 2017.
DOI: 10.1007/978-3-319-66706-5_5

correct in that it preserves the input-output behavior of the original program; however, it is insecure.

In recent work [6], we formulate a notion of a secure program transformation in terms of information flow (precisely, non-interference as in [7]) and show that checking the security of a dead-store elimination after the fact is undecidable in general. We also define a method which limits the removed dead stores to those where removal provably preserves security. In that paper it is also shown that the static single assignment (SSA) transformation is insecure. The technique used for securing dead-store elimination unfortunately does not apply to SSA. The question of how to secure SSA was left open. In this work, we present a mechanism to secure the SSA transformation.

```
void foo()
{
  int x;

  x = read_password();
  use(x);
  x = 0;  // clear password
  other();
  return;
}
```

```
void foo()
{
  int x1,x2;

  x1 = read_password();
  use(x1);
  x2 = 0;
  other();
  return;
}
```

Fig. 1. C program illustrating the insecurity of SSA transformation, from [6]

An example of how SSA may cause an information leak is shown in Fig. 1, taken from [6]. The source program is the password-reading program described above. The SSA transform introduces fresh names `x1` and `x2` for the assignments to `x`. Suppose that `x1` and `x2` are assigned distinct registers. The assignment to `x2` then has no effect and at the call to function `other`, the password is in the clear, stored in the register assigned to `x1`. Suppose further that there is a vulnerability in the function `other` by which an attacker can gain control of the program. The attacker can then read off the password, which is either in the register assigned to `x1`, or is stored on the call stack. This is a new information leak, one that is not present in the original program.

The leak can be prevented if `x1` and `x2` are always allocated the same register which cannot, however, be guaranteed. Moreover, it is inefficient and not always correct to forcibly clear any tainted data before an untrusted function call. This is because a sound taint analysis is generally over-approximate: variables that are declared tainted may, in fact, always contain either non-sensitive data, or sensitive data that is used after the function call.

Our method, therefore, does not modify the program in any essential manner. The unSSA transform groups together related SSA variables and renames every variable in a group G to a single fresh variable, say z_G. A register allocator is thus forced to assign a single register to the group (subject to live range splitting, which we discuss at the end of the paper). For the example program, `x1` and `x2` are placed in the same group so the renaming, in effect, restores the original program.

As grouping and renaming destroys the single assignment property of SSA, this transformation must be placed in the compiler only after all SSA-dependent transformations have been performed. This introduces a key problem. A modern compiler first converts a source program P to its SSA form, say Q_0, then applies a series of SSA-to-SSA optimizations, which result in equivalent but syntactically different intermediate programs $Q_1, \ldots, Q_n$. The unSSA conversion must, therefore, be applied to the final program Q_n, but block leaks introduced in the initial conversion to Q_0. Doing so correctly requires preserving leakage-relevant information through the series of SSA optimizations, which is done with the help of refinement proofs for each transformation. The unSSA transform uses the preserved information to determine a proper grouping of variables in Q_n. Although it is helpful for register allocation to produce small groups, we show that finding the optimal partitioning is undecidable. The unSSA transformation thus relies on sound but approximate analysis information to define the grouping.

The unSSA transform converts the SSA program Q_n to a non-SSA program R; the executable program X is then created by register allocation on R. The overall correctness claim shows that the object code X is at least as secure as the original program P. This is a *relative security* claim: one obtains only that any information leak in X has a corresponding leak in P, *not* that X is free of information leaks. It is analogous to the claim of compiler correctness, which also shows only that every input-output behavior of X can be found in P; not that X is correct in an absolute sense with respect to a specification.

To summarize, the paper studies the important question of making certain that a compiler transformation does not introduce new information leaks. We show that fresh leaks introduced by conversion to SSA form can be blocked by a suitable unSSA transformation, which groups SSA variables into equivalence classes. We show that finding the optimal grouping is, unfortunately, undecidable; hence, our algorithm relies on approximate taint and control-flow information. We also show that leaks may be introduced during register allocation, in particular during live-range splitting, and suggest a simple mechanism to block such a leak. The result is a secure end-to-end compilation.

2 Background

This section contains background on information leakage and taint analysis. Several basic definitions are taken from [6].

Program Syntax and Semantics. As illustrated in the introductory example, the SSA transformation leaks information when sensitive data is retained in registers that can be accessed in a nested procedure call. We can thus consider the point of invocation of an untrusted procedure as a potential *leak point* and require that any leak through a leak point in the final program is a leak that occurs in the source. To simplify the formal development and bring out the key features of the proposed method, the formal development is in terms of structured WHILE programs over integer variables, defined by the syntax below. The program operates on a set of input and state variables. Input variables are partitioned into H ("high security") and L ("low security") variables. All state variables are considered to be low security variables.

$x \in \mathbb{X}$ — variables
$e \in \mathbb{E} ::= c \mid x \mid f(e_1, \ldots, e_n)$ — expressions: f is a function, c a constant
$g \in \mathbb{G}$ — Boolean conditions on $\mathbb{X}$
$S \in \mathbb{S} ::= \mathsf{skip} \mid \mathsf{out}(e) \mid x := e \mid \|i : v_i := \phi(v_{i,A}, v_{i,B}) \mid S_1; S_2 \mid$
$\mathsf{if}\ g\ \mathsf{then}\ S_1\ \mathsf{else}\ S_2\ \mathsf{fi} \mid \mathsf{while}\ g\ \mathsf{do}\ S\ \mathsf{od}$ — statements

A program can be represented by its *control flow graph* (CFG). (The conversion is standard, and omitted.) A node of the CFG represents a program location, and an edge is labeled with a guarded command, of the form "$g \rightarrow a$", where g is a Boolean predicate and a is a primitive statement, one of skip, out (output), or assignment. A special node, entry, with no incoming edges, defines the initial program location, while a special node, exit, defines the final program location. Values for input variables are specified at the beginning of the program and remain constant throughout execution.

Dominance. Node n of a CFG *post-dominates* node m if all paths in the CFG from m to the exit node pass through n.

Program Semantics. The semantics of a program is defined in the standard manner. A *program state* s is a triple (m, e, p), where m is a CFG node, referred to as the *location* of s; if m is not the entry node, then e is the entry edge, (k, m) for some k, and p is a function that maps each variable to an integer value. The function p can be extended to evaluate an expression in the standard way (omitted). An *initial* state has the form $(\mathsf{entry}, \perp, p)$ where $p(x) = 0$ for all state variables x. A *final* state has the form (exit, e, p).

A pair of states, $(s = (m, e, p), t = (n, f, q))$ is in the *transition relation* if $f = (m, n)$ is an edge of the CFG, and for the guarded command $g \rightarrow a$ on that edge, the guard g holds of p, and the function $q(y)$ is identical to $p(y)$ for all variables y other than those modified by the statement a, for which it is defined as follows. If a is an assignment $x := e$, the only variable modified is x and $q(x)$ equals $p(e)$. For the assignment $\|i : v_i := \phi(v_{i,A}, v_{i,B})$, the variables modified are the v_i's, and $q(v_i)$ is given by $p(v_{i,A})$, if $e = A$, and by $p(v_{i,B})$, if $e = B$. For skip and out statements, $q = p$.

The guard predicates for all of the outgoing edges of a node form a partition of the state space, so that a program is *deterministic* and *deadlock-free*. A *execution trace* of the program (referred to in short as a trace) from state s is a sequence of states $s_0 = s, s_1, \ldots$ such that adjacent states are connected by the transition relation. A *computation* is a trace from the initial state. A computation is *terminating* if it is finite and the last state has the exit node as its location.

Information Leakage. Information leakage is defined using the standard concept of *non-interference* (cf. [3,7]). A program P is said to *leak* information if there is a pair of H-input values $\{a, b\}$, with $a \neq b$, and an L-input c such that the computations of P on inputs $(H = a, L = c)$ and $(H = b, L = c)$ either (a) differ in the sequence of output values, or (b) both terminate but differ in the value of one of the L-variables at their *final* states. We call (a, b, c) a *leaky triple* for program P.

Taint Proofs. Leakage is approximated by the notion of taint. Each variable in a program is marked as either "tainted" or "untainted". High inputs are always tainted, low inputs are always untainted. The correctness of these markings is expressed as a taint proof. Each program point is decorated with a taint assertion E, a function from variables to taint values. In earlier work [6], we define a sound taint proof system in the style of the Volpano-Irvine-Smith proof system [19], which sets up consistency conditions on these taint assertions. The soundness of the proof system implies that a leak cannot occur through any untainted variable. On the other hand, the fact that a variable is tainted does not necessarily imply that there is a leak through that variable.

Correct Transformation. For simplicity, we only consider program transformations which do not alter the set of input variables. A transformation from program P to program Q may alter the code of P or the set of state variables. The transformation is *correct* if, for every input value a, the execution of Q on a has a corresponding execution of P on a with an identical sequence of output values. Termination is considered an output, so that a terminating execution of Q must have a matching terminating execution of P. A correct transformation thus offers the relative correctness guarantee that every input-output behavior of Q is present in P. It does not assure the correctness of either program with respect to a specification.

Secure Transformation. A transformation is *secure* if the set of leaky triples for Q is a subset of the leaky triples for P. A secure transformation ensures relative security, i.e., that Q is not more leaky than P. It does not ensure that either P or Q are free of information leaks. Suppose that a transformation from P to Q is correct. For any leaky triple (a, b, c) for Q, if the computations of Q from inputs $(H = a, L = c)$ and $(H = b, L = c)$ differ in their output, this difference must also (by correctness) appear in the corresponding computations in P. Hence, the only way in which Q can be less secure than P is if the computations on inputs $(H = a, L = c)$ and $(H = b, L = c)$ terminate in Q with different L-values, but the corresponding P-computations (which must terminate, too, by correctness) have identical L-values.

The SSA Transformation. A program P is converted to its SSA form Q essentially by replacing each assignment to a variable x with a fresh name, say x_i for the i'th assignment. ϕ-functions are inserted at merge points to combine values that reach that point from different branches of a conditional or while statement. Not all merge points need a ϕ function; efficient algorithms to determine the optimal placement of ϕ functions are given in [5,18]. To illustrate the SSA transform by an example, consider the programs shown in Fig. 2. The program on the left is transformed to the program on the right. In the process, variable x is given three versions: $x1$, $x2$ and $x3$, and ϕ-functions are inserted at the start of the loop to merge the values of $x1, x3$ into $x2$, and of $i1, i3$ into $i2$.

```
for (i=0, x=0; i < N; i++)
{
  x = x+i;
}
```

```
i1 = 0;
x1 = 0;
loop:
     i2 = phi(i1,i3),
  || x2 = phi(x1,x3);
  if (i2 >= N) goto end;
  x3 = x2 + i2;
  i3 = i2 + 1;
  goto loop;
end:
```

Fig. 2. Illustrating the SSA transformation.

3 Securing SSA

The problem addressed in this work is stated precisely as follows. A program P is converted by a compiler to its SSA form, Q_0, which is transformed by a series of SSA-to-SSA optimizations through intermediate programs $Q_1, \ldots, Q_n$. The conversion from P to Q_0 may introduce new leaks, as illustrated in the introduction. The goal is to block these new leaks via a new, final transform, called the "unSSA" transform, which converts Q_n into a program R that is at least as secure as P. We use this naming convention throughout the section.

3.1 An Overview

The essential idea behind the unSSA transform can be understood by considering the changes that the SSA transformation makes in converting P to Q_0. A variable x of P is represented by several versions, say $x_1, x_2, \ldots, x_k$ in Q_0. Programs P and Q_0 have identical control-flow graphs and are observationally equivalent: the bisimulation relation is that at each common program point p, the value of a variable x at point p in P equals the value of one of its versions, x_i, at point p in Q, where the index i is a function of the location p.

Each version of x in Q_0 represents an assignment to x in P. This exposes all intermediate values of x and is the source of the new leaks, as illustrated in the introduction. In order to block such leaks, one has to reverse the SSA transformation, and assign multiple variants of x the same name. This is done by partitioning the variants of x into groups and rewriting the name of every variable in a group, say G, to a fresh name, say z_G.

The grouping must, however, be done carefully. One option is to group all variants of x into a single class, in which case the result is a program isomorphic to the original P. But that negates an important advantage of the SSA conversion. The conversion naturally splits the live range of a variable x (the extent to which it is live, or used) into disjoint sub-ranges for $x_1, x_2, \ldots, x_k$, reducing interference and improving register allocation. Ideally, one would like to choose a partition that is as fine as possible but no finer: i.e., it should maximize the number of independent groups. This, unfortunately, is undecidable in general.

Theorem 1. *It is undecidable to determine whether two instances of a variable must be grouped together.*

Proof: Consider an arbitrary program P. For a fresh high-security input h and a fresh low security state variable l, define the program $Q(h)$ as $P; l := h; l := 0$. Its SSA form is $\tilde{P}; l_1 := h; l_2 := 0$, where $\tilde{P}$ is the SSA form of P. The SSA transformation of Q leaks the value of h if, and only if, P terminates. Hence $\{l_1, l_2\}$ must be grouped together if, and only if, P terminates. **EndProof.**

The naming scheme followed in Q_0 holds clues to the origin of a variable: for instance, x_8 is a variant of the original variable x. This facilitates grouping: x_8 is never to be grouped with, say, y_3. Subsequent transformations, may, however, alter the set of variables and modify control flow, making it difficult to recover the origin of a variable. If, for example, variables x_8 and y_3 are renamed to u, v, respectively, it is no longer clear from the names that u and v should not be in the same group. A key problem that must be resolved, therefore, is the discovery of the relationships between the variables of the final program Q_n and the variables of Q_0, so that the grouping in Q_n can be done correctly. Our solution is to utilize the refinement relations that connect successive programs Q_i and Q_{i+1}. These relations implicitly hold information that relate variables across transformations. The sketch of the overall procedure is as follows.

- Each transformation from Q_i to Q_{i+1} is witnessed by a refinement relation, ξ_i. From this, one identifies a "core" set of variables, C_i, for each Q_i. The core set is defined so that any leak through the core variables of Q_{i+1} induces a leak via the core variables of Q_i.
  The core set C_0 for Q_0 is defined by the bisimulation relation between P and Q_0. For each variable x of P, its variant x_i is in the core set C_0 if x_i is related to x by the bisimulation at the exit node. (In the introductory example, the core set is $\{x_2\}$.) By transitivity, a leak via the final core set C_n induces a leak in P.
- The variables in Q_n are partitioned into groups, each with a representative variable that is either a core variable, or an untainted non-core variable. The unSSA transform converts Q_n to R by renaming all occurrences of a variable in a group G to the name of the representative of G.
  Additional properties are required to ensure the existence of such a partitioning, and to ensure the correctness of renaming. Those properties, labeled (P1)–(P3) below, hold for program Q_0 and must be preserved by each transformation.

The constructions guarantee that correctness is preserved when passing from P to R. They also ensure end-to-end security: a leak in R translates to a leak via the core variables of Q_n, which translates to a leak in P. The requirement that properties (P1)–(P3) are preserved across transformations potentially constraints the set of transformations that can be applied. We show that several common transformations do meet those conditions. The rest of this section defines these concepts and properties and gives a proof of the claimed result.

3.2 Core Sets

A "core" set of Q_{i+1} relative to Q_i is a subset X of the variables of Q_{i+1} such that if two end-states of Q_{i+1} differ in the value of some variable in X, the corresponding low end-states of Q_i differ in the value of some variable in the core set C_i of Q_i. Given the core set C_i of Q_i, a set X is a core set of Q_{i+1} if it meets the following constraint.

$$[\xi_i(t,s) \wedge \mathsf{final}_{i+1}(t) \wedge \xi_i(t',s') \wedge \mathsf{final}_{i+1}(t') \wedge s =_{C_i} s' \Rightarrow t =_X t'] \quad (1)$$

In the formulation, the predicate $\mathsf{final}_i(t)$ holds of a state if its location is the exit node of program Q_i; the relation ξ_i is a refinement relation from Q_{i+1} to Q_i; and the relation $=_Y$ represents equality of states on the set Y of variables. I.e., $t =_X t'$ is short for $t[x] = t'[x]$, for all $x \in X$. Informally, the constraint says that a leak in Q_{i+1} that is witnessed by end-states t, t' which differ on some variable in X has a corresponding leak in Q_i, with end states s, s' that differ in some variable of C_i.

It is easy to see from the constraint that if X and Y are core sets, so is $X \cup Y$; and if X is a core set and Y a subset of X, then Y is a core set. By closure under union, there is a largest core set. By closure under subset, the largest core set can be calculated as the set of variables u of Q_{i+1} for which the constraint holds with $X = \{u\}$. Thus, the largest core set of Q_{i+1} relative to C_i, denoted C_{i+1}, can be determined with a linear number of validity checks, one for each variable in Q_{i+1}.

The core set C_0 is defined in Sect. 3.1. Starting with C_0, one can successively determine the core sets $C_1, C_2, \ldots, C_n$ using the construction procedure above for the programs $Q_1, Q_2, \ldots, Q_n$. The main consequence of the core-set definition is the following theorem.

Lemma 1. *For every i, a leak in Q_{i+1} via its core set C_{i+1} has a corresponding leak in Q_i via its core set C_i.*

Proof: Consider a leaky triple (a, b, c) for Q_{i+1}. Let the induced computations on the inputs $(H = a, L = c)$ and $(H = b, L = c)$ be σ_a and σ_b. As the leak is through C_{i+1}, the final states of these computations, say t_a and t_b, differ for some variable in C_{i+1}. By the refinement relation ξ_i, there are corresponding computations δ_a and δ_b of Q_i whose final states, s_a and s_b, are related to t_a and t_b, respectively, by ξ_i. From implication (1), s_a and s_b differ in C_i; thus, there is a leak in Q_i via C_i. **EndProof.**

Theorem 2. *Any leak in Q_n via its core set C_n has a corresponding leak in P.*

Proof: Using Lemma 1, by induction on the length of the Q sequence, one obtains that a leak in Q_n via C_n corresponds to a leak in Q_0 via C_0. By the definition of C_0, this induces a leak in P. **EndProof.**

3.3 Grouping Variables

While Theorem 2 ensures that a leak through a core set is reflected as a leak in P, it does not cover leaks via non-core variables in Q_n. (In the introductory example, the variable x_1 through which the password is leaked is a non-core variable.) To stop such leaks, the unSSA transform partitions variables of Q_n into groups. Each variable is given the name of its representative, which is either a core variable or an untainted non-core variable. The grouping must be such that (1) it preserves correctness; and (2) it is as lax as possible, i.e., the number of groups is large, to give the register allocator more freedom.

We satisfy these requirements by requiring the following property: for each program Q_i, there is a taint proof and a partition of its variables into classes such that

- (P1) Each class of the partition has a representative variable, which is either a core variable or an untainted non-core variable
- (P2) The variables in a class have mutually disjoint live ranges, assuming that the core variables C_i are live at the end point (Variables with mutually disjoint live-ranges are said to be *interference-free.*)
- (P3) The definition of the representative variable in a class post-dominates the live range of any other variable in its class

These properties hold of the core set C_0 of the initial SSA program, Q_0. The partition has a class for each variable x of the original program P. The class associated with x holds all variants $x_1, \ldots, x_k$ of x in Q_0. The representative of each class is the variant that is in the core set C_0, which satisfies (P1). Property (P2) holds as the variants of x have disjoint live ranges by definition. Property (P3) holds as the members of C_0 are chosen based on the bisimulation between P and Q_0 at the final states.

We show that these properties, applied to Q_n, suffice to define a correct, secure unSSA transform. We then give sufficient conditions which ensure that a transformation preserves (P1)–(P3). Since the properties hold of Q_0, any series of transformations which preserve those properties results in a Q_n to which the unSSA transformation can be applied.

3.4 The unSSA Transform

The unSSA transformation from Q_n to R operates as follows:

1. Construct the core set C_n
2. Perform a taint analysis of Q_n

3. Partition the variables of Q_n into groups such that properties (P1)–(P3) defined above are satisfied
4. For each class Y, create a fresh variable, r_Y, and rename each occurrence of a variable in Y with r_Y

The result is the program R.

Theorem 3. *The unSSA transformation is correct.*

Proof Sketch: The variables in each class are interference-free by (P2). Renaming the variables in class Y with a fresh variable, r_Y, is analogous to the allocation of a physical register to a group of interference-free variables. Correctness thus follows from a standard bisimulation property of register allocation (cf. [16]): the control flow graphs of Q_n and R are isomorphic, and at a point p, the value of r_Y in program R equals the value of a specific variable of class Y in Q_n. **EndProof.**

Properties (P1)–(P3) can, in fact, be established through standard coloring algorithms used for register allocation. The interference graph is built from all variables. Fix a set of representative variables, which include all core variables and some untainted non-core variable names. An interference edge between variables x and y indicates that either the live ranges of x and y intersect, or that x is a representative variable that does not dominate y. The representative variables form the set of colors, and are each colored with their own color. The set of variables that are colored with variable v form the group for v. By construction, there are no edges between variables colored v, so those variables have mutually disjoint live ranges and the representative variable dominates all others.

Theorem 4. *Any leak in program R induces a corresponding leak in P.*

Proof: Let (a, b, c) be a leaky triple for program R. Thus, the computations σ_a and σ_b from respective inputs $(H = a, L = c)$ and $(H = b, L = c)$ differ at their final states in the value of some variable of R, say r_Y. Consider the corresponding computations, δ_a and δ_b, of program Q_n. Suppose r_Y corresponds to a class Y of variables in Q_n. By the bisimulation relation for register allocation described in the proof of Theorem 3, at each point, the value of r_Y on σ_a (σ_b) equals the value of a specific variable in class Y at the corresponding point on δ_a (δ_b). Assume that r_Y corresponds to variable $u \in Y$ at the end node, then the value of u is different at the end of σ_a and σ_a, hence u cannot be untainted. By (P3), u must be the representative variable in Y. By (P1), as u is a representative and tainted, it must be a core variable of Q_n. Therefore, δ_a and δ_b differ in the value of a core variable of Q_n. By Theorem 2, this leak in Q_n via a core variable has a corresponding leak in P. **EndProof.**

3.5 Preserving the Partitioning Properties

The previous theorems assume that a partitioning of Q_n with properties (P1)–(P3) can be established. As shown, these properties hold for the initial SSA program Q_0. We provide sufficient conditions on SSA-to-SSA transformations which preserve these properties, and show in the following section that these conditions hold for common transformations such as constant propagation and loop unrolling.

The conditions require establishing a simulation relation, ν_i, between the CFG's of Q_{i+1} and Q_i that preserve variable definitions and uses, according to a mapping μ from variables of Q_{i+1} and Q_i. Note that this simulation relation is structural, and thus different from the ξ_i relation referred to earlier, which is on the semantics of the programs.

- (C1) If y is a core or untainted non-core variable of Q_i, there is x such that $\mu(x) = y$ and x is a core or untainted non-core variable of Q_{i+1}
- (C2) The simulation relation ν_i from the CFG of Q_{i+1} to the CFG of Q_i preserves variable definitions and uses. I.e., for any variable x of Q_{i+1}, if x is defined on an edge (n, n') and n is simulated by m, then $\mu(x)$ is defined on the simulating edge (m, m'), and similarly for uses of x

Lemma 2. *Consider a transformation from Q_i to Q_{i+1} which satisfies conditions (C1)–(C2). If variables x, y interfere in Q_{i+1}, then $\mu(x), \mu(y)$ interfere in Q_i.*

Proof: We use the fact that both Q_i and Q_{i+1} are in SSA form. For SSA programs, as shown in [10], variables x and y interfere if, and only if, the definition of one of the variables, say x, dominates the definition of y, and x is live at y. Thus, there is a path in the CFG of Q_{i+1} from definition of x through the definition of y to a use of x. By (C2), this has a simulating path in Q_i which preserves defs and uses; thus, the corresponding path in Q_i starts at the definition of $\mu(x)$, passes through the definition of $\mu(y)$ to a use of $\mu(x)$. Hence, $\mu(x)$ and $\mu(y)$ interfere in Q_i. **EndProof.**

Theorem 5. *Consider a transformation from Q_i to Q_{i+1} which satisfies conditions (C1)–(C2). If Q_i satisfies (P1)-(P3), so does Q_{i+1}.*

Proof: Consider variables x, y to be equivalent in Q_{i+1} if $\mu(x)$ and $\mu(y)$ are equivalent in Q_i. For a class C of Q_{i+1}, let D be the class of Q_i that the members of C are mapped to by μ. Let d be the representative of D. By (P1), d is either a core variable or an untainted non-core variable. By (C1), there is a variable c such that $\mu(c) = d$ and c is a core or untainted non-core variable; this variable must be in class C. Pick one such c as the representative of class C. This establishes (P1).

Now consider variables x, y in C. Then $\mu(x), \mu(y)$ are in D and are, therefore, non-interfering. By the converse of Lemma 2, x and y are non-interfering, establishing (P2). Finally, let x be any variable in C other than the representative c. Consider a path σ in the CFG of Q_{i+1} from a use of x to the exit node. By (C2), there is a simulating path γ from a use of $\mu(x)$ to the exit node. By (P3) for Q_i, γ must pass through an edge e that defines the core variable $\mu(c)$. Hence, the edge corresponding to e on σ defines c. Therefore, every use of x is post-dominated by the definition of c, establishing (P3). **EndProof.**

4 Example Transformations

We give examples of compiler optimizations which preserve properties (P1)–(P3).

4.1 Constant Propagation and Folding

This transformation replaces expressions that have a constant value with the value. This is illustrated with the programs in Fig. 3. The original program P is in the top left corner, and has a constant secret value. The SSA transform yields program Q_0 that is in the top right, with core set is $\{x2\}$. Constant propagation and folding optimizes Q_0 to Q_1 that is in the bottom left. In Q_1, the core set is unchanged and $x1$ can be grouped with $x2$. After the unSSA transform, the result is program R in the bottom right, where the information leak introduced by SSA from variable $x1$ is revoked.

```
void foo()
{
  int x;

  x = secret;
  use(x);
  x = 0;
}
```

```
void foo()
{
  int x1, x2;

  x1 = secret;
  use(x1);
  x2 = 0;
}
```

```
void foo()
{
  int x1, x2;

  x1 = secret;
  use(secret);
  x2 = 0;
}
```

```
void foo()
{
  int x2;

  x2 = secret;
  use(secret);
  x2 = 0;
}
```

Fig. 3. C program illustrating constant propagation and folding

In general, consider a program Q_{i+1} that is obtained from Q_i through constant propagation and folding. The control-flow and variables are unchanged in the transformation. Suppose that there is a taint proof and a partition of variables in Q_i that satisfies (P1)–(P3). First, note that the same taint proof carries over to Q_{i+1}. To see this, consider a statement $x := e$ that is replaced with $x := \bar{e}$, where $\bar{e}$ is obtained by replacing variables in e with their constant values, and folding any constant expressions. Then a taint triple $\{E\}x := e\{F\}$ is valid in Q_i if $E(e) \sqsubseteq F(x)$ and $E(y) \sqsubseteq F(y)$, for all other variables y. As replacing variables with constants can only lead to a stronger taint value, it is the case that $E(\bar{e}) \sqsubseteq E(e)$; hence, $E(\bar{e}) \sqsubseteq F(x)$ by transitivity. Let the function μ be the identity function. As the set of core variables and the taint proof is identical in both programs, condition (C1) holds. Let ν be the identity relation on the control-flow graph nodes; then ν is a simulation which respects uses and defs of variables, establishing (C2). By Theorem 5, conditions (P1)–(P3) are preserved across the transformation.

4.2 Loop Unrolling

Loop unrolling is a transformation that replicates the body of a loop. We consider the basic case in Fig. 4, where the original loop is executed an even number of times, and the unrolling factor is 2. The program in the top-left is the original program P, and the program in the top-right is the SSA transformed program Q_0 whose core set is $\{i2, x2\}$. After loop unrolling, the program Q_1 in the bottom-left is generated, with the same core set. In the course of unrolling the body of the loop, all statements are duplicated and the phi-assignment and the test of the loop condition are simplified. The variable partition groups all variants of i together, and all variants of x together, as the corresponding live ranges are disjoint. Renaming the variables in each group and simplifying the resulting statements, one obtains the program R in the bottom-right, which is as secure as the original program P.

Loop unrolling preserves the set of variables and the core set, introducing new variables only inside the loop being unrolled. Suppose that there is a taint proof and a partitioning that satisfies properties (P1)–(P3) for program Q_i. Then the taint proof carries over essentially unchanged to the unrolled loop. In place of the original taint invariant I for the loop, one has the extended taint invariant I', where $I'(x) = I(x)$ for any original variable x, and $I'(x') = I(x)$, for the copy x' of variable x which is introduced in the unrolling. Other taint assertions are unchanged. Let μ be the function defined by $\mu(x) = x$, if x is an original variable, and $\mu(x') = x$, if x' is the copy of x introduced in the unrolling. As core variables and taints are unaffected by the transformation, condition (C1) holds with this definition of μ. Let ν be the relation which connects control-flow nodes in the copy of the loop body with their original nodes. One may verify that ν is a simulation which preserves defs and uses according to μ, establishing (C2). In the example above, `x4` is a copy of `x2` so $\mu(x4) = x2$. The transition defining `x4` in Q_{i+1} is matched by the transition defining `x2` in Q_i; similarly, the definition of `x5` is matched by the transition defining `x3`. By Theorem 5, conditions (P1)–(P3) are preserved across the loop unrolling transformation.

4.3 Secure DSE

The transformations considered so far preserve (P1)–(P3) but do not make use of the properties in defining the transformation itself. This section proposes a novel dead store elimination (DSE) transformation for SSA programs which does both. Similar to the DSE transformation introduced in [6], this is a heuristic to determine whether it is secure to remove a certain dead store. To be precise, for a SSA program Q_i satisfying partitioning properties (P1)–(P3), the transformation

```
void foo()
{
  int i, x;

  x = 0;
  for(i = 0; i < 2*K; i++)
  {
    x = f(x,i);
  }

  return;
}
```

```
void foo()
{
  int i1,i2,i3,
      x1,x2,x3;

  x1 = 0;
  i1 = 0;
  loop:
    x2 = phi(x1, x3) ||
    i2 = phi(i1, i3);
    if(i2 >= 2*K) goto end;
    x3 = f(x2,i2);
    i3 = i2 + 1;
    goto loop;
  end:

  return;
}
```

```
void foo()
{
  int i1,i2,i3,i4,i5,
      x1,x2,x3,x4,x5;

  x1 = 0;
  i1 = 0;
  loop:
    x2 = phi(x1, x5) ||
    i2 = phi(i1, i5);
    if(i2 >= 2*K) goto end;
    x3 = f(x2,i2);
    i3 = i2 + 1;
    x4 = x3 ||   // phi
    i4 = i3;
    skip;        // test
    x5 = f(x4,i4);
    i5 = i4 + 1;
    goto loop;
  end:

  return;
}
```

```
void foo()
{
  int i2, x2;

  x2 = 0;
  i2 = 0;
  loop:
    if(i2 >= 2*K) goto end;
    x2 = f(x2,i2);
    i2 = i2 + 1;
    x2 = f(x2,i2);
    i2 = i2 + 1;
    goto loop;
  end:

  return;
}
```

Fig. 4. C program illustrating loop unrolling

removes a dead assignment "$x := e$" is removed if either the partition containing x has size 1, or x is not a representative variable for its partition.

Lemma 3. *The single-step DSE transformation preserves (P1)–(P3).*

Proof: Consider a taint proof for program Q_i. Let E be the taint assertion just before the dead assignment to x. As Q_i is in SSA form, this is the only assignment to x. As it is dead, x is never referenced in Q_i. At all points in Q_{i+1}, let the taint status of x be "untainted". As x is never referenced in Q_i, this change does not affect the taint status of any other variable. As x is never modified in Q_{i+1}, it is correct to assert that x is untainted throughout.

Suppose the variables in Q_i are partitioned into classes $Y_1, Y_2, \ldots, Y_m$, and variable x comes from class Y_k. If the size of Y_k is 1, then the original partitioning is valid for Q_{i+1}, and clearly satisfies the properties (P1)–(P3). Otherwise, the size of Y_k is larger than 1 and x is not the representative of Y_k. Let $Y'_k = Y_k \backslash \{x\}$, and let $Y''_k = \{x\}$ be the new classes that are introduced. Clearly, Y''_k satisfies (P1)–(P3). We now consider Y'_k. The representative for this class is the representative for Y_k. It is easy to check that properties (P1)–(P3) hold for Y'_k. **EndProof.**

Theorem 6. *The DSE transformation preserves properties (P1)–(P3).*

Proof: The actual DSE transformation is a sequence of steps, each of which removes only one dead store. Then, this theorem follows immediately from the preservation of partitioning properties in each step shown in Lemma 3. **End-Proof.**

In the introductory example, x_2 is the representative variable of its class, hence the dead assignment to x_2 will not be removed by this transformation. Another example is introduced in Fig. 5. The original program P is on the left, and the program Q_0 on the right is the corresponding SSA transformed program whose core set is $\{x_3\}$. There are two non-trivial valid partitions of the three variables of Q_0:

(1) $\{x_1, x_3\}$, $\{x_2\}$: the core variable x_3 is selected as the representative variable of tainted non-core variable x_1. In this case, the dead assignment to x_2 will be removed, since x_2 is from a class of size 1. After assigning a fresh variable name to both x_1 and x_3 by the unSSA transformation, the final program will be as secure as the original program P.

(2) $\{x_1, x_2\}$, $\{x_3\}$: the untainted non-core variable x_2 is selected as the representative variable of tainted non-core variable x_1. In this case, the dead assignment to x_3 will be removed, since x_3 is from a class of size 1. After assigning a fresh variable name to both x_1 and x_2 by unSSA transformation, no information about password could be leaked and the final program becomes more secure than the original program P.

```
void foo()
{
  int x;

  x = read_password();
  use(x);
  x = 0;
  x = read_password2();
  return;
}
```

```
void foo()
{
  int x;

  x1 = read_password();
  use(x1);
  x2 = 0;
  x3 = read_password2();
  return;
}
```

Fig. 5. C program illustrating secure DSE

5 Related Work and Conclusions

The SSA transformation is a standard component of modern compilers, including LLVM and GCC. It continues to be extensively investigated, for its properties and applications to optimization (cf. the "SSA Book" [1]). The fact that it introduces information leaks was noted in our earlier work [6]. In this work, we investigate the question of SSA leaks in some depth, and offer a procedure that blocks the newly introduced leaks by partially reversing the SSA transformation prior to register allocation. Existing work on secure compilation (cf. [8,13]) does not apply to the SSA problem. To the best of our knowledge, the insecurity of SSA and the design of mechanisms that remedy it has not been investigated in the literature. The SWIPE algorithm [9] is a source-to-source transformation which introduces instructions that erase potentially sensitive data after the last use of such data. While the transformation enhances security at the source level, the effect of the new erasure instructions may be negated by the compiler's internal SSA conversion, as illustrated by the introductory example.

The major technical difficulty is to connect the leakage that may occur in a program obtained by a series of optimizations to the leakage introduced by the original conversion to SSA form. Our method tracks these connections using the refinement relations that witness each transformation. Further constraints are needed to ensure that the grouping of variables in the unSSA transformation is correct. We give sufficient conditions to show that transformations preserve those constraints, which do hold of the original SSA program, and demonstrate that some common transformations meet these conditions. Loosening the conditions to accommodate more transformations is an important subject for future work.

This work considers a formulation of security that is binary: either a triple is leaky or it is not. This ignores the information content of a leak, making no distinction between, say, the leak of an entire password and the leak of a single character of the password. It is difficult to formulate and analyze the quantitative information content of a leak (cf. [17] for a survey) but one may consider qualitative, knowledge-based formulations (cf. [2]) that are easier to analyze. The construction of a theory that lets one reason about the reduction of the information content of leaks across transformations is an important topic for further research.

This work has not investigated the security of register allocation, which follows the unSSA transform. In LLVM, allocation is done after a straightforward lifting of the program out of SSA form by eliminating phi-functions. Although allocation directly on SSA form is also possible [14], the unSSA transform already produces a non-SSA form program, so those techniques cannot be applied.

Register allocation algorithms, in the main, decide to allocate the live range of a variable either to memory ("spilling") or to a register. Those operations do not introduce a security leak. However, in order to better pack live ranges, an allocator may decide to break up the live range of a variable. This has an effect similar to that of the SSA transform: for instance, the live range of x in the introductory example could be broken up into ranges that correspond to those of the SSA variables x_1 and x_2. These sub-ranges are individually allocated to either registers or memory. In order to preserve security, the allocator should either disable splitting (which could reduce performance) or insert code that clears unused register or memory locations. For example, suppose the range for x is divided up into three sections, corresponding to fresh variables x_1, x_2 and x_3, and x_1 is allocated register A; x_3 is allocated register B; while x_2 is spilled to memory. If x_1 may hold a taint, then the contents of A should be cleared after they are copied to memory. Similarly, when the content in memory is copied to B at the start of x_3, the memory entry should be cleared. Adding those instructions also introduces overhead. However, as splitting is usually attempted around loops [4], it is possible that this overhead is not as considerable as that induced by entirely avoiding splitting. These questions need to be further investigated in an experimental setting.

Acknowledgements. Kedar Namjoshi was supported, in part, by grant CCF-1563393 from the National Science Foundation. We thank our colleagues at Bell Labs and UIC for helpful comments on this work.

References

1. Static single assignment book. http://ssabook.gforge.inria.fr/latest/book.pdf
2. Askarov, A., Chong, S.: Learning is change in knowledge: knowledge-based security for dynamic policies. In: Chong, S. (ed.) 25th IEEE Computer Security Foundations Symposium, CSF 2012, Cambridge, MA, USA, 25–27 June 2012, pp. 308–322. IEEE Computer Society (2012)
3. Bell, D., LaPadula, L.: Secure computer systems: mathematical foundations, vol. 1-III. Technical report ESD-TR-73-278, The MITRE Corporation (1973). 17
4. Cooper, K.D., Simpson, L.T.: Live range splitting in a graph coloring register allocator. In: Koskimies, K. (ed.) CC 1998. LNCS, vol. 1383, pp. 174–187. Springer, Heidelberg (1998). doi:10.1007/BFb0026430
5. Cytron, R., Ferrante, J., Rosen, B.K., Wegman, M.N., Zadeck, F.K.: Efficiently computing static single assignment form and the control dependence graph. ACM Trans. Program. Lang. Syst. **13**(4), 451–490 (1991)

6. Deng, C., Namjoshi, K.S.: Securing a compiler transformation. In: Rival, X. (ed.) SAS 2016. LNCS, vol. 9837, pp. 170–188. Springer, Heidelberg (2016). doi:10.1007/978-3-662-53413-7_9
7. Denning, D.E., Denning, P.J.: Certification of programs for secure information flow. Commun. ACM **20**(7), 504–513 (1977)
8. D'Silva, V., Payer, M., Song, D.X.: The correctness-security gap in compiler optimization. In: 2015 IEEE Symposium on Security and Privacy Workshops, SPW 2015, San Jose, CA, USA, 21–22 May 2015, pp. 73–87. IEEE Computer Society (2015)
9. Gondi, K., Bisht, P., Venkatachari, P., Sistla, A.P., Venkatakrishnan, V.N.: SWIPE: eager erasure of sensitive data in large scale systems software. In: Bertino, E., Sandhu, R.S. (eds.) Second ACM Conference on Data and Application Security and Privacy, CODASPY 2012, San Antonio, TX, USA, 7–9 February 2012, pp. 295–306. ACM (2012)
10. Hack, S.: Interference graphs of programs in SSA form. Technical report 2005–15, Universität Karlsruhe, June 2005
11. Le, V., Afshari, M., Su, Z.: Compiler validation via equivalence modulo inputs. In: O'Boyle, M.F.P., Pingali, K. (eds.) ACM SIGPLAN Conference on Programming Language Design and Implementation, PLDI 2014, Edinburgh, UK, 09–11 June 2014, pp. 216–226. ACM (2014)
12. Leroy, X.: Formal verification of a realistic compiler. Commun. ACM **52**(7), 107–115 (2009)
13. Patrignani, M., Garg, D.: Secure compilation and hyperproperty preservation. In: CSF (2017, to appear)
14. Pereira, F.M.Q., Palsberg, J.: SSA elimination after register allocation. In: Moor, O., Schwartzbach, M.I. (eds.) CC 2009. LNCS, vol. 5501, pp. 158–173. Springer, Heidelberg (2009). doi:10.1007/978-3-642-00722-4_12
15. Pnueli, A., Shtrichman, O., Siegel, M.: The Code Validation Tool (CVT)- automatic verification of a compilation process. Softw. Tools Technol. Transf. **2**(2), 192–201 (1998)
16. Rideau, S., Leroy, X.: Validating register allocation and spilling. In: Gupta, R. (ed.) CC 2010. LNCS, vol. 6011, pp. 224–243. Springer, Heidelberg (2010). doi:10.1007/978-3-642-11970-5_13
17. Smith, G.: Recent developments in quantitative information flow (invited tutorial). In: 30th Annual ACM/IEEE Symposium on Logic in Computer Science, LICS 2015, Kyoto, Japan, 6–10 July 2015, pp. 23–31. IEEE (2015)
18. Sreedhar, V.C., Gao, G.R.: A linear time algorithm for placing phi-nodes. In: Cytron, R.K., Lee, P. (eds.) Conference Record of POPL 1995: 22nd ACM SIGPLAN-SIGACT Symposium on Principles of Programming Languages, San Francisco, California, USA, 23–25 January 1995, pp. 62–73. ACM Press (1995)
19. Volpano, D.M., Irvine, C.E., Smith, G.: A sound type system for secure flow analysis. J. Comput. Secur. **4**(2/3), 167–188 (1996)
20. Yang, X., Chen, Y., Eide, E., Regehr, J.: Finding and understanding bugs in C compilers. In: Hall, M.W., Padua, D.A. (eds.) Proceedings of the 32nd ACM SIGPLAN Conference on Programming Language Design and Implementation, PLDI 2011, San Jose, CA, USA, 4–8 June 2011, pp. 283–294. ACM (2011)

Relative Store Fragments for Singleton Abstraction

Leandro Facchinetti[1], Zachary Palmer[2(✉)], and Scott F. Smith[1]

[1] Department of Computer Science, The Johns Hopkins University, Baltimore, USA
{leandro,scott}@jhu.edu

[2] Department of Computer Science, Swarthmore College, Swarthmore, USA
zachary.palmer@swarthmore.edu

Abstract. A *singleton abstraction* occurs in a program analysis when some results of the analysis are known to be exact: an abstract binding corresponds to a single concrete binding. In this paper, we develop a novel approach to constructing singleton abstractions via *relative store fragments*. Each store fragment is a *locally* exact store abstraction in that it contains only those abstract variable bindings necessary to address a particular question at a particular program point; it is *relative* to that program point and the point of view may be shifted. We show how an analysis incorporating relative store fragments achieves flow-, context-, path- and must-alias sensitivity, and can be used as a basis for environment analysis, without any machinery put in place for those specific aims. We build upon recent advances in *demand-driven* higher-order program analysis to achieve this construction as it is fundamentally tied to demand-driven lookup of variable values.

1 Introduction

A *singleton abstraction* [Mig10b], also known as a *must analysis* [Mid12], is a common thread found across advanced program analyses: some results of the analysis are known to be exact, meaning the abstraction set is in fact a singleton in those cases. Singleton abstractions have traditionally been used in must-alias analyses for first-order programs, e.g. [CWZ90]. For higher-order programs they have been used in lightweight closure conversion [SW97] in must-alias analysis [JTWW98], and abstract garbage collection has been used to produce singleton abstractions [MS06b].

This paper develops a novel approach to constructing singleton abstractions using *relative store fragments*. Unlike stores in traditional abstract interpretation, these are *fragments* in that they contain information about a *subset* of the store necessary to address a particular analysis question; there is no global store. Instead of storing binding information in terms of global calling context, these fragments express binding information *relative* to a particular point in the program using call path difference information similar to CFA frame strings [MS06a, GM17].

Facchinetti is supported by a CAPES Fellowship, process number 13477/13-7.

F. Ranzato (Ed.): SAS 2017, LNCS 10422, pp. 106–127, 2017.
DOI: 10.1007/978-3-319-66706-5_6

In this paper we define *Demand-driven Relative Store Fragment analysis*, abbreviated DRSF. DRSF incorporates relative store fragments to achieve flow-, context-, path- and must-alias sensitivity, and can be used as a basis for environment analysis [Shi91, BFL+14, GM17], without any extra machinery put in place for those specific aims. We define for this analysis an algebra of relative store fragment composition and relativization to combine these fragments in the process of answering control- and data-flow questions. We now briefly describe some dimensions of DRSF's expressiveness.

Path Sensitivity: Path-sensitivity is well-known as an important dimension of expressiveness in program analyses [BA98, DLS02, XCE03, DMH15, THF10]. Path-sensitive analyses observe control-flow decisions and use this information to refine their results. DRSF's store fragments are naturally conducive to path sensitivity: the values of variables used to dictate control flow are recorded in store fragments and used to discard impossible control flow combinations.

Must-alias Analysis: The original purpose of singleton analyses was to extract must-alias properties [CWZ90, JTWW98]. The case where a variable must (not just may) alias another means an assignment to one must (not just may) also affect the other. We can additionally use our singleton store abstraction to achieve must-alias properties over a mutable heap.

Context Sensitivity: Another pleasant aspect of the theory is that context-sensitivity [Shi91] also comes "for free": the call path annotations on variables additionally disambiguate contexts. Creating a multiplicity of store fragments is expensive, but the multiple purposes they may be put to allows the effort to be amortized. Along with standard k-CFA style context sensitivity [Shi91], CPA-style context-sensitivity [Age95, Bes09, VS10] also naturally emerges.

Environment Analysis: While we are primarily focused on fundamentals and not on potential clients of the analysis, the environment problem is a classic stress test for higher-order program analyses [Shi91, BFL+14, GM17] and DRSF can be used a basis to address that problem.

The Context: Demand-Driven Higher-Order Analysis. We work in the context of DDPA, a demand-driven higher-order analysis [PS16] which applies ideas of first-order demand-driven analyses [Rep94, DGS97, SR05] to higher-order programs. DDPA incorporates filters on data lookup for some path-sensitivity but lacks "alignment": it considers each variable separately.

Results. This paper is a proof-of-concept study of DRSF: we give a complete definition of the analysis for a simple functional language, prove some basic properties, and describe an implementation with additional features including a mutable heap. While we establish that the algorithm has an exponential worst-case, in practice on benchmarks it has reasonable performance.

2 Overview

In this section we will present a series of examples that illustrate the concepts behind DRSF. The analysis builds on DDPA [PS16], and basic features of that analysis will be introduced as we go.

2.1 A Simple Example Illustrating Path-Sensitivity

We start with a very simple program in an ML-like language:

```
let b = coin_flip () in
let x =
  if b then 4 else "dr" in
let y =
  if b then 5 else "sf" in
x + y
```

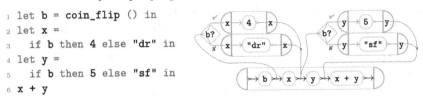

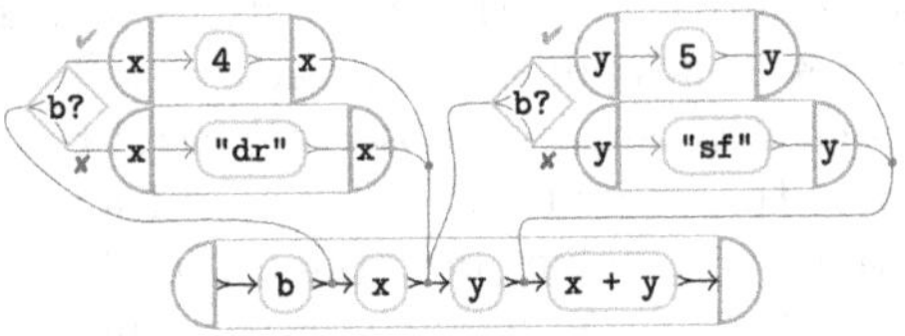

The `coin_flip` primitive non-deterministically returns either `true` or `false`. Operator `+` is overloaded to append strings; it is not defined when the operand types mismatch – i.e., there is no implicit coercion *à la* JavaScript. This program never has a type mismatch: the types of `x` and `y` are aligned by `b`. To observe that addition is safe in this program, an analysis must observe this alignment. Using $\hat{\circ}$ for the abstract entity corresponding to a concrete $\circ$, the analysis must show $\hat{\texttt{x}} = \{\widehat{4}\}$ and $\hat{\texttt{y}} = \{\widehat{5}\}$ occur together (and similarly for the strings), and, more importantly, prove that $\hat{\texttt{x}} = \{\widehat{4}\}$ and $\hat{\texttt{y}} = \{\widehat{\texttt{"sf"}}\}$ do not co-occur. DRSF is *path-sensitive*: it preserves this connection. We now outline how this is accomplished.

Both DDPA and DRSF construct a Control-Flow Graph (CFG) of the program; the CFG constructed by DRSF here appears to the right of the code. Given a (perhaps partial) CFG, the analyses answer questions of the type "what are the possible abstract values that reach *this* variable at *this* program point?" The analyses perform a lookup by traversing the CFG backward, in the direction opposite to control-flow, until they find a definition, in the tradition of demand-driven program analyses [Rep94, DGS97, SR05, HT01, PS16]. For example, if asked "what are the possible abstract values for `b` at the end of the program?" the analyses would initiate a lookup at the CFG node representing the end of the program and traverse the graph backward with respect to control-flow to reach the clause `b = coin_flip ()`, producing the result $\hat{b} = \{\widehat{\texttt{true}}, \widehat{\texttt{false}}\}$.

There are two complications in building demand-driven analyses for higher-order languages: the first is preventing unbounded search along cyclic paths in a CFG; the second is building the CFG itself, because higher-order functions determine control-flow, so data-flow and control-flow are intertwined. To address the former, DDPA and DRSF encode the CFG traversal in terms of a *PDA reachability* problem, building on ideas in [JSE+14, EMH10, BEM97]. For CFG construction, the analyses can perform lookups on partial CFGs and let the results inform the incremental construction of the full CFG.

The CFG above illustrates this process on our running example. The black and brown edges represent control flow, with black edges determined directly from program syntax, and brown edges introduced by the analysis. Initially, only the bottom-most spine exists, representing the statements at the top level. The analysis first wires in the upper-left widget for the conditional returning `x`: a lookup of `b` shows it can be `true` and so the `4` node is wired in. Since the lookup of `b` can also be `false` the `"dr"` node is also wired in. Similarly the branches of the `y` conditional are wired in one by one. In general, both DDPA and DRSF construct the CFG in a forward manner but use reverse lookup through the (partial) CFG to find potential values which can inform CFG construction. By induction, all the information necessary to resolve control-flow at a program point is already available in the partial CFG when the program point is considered.

With the complete CFG it is possible to look up the potential values of final expression `x + y`. This, in turn, requires the lookups of variables `x` and `y`. The key difference between DDPA and DRSF is in how the analyses answer to these lookups. DDPA produces only sets of abstract values: $\hat{\texttt{x}}$'s result is $\{\widehat{4}, \widehat{\texttt{"dr"}}\}$ and $\hat{\texttt{y}}$'s result is $\{\widehat{5}, \widehat{\texttt{"sf"}}\}$; any path-sensitivity has been lost by the form of the output. DRSF, in addition to abstract values, produces *abstract store sets* associated with them: $\hat{\texttt{x}}$'s store set is $\{\langle\widehat{4}, \{\hat{\texttt{b}} \mapsto \widehat{\texttt{true}}, \hat{\texttt{x}} \mapsto \widehat{4}\}\rangle, \langle\widehat{\texttt{"dr"}}, \{\hat{\texttt{b}} \mapsto \widehat{\texttt{false}}, \hat{\texttt{x}} \mapsto \widehat{\texttt{"dr"}}\}\rangle\}$ and $\hat{\texttt{y}}$'s store set is $\{\langle\widehat{5}, \{\hat{\texttt{b}} \mapsto \widehat{\texttt{true}}, \hat{\texttt{y}} \mapsto \widehat{5}\}\rangle, \langle\widehat{\texttt{"sf"}}, \{\hat{\texttt{b}} \mapsto \widehat{\texttt{false}}, \hat{\texttt{y}} \mapsto \widehat{\texttt{"sf"}}\}\rangle\}$. Observe that each individual store in the store set contain singletons representing a potential slice of the runtime; it is a pair of a value and the mappings for each variable that led to that value. The key advantage of DRSF is that, to compute the addition, a *store merge* is performed on the store sets for $\hat{\texttt{x}}$ and $\hat{\texttt{y}}$. This store merge operation eliminates impossible stores; for example, it discards the combination of $\hat{\texttt{x}} \mapsto \widehat{4}$ and $\hat{\texttt{y}} \mapsto \widehat{\texttt{"sf"}}$ *because the corresponding abstract stores disagree on their values for* $\hat{\texttt{b}}$. The set of stores can be non-deterministic, but each store contains singletons which agree on all mappings. This can be used to solve a whole class of issues concerning correlation between bindings, such as *fake rebinding* [VS10].

One important aspect of abstract stores is that they are not absolute for the whole program, but *relative* to the program point in which the lookup initiated. They are also *fragments*: only the variables incident on the current lookup need be included. This latter property will be made clear in the subsequent examples.

2.2 A Simple Example of Context-Sensitivity

The following example illustrates a use of higher-order functions:

```
let f = fun _ -> 4 in
let g = fun _ -> "s" in
let c = fun h -> h () in
let x = c f in
let y = c g in
x
```

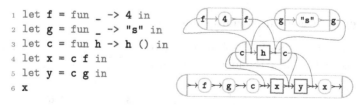

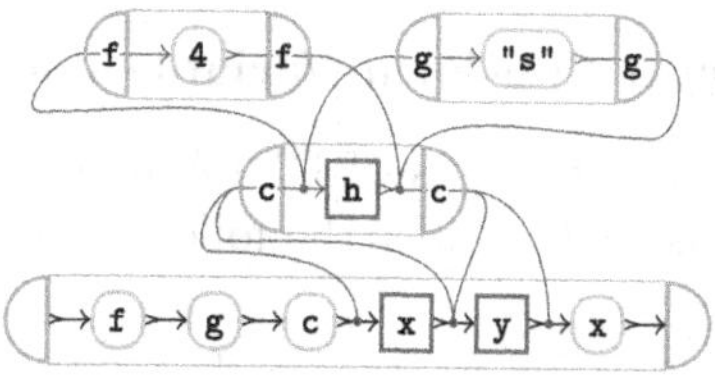

To look up `x` from the end of the program assuming the full CFG has been previously constructed, DRSF traverses the CFG in reverse from the program end.

Walking backward, call site `x` in line 4 is the source of the result; the analysis must then proceed in reverse into `c`'s body, whereupon it finds a call to `h`. At this point it must find which functions `h` could be; `h` is a parameter to `c`, so DRSF has to exit its body to look for the arguments that could have been passed in.

Now, the analysis faces a dilemma: there are two wirings to `c`'s body in the CFG. One is at `x`, where `h` is bound to `f`; the other is at `y`, where `h` is bound to `g`. The former wiring matches the execution we are tracing but, in a naive walk back through the CFG, this information has been lost.

DRSF achieves context-sensitivity via *traces* attached to variables to indicate the relative call stack context the variable was found in. When `f` is looked up from the perspective of the top-level program, the trace is empty: $[]$. The result of this lookup is $\hat{\mathtt{f}} = \{\langle \widehat{\mathtt{fun_4}}, \{\hat{\mathtt{f}}@[] \mapsto \widehat{\mathtt{fun_4}}\}\rangle\}$: trace $[]$ indicates that the definition of $\hat{\mathtt{f}}$ was found in the same calling context as where the question was asked.

During our lookup of `x`, however, we must find a store fragment for $\hat{\mathtt{h}}$, the parameter of the $\hat{\mathtt{c}}$ function, from *inside* of that function's body. $\hat{\mathtt{h}}$ is defined in terms of $\hat{\mathtt{f}}$, but that definition occurs in the same calling context as $\hat{\mathtt{c}}$'s call site; that is, we must go to where $\hat{\mathtt{c}}$ is called to find the value of $\hat{\mathtt{f}}$. One caller of $\hat{\mathtt{c}}$ is site $\hat{\mathtt{x}}$ and we use the trace $[\llparenthesis\hat{\mathtt{x}}]$ to describe that $\hat{\mathtt{x}}$ is the caller of the program point where our lookup started. Thus, one store we can obtain in looking up $\hat{\mathtt{h}}$ from within `c` is $\langle \widehat{\mathtt{fun_4}}, \{\hat{\mathtt{f}}@[\llparenthesis\hat{\mathtt{x}}] \mapsto \widehat{\mathtt{fun_4}}, \hat{\mathtt{h}}@[] \mapsto \widehat{\mathtt{fun_4}}\}\rangle$. Similarly, if we consider that $\hat{\mathtt{c}}$ can be called from site $\hat{\mathtt{y}}$, we obtain another potential store: $\langle \widehat{\mathtt{fun_s}}, \{\hat{\mathtt{g}}@[\llparenthesis\hat{\mathtt{y}}] \mapsto \widehat{\mathtt{fun_s}}, \hat{\mathtt{h}}@[] \mapsto \widehat{\mathtt{fun_s}}\}\rangle$.

Now recall that, in the path we were originally taking to search for `x`, we had entered `h` via call site `x`. So, to relativize the above stores to the top level of the program, we must append a $\rrparenthesis\hat{\mathtt{x}}$ to the trace on all store variables. This gives stores containing $\{\hat{\mathtt{f}}@[\llparenthesis\hat{\mathtt{x}}, \rrparenthesis\hat{\mathtt{x}}] \mapsto \widehat{\mathtt{fun_4}}, \hat{\mathtt{h}}@[\rrparenthesis\hat{\mathtt{x}}] \mapsto \widehat{\mathtt{fun_4}}\}$ and $\{\hat{\mathtt{g}}@[\llparenthesis\hat{\mathtt{y}}, \rrparenthesis\hat{\mathtt{x}}] \mapsto \widehat{\mathtt{fun_s}}, \hat{\mathtt{h}}@[\rrparenthesis\hat{\mathtt{x}}] \mapsto \widehat{\mathtt{fun_s}}\}$. Trace $[\llparenthesis\hat{\mathtt{x}}, \rrparenthesis\hat{\mathtt{x}}]$ is a no-op which cancels out to $[]$. On the other hand, $[\llparenthesis\hat{\mathtt{y}}, \rrparenthesis\hat{\mathtt{x}}]$ is a *contradiction* since call and return do not align and it means this latter store can be *eliminated* and only the former is sound. So, the lookup of $\hat{\mathtt{x}}$ yields only the result of $\hat{\mathtt{x}}$; this demonstrates context-sensitivity.

Our call string logic is related to CFA's delta frame strings [MS06a, GM17]. Note that trace-based context-sensitivity also influences path-sensitivity: DRSF is path-sensitive for sources of non-determinism not related to loss of context sensitivity: user input, `coin_flip`, integer comparisons in which precision was lost, and so on. We will see later that, just as in kCFA, the loss of context-sensitivity takes a toll path-sensitivity as well.

2.3 Precise Non-local Variable Lookup

One of the key features of DDPA inherited by DRSF is precision in non-local variable lookup. Consider the following program.

```
let f = fun x ->
  let g = fun y -> x in g
in
let a = f 0 in
let b = a 5 in
b
```

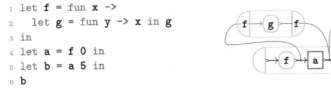

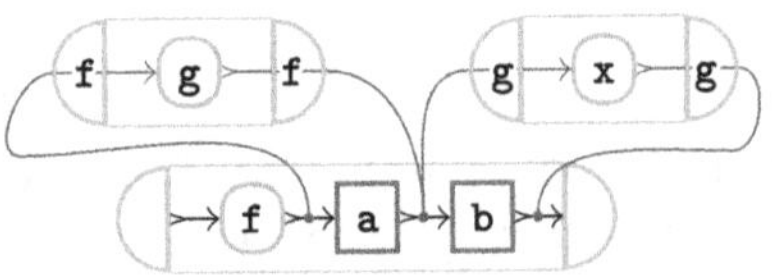

To look up `b` from the end of the program, DRSF first finds `b = a 5` so the function in `a` must be entered in reverse to find the value. `a` itself is a closure over the function `g`, so it then has to look up `g`'s return value, `x`. But if the analysis continues traversing the CFG backward with respect to control-flow looking for `x`, it comes back to the call site `b` and proceeds to skip over `a` and `f`, failing to find `x` at the start of the program. DRSF solves this problem with a *statically-scoped* search for non-locals in the style of *access links* in compiler implementations.

So, at the point where we were looking up `x` above, DRSF first must look up the *definition of the function that was applied*, `g`, and resume search for `x` from there as that is where `x`'s definition lexically occurs. Searching for `g` from within call site `b`, it is the return value from call site `a` which continues the search into `f`'s body. At that point, it finds `g`'s definition, and can resume lookup for `x` from that CFG location, where it finds that `x` is the function parameter. So DRSF returns to the call site `a` and finds the argument `0`, which leads to result $\hat{b} = \{\widehat{0}\}$.

2.4 Must-Alias Analysis

Each relative store contains singletons and this property naturally leads to must-alias analysis expressiveness. Consider the following program.

```
let f = fun rx -> rx := "dr" in
let r1 = ref 4 in
let r2 = r1 in
f r2;
!r1 + "sf"
```

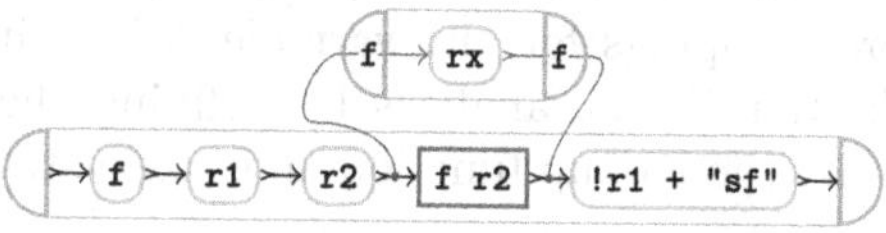

In looking up `r1`, we encounter a call to `f`. Since this is a stateful lookup unlike earlier lookups above, we must examine the `f` call for side effects; we discover that it sets its parameter `rx`. If we knew that `rx` *must* be an alias for `r1` we would have found the most recent assignment to `rx`, so this condition is checked. Searching for `rx` shows it *must* be `r2`, which in turn *must* be `r1`. So, there is only one viable store here and in it `"dr"` is the most recent assignment to `r1`. Therefore `!r1` always returns a string.

These small examples illustrate DRSF's expressiveness. Fortunately, the principles of the analysis are general: precision is retained on less trivial examples we run through the implementation in Sect. 4.1. The next step is to formalize the analysis to make its meaning precise.

3 The Analysis

We formally analyze the grammar of the language in Fig. 1. All expressions in this language are in A-normal form [FSDF93] to better align the expressions and the analysis; we also require that every variable declaration is unique. This grammar is a small subset of the implemented language; we leave out deep pattern matching, state, and atomic data and operators. The operational semantics for this simplistic call-by-value language is straightforward and is not given here for space reasons. For this discussion, it bears mentioning that conditional clause bodies are functions; when the condition is matched (or not matched), we call the appropriate function with the matched argument.

$e ::= [c, \ldots]$	*expressions*	$r ::= \{\ell = x, \ldots\}$	*records*
$c ::= x = b$	*clauses*	$f ::= \texttt{fun}\ x\ \texttt{->}\ (\,e\,)$	*functions*
$b ::= v \mid x \mid x\ x \mid x \sim p\ ?\ f : f \mid x.\ell$	*clause bodies*	x	*variables*
$v ::= r \mid f$	*values*	ℓ	*labels*
$p ::= \{\ell, \ldots\} \mid \texttt{fun} \mid \texttt{any}$	*patterns*		

Fig. 1. Expression Grammar

As in the previous section, we express the abstraction of a construct $\circ$ as $\hat{\circ}$. In this simple language, these constructs are in fact identical; we use two distinct forms for readability only.

The DRSF analysis incrementally constructs a control flow graph, a process which relies heavily upon a variable-value lookup function. Given a variable and a point in the program, this lookup function generally produces relative store fragments which indicate possible (abstract) values for that variable as well as store mappings for any variables which influenced this decision. We begin our definition of the analysis by defining these relative store fragments and then specify the lookup function and single-step CFG construction operation in turn.

3.1 Relative Store Fragments

The grammar for the analysis store constructs is given in Fig. 2. We further restrict $\hat{\Psi}$ such that there cannot be two mappings $\hat{\psi}/\hat{\psi}'$ with the same $\hat{\rho}$, provided $\hat{\rho} = \hat{x}@\hat{\Delta}$ and $\hat{\Delta}$ is a full trace. And, we impose an invariant that for any rooted store $\langle \hat{\psi}, \hat{\Psi} \rangle$, $\hat{\psi} \in \hat{\Psi}$.

$\hat{\rho} ::= \hat{x}@\hat{\Delta}$	*relative trace variable*	$\hat{\sigma} ::= \langle \hat{\psi}, \hat{\Psi} \rangle$	*rooted store*
$\hat{\Delta} ::= [\hat{\delta}, \ldots] \mid (\hat{\delta}, \ldots]$	*full and partial relative traces*	$\hat{\Psi} ::= \{\hat{\psi}, \ldots\}$	*raw store*
$\hat{\delta} ::= (\!|\hat{c} \mid |\!)\hat{c}$	*relative trace part*	$\hat{\psi} ::= \hat{\rho} \mapsto \hat{v}$	*store mapping*

Fig. 2. Abstract Store Grammar

A lookup of a variable in the DRSF analysis does not just produce a set of abstract values; it more generally returns a set of *store fragments* $\hat{\sigma}$ paired with locations where they are found (discussed in Sect. 3.2). Each store fragment $\hat{\sigma}$ is a *rooted store* because it includes a *root mapping* $\hat{\rho} \mapsto \hat{v}$ indicating the abstract value $\hat{v}$ of the looked-up variable (in the Overview we elided the "$\hat{\rho} \mapsto$" on the root mapping for simplicity), as well as a *raw store* $\hat{\Psi}$ of mappings for all other relevant variables in context. Mappings $\hat{\psi}$ do not map raw variables $\hat{x}$ to values:

they map *trace-relative* variables $\hat{\rho} = \hat{x}@\hat{\Delta}$ to values, with the traces $\hat{\Delta}$ defining the context where the variable was defined relative to the current context.

Relative traces come in two forms. The first form is a *full trace* $[\dots]$ which is precise: it describes exactly from where the result of lookup is obtained. The second form $(\dots]$ is a *partial trace* which represents a lossy suffix of the former, trimmed to allow the analysis to terminate. We formally define a trimming operation on relative traces here which retains only the rightmost k elements:

Definition 1. *We define* $(\hat{\Delta})\lceil^k$ *such that*

$$[\hat{\delta}_n, \dots, \hat{\delta}_1]\lceil^k = \begin{cases} [\hat{\delta}_n, \dots, \hat{\delta}_1] & \textit{when } n \leq k \\ (\hat{\delta}_k, \dots, \hat{\delta}_1] & \textit{otherwise} \end{cases} \qquad (\hat{\delta}_n, \dots, \hat{\delta}_1]\lceil^k = (\hat{\delta}_{\min(k,n)}, \dots, \hat{\delta}_1]$$

We are using standard notation $[a_1, \dots, a_n]$ for regular lists and $\hat{\Delta} \,||\, \hat{\Delta}'$ for list append. Relative traces are list-like, so it is convenient to use similar notation to our lists when considering list suffixes; for instance, we may write $\hat{\Delta} = \hat{\Delta}' \,||\, [\hat{\delta}]$ to indicate that $\hat{\delta}$ is the last item of the trace $\hat{\Delta}$. Because traces may be partial, however, we only use this notation when the trace is the left operand and the right operand is a simple list of trace parts.

We also define here two convenience routines for creating rooted stores and extracting the underlying value from them:

Definition 2.

1. *We define* $\langle\!|\hat{x}, \hat{v}|\!\rangle$*, the "store creation" operation, as* $\langle \hat{x}@[] \mapsto \hat{v}, \{\hat{x}@[] \mapsto \hat{v}\}\rangle$.
2. *We define* $(\!|\hat{\sigma}|\!)$*, the "store read" operation, as* $(\!|\langle \hat{\rho} \mapsto \hat{v}, \hat{\Psi}\rangle|\!) = \hat{v}$.

Trace Suffixing. Raw stores $\hat{\Psi}$ map *relative trace variables* to values. As indicated in Fig. 2, each relative trace variable is a pairing between a variable and a *relative trace* which describes the location of that variable relative to the current program stack. If a value was originally constructed outside of the current function, for instance, the trace $[\lhd\hat{c}]$ indicates that the call site $\hat{c}$ was pushed onto the stack since the value was bound. If lookup found a value originally bound inside of a function that has since returned, the trace may contain $[\rhd\hat{c}]$.

As every mapping in a store is relative to the current position of variable lookup, we must uniformly modify these traces as lookup moves between function calls. We begin by defining an operation which suffixes an existing relative trace with a new stack operation. This may cancel redundant values: $[\lhd\hat{c}, \rhd\hat{c}]$ enters and exits a function from the same call site and so is a no-op. Trace suffixing may also fail on impossible stack transformations: $[\lhd\hat{c}, \rhd\hat{c}']$ for $\hat{c} \neq \hat{c}'$ returns to a point not the calling point, an impossibility.

We now define a trace suffixing operation to formalize the above. Traces longer than a given k are trimmed to partial traces of the form $(\dots]$ by truncating the front of the list. This prevents traces from growing arbitrarily long and allows stores to keep finite context, as described above. We represent suffix failure in impossible cases by leaving the operation undefined.

Definition 3. *For each $k \geq 0$, trace suffixing $\ltimes_k$ is defined as follows:*

$$
\begin{array}{llll}
[] \ltimes_k \hat{\delta} & = [\hat{\delta}]\lceil^k & (] \ltimes_k \hat{\delta} & = (\hat{\delta}]\lceil^k \\
\hat{\Delta} \,||\, [\triangleleft\hat{c}] \ltimes_k \triangleright\hat{c} & = \hat{\Delta} & \hat{\Delta} \,||\, [\triangleleft\hat{c}_1] \ltimes_k \triangleright\hat{c}_2 & \text{is undefined if } \hat{c}_1 \neq \hat{c}_2 \\
\hat{\Delta} \,||\, [\triangleleft\hat{c}_1] \ltimes_k \triangleleft\hat{c}_2 & = (\hat{\Delta} \,||\, [\triangleleft\hat{c}_1, \triangleleft\hat{c}_2])\lceil^k & \hat{\Delta} \,||\, [\triangleright\hat{c}] \ltimes_k \hat{\delta} & = (\hat{\Delta} \,||\, [\triangleright\hat{c}, \hat{\delta}])\lceil^k
\end{array}
$$

We extend the trace suffixing operator to operate on pairs of traces. We allow $n = 0$ and/or $m = 0$ below.

$$
\begin{array}{l}
\hat{\Delta} \ltimes_k [\hat{\delta}_1, \ldots, \hat{\delta}_n] = \hat{\Delta} \ltimes_k \hat{\delta}_1 \ltimes_k \ldots \ltimes_k \hat{\delta}_n \\
\hat{\Delta} \ltimes_k (\hat{\delta}_1, \ldots, \hat{\delta}_n] = (\hat{\delta}_1, \ldots, \hat{\delta}_n]\lceil^k
\end{array}
$$

Observe that traces are *pop/push-bitonic* [Mig07] in that they have the form $[\triangleright\hat{c}_1, \ldots \triangleright\hat{c}_n, \triangleleft\hat{c}_1, \ldots \triangleleft\hat{c}_m]$ for $n, m \geq 0$.

Trace suffixing homomorphically extends to stores and other entities.

Definition 4. *We extend trace suffixing to variables, mappings, raw stores, and rooted stores as follows:*

$$
\begin{array}{rlrl}
(\hat{x}@\hat{\Delta}) \ltimes_k \hat{\delta} & = \hat{x}@(\hat{\Delta} \ltimes_k \hat{\delta}) & (\hat{x}@\hat{\Delta}) \ltimes_k \hat{\Delta}' & = \hat{x}@(\hat{\Delta} \ltimes_k \hat{\Delta}') \\
(\hat{\rho} \mapsto \hat{v}) \ltimes_k \hat{\delta} & = (\hat{\rho} \ltimes_k \hat{\delta}) \mapsto \hat{v} & (\hat{\rho} \mapsto \hat{v}) \ltimes_k \hat{\Delta} & = (\hat{\rho} \ltimes_k \hat{\Delta}) \mapsto \hat{v} \\
\hat{\Psi} \ltimes_k \hat{\delta} & = \left\{ \hat{\psi} \ltimes_k \hat{\delta} \middle| \hat{\psi} \in \hat{\Psi} \right\} & \hat{\Psi} \ltimes_k \hat{\Delta} & = \left\{ \hat{\psi} \ltimes_k \hat{\Delta} \middle| \hat{\psi} \in \hat{\Psi} \right\} \\
\langle \hat{\psi}, \hat{\Psi} \rangle \ltimes_k \hat{\delta} & = \langle \hat{\psi} \ltimes_k \hat{\delta}, \hat{\Psi} \ltimes_k \hat{\delta} \rangle & \langle \hat{\psi}, \hat{\Psi} \rangle \ltimes_k \hat{\Delta} & = \langle \hat{\psi} \ltimes_k \hat{\Delta}, \hat{\Psi} \ltimes_k \hat{\Delta} \rangle
\end{array}
$$

Note that in each case above if any of the $\ltimes_k$ on the right are undefined, the suffixing operation on the left is taken to be undefined.

To illustrate how the "undefinedness" of trace suffixing is fully propagated, $\hat{x}@[\triangleleft\hat{c}_1] \ltimes_k \triangleright\hat{c}_2$ and $\{\hat{x}@[\triangleleft\hat{c}_1] \mapsto \hat{v}, \ldots\} \ltimes_k \triangleright\hat{c}_2$ are both undefined if $\hat{c}_1 \neq \hat{c}_2$. Hereafter we will take k to be fixed and abbreviate $\ltimes_k$ as $\ltimes$.

Store Merge. Some lookup operations in DRSF require a *subordinate lookup*. For example, before proceeding from a call site into a function body, we must perform a lookup to make sure that function is called at this site. A key feature of DRSF is how stores from lookups can be *merged*: formally, $\hat{\Psi}_1 \oplus \hat{\Psi}_2$. Any store that represents an inconsistent run-time state can be eliminated in $\oplus$. There are two conditions which cause store merge to fail. First, a *variable* could be inconsistent: one store maps `x` to an integer while the other maps `x` to a record. Second, the *call stack* implied by the store could be inconsistent, for example one store contains $\mathtt{r}@[\triangleright\mathtt{x}, \triangleleft\mathtt{y}]$ and the other contains $\mathtt{r}@[\triangleright\mathtt{x}, \triangleleft\mathtt{z}]$: these constraints cannot simultaneously be satisfied and merge fails.

We now define store merge. The first condition – merging inconsistent variables – is implicitly addressed by the manner in which we propagate the undefined cases of the definitions above. To handle the second condition, we must define an auxiliary trace relation $\hat{\Delta}_1 \simeq \hat{\Delta}_2$ and apply it to stores.

Definition 5. *1. We define the* trace consistency relation $\hat{\Delta}_1 \bumpeq \hat{\Delta}_2$ *to hold iff there exist some* $\hat{\Delta}'_0$, $\hat{\Delta}'_1$, *and* $\hat{\Delta}'_2$ *such that the following hold:*
 - *No terms of the form* $(\!|\hat{c}$ *appear in* $\hat{\Delta}'_0$, $\hat{\Delta}'_1$, *or* $\hat{\Delta}'_2$;
 - $\hat{\Delta}_1 \ltimes \hat{\Delta}'_0 = \hat{\Delta}'_1$, *and* $\hat{\Delta}_2 \ltimes \hat{\Delta}'_0 = \hat{\Delta}'_2$.

2. Two stores $\hat{\Psi}_1$ *and* $\hat{\Psi}_2$ *are* trace consistent *(written* $\hat{\Psi}_1 \bumpeq \hat{\Psi}_2$*) iff* $\forall (\hat{x}_1@\hat{\Delta}_1) \mapsto \hat{v}_1 \in \hat{\Psi}_1, (\hat{x}_2@\hat{\Delta}_2) \mapsto \hat{v}_2 \in \hat{\Psi}_2.\ \hat{\Delta}_1 \bumpeq \hat{\Delta}_2$.

3. The merge $\hat{\Psi}_1 \oplus \hat{\Psi}_2$ *of two unrooted stores* $\hat{\Psi}_1$ *and* $\hat{\Psi}_2$ *is the union of their mappings,* $\hat{\Psi}_1 \cup \hat{\Psi}_2$, *provided the following conditions hold:*
 - *For all* $\hat{\rho} \mapsto \hat{v}_1 \in \hat{\Psi}_1$ *and* $\hat{\rho} \mapsto \hat{v}_2 \in \hat{\Psi}_2$, *if* $\hat{\rho}$ *of form* $\hat{x}@[\ldots]$ *then* $\hat{v}_1 = \hat{v}_2$
 - $\hat{\Psi}_1 \bumpeq \hat{\Psi}_2$

If these conditions do not hold, then $\hat{\Psi}_1 \oplus \hat{\Psi}_2$ *is undefined.*

Two forms of merge for rooted stores are used in DRSF and we make explicit definitions for readability. *Parallel store merge* $\hat{\sigma}_1 \leftleftarrows \hat{\sigma}_2$ merges two stores computed from the same reference point and the root of the merged store is set to the root of $\hat{\sigma}_1$. *Serial store merge* $\hat{\sigma}_1 \looparrowleft \hat{\sigma}_2$ merges stores whilst offsetting the reference point of the first store by the reference point of the second. This adjustment is used to support the non-local lookups described in Sect. 2.3.

Definition 6. *1. The* parallel store merge *operation* $\leftleftarrows$ *is defined as follows:*
$\langle \hat{\psi}_1, \hat{\Psi}_1 \rangle \leftleftarrows \langle \hat{\psi}_2, \hat{\Psi}_2 \rangle = \langle \hat{\psi}_1, \hat{\Psi}_1 \oplus \hat{\Psi}_2 \rangle$

2. The serial store merge *operation,* $\looparrowleft$, *is defined as follows:*
$\hat{\sigma} \looparrowleft \langle \hat{x}@\hat{\Delta} \mapsto \hat{v}, \hat{\Psi} \rangle = (\hat{\sigma} \ltimes \hat{\Delta}) \leftleftarrows \langle \hat{x}@\hat{\Delta} \mapsto \hat{v}, \hat{\Psi} \rangle$

These operations are undefined when any of the component operations are undefined.

Singleton Abstractions. At this point we have all the tools necessary to construct and utilize singleton abstractions in the analysis. Each mapping in a relative store fragment includes a relative trace $\hat{\Delta}$ which is either partial or full. Full traces describe in the analysis a set of memory locations at run-time that share a property, for example, closures over the same lambda or records with the same fields corresponding to the same variables. The conditions for unrooted store merge $\oplus$ (and, by extension, the store merge operations $\leftleftarrows$ and $\looparrowleft$) are then used to identify and discard cases in which stores have immediately dissonant values for full-trace bindings.

Note that immediate dissonance is only evident for values in which the concrete-to-abstract mapping is one-to-one, as is the case for our functions and records. When extending DRSF to other kinds of values (for example, numbers and strings) the analysis must conservatively assume dissonance whenever the abstract values fall out of the range for which the concrete-to-abstract mapping is one-to-one. For those values within the one-to-one mapping, subsequent lookups of e.g. function non-locals or record fields can be used to check for dissonance deeply within a structure. By induction, when these lookups reach the leaves of these data structures, they prove that *a chain of full-trace bindings represent singleton abstractions.* This allows the analysis we define below to be a basis for expressing singleton abstractions, though using DRSF to develop e.g. an environment analysis is beyond the scope of this paper.

3.2 Lookup over Control Flow Graphs

Before defining variable lookup for the analysis, we must formally define the control flow graphs described in Sect. 2. The grammar appears in Fig. 3. Recall that our simplified language is A-normalized and each variable declaration is unique. Each $\hat{a}$ is a program clause (a program point in Overview terminology) and each $\hat{a} \lll \hat{a}$ is a CFG edge (a brown or black arrow in the Overview CFGs) collected into set $\hat{G}$, the full CFG. Variable lookup produces a set of *positioned* stores $\hat{\Phi}$, which are relative store fragments together with a reference point for them. This reference point is used to support the statically scoped search described in Sect. 2.3.

$$
\begin{array}{rcll}
\hat{a} & ::= & \hat{c} \mid \hat{x} \overset{\llparenthesis\hat{c}}{=} \hat{x} \mid \hat{x} \overset{\rrparenthesis\hat{c}}{=} \hat{x} \mid \textsc{Start} \mid \textsc{End} & \textit{abstract annotated clauses} \\
\hat{g} & ::= & \hat{a} \lll \hat{a} & \textit{control flow edges} \\
\hat{G} & ::= & \{\hat{g}, \ldots\} & \textit{control flow graphs} \\
\hat{\phi} & ::= & \langle \hat{a}, \hat{\sigma} \rangle & \textit{positioned store} \\
\hat{\Phi} & ::= & \{\hat{\phi}, \ldots\} & \textit{positioned store set}
\end{array}
$$

Fig. 3. DRSF Analysis Grammar

For notational purposes, we overload each operation on stores $\hat{\sigma}$ to positioned stores $\hat{\phi}$; for instance, we let $\langle \hat{a}, \hat{\sigma} \rangle \ltimes \hat{\delta} = \langle \hat{a}, \hat{\sigma} \ltimes \hat{\delta} \rangle$ and $\llparenthesis \langle \hat{a}, \hat{\sigma} \rangle \rrparenthesis = \llparenthesis \hat{\sigma} \rrparenthesis$. We overload each such operation to sets of $\hat{\phi}$; for example, $\hat{\Phi} \ltimes \hat{\delta} = \{\hat{\phi} \ltimes \hat{\delta} \mid \hat{\phi} \in \hat{\Phi}\}$.

Let $\textsc{Match}(\hat{v}, \hat{p})$ be the natural shallow pattern match relation between a value and a pattern. Let $\mathrm{RV}(e)$ be the last variable defined in an expression: $\mathrm{RV}([\ldots, \hat{x} = \hat{b}]) = \hat{x}$.

We are finally in a position to define variable lookup $\hat{G}(\hat{a}, \hat{x})$, a function returning the set of positioned stores that give a value to $\hat{x}$ from the perspective of program point $\hat{a}$.

Definition 7. *For CFG $\hat{G}$, let $\hat{G}(\hat{a}_0, \hat{x})$ be the function returning the least set of positioned stores $\hat{\Phi}$ for some $\hat{a}_1 \overset{\hat{G}}{\lll} \hat{a}_0$ satisfying the following clauses:*

1. ***Variable search***
   (a) VALUE DISCOVERY
   If $\hat{a}_1 = (\hat{x} = \hat{v})$ *then* $\langle \hat{a}_1, \llparenthesis \hat{x}, \hat{v} \rrparenthesis \rangle \in \hat{\Phi}$.
   (b) VALUE ALIAS
   If $\hat{a}_1 = (\hat{x} = \hat{x}')$ *then* $\hat{G}(\hat{a}_1, \hat{x}') \subseteq \hat{\Phi}$.
   (c) CLAUSE SKIP
   If $\hat{a}_1 = (\hat{x}' = b)$ *and* $\hat{x}' \neq \hat{x}$, *then* $\hat{G}(\hat{a}_1, \hat{x}) \subseteq \hat{\Phi}$.
2. ***Function wiring***
   (a) FUNCTION ENTER: PARAMETER VARIABLE
   If $\hat{a}_1 = (\hat{x} \overset{\hat{c}\llparenthesis}{=} \hat{x}')$ *and* $\hat{c} = (\hat{x}''_1 = \hat{x}''_2\ \hat{x}')$, $\langle \hat{a}', \hat{\sigma} \rangle \in \hat{G}(\hat{a}_1, \hat{x}''_2)$, *then* $(\hat{G}(\hat{a}_1, \hat{x}') \leftleftarrows \hat{\sigma}) \ltimes \llparenthesis\hat{c} \subseteq \hat{\Phi}$.

(b) FUNCTION EXIT: RETURN VARIABLE

If $\hat{a}_1 = (\hat{x} \overset{\rrbracket\hat{c}}{=} \hat{x}')$, $\hat{c} = (\hat{x}\,\texttt{=}\,\hat{x}''_2\ \hat{x}'{}_3)$, $\langle \hat{a}'_1, \hat{\sigma}_1\rangle \in \hat{G}(\hat{c}, \hat{x}''_2)$, $\langle \hat{a}'_2, \hat{\sigma}_2\rangle \in \hat{G}(\hat{c}, \hat{x}''_3)$, $(\texttt{fun}\ \hat{x}''_4\ \texttt{->}\ (\ \hat{e}\ )) = (\!|\hat{\sigma}|\!)$, *and* $\mathrm{RV}(\hat{e} = \hat{x}')$, *then*
$((\hat{G}(\hat{a}_1, \hat{x}') \ltimes \rrbracket\hat{c}) \leftleftarrows \hat{\sigma}_1 \leftleftarrows \hat{\sigma}_2) \subseteq \hat{\Phi}$.

(c) FUNCTION ENTER: NON-LOCAL VARIABLE

If $\hat{a}_1 = (\hat{x}'' \overset{\llbracket\hat{c}}{=} \hat{x}')$, $\hat{c} = (\hat{x}''_1\,\texttt{=}\,\hat{x}'{}_2\ \hat{x}')$, $\hat{x}'' \neq \hat{x}$, *and* $\langle \hat{a}'_1, \hat{\sigma}_1\rangle \in \hat{G}(\hat{a}_1, \hat{x}''_2)$, $\langle \hat{a}'_2, \hat{\sigma}_2\rangle \in \hat{G}(\hat{a}_1, \hat{x}')$, *then*
$((\hat{G}(\hat{a}'_1, \hat{x}) \hookleftarrow_{P} \hat{\sigma}_1) \leftleftarrows \hat{\sigma}_2 \ltimes \llbracket\hat{c}) \subseteq \hat{\Phi}$.

3. ***Conditional wiring***

(a) CONDITIONAL ENTER: PARAMETER POSITIVE

If $\hat{a}_1 = (\hat{x}' \overset{\llbracket\hat{c}}{=} \hat{x}_1)$, $\hat{c} = (\hat{x}_2\,\texttt{=}\,\hat{x}_1\,\texttt{\char`~}\,\hat{p}\,\texttt{?}\,\hat{f}_1 : \hat{f}_2)$, $\hat{f}_1 = \texttt{fun}\,\hat{x}'\ \texttt{->}\,(\ \hat{e}\ )$, *and* $\hat{x} \in \{\hat{x}', \hat{x}_1\}$, *then*
$\{\hat{\phi} | \hat{\phi} \in \hat{G}(\hat{a}_1, \hat{x}_1) \wedge \textsc{Match}((\!|\hat{\phi}|\!), \hat{p})\} \subseteq \hat{\Phi}$.

(b) CONDITIONAL ENTER: PARAMETER NEGATIVE

If $\hat{a}_1 = (\hat{x}' \overset{\llbracket\hat{c}}{=} \hat{x}_1)$, $\hat{c} = (\hat{x}_2\,\texttt{=}\,\hat{x}_1\,\texttt{\char`~}\,\hat{p}\,\texttt{?}\,\hat{f}_1 : \hat{f}_2)$, $\hat{f}_2 = \texttt{fun}\,\hat{x}'\ \texttt{->}\,(\ \hat{e}\ )$, *and* $\hat{x} \in \{\hat{x}', \hat{x}_1\}$, *then*
$\{\hat{\phi} | \hat{\phi} \in \hat{G}(\hat{a}_1, \hat{x}_1) \wedge \neg\textsc{Match}((\!|\hat{\phi}|\!), \hat{p})\} \subseteq \hat{\Phi}$.

(c) CONDITIONAL ENTER: NON-PARAMETER POSITIVE

If $\hat{a}_1 = (\hat{x}' \overset{\llbracket\hat{c}}{=} \hat{x}_1)$, $\hat{c} = (\hat{x}_2\,\texttt{=}\,\hat{x}_1\,\texttt{\char`~}\,\hat{p}\,\texttt{?}\,\hat{f}_1 : \hat{f}_2)$, $\hat{f}_1 = \texttt{fun}\,\hat{x}'\ \texttt{->}\,(\ \hat{e}\ )$, $\hat{x} \notin \{\hat{x}', \hat{x}_1\}$, $\langle \hat{a}', \hat{\sigma}\rangle \in \hat{G}(\hat{c}, \hat{x}_1)$, *and* $\textsc{Match}((\!|\hat{\sigma}|\!), \hat{p})$, *then*
$(\hat{G}(\hat{a}_1, \hat{x}) \leftleftarrows \hat{\sigma}) \subseteq \hat{\Phi}$.

(d) CONDITIONAL ENTER: NON-PARAMETER NEGATIVE

If $\hat{a}_1 = (\hat{x}' \overset{\llbracket\hat{c}}{=} \hat{x}_1)$, $\hat{c} = (\hat{x}_2\,\texttt{=}\,\hat{x}_1\,\texttt{\char`~}\,\hat{p}\,\texttt{?}\,\hat{f}_1 : \hat{f}_2)$, $\hat{f}_2 = \texttt{fun}\,\hat{x}'\ \texttt{->}\,(\ \hat{e}\ )$, $\hat{x} \notin \{\hat{x}', \hat{x}_1\}$, $\langle \hat{a}', \hat{\sigma}\rangle \in \hat{G}(\hat{c}, \hat{x}_1)$, *and* $\neg\textsc{Match}((\!|\hat{\sigma}|\!), \hat{p})$, *then*
$(\hat{G}(\hat{a}_1, \hat{x}) \leftleftarrows \hat{\sigma}) \subseteq \hat{\Phi}$.

(e) CONDITIONAL EXIT: RETURN POSITIVE

If $\hat{a}_1 = (\hat{x} \overset{\rrbracket\hat{c}}{=} \hat{x}')$, $\hat{c} = (\hat{x}\,\texttt{=}\,\hat{x}_1\,\texttt{\char`~}\,\hat{p}\,\texttt{?}\,\hat{f}_1 : \hat{f}_2)$, $\hat{f}_1 = \texttt{fun}\,\hat{x}''\ \texttt{->}\,(\ \hat{e}\ )$, $\mathrm{RV}(\hat{e}) = \hat{x}'$, $\langle \hat{a}', \hat{\sigma}\rangle \in \hat{G}(\hat{c}, \hat{x}_1)$, *and* $\textsc{Match}((\!|\hat{\sigma}|\!), \hat{p})$, *then*
$(\hat{G}(\hat{a}_1, \hat{x}') \leftleftarrows \hat{\sigma}) \subseteq \hat{\Phi}$.

(f) CONDITIONAL EXIT: RETURN NEGATIVE

If $\hat{a}_1 = (\hat{x} \overset{\rrbracket\hat{c}}{=} \hat{x}')$, $\hat{c} = (\hat{x}\,\texttt{=}\,\hat{x}_1\,\texttt{\char`~}\,\hat{p}\,\texttt{?}\,\hat{f}_1 : \hat{f}_2)$, $\hat{f}_2 = \texttt{fun}\,\hat{x}''\ \texttt{->}\,(\ \hat{e}\ )$, $\mathrm{RV}(\hat{e})$ $\hat{x}'$, $\langle \hat{a}', \hat{\sigma}\rangle \in \hat{G}(\hat{c}, \hat{x}_1)$, *and* $\neg\textsc{Match}((\!|\hat{\sigma}|\!), \hat{p})$, *then*
$(\hat{G}(\hat{a}_1, \hat{x}') \leftleftarrows \hat{\sigma}) \subseteq \hat{\Phi}$.

4. ***Record projection***

(a) RECORD PROJECTION

If $\hat{a}_1 = (\hat{x}\,\texttt{=}\,\hat{x}'.\ell)$, $\langle \hat{a}', \hat{\sigma}\rangle \in \hat{G}(\hat{a}, \hat{x}'_1)$, $(\!|\hat{\sigma}|\!) = \hat{r}$, *and* $(\ell\,\texttt{=}\,\hat{x}'') \in \hat{r}$, *then*
$(\hat{G}(\hat{a}', \hat{x}'') \hookleftarrow_{P} \hat{\sigma}) \subseteq \hat{\Phi}$.

We will write $\hat{v} \in \hat{G}(\hat{c}, \hat{x})$ as an abbreviation for $\hat{v} = (\!|\hat{\phi}|\!)$ for some $\hat{\phi} \in \hat{G}(\hat{c}, \hat{x})$.

Understanding Lookup. There is a lot going on in Definition 7. To better understand the clauses, we will trace the lookup example of Sect. 2.2. Below is that example translated to the formal A-normalized grammar we use in this section, retaining integer and string data from the original example for clarity. (Note that there is only one of each, so singleton properties hold.) The diagram to the right is the final CFG produced by the wiring rules described in Sect. 3.3 below; here we illustrate variable lookup on this final CFG.

```
f = fun a -> ( r = 4 );
g = fun b -> ( s = "s" );
c = fun h -> ( t = h true );
x = c f;
y = c g;
z = x;
```

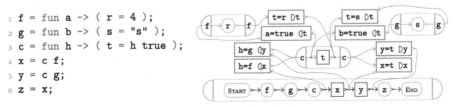

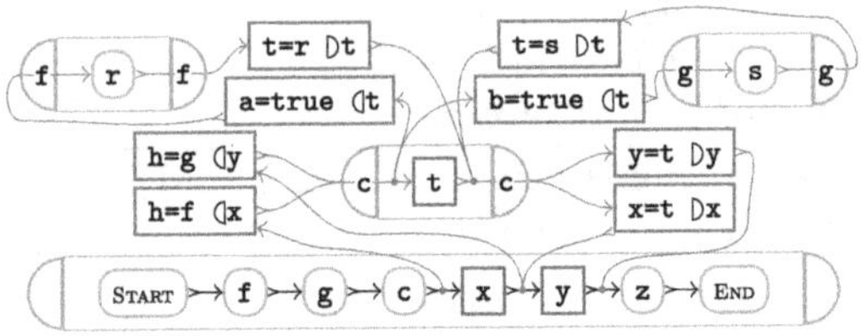

There are a few differences between this CFG and the informal presentation of Sect. 2.2 – this CFG precisely matches the dependency graph notation of Fig. 3. Each black or brown arrow-tipped edge in the CFG corresponds to a dependency $\hat{a} \ll \hat{a} \in \hat{G}$, for $\hat{G}$ being the whole CFG. The green half circles are only block delimiters for readability and do not correspond to nodes – the brown wiring edges go through them. The rectangular brown nodes are the wiring nodes $\hat{x} \overset{(\!|\hat{c}}{=} \hat{x}'$ and $\hat{x} \overset{|\!)\hat{c}}{=} \hat{x}'$ of the $\hat{a}$ grammar, and the whole CFG starts at node START and ends with END. The program is in ANF and all program points have names (except for the dummy argument in the function call at `t`); the result of function `f`, for instance, is named `r`.

Recall from the overview that we desire to look up the final value, $\hat{\mathtt{z}}$, from the end of the program: $\hat{G}(\text{END}, \hat{\mathtt{z}})$. (We coventionally begin the search not at the indicated node, e.g. END here, but at any predecessors to this node). Looking back from END, we see `z` defined as `x`; rule 1b of Definition 7 tells us to first continue by looking up $\hat{\mathtt{x}}$ from $\hat{\mathtt{z}}$: $\hat{G}(\hat{\mathtt{z}}, \hat{\mathtt{x}})$. (We will use the variable – $\hat{\mathtt{z}}$ here – alone as shorthand for its clause). We proceed lookup with rule 1c, which allows us to skip the clause `y = c g` as it does not affect $\hat{\mathtt{x}}$. Our lookup is then $\hat{G}(\hat{\mathtt{y}}, \hat{\mathtt{x}})$.

From $\hat{\mathtt{y}}$, rule 2b applies, which first entails looking up both function $\hat{\mathtt{c}}$ and argument $\hat{\mathtt{f}}$ from point $\hat{\mathtt{x}}$; these two lookups are both straightforward under the variable search rules 1a and 1c. Each returns a store which then gets parallel-merged to $\langle \hat{\mathtt{c}}@[] \mapsto \widehat{\mathtt{fun_h}}, \{\hat{\mathtt{c}}@[] \mapsto \widehat{\mathtt{fun_h}}, \hat{\mathtt{f}}@[] \mapsto \widehat{\mathtt{fun_4}}\}\rangle$. Continuing, it remains to look up $\hat{\mathtt{t}}$ from the wiring node, suffix the result with the trace $[|\!)\hat{\mathtt{x}}]$, and merge that result with the aforementioned store. Note that this merge requires all three to be in sync, a key to giving us path- and context-sensitivity.

The fact that we align the argument lookup in particular corresponds with what CPA [Age95, Bes09, VS10] achieves. CPA separately analyzes function calls with differing types of arguments. DRSF does so as well by creating for each argument type a distinct relative store fragment (the result of the lookup of $\hat{G}(\hat{c}, \hat{x}_3'')$ in rule 2b). This alignment requires only one operation and no special machinery in DRSF, as relative store fragments are already used to model many other kinds of inter-binding relationships as well.

We now tackle the lookup of $\hat{\texttt{t}}$. We begin by exploring call site $\texttt{t = h true}$: again, rule 2b applies. Here, there are two candidate wiring nodes: $\texttt{t} \overset{\rangle\texttt{t}}{=} \texttt{r}$ and $\texttt{t} \overset{\rangle\texttt{t}}{=} \texttt{s}$; both are possible, as either $\widehat{\texttt{fun}_4}$ or $\widehat{\texttt{fun}_\texttt{s}}$ may reach this call site. By rule 1a, looking back through node $\texttt{t} \overset{\rangle\texttt{t}}{=} \texttt{r}$ yields $\widehat{\texttt{int}}$ while node $\texttt{t} \overset{\rangle\texttt{t}}{=} \texttt{s}$ yields $\widehat{\texttt{string}}$. Clearly only the $\widehat{\texttt{int}}$ is possible at run-time. What does DRSF do here?

Lookup in DRSF can in general produce multiple (singleton) stores representing multiple abstract values. The lookup $\hat{G}(\texttt{t} \overset{\rangle\texttt{t}}{=} \texttt{r}, \hat{\texttt{r}})$ produces the store $\langle \hat{\texttt{r}}@[] \mapsto \widehat{\texttt{int}}, \{\hat{\texttt{r}}@[] \mapsto \widehat{\texttt{int}}\}\rangle$, which is then suffixed with $\rangle\hat{\texttt{t}}$. The resulting store $\langle \hat{\texttt{r}}@[\rangle\hat{\texttt{t}}] \mapsto \widehat{\texttt{int}}, \{\hat{\texttt{r}}@[\rangle\hat{\texttt{t}}] \mapsto \widehat{\texttt{int}}\}\rangle$ is then merged with the store used to verify that $\widehat{\texttt{fun}_4}$ could be called at this site, yielding $\langle \hat{\texttt{r}}@[\rangle\hat{\texttt{t}}] \mapsto \widehat{\texttt{int}}, \{\hat{\texttt{r}}@[\rangle\hat{\texttt{t}}] \mapsto \widehat{\texttt{int}}, \hat{\texttt{f}}@[\langle\hat{\texttt{x}}] \mapsto \widehat{\texttt{fun}_4}\}\rangle$. At this point, the lookup of $\hat{\texttt{t}}$ is complete and trace $[\rangle\hat{\texttt{x}}]$ can finally be suffixed to this result, giving $\langle \hat{\texttt{r}}@[\rangle\hat{\texttt{t}}, \rangle\hat{\texttt{x}}] \mapsto \widehat{\texttt{int}}, \{\hat{\texttt{r}}@[\rangle\hat{\texttt{t}}, \rangle\hat{\texttt{x}}] \mapsto \widehat{\texttt{int}}, \hat{\texttt{f}}@[] \mapsto \widehat{\texttt{fun}_4}, \hat{\texttt{c}}@[] \mapsto \widehat{\texttt{fun}_\texttt{h}}\}\rangle$ for $\hat{\texttt{x}}$.

The lookup $\hat{G}(\texttt{t} \overset{\rangle\texttt{t}}{=} \texttt{s}, \hat{\texttt{s}})$, demonstrates how store merging prunes impossible paths. This lookup produces the store $\langle \hat{\texttt{s}}@[] \mapsto \widehat{\texttt{string}}, \{\hat{\texttt{s}}@[] \mapsto \widehat{\texttt{string}}\}\rangle$, which we then suffix and merge as we did above to yield $\langle \hat{\texttt{s}}@[\rangle\hat{\texttt{t}}] \mapsto \widehat{\texttt{string}}, \{\hat{\texttt{s}}@[\rangle\hat{\texttt{t}}] \mapsto \widehat{\texttt{string}}, \hat{\texttt{g}}@[\langle\hat{\texttt{y}}] \mapsto \widehat{\texttt{fun}_\texttt{s}}\}\rangle$. Next, this store should be suffixed with $\rangle\hat{\texttt{x}}$ to adjust the perspective to be back out of the $\hat{\texttt{x}}$ call site, but this is *undefined*: the suffixing $\hat{\texttt{g}}@[\langle\hat{\texttt{y}}] \ltimes \rangle\hat{\texttt{x}}$, is undefined because reading in the forward-running direction it indicates a call at site $\hat{\texttt{y}}$ but which returns to site $\hat{\texttt{x}}$, an impossibility at run-time. So, this store is eliminated at the merge, and lookup of $\hat{G}(\textsc{End}, \hat{\texttt{z}})$ yields only the $\widehat{\texttt{int}}$ store described above.

Conditionals and records are variations on how functions are handled: the CFG is traversed in reverse, and stores are merged and relativized along the way as necessary. The parallel merges in conditional lookup give path-sensitivity on the conditional value: only aligned stores can merge.

3.3 Abstract Evaluation

We now present the single-step abstract evaluation relation which incrementally adds edges to build a full CFG. The above lookup function is the key subroutine.

Active nodes. To preserve standard evaluation order, we define the notion of an Active *node* node: only nodes with all previous nodes already executed can fire. This serves a purpose similar to an evaluation context in operational semantics.

Definition 8. $\textsc{Active}(\hat{a}', \hat{G})$ *iff path* $\{\textsc{Start} \ll \hat{a}_1, \ldots, \hat{a}_i \ll \hat{a}_{i+1}, \ldots, \hat{a}_n \ll \hat{a}'\} \subseteq \hat{G}$ *such that no* $\hat{a}_i$ *is of one of the forms* $\hat{x} = \hat{x}'\ \hat{x}''$ *or* $\hat{x} = \hat{x}' \sim \hat{p}\, ?\, \hat{f} : \hat{f}'$.

Wiring. Function application requires the concrete function body to be "wired" into the call site:

Definition 9. *Let* $\textsc{Wire}(\hat{c}, \texttt{fun}\ \hat{x}_0 \texttt{->} \hat{e}, \hat{x}_1, \hat{x}_2)$
$= \{\hat{c}' \ll (\hat{x}_0 \overset{\langle\hat{c}}{=} \hat{x}_1) \mid \hat{c}' \overset{\hat{G}}{\ll} \hat{c}\} \cup \{(\hat{x}_0 \overset{\langle\hat{c}}{=} \hat{x}_1) \ll \hat{e} \ll (\hat{x}_2 \overset{\rangle\hat{c}}{=} \mathrm{RV}(\hat{e}))\} \cup \{(\hat{x}_2 \overset{\rangle\hat{c}}{=} \mathrm{RV}(\hat{e})) \ll \hat{c}' \mid \hat{c} \overset{\hat{G}}{\ll} \hat{c}'\}$.

$\hat{c}'$ here is the call site, and we are wiring in function body $\hat{e}$ at this site.

$$\frac{\textsc{Application} \quad \hat{c} = (\hat{x}_1 = \hat{x}_2\ \hat{x}_3) \qquad \textsc{Active}(\hat{c}, \hat{G}) \qquad \hat{f} \in \hat{G}(\hat{c}, \hat{x}_2) \qquad \hat{G}(\hat{c}, \hat{x}_3) \neq \emptyset}{\hat{G} \longrightarrow^1 \hat{G} \cup \textsc{Wire}(\hat{c}, \hat{f}, \hat{x}_3, \hat{x}_1)}$$

$$\frac{\textsc{Record Conditional True} \quad \hat{c} = (\hat{x}_1 = \hat{x}_2 \sim \hat{p}\ ?\ \hat{f}_1 : \hat{f}_2) \qquad \textsc{Active}(\hat{c}, \hat{G}) \qquad \exists \hat{\phi} \in \hat{G}(\hat{c}, \hat{x}_2).\ \textsc{Match}((\!|\hat{\phi}|\!), \hat{p})}{\hat{G} \longrightarrow^1 \hat{G} \cup \textsc{Wire}(\hat{c}, \hat{f}_1, \hat{x}_2, \hat{x}_1)}$$

$$\frac{\textsc{Record Conditional False} \quad \hat{c} = (\hat{x}_1 = \hat{x}_2 \sim \hat{r}\ ?\ \hat{f}_1 : \hat{f}_2) \qquad \textsc{Active}(\hat{c}, \hat{G}) \qquad \exists \hat{\phi} \in \hat{G}(\hat{c}, \hat{x}_2).\ \neg\textsc{Match}((\!|\hat{\phi}|\!), \hat{p})}{\hat{G} \longrightarrow^1 \hat{G} \cup \textsc{Wire}(\hat{c}, \hat{f}_2, \hat{x}_2, \hat{x}_1)}$$

Fig. 4. Abstract Evaluation Rules

Next, we define the abstract small-step relation $\longrightarrow^1$ on graphs; see Fig. 4. The evaluation rules end up being straightforward after the above preliminaries. For application, if $\hat{c}$ is an ACTIVE call site, lookup of the function variable $\hat{x}_2$ returns function body $\hat{f}$ and *some* value $\hat{v}$ can be looked up at the argument position, we may wire in $\hat{f}$'s body to this call site. Note that $\hat{v}$ is only observed here to constrain evaluation order to be call-by-value. The case clause rules are similar. We define the small step relation $\longrightarrow^1$ to hold if a proof exists in the system in Fig. 4. We write $\hat{G}_0 \longrightarrow^* \hat{G}_n$ to denote $\hat{G}_0 \longrightarrow^1 \hat{G}_1 \longrightarrow^1 \ldots \longrightarrow^* \hat{G}_n$.

Now we can finally put it all together to analyze a program. We define a typical program abstraction function EMBED(e) to denote the lifting of an expression e into a CFG $\hat{G}$:

Definition 10. *EMBED$([c_1, \ldots, c_n])$ is the graph $\hat{G}_0 = \{\textsc{Start} \ll \hat{c}_1, \ldots, \hat{c}_i \ll \hat{c}_{i+1}, \ldots, \hat{c}_n \ll \textsc{End}\}$, where each $\hat{c}_i = c_i$.*

This initial graph is simply the linear sequence of clauses in the "main program". The *DRSF Analysis* for a program e is then graph $\hat{G}$ where EMBED$(e) \longrightarrow^* \hat{G}$ and $\hat{G}$ can only further step to itself.

3.4 DRSF Soundness

Soundness of DRSF is proven in two steps: we first demonstrate equivalence between a standard small step operational semantics and a *graph-based* operational semantics [PS16]; we then show that DRSF conservatively approximates the latter. We begin by overloading $\longrightarrow^1$ to a canonical small step evaluation relation on expressions e (straightforward and elided for reasons of space). Next, we define a graph-based operational semantics using ωDRSF: DRSF where trace concatenation $\ltimes$ never loses information (and so never produces partial traces). We use unhatted analogues of the grammars in Figs. 2 and 3 for ωDRSF entities. We also overload the operators on traces and stores to work similarly on the unhatted grammar, where trace concatenation has no maximum trace length.

We align these two operational semantics by defining a bisimulation $e \cong G$ and showing that it holds throughout evaluation. Key to this bisimulation is an alignment between the freshenings of bound variables in e and the traces in the mappings of concrete store fragments in G. We state the equivalence of these operational semantics as follows:

Lemma 1 (Equivalence of Operational Semantics). *For any* $e \cong G$*:*
if $e \longrightarrow^1 e'$ *then* $G \longrightarrow^* G'$ *such that* $e' \cong G'$*; and*
if $G \longrightarrow^1 G'$ *then* $e \longrightarrow^* e'$ *such that* $e' \cong G'$*.*

The discrepancy in the number of steps arises in how the operational semantics process variable aliasing. The small step operational semantics processes aliases eagerly while ωDRSF need not step for variable aliases (due to demand-driven lookup).

Given the equivalence of these operational semantics, we now show kDRSF simulates ωDRSF. We do this via a simulation relation $\preccurlyeq$ defined from each non-hatted term to its hatted analogue. The only non-trivial case here is that of traces, in which a full trace is simulated by the partial trace of any of its suffixes (e.g. $[\rhd x_1, \lhd x_2] \preccurlyeq (\lhd \hat{x}_2])$.

Lemma 2 (Simulation). *If* $G \preccurlyeq \hat{G}$ *and* $G \longrightarrow^1 G'$*, then* $\hat{G} \longrightarrow^* \hat{G}'$ *such that* $G' \preccurlyeq \hat{G}'$*.*

Lemma 2 is proven by establishing a Galois connection between ωDRSF and kDRSF following standard techniques [CC77,NNH99,VHM10,Mig10a]. Soundness of the overall analysis is an immediate corollary of the above two lemmas.

3.5 DRSF Complexity

DRSF as presented above has exponential worst-case complexity, but this can be mitigated. We now outline a proof of this property to understand its singular cause. Fortunately, our initial experiments suggest that this worst case is not common in practice; see Sect. 4.

DRSF's complexity is shown by bounding the size of $\hat{G}$ produced by the abstract evaluation rules of Fig. 4. We begin by counting the forms of the grammar in Fig. 2. Restricting that grammar to the program being analyzed and to traces of length at most k, we observe there are a polynomial number of forms of $\hat{\delta}$, $\hat{\Delta}$, $\hat{\rho}$, and $\hat{\psi}$.

The exponential growth of DRSF lies in the definition of $\hat{\Psi}$, which admits any subset of the $\hat{\psi}$ forms above. This leads us to the following key Lemma:

Lemma 3 (Exponential Raw Store Growth). *Restrict the grammar of Fig. 2 to contain only clauses, values, and variables appearing within* $\hat{e}$ *and only traces of length at most* k*. Let* $|L_{\hat{\Psi}}|$ *be the number of values of form* $\hat{\Psi}$ *and let* $|L_{\hat{\sigma}}|$ *be the number of values of form* $\hat{\sigma}$*. Then* $|L_{\hat{\Psi}}|$ *and* $|L_{\hat{\sigma}}|$ *are* $O(2^{n^{k+2}})$*.*

The rest of the proof demonstrates that DRSF is polynomial in $|L_{\hat{\sigma}}|$. Definition 7's lookup operation is reduced to a reachability problem on a push-down automaton [PS16] (which is polynomial in the size of the automaton [BEM97]) and the abstract evaluation relation $\hat{G} \longrightarrow^1 \hat{G}'$ is shown to be confluent, bounding the number of lookups to a polynomial of $|L_{\hat{\sigma}}|$. This leads us to:

Theorem 1 (DRSF Analysis Complexity). *The DRSF analysis of a program e is computable in time polynomial in* $|L_{\hat{\sigma}}|$.

3.6 Weakening DRSF

While the exponential case of DRSF appears to be uncommon, it may ultimately be necessary to apply weakenings to guarantee polynomial behavior. A full exploration of such weakenings is beyond the scope of this paper, but we outline one such weakening here.

Consider adding a "time-to-live" index to each mapping. Mappings with TTL are written $\hat{\rho} \overset{\ell}{\mapsto} \hat{v}$, where $\ell \in \mathbb{N}$. Each singleton store creates its single mapping with ℓ equal to some fixed value d. Finally, the raw store merge operation $\oplus$ decreases the value of each mapping's ℓ, and discards mappings with $\ell = 0$. When merging two mappings with the same $\hat{\rho}$ and $\hat{v}$, the maximum ℓ is retained.

With this TTL index, it is possible to prove no raw store can be created with a number of mappings greater than 2^d. Since d is a fixed constant, this bounds the number of mappings per raw store to be fixed. With only polynomially many stores, it follows from a lemma similar to Lemma 3 that $|L_{\hat{\sigma}}|$ is also polynomial, and by Theorem 1, the analysis with TTL is polynomial.

4 Implementation

An implementation of DRSF is available on GitHub[1] which additionally includes binary operators, deep pattern matching, and state as well as integers and strings for basic values. The abstraction function maps all integers and strings to the same abstract integer and abstract string, so the singleton abstractions are lost for them. The implementation proceeds as described in Sect. 3.5: lookups are performed by reduction to a reachability problem on a push-down automaton just as in DDPA [PS16]. We improve on previous reachability algorithms [BEM97, JSE+14, EMH10] by generalizing over patterns appearing in the automaton which arise due to the form of DRSF's lookup definition. We also rely upon the confluence of abstract evaluation to reuse work performed during lookup, even across lookup invocations.

4.1 Evaluation

To evaluate the performance of DRSF, we benchmarked it against an implementation of DDPA [PS16, PF16]. The analysis client in these experiments answers the question "what are all possible values for all variables at the top level of the program?" We used this client to compare both running times and precision.

[1] https://github.com/JHU-PL-Lab/odefa/tree/sas2017-drsf.

The test cases were taken from other higher-order program analysis evaluations [GLA+16, JLMVH13]. These Scheme programs were automatically translated to our core language. Many of these benchmarks are moderate sized programs which represent real-world uses.[2] Others are micro-benchmarks designed to stress particular aspects of the analysis.[3]

We conducted three experiments to measure the performance of the analyses.[4] For a monomorphic baseline we selected $k = 0$. For the second and third experiments, we selected $k = 2$ and $k = 4$ somewhat arbitrarily: on several of the benchmarks, $k = 4$ gave full precision, and $k = 2$ is a midpoint. The results are shown in Fig. 5.

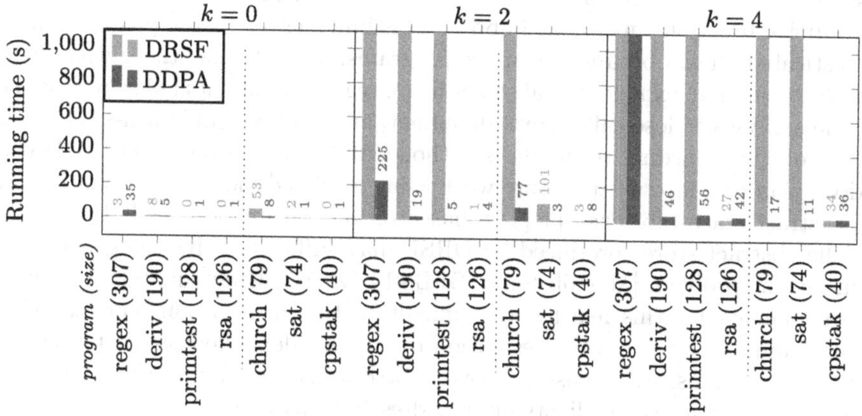

Fig. 5. The benchmark results. Numerical labels on bars are running times. Unlabeled bars timed out after 30 min. Numbers in parentheses are program point counts. The dotted lines separate the real-world programs from the micro-benchmarks.

DDPA is faster in all test cases, with a few exceptions, in which the difference between DDPA and DRSF is negligible. This is an expected result when comparing a polynomial analysis (DDPA) to an exponential one (DRSF). Both `regex` and `deriv` involve recursive functions operating on symbols and lists of symbols, which we encode as records in DRSF. We conjecture that DRSF's performance degenerates in these cases because they contain recursive functions, which is a

[2] `regex` is a regular expression engine using derivatives; `rsa` performs the RSA encryption algorithm; `primtest` is the Fermat primality testing algorithms; and `deriv` performs symbolic derivation of an equation.

[3] `sat` is a SAT solver, which stresses path- and context-sensitivity; `cpstak` is the TAK micro-benchmark in continuation-passing style, which stresses nested function calls and non-local lookups; and `church` tests the distributive property of multiplication over addition on Church numerals which includes polymorphic recursive functions and a massive number of function calls, stressing the function-wiring part of the analysis.

[4] Intel(R) Xeon(R) CPU E31220 @ 3.10 GHz, 8 GB of RAM, Debian GNU/Linux 8.8.

know weak spot in both analyses. The `regex` test case triggers this bad behavior more intensively because it includes a set of mutually recursive functions, which causes even DDPA to time out.

Besides the test cases we ran for performance measurement, we also tested the implementation with micro-benchmarks which serve primarily to exercise context-, path- and flow-sensitivity, as well as the capacity to precisely approximate the heap state with must-alias analysis. For most test cases, DRSF loses no precision other than value abstraction (e.g. $\mathtt{5} \mapsto \widehat{\mathtt{int}}$) given a sufficient k. Our implementation confirms the expressiveness improvements predicted in theory; for example, DDPA loses precision in the program from Sect. 2.1, and DRSF approximates it exactly, due to path-sensitivity. Further empirical expressiveness evaluations are left for future work due to the significant loss of precision in recursive functions, mentioned above. This impedes the development of more sophisticated clients because recursive programs, in particular those with polymorphic recursion, exhaust the abstract heap, regardless of our choice for k, causing the analyses to lose call-return alignment, and context- and path-sensitivity. This problem regarding recursion is orthogonal to the advancements in DRSF and we plan to address it in future work using a refined model of finitization for the abstract traces, for example, one based on regular expressions [GLA+16].

The abstract stores produced by DRSF may suffice to solve the generalized environment problem [Mig10b, Shi91, BFL+14, GM17]. Unfortunately, the most relevant clients for this feature are difficult to test in isolation. For example, Super-β inlining exercises the resolution of circular dependencies that occur in recursive programs. As discussed above, DRSF loses precision in those cases, so we plan to evaluate these clients after addressing this weakness.

Finally, we attempted to compare DRSF to state-of-the-art forward analyses including P4F [GLA+16] and OAAM [JLMVH13]. Unfortunately, these analyses are too different from DRSF to draw any significant conclusion. OAAM's reference implementation does not support $k > 0$ resulting in lower precision but faster running times. DRSF runs faster than the P4F reference implementation, but the latter was designed for correctness and not performance so this is arguably not a fair comparison.

5 Related Work

Anodization [Mig10b] aims for singleton abstraction by separating bindings so that there is only one concrete binding per abstract binding, making a structure similar to our relative store fragments. Anodization does not create local, relativized stores like we do here and is not a demand-driven analysis. It also has not been implemented or analyzed for complexity. Other higher-order analyses that incorporate a form of singleton abstraction include [JTWW98, SW97]; the former is carefully engineered to achieve a quartic time bound but is focused on must-alias analysis and lacks path- or general context-sensitivity.

CFA's delta frame strings [MS06a, GM17] are very similar in structure to our relative traces, but due to differences in forward- and reverse-analyses they are incorporated into the analysis quite differently. In DRSF they are placed on variables on the store to singularize them; in CFA they are part of the state. Moreover, CFA defines an abstraction for frame strings which loses more information than DRSF; for example, it discards the order of invocations of different procedures. A recent CFA extension [GM17] shows how the environment problem can be solved, but there is no implementation or evaluation.

There are many different approaches to building path-sensitivity into program analyses. Early work on path-sensitivity directly built the logic into an analysis [BA98]; subsequently, path-sensitivity was was implemented using SMT model-checkers over boolean-valued programs [DLS02, XCE03]. Some higher-order type systems contain analogues of path-sensitive precision [THF10]. Recent work shows how path sensitivity can be viewed as one of several orthogonal dimensions of analysis expressiveness along with context- and flow-sensitivity [SDM+13, DMH15]. In the first-order abstract interpretation literature, trace partitioning techniques give an added expressiveness that is related to DRSF traces [HT98, Bou92] – like DRSF these techniques add path information to the analysis state and path-sensitivity becomes an emergent property.

DRSF's store fragments are related to the heap fragments of separation logic [Rey02]: there are many partial stores for different program contexts which are merged. This analogy with separation logic is only high level since we are comparing first-order program logics to higher-order program analyses, but it points to potential applicability of store fragments to higher-order program logics.

We build on the DDPA higher-order demand-driven analysis [PS16]. Other demand-driven higher-order analyses include [RF01, FRD00, SDAB16], but these are flow-insensitive; they as well as DDPA lack a singleton abstraction. In [PS16] call-return alignment can fully replace the need for an explicit context-sensitivity mechanism, but it requires an explicit call stack. This comes for free in DRSF since it is embedded in the store variable traces.

The exponential problem we run into here is a fundamental issue in path-sensitive analyses. DRSF attemps to infer when path sensitivity is needed, erring on the side of precision rather than performance. SMT solvers are useful in [DLS02, XCE03] in part for their ability to handle a large state-space search.

6 Conclusions

In this paper we develop a general notion of singleton abstraction, *relative store fragments*, that cuts across many of the classic expressiveness dimensions of higher-order program analysis: the resulting analysis, DRSF, exhibits flow-, context-, path- and must-alias sensitivity solely through an accurate and compositional singleton abstraction. We give a formal definition of DRSF, sketch its soundness and complexity, and report on initial results from an implementation.

Future Work. While DRSF is usually avoiding its exponential worst-case complexity in practice, this issue will need to be addressed in a more realistic implementation. Also, like DDPA and other analyses such as kCFA, DRSF finitely unrolls recursive cycles and this usually adds no expressiveness as the analysis contour depth k gets larger, but can adversely affect running times; we plan to study how to avoid k-unrolling of recursive cycles when it is not helpful.

Acknowledgments. The authors thank the anonymous reviewers for helpful suggestions which improved the final version of the paper.

References

[Age95] Agesen, O.: The cartesian product algorithm. In: Tokoro, M., Pareschi, R. (eds.) ECOOP 1995. LNCS, vol. 952, pp. 2–26. Springer, Heidelberg (1995). doi:10.1007/3-540-49538-X_2

[BA98] Bodík, R., Anik, S.: Path-sensitive value-flow analysis. In: POPL (1998)

[BEM97] Bouajjani, A., Esparza, J., Maler, O.: Reachability analysis of pushdown automata: application to model-checking. In: Mazurkiewicz, A., Winkowski, J. (eds.) CONCUR 1997. LNCS, vol. 1243, pp. 135–150. Springer, Heidelberg (1997). doi:10.1007/3-540-63141-0_10

[Bes09] Besson, F.: CPA beats ∞-CFA. In: Proceedings of the 11th International Workshop on Formal Techniques for Java-like Programs (2009)

[BFL+14] Bergstrom, L., Fluet, M., Le, M., Reppy, J., Sandler, N.: Practical and effective higher-order optimizations. In: ICFP (2014)

[Bou92] Bourdoncle, F.: Abstract interpretation by dynamic partitioning. J. Funct. Program **2**, 407–423 (1992)

[CC77] Cousot, P., Cousot, R.: Abstract interpretation: a unified lattice model for static analysis of programs by construction or approximation of fixpoints. In: POPL (1977)

[CWZ90] Chase, D.R., Wegman, M., Zadeck, F.K.: Analysis of pointers and structures. In: PLDI (1990)

[DGS97] Duesterwald, E., Gupta, R., Soffa, M.L.: A practical framework for demand-driven interprocedural data flow analysis. ACM Trans. Program. Lang. Syst. **19**(6), 992–1030 (1997)

[DLS02] Das, M., Lerner, S., Mark Seigle, E.S.P.: Path-sensitive program verification in polynomial time. In: PLDI (2002)

[DMH15] Darais, D., Might, M., Van Horn, D.: Galois transformers and modular abstract interpreters. In: OOPSLA (2015)

[EMH10] Earl, C., Might, M., Van Horn, D.: Pushdown control-flow analysis of higher-order programs. In: Workshop on Scheme and Functional Programming (2010)

[FRD00] Fähndrich, M., Rehof, J., Das, M.: Scalable context-sensitive flow analysis using instantiation constraints. In: PLDI (2000)

[FSDF93] Flanagan, C., Sabry, A., Duba, B.F., Felleisen, M.: The essence of compiling with continuations. In: PLDI (1993)

[GLA+16] Gilray, T., Lyde, S., Adams, M.D., Might, M., Van Horn, D.: Pushdown control-flow analysis for free. In: POPL (2016)

[GM17] Germane, K., Might, M.: A posteriori environment analysis with pushdown Delta CFA. In: POPL (2017)

[HT98] Handjieva, M., Tzolovski, S.: Refining static analyses by trace-based partitioning using control flow. In: Static Analysis Symposium (1998)

[HT01] Heintze, N., Tardieu, O.: Demand-driven pointer analysis. In: PLDI (2001)

[JLMVH13] Johnson, J.I., Labich, N., Might, M., Van Horn, D.: Optimizing abstract abstract machines. In: ICFP (2013)

[JSE+14] Johnson, J.I., Sergey, I., Earl, C., Might, M., Van Horn, D.: Pushdown flow analysis with abstract garbage collection. In: JFP (2014)

[JTWW98] Jagannathan, S., Thiemann, P., Weeks, S., Wright, A.K.: Single and loving it: must-alias analysis for higher-order languages. In: POPL (1998)

[Mid12] Midtgaard, J.: Control-flow analysis of functional programs. ACM Comput. Surv. **44**, 10:1–10:33 (2012)

[Mig07] Might, M.: Environment analysis of higher-order languages. PhD thesis, Georgia Institute of Technology (2007)

[Mig10a] Might, M.: Abstract interpreters for free. In: Proceedings of the 17th International Conference on Static Analysis (2010)

[Mig10b] Might, M.: Shape analysis in the absence of pointers and structure. In: Barthe, G., Hermenegildo, M. (eds.) VMCAI 2010. LNCS, vol. 5944, pp. 263–278. Springer, Heidelberg (2010). doi:10.1007/978-3-642-11319-2_20

[MS06a] Might, M., Shivers, O.: Environment analysis via ΔCFA. In: POPL (2006)

[MS06b] Might, M., Shivers, O.: Improving flow analyses via ΓCFA: abstract garbage collection and counting. In: ICFP, Portland, Oregon (2006)

[NNH99] Nielson, F., Nielson, H.R., Hankin, C.: Principles of Program Analysis. Springer, New York (1999)

[PF16] Palmer, Z., Facchinetti, L.: DDPA implementation. https://github.com/JHU-PL-Lab/odefa/tree/sas2017-ddpa (2016)

[PS16] Palmer, Z., Smith, S.: Higher-order demand-driven program analysis. In: ECOOP (2016)

[Rep94] Reps, T.: Demand interprocedural program analysis using logic databases. In: Application of Logic Databases (1994)

[Rey02] Reynolds, J.: Separation logic: a logic for shared mutable data structures. In: LICS (2002)

[RF01] Rehof, J., Fähndrich, M.: Type-base flow analysis: from polymorphic subtyping to CFL-reachability. In: POPL. Springer, New York (2001)

[SDAB16] Späth, J., Do, L.N.Q., Ali, K., Bodden, E.: Demand-driven flow- and context-sensitive pointer analysis for Java. In: ECOOP, Boomerang (2016)

[SDM+13] Sergey, I., Devriese, D., Might, M., Midtgaard, J., Darais, D., Clarke, D., Piessens, F.: Monadic abstract interpreters. In: PLDI (2013)

[Shi91] Shivers, O.: Control-flow analysis of higher-order languages. PhD thesis, Carnegie-Mellon University (1991). TR CMU-CS-91-145

[SR05] Saha, D., Ramakrishnan, C.R.: Incremental and demand-driven points-to analysis using logic programming. In: PPDP (2005)

[SW97] Steckler, P.A., Wand, M.: Lightweight closure conversion. ACM Trans. Program. Lang. Syst. **19**, 48–86 (1997)

[THF10] Tobin-Hochstadt, S., Felleisen, M.: Logical types for untyped languages. In: ICFP (2010)

[VHM10] Van Horn, D. Might, M.: Abstracting abstract machines. In: ICFP (2010)

[VS10] Vardoulakis, D., Shivers, O.: CFA2: a context-free approach to control-flow analysis. In: European Symposium on Programming (2010)

[XCE03] Xie, Y., Chou, A., Engler, D.: Using symbolic, path-sensitive analysis to detect memory access errors. In: ESEC/FSE, Archer (2003)

Loop Invariants from Counterexamples

Marius Greitschus(✉), Daniel Dietsch(✉), and Andreas Podelski(✉)

University of Freiburg, Freiburg im Breisgau, Germany
{greitsch,dietsch,podelski}@informatik.uni-freiburg.de

Abstract. We propose a new approach to software model checking where we integrate abstract interpretation and trace abstraction. We use abstract interpretation to derive loop invariants for the path program corresponding to a given spurious counterexample. A path program is the smallest subprogram that still contains a given path in the control flow graph. We use the principle of trace abstraction to construct an overall proof. The key observation of our approach is that proofs by abstract interpretation on individual program fragments can be composed directly if we use the framework of trace abstraction (in trace abstraction, composing proofs amounts to a set-theoretic operation, i.e., set union). We implemented our approach in the open-source software model checking framework Ultimate. Our evaluation shows that we can solve up to 40% more benchmarks.

1 Introduction

When trying to prove the correctness of a program, finding useful abstractions in form of state assertions is the most important part of the process [15,20]. In this context, usefulness is about being able to prove correctness as efficiently as possible. Hence, in order to be able to analyze large programs, it is important to find state assertions automatically. The class of methods based on abstract interpretation [12] is well-known for being able to find state assertions automatically. Abstract interpretation computes an over-approximation of a program's states by using an up-front and largely program-independent abstraction. Many such abstractions exist [7,13,23,24] and all of them are useful, because they give rise to different kinds of state assertions that can be used to prove the correctness of different kinds of programs. It is the strength of abstract interpretation that it always terminates and always computes a fixpoint in the selected abstraction. If the program contains loops, the computed fixpoint also contains a loop invariant which allows for an easy abstraction of loops. While abstract interpretation scales favorably with the size of the program, the computed over-approximation is often not precise enough to be useful to prove the correctness of a program.

Another way of proving program correctness is to use software model checking tools like Blast [6], SLAM [3], and more recently, CPAchecker [9] and Ultimate Automizer [17], that follow the counterexample-guided abstraction refinement (CEGAR) approach [11]. In CEGAR, an abstraction is continuously refined by synthesizing state assertions from paths through the control flow graph

F. Ranzato (Ed.): SAS 2017, LNCS 10422, pp. 128–147, 2017.
DOI: 10.1007/978-3-319-66706-5_7

of the program that (1) are not contained in the current abstraction, (2) can reach an error location, and (3) are not executable. By extracting state assertions from those paths, the abstraction can be refined to fit the program at hand, which allows the user a greater amount of flexibility because he does not need to decide beforehand on a suitable abstraction. The path analysis has to be precise, i.e., it has to ensure that paths that represent real errors can be identified. Unfortunately, this precision causes the analysis to often produce state assertions that are not loop invariants, thus forcing the CEGAR algorithm to unwind loops of the program. If this happens, the algorithm may not be able to refine the abstraction at all, e.g., because the loop of the analyzed program can be unwound infinitely often.

In this paper we propose a unification of both techniques, abstract interpretation and CEGAR-based software model checking, such that both can benefit from their strengths: we use abstract interpretation to find loop invariants, an interpolating SMT solver to analyze single paths, and we combine both in a CEGAR-based abstraction refinement loop. We implemented our approach in the tool Ultimate Taipan which uses a CEGAR loop to iteratively refine an abstraction of an input program in the form of a control flow graph with the help of state assertions deduced from the analysis of *path programs* with abstract interpretation.

1.1 Example

Consider the example program $\mathcal{P}_1$ in Fig. 1 and its corresponding control flow graph. We are interested in proving that the error location of $\mathcal{P}_1$'s control flow graph (see Fig. 1b), ℓ_7, is unreachable. A CEGAR-based approach to generate the proof by iteratively refining an abstraction of the program begins with picking

```
int x:=0, y:=1000;
while(*){
  if (x < 100) {
    x:=x+1;
    y:=y-1;
  } else {
    x:=x+2;
    y:=y-2;
  }
}
if (x==1000) {
  assert y<=0;
}
```

(a) C code.

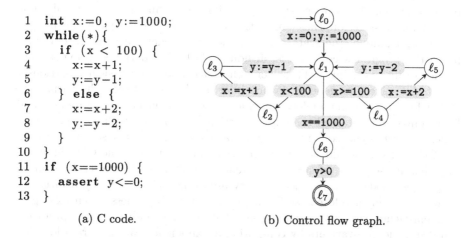

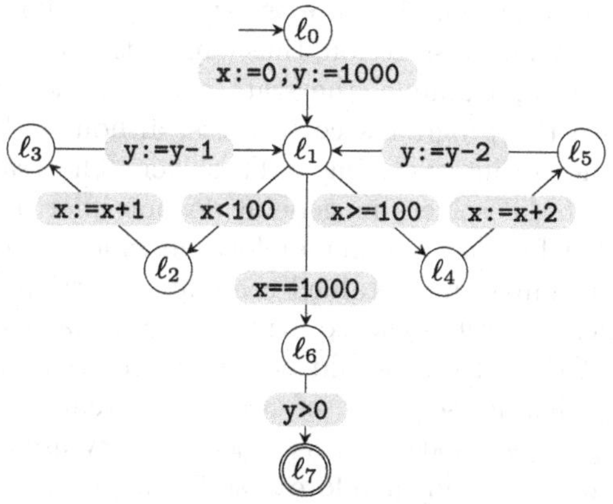

(b) Control flow graph.

Fig. 1. Example program $\mathcal{P}_1$ with its source code and its corresponding control flow graph (CFG). The location ℓ_0 of the CFG is the initial location, ℓ_7 is the error location.

a sequence of statements from the CFG, which starts in the initial location and ends in an error location. Next, an analysis decides whether the selected sequence of statements is executable or not, and if not, the abstraction is refined such that this particular sequence is no longer contained.

Assume that in the first iteration, the shortest sequence of statements τ_1 from the initial location ℓ_0 to the error location ℓ_7 is picked.

τ_1 : `x:=0;y:=1000` `x==1000` `y>0`

This sequence of statements is not executable, because the first two statements contradict each other. A possible proof for this contradiction consists of the following sequence of state assertions.

true `x:=0;y:=1000` $x = 0 \wedge y = 1000$ `x==1000` *false* `y>0` *false*

This sequence of state assertions allows the CEGAR tool to refine its abstraction such that τ_1 is removed from it. In the next iteration, we assume that τ_2 is selected.

τ_2 : `x:=0;y:=1000` `x<100` `x:=x+1` `y:=y-1` `x==1000` `y>0`

Again, this sequence of statements is not executable. For example, the statements `x:=0;y:=1000` , `x:=x+1` , and `x==1000` contradict each other for which we can extract the following proof.

true `x:=0;y:=1000` $x = 0 \wedge y = 1000$ `x<100` $x = 0 \wedge y = 1000$ `x:=x+1` $x = 1 \wedge y = 1000$ `y:=y-1` $x = 1 \wedge y = 999$ `x==1000` *false* `y>0` *false*

We could continue in this fashion until we have constructed a proof for each unwinding of the while loop of $\mathcal{P}_1$. However, we would prefer to obtain other proofs that contain state assertions that allow us to find a more general refinement of our abstraction, thus eliminating the need for multiple loop unwindings.

In our example, the state assertions are not general enough to efficiently prove the program's correctness, although they were obtained using a state-of-the-art interpolating SMT solver. The reason we obtain such assertions is that SMT solvers in general do not infer a relation between the variables `x` and `y` for any number of loop unwindings from sequences of statements. If, for example, we obtained the state assertion $x \geq 0 \wedge y \leq 1000 \wedge x + y = 1000$, which is a relational constraint over variables `x` and `y`, in the second iteration, the CEGAR tool would be able to refine its abstraction of the CFG in such a way that no sequence of statements remains that leads to the error location. $x \geq 0 \wedge y \leq 1000 \wedge x + y = 1000$ is very useful because it is a loop invariant at location ℓ_1, and therefore is sufficient to prove the correctness of our example.

Approaches based on static program analysis, such as abstract interpretation, can deduce loop invariants by computing a fixpoint for each program location. In our example, an abstract interpreter that uses a relational abstract domain,

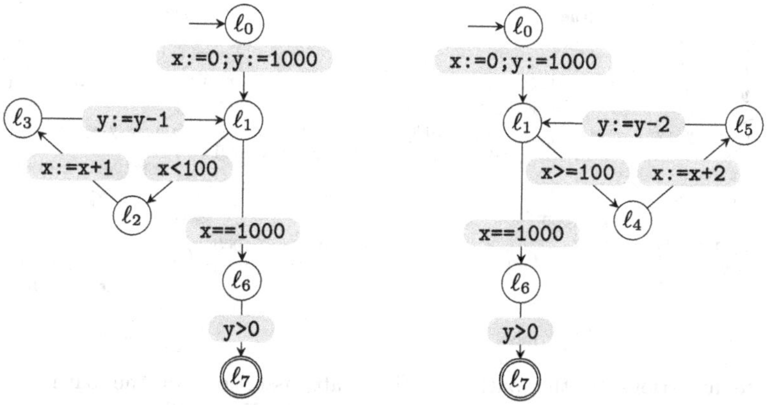

(a) The path program corresponding to the left branch of the if-statement, computed from the sequence of statements τ_2.

(b) The path program corresponding to the right branch of the if-statement.

Fig. 2. The two path programs computed for $\mathcal{P}_1$.

e.g. octagons [21], would suffice. However, such an analysis of the whole program may not be able to find an invariant strong enough to prove the program to be correct.

In this paper, we propose to improve the precision by not analyzing the whole program, but just a fragment of it. We can compute such a fragment by projecting the CFG of the program to the statements occurring in the selected sequence of statements. The resulting CFG is called a *path program* [8]. Figure 2a shows the path program computed from $\mathcal{P}_1$ and the sequence of statements τ_2. We can now calculate the fixpoint of, e.g., an octagon-based abstraction for this path program, which then yields the state assertions shown in Fig. 3a. The state assertion at ℓ_1 contains a loop invariant strong enough to prove correctness of the path program in the second iteration of the CEGAR loop. The CEGAR tool removes the program fragment covered by this path program from its abstraction of the program, such that the resulting abstraction only contains sequences of statements that lead through the other branch of the `if`-statement inside the loop. Thus, in iteration 3, we obtain the path program depicted in Fig. 2b from one of those sequences. After computing the corresponding state assertions with abstract interpretation (see Fig. 3b), the CEGAR tool will remove this path program from the program abstraction, thus removing all sequences of statements that lead to the error location. In general, the chosen abstraction may not be precise enough to find a useful invariant. In this case, we fall back to a conventional analysis of a single trace s.t. the CEGAR loop is guaranteed to remove at least a single error trace.

In the following, we present our approach that combines the analysis of single sequences of statements and the analysis of path programs in an

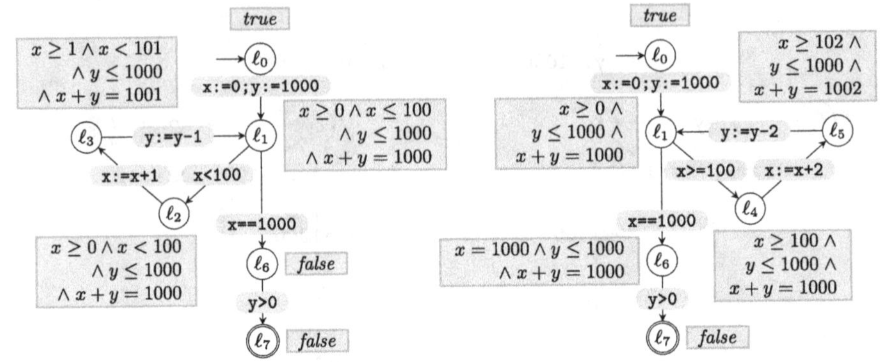

(a) State assertions of the path program from Figure 2a.

(b) State assertions of the path program from Figure 2b.

Fig. 3. State assertions computed for both path programs of Fig. 2.

automata-theoretic setting. We focus on obtaining loop invariants with abstract interpretation if possible, but can fall back on the analysis of single traces if the computed abstraction is too weak to prove infeasibility of a trace.

2 Preliminaries

In this section, we present our understanding of programs and their semantics, give a brief overview over abstract interpretation, and explain the trace abstraction algorithm which we use as basis of our approach.

Programs and Traces. We consider a simple programming language whose statements are assignment, assume, and sequential composition. We use the syntax that is defined by the grammar

$$\texttt{s} ::= \texttt{assume bexpr} \mid \texttt{x:=expr} \mid \texttt{s;s}$$

where *Var* is a finite set of program variables, $\texttt{x} \in \mathit{Var}$, `expr` is an expression over *Var* and `bexpr` is a Boolean expression over *Var*. For brevity we use `bexpr` to denote the assume statement `assume bexpr`.

We represent a *program* over a given set of statements *Stmt* as a labeled graph $\mathcal{P} = (\mathit{Loc}, \delta, \ell_0)$ with a finite set of nodes *Loc* called locations, a set of edges labeled with statements, i.e., $\delta \subseteq \mathit{Loc} \times \mathit{Stmt} \times \mathit{Loc}$, and a distinguished node $\ell_0 \in \mathit{Loc}$ which we call the initial location.

We call a sequence of statements $\tau = \texttt{s}_0\texttt{s}_1\texttt{s}_2 \ldots \in \mathit{Stmt}^*$ a *trace of the program* $\mathcal{P}$ if τ is the edge labeling of a path that starts at the initial location ℓ_0. We define the set of all program traces formally as follows.

$$T(\mathcal{P}) = \{\texttt{s}_0\texttt{s}_1 \ldots \in \mathit{Stmt}^* \mid \exists \ell_1, \ell_2, \ldots \bullet (\ell_i, \texttt{s}_i, \ell_{i+1}) \in \delta, \text{ for } i \geq 0\}$$

Note that each trace starts in the unique initial location ℓ_0, i.e., for the first transition of a trace we only require that ℓ_1 of $(\ell_0, \mathtt{s}_0, \ell_1)$ exists.

Let $\mathcal{D}$ be the set of values of the program's variables. We denote a concrete program state c as a function $c : \mathit{Var} \to \mathcal{D}$ that maps program variables to values. We use $\mathcal{C}$ to denote the set of all concrete program states. Each statement $\mathtt{s} \in \mathit{Stmt}$ defines a binary relation $\rho_{\mathtt{s}}$ over concrete program states which we call the *successor relation*. Let Expr be the set of all expressions over the program variables Var. We assume a given interpretation function $\mathcal{I} : \mathit{Expr} \times (\mathit{Var} \to \mathcal{D}) \to \mathcal{D}$ and define the relation $\rho_{\mathtt{s}} \subseteq \mathcal{C} \times \mathcal{C}$ inductively as follows:

$$\rho_{\mathtt{s}} = \begin{cases} \{(c, c') \mid \mathcal{I}(\mathtt{bexpr})(c) = \mathit{true} \text{ and } c = c'\} & \text{if } \mathtt{s} \equiv \mathtt{assume\ bexpr} \\ \{(c, c') \mid c' = c[\mathtt{x} \mapsto \mathcal{I}(\mathtt{expr})(c)]\} & \text{if } \mathtt{s} \equiv \mathtt{x{:}{=}expr} \\ \{(c, c') \mid \exists c'' \bullet (c, c'') \in \rho_{\mathtt{s}_1} \text{ and } (c'', c') \in \rho_{\mathtt{s}_2}\} & \text{if } \mathtt{s} \equiv \mathtt{s}_1; \mathtt{s}_2 \end{cases}$$

Given a trace $\tau = \mathtt{s}_0\mathtt{s}_1\mathtt{s}_2\ldots$, a sequence of concrete program states $\pi = c_0c_1c_2\ldots$ is called a *program execution of trace* τ if each successive pair of concrete program states is contained in the successor relation of the corresponding statement of the trace, i.e., $(c_i, c_{i+1}) \in \rho_{\mathtt{s}_i}$ for $i \in \{0, 1, \ldots\}$. We call a trace τ *infeasible* if it does not have any program execution, otherwise we call τ *feasible*.

Path Programs [8]. Given the program $\mathcal{P} = (\mathit{Loc}, \delta, \ell_0)$ over the set of statements Stmt and the trace $\tau = \mathtt{s}_0\mathtt{s}_1\ldots$ of $\mathcal{P}$, the path program $\mathcal{P}_\tau = (\mathit{Loc}_\tau, \delta_\tau, \ell_{0_\tau})$ is defined as follows.

- The set of program locations Loc_τ consists of the locations on the path of $\mathcal{P}$ which is labeled by the trace τ, i.e., $\mathit{Loc}_\tau = \{\ell \mid \ell \in \mathit{Loc} \wedge \exists \mathtt{s}_i \in \tau \textit{ s.t. } (\ell, \mathtt{s}_i, \ell') \in \delta \vee (\ell', \mathtt{s}_i, \ell) \in \delta)\}$,
- the transition relation δ_τ consists of the transitions that lie on the path, i.e., $\delta_\tau = \{(\ell, \mathtt{s}_i, \ell') \mid \mathtt{s}_i \in \tau \wedge (\ell, \mathtt{s}_i, \ell') \in \delta\}$, and
- the initial location ℓ_{0_τ} is the initial location of the path, i.e., $\ell_{0_\tau} = \ell_0$.

Abstract Interpretation. Abstract interpretation [12] is a well-known static analysis technique that computes a fixpoint of abstract values of an input program's variables for each program location. This fixpoint is an over-approximated abstraction of the program's concrete behavior. To this end, abstract interpretation uses an abstract domain defining allowed abstract values of the program's variables in the form of a complete lattice.

Formally, an abstract domain is defined as follows. Let $L = (\sqsubseteq, \sqcup, \sqcap, \bot, \top)$ be a complete lattice, i.e. a partially ordered set with partial ordering relation $\sqsubseteq$, such that for all $a, b \in L$, a and b have a least upper bound $a \sqcup b$ and a greatest lower bound $a \sqcap b$, and every subset $X \subseteq L$ has a least upper bound $\sqcup X$ and a greatest lower bound $\sqcap X$. The least element of L is $\bot = \sqcup\emptyset$, and the greatest element of L is $\top = \sqcup L$. For two lattices $L_1 = (\sqsubseteq_1, \sqcup_1, \sqcap_1, \bot_1, \top_1)$ and $L_2 = (\sqsubseteq_2, \sqcup_2, \sqcap_2, \bot_2, \top_2)$, $\alpha : L_1 \to L_2$ is called an *abstraction function* and $\gamma : L_2 \to L_1$ is called a *concretization function* if and only if $\forall x \in L_1, \forall y \in L_2 \centerdot \alpha(x) \sqsubseteq_2 y \iff x \sqsubseteq_1 \gamma(y)$.

An *abstract domain* is a tuple $A^\# = (\mathcal{D}^\#, \nabla, \alpha, \gamma)$, where $\mathcal{D}^\#$ is a complete lattice representing the domain of possible abstract values, $\nabla : \mathcal{D}^\# \times \mathcal{D}^\# \rightarrow \mathcal{D}^\#$ is a *widening operator*, and $\alpha : \mathcal{D} \rightarrow \mathcal{D}^\#$ and $\gamma : \mathcal{D}^\# \rightarrow \mathcal{D}$ are the abstraction function and the concretization function, respectively, which map concrete values of the complete lattice of values of a program's variables $\mathcal{D}$ to abstract values and vice versa. An *abstract program state* is a function $\sigma : \mathit{Var} \rightarrow \mathcal{D}^\#$ which assigns each variable occurring in the program an abstract value. We use S to denote the set of all abstract program states of the program. Given a concrete state $c \in \mathcal{C}$, we use $\sigma = \alpha(c)$ to denote the application of α to every value of every variable in c in order to obtain the corresponding abstract state $\sigma \in S$.

The fixpoint computation algorithm traverses the input program and assigns to each location of the program an abstract state by iteratively applying an *abstract transformer*, $\mathit{post}^\# : S \times \mathit{Stmt} \rightarrow S$, starting at the initial location. This abstract transformer computes an *abstract post state* for a given abstract state and a statement, i.e., it computes the effect a statement has on a given abstract state. In case of branching in the program, the fixpoint computation algorithm may choose to either merge the states at the join point of the branches with the join operator $\sqcup$ defined by the complete lattice of abstract values in the abstract domain, or to keep an arbitrary number of disjunctive abstract states. In the latter case, precision is increased at the cost of additional computations due to more abstract states in the abstraction.

The fixpoint computation algorithm is guaranteed to achieve progress and to eventually terminate. Progress is achieved by the application of the widening operator ∇, defined by the abstract domain: when the fixpoint computation algorithm traverses the statements of a loop, an infinite repetition of the application of the abstract transformer to the loop's statement is avoided by widening the approximation of the loop's body.

Upon termination, an over-approximated abstraction of the program is guaranteed to have been computed. The resulting abstraction is represented as a mapping $\mathit{fp} : \mathit{Loc} \rightarrow 2^S$, which maps to each location a disjunctive set of abstract states.

Trace Abstraction. The trace abstraction algorithm [18,19] is a CEGAR-based software model checking approach that proves the correctness of a program $\mathcal{P}$ by partitioning the set of possible error traces in feasible and infeasible traces. In the following, we briefly explain this approach. Consider the trace abstraction algorithm shown in Fig. 4. The input program $\mathcal{P}$ over the set of statements *Stmt* is first translated into a *program automaton* $\mathcal{A}_\mathcal{P}$, which encodes the correctness property of $\mathcal{P}$ by marking some of its locations as error locations. Those error locations serve as the accepting states of the program automaton $\mathcal{A}_\mathcal{P}$, and the set of statements *Stmt* as its alphabet. By construction, the language of the program automaton represents all traces of $\mathcal{P}$ that reach an error location.

The goal of the algorithm is to iteratively construct a *data automaton* $\mathcal{A}_\mathcal{D}$ whose language only consists of infeasible traces. If the language of the data automaton contains the language of the program automaton, we know that all

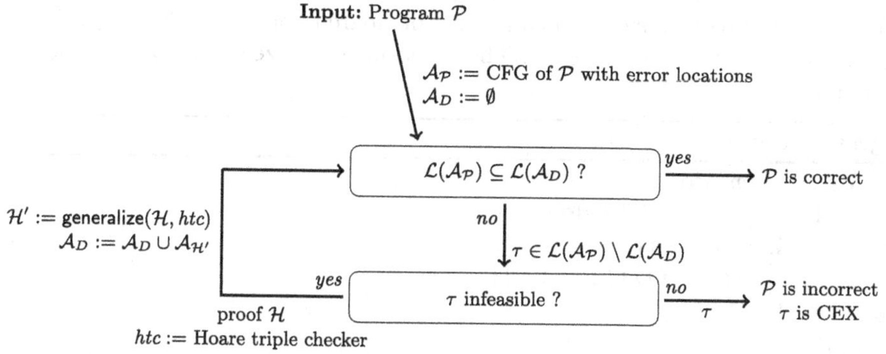

Fig. 4. The trace abstraction software model checking algorithm.

traces of the program that may reach an error location are infeasible, and thus the program is correct. Whenever the language of the data automaton does not contain the language of the program automaton, there exists a trace τ for which we do not know if it is infeasible and which reaches an error location. If the trace τ is feasible, it represents at least one valid program execution that can reach an error location. Hence, τ is a valid counterexample. If the trace τ is infeasible, a proof of infeasibility of τ in form of a set of Hoare triples $\mathcal{H}$ is constructed. The algorithm then constructs from this set a new data automaton, whose language contains the language of the old data automaton and at least τ as a new word. Only adding one trace in a single iteration is in most cases not sufficient, because, e.g., programs with loops contain infinitely many traces. Therefore, the trace abstraction algorithm constructs a data automaton not only from the trace τ, but from a set of Hoare triples $\mathcal{H}$. Additionally, before constructing the data automaton, the algorithm tries to generalize the proof $\mathcal{H}$ by adding more valid Hoare triples to it.

More formally, a data automaton is a *Floyd-Hoare automaton* [14,19]. A Floyd-Hoare automaton $\mathcal{A} = (Q, \delta, q_0, F)$ is an automaton over the alphabet of the program's statements *Stmt* together with a mapping that assigns to each state $q \in Q$ a state assertion φ_q such that the following holds:

- The initial state is annotated by the state assertion *true*,
- for each transition $(q, \mathtt{s}, q') \in \delta$ the triple $\{\varphi_q\}\, \mathtt{s}\, \{\varphi_{q'}\}$ is a valid Hoare triple, and
- each accepting state $q \in F$ is annotated by the state assertion *false*.

The generalization of a proof $\mathcal{H}$ is performed by a function generalize : $\mathcal{H} \times htc \rightarrow \mathcal{H}$ for a program $\mathcal{P}$ over a set of statements *Stmt*, where

- $\{\varphi_q\}\, \mathtt{s}\, \{\varphi_{q'}\} \in \mathcal{H}$ is a set of valid Hoare triples, and
- $htc : \mathcal{H} \rightarrow \{\top, \bot, ?\}$ is a function that determines whether a given Hoare triple is valid, invalid, or unknown.

The set of all predicates contained in a set of Hoare triples $\mathcal{H}$ is $Pred(\mathcal{H}) := \{\varphi \mid \{\psi\}\, \mathsf{s}\, \{\varphi\} \in \mathcal{H} \text{ or } \{\varphi\}\, \mathsf{s}\, \{\psi\} \in \mathcal{H}\}$. The function generalize generalizes a proof $\mathcal{H}$ as follows.

```
generalize(H, htc)
for s ∈ Stmt do
    for φ, φ' ∈ Pred(H) do
        if htc({φ} s {φ'}) = ⊤ then
            H := H ∪ {{φ} s {φ'}}
    end
end
```

If the set of predicates $Pred(\mathcal{H})$ of a proof $\mathcal{H}$ contains the predicates $true$ and $false$, we can construct a Floyd-Hoare automaton $\mathcal{A}_{\mathcal{H}} = (Q, \delta, q_0, F)$ from it as follows.

- The set of locations Q consists of one location for each predicate $\varphi \in Pred(\mathcal{H})$, i.e., $Q = \{q \mid \varphi_q \in Pred(\mathcal{H})\}$,
- the set of transitions δ contains one transition for each Hoare triple in $\mathcal{H}$, i.e. $\delta = \{(q, s, q') \mid \{\varphi_q\}\, \mathsf{s}\, \{\varphi_{q'}\}\}$,
- the initial location q_0 is the location labeled with $true$, and
- the set of accepting states F contains only the location labeled with $false$.

3 Algorithm

In this section, we present our software model checking algorithm and the basic idea behind it. Our approach is centered around an automata-theoretic counterexample-guided trace partitioning approach. Figure 5 shows a simplified

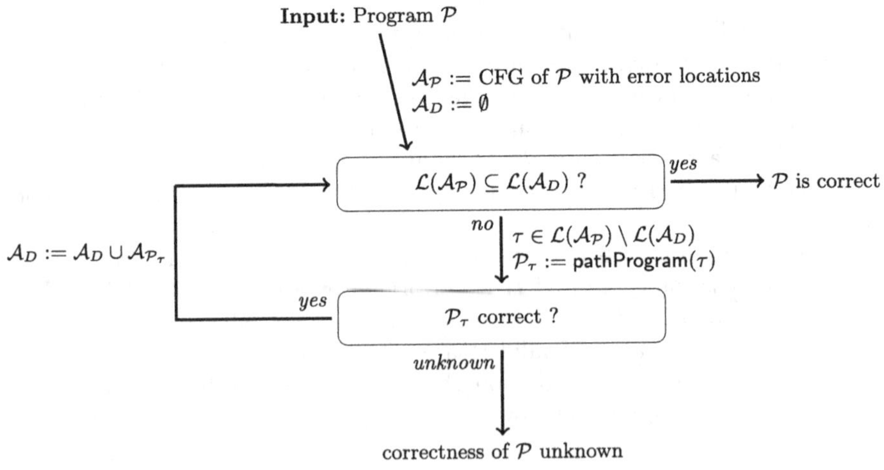

Fig. 5. The basic idea behind our software model checking approach.

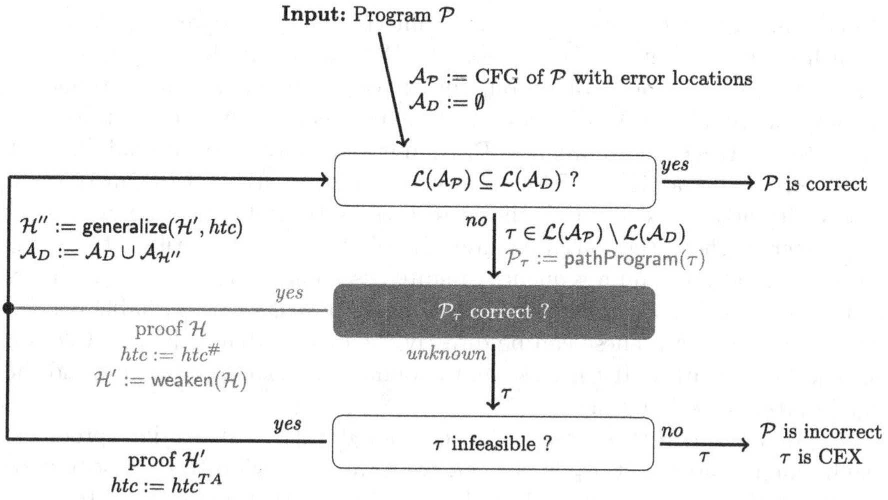

Fig. 6. Our complete software model checking algorithm. The differences to Fig. 4 are highlighted in blue.

version of our algorithm that already integrates trace abstraction, abstract interpretation and path programs. Similar to trace abstraction, we translate the input program $\mathcal{P}$ into a program automaton $\mathcal{A_P}$ and try to find a data automaton $\mathcal{A}_D$ that represents only infeasible traces. As long as we did not cover all traces represented by $\mathcal{A_P}$, we continue to update $\mathcal{A}_D$ and pick a not yet covered trace τ from the uncovered part of $\mathcal{A_P}$. But instead of directly analysing the trace τ, we construct a path program $\mathcal{P}_\tau$. Next, we use abstract interpretation to compute a fixpoint of $\mathcal{P}_\tau$ and to determine whether $\mathcal{P}_\tau$ is correct, i.e., if the error location of $\mathcal{P}_\tau$ is reachable. Using the path program of τ allows us to analyze multiple traces of $\mathcal{P}$ at once. If abstract interpretation is able to show correctness of the path program $\mathcal{P}_\tau$, we directly add the program (automaton) $\mathcal{P}_\tau$ to the data automaton $\mathcal{A}_D$, because we now know that all traces of $\mathcal{P}_\tau$ are infeasible. In contrast to trace abstraction, this step does not create a Floyd-Hoare automaton, since $\mathcal{P}_\tau$ is added to $\mathcal{A}_D$ instead of first producing a proof an then constructing an automaton from it.

Since abstract interpretation is used to determine correctness of the constructed path programs, the result may also be "unknown". In this case, our simple algorithm cannot deduce any information about the correctness of $\mathcal{P}_\tau$ and thus, also not about the correctness of $\mathcal{P}$. To avoid this problem, we extend our basic algorithm with the analysis of single traces as a fallback.

Figure 6 shows our full software model checking algorithm. Our algorithm retains the precision of software model checking but also utilizes abstract interpretations ability to find loop invariants to prevent divergence due to loop unwinding. As it is based on trace abstraction, we extended Fig. 4 and highlighted all new parts in blue. As with our simplified algorithm and with trace abstraction, we try to construct a data automaton that represents all traces of which we know that they are infeasible. We know that the program is safe when all traces of the program automaton are contained in the data automaton. Whenever we find a trace τ of $\mathcal{P}$ for which we not yet know whether it is feasible or not, we construct a path program $\mathcal{P}_\tau$ from it and analyse this instead. We first try to find an abstraction of $\mathcal{P}_\tau$ with abstract interpretation. If the abstraction is not sufficiently coarse to prove the correctness of the path program, we use an SMT solver to check the initial counterexample trace τ for infeasibility. If τ is infeasible, we also obtain a sequence of state assertions – either by Craig interpolation or by using a combination of strongest post and unsatisfiable cores – from the SMT solver. These can be directly used to construct the proof $\mathcal{H}$ and continue the algorithm. If τ is feasible, we found a valid counterexample and the original program $\mathcal{P}$ is unsafe.

In the case where the abstraction computed with abstract interpretation is sufficient to show that $\mathcal{P}_\tau$ is correct, we have to provide trace abstractions generalize function with a proof $\mathcal{H}$ and a function *htc* that can be used to check additional Hoare triples for validity. The next subsection describes how we initially obtain $\mathcal{H}$ from the abstraction and how our *htc* function works. Afterwards we explain in Sect. 3.2 how we optimize the initial proof $\mathcal{H}$ with the function weaken such that we get a more general proof that still contains all loop invariants for the path program.

3.1 Proofs from Fixpoints

After abstract interpretation proves the path program $\mathcal{P}_\tau$ safe, we need to construct a proof of infeasibility $\mathcal{H}$ from the computed fixpoints. For this construction we depend on some function p that converts an abstract state to a predicate without any loss of precision. Note that in general, it might not be possible to express a particular abstract domain as a SMT-compatible predicate, e.g., because there might be no suitable theory available. Given a function p, we construct the proof $\mathcal{H}$ for a path program $\mathcal{P}_\tau = (Loc, \delta, l_0)$ and an abstraction *fp* as follows.

First, we compute a state assertion φ_ℓ for each location ℓ of $\mathcal{P}_\tau$ by taking the disjunction of all abstract states resulting from an application of *fp* on ℓ:

$$\varphi_\ell = \bigvee_{\sigma_i^\ell \in fp(\ell)} p(\sigma_i^\ell)$$

Then, we construct Hoare triples by collecting all φ_ℓ along the transition relation δ, i.e., $\mathcal{H} = \{\{\varphi_\ell\}\, \mathtt{s}\, \{\varphi_{\ell'}\} \mid (\ell, \mathtt{s}, \ell') \in \delta\}$.

In the original trace abstraction algorithm, the next step is the generalization of the proof with generalize and *htc*. The function *htc* is implemented by letting an SMT solver decide whether the Hoare triple is valid or not. Because the state assertions computed by abstract interpretation usually contain many conjuncts, SMT solver queries that involve them can be quite slow. Therefore, we use a different *htc* function, namely $htc^\#$. As each state assertion φ_ℓ in $Pred(\mathcal{H})$ is

Table 1. Transition relation δ with labeling for the generalized data automaton of the path program from Sect. 1.1.

δ	Labeling
(ℓ_0, ℓ_0)	*Stmt*
(ℓ_0, ℓ_1)	`x:=0;y:=1000`
(ℓ_1, ℓ_0)	*Stmt*
(ℓ_1, ℓ_1)	*Stmt* \ { `x:=x+1` , `x:=x+2` , `y:=y-1` , `y:=y-2` }
(ℓ_1, ℓ_2)	{ `x:=0;y:=1000` , `x<100` , `x==1000` }
(ℓ_1, ℓ_3)	{ `x==1000` }
(ℓ_1, ℓ_4)	{ `x==1000` }
(ℓ_2, ℓ_0)	*Stmt*
(ℓ_2, ℓ_1)	*Stmt* \ { `x:=x+1` , `x:=x+2` , `y:=y-1` , `y:=y-2` }
(ℓ_2, ℓ_2)	*Stmt* \ { `x:=x+1` , `x:=x+2` , `y:=y-1` , `y:=y-2` }
(ℓ_2, ℓ_3)	{ `x>=100` , `x==1000` , `x:=x+1` }
(ℓ_2, ℓ_4)	{ `x>=100` , `x==1000` }
(ℓ_3, ℓ_0)	*Stmt*
(ℓ_3, ℓ_1)	{ `x:=0;y:=1000` , `x==1000` , `y:=y-1` }
(ℓ_3, ℓ_2)	{ `x:=0;y:=1000` , `x==1000` }
(ℓ_3, ℓ_3)	*Stmt* \ { `x:=x+1` , `x:=x+2` , `y:=y-1` , `y:=y-2` }
(ℓ_3, ℓ_4)	{ `x:=0;y:=1000` , `x==1000` }
(ℓ_4, ℓ_4)	*Stmt*

constructed from a set of abstract states $fp(\ell)$ at the location ℓ, we can use the abstract transformer $post^\#$ instead of an SMT query. For each candidate Hoare triple $\{\varphi_\ell\}\,\mathtt{s}\,\{\varphi_{\ell'}\}$ in $\mathcal{H}$ we check whether each abstract successor state of φ_ℓ is contained by one of the abstract states in $\varphi_{\ell'}$. If the following formula is valid for the given Hoare triple, the Hoare triple itself is valid.

$$\forall \sigma_i^l \in fp(\ell) \,.\, \left(post^\#(\sigma_i^l, \mathtt{s}) = \sigma_i^{\ell''} \wedge \exists \sigma_i^{\ell'} \in fp(\ell') \,.\, \left(\sigma_i^{\ell''} \subseteq \sigma_i^{\ell'}\right)\right)$$

The construction of a data automaton from a proof of infeasibility $\mathcal{H}$ for a path program is then conducted as described in Sect. 2. Note that by construction, we retain the property of Floyd-Hoare automata, that for each transition $(q, \mathtt{s}, q') \in \delta_{AI}$ the triple $\{\varphi_q\}\,\mathtt{s}\,\{\varphi_{q'}\}$ is a valid Hoare triple. Therefore, the automaton accepts at least all the traces represented by the path program. Table 2 shows the locations and Table 1 the transition relation of the data automaton constructed in this fashion for the example path program from Sect. 1.1.

3.2 Weakening of State Assertions

A state assertion φ_ℓ, derived from a set of abstract states $fp(\ell)$, might be very large, depending on the precision of the abstract domain. For example, let $fp(\ell) =$

Table 2. Locations of the generalized data automaton of the path program from Sect. 1.1. ℓ_0 is the initial location, ℓ_4 is an accepting state.

Loc	Labeling
ℓ_0	*true*
ℓ_1	$x \geq 0 \wedge x \leq 100 \wedge\ y \leq 1000 \wedge\ x + y = 1000$
ℓ_2	$x \geq 0 \wedge x < 100 \wedge\ y \leq 1000 \wedge\ x + y = 1000$
ℓ_3	$x \geq 1 \wedge x < 101 \wedge\ y \leq 1000 \wedge\ x + y = 1001$
ℓ_4	*false*

$\{(x \in [0; 10], y \in [-100; 100])\}$ be an abstract state that stores interval values of variables. Then, the state assertion $\varphi_\ell = x \geq 0 \wedge x \leq 10 \wedge y \geq -100 \wedge y \leq 100$ already contains four conjunctive terms for two variables that are present in q. A more precise abstract domain, e.g., the relational domain based on octagons, not only stores the bounds for each value interval per variable, but also the relations between all pairs of variables. A corresponding state assertion thus grows quadratically with the number of variables. The size of the state assertions, i.e., the number of conjunctive terms, is crucial for the runtime of various operations. We already mentioned that using an SMT solver to check whether a Hoare triple is valid is too expensive because of the size of the state assertions. But the application of $post^\#$ also scales unfavorably with the number of variables in an abstract state; for example, calculating the closure of an octagon matrix requires cubic time relative to the number of variables.

The predicates (i.e., the pre- and postconditions of the Hoare triples) of the proof $\mathcal{H}$ we obtained from abstract interpretation are still backed by abstract states. Hence we are interested in reducing the number of variables in those states and thus the number of conjuncts in the predicates as much as possible while still retaining the proof of correctness for the path program.

Our approach contains a simple method to achieve such a reduction, namely the function weaken that takes a set of Hoare triples and yields a set of Hoare triples. weaken uses a simple data-flow based analysis to remove variables and still retain the proof. It also exploits the fact that the proofs we obtain have a certain form. Because they correspond to traces, they can be represented as a joined sequence of Hoare triples

$$\mathcal{H} = \{\varphi_0\}\, \mathtt{s}_0\, \{\varphi_1\}\, \mathtt{s}_1 \ldots \{\varphi_n\}\, \mathtt{s}_n\, \{\varphi_{n+1}\}$$

where $\varphi_0 = \mathit{true}$ and $\varphi_{n+1} = \mathit{false}$. Note that the proofs for path programs also have this form, because we can just use the trace from which the path program was constructed. We only have to consider the case that at least one φ_i is equal to φ_j. We preserve all loop invariants because any unrolling of the loop is enough to reason about the inductivity of a loop invariant. Assuming this form for $\mathcal{H}$, the function weaken implements the following algorithm.

weaken($\mathcal{H}$)

1 $K := \emptyset$, $\mathcal{H}' := \emptyset$, $\hat{\mathcal{H}} :=$ reverse sequence of Hoare triples in $\mathcal{H}$
2 **for** $\{\varphi\}\, s\, \{\varphi'\} \in \hat{\mathcal{H}}$ **do**
3 $\quad W_{\mathtt{s}} :=$ All variables only written in s, $R_{\mathtt{s}} :=$ All variables read in s
4 $\quad K := K \setminus W_{\mathtt{s}}$
5 $\quad K_{\mathtt{s}} := R_{\mathtt{s}} \cup K$
6 $\quad \hat{\varphi} := \varphi$ without conjuncts that contain only variables not in $K_{\mathtt{s}}$
7 $\quad K := K \cup Var(\hat{\varphi})$
8 $\quad \mathcal{H}' := \mathcal{H}' \cup \{\{\hat{\varphi}\}\, \mathtt{s}\, \{\varphi'\}\}$
9 **end**

The algorithm first initializes a set K of variables that should not be removed in line 1. Then, it iterates backwards over the set of Hoare triples $\mathcal{H}$ that is in the form described above. The important aspects are the updates of the set of variables that should not be removed, K, in line 4 and 7, and the computation of a new Hoare-triple in line 6. In line 4, we remove all variables that are written in the current statement from the set of variables that should not be removed. The reasoning being that we do not need to keep information about variables that will change as consequence of the execution of the current statement. In line 6 the algorithm transforms each Hoare triple by removing all conjuncts from the precondition that contain only variables that are not read in the current statement and are not in the set of variables that should not be removed. In line 7, we add all variables now occurring in the new precondition to the set of variables that should not be removed.

The resulting Hoare triple is still valid because the post-condition can only contain information about variables that still have to be kept or were written in the current statement.

4 Implementation and Evaluation

In this section, we present the implementation and evaluation of our approach.

We implemented our algorithm in ULTIMATE, an open-source program analysis framework[1]. The resulting tool, ULTIMATE TAIPAN, is based on ULTIMATE AUTOMIZER[2], a state-of-the-art software model checker that implements trace abstraction (see Sect. 2). ULTIMATE TAIPAN extends ULTIMATE AUTOMIZER and ULTIMATE with an own fixpoint computation engine based on abstract interpretation, various abstract domains and methods for the extraction and creation of path programs. Our engine currently supports sets of octagons [21] as relational abstraction, sets of intervals and sets of divisibility congruences [16] as non-relational abstractions. It also allows for parameterized combinations of these domains. We currently do not support arrays, bitvectors and floats.

[1] https://ultimate.informatik.uni-freiburg.de.

[2] https://ultimate.informatik.uni-freiburg.de/automizer.

Our implementation of ULTIMATE TAIPAN also uses two small optimizations:

- We only compute a path program and use abstract interpretation when the trace τ contains a loop. If the trace contains only straight-line code, the analysis with SMT solvers is usually faster and provide more general state assertions.
- We cache the path programs we already analyzed to prevent re-analyzing path programs for which the used abstract domain was too weak to provide a proof. This may happen if both, abstract interpretation and SMT-based analysis, were unable to find a loop invariant for the path program and the algorithm unrolls a loop. In this case, instead of re-analyzing an already analyzed path program, the abstract interpretation module reports unknown and the algorithm continues.

In our evaluation we compare ULTIMATE AUTOMIZER (AUTOMIZER) with two variants of ULTIMATE TAIPAN (TAIPAN and LAZYTAIPAN). The three configurations differ only in the way they obtain state assertions from traces. In each iteration, they al try multiple methods to obtain state assertions that are loop invariants for the path program induced by the trace. These methods are applied one after another. If one method fails to provide loop invariants, the next method is used. If all methods fail to provide loop invariants, but some of them could show infeasibility, the abstraction is refined with all of the state assertions obtained. If no method could show infeasibility (or feasibility), the tools abort and return "Unknown" as the final result.

The first method is for all configurations an application of the SMT solver SMTINTERPOL [10] using Craig interpolation. This SMT solver is tightly integrated into ULTIMATE and can thus be called very efficiently.

Next, the three configurations use either the interpolation engine of the two SMT solvers Z3 [22] and CVC4 [4] on the trace, or our abstract interpretation engine on the path program induced by the trace. Only the order of these methods differs.

- AUTOMIZER tries Z3 followed by CVC4,
- TAIPAN tries abstract interpretation followed by Z3 and then CVC4, and
- LAZYTAIPAN tries Z3 followed by CVC4 and lastly abstract interpretation.

For our evaluation we applied the three configurations to C programs taken from the SV-COMP 2017 [5] repository[3]. Each of the verification tasks in SV-COMP reachability category contains one error location, which is either reachable or unreachable. We concentrated on two subcategories, namely "ReachSafety-Loops" (Loops) and "ReachSafety-ECA" (ECA). We chose these categories because they represent control-intensive programs that do not contain arrays, floats or bitvectors. One main difference between the two sets is in size. While Loops contains files with 8 to 1644 lines of code, ECA's samples range from 591 to 185053 lines of code. Loops also contains programs with more intricate loop invariants requiring relations between variables, while ECA is very control-intensive with many branches in a single loop. We used all 159 examples from Loops and 200 random examples from ECA. All benchmarks were run on

[3] https://github.com/sosy-lab/sv-benchmarks/releases/tag/svcomp17.

Table 3. The evaluation results. The complete benchmark set contained 359 samples (column "#"). Each cell in the column "Succ." contains the number of samples this particular setting could solve. Each cell in the column "Excl." shows how many samples were solved *exclusively* by this setting. The row "Portfolio" shows how many benchmarks could be solved by any of the settings, and the row "Common" shows how many benchmarks could be solved by all of them.

	Total			ECA			Loops		
	#	Succ.	Excl.	#	Succ.	Excl.	#	Succ.	Excl.
LazyTaipan	359	145	0	200	47	0	159	98	0
Automizer	359	124	17	200	34	12	159	90	5
Taipan	359	176	30	200	77	30	159	99	0
Portfolio	359	193	-	200	89	-	159	104	-
Common	359	106	-	200	22	-	159	84	-

an Intel Core i7-2600 with 3.40 GHz using a timeout of 90 s and a memory limit of 4 GB for the tool itself and 2 GB for the SMT solver.

Table 3 shows the results of the evaluation. Out of the 359 input programs, the default trace abstraction variant Automizer was able to solve 124 programs compared to 145 solved by LazyTaipan and 176 solved by Taipan. The clear advantage is visible in both benchmarks sets. Nevertheless, the Ultimate Automizer setting can solve 17 settings exclusively, 12 of them in ECA. These examples are due to cases where the fixpoint calculation lost precision because of branching.

Figure 7 shows four metrics collected during the evaluation. The top left hand chart shows the runtime in $\log(s)$ for all individual benchmark programs, ordered by time. It shows that Taipan was not only able to solve the most samples, but also took a comparable amount of time.

On the top right hand side in Fig. 7 the number of refinements in the CEGAR loop is shown. This number indicates how often a new data automaton was constructed during the refinement step. The graph shows that the number of iterations are very similar for all three configurations. They only differ in their offset. This corresponds to the importance of loop invariants: Each benchmark requires a number of loop invariants that if found, solve the benchmark. If one path program remains without loop invariant, all three approaches diverge.

The middle left hand chart of Fig. 7 shows the number of iterations in which a path program was constructed and analyzed with abstract interpretation. Depending on the setting, this was done early (Taipan) or late (LazyTaipan) during an iteration. Approximately 40 (resp. 60) examples could be solved using the interpolating SMT solvers alone, but for the remaining ones abstract interpretation was required to infer suitable state assertions. In many cases, only a single abstract interpretation iteration was necessary for solving the sample – all other parts of the proof could be provided by the SMT solvers.

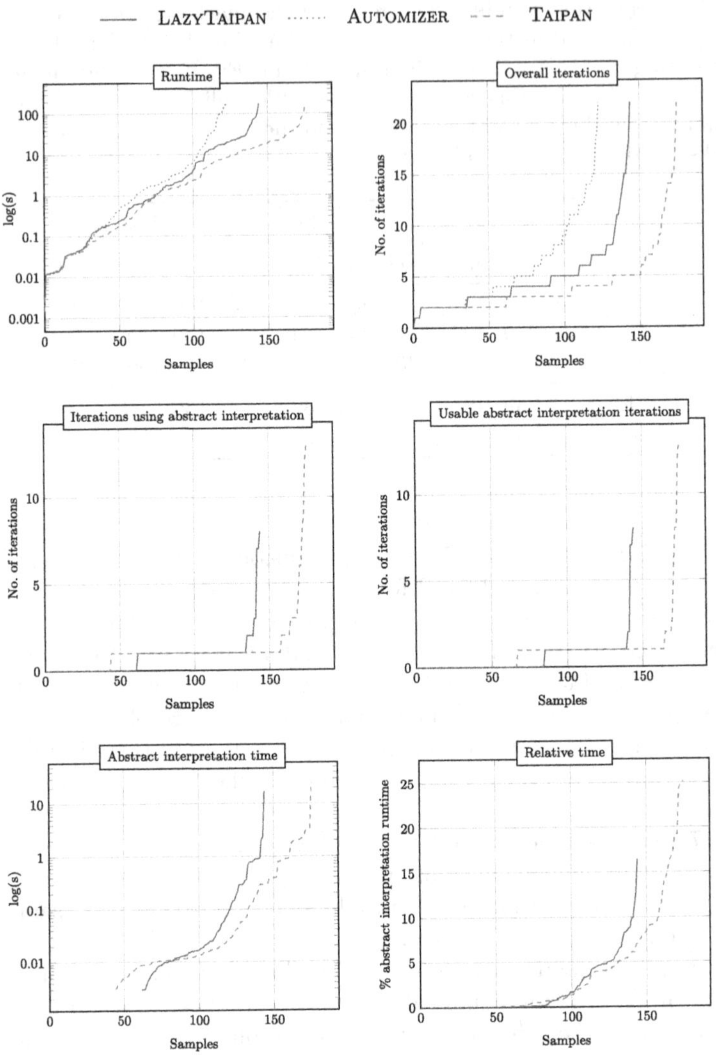

Fig. 7. Statistics collected during the execution of the benchmarks. All plots show the measured data on the y-axis and range over the samples on the x-axis. The order of the samples is sorted by the measurement value for each plot. This allows us to show trends but also prevents the comparison of single samples. The upper-left chart "Runtime" compares the total runtime of the different settings. The upper-right chart "Overall iterations" compares the number of iterations, the middle-left chart "Iterations using abstract interpretation" compares the number of iterations were abstract interpretation was applied to path programs with loops, and the middle-right chart "Useable abstract interpretation iterations" shows the number of refinements were abstract interpretation computed a proof for the infeasibility of the path program. Finally, the lower-left and lower-right charts "Abstract interpretation time" and "Relative time" show the absolute amount of time and the time relative to the overall time that the fixpoint computation took.

The middle right hand chart shows the number of iterations in which abstract interpretation could prove the infeasibility of the path program. Compared to the total number of abstract interpretation refinements, this was in roughly 70% of the benchmarks the case.

One observation from our experiments is that the analysis of a path program with abstract interpretation takes significantly more time than the analysis of a single trace with an SMT solver. In the current state, this may be an artifact of the implementation and we believe this can be improved further.

The results of our evaluation show that TAIPAN outperforms in particular the AUTOMIZER variant without abstract interpretation substantially. Trying to delay the more expensive analysis of path programs as we have done with the setting LAZYTAIPAN is not helpful, as one may expect. One reason for this is that for difficult traces, the solvers also may take a long time and then only provide unsuitable state assertions.

5 Related Work

In their work on Craig Interpretation [1,2], Albarghouthi et al. use a CEGAR-based approach with abstract interpretation to refine infeasible program traces. In contrast to our work, they use abstract interpretation to compute an initial abstraction of the whole program. Then, a trace to an error location is picked from the abstraction, instead of the original program, and analyzed using a bounded model checker. If the trace is infeasible, this results in a set of state assertions, which may be too precise, i.e., non-inductive, to be used to refine the initial abstraction. Abstract interpretation is used again, this time to weaken the found state assertions in an attempt to achieve inductivity before refinement of the last abstraction is done and the next iteration begins. Because the analysis is done on an abstraction dependent on the fixpoint computed by abstract interpretation, many iterations are needed in the worst case to identify infeasible program traces. The fact that we are using abstract interpretation to compute fixpoints of path programs which are a subset of the original program, instead of an abstraction, allows us to circumvent the problem that an abstraction of the whole program might be too weak to prove the program to be correct. Additionally, we often eliminate the need to use expensive model checking techniques to refine the abstraction iteratively. Therefore, our generalization with abstract interpretation is more localized and more precise than an abstraction obtained by analyzing the whole program.

Beyer et al. use path programs in a CEGAR approach to compute invariants of locations in a control flow graph of a program [8]. The refinement of the abstraction is done by using a constrained-based invariant synthesis algorithm which computes an invariant map, mapping predicates forming invariants to locations of the path program. Those invariants are excluding already visited parts from the original program. This is done until a counterexample for the program's correctness has been found or the program has been proven to be correct. In contrast to our work, their approach uses an interpolant generator to generate the invariant mapping, whereas we use both, an interpolant generator and a fixpoint computation engine to obtain suitable state assertions. In addition, their approach is only able to synthesize loop invariants by using invariant templates which are parametric assertions over program variables, present in each location of the program. Although they propose to use other approaches to generate invariants, including abstract interpretation, they do not present a combination of those methods.

6 Conclusion

In this paper, we presented a CEGAR approach that benefits from the precision of trace abstraction and the scalability of abstract interpretation. We use an automata theoretical approach to pick traces from a program automaton which are checked for infeasibility. If the trace is infeasible, we construct a path program and compute an abstraction of the path program by using abstract interpretation. With the help of this abstraction, we are guaranteed to obtain state assertions, in particular loop invariants, which help us to exclude a generalization of the found infeasible trace from the program. Because abstract interpretation may yield an abstraction which is not precise enough to synthesize usable loop invariants, we use the default precise trace abstraction approach as a fallback.

Our experiments show that by using abstract interpretation to generate loop invariants of path programs, we are able to prove a substantial larger set of benchmark programs.

References

1. Albarghouthi, A., Gurfinkel, A., Chechik, M.: Craig interpretation. In: Miné, A., Schmidt, D. (eds.) SAS 2012. LNCS, vol. 7460, pp. 300–316. Springer, Heidelberg (2012). doi:10.1007/978-3-642-33125-1_21
2. Albarghouthi, A., Li, Y., Gurfinkel, A., Chechik, M.: Ufo: a framework for abstraction- and interpolation-based software verification. In: Madhusudan, P., Seshia, S.A. (eds.) CAV 2012. LNCS, vol. 7358, pp. 672–678. Springer, Heidelberg (2012). doi:10.1007/978-3-642-31424-7_48
3. Ball, T., Rajamani, S.K.: The SLAM toolkit. In: Berry, G., Comon, H., Finkel, A. (eds.) CAV 2001. LNCS, vol. 2102, pp. 260–264. Springer, Heidelberg (2001). doi:10.1007/3-540-44585-4_25
4. Barrett, C., Conway, C.L., Deters, M., Hadarean, L., Jovanović, D., King, T., Reynolds, A., Tinelli, C.: CVC4. In: Gopalakrishnan, G., Qadeer, S. (eds.) CAV 2011. LNCS, vol. 6806, pp. 171–177. Springer, Heidelberg (2011). doi:10.1007/978-3-642-22110-1_14
5. Beyer, D.: Reliable and reproducible competition results with benchexec and witnesses (report on SV-COMP 2016). In: Chechik, M., Raskin, J.-F. (eds.) TACAS 2016. LNCS, vol. 9636, pp. 887–904. Springer, Heidelberg (2016). doi:10.1007/978-3-662-49674-9_55
6. Beyer, D., Henzinger, T.A., Jhala, R., Majumdar, R.: The software model checker BLAST. STTT 2007 **9**(5–6), 505–525 (2007)

7. Beyer, D., Henzinger, T.A., Majumdar, R., Rybalchenko, A.: Invariant synthesis for combined theories. In: Cook, B., Podelski, A. (eds.) VMCAI 2007. LNCS, vol. 4349, pp. 378–394. Springer, Heidelberg (2007). doi:10.1007/978-3-540-69738-1_27
8. Beyer, D., Henzinger, T.A., Majumdar, R., Rybalchenko, A.: Path invariants. In: PLDI 2007, pp. 300–309 (2007)
9. Beyer, D., Keremoglu, M.E.: CPA checker: a tool for configurable software verification. In: CAV 2011, pp. 184–190 (2011)
10. Christ, J., Hoenicke, J., Nutz, A.: SMTInterpol: an interpolating SMT solver. In: Donaldson, A., Parker, D. (eds.) SPIN 2012. LNCS, vol. 7385, pp. 248–254. Springer, Heidelberg (2012). doi:10.1007/978-3-642-31759-0_19
11. Clarke, E., Grumberg, O., Jha, S., Lu, Y., Veith, H.: Counterexample-guided abstraction refinement. In: CAV 2000, pp. 154–169 (2000). http://dx.doi.org/10.1007/10722167_15
12. Cousot, P., Cousot, R.: Abstract interpretation: a unified lattice model for static analysis of programs by construction or approximation of fixpoints. In: POPL 1977, pp. 238–252 (1977). http://doi.acm.org/10.1145/512950.512973
13. Cousot, P., Halbwachs, N.: Automatic discovery of linear restraints among variables of a program. In: POPL 1978, pp. 84–96 (1978). http://doi.acm.org/10.1145/512760.512770
14. Dietsch, D.: Automated verification of system requirements and software specifications. Ph.D. thesis, University of Freiburg (2016)
15. Floyd, R.W.: Assigning meanings to programs. Math. Aspects Comput. Sci. **19**(19–32), 1 (1967)
16. Granger, P.: Static analysis of linear congruence equalities among variables of a program. In: Abramsky, S., Maibaum, T.S.E. (eds.) TAPSOFT 1991. LNCS, vol. 493, pp. 169–192. Springer, Heidelberg (1991). doi:10.1007/3-540-53982-4_10
17. Heizmann, M., Christ, J., Dietsch, D., Ermis, E., Hoenicke, J., Lindenmann, M., Nutz, A., Schilling, C., Podelski, A.: Ultimate automizer with SMTInterpol. In: Piterman, N., Smolka, S.A. (eds.) TACAS 2013. LNCS, vol. 7795, pp. 641–643. Springer, Heidelberg (2013). doi:10.1007/978-3-642-36742-7_53
18. Heizmann, M., Hoenicke, J., Podelski, A.: Refinement of trace abstraction. In: Palsberg, J., Su, Z. (eds.) SAS 2009. LNCS, vol. 5673, pp. 69–85. Springer, Heidelberg (2009). doi:10.1007/978-3-642-03237-0_7
19. Heizmann, M., Hoenicke, J., Podelski, A.: Software model checking for people who love automata. In: Sharygina, N., Veith, H. (eds.) CAV 2013. LNCS, vol. 8044, pp. 36–52. Springer, Heidelberg (2013). doi:10.1007/978-3-642-39799-8_2
20. Hoare, C.A.R.: An axiomatic basis for computer programming. Commun. ACM **12**(10), 576–580 (1969)
21. Miné, A.: The octagon abstract domain. High. Order Symbolic Comput. **19**(1), 31–100 (2006). http://dx.doi.org/10.1007/s10990-006-8609-1
22. Moura, L., Bjørner, N.: Z3: an efficient SMT solver. In: Ramakrishnan, C.R., Rehof, J. (eds.) TACAS 2008. LNCS, vol. 4963, pp. 337–340. Springer, Heidelberg (2008). doi:10.1007/978-3-540-78800-3_24
23. Sagiv, S., Reps, T.W., Wilhelm, R.: Parametric shape analysis via 3-valued logic. In: POPL 1999, pp. 105–118 (1999). http://doi.acm.org/10.1145/292540.292552
24. Sankaranarayanan, S., Sipma, H.B., Manna, Z.: Scalable analysis of linear systems using mathematical programming. In: VMCAI 2006, pp. 25–41 (2005). http://dx.doi.org/10.1007/978-3-540-30579-8_2

A Context-Sensitive Memory Model for Verification of C/C++ Programs

Arie Gurfinkel[1] and Jorge A. Navas[2(✉)]

[1] University of Waterloo, Waterloo, Canada
arie.gurfinkel@uwaterloo.ca
[2] SRI International, Menlo Park, USA
jorge.navas@sri.com

Abstract. Verification of low-level C/C++ requires a precise memory model that supports type unions, pointer arithmetic, and casts. We present a new memory model that splits memory into a finite set of disjoint regions based on a pointer analysis. The main contribution is a field-, array- and context-sensitive pointer analysis tailored to verification. We have implemented our memory model for the LLVM bitcode and used it on a C++ case study and on SV-COMP benchmarks. Our results suggests that our model can reduce verification time by producing a finer-grained partitioning in presence of function calls.

1 Introduction

Verification of low-level C and C++ programs (e.g., OS drivers, flight control systems) often requires a low-level modeling of the heap that supports *type-unsafe* features such as type unions, pointer arithmetic, and pointer casts. The more detailed the memory model the more precise the analysis. However, extra details often increase the computational cost of the analysis.

A memory model defines the semantics of pointers. The standard C/C++ memory model (also called *block-level*) interprets a pointer as a pair (id, o) where id is an identifier that uniquely defines a memory region and o defines the byte in the region being point to. The number of regions is unbounded. On the other hand, in the *flat* or *byte-level* model used by most execution platforms there is a single memory region (i.e., the memory) and every allocation returns a new offset in that region. For verification purposes, we adopt a memory model similar to that of C/C++ but ensuring a finite number of memory regions.

We say that a memory model is *context-sensitive* (*context-insensitive*) if memory is divided into finitely many global regions and every pointer points

This material is based upon work supported by the Defense Advanced Research Projects Agency (DARPA) and Space and Naval Warfare Systems Center Pacific (SSC Pacific) under Contract No. N66001-15-C-4061. Any opinions, findings and conclusions or recommendations expressed in this material are those of the author(s) and do not necessarily reflect the views of the DARPA or SSC Pacific. This work has been also supported in part by NSF grant 1528153.

F. Ranzato (Ed.): SAS 2017, LNCS 10422, pp. 148–168, 2017.
DOI: 10.1007/978-3-319-66706-5_8

```
void f(int* x,int* y) {
  *x = 1;
  *y = 2;
}
void g(int* p,int* q,int* r,int* s) {
  f(p,q);
  f(r,s);
}
```

(a) C-like fragment

(b) Context-sensitive	(c) Context-insensitive	(d) Our approach
$f(x, y, A_x, A_y, A'_x, A'_y)$	$f(x, y, A_{xy}, A''_{xy})$	$f(x, y, A_{xy}, A''_{xy})$
$A'_x = A_x[x \leftarrow 1]$	$A'_{xy} = A_{xy}[x \leftarrow 1]$	$A'_{xy} = A_{xy}[x \leftarrow 1]$
$A'_y = A_y[y \leftarrow 2]$	$A''_{xy} = A'_{xy}[y \leftarrow 2]$	$A''_{xy} = A'_{xy}[y \leftarrow 2]$
$g(\ldots)$	$g(\ldots)$	$g(\ldots)$
$f(p, q, A_{pq}, A_{pq}, A'_{pq}, A'_{pq})$	$f(p, q, A_{pqrs}, A'_{pqrs})$	$f(p, q, A_{pq}, A'_{pq})$
$f(r, s, A_r, A_s, A'_r, A'_s)$	$f(r, s, A'_{pqrs}, A''_{pqrs})$	$f(r, s, A_{rs}, A'_{rs})$

Fig. 1. Several translations to a side-effect free language if p and q may alias.

to a region that does (not) depend on the call paths leading to the allocation of the region. A context-sensitive memory model might scale more than its context-insensitive counterpart because it induces a finer-grained memory partitioning so that verification conditions can be solved more efficiently.

This paper presents a new context-sensitive memory model for verification of C/C++ programs. Like other memory models (e.g., [19,21]) our model divides memory into disjoint regions based on the information computed by a pointer analysis. Unlike these works, our memory model produces a finer-grained partitioning in the presence of function calls.

Our main technical contribution is a context, field, and array-sensitive pointer analysis for C/C++ which disambiguates the heap in a way that a side-effect free version of the program can be obtained from which modular verification conditions can be generated. A standard approach (e.g., SMACK [18], SEAHORN [11], CBMC [7], ESBMC [10], and CASCADE [22]) to transforming an imperative program to a side-effect-free form is to map each pointer p to a symbolic memory region M_p using a pointer analysis. Then, each M_p is replaced by a logical array A_p and memory accesses are replaced by array stores and selects to A_p. Each array store on A_p produces a new version of A'_p representing the array after the execution of the memory write. This encoding is straightforward for intra-procedural code. However, a precise modular encoding is more challenging.

Consider the snippet of C on Fig. 1(a) and three translations to a side-effect free program[1] on Fig. 1(b–d) using three flow-insensitive pointer analyses:

[1] Logic-based verifiers require to generate verification conditions in a side-effect free form so that they can be solved by SMT solvers. In this paper, we focus on how to provide precise points-to information to produce a sound translation to such a form. The syntax and semantics of the language and construction of VCs are beyond the scope of this paper. We refer readers to e.g., [11,18] and their references for details.

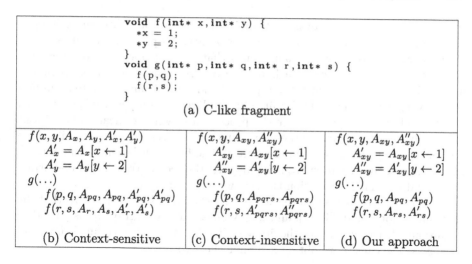

(b) a context-sensitive analysis, (c) context-insensitive, and (d) our technique. Assume that at the entry of the procedure g variables p and q may alias.

Memory has been disambiguated such that each accessed memory region is passed explicitly to each call. Each logical array A_S denotes a memory region to which all pointers in S point to. Non-primed and primed names denote input and output versions, respectively. Intuitively, the larger the number of non-primed array variables the more efficient the process of solving verification conditions may be because more disjointness information between regions is available to the solver. Let us focus on the procedure g. The first translation produces three non-primed array variables: A_{pq}, A_r, and A_s, the second translation one array: A_{pqrs}, and the third translation two arrays: A_{pq} and A_{rs}.

However, closer inspection to the first translation in Fig. 1(b) reveals that the encoding is not sound. Since p and q may alias, the same array A_{pq} is passed to the 3rd and 4th arguments at the first callsite of f in g. The encoding is unsound because at the callsite we obtain a similar effect to:

$$H'_{pq} = H_{pq}[p \leftarrow 1] \text{ and } H'_{pq} = H_{pq}[q \leftarrow 2]$$

i.e., the update of p is lost, instead of the correct

$$H'_{pq} = H_{pq}[p \leftarrow 1] \text{ and } H''_{pq} = H'_{pq}[q \leftarrow 2]$$

where both updates of p and q are preserved.

This example shows that an arbitrary context-sensitive pointer analysis cannot be directly leveraged for modular verification without being unsound unless the analysis ensures the following correctness condition **CC**: *"no two disjoint memory regions modified in a function can be aliased at any particular call site"*.

A simple solution adopted by verifiers such as SMACK and SEAHORN is to give up the precision of a context-sensitive pointer analysis and use a context-insensitive one. The resulting translation is shown in Fig. 1(c). A more precise but incomplete approach adopted by Hubert and Marché [12] exploits context-sensitivity if **CC** holds and returns inconclusive results otherwise. Moy [17] refines Hubert and Marché's approach by generating function contracts that ensure that **CC** holds, rejecting programs for which it does not.

We argue that none of these solutions is fully satisfactory. Instead, our approach consists of reusing existing pointer analysis technology and adapting it to verification. Pointer analyses have been studied for decades and, thus, we want to leverage existing advances as much as possible. For this reason, our pointer analysis is inspired by *Data Structure Analysis (DSA)* [15]. DSA is a context, field-sensitive pointer analysis that represents the heap explicitly. Moreover, DSA supports *type-unsafe* C/C++ code and it scales to large code bases. However, context-sensitivity cannot be directly exploited because DSA does not ensure **CC**. We also observed that DSA is very imprecise when modeling consecutive sequences of bytes (e.g., C arrays) which complicates the verification of some programs such as our C++ case study. Last, but not less important, our experience with the public implementation of DSA [1] is that it is full of corner cases and it is very hard to reason about its correctness. Our goal is to develop a new

```
class X {
   X() {....}
};

class Y: public X {
   Y(): X() {....}
};

class Z: public X {
   Z(): X() {....}
};

Y* y = new Y();
Z* z = new Z();
```

```
% Constructor for Y
_Y_c(this) {
   _X_c(this);
   ...
}
% Constructor for Z
_Z_c(this) {
   _X_c(this);
   ...
}

% Y y = new Y();
y = _Znwm(sizeof(Y));
_Y_c(y);

% Z z = new Z();
z = _Znwm(sizeof(Z));
_Z_c(z);
```

Fig. 2. A C++ fragment and its translation to a low-level IR form.

pointer analysis that enjoys the same benefits as DSA while producing a sound and context-sensitive static partitioning of the heap required for verification. Unlike [15], we provide a more rigorous formalization of the analysis from which a proof of correctness can follow.

Coming back to our example, the side-effect free program obtained with our analysis is shown on Fig. 1(d). The translation is sound yet more precise than using a context-insensitive analysis since we do not merge the regions A_{pq} and A_{rs} passed to each call to `f`, and, thus, it is still context-sensitive. It is worth mentioning that the more different heap call patterns there are for a function, the fewer opportunities to partition the heap into smaller regions. This problem can be addressed by cloning functions with different call patterns. However, this is orthogonal to our approach and was not necessary during our experimental evaluation.

Although it is folklore that context-sensitivity is beneficial for analysis, it is particularly important for verification of C++ programs. Consider the snippet of C++ on the left in Fig. 2, where classes `Y` and `Z` are sub-classes of `X`. This fragment allocates memory for two objects of class `Y` and `Z`. We omit all class methods except the constructors. The constructors of `Y` and `Z` call the constructor of the base class `X`. We show on the right in Fig. 2 a translation to a low-level intermediate representation (IR) without C++ features that resembles LLVM [14] IR. Each object allocation (`_znwm` is the C++ mangled name for the `new` operator) is followed by a call to the corresponding constructor `_Y_c` and `_Z_c` which in turn calls `_X_c`. As a result, `_X_c` is called twice: one from `_Y_c` and another from `_Z_c`. The key observation is that a context-insensitive pointer analysis will merge `y` and `z` into the same alias set, collapsing the whole hierarchy into a large alias set. However, a context-sensitive pointer analysis will not merge them since it can distinguish between different calls to the constructor `_X_c`.

In summary, the paper makes the following contributions: (1) It presents a new context- and field-sensitive pointer analysis that (a) is based on a new concept of a *simulation relation* between graphs that allows to produce sound modular verification conditions and, unlike DSA, reason formally about proof of correctness, and (b) is *array-sensitive*; (2) The analysis is implemented[2] operating on LLVM bitcode and integrated in SeaHorn; and (3) It has been evaluated on the flight control component of the Core Autonomous Safety Software (CASS) of an Autonomous Flight Safety System written in C++ and on C benchmarks from the Software Verification Competition (SV-COMP). We show that it reduces verification times by producing a finer-grained memory partitioning.

2 Syntax and Concrete Memory Model

Consider a simple imperative language shown in Fig. 3. It captures the core pointer arithmetic of C/C++ at the function level. The variables $p, q \in \mathcal{V}_\mathcal{P}$ denote pointer variables, $m \in \mathcal{V}_\mathcal{I}$ denotes integer variables, the symbols c, d denote integer constants, and x denotes either a pointer or integer variable. The set of program variables is denoted by $\mathcal{V}$. We restrict variables to pointer and integer types $\mathcal{V} = \mathcal{V}_\mathcal{P} \cup \mathcal{V}_\mathcal{I}$ and we assume that they are disjoint, $\mathcal{V}_\mathcal{P} \cap \mathcal{V}_\mathcal{I} = \emptyset$. The set of statements is denoted by $\mathbb{S}$. Each statement is assigned a unique label $\ell \in \mathbb{L}$.

$$
\begin{array}{lll}
S & ::= & p = \&\mathtt{x} \mid p = \mathbf{malloc}(...) \\
 & & p = q + (c \times m) + d \quad (c \geq 0) \\
 & & p = *\mathtt{q} \mid *\mathtt{p} = q \\
 & & S; S \\
 & & \mathsf{if}\ (Cond)\ \mathsf{then}\ S\ \mathsf{else}\ S \\
 & & \mathsf{while}\ (Cond)\ \mathsf{do}\ S \\
Cond & ::= & p = q \mid p \neq q
\end{array}
$$

Fig. 3. Syntax of pointer operations

A *cell* c is a pair (id, o) where id is a unique identifier of a memory object of size sz and o is byte offset in id, $0 \leq o < sz$. The set of all concrete objects is denoted by $\mathcal{O}_\mathbb{C}$ and we use $\mathcal{C}_\mathbb{C}$ to denote the set of all possible concrete cells. Note that the cardinality of $\mathcal{C}_\mathbb{C}$ is unbounded since the number of concrete objects in the heap is unbounded. Memory is represented by a *concrete points-to graph*. A concrete points-to graph is a triple $\langle V, E, \sigma \rangle$, where:

- $V \subseteq \mathcal{C}_\mathbb{C}$ is a set of concrete cells;
- $E \subseteq \mathcal{C}_\mathbb{C} \times \mathcal{C}_\mathbb{C}$ is a set of edges denoting that a source cell points to target cell.
- The environment $\sigma : \mathcal{V}_\mathcal{P} \mapsto \mathcal{C}_\mathbb{C}$ maps pointer variables to cells. We write $\mathsf{dom}(\sigma)$ for the domain of σ, that is, the set of variables for which it is defined.

[2] It is publicly available at https://github.com/seahorn/sea-dsa.

```
typedef struct list{
  struct list *n;
  int e;
} ll;
ll* mkList(int s,int e){
 if (s <= 0)
   return NULL;
 ll*p=malloc(sizeof(ll));
 p->e=e;
 p->n=mkList(s-1,e);
 return p;
}
void main(){
 ll* a[4]; int i;
 for(i=0;i<4;i++)
   a[i] = mkList(2,0);
}
```

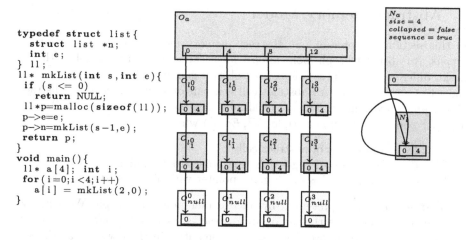

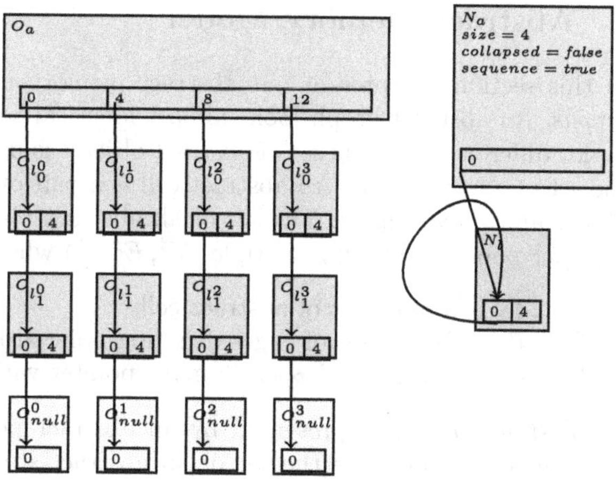

Fig. 4. C snippet (left), concrete (center), and abstract points-to graphs (right).

The symbol $\mathcal{G}_{\mathbb{C}}$ denotes the set of all concrete points-to graphs. Concrete graphs are *functional* in the sense that for each source cell there is at most one target cell. For convenience, we will write $c_2 = E(c_1)$ and $E(c_3) = c_4$ to refer to $c_1 \rightarrow c_2 \in E$ and $E \setminus \{c_3 \rightarrow \_\} \cup \{c_3 \rightarrow c_4\}$, respectively.

Example 1 (Concrete points-to graph). The middle of Fig. 4 depicts the cells and edges of a concrete points-to graph from a simplified fragment extracted from the CASS code. The program initializes each array element of size four to a new linked list of two memory objects which is dynamically allocated by the function mkList. The array is represented by a concrete object O_a of size 16 (assuming four bytes per pointer). The variable a points to the first cell $(O_a, 0)$. For each cell (O_a, i) $(i \in \{0, 4, 8, 12\})$ there is an edge to the first cell of each linked list: $(O^0_{l_0}, 0)$, $(O^1_{l_0}, 0)$, $(O^2_{l_0}, 0)$, and $(O^3_{l_0}, 0)$. The size of each list object is 8 (assuming integers occupy 4 bytes as well). Finally, each of the lists has an edge to a special concrete object $O^{i\in\{0,1,2,3\}}_{null}$ that represents a null terminator. ■

A *concrete state* is a triple $\langle g, \pi, l\rangle$ where $g \in \mathcal{G}_{\mathbb{C}}$ is a concrete points-to graph, $\pi : \mathcal{V}_{\mathcal{I}} \mapsto \mathbb{Z}$ is an environment mapping integer variables to values, and $l \in \mathbb{L}$ is the label of the next statement to be executed.

We do not give the concrete semantics of our language since it is standard. We only point out that the semantics of a *taken-address* variable (i.e., `p = &x`) creates a new memory object but always the same for the same variable, and **malloc** returns non-deterministically a fresh memory object from the (infinite) set of unallocated objects. Note that, *re-incarnation* of freed memory cannot be modeled in our semantics. For instance, in the following sequence of statements: `p = malloc(...); q = p; free(p); r = malloc(...)`, the pointer variable `r` cannot be aliased with `q`.

3 Abstract Memory Model

In this section, we present our abstract memory model via *abstract points-to graphs*. An abstract graph looks almost identical to a concrete graph with the major difference that the set of abstract objects is finite. The symbol $\mathcal{C}_{\mathbb{A}}$ denotes the set of abstract cells. An abstract cell is a pair of an identifier of an abstract object and a byte offset. The set of all abstract objects is denoted by $\mathcal{O}_{\mathbb{A}}$. An abstract points-to graph is a triple $\langle V^{\sharp}, E^{\sharp}, \sigma^{\sharp} \rangle$ where:

- $V^{\sharp} \subseteq \mathcal{C}_{\mathbb{A}}$ is a finite set of abstract cells.
- $E^{\sharp} \subseteq \mathcal{C}_{\mathbb{A}} \times \mathcal{C}_{\mathbb{A}}$ is a set of edges denoting points-to relations.
- The environment $\sigma^{\sharp} : \mathcal{V}_{\mathcal{P}} \mapsto \mathcal{C}_{\mathbb{A}}$ maps pointer variables to abstract cells.

An *abstract state* is represented by an abstract points-to graph. We will use the symbol $\mathbb{A}$ to denote the set of all abstract states. Note that our abstract semantics over-approximates the concrete semantics in three ways: (a) the set of objects is finite, (b) the abstract semantics is flow insensitive, and (c) it does not keep track of an environment for integer variables. To keep the number of objects finite, each abstract object maintains the following information:

- whether the abstract object is *collapsed* meaning that all cells from this object have been merged into a single one (i.e., field-sensitivity is lost). The function $\mathsf{isCollapsed} : \mathcal{O}_{\mathbb{A}} \mapsto \mathbb{B}$ serves to denote such objects;
- whether an abstract object represents a sequence of an unknown number of consecutive bytes (e.g., C arrays). The function $\mathsf{isSeq} : \mathcal{O}_{\mathbb{A}} \mapsto \mathbb{B}$ denotes such objects;
- a *size* that over-approximates the size of every concrete object represented by the abstract object. The function $\mathsf{size} : \mathcal{O}_{\mathbb{A}} \mapsto \mathbb{N}$ maps objects to their sizes:
  - if $\mathsf{isCollapsed}(n)$ then $\mathsf{size}(n) = 1$;
  - if $\mathsf{isSeq}(n)$ then $\mathsf{size}(n) = k$ represents that the actual size is some value in the set $\{k \times N \mid N \in \mathbb{N}, k > 0\}$ (i.e., positive multiple of k);
  - otherwise, it returns the value of the largest offset accessed so far plus the size of the field indexed by that offset.

  It is worth mentioning that the size of an abstract object is computed based on its *use* and not based on the allocation. Therefore, the values returned by size change during the analysis.

Example 2 (Abstract points-to graph). The right of Fig. 4 depicts the cells and edges of an abstract points-to graph. The whole array is abstracted to an object N_a marked as a sequence of consecutive bytes whose unknown size is multiple of 4 (e.g., $4, 8, 12, 16, 20, \ldots$). The abstraction loses the fact that the original array had exactly four elements of four bytes each. The linked lists are also abstracted. Each list is abstracted by a single object N_l that has two fields at offsets 0 and 4. There is a loop edge at $(N_l, 0)$ that means we have lost track of the exact list size. Moreover, the abstraction loses the fact that the linked lists are null-terminated. Note that in spite of this loss of precision, this abstraction is able to preserve the fact that the array and the linked lists point to two disjoint memory regions which is a very valuable information while solving the verification conditions. ■

Simulation Relation Between Graphs. We now introduce the fundamental concept of a simulation relation between points-to graphs. First, we define two helper functions. Given an object n' and a set of edges E, $\mathsf{Links}(n', E)$ returns a sequence of numerical offsets $(o_n)_{n \in \mathbb{N}}$ such that $(o_n) = o$ if $(n', o) \to c \in E$. Function $\oplus_n : \mathbb{N} \times \mathbb{N} \mapsto \mathbb{N}$ adds numerical offsets and adjusts them depending on object n flags as follows:

$$o_1 \oplus_n o_2 = \begin{cases} 0 & \text{if } \mathsf{isCollapsed}(n) \\ (o_1 + o_2) \,\%\, \mathsf{size}(n) & \text{if } \mathsf{isSeq}(n) \\ o_1 + o_2 & \text{otherwise} \end{cases}$$

We say that there is a *simulation relation* between two abstract graphs $\langle V_1^\sharp, E_1^\sharp, \sigma_1^\sharp \rangle$ and $\langle V_2^\sharp, E_2^\sharp, \sigma_2^\sharp \rangle$ if $\exists \rho \subseteq \mathcal{C}_\mathbb{A} \times \mathcal{C}_\mathbb{A}.\ \forall p \in \mathsf{dom}(\sigma_1^\sharp).\ (\sigma_1^\sharp(p), \sigma_2^\sharp(p)) \in \rho$, and for all $((n_1, o_1), (n_2, o_2)) \in \rho$:

- if $(o_1 \leq o_2 \wedge o_1 > 0)$ then $((n_1, 0), (n_2, o_2 - o_1)) \in \rho$
- else

$$\begin{array}{lr} ((o_1 \leq o_2) \wedge o_1 = 0) & \wedge \\ \mathit{compatible}(n_1, n_2, o_2) & \wedge \\ \forall o \in \mathsf{Links}(n_1, E_1^\sharp).(E_1^\sharp((n_1, o)), E_2^\sharp((n_2, o_2 \oplus_{n_2} o))) \in \rho & \end{array}$$

where

$$\mathit{compatible}(n_1, n_2, o) = \begin{cases} \mathit{true} & \text{if } (\mathsf{isCollapsed}(n_2)) \\ \mathit{false} & \text{if } (\mathsf{isCollapsed}(n_1)) \\ \mathit{false} & \text{if } (\mathsf{isSeq}(n_1) \wedge \neg\ \mathsf{isSeq}(n_2)) \\ (o = 0 \wedge & \text{if } (\mathsf{isSeq}(n_2)) \\ \ \mathsf{size}(n_1) \geq \mathsf{size}(n_2) \wedge & \\ \ \mathsf{size}(n_1) \,\%\, \mathsf{size}(n_2) = 0) & \\ n_1 = n_2 \implies o = 0 & \text{otherwise} \end{cases}$$

We can adapt the definition of a simulation relation to a relation between a concrete and abstract graph. For that, we only need to extend $\mathsf{isCollapsed}(n)$ and $\mathsf{isSeq}(n)$ to return *false* for any concrete object n, and let $\mathsf{size}(n)$ denote the allocated size of n[3]. Given a concrete graph $g_c \in \mathcal{G}_\mathbb{C}$ and an abstract graph $g_a \in \mathcal{G}_\mathbb{A}$, we use the notation $g_c \preceq g_a$ to say that there is a simulation relation between g_c and g_a.

Concretization and Ordering of Abstract Graphs. The meaning of an abstract graph is given by the function $\gamma : \mathcal{G}_\mathbb{A} \mapsto 2^{\mathcal{G}_\mathbb{C}}$ and it is defined as $\gamma(g_a) =$

[3] For simplicity, we choose not to modify the definition of a concrete object to include its size.

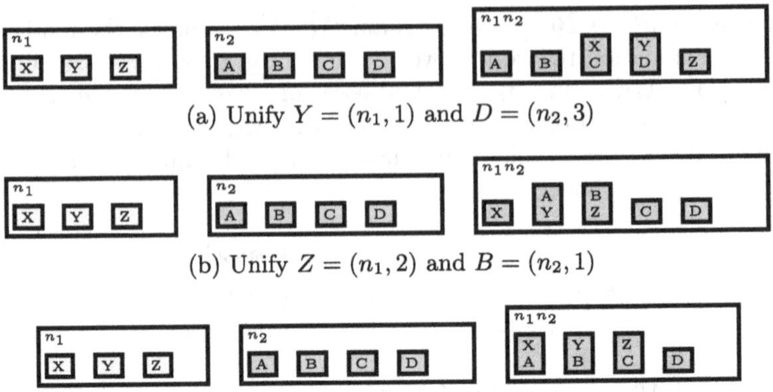

(a) Unify $Y = (n_1, 1)$ and $D = (n_2, 3)$

(b) Unify $Z = (n_1, 2)$ and $B = (n_2, 1)$

(c) Unify $Y = (n_1, 1)$ and $B = (n_2, 1)$

Fig. 5. Unification examples with all fields of size one.

$\{g_c \in \mathcal{G}_\mathbb{C} \mid g_c \preceq g_a\}$. Moreover, a simulation relation defines an ordering between abstract graphs such that $g \sqsubseteq_{\mathcal{G}_\mathbb{A}} g'$ if and only if there exists a simulation relation between g and g'.

Remark. The concept of a simulation relation between abstract graphs also plays an essential role for the analysis of procedures (see Sect. 4).

Example 3 (Simulation relation between a concrete and abstract graph). Coming back to Fig. 4, let the environments $\{p \mapsto (O_a, 0)\}$ and $\{p \mapsto (N_a, 0)\}$ together with the cells and edges shown in Fig. 4 (center) and (right), form the concrete g_C and abstract g_A graphs, respectively. There is a simulation relation ρ between g_C and g_A, defined as follows:

$$
\begin{aligned}
\rho = \{\ & ((O_a, 0), (N_a, 0)),\\
& ((O_{l_0^0}, 0), (N_l, 0)), \ldots, ((O_{l_0^3}, 0), (N_l, 0)),\\
& ((O_{l_1^0}, 0), (N_l, 0)), \ldots, ((O_{l_1^3}, 0), (N_l, 0)),\\
& ((O^0_{null}, 0), (N_l, 0)), \ldots, ((O^3_{null}, 0), (N_l, 0))\ \}
\end{aligned}
$$

To show that ρ is a simulation relation, it suffices to show that $((O_a, 0), (N_a, 0)) \in \rho$. Since $o_1 = 0$ and $o_2 = 0$ the "else" branch is triggered. The first conjunct holds trivially. Then, we need to check whether *compatible*$(O_a, N_a, 0)$ holds. Since O_a is a concrete object, we have that $\mathsf{isSeq}(O_a) = false$, but $\mathsf{isSeq}(N_a) = true$. Thus, the forth "if" in the definition of *compatible* is applicable. Since $\mathsf{size}(O_a) = 16$ and $\mathsf{size}(N_a) = 4$ the condition holds. Next, we check that ρ includes the pairs of cells $(E((n_1, 0)), E((n_2, 0 \oplus_{n_2} 0)))$,..., $(E((n_1, 12)), E((n_2, 12 \oplus_{n_2} 0)))$, which, after substitution, become $((O_{l_0^0}, 0), (N_l, 0))$,..., $((O_{l_0^3}, 0), (N_l, 0))$. We only show that $((O_{l_0^0}, 0), (N_l, 0)) \in \rho$ since the other pairs are identical. Again, the "else" branch is triggered together with the forth "if" from the *compatible* definition but with $\mathsf{isSeq}(O_{l_0^0}) = false$, $\mathsf{size}(O_{l_0^0}) = 8$, $\mathsf{isSeq}(N_l) = true$, and $\mathsf{size}(N_l) = 8$. Thus, the conditions hold. Finally, we need to check that $E((O_{l_0^0}, 0)) \equiv (O_{l_1^0}, 0)$ is simulated by $E((N_l, 0)) \equiv (N_l, 0)$. Hence, we can conclude that g_C is a concretization of g_A. ■

Another key concept in our memory model is an operation unifyCells that given two cells (n_1, o_1) and (n_2, o_2) creates a new cell (and possibly a new object) (n_3, o_3) that abstracts them both (i.e., (n_3, o_3) simulates both (n_1, o_1) and (n_2, o_2)). Conceptually, the operation replaces the objects n_1 and n_2 by a new object that is an abstraction of both of them. In practice, this is done by destructively updating the objects in the points-to graph. The pseudo-code for unifyCells is given in Fig. 6. We use unifyCells to combine cells in the graph and to combine points-to graphs as needed by the abstract semantics.

The idea is to *embed* one cell into another, possibly modifying them and all their reachable cells in the graph. If this is not possible then the cells are collapsed and field-sensitivity is lost. Given two cells $c_1 = (n_1, o_1)$ and $c_2 = (n_2, o_2)$ let us assume that $o_1 < o_2$ as shown in Fig. 5(a). The solution is to embed object n_1 in n_2 such that the memory location referred to by (n_2, o_2) is the same as that referred to by (n_1, o_1). This is achieved by adjusting $(n_1, 0)$ to $(n_2, o_2 - o_1)$. Then, each (n_1, o_i) can be mapped to $(n_2, o_2 - o_1 + o_i)$. In particular, (n_1, o_1) becomes (n_2, o_2). The case where $o_2 < o_1$ is symmetric (Fig. 5(b)), otherwise, if $o_1 = o_2$ the we can choose arbitrarily to embed one into the other (Fig. 5(c)). unifyCells at lines 1–6 decides which cell is embedded into and the offset adjustments.

unifyNodes unifies in place all cells of n_1 starting at offset 0 with all cells of n_2 starting at offset o. If possible it will redirect all the incoming edges of n_1 to n_2 by shifting them by o and unify recursively all the outgoing edges (see redirectEdges). After that, it destroys n_1 (and all its cells) and keeps n_2. The pseudo-code is more involved because it also checks for conditions where the objects must be collapsed:

1. If n_1 is collapsed but n_2 is not (Line 8): we need to collapse n_2 and redirect edges.
2. If n_1 is a sequence but n_2 is not (Line 11): check if we can embed the non-sequence n_2 into the sequence object n_1, which is handled by the next case.
3. If n_1 is a non-sequence and n_2 is a sequence (Line 16): try to modify n_1 into a sequence object and continue with the unification. We will explain this case through an example. Assume the size of n_2 is 4, meaning that it represents a memory region of size $4 \times C$ for some constant C. If the size of n_1 is divisible by 4, then we can convert n_1 into a sequence. If the size of n_1 is smaller than 4, we can embed it into n_2 by redirecting all the edges. If neither of the two conditions hold, we collapse n_1 and n_2.
4. if n_1 and n_2 are both sequences (Line 22): try to embed the larger one into the smaller one. We might collapse if the sizes of the sequences are not compatible or if we try to unify at non-zero offsets.

Assume a functional version of unifyCells denoted as unifyCells^{F} that copies the input graph into g', perform unifyCells on g', and returns g'. The correctness of our approach follows from the following result.

```
unifyCells((n1, o1), (n2, o2), g)
  if (o1 < o2)
      unifyNodes (n1, n2, o2 − o1, g)
  elif (o2 < o1)
      unifyNodes (n2, n1, o1 − o2, g)
  else
      unifyNodes (n1, n2, 0, g)

% Embed in-place object n1 into object n2
% at offset o
unifyNodes(n1, n2, o, g)
  o' = o ⊕_n2 0
  if (isCollapsed(n1) ∧ ¬ isCollapsed(n2))
      return collapse(n1, n2, o', g)
  elif ¬ isCollapsed(n1) ∧ ¬ isCollapsed(n2)
      if (isSeq(n1) ∧ ¬ isSeq(n2))
         if (o' = 0)
            return unifyNodes(n2, n1, 0, g)
         else
            return collapse(n1, n2, o', g)
      elif (¬ isSeq(n1) ∧ isSeq(n2))
         if (size(n1) % size(n2) = 0)
            isSeq(n1) = true
            return unifyNodes(n1, n2, o, g)
         elif (size(n1) + o' > size(n2))
            return collapse(n1, n2, o', g)
      elif (isSeq(n1) ∧ isSeq(n2))
         if (size(n1) < size(n2))
            return unifyNodes(n2, n1, 0, g)
         elif ((size(n2) % size(n1) ≠ 0) ∨
               (o ⊕_n1 0 > 0))
            return collapse(n1, n2, o', g)
  if (n1 = n2 ∧ o' > 0) collapseNode(n2, g)
  redirectEdges(n1, n2, o', g)

% Move all edges from/to n1's cells
% to n2 and destroy n1
redirectEdges(n1, n2, o, ⟨V♯, E♯, σ♯⟩)
  foreach c1 → (n1, i) ∈ E♯
      E♯(c1) = (n2, o ⊕_n2 i)
      foreach p ∈ dom(σ♯)∧
                σ♯(p) = (n1, i)
         σ♯[p ↦ (n2, o ⊕_n2 i)]
  foreach (n1, i) → c ∈ E♯
      if (n2, o ⊕_n2 i) → c' ∈ E♯
         unifyCells(c, c', ⟨V♯, E♯, σ♯⟩)
      else
         E♯((n2, o ⊕_n2 i)) = c
  V♯ = V♯ \ {n1}
  E♯ = E♯ \ {e ∈ E♯ | e and n1
             are incident}

% n loses all its field-sensitivity
collapseNode(n, ⟨V♯, E♯, σ♯⟩)
  c = (mkNode(), 0)
  foreach o ∈ Links(n, E♯)
      unifyCells(c, (n, o), ⟨V♯, E♯, σ♯⟩)
      E♯ = E♯ \ {(n, o) → _}
  size(n) = 1
  isCollapsed(n) = true
  E♯((n, 0)) = c

% Collapse n2 and redirect n1 to n2
collapse(n1, n2, o, g)
  collapseNode(n2, g)
  redirectEdges(n1, n2, o, g)
```

Fig. 6. Unification of two cells

Lemma 1. *For all abstract graphs* $g \equiv \langle V^\sharp, E^\sharp, \sigma^\sharp \rangle \in \mathcal{G}_{\mathbb{A}}$ *and for all* $c, c' \in V^\sharp$. *Let* g' *be the result of* $\mathsf{unifyCells}^{\mathsf{F}}(c, c', g)$. *Then, there always exists a simulation relation between* g *and* g'.

Proof. By structural induction over unifyCells and unifyNodes functions.

This lemma says that the result of unifying two cells produces always a new abstract graph whose concretization is always a superset of the concretization of the graphs before the unification took place. Moreover, note that once our analysis decides to merge two cells they can never be split again. This is also true during the analysis of function calls.

```
⟦S⟧𝔸(⟨V♯, E♯, σ♯⟩)
49: switch (S)
50:   l : p = &x:
51:     n = mkNode(x)
52:     unify(p, (n, 0), ⟨V♯, E♯, σ♯⟩)
53:     return ⟨V♯ ∪ {n}, E♯, σ♯⟩
54:   l : p = malloc(...):
55:     n = mkNode(l)
56:     unify(p, (n, 0), ⟨V♯, E♯, σ♯⟩)
57:     return ⟨V♯ ∪ {n}, E♯, σ♯⟩
58:   l : p = q + (c × m) + d:
59:     (n, o) = σ♯(q)
60:     if (isCollapsed(n))
61:       collapsePointer(p, ⟨V♯, E♯, σ♯⟩)
62:     elif (c = 0 ∧ ¬ isSeq(n))
63:       sz_field = sizeof(typeof(n, o + d))
64:       sz = o + d + sz_field
65:       updateSize(n, sz, ⟨V♯, E♯, σ♯⟩)
66:       unify(p, (n, o + d), ⟨V♯, E♯, σ♯⟩)
67:     else
68:       isSeq(n) = true
69:       sz_gcd = gcd(size(n), c)
70:       updateSize(n, sz_gcd, ⟨V♯, E♯, σ♯⟩)
71:       unify(p, (n, o), ⟨V♯, E♯, σ♯⟩)
72:     break
73:   l : q = *p:
74:   l : *p = q:
75:     unifyCells(E♯(σ♯(p)), σ♯(q), ⟨V♯, E♯, σ♯⟩)
76:   default:
77: return ⟨V♯, E♯, σ♯⟩

unify(p, c, ⟨V♯, E♯, σ♯⟩)
78: if p ∉ dom(σ♯)
79:   σ♯[p ↦ c]
80: else
81:   unifyCells(σ♯(p), c, ⟨V♯, E♯, σ♯⟩)

collapsePointer(p, g)
82: n = mkNode()
83: collapseNode(n, g)
84: unify(p, (n, 0), g)

updateSize(n, sz, g)
85: if (isSeq(n) ∧ size(n) ≠ sz)
86:   collapseNode(n, g)
87: elif (¬isSeq(n) ∧ sz > size(n))
88:   size(n) = sz
```

Fig. 7. Abstract semantics of the atomic pointer operations.

We can now define the abstract semantics for our core pointer language in Fig. 7 by means of the function $[\![\cdot]\!]_{\mathbb{A}} : \mathbb{S} \mapsto (\mathbb{A} \mapsto \mathbb{A})$. We only show the abstract semantics of the atomic pointer operations and postpone the analysis of function calls to the next section.

The analysis creates a new object the first time a taken-address variable (line 50) is accessed or when a new allocation occurs (line 54). In this case, a fresh cell consisting of the new object and a zero-offset is unified with the cell of the left-hand side (if any). The analysis of a memory load (line 73) or store (line 74) is done in the same way: the dereference of a pointer p requires us to find the target cell of the edge whose source is the cell of p and unify it with the cell of the non-dereferenced pointer (line 75). The analysis of pointer casts and pointer arithmetic at line 58 is more involved and consists of three main cases:

1. *(collapse)* if the object of the base pointer q is already collapsed then the object of the left-hand side is also collapsed;

2. *(pointer casts, address of a struct field or a constant array index)* if the object of q is not a sequence and its offset can be statically determined (i.e., the statement can be simplified to $p = q + d$) then the cell of p is unified to the cell $(n, o + d)$ where (n, o) is the cell of q. Moreover, the size of n might grow if the accessed offset $o + d$ plus the size of the indexed field is greater than its current size.
3. *(address of a symbolic array index)* the cell of q is unified with the cell of p after marking the object of q as a sequence. Again, we might need to update the size of the object of q. Since the object is a sequence, the new size is the *greatest common divisor (gcd)* of the old size and c.

Finally, we lift $[\![S]\!]_{\mathbb{A}}(g)$ to a function F, denoted by $[\![F]\!]_{\mathbb{A}}(g)$, as the application of $[\![S]\!]_{\mathbb{A}}$ to each statement S in F starting from the abstract graph g.

Example 4 (Comparing with DSA). Consider the program in Fig. 4. The DSA algorithm described in [15] is array-insensitive. DSA creates an object N_a after the stack allocation `11 * a[4]` and since the allocation size is statically known it decides that the size of N_a is 16 (assuming 4 bytes per pointer). Then, during the analysis of `a[i] = mkList(...)` it notices that there is a symbolic access to object N_a at some unknown offset. Although it knows that the size of the accessed element is 4, it loses all field-sensitivity since $4 \neq 16$.

After the array allocation our analysis creates a cell $(N_a, 0)$ where $\mathsf{isSeq}(N_a) = \mathsf{isCollapsed}(N_a) = \mathit{false}$ and $\mathsf{size}(N_a) = 16$. Next, the analysis `a[i] = mkList(...)` requires us to compute the address p_a of the array index which is translated to $p_a = a + (4 \times i) + 0$. Since the size of the array index is $c = 4 \neq 0$, the else branch at line 67 in Fig. 7 is applicable. As a result, $\mathsf{isSeq}(N_a) = \mathit{true}$ and $\mathsf{size}(N_a) = \mathsf{gcd}(16, 4) = 4$. Thus, our analysis first assigns a fixed size to N_a after its allocation (similar to DSA) but then it decides by its use that N_a is a non-empty sequence of bytes whose size is divisible by 4.

The same result would be obtained if the loop was unrolled. However, if the size of the array was not known then DSA would not have collapsed the abstract object. However, the pattern exemplified by our snippet of having a small array simulating a struct is actually common in our C++ case study and there the impact of collapsing is much worse since this kind of arrays are embedded in complex C++ objects. ■

4 A Context-Sensitive Abstract Memory Model

In this section, we describe how we extend the intra-procedural pointer analysis described in Sect. 3 to support more precisely function calls so that it can be leveraged to produce a side-effect free form useful for verification.

We do not define the syntax and concrete semantics of function calls as they are standard. We fix some notation and define some helper functions needed by our analysis. For a given function call (or *callsite*) cs we refer to f_{callee} and f_{caller} as the callee function and the function where cs is executed, respectively. We assume functions $\mathsf{callee}(cs)$ and $\mathsf{caller}(cs)$ that return f_{callee} and f_{caller},

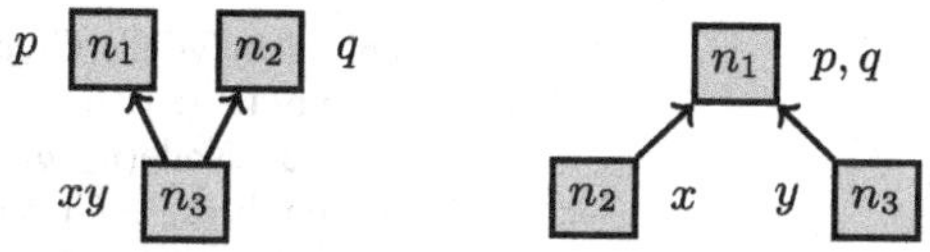

Fig. 8. Problematic aliasing patterns when `f(p,q)` calls to `f(x,y)`

respectively. We also assume functions formals(cs) and actuals(cs) that return the formal parameters of f_{callee} and the actual parameters of the call, respectively.

Our algorithm works in three phases. We start by describing the first two phases of the algorithm which are more straightforward and postpone the third one to the end of the section. The procedure cloneSummaries on the bottom left in Fig. 9 describes the first and second phase of our inter-procedural algorithm. First, each function f is analyzed in isolation while its abstract graph (a.k.a *function summary*) is computed. This phase is the only one that analyzes f's statements. If there is a recursive call then all the functions in the same *Strongly Connected Component (SCC)* will be analyzed in an intra-procedural manner. This has not been a problem in practice since our benchmarks have few recursive functions (e.g., our C++ case study has no recursive calls). Second, the *call graph* is traversed in reverse topological order exploring all callees before their callers. At each callsite the callee's graph is *cloned* into the caller's abstract graph while the objects of the formal and actual parameters are unified. This is done by the procedure cloneAndUnifyCells.

Therefore, *heap cloning* is how our analysis achieves context-sensitivity while being fully modular. Coming back to Fig. 1(a). Although `p` and `q` are aliased, they are disjoint from `r` and `s`. Thus, our analysis can distinguish each call to `f` without merging the cells of the first call to `f` (`p` and `q`) with the cells of the second call (`r` and `s`).

After completion of cloneSummaries, each cell pointed by the callee's formal parameters can be aliased with at most one cell from the caller's actual parameters and thus, scenarios such as the one illustrated on the left in Fig. 8 are not possible[4]. The pattern on the right is still possible: a cell in the caller can be the target of two different cells in the callee (i.e., **CC** does not hold). The example in Fig. 1(b) illustrated how this situation precludes pointer analyses to be used for obtaining sound side-effect-free programs.

The main purpose of the third phase of our algorithm is to ensure that the two patterns depicted in Fig. 8 are not possible. This phase is done by the **while** loop in procedure CSAnalysis on the left in Fig. 9.

At this point, the analysis has cloned all summaries by calling the procedure cloneSummaries (line 1). As a result, each cell originated from the callee's formal parameters cannot be mapped to two distinct cells in the caller graph. The reason is that cloneSummaries calls unifyCells for each pair of formal-actual parameters. On the left in Fig. 8, the cell $(n_3, 0)$ is unified with $(n_1, 0)$ from the pair (x, p).

[4] For simplicity, we assume in Fig. 8 all cells have zero offsets.

```
CSAnalysis(cg)
1:  cloneSummaries(cg)
2:  W = {cs | cs ∈ cg}
3:  while W ≠ ∅
4:      W = W \ {cs}
5:      g ≡ ⟨_, _, σ♯_callee⟩ = G[callee(cs)]
6:      g′ ≡ ⟨_, _, σ♯_caller⟩ = G[caller(cs)]
7:      C = {σ♯_callee(p) | p ∈ formals(cs)}
8:      C′ = {σ♯_caller(p) | p ∈ actuals(cs)}
9:      if (propagate(formals(cs), g, g′) =↓)
10:         cloneAndUnifyCells(C′, g′, C, g)
11:         W∪= uses(callee(cs))∪
                defs(callee(cs))
12:     elif (propagate(formals(cs), g, g′) =↑)
13:         cloneAndUnifyCells(C, g, C′, g′)
14:         W∪= uses(caller(cs))∪
                defs(caller(cs))

cloneSummaries(cg)
15: foreach scc in reverse topological
        order of cg
16:     g_scc = ⟨∅, ∅, []⟩
17:     foreach (f ∈ scc)  [[f]]_A(g_scc)
18:     foreach (f ∈ scc)  G[f] = g_scc
19:     foreach callsite cs ∈ scc
20:         ⟨V♯_1, E♯_1, σ♯_1⟩ = G[callee(cs)]
21:         ⟨V♯_2, E♯_2, σ♯_2⟩ = G[caller(cs)]
22:         C_1 = {σ♯_1(p) | p ∈ formals(cs)}
23:         C_2 = {σ♯_2(p) | p ∈ actuals(cs)}
24:         cloneAndUnifyCells(C_1, ⟨V♯_1, E♯_1, σ♯_1⟩,
                               C_2, ⟨V♯_2, E♯_2, σ♯_2⟩)

cloneAndUnifyCells(C_1, g_1, C_2, g_2)
25: foreach ((n_1, o_1) ∈ C_1)
26:     cloneNode(n_1, g_1, g_2)
27: foreach (c_1 ∈ C_1 ∧ c_2 ∈ C_2)
28:     unifyCells(c_1, c_2, g_2)

% Clone object n into graph tg
cloneNode(n, ⟨V♯, E♯, σ♯⟩, ⟨V♯_tg, E♯_tg, σ♯_tg⟩)
29: if (n ∈ V♯_tg) return
30: V♯_tg = V♯_tg ∪ {n}
31: foreach (p ∈ dom(σ♯) ∧ σ♯(p) = (n, o))
32:     σ♯_tg[p ↦ (n, o)]
33: foreach ((n, o) → (n′, o′)) ∈ E♯
34:     cloneNode(n′, ⟨V♯, E♯, σ♯⟩,
                  ⟨V♯_tg, E♯_tg, σ♯_tg⟩)
35:     E♯_tg(n, o) = (n′, o′)

propagate(roots, g, g′)
36: Let R be a simulation relation between
      g and g′ projected onto roots
37: if R is an injective function
38:     return none
39: elif R is a function
40:     return ↓
41: else
42:     return ↑
```

Fig. 9. Our Context-Sensitive Pointer Analysis for Verification. cg is the program call graph and G is a global variable that maps functions to abstract graphs.

Then, the cell $(n_3, 0)$ is unified with $(n_2, 0)$ from the other pair (y, q). After these unifications, x, y, p, q point to the same cell.

Next, we scan all the function calls in the program and build a simulation relation $\mathcal{R}$ between the f_{callee}'s graph and f_{caller}'s graph but only considering cells[5] that are reachable from f_{callee}'s actual parameters. A key insight is that we can use $\mathcal{R}$ to find out whether two distinct cells in the callee can be mapped to the same cell in the caller ($\mathcal{R}$ is not an injective function). This is the case depicted on the right in Fig. 8. If this is not possible (i.e., $\mathcal{R}$ is an injective function) then we are done with this callsite. Otherwise, we require a *top-down propagation* by unifying cells from f_{caller}'s actual parameters with the ones from f_{callee}'s formals parameters (line 9). For instance, in Fig. 1(a) the call `f(p,q)` forces our

[5] In fact, we only need to consider cells that can be modified. Our implementation considers this optimization.

analysis to unify the cells of x and y with the cell of p and q resulting in a single array variable A_{xy} in the translation in Fig. 1(d). After a top-down propagation occurs, it is possible that a cell in the callee is now mapped to more than one cell in the caller. The simulation relation between callee and caller is then not a function anymore. This can be fixed by performing a *bottom-up propagation* that unifies the cells of f_{callee}'s formal parameters and f_{caller}'s actual parameters (line 12). Either way, after unification occurs during the analysis of a callsite, we must update our worklist by adding other callsites that might be affected. If a top-down (bottom-up) propagation was performed then we need to revisit all the function calls where f_{callee} (f_{caller}) is the callee (uses) and all callsites defined in f_{callee} (f_{caller}) denoted by defs.

Finally, it is worth mentioning that this propagation phase does not affect the modularity of our analysis since only cells from summary graphs and those involved at the callsites are considered. Each function is still analyzed only once by the cloneSummaries procedure.

Correctness and Termination. Upon completion for every callsite the simulation relation between the callee and caller graph is an injective function. This condition suffices to ensure that no two cells in a function can be equal for any call. Termination is straightforward since in the worst case the algorithm will merge all the cells between callee's formal parameters and caller's actual parameters. Since the number of cells is finite, this process must terminate.

Limitations. We assume that programs are *complete* and thus, every callee function is known (or *resolved*) at compile time. Although resolving callsites is non-trivial, we consider it an orthogonal problem. We can apply the solution adopted by DSA [15] based on a top-down traversal of the call graph after the bottom-up one. A less precise but simpler solution is to replace each unresolved call by a non-deterministic call to one of the possible functions whose type signature match. For our experiments, the latter solution was precise enough.

5 Experimental Evaluation

We have implemented our pointer analysis[6] with full support for LLVM bitcode and integrated it in SeaHorn [2]. For comparison, we have also integrated in SeaHorn the public implementation of DSA [1]. We use the context-insensitive version of DSA since we cannot use its context-sensitivity without being unsound. Note that the precision of SeaHorn (i.e., number of false positives) does not depend on the underlying pointer analysis. However, its scalability will be greatly affected as our results show. All experiments were carried out on a 3.5 GHz Intel Xeon processor with 16 cores and 64 GB on a Linux machine.

Results on C SV-COMP Benchmarks. We ran SeaHorn on all 2,326 programs from the SV-COMP'17 sub-category DeviceDrivers64[7]. This collection of

[6] The pointer analysis is available from https://github.com/seahorn/sea-dsa.

[7] Accessed https://github.com/sosy-lab/sv-benchmarks with sha `879e141f11348e49591738d3e11793b36546a2d5`.

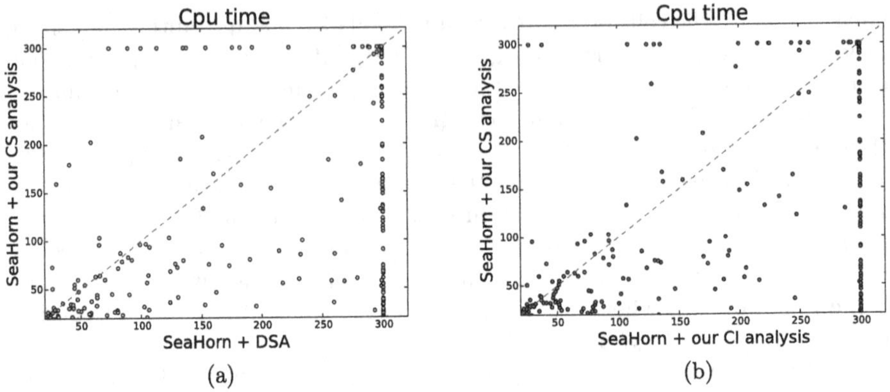

Fig. 10. CPU time spent by SEAHORN on DeviceDrivers64: (a) comparing DSA (SEAHORN + DSA) and our analysis (SEAHORN + our CS analysis), and (b) comparing our analysis without (CI) context-sensitivity with (CS) context-sensitivity.

programs corresponds to Linux device drivers and its verification requires low-level modeling of pointers.

Figure 10(a) compares the impact of using DSA (x-axis) and our analysis (y-axis) on the CPU time spent by SEAHORN with a timeout of 5 min and 4 GB memory limit. The scattered plot shows that in the majority of the cases, our analysis speeds up verification. Moreover, using our analysis SEAHORN was able to prove 81 more programs. Nevertheless, the plot indicates that our analysis is not always more beneficial than DSA. We investigated whether this occasional negative impact was due to timeouts in our pointer analysis. We compared the analysis time of DSA and our pointer analysis and differences were negligible. Both analyses were able to analyze each program in less than two seconds. Another possible explanation is in the use of SPACER [13] as back end in SEAHORN. SPACER is an SMT-based model checker and, thus, regardless of the memory model it always depends on the unpredictable nature of SMT solvers. We suspect that having more array variables (produced by our analysis) may have a negative impact if they are irrelevant to the property.

Since DSA and our analysis are different implementations, we also compare our analysis with and without context-sensitivity. Figure 10(b) shows the results of this comparison. We observe again that context-sensitivity often boosts SEAHORN during the verification process. Moreover, this comparison suggests our implementation is robust since the results are consistent with the previous experiment.

Case Study: Checking Buffer Overflow in C++ CASS Code. We have evaluated our analysis to verify absence of buffer overflows on the flight control system of the Core Autonomous Safety Software (CASS) of an Autonomous

Table 1. Preliminary results on proving absence of buffer overflows in CASS.

	Nodes	Collapsed	Max Node Density	Safe Alloc. Sites	Time (s)
SEAHORN + DSA	258	49%	0.8	49	33,119
SEAHORN + our CS	12,789	4%	0.13	73	31,102

Flight Safety System. CASS[8] is written in C++ using standard C++ 2011 and following MISRA C++ 2008. It follows an object-oriented style and makes heavy use of dynamic arrays and singly-linked lists. CASS uses two custom libraries: one to manipulate strings and another for using associative containers (`map`). We did not consider these two libraries for our evaluation.

Instead of proving that all memory accesses are in-bounds by running SEAHORN once on an instrumented program[9] with all the properties, we split the set of accesses into multiple subsets so that we can run in parallel multiple instances of SEAHORN on a smaller number of memory accesses. We first identify all heap and stack allocation sites in the program. Each allocation site is a unique identifier of each LLVM instruction that allocates memory (e.g., `alloca`, `malloc`, etc.). Let k be the (finite) number of allocation sites. We run k instances of SEAHORN on an instrumented program that only checks for memory accesses from regions that are allocated by the allocation site of interest. This information is provided conservatively by the pointer analysis. The purpose of this methodology is twofold: (1) we can exploit parallelism, and (2) more importantly, we group memory accesses by allocation sites hoping that they can share the same proof.

Table 1 shows the results of running SEAHORN on CASS. Column Nodes is the number of nodes in the graph. If the pointer analysis is context-insensitive there is only one graph, otherwise it is the sum of all graphs. The larger is the number of nodes the finer is the partitioning induced by the pointer analysis. Column Collapsed is the percentage of the nodes for which the analysis lost all the field-sensitivity. We define *density* of a node n as the number of memory accesses from pointers that point to n divided by the total number of accesses. Column Max Node Density is the maximum density value: the smaller, the better. Column Safe Alloc. Sites is the number of allocation sites proven safe by SEAHORN. An allocation site is considered proven if all its memory accesses are proven safe. Finally, Time is the accumulated time in seconds of proving all allocation sites. We set a timeout of 100 s per allocation site and 4 GB memory

[8] CASS is owned NASA and is not publicly available. It is 13,460 LOC (excluding blanks/comments).

[9] How to instrument effectively a program for proving memory safety is beyond the scope of this paper. SeaHorn provides several LLVM bitcode transformations that insert assertions such that the transformed bitcode is free of buffer overflows if all assertions hold. For our experiments, we used one that stores non-deterministically the offset and size of a pointer. This instrumentation is simple and relies on the solver to resolve the non-determinism to make sure all pointers are properly checked.

limit. The total number of allocation sites is 357 and the number of memory accesses is 3,946.

The results show that context-sensitivity is extremely important for precise memory analysis of C++ programs. In particular, the number of collapsed nodes for which field sensitivity is lost has decreased significantly. The results also show a positive impact on verification, both in number of memory accesses proven safe and on the time. Yet, there is still a significant number of memory access that remains unproved within our time limit.

6 Related Work

Rakamaric et al. [19] and Wang et al. [21] present memory models that resemble ours. These models used in SMACK and CASCADE, respectively, are based on a static partitioning of memory using an unification-based pointer analysis. [19] rely on DSA and propose a variant of the Burstall model [5] by combining unification with a static analysis that can infer types conservatively. [21] propose a cell-based model similar to [19] but unification and type inference are performed simultaneously producing finer-grained partitions. Both [19] and [21] identify arrays based on their allocations rather than their uses as our model does. Therefore, at the function level these models and ours are incomparable. More importantly, both [19] and [21] are context-insensitive. CBMC [7] and ESBMC [10] similarly split memory into a finite set of regions using a pointer analysis. However, the model is field- and context-insensitive and it does not support symbolic array accesses.

HAVOC [6,9] uses a byte-level memory model augmented with another map that assigns types to memory offsets. This memory model is more precise than ours but much less efficient. VCC [8] is based on a typed object memory model that is sound and complete for type-unsafe C programs. However, the model introduces *quantified* axioms that can be challenging for the verifier. FRAMA-C[10] provides the JESSIE plugin[11] that translates C programs into verification conditions using a weakest precondition calculus. JESSIE is based on a *"byte-level block"* memory model [17] which can be seen as a hybrid between the byte-level model and ours by replacing the pair (id, o) with (a, o) where a is an address. This model relies on a pointer analysis to partition memory and it is context-sensitive, but it requires to add extra axioms to ensure that the analysis of function calls is sound. Unlike VCC and JESSIE models our model does not add any extra axioms. Ours is at much higher level of abstraction than these models. Abstract graph objects become logical arrays only during the generation of verification conditions and it is the underlying solver the one that will introduce select/store axioms as needed during the solving of those verification conditions.

[10] https://frama-c.com/.

[11] FRAMA-C provides another plugin called VC for C programs, complementary to JESSIE, with three different memory models: Hoare (unsound with pointers), Typed based on Burstall's model that does not support casts, and Byte which is a byte-level memory model.

Venet [20] proposes a model by combining Andersen's pointer analysis [3] with a numerical abstraction of offsets. This model supports dynamic memory allocation by mapping allocations to *timestamps*. Miné [16] presents a precise cell-based memory model (limited to programs without dynamic allocation) which represents pointers flow-sensitively as well as precise numerical relationships between offsets. This model can also reason about memory *contents*. Although more precise than ours, these two models rely on expensive numerical abstractions. Moreover, their designs fulfill a different purpose. Our goal is to produce a static memory partitioning from which we can generate verification conditions that can be solved efficiently. Instead, they produce an accurate modeling of memory from which they can prove directly properties without external solvers. More recently, Balatsouras and Smaragdakis [4] propose a new structure-sensitive pointer analysis for C/C++ programs based on LLVM. Similar to ours, this analysis can be used to perform static memory partitioning. However, the analysis is context-insensitive and its field and array-sensitivity is limited to constant pointer offsets.

7 Conclusion

The paper presents a new context-sensitive memory model for verification of C/C++. This model relies on a *field-*, *array-*, and *context-sensitive* pointer analysis tailored for generating verification conditions. The notion of *simulation relation* between points-to graphs plays a major role during the analysis of function calls. Our results suggest that our memory model can often produce a finer-grained partition of memory for programs with procedures and that this results in faster verification times.

References

1. Data Structure Analysis (DSA) implementation. https://github.com/seahorn/llvm-dsa
2. SeaHorn Verification Framework. http://seahorn.github.io/
3. Andersen, L.O.: Program analysis and specialization for the C Programming language. Technical report (1994)
4. Balatsouras, G., Smaragdakis, Y.: Structure-sensitive points-to analysis for C and C++. In: Rival, X. (ed.) SAS 2016. LNCS, vol. 9837, pp. 84–104. Springer, Heidelberg (2016). doi:10.1007/978-3-662-53413-7_5
5. Burstall, R.M.: Some techniques for proving correctness of programs which alter data structures. In: Machine Intelligence (1972)
6. Chatterjee, S., Lahiri, S.K., Qadeer, S., Rakamarić, Z.: A reachability predicate for analyzing low-level software. In: Grumberg, O., Huth, M. (eds.) TACAS 2007. LNCS, vol. 4424, pp. 19–33. Springer, Heidelberg (2007). doi:10.1007/978-3-540-71209-1_4
7. Clarke, E., Kroening, D., Lerda, F.: A tool for checking ANSI-C Programs. In: Jensen, K., Podelski, A. (eds.) TACAS 2004. LNCS, vol. 2988, pp. 168–176. Springer, Heidelberg (2004). doi:10.1007/978-3-540-24730-2_15

8. Cohen, E., Moskal, M., Tobies, S., Schulte, W.: A precise yet efficient memory model for C. Electr. Notes Theor. Comput. Sci. **254**, 85–103 (2009)
9. Condit, J., Hackett, B., Lahiri, S.K., Qadeer, S.: Unifying type checking and property checking for low-level code. In: POPL, pp. 302–314 (2009)
10. Cordeiro, L., Fischer, B., Marques-Silva, J.: SMT-based bounded model checking for embedded ANSI-C software. IEEE Trans. Softw. Eng. **38**(4), 957–974 (2012)
11. Gurfinkel, A., Kahsai, T., Komuravelli, A., Navas, J.A.: The SeaHorn verification framework. In: Kroening, D., Păsăreanu, C.S. (eds.) CAV 2015. LNCS, vol. 9206, pp. 343–361. Springer, Cham (2015). doi:10.1007/978-3-319-21690-4_20
12. Hubert, T., Marche, C.: Separation analysis for deductive verification. In: HAV (2007)
13. Komuravelli, A., Gurfinkel, A., Chaki, S., Clarke, E.M.: Automatic abstraction in SMT-based unbounded software model checking. In: Sharygina, N., Veith, H. (eds.) CAV 2013. LNCS, vol. 8044, pp. 846–862. Springer, Heidelberg (2013). doi:10.1007/978-3-642-39799-8_59
14. Lattner, C., Adve, V.S.: LLVM: a compilation framework for lifelong program analysis & transformation. In: CGO, pp. 75–88 (2004)
15. Lattner, C., Adve, V.S.: Automatic pool allocation: improving performance by controlling data structure layout in the heap. In: PLDI, pp. 129–142 (2005)
16. Miné, A.: Field-sensitive value analysis of embedded C programs with union types and pointer arithmetics. In: LCTES, pp. 54–63 (2006)
17. Moy, Y.: Automatic modular static safety checking for C Programs. Ph.D. thesis, Université Paris-Sud (2009)
18. Rakamarić, Z., Emmi, M.: SMACK: decoupling source language details from verifier implementations. In: Biere, A., Bloem, R. (eds.) CAV 2014. LNCS, vol. 8559, pp. 106–113. Springer, Cham (2014). doi:10.1007/978-3-319-08867-9_7
19. Rakamarić, Z., Hu, A.J.: A scalable memory model for low-level code. In: Jones, N.D., Müller-Olm, M. (eds.) VMCAI 2009. LNCS, vol. 5403, pp. 290–304. Springer, Heidelberg (2008). doi:10.1007/978-3-540-93900-9_24
20. Venet, A.: A scalable nonuniform pointer analysis for embedded programs. In: Giacobazzi, R. (ed.) SAS 2004. LNCS, vol. 3148, pp. 149–164. Springer, Heidelberg (2004). doi:10.1007/978-3-540-27864-1_13
21. Wang, W., Barrett, C., Wies, T.: Partitioned memory models for program analysis. In: Bouajjani, A., Monniaux, D. (eds.) VMCAI 2017. LNCS, vol. 10145, pp. 539–558. Springer, Cham (2017). doi:10.1007/978-3-319-52234-0_29
22. Wang, W., Barrett, C., Wies, T.: Cascade 2.0. In: McMillan, K.L., Rival, X. (eds.) VMCAI 2014. LNCS, vol. 8318, pp. 142–160. Springer, Heidelberg (2014). doi:10.1007/978-3-642-54013-4_9

Effect Summaries for Thread-Modular Analysis

Sound Analysis Despite an Unsound Heuristic

Lukáš Holík[1], Roland Meyer[2], Tomáš Vojnar[1], and Sebastian Wolff[2,3(✉)]

[1] FIT BUT, IT4Innovations Centre of Excellence, Brno, Czech Republic
[2] TU Braunschweig, Braunschweig, Germany
sebastian.wolff@tu-bs.de
[3] Fraunhofer ITWM, Kaiserslautern, Germany

Abstract. We propose a novel guess-and-check principle to increase the efficiency of thread-modular verification of lock-free data structures. We build on a heuristic that guesses candidates for stateless effect summaries of programs by searching the code for instances of a copy-and-check programming idiom common in lock-free data structures. These candidate summaries are used to compute the interference among threads in linear time. Since a candidate summary need not be a sound effect summary, we show how to fully automatically check whether the precision of candidate summaries is sufficient. We can thus perform sound verification despite relying on an unsound heuristic. We have implemented our approach and found it up to two orders of magnitude faster than existing ones.

1 Introduction

Verification of concurrent, lock-free data structures has recently received considerable attention [2,3,14,28,29]. Such structures are both of high practical relevance and, at the same time, difficult to write. A common correctness notion in this context is *linearizability* [15], which requires that every concurrent execution can be linearized to an execution that could also occur sequentially. For many data structures, linearizability reduces to checking control-flow reachability in a variant of the data structure that is augmented with observer automata [2]. This control-flow reachability problem, in turn, is often solved by means of *thread-modular analysis* [4,19]. Our contribution is on improving thread-modular analyses for verifying linearizability of lock-free data structures.

Thread-modular analyses compute the least solution to a recursive equation

$$X \;=\; X \cup \mathit{seq}(X) \cup \mathit{interfere}(X)\,.$$

This work was supported by the Czech Science Foundation project 16-24707Y, the BUT FIT project FIT-S-17-4014, the IT4IXS: IT4Innovations Excellence in Science project (LQ1602), and by the German Science Foundation (DFG) project R2M2. The full version is available as technical report [16].

R. Meyer–A part of the work was done when the author was at Aalto University.

F. Ranzato (Ed.): SAS 2017, LNCS 10422, pp. 169–191, 2017.
DOI: 10.1007/978-3-319-66706-5_9

The domain of X are sets of *views*, partial configurations reflecting the perception of a single thread about the shared heap. Crucially, thread-modular analyses abstract away from the correlation among the views of different threads. Function $seq(X)$ computes a sequential step, the views obtained from X by letting each thread execute a command on its own views. This function, however, does not reflect the fact that a thread may change a part of the shared heap seen by others. Such interference steps are computed by $interfere(X)$. It is this function that we improve on. Before turning to the contribution, we recall the existing approaches and motivate the need for more work.

In the *merge-and-project* approach to interference (e.g., [4,11,19,22]), a merge operation is applied on every two views in X to determine all merged views consistent with the given ones. On each of the consistent views, one thread performs a sequential step, and the result is projected to what is seen by the other thread. The approach has problems with efficiency. The number of merge operations is exactly the square of the number of views in the fixed point. In addition, every merge of two views is expensive. It has to consider all consistent views whose number can be exponential in the size of the views.

The *learning* approach to interference [24,34] derives, via symbolic execution, a symbolic update pattern for the shared heap. The learning process is integrated into the fixed-point computation, which incurs an overhead. Moreover, the number of update patterns to be learned is bounded only by the number of reachable views. An interference step applies the learned update patterns to all views, which again is quadratic in the number of views. Moreover, although update patterns abstract away from thread-local information, computing each application still requires a potentially expensive matching. There are, however, fragments of separation logic with efficient entailment [7].

What is missing is an *efficient* approach to computing interferences among threads.

Main Ideas of the Contribution. We propose to compute $interfere(X)$ by means of so-called *effect summaries*. An effect summary for a method M is a *stateless* program Q_M which over-approximates the effects that M has on the shared heap. With such summaries at hand, the interference step can be computed in linear time by executing the method summaries Q_M for all methods M on the views in the current set X. This is a substantial improvement in efficiency over merge-and-project and learning techniques, which require time roughly quadratic in the size of the fixed-point approximant, X, and possibly exponential in the size of views.

Technically, *statelessness* is defined as atomicity and absence of persistent local state. We found both requirements typically satisfied by methods of lock-free data structures. For our approach, this means stateless summaries are likely to exist (which is confirmed by our experiments). The reason why the atomicity requirement holds is that the methods have to preserve the integrity of the data structure under interleavings. The absence of persistent state holds since interference by other threads may invalidate local state at any time.

We propose a heuristic to compute, from a method M, a stateless program Q_M which is a candidate for being an effect summary of M. Whether or not this candidate is indeed a summary of M is checked on top of the actual analysis, as discussed below. Our heuristic is based on looking for occurrences of a programming idiom common in lock-free data structures which we call *copy-and-check blocks*. Such a block is a piece of code that, despite lock-free execution, appears to be executed atomically. Roughly, we identify each such block and turn it into an atomic program.

Programmers achieve the above mentioned atomicity of copy-and-check blocks by first creating a local copy of a shared variable, performing some computation over it, checking whether the copy is still up-to-date and, if so, publishing the results of the computation to the shared heap. A classic implementation of such blocks is based on *compare-and-swap* (CAS) instructions. In this case, for a local variable `t` and a shared variable `T`, the copy-and-check block typically starts with an assignment `t = T` and finishes with executing `CAS(T,t,x)` which atomically checks whether `t == T` holds and, if so, changes the value of `T` to `x`. Hereafter, we will denote such blocks as *CAS blocks*, and we will concentrate on them since they are rather common in practice [8,23,31]. However, we note that the same principle can be used to handle other kinds of copy-and-check blocks, e.g., those based on the *load-link/store-conditional* (LL/SC) mechanism.

The idea of program analyses to employ the intended behavior of CAS blocks by treating them as atomic is quite natural. The reason why it is not common practice is that this approach is not sound in general. The atomicity may be introduced too coarsely, and, as a result, an *interfere*(X) implementation based on the guessed candidate summaries may miss interleavings present in the actual program. For our analysis, this means that its soundness is conditional upon the fact that the candidate summaries used are indeed proper effect summaries. It must be checked that they are stateless and that they cover all effects on the shared heap. We propose a fully automatic and efficient way of performing those checks. To the best of our knowledge, we are the first to propose such checks.

To check whether candidate summaries indeed cover the effects of the methods for which they were constructed, the idea is to let the methods execute under any number of interferences with the candidate summaries and see if some effect not covered by the candidate summaries can be obtained. Formally, we use the program $Q = \bigoplus_i Q_{M_i}$, which executes a non-deterministically chosen candidate summary Q_{M_i} of a method M_i, execute the Kleene iteration Q^* in parallel with each method M, and check whether the following inclusions holds:

$$\mathit{Effects}(M \parallel Q^*) \subseteq \mathit{Effects}(Q^*).$$

If this inclusion holds, Q^* covers the actual interference all methods may cause. Hence, our novel implementation of *interfere*(X) explores all possible interleavings. The cost of the inclusion test is asymptotically covered by that of computing the fixed point, and practically negligible. It can be checked in linear time (in the size of the fixed point) by performing, for every view in X, a sequential step and testing whether the effect of the step can be mimicked by the candidate summaries. It is worth pointing out the cyclic nature of our reasoning: we use the candidate summaries to prove their own correctness.

Statelessness is an important aspect in the above process. It guarantees that the sequential iteration of Q^* explores the overall interference the methods of the data structure cause. As we are interested in parametric verification, the overall interference is, in fact, the one produced by an unbounded number of concurrent method invocations. Hence, computing this interference using candidate summaries requires us to analyse the program $\prod^\infty Q$, which is a parallel composition of arbitrarily many Q instances. However, statelessness guarantees that each of these instances executes atomically without retaining any local state. While the atomicity ensures that the concurrent Q instances cannot overlap, the absence of local state ensures that Q instances cannot influence each other, even if executed consecutively by the same thread. Hence, we can use a single thread executing the iteration Q^* in order to explore the interference caused by $\prod^\infty Q$. This justifies the usage of Q^* for the effect coverage above. The check for statelessness is similar to the one of effect coverage. If both tests succeed, the analysis information is guaranteed to be sound.

Overview of the Approach, Its Advantages, and Experimental Evaluation. Overall, our thread-modular analysis proceeds as follows. We employ the CAS block heuristic to compute candidate summaries. We use these candidates to determine the interferences in the fixed-point computation. Once the fixed point has been obtained, we check whether the candidates are valid summaries. If so, the fixed point contains sound information, and can be used for verification (or, an on-the-fly computed verification result can be used). Otherwise, verification fails. Currently, we do not have a refinement loop because it was not needed in our experiments.

Our method overcomes the limitations of the previous approaches as follows. The summary program, Q, is quadratic in the syntactic size of the program—not in the size of the fixed point. The interference step executes the summary on all views in the current set X, which means an effort linear rather than quadratic in the fixed-point approximant. Moreover, Q is often acyclic and hence needs linear time to execute, as opposed to the worst case exponential merge or match. In our benchmarks, we needed at most 5 very short summaries, usually around 3–5 lines of code each. The computation of candidate summaries (based on cheap and standard static analyses) and their check for validity are separated from the fixed point, and the cost of both operations is negligible. We stress that our fixed point as well as the validity check do not rely on the actual algorithm used to compute the summary.

We implemented our thread-modular analysis with effect summaries on top of our state-of-the-art tool [14] based on thread-modular reasoning with merge-and-project. We applied the implementation to verify linearizability in a number of concurrent list implementations. Compared to [14], we obtain a speed-up of two orders of magnitude. Moreover, we managed to infer stateless effect summaries for all our case studies except the DGLM queue [8] under explicit memory management (where one needs to go beyond statelessness). However, we are not aware of any automatic approach that would be able to verify linearizability of this algorithm.

2 Effect Summaries on an Example

The main complication for writing lock-free algorithms is to guarantee robustness under interleavings. The key idea to tackle this issue is to use a specific update pattern, namely the CAS-blocks discussed in Sect. 1. We now show how CAS blocks are employed in Treiber's lock-free stack implementation under garbage collection, the code of which is given in Listing 1. The `push` method implements a CAS block by: (1) copying the top of stack pointer, `top = ToS`, (2) linking the `node` to be inserted to the current top of stack, `node.next = top`, and (3) making `node` the new top of stack in case no other thread changed the shared state, `CAS(ToS,top,node)`. Similarly, `pop` proceeds by: (1) copying the top of stack pointer, `top=ToS`, (2) querying its successor, `next=top.next`, and (3) swinging `ToS` to that successor in case the stack did not change, `CAS(ToS,top,next)`.

```
struct Node { data_t data; Node next; }
shared Node ToS;

void push(data_t in) {
    Node node = new Node(in);
    while (true) {
        Node top = ToS;
        node.next = top;
        if(CAS(ToS, top, node)){
            return;
}   }   }

S1: atomic {
    /* push */
    Node node = new Node(*);
    node.next = ToS;
    ToS = node;
}
```

```
bool pop(data_t& out) {
    while (true) {
        Node top = ToS;
        if(top == NULL){
            return false;
        }
        Node next = top.next;
        if(CAS(ToS, top, next)){
            out = top.data;
            return true;
}   }   }

S2: atomic {
    /* pop */
    assume(ToS != NULL);
    ToS = ToS.next;
} S3: atomic { /* skip */ }
```

Listing 1. Pseudo code of the Treiber's lock-free stack [31] and its effect summaries.

Following the CAS-block idiom, the only statements modifying the shared heap in Treiber's stack are the CAS operations. Hence, we identify three types of effects on the shared heap. First, a successful CAS in `push` makes `ToS` point to a newly allocated cell that, in turn, points to the previous value of `ToS`. Second, a successful CAS in `pop` moves `ToS` to its successor `ToS.next`. Since we assume garbage collection, the removed element is not freed but remains in the shared heap until collected. Third, the effect of any other statement on the shared heap is the identity.

With the effects of Treiber's stack identified, we can turn towards finding an approximation. For that, consider the program fragments from Listing 1: `S1` covers the effects of the CAS in `push`, `S2` covers the effects of the CAS in `pop`, and, lastly, `S3` produces the identity-effect covering all remaining statements. Then, the summary program is $Q = \texttt{S1} \oplus \texttt{S2} \oplus \texttt{S3}$.

To obtain the non-trivial summaries `S1` and `S2`, it suffices to concentrate on the block of code between the `top = ToS` assignment and the subsequent `CAS(ToS, top, _)` statement. Without going into details (which will be provided in Sect. 5), the summaries result from considering the code between the two statements atomic, performing simplification of the code under this atomicity assumption, and including some purely local initialization and finalization code (such as the allocation in the `push` method).

3 Programming Model

A concurrent program P is a parallel composition of threads T. The threads are while-programs formed using sequential composition, non-deterministic choice, loops, atomic blocks, skip, and primitive commands. The syntax is as follows:

$$P ::= T \mid P \| P \qquad T ::= T_1;T_2 \mid T_1 \oplus T_2 \mid T^* \mid \texttt{atomic}\, T \mid \textbf{skip} \mid C\,.$$

We use $Thrd$ for the set of all threads. We also write P^* to mean a program P with the Kleene star applied to all threads. The syntax and semantics of the commands in C are orthogonal to our development. We comment on the assumptions we need in a moment.

We assume programs whose threads implement methods from the interface of the lock-free data structure which is to be verified. The fact that, at runtime, we may find an arbitrary (finite) number of instances of each of the threads corresponds to an arbitrary number of concurrent method invocations. The verification task is then formulated as proving a designated shared heap unreachable in all instantiations of the program. Since thread-modular analyses simultaneously reason over all instantiations of the program, we refrain from making this parameterization more explicit. Instead, we consider program instances simply as programs with more copies of the same threads.

We model heaps as partial and finite functions $h\colon Var \cup \mathbb{N} \nrightarrow \mathbb{N}$. Hence, we do not distinguish between the stack and the heap, and let the heap provide valuations for both the program variables from Var and the memory cells from $\mathbb{N}$. We use $\mathbb{H}$ for the set of all heaps. Initially, the heap is empty, denoted by emp with $dom(emp) = \varnothing$. We write $\bot$ if a partial function is undefined for an argument: $h(e) = \bot$ if $e \notin dom(h)$.

We assume each thread has an identifier from $Tid \subseteq \mathbb{N}$. A *program state* is a pair (s, cf) where $s \in \mathbb{H}$ is the shared heap and $cf\colon Tid \rightarrow Thrd \times \mathbb{H}$ maps the thread identifiers to *thread configurations*. A thread configuration is of the form (T, o) with $T \in Thrd$ and $o \in \mathbb{H}$ being a heap owned by T. If $cf = \{i \rightarrow (T, o)\}$ contains a single mapping, we write simply $(s, (T, o))$.

Our development crucially relies on having a notion of separation between the shared heap s and the owned heap o of a thread T. However, the actual definitions of what is owned and what shared are a parameter to our development. We just require the separation to respect disjointness of the shared and owned heaps and to be defined such that it is preserved across execution of program statements. The latter is formalized below in Assumption 1. To render disjointness formally, we say that a state $(s,\ cf)$ is *separated*, denoted by $separate(s,\ cf)$, if, for every $i_1, i_2 \in dom(cf)$ with $cf(i_j) = (T_{i_j},\ o_{i_j})$ and $i_1 \neq i_2$, we have $dom(s) \cap dom(o_{i_j}) \cap \mathbb{N} = \varnothing$ and $dom(o_{i_1}) \cap dom(o_{i_2}) \cap \mathbb{N} = \varnothing$. Note that, in order to allow for thread-local variables, the heaps need to be disjoint only on memory cells (but not on variables), thus the additional intersection with $\mathbb{N}$.

We use $\rightarrow$ to denote *program steps.* The sequential semantics of threads is as expected for sequential composition, choice, loops, and skip. An atomic block `atomic` T summarizes a computation of the underlying thread T into a single program step. The semantics of primitive commands depends on the actual set C. We do not make it precise but require it to preserve separation in the following sense.

Assumption 1. *For every step $(s,\ (T,\ o)) \rightarrow (s',\ (T',\ o'))$ with $separate(s,\ (T,\ o))$, we have $separate(s',\ (T',\ o'))$.*

The semantics of a concurrent program incorporates the requirement for separation into its transition rule. A thread may only update the shared heap and those parts of the heap it owns. No other parts can be modified. Therefore, we let threads execute in isolation and ensure that the combined resulting state is separated:

$$\frac{(s,\ cf(i)) \rightarrow (s',\ cf'_I) \qquad cf' = cf[i \rightarrow cf'_I] \qquad separate(s',\ cf')}{(s,\ cf) \rightarrow (s',\ cf')} \ (\text{PAR})$$

Although a precise notion of separation is not needed for the development of our approach in Sect. 4, we give, for illustration, the notion we use in our implementation and experiments. In the case of garbage collection (like in Java), the owned heap of a thread includes, as usual, its local variables and cells accessible from these variables, which were allocated by the thread but never made accessible through the shared variables. The shared heap then contains the shared variables, all cells that were once made accessible from them, as well as cells waiting for garbage collection. For the case of explicit memory management, we need a more complicated mechanism of ownership transfer where a shared cell can become owned again. We propose such a mechanism in Sect. 6.

We assume the computation of the program under scrutiny to start from an initial state $init_P = (\mathsf{s}_{\text{init}},\ cf_{init,P})$ where s_{init} is the result of an initialization procedure. The initial thread configurations, denoted by $cf_{init,T}$, are of the form (T, emp). The initialization procedure is assumed to be part of the input program. We are interested in the shared heaps reachable by program P from its initial state:

$$SH(P) := \{s \mid \exists\ cf.\ init_P \rightarrow^* (s,\ cf)\}.$$

In what follows, we assume that the correctness of a program P can be read of its reachable shared heaps, $SH(P)$. For this, some instrumentation of P might be needed. Such instrumentations are possible for a variety of properties. In particular, the instrumentation with observer automata from Sect. 1 allows one to check for linearizability.

4 Interference via Summaries

We now present our new approach to computing the effect of thread interference steps on the shared heap (corresponding to evaluating the expression *interfere*(X) from Sect. 1 for a set of views X) in a way which is suitable for concurrency libraries. In particular, we introduce a notion of a *stateless effect summary* Q: a program whose repeated execution is able to produce all the effects on the shared heap that the program under scrutiny, P, can produce. With a stateless effect summary Q at hand, one can compute *interfere*(X) by repeatedly applying Q on the views in X until a fixed point is reached. Here, statelessness assures that Q is applicable repeatedly without any need to track its local state.

Later, in Sect. 5, we provide a heuristic for deriving *candidates* for stateless effect summaries. Though our experiments show that the heuristic we propose is very effective in practice, the candidate summary that it produces is not guaranteed to be an effect summary, i.e., it is not guaranteed to produce all the effects on the shared heap that P can produce. A candidate summary which is not an effect summary is called *unsound*. To guarantee soundness of our approach even when the obtained candidate summary is unsound, we provide a test of soundness of candidate summaries. Interestingly, as we prove, it is the case that even (potentially) unsound candidate summaries can be used to check their own soundness—although this step appears to be cyclic reasoning.

4.1 Stateless Effect Summaries

We start by formalizing the notion of statelessness. Intuitively, a thread is stateless if it terminates after a single step and disposes its local heap. Formally, we say that a thread T of a program Q is *stateless* if, for all reachable shared heaps $s \in SH(Q^*)$ and all transitions $(s,\ cf_{init,T}) \rightarrow (s',\ cf)$, we have $cf = (\texttt{skip}, emp)$. A program Q is stateless if so are all its threads. Note that statelessness should hold from all reachable shared heaps rather than from just all heaps. While an atomic execution to `skip` would be easy to achieve from all heaps, a clean-up yielding *emp* can only be achieved if we have control over the thread-local heap. Also note that statelessness basically requires a thread to consist of a top-level atomic block to ensure termination in a single step.

For an example, consider the summary `S1` of `push` in Treiber's stack from Listing 1. It is stateless because (1) the top-level `atomic` block ensures execution in a single step, and (2) the allocated node is published, i.e., moved from the owned heap to the shared heap.

Next, we define the *effects* of a program P, denoted by $EF(P) \subseteq \mathbb{H} \times \mathbb{H}$, to be the set $EF(P) = \{(s,\ s') \mid init_P \rightarrow^* (s,\ cf) \rightarrow (s',\ cf')\}$. This set generalizes the reachable shared heaps, $SH(P)$: it contains all atomic (single-step) updates P performs on the heaps from $SH(P)$.

In Treiber's stack, as discussed in Sect. 2, the updates performed by the CAS statements are effects. The remaining statements also yield effects. However, since they do not modify the shared heap, they produce the identity effect.

Altogether, a program Q is a *(stateless) effect summary* of P if it is stateless and $EF(T \parallel Q^*) \subseteq EF(Q^*)$ holds for all threads $T \in P$. We refer to this inclusion as the *effect inclusion*. Intuitively, it states that Q^* subsumes all the effects T may have under interference with Q^*. The lemma below shows that the effect inclusion can be used to check whether a candidate summary is indeed an effect summary. Moreover, the check can deal with the different threads separately.

Lemma 1. *If Q is stateless and $EF(T \parallel Q^*) \subseteq EF(Q^*)$ holds for all $T \in P$, then we have $EF(P) \subseteq EF(P \parallel Q^*) \subseteq EF(Q^*)$.*

In what follows, we describe our novel thread-modular analysis based on effect summaries. We assume that, in addition to the program P under scrutiny, we have a program Q which is a candidate for being a summary of P (obtained, e.g., by the heuristic that we provide in Sect. 5). In Sect. 4.2, we first provide a fixed-point computation where the interference step is implemented by a repeated application of the candidate summary Q. We show that if the candidate summary Q is an effect summary, then the fixed point we compute is a conservative over-approximation of the reachable shared heaps of P. Next, in Sect. 4.3, we show that the fact whether or not Q is indeed an effect summary of P can be checked efficiently on top of the computed fixed point (even though the fixed point need not over-approximate the reachable shared heaps of P).

In the case that the test of Sect. 4.3 fails, Q is not an effect summary of P, and our verification fails with no definite answer. As future work, one could think of proposing ways of patching the summaries based on feedback from the failed test. Then, along the lines of [5,6], the previously computed, unsound state space can be reused: one applies the newly added summaries to the already explored states and continues with the analysis afterwards. However, in our experiments, using the heuristic computation of candidate summaries proposed in Sect. 5, this situation has not happened for any program where a stateless effect summary exists. In the only experiment where our approach failed (the DGLM queue under explicit memory management, which has not been verified by any other fully automatic tool), the notion of stateless effect summaries itself is not strong enough. Hence, a perhaps more interesting question for future work is how to further generalize the notion of effect summaries.

4.2 Summaries in the Fixed-Point Computation

To explore the reachable shared heaps of a program P, we suggest a thread-modular analysis which explores the reachable states of the threads $T \in P$ in isolation. To account for the possible thread interleavings of the original program, we apply interference steps to the threads T by executing the provided summary Q. Conceptually, this process corresponds to exploring the state space of the two-thread programs $T \parallel Q^*$ for all syntactically different threads $T \in P$. Technically, we collect the reachable states of those programs in the following least fixed point:

$$X_0 = \{(s_{\text{init}}, (T, emp)) \mid T \in P\}$$
$$X_{i+1} = X_i \cup seq(X_i) \cup interfere(X_i)\ .$$

Since Q^* has no internal state, the analysis only keeps the thread-local configurations of the threads T. Functions $seq(\cdot)$ and $interfere(\cdot)$ compute sequential steps (steps of T) and interference steps (steps of Q^*), respectively, as follows:

$$\begin{aligned} seq(X_i) &= \{(s', cf') \mid \exists\,(s, cf) \in X_i.\ (s, cf) \rightarrow (s', cf')\} \\ interfere(X_i) &= \{(s', cf\ ) \mid separate(s', cf)\ \wedge\ \exists\, s, cf'. \\ &\qquad\qquad (s, cf) \in X_i\ \wedge\ (s, cf_{init,Q}) \rightarrow (s', cf')\}\ . \end{aligned}$$

Function $seq(X_i)$ is standard. For $interfere(X_i)$ we apply Q to each configuration $(s, cf) \in X_i$ by letting it start from the shared heap s and its initial thread-local configuration $cf_{init,Q}$. Then we extract the updated shared heap, s', resulting in the post configuration (s', cf). Altogether, this procedure applies to the views in X_i the shared heap updates dictated by Q. The thread-local configurations, cf, of threads T are not changed by interference. This locality follows from the separation.

The following lemma states that the set of shared heaps collected from the above fixed point is indeed the set of reachable shared heaps of all $T \parallel Q^*$. Let X_k be the fixed point and define $\mathcal{R} = \{s \mid \exists cf.\,(s, cf) \in X_k\}$.

Lemma 2. *If Q is a summary of P, then $\mathcal{R} = \bigcup_{T \in P} SH(T \parallel Q^*)$.*

With the state space exploration in place, we can turn towards a soundness result of our method: given an appropriate summary Q, the fixed-point computation over-approximates the reachable shared heaps of P.

Theorem 1. *If Q is a summary of P, then we have $SH(P) \subseteq SH(Q^*) = \mathcal{R}$.*

The rationale behind the theorem is as follows. Relying on Q being a summary of P provides the effect inclusion. So, Lemma 1 yields $EF(P \parallel Q^*) \subseteq EF(Q^*)$. From the definition of effects we can then conclude $SH(P \parallel Q^*) \subseteq SH(Q^*)$. Thus, we have $SH(P) \subseteq SH(Q^*)$ because $SH(P) \subseteq SH(P \parallel Q^*)$ is always true. This shows the first inclusion. Similarly, the effect inclusion gives $SH(T \parallel Q^*) \subseteq SH(Q^*)$ by the definition of reachability. Hence, we conclude using Lemma 2.

4.3 Soundness of Summarization

Soundness of our method, as stated by Theorem 1 above, is conditioned by Q being a summary of P. In our framework, Q is heuristically constructed and there is no guarantee that it really summarizes P. Hence, for our analysis to be sound, we have to check summarization; we have to establish (1) the effect inclusion, and (2) statelessness of Q. To that end, we check that (1) every update T performs on the shared heap in the system $T \parallel Q^*$ can be mimicked by Q, and that (2) every execution of Q terminates in a single step and does not retain persistent local state. We implement those checks on top of the fixed point, X_k, as follows:

$$\begin{aligned} &\forall\,(s, cf) \in X_k\ \forall\, s', cf', i\ \exists cf''. \\ &\qquad (s, cf) \rightarrow (s', cf') \implies (s, cf_{init,Q}) \rightarrow (s', cf'') && \text{(CHK-MIMIC)} \\ &\qquad \wedge (s, cf_{init,Q}(i)) \rightarrow (s', cf') \implies cf' = (\mathtt{skip}, emp) && \text{(CHK-STATELESS)} \end{aligned}$$

The above properties indeed capture our intuition. The former, (CHK-MIMIC), states that, for every explored T-step of the form $(s, cf) \rightarrow (s', cf')$, the effect (s, s') is also an effect of Q. That is, executing Q starting from s yields s'. This establishes the effect inclusion as required by Lemma 1. The latter check, (CHK-STATELESS), states that every thread of Q must terminate in a single step and dispose its owned heap. This constraint is relaxed to those shared heaps which have been explored during the fixed-point computation. That is, it ensures statelessness of Q on all heaps from $\mathcal{R}$. The key aspect is to guarantee that $\mathcal{R}$ includes $SH(Q^*)$ as required by the definition. We show that this inclusion follows from the check.

The above checks rely on the fixed point, which, in turn, is computed using the candidate summary Q. That is, we use Q to prove its own correctness. Nevertheless, our development results in a sound analysis as stated by the following theorem.

Theorem 2. *The fixed point X_k satisfies (*CHK-MIMIC*) and (*CHK-STATELESS*) if and only if Q is a summary of P.*

5 Computing Effect Summaries

We now provide our heuristic for computing effect summaries. It is based on CAS blocks between an assignment `t=T`, denoted as *checked assignment*, and a CAS statement `CAS(T,t,x)`, denoted as *checking CAS* below. Since we compute a summary for each such block, the number of summaries is at most quadratic in the size of the input.

In what follows, consider some method M given by its control-flow graph (CFG) $G = (V, E, v_{init}, v_{final})$. The CFG has a unique initial and a unique final state, which we will use in our construction. Return commands are assumed to lead to the final state. As we are only interested in the effect on the shared heap, we drop return values from return commands. Likewise, we skip assignments to output parameters unless they are important for the flow of control in M. We assume the summaries to execute with non-deterministic input values, and so we replace every input parameter with a symbolic value $*$. Conditionals, loops, and CAS commands are represented by two edges, for the successful and failing execution, respectively. Let $e_{asgn} := (v_{asgns}, \texttt{t=T}, v_{asgnt})$ be the CFG edge of the checked assignment, and let the successful branch of the checking CAS be $e_{cas} := (v_{cas}, \texttt{CAS(T,t,x)}, v_{cassuc})$. Next, let $e_{asgn'} := (v_{asgns}, \texttt{t=T}, v_{asgnt'})$ be a copy of the checked assignment to be used as the beginning of the CAS block, and let $e_{cas'} := (v_{cas}, \texttt{CAS(T,t,x)}, v_{cassuc'})$ be a copy of the checking CAS to be used as the end of the CAS block. Here, $v_{asgnt'}$ and $v_{cassuc'}$ are fresh nodes.

To give a concise description of effect summaries, the following shortcuts will be helpful. We write $rand(G)$ for the CFG obtained from G by replacing each occurrence of a shared variable by a non-deterministic value $*$. By $G - S$, we mean the CFG obtained from G by dropping all edges carrying commands from the set S. Given nodes v_1 and v_2, we denote by $G(v_1, v_2)$ the CFG obtained from G by making v_1/v_2 the initial/final node, respectively. Given two CFGs G

and G', we define $G; G'$ as their disjoint union where the single final state of G is merged with the single initial state of G'. Finally, we allow compositions $e; G$ and $G; e$ of a CFG G with a single edge e, by viewing e as a CFG consisting of a single edge with the initial/final nodes being the initial/final nodes of e, respectively.

The construction of the summary proceeds in two steps. First we identify the CAS block and create the control-flow structure, then we clean it up using data flow analysis and generate the final code of the summary. Note that the clean-up step is optional but generates a concise form beneficial for verification.

Step 1: Control-flow structure. A summary consists of an initialization phase, followed by the CAS block, and a finalization phase. The first step results in the CFG

$$G_{init}; G_{block}; G_{final} .$$

The guiding theme of the construction is to preserve all sequences of commands that may lead through the CAS block.

In the initialization phase, which is intended for purely local initialization, the method is assumed to be interrupted by other threads in the sense that the values of shared pointers may spontaneously change. Therefore, we replace all dependencies on shared variables by non-deterministic assignments. Moreover, all return commands are removed since we have not yet passed the CAS block. Eventually, when arriving at the v_{asgns} location, the summary non-deterministically guesses that the CAS block should begin, and so the control is transferred to it via the $e_{asgn'}$ edge. Hence, the initialization is:

$$G_{init} \;:=\; (rand(G) - \{\texttt{return}\})(v_{init}, v_{asgns}) .$$

The CAS block begins with the $e_{asgn'}$ edge, i.e., with the checked assignment, and ends with the $e_{cas'}$ edge, i.e., the checking CAS statement. From the CAS block, we remove all control-flow edges with assignments `t=T` as we fixed the checked assignment when entering the CAS block (other assignments of the form `t=T`, if present, will give rise to other CAS blocks; and a repeated execution of the same checked assignment then corresponds to a repeated execution of the summary). We also remove the return commands as the finalization potentially still has to free owned heap. Failing executions of the checking CAS do not leave the CAS block (and typically get stuck due to the removed checked assignments). Successful executions may leave the CAS block, but do not have to. Eventually, the summary guesses the last successful execution of the checking CAS and enters the finalization phase. Hence, we get the following code:

$$G_{block} \;:=\; e_{asgn'}; ((G - \{\texttt{return}, \texttt{t=T}\})(v_{asgnt}, v_{cas})); e_{cas'} .$$

Sometimes, the checked assignment can use local variables assigned prior to the checked assignment. In such a case, we add edges with these assignments before the $e_{asgn'}$ edge. This happens, e.g., in the enqueue procedure of Michael&Scott's lock-free queue where the sequence `tail=Tail;next=tail.next` is used. If the checked assignment is `next=tail.next`, we start G_{block} with edges containing `tail=Tail` and `next=tail.next`.

```
// Initialization
while (true) {
  if (*) goto L1;
  Node top=*;
  if (top==NULL){
    STOP;
  }
  Node next=top.next;
  if(CAS(*,top,next)){
    out=top.data;
    STOP;
  }
}
STOP;
```

```
// CAS block
L1:Node top=ToS;
goto L2;
while (true) {
  STOP;
  L2:if(top==NULL){
    STOP;
  }
  Node next=top.next;
  if(*) goto L3;
  if(CAS(ToS,top,next)){
    out=top.data;
    STOP;
  }
}
STOP;
L3:if(CAS(ToS,top,next))
   goto L4;
```

```
// Finalization
while (true) {
  Node top=*;
  if(top==NULL){
    return;
  }
  Node next=top.next;
  if(CAS(*,top,next)){
    L4:out=top.data;
    return;
  }
}
```

Fig. 1. Step 1 in the summary computation for the pop method in Treiber's stack.

The finalization phase, again, cannot rely on shared variables. However, here, we preserve the return statements to terminate the execution:

$$G_{final} := rand(G)(v_{cassuc}, v_{final}) .$$

Figure 1 illustrates the construction on the pop method in Treiber's stack. Instead of a CFG, we give the source code. STOP represents deleted edges and the fact that we cannot move from one phase to another not using the new edges.

Step 2: Cleaning-up and summary generation. We perform *copy propagation* using a must analysis that propagates an assignment y=x to subsequent assignments z=y, resulting in z=x. That it is a must analysis means the propagation is done only if z=y definitely has to use the value of y that stems from the assignment y=x. Moreover, we perform the copy propagation assuming that the entire summary executes atomically. For the initialization phase, the result is that the non-deterministic values for shared variables propagate through the code. Similarly, for the CAS block, the shared variables themselves propagate through the code. For the finalization phase, non-deterministic values propagate only in the case when a local variable does not receive its value from the CAS block. As a result, after the copy propagation, the CAS and the finalization block may contain conditionals that are constantly true or constantly false. We replace those that evaluate to true by skip and remove the edges that evaluate to false. The result of the copy propagation is illustrated in Fig. 2.

Subsequently, we perform a *live variables analysis*. A variable is live if it may occur in a subsequent conditional or on the right-hand side of a subsequent assignment. Otherwise, it is dead. We remove all assignments to dead variables including output parameters. In our running example, all assignments to local variables as well as to the output parameter can be removed.

Next, we remove code that is *unreachable*, *dead*, or *useless*. Unreachable code can appear due to the modifications of the CFG. Dead code does not lead to

```
// Initialization
while (true) {
  if (*) goto L1;
  Node top=*;
  if(*){
    STOP;
  }
  Node next=*;
  if(*){
    out=*;
    STOP;
  }
}
STOP;
```

```
// CAS block
L1:Node top=ToS;
   goto L2;
while (true) {
  STOP;
  L2:if(ToS==NULL){
    STOP;
  }
  Node next=ToS.next;
  if(*) goto L3;
  ToS=ToS.next;
  out=ToS.data;
  STOP;
}
STOP;
L3:if(CAS(ToS,ToS,ToS.next))
   goto L4;
```

```
// Finalization
while (true) {
  Node top=*;
  if(*){
    return;
  }
  Node next=*;
  if(*){
    L4:out=ToS.data;
    return;
  }
}
```

Fig. 2. Copy propagation within the summary computation for pop in Treiber's stack.

the final location. Useless code does not have any impact on the values of the variables used, which can concern even (possibly infinite) useless loops.

Finally, the resulting code is wrapped into an `atomic` block, and conditionals are replaced by `assume` statements. For the `pop` method in Treiber's stack, we get the summary `S2` given in Listing 1.

6 Generalization to Explicit Memory Management

We now generalize our approach to explicit memory management. The problem is that the separation between the shared and owned heap is difficult to define and establish in this case. Ownership as understood in garbage collection, where no other thread can access a cell that was allocated by a thread but not made shared, does not exist any more. Memory can be freed and *reallocated*, with other threads still holding (dangling) pointers to it. These threads can read and modify that memory, hence the allocating thread does not have strong guarantees of exclusivity. However, programmers usually try to prevent effects of accidental reallocations: threads are designed to *respect ownership*. That is, a thread should be allowed to execute *as if* it had exclusive access to the memory it owns.

Our development is parameterized by a notion of separation between the shared and owned heap. To generalize the results, we provide a new notion of ownership suitable for explicit memory management. However, the new notion is not guaranteed to be preserved by the semantics. Instead, we include into our fixed-point computation a check that the program respects this ownership, and give up the analysis if the check fails.

To understand how the heap separation is influenced by basic pointer manipulations, we consider the following set of commands C:

$$x = \texttt{malloc},\ x = \texttt{free},\ x = y,\ x = y.sel_i,\ x.sel_i = y\ .$$

Here, x, y are program variables and $sel_0, \ldots, sel_n$ are selectors, from which the first, say m, are *pointer selectors* and the rest are *data selectors*. Command

$x = \texttt{malloc}$ allocates a *record*, a free block of addresses $a+0, \ldots, a+n$, and sets $h(x)$ to a. Command $x = \texttt{free}$ frees the record $h(x)+0, \ldots, h(x)+n$. Selectors correspond to field accesses: $x.sel_i$ refers to the content of $a+i$ if x points to a. The remaining commands have the expected meaning.

6.1 Heap Separation

We work with a three-way partitioning of the heap into *shared*, *owned*, and *free* addresses. Free are all addresses that are fresh or have been freed and not reallocated. Shared is every address that is *reachable* from the shared variables and not free. The reachability predicate, however, requires care. First, we must obviously generalize reachability from the first memory cell of a record to the whole record. Second, we must not use *undefined* pointers for reachability. A pointer is undefined if it was propagated from uninitialized or uncontrolled memory. Letting the shared heap propagate through such values would make it possible for the entire allocated heap to be shared (since undefined pointers can have an arbitrary value). Then, owned is the memory which is not shared nor free. The owned memory is partitioned into disjoint blocks that are *owned by individual threads*. A thread gains ownership by moving memory into the owned part, and loses it when the memory is removed from the owned part. The actions by which a thread can gain ownership are (1) allocation and (2) breaking reachability from shared variables by an update of a pointer or a shared variable (*ownership transfer*). An *ownership violation* is then a modification of a thread's owned memory by another thread. This can in particular be (1) freeing or publishing the owned memory or (2) an update of a pointer therein. A program respects ownership if it cannot reach an ownership violation.

Let us discuss these concepts formally. We use $\bot$ to identify free cells. That is, in a heap h address a is free if $h(a) = \bot$ (also written $a \notin dom(h)$). A record is free if so are all its cells. Consequently, the free command sets all cells of a record to $\bot$. The shared heap is identified by reachability through defined pointers starting from the shared variables. For undefined pointers we use the symbolic value udef. Initially, all variables are undefined. Moreover, we let allocations initialize the selectors of records to udef. We use a value distinct from $\bot$ to detect ownership violations by checking whether $\bot$ is reachable from the shared heap (see below). Value udef is explicitly allowed to be reachable (this may be needed for list implementations where selectors of sentinel nodes are not initialized). Let $Ptrs$ be the shared pointer variables. Then, the addresses of the shared records in a heap h, denoted by $records(h) \subseteq \mathbb{N} \cup \{\bot\}$, are collected by the following fixed point (where the *address of a record* is its lowest address):

$$S_0 = \{a \mid \exists x \in Ptrs \,.\, h(x) = a \neq \texttt{udef}\}$$
$$S_{i+1} = \{b \mid \exists a \in S_i \, \exists k.\; a \neq \bot \;\wedge\; 0 \leq k < m \;\wedge\; h(a+k) = b \neq \texttt{udef}\}$$

All addresses within the shared records are shared. The remaining cells, i.e., those that are neither free nor shared, are owned. This definition establishes a sufficient separation for Assumption 1. It is automatically lifted to the concurrent setting by Rule (PAR) following the intuition from above.

It remains to detect ownership violations, which occur whenever a thread modifies cells owned by other threads. Due to the separation integrated into Rule (PAR), threads execute with only the shared heap and their owned heap being visible. The remainder of the heap is cut away. By choice of $\bot$ to identify free cells, the cut away part appears free to the acting thread. In particular, the parts owned by other threads appear free. Hence, in order to avoid ownership violations, a thread must not modify free cells. To that end, an ownership violation occurs if (A) a free cell is freed again, (B) a free cell is written to, or (C) a free cell is published to the shared heap. For (A) and (B) we extend the semantics of commands to raise an ownership violation if a free cell is manipulated. For (C) we check for every program step whether it results in a shared heap where $\bot$ is made reachable.

Formally, we have the following rules.

$$\frac{\exists\, sel\,.\,(s \uplus o)(x).sel \notin dom(s \uplus o)}{(s,\, (x = \texttt{free},\, o)) \rightarrow violation}\ \text{(A)} \qquad \frac{(s \uplus o)(x).sel \notin dom(s \uplus o)}{(s,\, (x.sel = y,\, o)) \rightarrow violation}\ \text{(B)}$$

$$\frac{(s,\, cf) \rightarrow (s',\, cf') \qquad \bot \in records(s')}{(s,\, cf) \rightarrow violation}\ \text{(C)}$$

Note that reading out free cells is allowed by the above rules. This is necessary because lock-free algorithms typically perform speculating reads and check only later whether the result of the read is safe to use. Moreover, note that our detection of ownership violations can yield false-positives. A cell may not be owned, yet an ownership violation is raised because it appears free to the thread. We argue that such false-positives are *desired* as they access truly free memory. Put differently: an ownership violation detected by the above rules is either indeed an ownership violation or an unsafe access of free memory, that is, a bug.

6.2 Ownership Transfer

The above separation is different from the one used under garbage collection in the earlier sections. When an address becomes unreachable from the shared variables, it is *transferred* into the acting thread's owned heap (although other threads may still have pointers to it). We introduce this ownership transfer to simplify the construction of summaries. The idea is best understood on an example.

Under explicit memory management, threads free cells that they made unreachable from the shared variables to avoid memory leaks. Consider, for example, the method pop in Treiber's stack (Listing 1). There, a thread updates the ToS variable making the former top of stack, say a, unreachable from the shared heap. In the version for explicit memory management, a is then freed before returning. If ownership was not transferred and address a stayed shared, then two summaries would be needed: one for the update of `ToS` and one for freeing a. However, a stateless version of the latter summary could not learn which address to free since it starts with the empty local heap and with a unreachable from the shared heap. If, on the other hand, ownership of a is transferred to the acting thread, then the former summary can include freeing a (which does not change the shared heap). Moreover, it is even forced to free a in order to remain stateless since a would otherwise persist in its owned heap.

We stress that our framework can be instantiated with other notions of separation, like an analogue of the one for garbage collection or the one of [14], which both do not have ownership transfer. This would complicate the reasoning in Sect. 4, but could lead to a more robust analysis (ownership transfer is prone to ownership violations).

6.3 ABA Prevention

Additionally, synchronization mechanisms can be incorporated into our approach. For instance, lock-free data structures may use *version counters* to prevent the *ABA problem* [23]: a variable leaves and returns to the same address, and an observer incorrectly concludes that the variable has never changed. A well-known scenario of this type causes stack corruption in a naive extension of Treiber's stack to explicit memory management [23]. To give the observer a means of detecting that a variable has been changed, pointers are associated with a counter that increases with every update.

In our analysis, such version counters must be persistent in the shared memory. Since this is an exception from the above definition of separation, a presence of version counters must be indicated by the user (e.g., the user specifies that the version counter of a pointer a is always stored at address $a+1$). The semantics is then adapted in such a way that (1) version counters remain in the shared heap upon freeing, (2) are retained in case of reallocations, and (3) are never transferred to a thread's owned heap. The modifications can be easily implemented, and are detailed in [16]. Last, the thread-modular abstraction has to be adjusted since keeping all counters ever allocated in every thread view is not feasible. One solution is to remember only the values of those counters that are attached to the allocated shared and the thread's own heap.

7 Experiments and Discussion

To substantiate our claim for practical benefits of the proposed method, we implemented the techniques from Sects. 4 and 6.[1] Therefore, we modified our previous linearizability checker [14] to perform our novel fixed-point computation. The modifications were straightforward leveraging the existing infrastructure.

Our findings are listed in Table 1. Experiments were conducted on an Intel Xeon E5-2670 running at 2.60 GHz. The table includes the running times (averaged over ten runs) and the number of explored views (the size of set X from

[1] Available at: https://github.com/Wolff09/TMRexp/releases/SAS17/.

Table 1. Experimental results: a speed-up of up to two orders of magnitude.

Program		Thread-modular [14]	Thread summaries
Coarse stack	GC	0.29s/343	0.03s/256
	MM	1.89s/1287	0.19s/1470
Coarse queue	GC	0.49/343	0.05s/256
	MM	2.34s/1059	0.98s/2843
Treiber's stack [31]	GC	1.99s/651	0.06s/458
	MM	25.5s/3175	1.64s/2926
Michael & Scott's queue [23]	GC	11.0s/1530	0.39s/1552
	MM	11700s/19742	102s/27087
DGLM queue [8]	GC	9.56s/1537	0.37s/1559
	MM	Unsafe (spurious)	Violation

Sect. 1). Our benchmarks include well-known data structures such as Treiber's lock-free stack [31], Michael&Scott's lock-free queue [23], and the lock-free DGLM queue [8]. We do not include lock-free set implementations due to limitations of the tool in handling data—not due to limitations of our approach. We ran each benchmark under garbage collection (GC), and explicit memory management (MM) with version counters. Additionally, we include for each benchmark a comparison between our novel fixed point using summaries and the optimized version of the classical thread-modular fixed point from [14].

Our experiments show that summaries provide a significant performance boost compared to classical interference. This holds true for both garbage collection and explicit memory management. For garbage collection, we experience a speed-up of one order of magnitude throughout the entire test suite. Although comparisons among different implementations are inherently unfair, we note that our tool compares favorably to competitors [2,3,33,34]. Under explicit memory management, the same speed-up is present for simple algorithms, like Treiber's stack. For slightly more complex implementations, like Michael&Scott's queue, we observe a more eminent speed-up of over two orders of magnitude. This speed-up is present even though the analysis explores a way larger search space than its classical counterpart. This confirms that our approach of reducing the complexity of interference steps rather than reducing the search space is beneficial for verification.

Unfortunately, we could not establish correctness of the DGLM queue under explicit memory management with neither of the fixed points. For the classical one, the reason was imprecision in the underlying shape analysis which resulted in spurious unsafe memory accesses. For our novel fixed point, the tool detected an ownership violation according to Sect. 6. While being correct, the DGLM queue indeed features such a violation. The update pattern in the deque method can result in freeing nodes that were made unreachable by other threads. The problematic scenario only occurs when the head of the queue overtakes the tail.

Despite the similarity, this behavior is not present in Michael&Scott's queue which is why it does not suffer from such a violation.

As hinted in Sect. 6, one could generalize our theory in such a way that no ownership transfer is required. Without ownership transfer, however, freeing cells becomes an effect of the shared heap which cannot be mimicked: a stateless summary cannot acquire a pointer to an unreachable cell and thus not mimic the free. Consequently, one has to relax the assumption of statelessness. This inflicts major changes on the fixed point from Sect. 4. Besides program threads, it would need to include threads executing stateful summaries. Moreover, one would need to reintroduce interference steps. However, only such interference steps are required where stateful summaries appear as the interfering thread. Hence, the number of interference steps is expected to be significantly lower than for ordinary interference. We consider a proper investigation of these issues an interesting subject for future work.

8 Related Work

We already commented on the two approaches of computing interference steps. The merge-and-project approach [4,11,19,22] suffers form low scalability and precision due to computing too many merge-compatible heaps. To improve precision of interference, works like [12,30,34] track additional thread correlations; ownership, for instance. However, keeping more information within thread states usually has a negative impact on scalability. Moreover, for the programs of our interest, those techniques were not applicable in the case of explicitly managed memory which does not provide exclusivity guarantees. Instead, [2,4] proposed to maintain views of two threads, allowing one to infer the context in which a views occurs. Since this again jeopardizes scalability, [14] tailored ownership towards explicit memory management. Still, computing interference remained quadratic in the size of the fixed point. Our approach improves dramatically on the efficiency of [14] while keeping its precision.

The learning approach in [32,34,35] and [24–26] performs a variant of rely/guarantee reasoning [18] paired with symbolic execution and abstract interpretation, respectively. In a fixed point, the interference produced by a thread is recorded and applied to other threads in consecutive iterations. This computes a symbolic representation of the inteference which is as precise as the underlying abstract domain (although the precision may be relaxed by further abstraction and hand-crafted joins). Our method improves on this in various aspects. First, we never compute the most precise interference information. Our summaries can be understood as a form of interpolant between the most precise approximation and the complement of the bad states. Second, our summaries are syntactic objects (program code) which are independent of the actual verification procedure and thus reusable. The learned interference may be reused only in the same abstract domain it was computed in. Third, we show how to lift our approach to explicit memory management what has not been done before. Fourth, our results are independent of the actual program semantics relying only on a small core language. Our development required to formulate the principles that libraries rely on (statelessness) which have not been made explicit elsewhere.

Another approach to make the verification of low-level implementations tractable is atomicity abstraction [1,9,10,20,27,28]. The core idea is to translate a given program into its specification by introducing and enlarging atomic blocks. The code transformations must be provably sound, with the soundness arguments oftentimes crafted for a particular semantics only. While generating summaries is closely related to making the program under scrutiny more atomic, we pursue a different approach. Our rewriting rules (i.e. the computation of summaries) do not need to be, and indeed are not, provably sound, which allows for much more freedom. Nevertheless, we guarantee a sound analysis. Our sanity checks can be understood as an efficient, fully automatic procedure to check whether or not the applied atomicity abstraction was sound. Additionally, we do not rely on a particular memory semantics.

Simulation relations are widely used for linearizability proofs [8,9,29,36] and verified compilation [17,21]. There, one establishes a simulation relation between a low-level program and a high-level program stating that the latter preserves the behaviors of the former. Verifying properties of the low-level program then reduces to verifying the same property for the high-level program. Establishing simulation relations, however, suffers from the same shortcomings as atomicity abstraction.

Finally, [13] introduces *grace periods*, an idiom similar to CAS blocks. It reflects the protocol used by a program to prohibit data corruption. During a grace period, it is guaranteed that a thread's memory is not freed. However, no method for checking conformance to such periods is given. That is, soundness of the analysis results cannot be checked when relying on grace periods whereas our sanity checks can efficiently detect unsound verification results.

9 Conclusion

We proposed a new approach for verifying lock-free data structures. The approach builds on the so-called CAS blocks (or, more generally, copy-and-check code blocks) which are commonly used when implementing lock-free data structures. We proposed a heuristic that builds stateless program summaries from such blocks. By avoiding many expensive merge-and-project operations, the approach can greatly increase the efficiency of thread-modular verification. This was confirmed by our experimental results showing that the implementation of our approach compares favorably with other competing tools. Moreover, our approach naturally combines with recently proposed reasoning about ownership to improve the precision of thread-modular reasoning, which allowed us to handle complex lock-free code efficiently even under explicit memory management. Of course, our heuristically computed stateless summaries can miss some reachable shared heaps, but, as a major part of our contribution, we proved that one can check whether this is the case on the generated state space. Hence, we can perform sound verification using a potentially unsound abstraction.

In the future, we would like to investigate CEGAR to include missing effects into our summaries. The main question here is how to refine the program code of a summary using an abstract representation of the missing effects. Further, it may be necessary to introduce stateful summaries in order to include certain effects, as revealed by the DGLM queue under explicit memory management. Moreover, in theory, our approach could increase not only efficiency but also precision compared with other approaches. This is due to the atomicity of the CAS blocks that could rule out interleavings that other approaches would explore. We have not found this confirmed in our experiments. Nevertheless, we find it worth investigating the theoretical and practical aspects of this matter in the future.

References

1. Abadi, M., Lamport, L.: The existence of refinement mappings. In: LICS. pp. 165–175. IEEE, Las Vegas (1988)
2. Abdulla, P.A., Haziza, F., Holík, L., Jonsson, B., Rezine, A.: An integrated specification and verification technique for highly concurrent data structures. In: Piterman, N., Smolka, S.A. (eds.) TACAS 2013. LNCS, vol. 7795, pp. 324–338. Springer, Heidelberg (2013). doi:10.1007/978-3-642-36742-7_23
3. Abdulla, P.A., Jonsson, B., Trinh, C.Q.: Automated verification of linearization policies. In: Rival, X. (ed.) SAS 2016. LNCS, vol. 9837, pp. 61–83. Springer, Heidelberg (2016). doi:10.1007/978-3-662-53413-7_4
4. Berdine, J., Lev-Ami, T., Manevich, R., Ramalingam, G., Sagiv, M.: Thread quantification for concurrent shape analysis. In: Gupta, A., Malik, S. (eds.) CAV 2008. LNCS, vol. 5123, pp. 399–413. Springer, Heidelberg (2008). doi:10.1007/978-3-540-70545-1_37
5. Beyer, D., Henzinger, T.A., Keremoglu, M.E., Wendler, P.: Conditional model checking: a technique to pass information between verifiers. In: SIGSOFT FSE. p. 57. ACM, New York (2012)
6. Christakis, M., Wüstholz, V.: Bounded abstract interpretation. In: Rival, X. (ed.) SAS 2016. LNCS, vol. 9837, pp. 105–125. Springer, Heidelberg (2016). doi:10.1007/978-3-662-53413-7_6
7. Cook, B., Haase, C., Ouaknine, J., Parkinson, M., Worrell, J.: Tractable reasoning in a fragment of separation logic. In: Katoen, J.-P., König, B. (eds.) CONCUR 2011. LNCS, vol. 6901, pp. 235–249. Springer, Heidelberg (2011). doi:10.1007/978-3-642-23217-6_16
8. Doherty, S., Groves, L., Luchangco, V., Moir, M.: Formal verification of a practical lock-free queue algorithm. In: FORTE. LNCS, vol. 3235, pp. 97–114. Springer, New York (2004)
9. Elmas, T., Qadeer, S., Sezgin, A., Subasi, O., Tasiran, S.: Simplifying linearizability proofs with reduction and abstraction. In: Esparza, J., Majumdar, R. (eds.) TACAS 2010. LNCS, vol. 6015, pp. 296–311. Springer, Heidelberg (2010). doi:10.1007/978-3-642-12002-2_25
10. Elmas, T., Qadeer, S., Tasiran, S.: A calculus of atomic actions. In: POPL. pp. 2–15. ACM, New York (2009)
11. Flanagan, C., Qadeer, S.: Thread-modular model checking. In: Ball, T., Rajamani, S.K. (eds.) SPIN 2003. LNCS, vol. 2648, pp. 213–224. Springer, Heidelberg (2003). doi:10.1007/3-540-44829-2_14

12. Gotsman, A., Berdine, J., Cook, B., Sagiv, M.: Thread-modular shape analysis. In: PLDI. pp. 266–277. ACM, New York (2007)
13. Gotsman, A., Rinetzky, N., Yang, H.: Verifying concurrent memory reclamation algorithms with grace. In: Felleisen, M., Gardner, P. (eds.) ESOP 2013. LNCS, vol. 7792, pp. 249–269. Springer, Heidelberg (2013). doi:10.1007/978-3-642-37036-6_15
14. Haziza, F., Holík, L., Meyer, R., Wolff, S.: Pointer race freedom. In: Jobstmann, B., Leino, K.R.M. (eds.) VMCAI 2016. LNCS, vol. 9583, pp. 393–412. Springer, Heidelberg (2016). doi:10.1007/978-3-662-49122-5_19
15. Herlihy, M., Wing, J.M.: Linearizability: A correctness condition for concurrent objects. ACM TOPLAS **12**(3), 463–492 (1990)
16. Holík, L., Meyer, R., Vojnar, T., Wolff, S.: Effect summaries for thread-modular analysis. CoRR abs/1705.03701 (2017). http://arxiv.org/abs/1705.03701
17. Jagannathan, S., Petri, G., Vitek, J., Pichardie, D., Laporte, V.: Atomicity refinement for verified compilation. In: PLDI, p. 27. ACM, New York (2014)
18. Jones, C.B.: Specification and design of (parallel) programs. In: IFIP, pp. 321–332 (1983)
19. Jones, C.B.: Tentative steps toward a development method for interfering programs. ACM TOPLAS **5**(4), 596–619 (1983)
20. Jonsson, B.: Using refinement calculus techniques to prove linearizability. Formal Asp. Comput. **24**(4–6), 537–554 (2012)
21. Leroy, X.: A formally verified compiler back-end. JAR **43**(4), 363–446 (2009)
22. Malkis, A., Podelski, A., Rybalchenko, A.: Thread-modular verification is cartesian abstract interpretation. In: Barkaoui, K., Cavalcanti, A., Cerone, A. (eds.) ICTAC 2006. LNCS, vol. 4281, pp. 183–197. Springer, Heidelberg (2006). doi:10.1007/11921240_13
23. Michael, M.M., Scott, M.L.: Nonblocking algorithms and preemption-safe locking on multiprogrammed shared memory multiprocessors. JPDC **51**(1), 1–26 (1998)
24. Miné, A.: Static analysis of run-time errors in embedded critical parallel C programs. In: Barthe, G. (ed.) ESOP 2011. LNCS, vol. 6602, pp. 398–418. Springer, Heidelberg (2011). doi:10.1007/978-3-642-19718-5_21
25. Miné, A.: Relational thread-modular static value analysis by abstract interpretation. In: McMillan, K.L., Rival, X. (eds.) VMCAI 2014. LNCS, vol. 8318, pp. 39–58. Springer, Heidelberg (2014). doi:10.1007/978-3-642-54013-4_3
26. Monat, R., Miné, A.: Precise thread-modular abstract interpretation of concurrent programs using relational interference abstractions. In: Bouajjani, A., Monniaux, D. (eds.) VMCAI 2017. LNCS, vol. 10145, pp. 386–404. Springer, Cham (2017). doi:10.1007/978-3-319-52234-0_21
27. Popeea, C., Rybalchenko, A., Wilhelm, A.: Reduction for compositional verification of multi-threaded programs. In: FMCAD, pp. 187–194. IEEE, New York (2014)
28. Rocha Pinto, P., Dinsdale-Young, T., Gardner, P.: TaDA: a logic for time and data abstraction. In: Jones, R. (ed.) ECOOP 2014. LNCS, vol. 8586, pp. 207–231. Springer, Heidelberg (2014). doi:10.1007/978-3-662-44202-9_9
29. Schellhorn, G., Derrick, J., Wehrheim, H.: A sound and complete proof technique for linearizability of concurrent data structures. ACM TOCL **15**(4), 31:1–31:37 (2014)
30. Segalov, M., Lev-Ami, T., Manevich, R., Ganesan, R., Sagiv, M.: Abstract transformers for thread correlation analysis. In: Hu, Z. (ed.) APLAS 2009. LNCS, vol. 5904, pp. 30–46. Springer, Heidelberg (2009). doi:10.1007/978-3-642-10672-9_5
31. Treiber, R.: Systems programming: coping with parallelism. Technical report RJ 5118, IBM (1986)

32. Vafeiadis, V.: Shape-value abstraction for verifying linearizability. In: Jones, N.D., Müller-Olm, M. (eds.) VMCAI 2009. LNCS, vol. 5403, pp. 335–348. Springer, Heidelberg (2008). doi:10.1007/978-3-540-93900-9_27
33. Vafeiadis, V.: Automatically proving linearizability. In: Touili, T., Cook, B., Jackson, P. (eds.) CAV 2010. LNCS, vol. 6174, pp. 450–464. Springer, Heidelberg (2010). doi:10.1007/978-3-642-14295-6_40
34. Vafeiadis, V.: RGSep action inference. In: Barthe, G., Hermenegildo, M. (eds.) VMCAI 2010. LNCS, vol. 5944, pp. 345–361. Springer, Heidelberg (2010). doi:10.1007/978-3-642-11319-2_25
35. Vafeiadis, V., Parkinson, M.: A marriage of rely/guarantee and separation logic. In: Caires, L., Vasconcelos, V.T. (eds.) CONCUR 2007. LNCS, vol. 4703, pp. 256–271. Springer, Heidelberg (2007). doi:10.1007/978-3-540-74407-8_18
36. Zhang, S.J., Liu, Y.: Model checking a lazy concurrent list-based set algorithm. In: SSIRI, pp. 43–52. IEEE, New York (2010)

Toward a Sound Analysis of Guarded LTI Loops with Inputs by Abstract Acceleration

Colas Le Guernic[1,2](✉)

[1] DGA Maîtrise de l'Information, Bruz, France
[2] Inria Rennes - Bretagne Atlantique, Rennes, France
colas.le-guernic@inria.fr

Abstract. In a POPL 2014 paper, Jeannet et al. showed that abstract acceleration is a relevant approach for general linear loops thanks to the Jordan decomposition of the linear transformer. Bounding the number of loop iterations involves interval-linear constraints. After identifying sources of over-approximation, we present some improvements over their method. First, we improve precision by using interval hulls in the Jordan parameters space instead of the state space, avoiding further interval arithmetic. Then, we show how to use conic hulls instead of interval hulls to further improve precision.

Furthermore, we extend their work to handle linear loops with bounded nondeterministic input. This was already attempted by Cattaruzza et al. in a SAS 2015 paper, unfortunately their method is unsound. After explaining why, we propose a sound approach to guarded LTI loops with bounded nondeterministic inputs by reduction to the autonomous case.

1 Introduction

Finding bounds on the values taken by variables is an essential step in program, and model, verification. Difficulties arise in the presence of loops. We are here specifically interested in loops whose body consists of a linear transformation on the program variables, with a linear exit condition. Such loops are pervasive in cyber-physical models as well as embedded codes.

If the number of steps is bounded, linear loops can be analyzed with iterative methods [12,15] or bounded model checking [4]. When no bound is known or small enough, invariants may be derived through abstract interpretation [7], with abstract domains tailored to some of the emergent nonlinear relations [8,18], or barrier certificates [17].

An alternative approach, abstract acceleration [9,10], aims at replacing the loop by a single abstract transformer. Jeannet et al. [11] proved the approach tractable for general linear loops. Cattaruzza et al. [5,6] tried to extend their result to general linear loops with bounded inputs, unfortunately their analysis is not clearly stated and based on unsound assumptions.

We describe our problem in more details and introduce some notations in Sect. 2. We then express, in Sect. 3, Jeannet et al.'s approach [11] in our setting.

F. Ranzato (Ed.): SAS 2017, LNCS 10422, pp. 192–211, 2017.
DOI: 10.1007/978-3-319-66706-5_10

This is more than just a reminder, in particular we clearly identify sources of over-approximation, and is necessary for the clarity of the rest of the paper. Our contributions to the abstract acceleration of loops without inputs are presented in Sect. 4 and experimentally evaluated in Sect. 5. Inputs are considered in Sect. 6 in which we first demonstrate the unsoundness of Cattaruzza et al. [5] approach before presenting our solution. Finally we discuss the impact of floating point computations in Sect. 7.

2 Preliminaries

We are interested in the approximation of invariants for linear time-invariant (LTI) loops over $\mathbb{R}$ of the form:

$$\begin{aligned}&\text{assume}(x \in X_0)\\&\text{while}(Gx \leq h) \quad x := Ax + B \cdot \text{Get}(U) + c\end{aligned}$$

where G, A, and B are matrices, c and h constant vectors, X_0 the initial set, and $\text{Get}(U)$ nondeterministically returns a fresh vector from the set U at each loop iteration.

Without loss of generality we can restrict ourselves to (see [13], Appendix 1):

$$\text{while}(Gx \leq 0) \quad x := Ax + \text{Get}(U) \qquad \text{with } 0 \in U. \tag{1}$$

Noting τ the effect of one loop iteration, abstract acceleration aims at finding a sound approximation of τ^*: $X_0 \mapsto \bigcup_{i=0}^{\infty} \tau^i(X_0)$.

We call Eq. (1) the loop representation of the problem. It can also be stated with a sequential representation:

$$X_{n+1} = A(X_n \cap \mathcal{G}) \oplus U \tag{2}$$

where $\mathcal{G}$ is the set $\{x \mid Gx \leq 0\}$, and $\oplus$ is the Minkowski sum: the sum of two sets is the set of the sums of elements of each set. Given an initial set X_0, we want to over-approximate $\mathcal{X} = \bigcup_{i=0}^{\infty} X_i$. Throughout this paper we will mainly use this last representation.

For the reader's sake, we now list the notations used throughout this paper:

- A is the matrix of the linear transformation performed in the loop body;
- $\mathcal{A}$ is the set $\{A^k \mid k \in \mathbb{N}\}$, and $\mathcal{A}_n = \{A^k \mid k \in \mathbb{N},\, k < n\}$;
- $\mathcal{B}$ denotes a box, or a product of intervals;
- d is the dimension of the system, $x \in \mathbb{R}^d$;
- $d' \leq d$ is the degree of the minimal polynomial of A;
- $\text{Vect}\,(\mathcal{A})$ is the vector space generated by $\mathcal{A}$;
- for a given basis $(M_0, \ldots, M_{d'-1})$ of $\text{Vect}\,(\mathcal{A})$, $m(n)$ is the vector describing A^n in that basis, $\mathcal{M}$ is the set $\left\{m \mid \exists k \in \mathbb{N},\, \sum_{i=0}^{d'-1} m_i M_i = A^k\right\}$, and $\mathcal{M}_n$ is $\left\{m \mid \exists k \in \mathbb{N},\, k < n,\, \sum_{i=0}^{d'-1} m_i M_i = A^k\right\}$;

- $\mathcal{X} = \bigcup_{k=0}^{\infty} X_k$ and $\mathcal{X}_n = \bigcup_{k=0}^{n-1} X_k$;
- N is the smallest index, if it exists, such that $\mathcal{X}_N = \mathcal{X}$;
- Π_i and $\Pi_{i,j}$ are orthogonal projections over the line generated by component i and the plane generated by components i and j respectively.
- for a given matrix A, $|A|$ is the matrix obtained by taking the absolute value of each component of A.
- for a given set S, $\overline{S}$ is an over-approximation of S, $\square(S)$ is its interval hull, $\boxdot(S) = \square(S \cup -S)$ is its centrally symmetric interval hull, and $\square_T(S)$ is the over-approximation of S by a polyhedron with template T.

3 Abstract Acceleration of LTI Systems Without Inputs

In this section we are interested in loops of the form:

$$\text{while}(Gx \leq 0) \quad x := Ax.$$

The next two subsections summarize the results of Jeannet et al. [11] using the sequential representation of the problem. For the sake of clarity we will not systematically cite their paper. In Sect. 3.3 we identify independent sources of over-approximations inherent to the method.

3.1 Linear Systems Without Guards

Without guards, the program becomes while($true$) $x := Ax$, and generates the sequence $X_{n+1} = AX_n$. Then: $\mathcal{X} = \bigcup_{i=0}^{\infty} A^i X_0$.

Considering $\mathcal{A} = \{A^i \mid i \in [0...\infty]\}$, one can compute $\mathcal{X}$ by applying $\mathcal{A}$ on X_0 element-wise: $\mathcal{X} = \mathcal{A}X_0 = \{Mx \mid M \in \mathcal{A}, x \in X_0\}$.

In order to render this representation effectively useful, Jeannet et al. [11] proceeds in three steps: express A^n as a nonlinear function of n; use this symbolic expression to tightly over-approximate $\mathcal{A}$ with a logahedron (a certain type of polyhedron) $\overline{\mathcal{A}}$; tightly over-approximate $\overline{\mathcal{A}}X_0$ with a polyhedron.

Symbolic Expression for $\mathcal{A}$. First let us remark that, following Cayley-Hamilton theorem, $\mathcal{A}$ lies in a subspace of $\mathbb{R}^{d \times d}$ of dimension $d' \leq d$. Thus, for a given basis $M_0, \ldots, M_{d'-1}$ of this subspace, and for any $n \in \mathbb{N}$, there exists a unique vector $m(n)$ such that:

$$A^n = \sum_{i=0}^{d'-1} m_i(n) M_i, \quad \text{and} \quad \mathcal{A} = \left\{ \sum_{i=0}^{d'-1} m_i M_i \mid m \in \mathcal{M} \right\}$$

where $\mathcal{M} = \{m(n) \mid n \in \mathbb{N}\}$.

In order to find a suitable basis, with an easy to represent and approximate $\mathcal{M}$, Jeannet et al. [11] suggest to use the Jordan decomposition of A: PJP^{-1} (see [13], Appendix 2, to get the intuition on a simple case or [11] for the full expression).

Tight Over-Approximation of $\mathcal{M}$. Since $\mathcal{A}$ is the image of $\mathcal{M}$ by a linear transformation, one can obtain a polyhedral over-approximation $\overline{\mathcal{A}}$ of $\mathcal{A}$ from a polyhedral over-approximation $\overline{\mathcal{M}}$ of $\mathcal{M}$:

$$\overline{\mathcal{A}} = \left\{ \sum_{i=0}^{d'-1} m_i M_i \mid m \in \overline{\mathcal{M}} \right\}.$$

Since each of the components of m are nonlinear, computing precisely supporting hyperplanes in arbitrary directions is hard. Jeannet et al. [11] restricts constraints to linear combinations of (almost) any two components and provides a way to compute the corresponding supporting hyperplane, leading to a logahedral approximation of $\mathcal{M}$.

Applying a *Set* of Linear Transformations. Jeannet et al. [11] suggest two approaches, but the one they recommend involves expressing $\mathcal{M}$ and X_0 with vertices (and rays) and multiplying them pairwise, leading to the best convex approximation of the result. They acknowledge that the exponential complexity in the dimension starts to show at dimension 8.

3.2 Linear Systems with Guards

We are now interested in the sequence: $X_{n+1} = A(X_n \cap \mathcal{G})$. Using the closed form of X_n we can deduce that:

$$\mathcal{X} = \bigcup_{n=0}^{\infty} A^n \left(X_0 \cap \bigcap_{i=0}^{n-1} \{x \mid GA^i x \leq 0\} \right).$$

Reduction to the Unguarded Case. In order to avoid this alternation of unions and intersections Jeannet et al. [11] over-approximate $\mathcal{X}$ with:

$$X_0 \cup A\left(\mathcal{A}\left(X_0 \cap \mathcal{G}\right) \cap \mathcal{G}\right)$$

which is equivalent to applying the unguarded acceleration to $X_0 \cap \mathcal{G}$ before applying the loop transformer, τ, once. In order to improve over this approximation Jeannet et al. [11] proposes to search for the first N such that $X_N \cap \mathcal{G} = \emptyset$. Then:

$$\mathcal{X} \subseteq X_0 \cup A\left(\mathcal{A}_N\left(X_0 \cap \mathcal{G}\right) \cap \mathcal{G}\right).$$

Bounding the Number of Steps. We want to find the smallest n such that $X_n \cap \mathcal{G}$ is empty, which is equivalent fo finding the smallest n such that:

$$\emptyset = X_0 \cap \bigcap_{i=0}^{n} \{x \mid GA^i x \leq 0\}.$$

Again, this might be hard to compute directly, instead Jeannet et al. [11] look for the smallest n such that $A^n(X_0 \cap \mathcal{G}) \cap \mathcal{G}$ is empty.

Moving to Vect($\mathcal{A}$). In order to do so, they express the problem in the vector space generated by $\mathcal{A}$:

$$\left(\sum_{i=0}^{d'-1} m_i(n)M_i\right)(X_0 \cap \mathcal{G}) \cap \mathcal{G} = \emptyset \iff m(n) \notin \mathcal{K}$$

where $\mathcal{K}$ is the set of $m \in \mathcal{M}$ such that the intersection is not empty:

$$\mathcal{K} = \mathcal{M} \cap \left\{ m \mid \exists x \in X_0 \cap \mathcal{G},\ \sum_{i=0}^{d'-1} m_i G M_i x \leq 0 \right\}.$$

The intersection with $\mathcal{M}$ is not necessary here but will be useful to constrain the over-approximations of $\mathcal{K}$. The other part of the definition of $\mathcal{K}$ is simply the set of parameters m such that the image by the corresponding linear transformation, $\sum_{i=0}^{d'-1} m_i M_i$, of at least one point of $X_0 \cap \mathcal{G}$ lies in $\mathcal{G}$.

We are now looking for the smallest n such that $m(n) \notin \mathcal{K}$. First they over-approximate $\mathcal{K}$ with a simpler convex set, then they look for a separating hyperplane.

Approximating $\mathcal{K}$. The first step consists in replacing the bilinear constraints with *interval-linear* constraints by substituting $X_0 \cap \mathcal{G}$ with its interval hull $\square(X_0 \cap \mathcal{G})$[1]:

$$\mathcal{K} \subseteq \mathcal{M} \cap \left\{ m \mid \sum_{i=0}^{d'-1} m_i G M_i \square(X_0 \cap \mathcal{G}) \leq 0 \right\}.$$

Then, linearization techniques exploiting the template approximation of $\mathcal{M}$ are applied to obtain a convex polyhedron:

$$\overline{\mathcal{K}} = \overline{\square_T(\mathcal{M}) \cap \left\{ m \mid \sum_{i=0}^{d'-1} m_i G M_i \square(X_0 \cap \mathcal{G}) \leq 0 \right\}}.$$

Approxmating N. Since $\overline{\mathcal{K}}$ is convex, $m(n)$ leaves $\overline{\mathcal{K}}$ as soon as one of its constraints is violated. Thus for each constraint $gx \leq h$ of $\overline{\mathcal{K}}$, we are looking for the smallest positive integer n such that $g \cdot m(n) > h$. Unfortunately this expression is nonlinear, and finding the smallest n for arbitrary g might be costly. Instead, Jeannet et al. [11] restricts the set of constraints to linear combinations of two components as in Sect. 3.1 by over-approximating $\overline{\mathcal{K}}$ with its template polyhedron $\square_T(\overline{\mathcal{K}})$. See [11] for technical details on how each minimization is performed.

[1] To be more precise, Jeannet et al. [11] substitute $P^{-1}(X_0 \cap \mathcal{G})$ by its interval hull in $PJ_iP^{-1}(X_0 \cap \mathcal{G})$, where P is the invertible matrix leading to the Jordan form of $A = PJP^{-1}$. Use of this transformation is not justified and its advantage is not clear.

3.3 Recap: Sources of Over-Approximation

We are interested in a conservative approximation of $\bigcup_{i=0}^{\infty} X_i$. This is done in two steps: first a bound N on the smallest n such that X_{n+1} is empty is computed, then $\bigcup_{i=0}^{N} X_i$ is over-approximated. None of these steps can be done exactly in a reasonable time, thus several approximations are performed to render the problem practical.

Bounding the number of steps:

Ignoring the guard: Instead of looking for the smallest n such that X_0 and $\bigcap_{i=0}^{n} \{x \mid GA^i x \leq 0\}$ have an empty intersection, we look for the smallest n such that $X_0 \cap \mathcal{G} \cap \{x \mid GA^n x \leq 0\}$ is empty, ignoring the influence of $\bigcap_{i=1}^{n-1} \{x \mid GA^i x \leq 0\}$.

Bounding $X_0 \cap \mathcal{G}$: The problem is then further simplified to transform bilinear constraints in $\mathcal{K}$ into interval-linear constraints. We look for the smallest n such that $\square(X_0 \cap \mathcal{G}) \cap \{x \mid GA^n x \leq 0\}$ is empty. This approximation is propagated and amplified by the use of interval arithmetic to approximate $\mathcal{K}$ with a set of interval-linear constraints.

Linearization: $\mathcal{K}$ is then further approximated to replace interval-linear constraints with linear constraints.

Bounding $\overline{\mathcal{K}}$: Finally, $\overline{\mathcal{K}}$ is tightly over-approximated with a template polyhedron (logahedron) so that minimizing n such that any of its constraint is violated becomes tractable.

We do not consider the over-approximation of $\mathcal{M}$ in the computation of $\mathcal{K}$ to be a source of error. Indeed, $\mathcal{M}$ here is only used to limit the error produced by the last two steps. If they did not produce errors, the quality of the approximation of $\mathcal{M}$ would have no incidence on the computed bound on the number of steps.

At last the minimization procedure itself may produce an over-approximation: for each constraint of $\square_T\left(\overline{\mathcal{K}}\right)$ it is not guaranteed to return a finite value, but if it does it is the minimum integer n such that $m(n)$ violate that constraint.

Approximating $\bigcup_{n=0}^{N} X_n$:

Ignoring the guard: Again, the first step is to ignore some of the influence of the guard: $\bigcup_{n=0}^{N} X_n = \bigcup_{n=0}^{N} A^n \left(X_0 \cap \bigcap_{i=0}^{n-1} \{x \mid GA^i x \leq 0\}\right)$ is over-approximated with $X_0 \cup \bigcup_{n=1}^{N} A^n \left(X_0 \cap \mathcal{G} \cap \{x \mid GA^{n-1} x \leq 0\}\right)$ expressed as $X_0 \cup A\left(\mathcal{A}_N\left(X_0 \cap \mathcal{G}\right) \cap \mathcal{G}\right)$.

Bounding $\mathcal{A}_N$: $\mathcal{A}_N$ is over-approximated with a logahedron: a template polyhedron whose constraints only involve two components at most. This over-approximation is tight, meaning that each face of $\square_T(\mathcal{A}_N)$ touches $\mathcal{A}_N$. The only room for improvement here lies in the choice of the directions of approximation and the ability to find tight bounds in arbitrary directions.

Bounding $\square_T(\mathcal{A}_N)(X_0 \cap \mathcal{G}) \cap \mathcal{G}$: This operation is already quite precise, indeed $\square_T(\mathcal{A}_N)(X_0 \cap \mathcal{G})$ is over-approximated by its convex hull. Yet, the quality of the approximation with respect to $\mathcal{A}_N(X_0 \cap \mathcal{G}) \cap \mathcal{G}$ is hard to evaluate.

Concerning complexity, the most costly operations are:

- The symbolic computation of the Jordan form of A.
- The product $\square_T(\mathcal{A}_N)(X_0 \cap \mathcal{G})$ done by computing the pairwise products of the vertices and rays generating $\square_T(\mathcal{A}_N)$ and $(X_0 \cap \mathcal{G})$.

4 Contributions to Abstract Acceleration of Linear Systems Without Inputs

The previous section offered an original presentation of the results of Jeannet et al. [11]. Moreover, we highlighted the different sources of over-approximation. In the current section we present our own contributions, focusing on the approximation of $\mathcal{K}$, the set used to bound the maximum number of iterations.

When the number of steps is finite, correctly bounding it can provide a great improvement on precision. This bound is computed by finding the smallest n such that $m(n) \notin \mathcal{K}$. Let us recall the expression for $\mathcal{K}$:

$$\mathcal{K} = \mathcal{M} \cap \left\{ m \mid \exists x \in X_0 \cap \mathcal{G},\ \sum_{i=0}^{d'-1} m_i G M_i x \leq 0 \right\}.$$

For the sake of presentation we will consider here that G is composed of only one constraint g. When G has multiple rows, each row can be treated independently, similarly to what is implicitly[2] done by Jeannet et al. [11].

Remark 1. Independent treatment of each constraint leads to a first approximation, indeed the set $\{m \mid \exists x \in X,\ f(g_0, m, x) \leq 0 \wedge f(g_1, m, x) \leq 0\}$ may be smaller than the intersection:

$$\{m \mid \exists x \in X,\ f(g_0, m, x) \leq 0\} \cap \{m \mid \exists x \in X,\ f(g_1, m, x) \leq 0\}.$$

In the first case, both constraints must be verified for the same x, in the second case, one can choose two different x. It can be partially overcome by considering linear combinations of constraints.

By noting L the matrix whose rows are the gM_i we can express $\mathcal{K}$ as:

$$\mathcal{K} = \mathcal{M} \cap \{m \mid \exists x \in X \cap \mathcal{G},\ m \cdot Lx \leq 0\}.$$

In the following subsections, we make the assumption that there is no x in $X_0 \cap \mathcal{G}$ such that $Lx = 0$, if there was, $\mathcal{K}$ would be equal to $\mathcal{M}$, and the number of steps would be unbounded.

[2] When approximating $\mathcal{K}$ with interval linear constraints the relation between the constraints parameters are lost.

4.1 Avoiding Interval Arithmetic

As presented earlier, the first step of the approximation of $\mathcal{K}$ is to replace bilinear with interval-linear constraints by first over-approximating $X \cap \mathcal{G}$ with its interval hull and then propagate those intervals by interval arithmetic:

$$\begin{aligned}\mathcal{K} &\subseteq \mathcal{M} \cap \{m \mid \exists x \in \square(X \cap \mathcal{G}),\, m \cdot Lx \leq 0\} \\ &\subseteq \mathcal{M} \cap \{m \mid m \cdot L\square(X \cap \mathcal{G}) \leq 0\}\end{aligned}$$

leading to a superset[3] of:

$$\mathcal{M} \cap \{m \mid m \cdot \square(L\square(X \cap \mathcal{G})) \leq 0\}\,.$$

Expressing $\sum_{i=0}^{d'-1} m_i G M_i x$ as $m \cdot Lx$ makes it clear that interval arithmetic can be avoided. Thus we suggest to use the interval hull of $L(X \cap \mathcal{G})$ directly:

$$\mathcal{K} \subseteq \mathcal{M} \cap \{m \mid \exists \ell \in \square(L(X \cap \mathcal{G}))\,,\, m \cdot \ell \leq 0\}$$

leading to a more precise approximation. $L(X \cap \mathcal{G})$ does not need to be computed explicitly, $\square(L(X \cap \mathcal{G}))$ can be computed directly by optimizing linear functions on $X \cap \mathcal{G}$ in the directions given by $L^\top$. The procedure is efficient even if L is not invertible.

Example 1. Starting from any point in the convex hull of $\{(1,0); (0,1)\}$, consider the loop: while$(x + y \leq 10)\{x := 2x;\, y := 2y\}$. Jeannet et al. [11] can not find any bound on the number of steps while our approach finds the correct one (see [13], Appendix 3.1, for details).

The improvement is not always that dramatic but the resulting bound is always at least as good as the one given by Jeannet et al. [11]. Indeed, their interval linear constraints are based on a superset of $\square(L\square(X \cap \mathcal{G}))$ while ours is based on $\square(L(X \cap \mathcal{G}))$ directly.

Furthermore, our method does not introduce any overhead in terms of time complexity. Indeed computing the interval hull of $L(X \cap \mathcal{G})$ or $X \cap \mathcal{G}$ both involve maximizing $2d'$ or $2d$ respectively linear functions over $X \cap \mathcal{G}$ as discussed earlier.

4.2 Avoiding Interval Hull

We are here again interested in the first step of the approximation of $\mathcal{K}$, replacing bilinear with interval-linear constraints.

In the previous section we were interested in what to get a product of intervals from, we got:

$$\mathcal{K} \subseteq \mathcal{M} \cap \{m \mid \exists \ell \in \square(L(X \cap \mathcal{G}))\,,\, m \cdot \ell \leq 0\}\,.$$

[3] Both sets would be equal if interval arithmetic did not amplify and propagate any approximation.

In this section we are interested in how to get a suitable product of intervals $\mathcal{B}$ such that:

$$\mathcal{K} \subseteq \mathcal{M} \cap \{m \mid \exists \ell \in \mathcal{B},\, m \cdot \ell \leq 0\}.$$

Intuitively the best way to get such a product of intervals is to take the interval hull: $\mathcal{B} = \square(L(X \cap \mathcal{G}))$. We will show that it is possible to use another box leading to a better approximation of $\mathcal{K}$. Let us first remark that:

$$m \cdot \ell \leq 0 \iff \exists \alpha \in \mathbb{R}^+,\, \alpha \neq 0 \wedge m \cdot (\alpha \ell) \leq 0.$$

Thus, if $0 \notin L(X_0 \cap \mathcal{G})$:

$$\mathcal{K} = \mathcal{M} \cap \{m \mid \exists \ell \in \angle(L(X_0 \cap \mathcal{G}))\,,\, \ell \neq 0 \wedge m \cdot \ell \leq 0\}$$

where $\angle(X) = \{\alpha \ell \mid \alpha \in \mathbb{R}^+,\, \ell \in X\}$ is the conic hull of X.

We will not use this conic representation directly, instead we will look for a product of intervals that generates a cone containing $\angle(X_0 \cap \mathcal{G})$, but not bigger (and hopefully smaller) than the cone generated by $\square(X_0 \cap \mathcal{G})$, leading to a better approximation of $\mathcal{K}$. Ideally, we would like to find a product of intervals generating the smallest possible cone. Unfortunately such a box does not necessarily exist. Instead, we will show how to compute a suitable subset of $\square(X_0 \cap \mathcal{G})$ and optimal degenerate boxes. First, let us characterize conic hulls of products of closed intervals.

Theorem 1. *For any product of closed intervals, its conic hull $\angle(\mathcal{B})$ is entirely determined by its projection on canonical planes.*

Proof. See [13], Appendix 4.

Algorithm 1. Interval hull subset.

Input: A nonempty set X in dimension d such that $0 \notin \square(X)$.
Output: A box B such that $\angle(X) \subseteq \angle(B)$ and $B \subseteq \square(X)$.

$S \leftarrow \emptyset^d$
for $i = 0$ to $d-2$ **do**
  for $j = i+1$ to $d-1$ **do**
    $(x, y) \leftarrow$ GET_PAIR(X, i, j)
    $S_i \leftarrow \square(S_i \cup \{x_0\} \cup \{y_0\})$
    $S_j \leftarrow \square(S_j \cup \{x_1\} \cup \{y_1\})$
  end for
end for
return S

Algorithm 1 exploits this characterization to compute a box $\mathcal{B}$ included in $\square(L(X_0 \cap \mathcal{G}))$ such that $\angle(L(X_0 \cap \mathcal{G}))$ is included in $\angle(\mathcal{B})$. The problem is projected on each of the $d(d-1)/2$ canonical planes, then solved by GET_PAIR which returns two points with minimal coordinates along the two half-lines (that may be colinear) delimiting the cone and on the frontier of the interval hull. The coordinates of those points are then used to update the full dimensional solution.

There are some subtleties in GET_PAIR. Applied on Fig. 1b it returns the coordinates of the bottom left and top left vertices of the box. But in situations similar to Fig. 1a, there are no half-lines delimiting the cone. Any pair of point whose interval hull is $[-\epsilon;\epsilon] \times [-\epsilon;\epsilon]$ for ϵ sufficiently small is suitable, but $[0;0] \times [0;0]$ does not span the whole plane. Still, GET_PAIR can safely return a pair of points generating $[0;0] \times [0;0]$. It will conflict with the output requirement of Algorithm 1, but not with the underlying goal of over-approximating $\mathcal{K}$. If we denote by $\mathcal{B}_\epsilon$ the box returned using a conservative GET_PAIR, and $\mathcal{K}_\epsilon$ the set: $\mathcal{M} \cap \{m \mid \exists \ell \in \mathcal{B}_\epsilon,\, m \cdot \ell \leq 0\}$, then: $\mathcal{K} \subseteq \bigcap_{\epsilon>0} \mathcal{K}_\epsilon \subseteq \mathcal{K}_0$. Indeed, since $\mathcal{B}_0$ is closed, for any m not in $\mathcal{K}$, there exists $\mu > 0$ such that for all $\ell \in \mathcal{B}_0$, $m \cdot \ell \geq \mu$. Thus there exists $\epsilon > 0$ such that m does not belong to $\mathcal{K}_\epsilon$, which implies that $\bigcap_{\epsilon>0} \mathcal{K}_\epsilon \subseteq \mathcal{K}_0$. Similar arguments allow to return the same value when the origin is on the frontier of the interval hull.

Moreover, if a delimiting half-line does not intersect the interval hull, then GET_PAIR can safely return a point with one infinite coordinate.

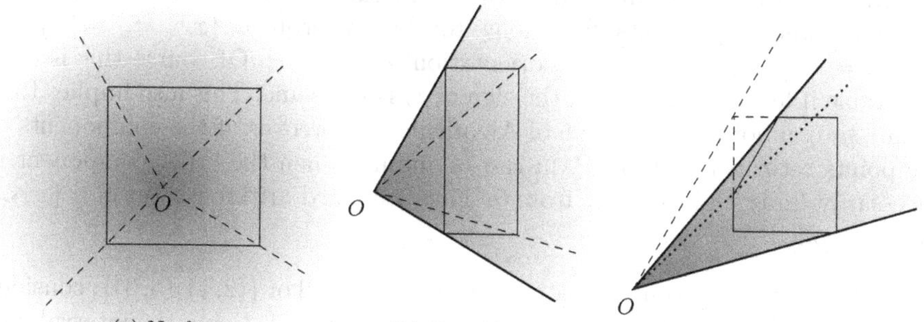

(a) No faces. (b) Two faces. (c) Iterative refinement.

Fig. 1. Projection of a product of intervals and its conic hull on a plane.

Another subtlety, concerns the projection of X on canonical planes. It can be costly and unnecessary. Instead, GET_PAIR takes as arguments X and the indices of the canonical vectors to project on. Starting from the conic hull of the interval hull of X, an approximation of the exact two-dimensional conic hull is iteratively refined by optimizing linear functions on the full dimensional X as illustrated in Fig. 1c.

Example 2. Starting from any point in the convex hull of $\{(2,1);(6,3)\}$, consider the loop: while$(-2x + y \leq 0)\{x := 0.9x;\ y := y\}$. Using the interval hull leads to a bound of 23 steps, while Algorithm 1 improves this bound to 13 (see [13], Appendix 3.2, for details).

Unfortunately, Algorithm 1 needs $\square(L(X_0 \cap \mathcal{G}))$ to be full dimensional in order to lead to any improvement and this is not always the case, especially for affine systems. Instead of finding a box included in $\square(L(X_0 \cap \mathcal{G}))$, Algorithm 2 computes an optimal flat box whose conic hull contains $L(X_0 \cap \mathcal{G})$.

Algorithm 2. Optimal flat box.

Input: A nonempty set X in dimension d and an index i such that $0 \notin \Pi_i \square(X)$.
Output: The smallest box B such that $\angle(X) \subseteq \angle(B)$ and, $B \subseteq \{x \mid x_i = 1\}$ or $B \subseteq \{x \mid x_i = -1\}$.

1: $S \leftarrow \emptyset^d$
2: $S_i \leftarrow \textsc{Sign}(\Pi_i \square(X))$
3: **for all** $j \neq i$ **do**
4: $\quad (x, y) \leftarrow \textsc{Get\_Pair}(X, i, j)$
5: $\quad S_j \leftarrow \square(S_j \cup \{x_1/|x_0|, y_1/|y_0|\})$
6: **end for**
7: **return** $\square(S)$

Similarly to Algorithm 1, Algorithm 2 makes use of GET_PAIR, and then scales the returned points to belong to the hyperplane $\{x \mid x_i = 1\}$, or $\{x \mid x_i = -1\}$ depending on the orientation of the cone. Of course this is only applicable if for all points in X, the sign of x_i is the same. This also implies that x_0 and y_0 can not be 0 on line 5 of Algorithm 2. Moreover, if the components of the points returned by GET_PAIR can be infinite, then the other component is necessarily finite and different from 0. Thus standard arithmetic on $\mathbb{R} \cup \{\pm\infty\}$ can be applied.

Example 3. Starting from any point in the convex hull of $\{(2, 1); (6, 3)\}$, consider the loop: while$(-2x + y - 0.1 \leq 0)\{x := 0.9x;\ y := y + 1\}$. Using the interval hull leads to a bound of 5 steps, Algorithm 1 cannot help us because $\square(L(X_0 \cap \mathcal{G}))$ is flat. Using Algorithm 2 optimizing the first component bounds the number of steps by 4. (see [13], Appendix 3.3, for details).

One might want to apply Algorithm 2 even if zero belongs to $\Pi_i \square(L(X_0 \cap \mathcal{G})$, as long as this set does not contain points of opposing signs. But then, the resulting $\overline{\mathcal{K}}$ is not guaranteed to be an over-approximation, and the resulting bound n has to be checked by optimizing the linear function $x \mapsto -L^\top m(n) \cdot x$ on $X_0 \cap \mathcal{G}$ in order to verify that there is no ℓ in $L(X_0 \cap \mathcal{G})$ such that $m(n) \cdot \ell \leq 0$.

As an example, consider the convex hull of $(0, 1)$ and $(2, -2)$. Its interval hull is $[0; 2] \times [-2; 1]$ and Algorithm 1 would return $[0; 0] \times [0; 0]$, then $\overline{\mathcal{K}} = \mathcal{M}$ and no bound on the number of iterations can be found. If instead one applies an adapted version of Algorithm 2 on the first component, the resulting box would be $[1; 1] \times [-1; \infty]$, only the half-line $[0; 0] \times]0; \infty]$ is missing from the resulting conic hull.

Algorithms 1 and 2 can be factorized to share the calls to GET_PAIR, resulting in a set of interval linear constraints. If one wants to perform only $d' - 1$

calls to GET_PAIR instead of $d'(d'-1)/2$, then we propose the following heuristic to choose the dimension i on which to apply Algorithm 2: first we filter out all indices such that 0 belongs to $\Pi_i \Box(X)$, then we only keep all indices corresponding to parameters associated with the eigenvalue λ of maximal norm, then choose one on the highest diagonal. The rational behind this heuristic is that at some point the associated parameter will grow faster than any other suitable one.[4]

Remark 2. Unless the system has been augmented with one nonnull dimension, it may happen that $0 \in \Box(L(X_0 \cap \mathcal{G}))$ even if $0 \notin L(X_0 \cap \mathcal{G})$. Then the only suitable cone generated by a product of interval spans the whole state space and a change of variable is necessary. Since $0 \notin L(X_0 \cap \mathcal{G})$, there exist a separating hyperplane between 0 and $L(X_0 \cap \mathcal{G})$, and a change of variable R such that $0 \notin \Box(RL(X_0 \cap \mathcal{G}))$ and we can use:

$$\mathcal{K} \subseteq \mathcal{M} \cap R^{\top} \{m \mid \exists \ell \in \Box(RL(X \cap \mathcal{G})), m \cdot \ell \leq 0\}.$$

Such a change of variable might also be useful to improve precision, in particular if $RL(X \cap \mathcal{G})$ is already a product of intervals.

4.3 Avoiding Interval-Linear Constraints

These last two improvements, *avoiding interval arithmetic* and *avoiding interval hull*, tackle the approximation errors introduced in the step designated as *Bounding* $X_0 \cap \mathcal{G}$ in Sect. 3.3 leading to interval linear constraints. The only requirement is that one can optimize linear functions over $X_0 \cap G$.

If X_0 is convex and $X_0 \cap G$ can be expressed as the Minkowski sum of a compact convex set $\mathcal{V}$ and the conic hull of a compact convex set $\mathcal{R}$, then it is relatively easy to show that for any $\alpha > 0$:

$$\angle(X_0 \cap G) = \angle(\text{CONVEXHULL}(\mathcal{V} \cup \alpha\mathcal{R})).$$

This can be used before applying Algorithms 1 or 2. If additionally, $\mathcal{V}$ and $\mathcal{R}$ are, or can be over-approximated by, compact polyhedra with a low number of vertices, then one can avoid interval linear constraints altogether. In fact $\angle(L(X_0 \cap \mathcal{G}))$ can be directly represented as a sum of rays:

$$\angle(L(X_0 \cap \mathcal{G})) = \left\{ \sum_i \alpha_i r_i | \forall i,\, \alpha_i \geq 0 \right\}.$$

Then for any $\ell = \sum_i \alpha_i r_i$ in $\angle(L(X_0 \cap \mathcal{G}))$:

$$m \cdot \ell \leq 0 \Leftrightarrow \sum_i \alpha_i m \cdot r_i \leq 0 \Longrightarrow \exists i,\, m \cdot r_i \leq 0.$$

[4] We use a similar heuristic in the experimental section to decide if an interval linear constraints can lead to a bound.

Indeed, if all elements in the sum were positive, the sum would be positive. This only works because we are considering one constraint at a time, if the comparison were multidimensional component-wise comparison, not being smaller than 0 would not imply being bigger than 0.

Thus:

$$\mathcal{K} \subseteq \bigcup_i \mathcal{M} \cap \{m \mid m \cdot r_i \leq 0\}.$$

The other direction is trivial since all r_i belong to $\angle(L(X_0 \cap \mathcal{G}))$.

$\mathcal{K}$ can be exactly[5] expressed as a union of half-spaces (intersected with $\mathcal{M}$). In other words, $\mathcal{K}$ is the complement in $\mathcal{M}$ of a polyhedron[6].

4.4 Iterative Improvement

As explained before, the number of iterations of the loop under consideration is the smallest n such that $m(n)$ does not belong to $\mathcal{K}$. Since $m(n)$ belongs to $\mathcal{M}$ by definition, the presence of $\mathcal{M}$ in the expression of $\mathcal{K}$ is superfluous. Nevertheless it helps bound the successive approximations needed to get a manageable expression for $\overline{\mathcal{K}}$. Once a bound N is found, one can restart the process (or continue with another constraints) expressing $\mathcal{K}$ as:

$$\mathcal{K} \subseteq \mathcal{M}_N \cap \{m \mid \exists \ell \in L(X \cap \mathcal{G}),\, m \cdot \ell \leq 0\}.$$

Taking $\mathcal{M}_N$ instead of $\mathcal{M}$ will improve subsequent approximations, and may lead to a smaller bound on the number of iterations.

5 Experimental Evaluation

Before considering loops with bounded inputs, let us evaluate the improvements presented so far. We only here focus on the techniques introduced in Sects. 4.1 and 4.2 because they have minimal requirements on X_0 and focus on one specific step that can be easily compared with Jeannet et al. [11] approach: deriving an interval linear constraint in order to bound the number of loop iterations.

We randomly generated 100 linear loops in several dimensions (2, 5, 10, 15, 20). To avoid diagonal systems we generated directly the Jordan form from a random partition of d. Then the guard and four different initial sets (balls for the 1, 2, and ∞ norms as well as a half-line, leading to an unbounded input set) were chosen such that all trajectories leave the guard after at most 32 steps, resulting in a total of 2000 instances.

We compared the performances of our own implementation of Jeannet et al. [11] algorithm with the improvement introduced in Sect. 4.1, a version of Algorithm 1 that returns a subset of the interval hull of $L(X_0 \cap \mathcal{G})$ and all

---

5 If there are several constraints, treating each constraint independently leads to an over-approximation.

6 Almost the dual cone of $L(X_0 \cap \mathcal{G})$.

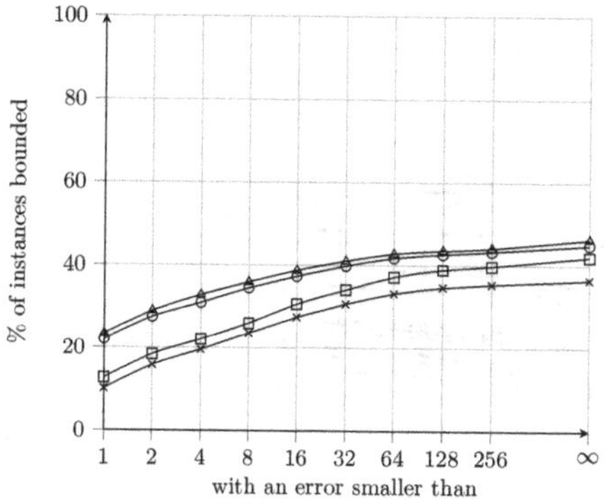

Fig. 2. Cumulative frequency of instances bounded by interval linear constraint(s) generated by: (×) Jeannet et al. [11], (□) Sect. 4.1, (○) Algorithm 2, and (△) Algorithm 1.

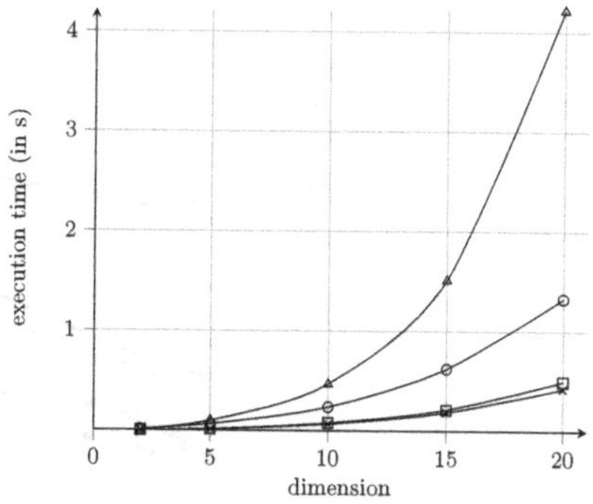

Fig. 3. Median execution time to generate an interval linear constraint using: (×) Jeannet et al. [11], (□) Sect. 4.1, (○) Algorithm 2, and (△) Algorithm 1.

possible flat boxes by factorizing calls to GET_PAIR at no visible additional cost as suggested at the end of Sect. 4.2, and a version of Algorithm 2 that returns the interval hull of $L(X_0 \cap \mathcal{G})$ and a box flat in the direction associated with the asymptotically bigger component as described at the end of Sect. 4.2.

The quality of the computed interval linear constraint is assessed by computing the first n such that $m(n)$ violates it, iteratively using exact arithmetic[7], and taking the difference with the exact bound. At some point, some components of $m(n)$ grows faster than all others and one may prove that the constraint will never be violated.

Results are shown in Fig. 2: Algorithms 1 and 2 can bound exactly more than one fifth of our instances, twice as many as Jeannet et al., and one third with an error smaller than 8 steps. Moreover, for instances that are bounded but not exactly, the error is a few orders of magnitude smaller, notice the log-scale for the x-coordinates. We also found bounds for instances that Jeannet et al. was unable to bound, representing almost 10% of our instances.

Computations were performed with a 2.5 GHz CPU and 6 Gb of memory using Python 3.5. As expected, Fig. 3 shows that Algorithm 2 has a complexity similar to Jeannet et al. but with a much higher constant, while Algorithm 1 suffers from an additional factor d.

Figure 4 illustrates the effect of dimension on precision. Note that Algorithm 2 in dimension 15 has a precision similar to Jeannet et al. approach in dimension 5.

[7] This is not how a bound N should be computed, and is only useful to asses the quality of the interval linear constraint.

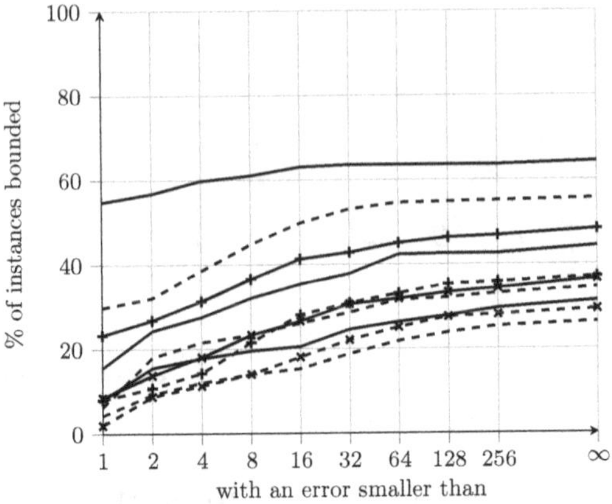

Fig. 4. Cumulative frequency of instances bounded by interval linear constraint(s) generated by: Jeannet et al. [11] (dashed), and Algorithm 2 (solid), in dimension 2, 5 (+), 10, 15 (×), and 20 (top to bottom).

6 Abstract Acceleration of LTI Systems with Inputs

In the previous section we introduced a few improvements over Jeannet et al. [11] techniques for the analysis of LTI loops with no inputs. We are now interested in loops of the form:

$$\text{while}(Gx \leq 0) \quad x := Ax + \text{Get}(U)$$

with Get(U) nondeterministically returning a fresh point in U at each loop iteration, and, without loss of generality, $0 \in U$.

Extending the work of Jeannet et al. [11] to systems with inputs has already been attempted in Cattaruzza et al. [5]. Unfortunately the method described is unsound. We will explain why in the next subsection before presenting a sound extension to systems with inputs, by reducing the problem to systems without inputs.

6.1 Unsoundness of Cattaruzza et al. SAS Paper

There are several issues with Cattaruzza et al. [5] paper and its extended version [6]. Among them, two clearly make the method unsound and another one exhibits this unsoundness.

The first one concerns the use of numerical algorithms to compute the Jordan form and is discussed in more details in Sect. 7.1. The second one is central to the method and can not be corrected easily. Almost all approximations are based on the following (wrong) assumption [5, p. 322]:

> Let $g_i = \sum_{j=1}^{p} a_{ij} v_j$, where v_j are generalised eigenvectors of A. [...]
>
> Then $A^n g_i = \sum_{j=1}^{p} \lambda_j^n a_{ij} v_j$ where λ_j is the corresponding eigenvalue of v_j.

Which amounts to forgetting about the upper-diagonal in the Jordan decomposition. It would only be true if the v_j were eigenvectors instead of generalized eigenvectors, but then g_i would not necessarily admit a decomposition over them.[8]

Last, the experimental results section presents a comparison between their method and LGG algorithm [16] on an example with no guards. In this context, LGG algorithm is known to perform a tight over-approximation [14]: the exact set touches all the faces of the computed approximation. Since they used octahedral abstractions, the projections of the sets computed by LGG on state variables coincide with the projection of the exact reachable set. Yet, their algorithm computes a set with a smaller range in one dimension, effectively missing some reachable states and exhibiting the unsoundness of the method.

6.2 Reduction to Systems Without Inputs

In order to tackle LTI loops with inputs, we will reduce the problem to LTI loops without inputs. Some over-approximations are necessary, and we try to limit them to over-approximation that are already present in the analysis of systems without inputs, starting with the influence of the guard, which is only considered at the first and last step. For the transient behavior, we ignore the guards, then:

$$X_n = AX_{n-1} \oplus U = A^n X_0 \oplus \bigoplus_{i=0}^{n-1} A^i U.$$

Lemma 1. *For any real matrix A and any set U, if we denote by $\square(.)$ the interval hull, $\boxdot(.)$ the centrally symmetric interval hull, and $|A|$ the matrix whose entries are the absolute value of the corresponding entries of A, we have:*

$$\bigoplus_{i=0}^{n-1} A^i U \subseteq \square\left(\left(\sum_{i=0}^{n-1} |A|^i\right) \boxdot(U)\right).$$

Proof. For any point $u \in U$ and any vector ℓ, it is relatively easy to show that: $A^i u \cdot \ell \leq |A|^i |u| \cdot |\ell|$. By denoting $u_{\max}$ the supremum, component-wise, of all $|u|$ for $u \in U$, we can further deduce that:

$$\forall \ell, \forall v \in \bigoplus_{i=0}^{n-1} A^i U,\ v \cdot \ell \leq \left(\sum_{i=0}^{n-1} |A|^i\right) u_{\max} \cdot |\ell|.$$

This set of constraints uniquely defines the set

$$\square\left(\left(\sum_{i=0}^{n-1} |A|^i\right) \boxdot(U)\right).$$

□

[8] The authors attempted a correction [6], unfortunately Eq. (16) is only true if all the k_{ij} are positive and the method is still unsound.

Let us know consider the following LTI system with no inputs:

$$Y_{k+1} = \begin{pmatrix} 0 & I & I & 0 \\ 0 & A & 0 & 0 \\ 0 & 0 & I & I \\ 0 & 0 & 0 & |A| \end{pmatrix} Y_k, \text{and}\, Y_0 = \begin{pmatrix} X_0 \\ AX_0 \\ \boxdot(U) \\ A\boxdot(U) \end{pmatrix}.$$

Then for any k, $X_k \subseteq \square\left(\begin{pmatrix} I & 0 & 0 & 0 \end{pmatrix} Y_k\right)$, as a direct consequence of Lemma 1.

The maximum number of iterations remains to be bounded. We can not directly use G, because it will only guarantee that Y_N is fully outside the guards while we are interested in $\square(Y_N)$. If one of the components of $\mathcal{X}$ is bounded and always has the same sign (which will necessarily be the case if the linear system was obtained from an affine system by adding one dimension) we denote by $\mathcal{B}$ the resulting band, then we define a new set of guards $\mathcal{G}'$ as the smallest cone containing the interval hull of the intersection between $\mathcal{G}$ and $\mathcal{B}$. This is still not enough, but if we consider each of the guards defined by $\mathcal{G}'$ independently, we can guarantee that if Y_N is outside of those guards, then $\square(Y_N)$ is outside of $\mathcal{G}$. Indeed, consider Fig. 1b, if the projection of $\mathcal{G}$ on the corresponding plane is delimited by the doted lines, and the bounds on the first component defined by the width of the rectangle, then for any set within the bounds and outside of the solid lines, its interval hull is outside of the dotted lines.

Thus a bound on the number of iteration before Y_n leaves $\mathcal{G}'$ also bounds the number of iteration before X_n leaves $\mathcal{G}$ and we can now use the method described in the first section for systems without inputs to analyse systems with inputs.

In order to limit the over-approximation, one should first perform a change of variables that isolate contracting stable subspaces of A, using a real jordan form, and/or limit the over-approximation induced by $\mathcal{G}'$.

It is to be noted that the resulting system's dimension is four times the initial system's. Nevertheless the high sparsity and redundancy of the resulting system, if correctly exploited, should lead to a moderate increase in computation time.

7 About Floating Point Numbers

Floating point numbers are an approximation of real numbers with a compact computer representation. When doing verification, one must take into account the errors introduced by their use in the verification process but also in the process to verify.

7.1 Mixing Floats and Symbolic Relations

One important relation for the method to work is that for any n, $A^n = PJ^nP^{-1}$. Jeannet et al. [11] ensure soundness by computing the Jordan decomposition symbolically, then enclosing P, J, and P^{-1} with interval matrices. Thus PJ^nP^{-1} represents a set of matrices containing the exact A^n.

Cattaruzza et al. [5] use a numerical algorithm to compute the Jordan form, which is much faster. Note that the Jordan decomposition is known to be numerically unstable. The authors still claim soundness by bloating the diagonal element of J with some constant $\delta_{\max} = |A - PJP^{-1}|$; it is not clear from the paper which norm is considered and the proof is left to the reader. Unfortunately, this bloating is not sufficient. Consider floating point numbers with a mantissa of size $2m$ such that $2^{2m} - 1$ and $2^{2m} + 2$ can be represented exactly but $2^{2m} + 1$ cannot. Then consider:

$$\begin{pmatrix} 1 + 2^{1-2m} & 1 \\ -2^{-4m} & 1 \end{pmatrix} = \begin{pmatrix} 1 & 1 \\ -2^{-2m} & 1 \end{pmatrix} \begin{pmatrix} 1 & 1 \\ 0 & 1 \end{pmatrix} \begin{pmatrix} 1 & -1 \\ 2^{-2m} & 1 \end{pmatrix}$$

All of these matrices can be represented exactly. With the notation $A = PJP'$ and interval arithmetic over floating point numbers one can verify that $A - (PJ)P' = 0$, thus no bloating is necessary according to Cattaruzza et al. [5]. Yet, for any $n > 1$, $A^n \neq PJ^nP'$. The reason why is that $PP' = P'P = (1 + 2^{-2m})I$ (which might be rounded to I using floating point numbers). The bloating they introduce is unsound, in particular because the authors do not seem to consider approximations in the matrices P and P^{-1}.

7.2 Loops with Floating Point Arithmetic

The use of floating point arithmetic in the process to verify is not an issue for Jeannet et al. [11], Cattaruzza et al. [5,6], or us, since we all consider loops involving real arithmetic only. A more realistic scenario in the context of program verification would be to consider floating point arithmetic which can have a dramatic effect especially when the floating point errors make the system stay longer in the body of the loop.

Again consider floating point numbers with a mantissa of size $2m$ such that $2^{2m} - 1$ and $2^{2m} + 2$ can be represented exactly but $2^{2m} + 1$ cannot. Then consider:

$$\text{while}(x - 2^m y \leq 0) \quad \begin{pmatrix} x \\ y \end{pmatrix} := \begin{pmatrix} 2^m & 1 \\ 0 & 2^m \end{pmatrix} \begin{pmatrix} x \\ y \end{pmatrix}$$

with $x_0 = 2^m$ and $y_0 = 1$. Depending on the rounding mode, this might loop until $x = +\infty$. Yet, Jeannet et al. [11] method returns $\left([2^m; 2^{2m} + 2], [1; 2^m]\right)$, which is correct with respect to an implementation of the considered loop using *real* numbers.

8 Conclusion

We proposed a novel sound approach to the unbounded reachability analysis of guarded LTI systems with inputs. A solution has already been presented [5,6], unfortunately several major issues makes it unsound as we have demonstrated in this paper.

Our approach is based on a reduction from the system with inputs to a system without inputs. This reduction is independent from the method used to solve the reduced system but we suggest to use abstract acceleration as described by Jeannet et al. [11] for which we have introduced several improvements, mainly involving the avoidance of interval arithmetic. Our improvements strictly increase the precision, potentially dramatically as illustrated by a few simple examples and an extensive experimentation. Moreover, our description of the work of Jeannet et al. [11] highlights various independent sources of over-approximation and paves the way for further improvements.

Nevertheless our reduction is accompanied by a fourfold increase of dimension and can not be efficiently exploited yet. One solution would be to take advantage of the sparsity of the resulting system. There are also opportunities to increase the efficiency of abstract acceleration in particular concerning the application of the set of linear transformations $\mathcal{A}$ to X_0, one could start with techniques developed for parametrized systems [2,3] and implemented in CORA [1], the cost in terms of precision remains to be evaluated.

If the approach is sound for machine integers, as long as no overflow occurs[9], future work should also focus on the use of floating point arithmetic in the loop body, considering only diagonalizable systems might be enough since the set of real matrices diagonalizable in $M_n(\mathbb{C})$ is dense in $M_n(\mathbb{R})$.

References

1. Althoff, M.: An introduction to CORA 2015. In: Frehse, G., Althoff, M. (eds.) 1st and 2nd International Workshop on Applied veRification for Continuous and Hybrid Systems, ARCH14-15. EPiC Series in Computing, vol. 34, pp. 120–151. EasyChair (2015)
2. Althoff, M., Krogh, B.H., Stursberg, O.: Analyzing reachability of linear dynamic systems with parametric uncertainties. In: Rauh, A., Auer, E. (eds.) Modeling, Design, and Simulation of Systems with Uncertainties. Mathematical Engineering, vol. 3, pp. 69–94. Springer, Heidelberg (2011). doi:10.1007/978-3-642-15956-5_4
3. Althoff, M., Le Guernic, C., Krogh, B.H.: Reachable set computation for uncertain time-varying linear systems. In: Proceedings of the 14th International Conference on Hybrid Systems: Computation and Control, HSCC 2011, NY, USA, pp. 93–102 (2011). http://doi.acm.org/10.1145/1967701.1967717
4. Biere, A., Cimatti, A., Clarke, E., Zhu, Y.: Symbolic model checking without BDDs. In: Cleaveland, W.R. (ed.) TACAS 1999. LNCS, vol. 1579, pp. 193–207. Springer, Heidelberg (1999). doi:10.1007/3-540-49059-0_14
5. Cattaruzza, D., Abate, A., Schrammel, P., Kroening, D.: Unbounded-time analysis of guarded LTI systems with inputs by abstract acceleration. In: Blazy, S., Jensen, T. (eds.) SAS 2015. LNCS, vol. 9291, pp. 312–331. Springer, Heidelberg (2015). doi:10.1007/978-3-662-48288-9_18
6. Cattaruzza, D., Abate, A., Schrammel, P., Kroening, D.: Unbounded-time analysis of guarded LTI systems with inputs by abstract acceleration (extended version). CoRR abs/1506.05607 (2015). http://arxiv.org/abs/1506.05607

[9] The corresponding constraint can be added to the loop guard.

7. Cousot, P., Cousot, R.: Abstract interpretation: a unified lattice model for static analysis of programs by construction or approximation of fixpoints. In: Conference Record of the Fourth ACM Symposium on Principles of Programming Languages, Los Angeles, California, USA, pp. 238–252. ACM (1977). http://doi.acm.org/10.1145/512950.512973
8. Feret, J.: Static analysis of digital filters. In: Schmidt, D. (ed.) ESOP 2004. LNCS, vol. 2986, pp. 33–48. Springer, Heidelberg (2004). doi:10.1007/978-3-540-24725-8_4
9. Gonnord, L., Halbwachs, N.: Combining widening and acceleration in linear relation analysis. In: Yi, K. (ed.) SAS 2006. LNCS, vol. 4134, pp. 144–160. Springer, Heidelberg (2006). doi:10.1007/11823230_10
10. Gonnord, L., Schrammel, P.: Abstract acceleration in linear relation analysis. Sci. Comput. Program. **93**, 125–153 (2014). http://dx.doi.org/10.1016/j.scico.2013.09.016
11. Jeannet, B., Schrammel, P., Sankaranarayanan, S.: Abstract acceleration of general linear loops. In: Proceedings of the 41st ACM SIGPLAN-SIGACT Symposium on Principles of Programming Languages, POPL 2014, NY, USA, pp. 529–540 (2014). http://dx.doi.org/10.1145/2535838.2535843
12. Kurzhanskiy, A.A., Varaiya, P.: Ellipsoidal techniques for reachability analysis of discrete-time linear systems. IEEE Trans. Automat. Contr. **52**(1), 26–38 (2007). http://dx.doi.org/10.1109/TAC.2006.887900
13. Le Guernic, C.: Toward a sound analysis of guarded LTI loops with inputs by abstract acceleration (extended version). https://hal.inria.fr/hal-01550767
14. Le Guernic, C.: Reachability analysis of hybrid systems with linear continuous dynamics. Ph.D. thesis, Université Joseph Fourier - Grenoble I (2009). https://tel.archives-ouvertes.fr/tel-00422569
15. Le Guernic, C., Girard, A.: Reachability analysis of hybrid systems using support functions. In: Bouajjani, A., Maler, O. (eds.) CAV 2009. LNCS, vol. 5643, pp. 540–554. Springer, Heidelberg (2009). doi:10.1007/978-3-642-02658-4_40
16. Le Guernic, C., Girard, A.: Reachability analysis of linear systems using support functions. Nonlinear Anal. Hybrid Syst. **4**(2), 250–262 (2010). IFACWorld-Congress2008. http://dx.doi.org/10.1016/j.nahs.2009.03.002
17. Prajna, S., Jadbabaie, A.: Safety verification of hybrid systems using barrier certificates. In: Alur, R., Pappas, G.J. (eds.) HSCC 2004. LNCS, vol. 2993, pp. 477–492. Springer, Heidelberg (2004). doi:10.1007/978-3-540-24743-2_32
18. Roux, P., Jobredeaux, R., Garoche, P., Feron, E.: A generic ellipsoid abstract domain for linear time invariant systems. In: Hybrid Systems: Computation and Control (part of CPS Week 2012), HSCC 2012, Beijing, China, 17–19 April 2012, pp. 105–114. ACM (2012). http://doi.acm.org/10.1145/2185632.2185651

Scalable Minimizing-Operators on Polyhedra via Parametric Linear Programming

Alexandre Maréchal(✉), David Monniaux, and Michaël Périn

Université Grenoble-Alpes, CNRS,
VERIMAG, 38000 Grenoble, France
{alex.marechal,david.monniaux,michael.perin}@univ-grenoble-alpes.fr
http://www-verimag.imag.fr/~monniaux/
http://www-verimag.imag.fr/~perin/

Abstract. Convex polyhedra capture linear relations between variables. They are used in static analysis and optimizing compilation. Their high expressiveness is however barely used in verification because of their cost, often prohibitive as the number of variables involved increases. Our goal in this article is to lower this cost.

Whatever the chosen representation of polyhedra – as constraints, as generators or as both – expensive operations are unavoidable. That cost is mostly due to four operations: conversion between representations, based on Chernikova's algorithm, for libraries in double description; convex hull, projection and minimization, in the constraints-only representation of polyhedra.

Libraries operating over generators incur exponential costs on cases common in program analysis. In the Verimag Polyhedra Library this cost was avoided by a constraints-only representation and reducing all operations to variable projection, classically done by Fourier-Motzkin elimination. Since Fourier-Motzkin generates many redundant constraints, minimization was however very expensive.

In this article, we avoid this pitfall by expressing projection as a parametric linear programming problem. This dramatically improves efficiency, mainly because it avoids the post-processing minimization.

We show how our new approach can be up to orders of magnitude faster than the previous approach implemented in the Verimag Polyhedra Library that uses only constraints and Fourier-Motzkin elimination, and on par with the conventional double description approach, as implemented in well-known libraries.

Keywords: Polyhedra · Parametric linear programming · Projection

1 The Challenge of Verification Using Polyhedra

Static analyzers establish the validity of assertions in programs by discovering inductive invariants that entail them. Analyzers based on abstract interpretation

This work was partially supported by the European Research Council under the European Union's Seventh Framework Programme (FP/2007-2013)/ERC Grant Agreement nr. 306595 "STATOR".

F. Ranzato (Ed.): SAS 2017, LNCS 10422, pp. 212–231, 2017.
DOI: 10.1007/978-3-319-66706-5_11

consider invariants within an *abstract domain* [5]. Invariants on numeric variables are of particular interest. They may entail that software produce no arithmetic overflow, no array index out of bounds—the user may be directly interested in such properties, or an optimizing compiler may discard runtime checks for violations that cannot occur. Furthermore, proofs of more complicated properties may use numerical invariants internally—for instance proofs of sorting algorithms need invariants on indices.

An example of abstract domain suitable for program states given by vectors of n numerical variables is the domain of products of n intervals; but such a domain cannot express relationships between variables. This hinders verification even if the final goal is to prove that a given variable lies within certain bounds, for instance to prove that a string length is less than a fixed buffer size: one may need to prove that the sum of the length of two strings is less than this size, thus a relation between these lengths.

The domain of *convex polyhedra* comprises sets of states defined by conjunctions of linear (in)equalities over the variables [6]. The analyzer needs to perform a variety of operations on these sets—least upper bound (convex hull, in the case of polyhedra), inclusion tests, projections, image and reverse image by program operations; also, in some cases, intersections and Minkowski sums. In addition to static analyzers, convex polyhedra are used inside highly optimizing compilers to reorganize loop nests [1].

Despite their expressiveness and 40 years of research, polyhedra are little used in verification because operations on polyhedra are still costly and do not scale to large programs [13]. Usually, they are restricted to a small subset of program variables such as loop indices [14]—including more variables would mean skyrocketing costs.

Most libraries for computing over convex polyhedra maintain a *double description*, both as *generators* (vertices, in the case of bounded polyhedra) or *constraints* (faces). A common case in program analysis is upper and lower bounds are known on all N variables—that is, the vector of variables lies within a distorted N-dimensional hypercube, which has 2^N vertices. This explains the reputation of polyhedra as unwieldy except in very low dimension, and motivated the design of the Verimag Verified Polyhedra Library (VPL) that operates on constraints-only representations [8,10]. An advantage of that approach is that it is easy to log enough information to independently check that the computed polyhedron includes the exact polyhedron that should be computed, which suffices for proving that static analysis is sound [9,10]; the certificate checker was implemented and proved correct in Coq.[1] The consequence is that many operations of the VPL, such as assignment, convex hull or Minkowski sum, were encoded as projection, finally performed by Fourier-Motzkin elimination [2]. Unfortunately, Fourier-Motzkin elimination generates numerous redundant constraints;

[1] Certifying a library in double description would have likely entailed implementing and proving in Coq the correctness of Chernikova's conversion algorithm from one representation to the other.

and even by incrementally removing them after each elimination of a variable, intermediate steps may create large lists of constraints.

In 2013, the overall performance of VPL [10] on typical verification benchmarks was on a par with that of double description libraries, though the timings on individual operations differed: some operations are faster than in double description, some are slower—all those involving projection, including convex hull. Projection by Fourier-Motzkin was the bottleneck.

Contribution. In this article we report on an algorithmic breakthrough that speeds up typical computations on polyhedra in constraints-only representation by several orders of magnitude when polyhedra becomes large (in number of relations) or dense (in number of variables involved in each relations). Scalability results from the inseparable combination of (i) the formulation of the projection via Parametric Linear Programming (PLP) (Sect. 3); (ii) the implementation of a PLP-solver over rationals, to get exact results (Sect. 5); (iii) a new normalization criterion, which ensures the absence of redundant constraints and saves the post-processing elimination of redundancy (Sect. 6). This normalization, its proof and a certifying implementation are the main contributions of this paper.[2]

We demonstrate the scalability by comparing timings of projections between the PLP-based algorithm, Fourier-Motzkin elimination and an existing library based on double description (Sect. 7).

Related work. The high cost of general convex polyhedra was long deplored. It motivated studying restricted classes of polyhedra, with simpler and faster algorithms, such as *octagons* [26]; and even these were found to be too slow, motivating recent algorithmic improvements [32]. We instead sought to conserve the domain of polyhedra as originally described [6,12], but with very different algorithms.

Our work was inspired by Howe et al.'s attempt to replace the Fourier-Motzkin elimination by a formulation as a Parametric Linear Optimization Problem (PLOP) [15], which they solved by an ad hoc algorithm. Unfortunately, their implementation is not available. We took a step further and developed a generic PLP-solver exploiting insights by [17,18]. Our solver, implemented in OCAML, works over rationals and generates COQ-certificates of correctness of its computations, similar to those in VPL [8–10].

Most libraries for computing over convex polyhedra for static analysis or compilation, including PolyLib,[3] Komei Fukuda's CDD,[4] the Parma Polyhedra Library,[5] the NEWPOLKA library included in Apron,[6] operate over the double description; see e.g. [28] for an introduction. The costliest and most complicated operation is the conversion from one representation to the other, using

[2] The VPL 0.2 is available at https://github.com/VERIMAG-Polyhedra/VPL.

[3] https://icps.u-strasbg.fr/polylib/.

[4] https://www.inf.ethz.ch/personal/fukudak/cdd_home/.

[5] http://bugseng.com/products/ppl/ [28].

[6] http://apron.cri.ensmp.fr/library/ [16].

Chernikova's algorithm [3,20]. It is rather easy to prune redundant items from one representation if one has the other, which explains the attractiveness of that approach. Its only drawback is that, as explained above, the generator representation is exponential in the dimension on very common and simple cases.

The explosive nature of the generator representation motivated approaches that detect when a polyhedron is a Cartesian product of polyhedra and compute generator representations separately for each element of the product, thereby avoiding exponential blowup in the case of the hypercube [13,31].

General texts on polyhedra and linear programming include [4,7,29].

2 Basics

Throughout the article, vectors are written in boldface lowercase, and matrices in boldface uppercase. An affine form over $\boldsymbol{x}$ is a linear combination plus constant of $x_1, ..., x_n$. For two vectors $\boldsymbol{a_\ell}$ and $\boldsymbol{x}$ of the same length, the dot product $\langle \boldsymbol{a_\ell}, \boldsymbol{x} \rangle = \sum_i a_{\ell i}\, x_i$ is a linear function of $\boldsymbol{x}$. Thus, we often use the notation $\boldsymbol{a_\ell}(\boldsymbol{x})$ instead of $\langle \boldsymbol{a_\ell}, \boldsymbol{x} \rangle$.

A *convex polyhedron*[7] is the set of points $\boldsymbol{x} = (x_1, \ldots, x_n) \in \mathbb{Q}^n$ that satisfy a conjunction (or a set) of linear constraints of the form $\boldsymbol{C_\ell} : \sum_{i=1}^{n} a_{\ell i}\, x_i \bowtie b_\ell$ where x_i are program variables, $a_{\ell i}$ and b_ℓ are constants in $\mathbb{Q}$, and $\bowtie \in \{\leq, =, \geq\}$. All constraints can be assumed to use only $\geq$.[8] Such a constraint is the ℓth row of a vector inequality $\boldsymbol{Ax} \geq \boldsymbol{b}$. We use $[\![\mathcal{P}]\!]$ to specifically refer to the set of points defined by the set of constraints $\mathcal{P}$. Given a polyhedron $[\![\mathcal{P}]\!] = \{\, \boldsymbol{x} \mid \boldsymbol{Ax} \geq \boldsymbol{b} \,\}$, the same system with strict inequalities defines $\mathring{\mathcal{P}}$, *the interior of* $\mathcal{P}$, and $\mathring{x}$ denotes a point of $[\![\mathring{\mathcal{P}}]\!] \stackrel{def}{=} \{\, \boldsymbol{x} \mid \boldsymbol{Ax} > \boldsymbol{b} \,\}$. In all the paper and without loss of generality, we focus on polyhedra with non-empty interior, meaning that equalities (explicit or implicit) are extracted and treated separately, as in most polyhedra libraries.

Before presenting our encoding of the projection operator as a PLOP, we start by recalling the fundamental Farkas' Lemma and Fourier-Motzkin's Algorithm for variable elimination.

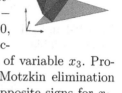

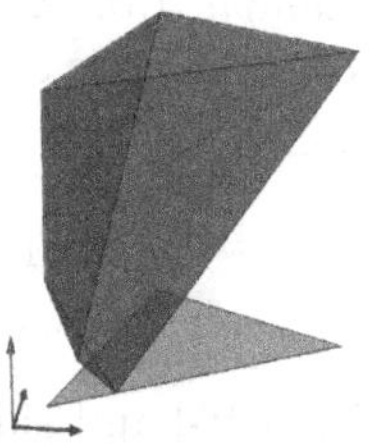

Example 1.1. The right-hand side figure shows the geometrical space defined by the polyhedron $\mathcal{P} = \{\boldsymbol{C_1} : -x_1 - 2x_2 + 2x_3 \geq -7, \boldsymbol{C_2} : -x_1 + 2x_2 \geq 1, \boldsymbol{C_3} : 3x_1 - x_2 \geq 0, \boldsymbol{C_4} : -x_3 \geq -10, \boldsymbol{C_5} : x_1 + x_2 + x_3 \geq 5\}$ and its projection on dimensions (x_1, x_2) resulting from the elimination of variable x_3. Projecting variable x_3 from $\mathcal{P}$ – noted $\mathcal{P}_{\backslash\{x_3\}}$ – by Fourier-Motzkin elimination consists in eliminating x_3 by combining constraints with opposite signs for x_3. Constraints that do not involve x_3 remain unchanged. This retains constraints

[7] We only deal with convex polyhedra. For readability, we will omit the adjective *convex* in the following.

[8] An equality $a = b$ corresponds to the conjunction of inequalities $a \geq b \wedge a \leq b$ and $a \leq b$ is equivalent to $-a \geq -b$.

C_2, C_3 and produces two new constraints: $C_1 + 2C_4 : -x_1 - 2x_2 \geq -27$ and $C_4 + C_5 : x_1 + x_2 \geq -5$. By Farkas' Lemma, the latter is redundant with respect to C_2 and C_3 as it can be expressed as a nonnegative combination of C_2, C_3.

Lemma 1 (Farkas' lemma [29, 7.1h, p. 93]). *A constraint C' is a logical consequence of a non-contradictory set of constraints $\mathcal{P} = \{C_1, \ldots, C_p\}$ iff there exists $\lambda_0, \ldots, \lambda_p \geq 0$ such that $C' = \lambda_0 + \sum_{i=1}^{p} \lambda_i C_i$, called a* Farkas decomposition *of C' on $\mathcal{P}$.*

Example 1.2. The combination $\frac{4}{5} C_2 + \frac{3}{5} C_3 : x_1 + x_2 \geq \frac{4}{5}$ is a logical consequence of C_2 and C_3 and it is a stronger condition than $C_4 + C_5 : x_1 + x_2 \geq -5$ since $\frac{4}{5} > -5$. Thus, the constraint $C_4 + C_5$ is redundant with respect to C_2 and C_3. Therefore the polyhedron $\mathcal{P}_{\backslash \{x_3\}}$ is only formed of three constraints $\{C_2, C_3, C_1 + 2C_4\}$.

3 Projection via Parametric Linear Programming

Naive Fourier-Motzkin elimination produces $O((\frac{|\mathcal{P}|}{2})^{2^k})$ constraints when eliminating k variables of a polyhedron with $|\mathcal{P}|$ constraints [30]. Most of them are redundant: indeed, the number of faces of the projected polyhedron is $O(|\mathcal{P}|^k)$ [27, Sect. 4.1].[9] Removing the redundant constraints is costly, even though there exists improved algorithms [21].

Jones et al. [17] then Howe et al. [15] noticed that the projection of a polyhedron can be expressed as a Parametric Linear Programming problem. In fact, PLP naturally arises when trying to generalize Fourier-Motzkin method to eliminate several variables simultaneously. In this article we achieve the work initiated by [15], whose goal was to compute the projected polyhedron without generating redundant constraints. Let us first explain their approach.

Example 1.3. As a consequence of Farkas lemma, any constraint implied by $\{C_1, \ldots, C_5\}$ is a nonnegative combination of them, written $\lambda_0 + \sum_{i=1}^{5} \lambda_i C_i$ with $\lambda_i \geq 0$, *i.e.*

$$\begin{aligned} &\lambda_0 + \lambda_1(-x_1 - 2x_2 + 2x_3) + \lambda_2(-x_1 + 2x_2) + \lambda_3(3x_1 - x_2) \\ &+ \lambda_4(-x_3) + \lambda_5(x_1 + x_2 + x_3) \;\; \geq \;\; -7\lambda_1 + \lambda_2 - 10\lambda_4 + 5\lambda_5 \end{aligned}$$

The left-hand side of the inequality can be rearranged to reveal the coefficient of each variable x_i and we can bring the right-hand side term of $\geq$ to the left.

$$\begin{aligned} \lambda_0 + (-\lambda_1 - \lambda_2 + 3\lambda_3 + \lambda_5)\, x_1 + (-2\lambda_1 + 2\lambda_2 - \lambda_3 + \lambda_5)\, x_2 \\ + (2\lambda_1 - \lambda_4 + \lambda_5)\, x_3 - (-7\lambda_1 + \lambda_2 - 10\lambda_4 + 5\lambda_5) \geq 0 \end{aligned} \tag{1}$$

Then, any instantiation of that inequality with λ_i canceling the coefficient of x_3, *i.e.* that satisfies (α) $2\lambda_1 - \lambda_4 + \lambda_5 = 0$, is an over-approximation of $\mathcal{P}_{\backslash \{x_3\}}$.

[9] This follows from McMullen's bound on the number of $n - k - 1$-faces of the polyhedron [24,25].

Indeed, it does not involve x_3 and, as a Farkas combination, it is by construction a logical consequence of $\mathcal{P}$. Constraints found by the FM elimination of x_3 correspond to the solutions $(\lambda_0, \ldots, \lambda_5) \in \{(0,0,1,0,0,0), (0,0,0,1,0,0), (0,1,0,0,2,0), (0,0,0,0,1,1)\}$ of Equation (α). Note that it is possible to eliminate several variables simultaneously by setting an elimination equation for each variable that must be discarded.

Here is a first formulation of a projection as a PLOP. We will refine it later, as it is not sufficient to avoid redundancies in the result. Given a polyhedron $\mathcal{P} = \{\, \boldsymbol{C_1} : \boldsymbol{a_1}(\boldsymbol{x}) \geq b_1, \ldots, \boldsymbol{C_p} : \boldsymbol{a_p}(\boldsymbol{x}) \geq b_p \,\}$ on variables $x_1, \ldots, x_n$, the projection of $\mathcal{P}$ by elimination of k variables $x_{e_1}, \ldots, x_{e_k}$ can be obtained as the solution of the optimization problem:

$$\left.\begin{array}{ll}\textbf{minimize the objective function} & \mathcal{Z}(\boldsymbol{x}) = \lambda_0 + \sum_{i=1}^{p} \lambda_i \times (\boldsymbol{a_i}(\boldsymbol{x}) - b_i) \\ \textbf{under the constraints} & (F)\ \lambda_0 \geq 0, ..., \lambda_p \geq 0 \\ & (\dagger)\ \sum_{i=0}^{p} \lambda_i = 1 \\ & (\alpha)\ \boldsymbol{\alpha_{e_1}}(\boldsymbol{\lambda}) = 0, ..., \boldsymbol{\alpha_{e_k}}(\boldsymbol{\lambda}) = 0 \end{array}\right\} \quad (2)$$

where $\boldsymbol{\alpha_i}(\boldsymbol{\lambda})$ denotes the coefficient of x_i in the reformulation of the objective as $\boldsymbol{\alpha_1}(\boldsymbol{\lambda}) \times x_1 + \ldots + \boldsymbol{\alpha_n}(\boldsymbol{\lambda}) \times x_n + \boldsymbol{\alpha_0}(\boldsymbol{\lambda})$. The unknowns λ_i are called the *decision variables*: the solver must find a solution for them. Note the inequalities (F) from Farkas' Lemma in addition to the (α) equations defining a projection. This problem has a *parametric objective*: the objective function depends on parameters $x_1, \ldots, x_n$ due to the terms $\boldsymbol{a_i}(\boldsymbol{x})$ in the coefficients of the decision variables. But once $x_1, \ldots, x_n$ are fixed, both the objective function and the constraints become linear in the decision variables, thus this problem belongs to *parametric linear programming.*

An additional constraint, here $\sum_i \lambda_i = 1$, is needed to prevent the solver from obtaining the optimal solution $\boldsymbol{\lambda} = \boldsymbol{0}$ which is always valid in a projection problem, whatever the parameter values. The $(\dagger)$ condition only excludes this useless null solution because any other solution can be scaled so that $\sum_i \lambda_i = 1$. The presence of λ_0 in the objective can seem useless and strange to readers who are familiar with linear programming: the solution $\lambda_0 = 1$ and $\lambda_1 = ... = \lambda_p = 0$ becomes feasible and generates a trivially redundant constraint $\boldsymbol{C_{triv}} : 1 \geq 0$. The role of λ_0 will become clear in Sects. 4 and 6.

Example 1.4. The elimination of x_3 via PLP is defined by two matrices: $\boldsymbol{O}$ is built from $[-\boldsymbol{b}|\boldsymbol{A}]^\intercal$ and encodes the objective. The other one captures the requirement (α) and $(\dagger)$. As usual in solvers, Farkas constraints (F) are left implicit.

$$
\left.
\begin{array}{ll}
\textbf{minimize the objective function} & \\
(1, x_1, x_2, x_3)^{\intercal} \overbrace{\left(\begin{array}{ccccccc} 0 & 1 & 7 & -1 & 0 & 10 & -5 \\ 0 & 0 & -1 & -1 & 3 & 0 & 1 \\ 0 & 0 & -2 & 2 & -1 & 0 & 1 \\ 0 & 0 & 2 & 0 & 0 & -1 & 1 \end{array}\right)}^{\boldsymbol{O}} \begin{pmatrix} 1 \\ \lambda_0 \\ \vdots \\ \lambda_5 \end{pmatrix} = \mathcal{Z}(\boldsymbol{x}) & \text{with columns } 2\text{–}7 = [-\boldsymbol{b}|\boldsymbol{A}]^{\intercal} \\
\textbf{under the constraints} \quad \underbrace{\left(\begin{array}{ccccccc} -1 & 1 & 1 & 1 & 1 & 1 & 1 \\ \hline 0 & 0 & 2 & 0 & 0 & -1 & 1 \end{array}\right)}_{\boldsymbol{\alpha}} \begin{pmatrix} 1 \\ \lambda_0 \\ \vdots \\ \lambda_5 \end{pmatrix} = \mathbf{0} & \text{first row } (\dagger)
\end{array}
\right\} \quad (3)
$$

This formulation of the projection is correct. Unfortunately, it may still generate redundant constraints: the solutions $(\lambda_0, \ldots, \lambda_5) \in \{(1,0,0,0,0,0), (0,0,1,0,0,0), (0,0,0,1,0,0), (0,\frac{1}{3},0,0,\frac{2}{3},0), (0,0,0,0,\frac{1}{2},\frac{1}{2})\}$ include the trivial constraint $1 \geq 0$ and $\frac{1}{2}\boldsymbol{C_4} + \frac{1}{2}\boldsymbol{C_5}$ which is equivalent to the redundant constraint $\boldsymbol{C_4} + \boldsymbol{C_5}$ found by Fourier-Motzkin elimination. We shall address this point in Sect. 6.

4 Polyhedra as Solutions of Parametric Linear Optimization Problems

In the previous section we encoded the projection of a polyhedron as a PLOP. For interpreting the result of a PLP-solver as a polyhedron we need to go one step further into the field of PLP and look at the solutions of a PLOP.

To summarize, Parametric Linear Programming is an extension of Linear Programming where the constants in the constraints or the coefficients in the objective function may be replaced by affine combinations of parameters [11]. In this article, we only deal with the case where parameters appear in the objective function. The general form of a PLOP that stems from projection is

$$
\left.
\begin{array}{l}
\textbf{minimize the objective function } \mathcal{Z}(\boldsymbol{x}) \stackrel{def}{=} \lambda_0 + \sum_{i=1}^{p} \lambda_i \times (\boldsymbol{a_i}(\boldsymbol{x}) - b_i) \\
\textbf{under the constraints } \lambda_0, ..., \lambda_p \geq 0, \ (\dagger) \ \sum_{i=0}^{p} \lambda_i = 1, \ \boldsymbol{\alpha\lambda} = \mathbf{0}
\end{array}
\right\} \quad (4)
$$

where $\boldsymbol{x}$ is the vector of parameters $(x_1, ..., x_n)$; $(\boldsymbol{a_i}(\boldsymbol{x}) - b_i)$ are *affine forms on the parameters*; and $\boldsymbol{\alpha}$ is a matrix. In a projection problem the system of equations $\boldsymbol{\alpha\lambda} = \mathbf{0}$ constrains the *decision variables* $\lambda_1, ..., \lambda_p$ but not λ_0.

The solution is a concave, piecewise affine function $\mathcal{Z}^{\star}$, mapping the parameters to the optimal solution:

$$
\mathcal{Z}^{\star} \stackrel{def}{=} \boldsymbol{x} \mapsto \begin{cases} \mathcal{Z}_1^{\star}(\boldsymbol{x}) & \text{if } \boldsymbol{x} \in \mathcal{R}_1 \\ \vdots & \\ \mathcal{Z}_r^{\star}(\boldsymbol{x}) & \text{if } \boldsymbol{x} \in \mathcal{R}_r \end{cases} \quad (5)
$$

Each piece is an affine form over $\boldsymbol{x}$, obtained by instantiating the objective function $\mathcal{Z}$ with a solution $\boldsymbol{\lambda}$; a piece can also be denoted by $\mathcal{Z}^\star_{\boldsymbol{\lambda}}$. Each $\mathcal{Z}^\star_i$ is associated to a *region of optimality* $\mathcal{R}_i$ that designates the set of $\boldsymbol{x}$ for which the minimum of $\mathcal{Z}^\star(\boldsymbol{x})$ is $\mathcal{Z}^\star_i(\boldsymbol{x})$. Regions of optimality are polyhedra; that will be clear in Sect. 5 when we will explain how they are computed by our solver (see Example 1.6). They form a *quasi-partition* of the space of parameters: their union covers $\mathbb{Q}^n$ and the intersection of *the interior* of two distinct regions is empty. They however do not form a partition because two regions $\mathcal{R}_i, \mathcal{R}_j$ may overlap on their frontiers; then, their solutions $\mathcal{Z}^\star_i, \mathcal{Z}^\star_j$ coincide on the intersection.

From optimal function to polyhedron. A PLOP can be thought of as a *declarative description of the projection operator.* The solution $\mathcal{Z}^\star$ can be interpreted as a polyhedron $\mathcal{P}^\star$ that is the projection of an input polyhedron $\mathcal{P}$. This requires some explanations:

- Due to the Farkas conditions $\lambda_0, ..., \lambda_p \geq 0$ which preserve the direction of inequalities, the objective function of PLOP (4), *i.e.* $\lambda_0 + \sum_{i=1}^{p} \lambda_i \times (\boldsymbol{a_i}(\boldsymbol{x}) - b_i)$ can be interpreted as a constraint implied by the input polyhedron $\mathcal{P} = \{\boldsymbol{C_1} : \boldsymbol{a_1}(\boldsymbol{x}) \geq b_1, ..., \boldsymbol{C_p} : \boldsymbol{a_p}(\boldsymbol{x}) \geq b_p\}$. Actually, for a given $\boldsymbol{\lambda}$, the statement $\mathcal{Z}^\star_{\boldsymbol{\lambda}}(\boldsymbol{x}) \geq 0$ is equivalent to the constraint

$$\lambda_0 + \sum_{i=1}^{p} \lambda_i \times \boldsymbol{a_i}(\boldsymbol{x}) \geq \sum_{i=1}^{p} \lambda_i \times b_i \tag{6}$$

- Minimizing the objective ensures that the λ_0-shift of the constraint will be minimal, meaning that the constraint $\mathcal{Z}^\star_{\boldsymbol{\lambda}}(\boldsymbol{x}) \geq 0$ will be tightly adjusted.
- The requirement $\boldsymbol{\alpha}\boldsymbol{\lambda} = \boldsymbol{0}$ captures the expected effect of the projection. Thus, any solution $\boldsymbol{\lambda}$ defines a constraint $\mathcal{Z}_{\boldsymbol{\lambda}}(\boldsymbol{x}) \geq 0$ of the polyhedron $\mathcal{P}^\star$.

Now recall that a polyhedron is a set of points that satisfy linear inequalities. Therefore, it is natural to define $[\![\mathcal{P}^\star]\!]$ as $\{\, \boldsymbol{x} \mid \mathcal{Z}^\star(\boldsymbol{x}) \geq 0 \,\}$. The following lemma proves that this set of points is a polyhedron.

Lemma 2. $\{\, \boldsymbol{x} \mid \mathcal{Z}^\star(\boldsymbol{x}) \geq 0 \,\} = \bigcap\limits_{k=1}^{r} \{\, \boldsymbol{x} \mid \mathcal{Z}^\star_k(\boldsymbol{x}) \geq 0 \,\}$

Proof. Let us prove the mutual inclusion.

($\subseteq$) Pick up a point $\boldsymbol{x'} \in \{\, \boldsymbol{x} \mid \mathcal{Z}^\star(\boldsymbol{x}) \geq 0 \,\}$. By definition of $\mathcal{Z}^\star$ as a piecewise function defined on the whole space of parameters, then there exists i such that $\boldsymbol{x'} \in \mathcal{R}_i$ and $\mathcal{Z}^\star(\boldsymbol{x'}) = \mathcal{Z}^\star_i(\boldsymbol{x'})$. It follows that $\mathcal{Z}^\star_i(\boldsymbol{x'}) \geq 0$ since $\boldsymbol{x'}$ belongs to the set of points where $\mathcal{Z}^\star$ is nonnegative. Moreover, the fact that $\boldsymbol{x'}$ belongs to $\mathcal{R}_i$ – the region of optimality of $\mathcal{Z}^\star_i$ in a minimization problem – ensures that $\mathcal{Z}^\star_k(\boldsymbol{x'}) \geq \mathcal{Z}^\star_i(\boldsymbol{x'})$ for all k and therefore, $\mathcal{Z}^\star_k(\boldsymbol{x'}) \geq 0$ for all k. Thus, $\boldsymbol{x'} \in \{\, \boldsymbol{x} \mid \mathcal{Z}^\star_k(\boldsymbol{x}) \geq 0 \,\}$ for all $k = 1...r$. Finally, $\boldsymbol{x'} \in \bigcap\limits_{k=1..r} \{\, \boldsymbol{x} \mid \mathcal{Z}^\star_k(\boldsymbol{x}) \geq 0 \,\}$.

($\supseteq$) Pick up a point $\boldsymbol{x}' \in \bigcap_{k=1}^{r} \{\, \boldsymbol{x} \mid \mathcal{Z}_k^\star(\boldsymbol{x}) \geq 0 \,\}$. Then, $\boldsymbol{x}'$ belongs to a least one $\mathcal{R}_i$ because the regions form a (pseudo) partition of the whole space of parameters $\mathbb{Q}^n$, thus $\bigcup_{k=1}^{r} \mathcal{R}_k = \mathbb{Q}^n$. Yet, the affine piece that defines $\mathcal{Z}^\star$ on $\boldsymbol{x}'$ is $\mathcal{Z}_i^\star$ and $\mathcal{Z}^\star(\boldsymbol{x}') = \mathcal{Z}_i^\star(\boldsymbol{x}')$. Moreover, all the affine pieces of $\mathcal{Z}^\star$ are nonnegative on $\boldsymbol{x}'$ since $\boldsymbol{x}' \in \bigcap_{k=1}^{r} \{\, \boldsymbol{x} \mid \mathcal{Z}_k^\star(\boldsymbol{x}) \geq 0 \,\}$. Then, in particular $\mathcal{Z}_i^\star(\boldsymbol{x}') \geq 0$ and the same goes for $\mathcal{Z}^\star(\boldsymbol{x}')$. Finally, $\boldsymbol{x}' \in \{\, \boldsymbol{x} \mid \mathcal{Z}^\star(\boldsymbol{x}) \geq 0 \,\}$.

Constructing the vector inequality $\boldsymbol{Z}^\star \ \boldsymbol{x} \ \geq \ \boldsymbol{b}^\star$ that defines the polyhedron $\mathcal{P}^\star$ is straightforward from the solution $\mathcal{Z}^\star$. If suffices to get rid of the regions of optimality and to interpret each affine piece of $\mathcal{Z}^\star$ as an inequality: $\{\, \boldsymbol{x} \mid \mathcal{Z}^\star(\boldsymbol{x}) \geq 0 \,\} =$ (by Lemma 2) $\bigcap_{k=1}^{r} \{\, \boldsymbol{x} \mid \mathcal{Z}_k^\star(\boldsymbol{x}) \geq 0 \,\} = \{\boldsymbol{x} \mid \bigwedge_{k=1}^{r} \mathcal{Z}_k^\star(\boldsymbol{x}) \geq 0\}$ $= \{\boldsymbol{x} \mid \bigwedge_{k=1}^{r} \langle \boldsymbol{z}_k^\star, \boldsymbol{x}\rangle - b_k^\star \geq 0\} = \{\, \boldsymbol{x} \mid \boldsymbol{Z}^\star \boldsymbol{x} \geq \boldsymbol{b}^\star \,\}$. Let us detail this construction.

Each piece $\mathcal{Z}_k^\star$ of the solution is an affine form over $\boldsymbol{x}$ and $\mathcal{Z}_k^\star(\boldsymbol{x}) \geq 0$ defines a constraint in the form (6) which can be written $\sum_{i=1}^{n} z_{ki}^\star \, x_i \geq b_k^\star$ *i.e.* $\langle \boldsymbol{z}_k^\star, \boldsymbol{x}\rangle \geq b_k^\star$ for some vector $\boldsymbol{z}_k^\star = (z_{k1}^\star, ..., z_{kn}^\star)$ and some constant $b_k^\star$. It follows from Lemma 2 that the set of points $\boldsymbol{x}$ where $\mathcal{Z}^\star(\boldsymbol{x})$ is nonnegative is a polyhedron defined by the vector inequality $\boldsymbol{Z}^\star \boldsymbol{x} \geq \boldsymbol{b}^\star$ where the rows of $\boldsymbol{Z}^\star$ are the vectors $\boldsymbol{z}_1^\star, \ldots, \boldsymbol{z}_r^\star$ and $\boldsymbol{b}^\star$ is the column vector $(b_1^\star, \ldots, b_r^\star)^\intercal$.

Example 1.5. On our running projection problem, the PLP-solver returns the following optimal function, and the instantiation of the decision variables λ_i that defines each affine piece:

$$\mathcal{Z}^\star \stackrel{def}{=} (x_1, x_2) \mapsto \begin{cases} \mathcal{Z}_2^\star : & -x_1 \ + 2x_2 \ - 1 \ \text{ on } \mathcal{R}_2 \ \ (\text{for } \lambda_2 = 1) \\ \mathcal{Z}_3^\star : & 3x_1 \ \ - x_2 \qquad \text{ on } \mathcal{R}_3 \ \ (\text{for } \lambda_3 = 1) \\ \mathcal{Z}_4^\star : & -\frac{1}{3}x_1 - \frac{2}{3}x_2 + 9 \ \text{ on } \mathcal{R}_4 \ \ (\text{for } \lambda_1 = \frac{1}{3},\ \lambda_4 = \frac{2}{3}) \\ \mathcal{Z}_5^\star : & \frac{1}{2}x_1 + \frac{1}{2}x_2 + \frac{5}{2} \ \text{ on } \mathcal{R}_5 \ \ (\text{for } \lambda_4 = \frac{1}{2},\ \lambda_5 = \frac{1}{2}) \\ \mathcal{Z}_1^\star : & 1 \ \text{ on } \mathcal{R}_1 \ \ (\text{for } \lambda_0 = 1) \end{cases}$$

from which we construct the polyhedron

$$\mathcal{P}^\star = \overbrace{\begin{pmatrix} -1 & 2 & 0 \\ 3 & -1 & 0 \\ -\frac{1}{3} & -\frac{2}{3} & 0 \\ \frac{1}{2} & \frac{1}{2} & 0 \\ 0 & 0 & 0 \end{pmatrix}}^{\boldsymbol{Z}^\star} \overbrace{\begin{pmatrix} x_1 \\ x_2 \\ x_3 \end{pmatrix}}^{\boldsymbol{x}} \geq \overbrace{\begin{pmatrix} 1 \\ 0 \\ -9 \\ -\frac{5}{2} \\ -1 \end{pmatrix}}^{\boldsymbol{b}^\star} = \left\{ \begin{array}{rl} \boldsymbol{C_2} : & -x_1 + 2x_2 \geq \ 1 \\ \boldsymbol{C_3} : & 3x_1 \ - x_2 \geq \ 0 \\ \frac{1}{3}\boldsymbol{C_1} + \frac{2}{3}\boldsymbol{C_4} : & -\frac{1}{3}x_1 - \frac{2}{3}x_2 \geq -9 \\ \frac{1}{2}\boldsymbol{C_4} + \frac{1}{2}\boldsymbol{C_5} : & \frac{1}{2}x_1 + \frac{1}{2}x_2 \geq -\frac{5}{2} \\ \boldsymbol{C_{triv}} : & 0 \geq -1 \end{array} \right\}$$

Variable x_3 does not appear anymore in the constraints of $\mathcal{P}^\star$ because its column in $\boldsymbol{Z}^\star$ is made of 0. The regions of optimality, shown on Fig. 1(*a*) form a pseudo-partition of the whole space of parameters (x_1, x_2): regions $\mathcal{R}_2, \ldots, \mathcal{R}_5$ are unbounded; the central triangle is the region $\mathcal{R}_1$ associated to the constant affine form $\mathcal{Z}_1^\star = 1$ which produces the trivial constraint $\boldsymbol{C_{triv}} : 1 \geq 0$. Each boundary of $\mathcal{P}^\star$ (shown as bold lines in the figure) is the intersection of a region of optimality $\mathcal{R}_i$ with the space where the associated affine form $\mathcal{Z}_i^\star$ evaluates to zero. We retrieve constraints equivalent to those of Example 1.1, except that the redundant constraint $\frac{1}{2}\boldsymbol{C_4} + \frac{1}{5}\boldsymbol{C_5}$ generated by $\mathcal{Z}_5^\star$ is still present. The drawing of the regions reveals that $\mathcal{Z}_5^\star$ does not vanish on its region of optimality, *i.e.* $[\![\mathcal{Z}_5^\star = 0]\!] \cap [\![\mathring{\mathcal{R}}_5]\!] = \emptyset$. Actually, this is true for any redundant constraint. Indeed, we will prove in Sect. 6 (Lemma 5) that $[\![\mathcal{Z}_i^\star = 0]\!] \cap [\![\mathring{\mathcal{R}}_i]\!] \neq \emptyset$ ensures the irredundancy of the constraint $\mathcal{Z}_i^\star \geq 0$ in $\mathcal{P}^\star$.

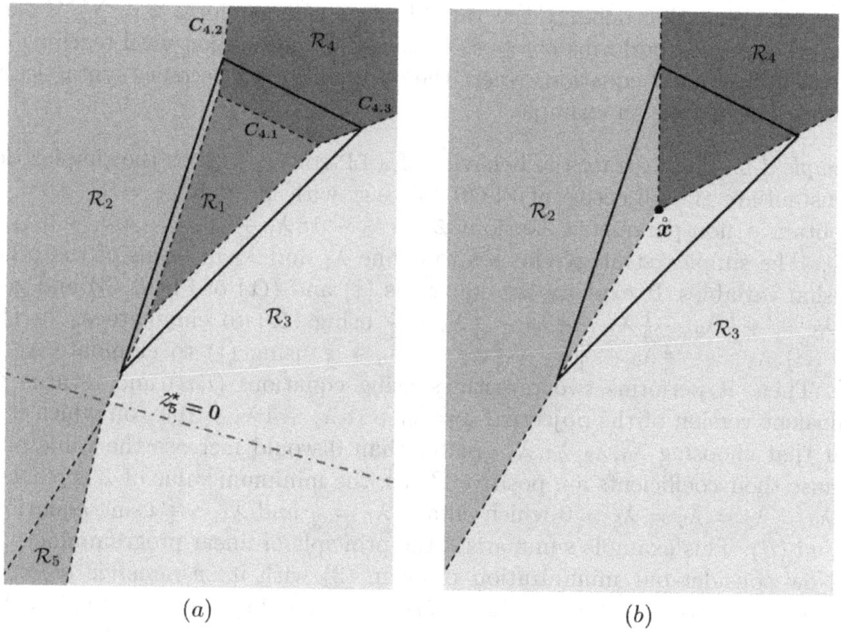

Fig. 1. The regions of optimality of the solution $\mathcal{Z}^\star$ of Example 1.5 obtained by solving PLOP (3). The bold lines are the boundaries of the projected polyhedron $\mathcal{P}^\star$. Figure (a) shows regions obtained when the PLOP contains the constraint $\sum_i \lambda_i = 1$. Figure (b) shows regions obtained when constraints are normalized on point $\mathring{x}$ (see Sect. 6).

5 Principle of a PLP-Solver

Due to space limitations we shall only sketch how our parametric linear programming solver works. It is based on a recent algorithm by Jones et al. [18] with some improvements: it uses a fast simplification of regions [23] and performs exact computations in rationals so as to avoid rounding errors.

This algorithm for solving a PLOP is a generalization of the simplex algorithm which can itself be seen as an extension of Gaussian elimination for solving a system of linear equations.

Gaussian elimination proceeds by rewriting: each equation defines a variable in terms of the other ones. This equation can be used to eliminate the variable from the other equations by substitution. This operation is called a pivot. Gauss pivoting strategy leads to an equivalent system in echelon form where un/satisfiability becomes trivial.

The simplex algorithm follows the same principle but differs in the selection of the variable to eliminate. First, each inequality $C_\ell : \sum_{i=1}^{n} a_{\ell i}\, x_i \leq b_\ell$ is changed into an equality $\sum_{i=1}^{n} a_{\ell i}\, x_i + x_{n+\ell} = b_\ell$ by introducing a variable $x_{n+\ell} \geq 0$ called a *slack variable*. Second, the objective function is added to the system as an extra equation defining the variable $\mathcal{Z}$ as a linear form $\mathcal{Z} = \sum_{i=1}^{n+r} o_i x_i$. Then, the simplex performs pivots as in Gaussian elimination until reaching an equivalent system of equations where the optimality of $\mathcal{Z}$ becomes syntactically obvious. Let us take an example.

Example 1.6. To illustrate the behavior of a LP-solver, such as the simplex, let us instantiate the objective of PLOP (3), e.g. with $x_1 = 5, x_2 = 11, x_3 = 1$, to obtain a non-parametric version: $\mathcal{Z} = \lambda_0 - 18\,\lambda_1 + 16\,\lambda_2 + 4\,\lambda_3 + 9\,\lambda_4 + 12\,\lambda_5$. The simplex strategy chooses to define λ_1 and λ_4 in terms of the other decision variables. It exploits the equations (†) and ($\boldsymbol{\alpha}$) of PLOP (3) and gets (i) $\lambda_1 = -\frac{1}{3}\lambda_0 - \frac{1}{3}\lambda_2 - \frac{1}{3}\lambda_3 - \frac{2}{3}\lambda_5 + \frac{1}{3}$ using ($\boldsymbol{\alpha}$) to eliminate λ_4 in (†), and (ii) $\lambda_4 = -\frac{2}{3}\lambda_0 - \frac{2}{3}\lambda_2 - \frac{2}{3}\lambda_3 - \frac{1}{3}\lambda_5 + \frac{2}{3}$ using (†) to eliminate λ_1 in ($\boldsymbol{\alpha}$). Then, it performs two rewritings using equations (i, ii) and returns an equivalent version of the objective $\mathcal{Z} = \lambda_0 + 16\,\lambda_2 + 4\,\lambda_3 + 21\,\lambda_5$ on which it is clear that choosing $\lambda_0, \lambda_2, \lambda_3, \lambda_5$ greater than 0 would increase the value of $\mathcal{Z}$ because their coefficients are positive. Thus, the minimum value of $\mathcal{Z}$ is reached for $\lambda_0 = \lambda_2 = \lambda_3 = \lambda_5 = 0$ which entails $\lambda_1 = \frac{1}{3}$ and $\lambda_4 = \frac{2}{3}$ using equations (i) and (ii). This example summarizes the principle of linear programming.

Now consider our minimization problem (3) with its *parametric objective* $\mathcal{Z}(x_1, x_2, x_3) = \lambda_1(-x_1 - 2\,x_2 + 2\,x_3 + 7) + \lambda_2(-x_1 + 2\,x_2 - 1) + \lambda_3(3\,x_1 - x_2) + \lambda_4(-x_3 + 10) + \lambda_5(x_1 + x_2 + x_3 - 5) + \lambda_0$. Our PLP-solver uses the previous instantiated problem to discover the useful pivots (i, ii). Then, it replays the same rewritings on the parametric version. Those operations are efficiently implemented using the matrix representation of (3): they boils down to the addition of combinations of rows of (†) and $\boldsymbol{\alpha}$ to those of $\boldsymbol{O}$. We end up with the following objective:

$$\underbrace{-\frac{1}{3}\,x_1 - \frac{2}{3}\,x_2 + 9}_{\mathcal{Z}_4^\star} + \lambda_0 \underbrace{\frac{1}{3}\,(x_1 + 2\,x_2 - 24)}_{\geq 0 : \boldsymbol{C_{4.1}}} + \lambda_2 \underbrace{\frac{2}{3}\,(-x_1 + 4\,x_2 - 15)}_{\geq 0 : \boldsymbol{C_{4.2}}}$$
$$+ \lambda_3 \underbrace{\frac{1}{3}\,(10\,x_1 - x_2 - 27)}_{\geq 0 : \boldsymbol{C_{4.3}}} + \lambda_5 \underbrace{\frac{1}{3}\,(5\,x_1 + 7\,x_2 - 39)}_{\geq 0 : \boldsymbol{C_{4.4}}}$$

We recognize the 4th piece of $\mathcal{Z}^\star$. The argument for optimality used in the non-parametric version can be generalized: The minimality of $\mathcal{Z}_4^\star$ holds if *the parametric coefficients of the remaining variables are nonnegative*, since increasing the values of $\lambda_0, \lambda_2, \lambda_3, \lambda_5$ (which must be nonnegative) would make the objective value grow. This condition defines the region of optimality $\mathcal{R}_4$ of $\mathcal{Z}_4^\star$ as the polyhedron $\{\boldsymbol{C_{4.1}}, \boldsymbol{C_{4.2}}, \boldsymbol{C_{4.3}}\}$, see Fig. 1(a). $\boldsymbol{C_{4.4}}$ is actually redundant with respect to $\boldsymbol{C_{4.1}}$, $\boldsymbol{C_{4.2}}$ and $\boldsymbol{C_{4.3}}$. It is thus eliminated from the representation of $\mathcal{R}_4$, and therefore does not appear on Fig. 1(a).

The PLP-solver then chooses an opposite sign condition of a parametric coefficient $\boldsymbol{C_{4.i}}$ – that means exploring an adjacent region by crossing a frontier – and selects a new instantiation point on this side of the constraint. The objective is then instantiated accordingly and submitted to the simplex which provides the meaningful pivots leading to another optimal affine form and its region of optimality. The benefit of PLP is that the exploration of one instance with the simplex is generalized into a whole region of optimality. The exploration goes on until the whole space of parameters has been covered by the union of regions: any new instantiation point falls in an already explored region.

6 Polyhedra in Minimal Form for Free

The previous sections showed how to compute the optimal solution of a PLOP and how to interpret the solution $\mathcal{Z}^\star$ as a polyhedron $\mathcal{P}^\star = \bigwedge_{k=1}^{r} \mathcal{Z}_k^\star(\boldsymbol{x}) \geq 0$. Still, the representation of $\mathcal{P}^\star$ may not be minimal: some constraints $\mathcal{Z}_k^\star(\boldsymbol{x}) \geq 0$ may be redundant in $\mathcal{P}^\star$. We could remove those redundancies afterwards but, as noticed by Howe et al. [15], it is highly preferable to prevent their generation by adding a *normalization constraint* to the PLOP. We adapt their intuition to our formulation of the problem and we bring the proof that it indeed avoids redundancies. This requires to make a detour via normalized solutions to explain the expected effect of a normalization constraint.

6.1 Normalizing the Projection PLOP

Let us normalize the function $\mathcal{Z}^\star$ so that it evaluates to 1 on a given point $\mathring{\boldsymbol{x}}$ in the interior of $\mathcal{P}^\star$. Formally, we consider a solution $\widetilde{\mathcal{Z}}^\star(\boldsymbol{x}) \stackrel{def}{=} \frac{\mathcal{Z}^\star(\boldsymbol{x})}{\mathcal{Z}^\star(\mathring{\boldsymbol{x}})}$ or equivalently $\forall k,\ \widetilde{\mathcal{Z}}_k^\star(\boldsymbol{x}) \stackrel{def}{=} \frac{\mathcal{Z}_k^\star(\boldsymbol{x})}{\mathcal{Z}_k^\star(\mathring{\boldsymbol{x}})}$. The key point of this transformation is that the space $[\![\mathcal{Z}^\star \geq 0]\!]$, which is the polyhedron $\mathcal{P}^\star$ of interest, is unchanged. The normalized solution $\widetilde{\mathcal{Z}}^\star$ will differ from the original one but must fulfills $[\![\widetilde{\mathcal{Z}}^\star \geq 0]\!] = [\![\mathcal{Z}^\star \geq 0]\!]$ which is true on the main functions if it holds on each of their pieces, *i.e.* $\forall k, [\![\widetilde{\mathcal{Z}}_k^\star \geq 0]\!] = [\![\mathcal{Z}_k^\star \geq 0]\!]$. The normalization preserves the nonnegativity space of each $\mathcal{Z}_k^\star$ because $\frac{1}{\mathcal{Z}_k^\star(\mathring{\boldsymbol{x}})}$ is a positive scalar: Indeed, $\mathring{\boldsymbol{x}}$ belongs to the interior of $\mathcal{P}^\star$, *i.e.* $[\![\bigwedge_k \mathcal{Z}_k^\star > 0]\!]$ by Lemma 2. The proof of this remark is given in Lemma 7, available in the appendix of the extended version of this paper [22].

Example 2. The transformation of the solution only changes the inclination of $\mathcal{Z}_k^\star$, not the space where they cross 0. This can easily be illustrated on one-variable constraints. Consider three constraints $\boldsymbol{C_1} : 2x \geq 5$, $\boldsymbol{C_2} : x \leq 12$ and a redundant one $\boldsymbol{C_3} : x \geq 2$, corresponding to three affine forms $\mathcal{Z}^\star_1(x) = 2x - 5$, $\mathcal{Z}^\star_2(x) = 12 - x$ and $\mathcal{Z}^\star_3(x) = x - 2$. On the left-hand side we plotted the functions $z = \mathcal{Z}^\star_i(x)$ for $i \in \{1, 2, 3\}$ and, on the right-hand side, their normalizations with respect to the point $\mathring{x} = 3$.

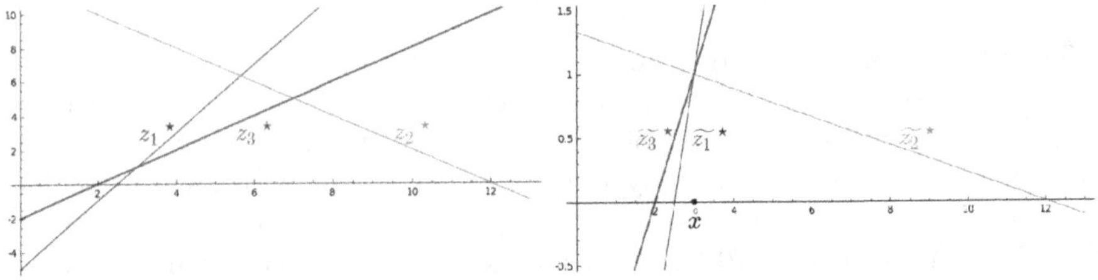

The most interesting consequence of the normalization is that *a constraint is redundant iff its normalized affine form is nowhere minimal.* This property does not hold on the non-normalized forms: although $\boldsymbol{C_3}$ is redundant *w.r.t.* $\boldsymbol{C_1}$ and $\boldsymbol{C_2}$, $\mathcal{Z}^\star_3$ is minimal *w.r.t.* $\mathcal{Z}^\star_1$ and $\mathcal{Z}^\star_2$ on $x \in [3, 7]$. On the contrary, considering the normalized forms, $\widetilde{\mathcal{Z}}^\star_3$ is no longer minimal, thus *it will be absent from the piecewise solution of a minimization problem.* One of our contribution is the proof of this result (Sect. 6.2).

Last, but not least, the normalized pieces are not computed *a posteriori* from the original solutions. They are obtained directly by enforcing the normalization of the objective through an additional constraint $\mathcal{Z}(\mathring{\boldsymbol{x}}) = 1$. Recall from (4) that the objective of the PLOP is $\mathcal{Z}(\boldsymbol{x}) \stackrel{def}{=} \lambda_0 + \sum_{i=1}^{p} \lambda_i \times (\boldsymbol{a_i}(\boldsymbol{x}) - b_i)$. Then, the *normalization constraint* becomes (‡) $\lambda_0 + \sum_{i=1}^{p} \lambda_i \times (\boldsymbol{a_i}(\mathring{\boldsymbol{x}}) - b_i) = 1$ where the $\boldsymbol{a_i}(\mathring{\boldsymbol{x}})$ are coefficients in $\mathbb{Q}$, obtained by evaluating the constraints of the input polyhedron at $\mathring{\boldsymbol{x}}$. The normalization constraint replaces the previous requirement (†) $\sum_i \lambda_i = 1$ in the PLOP: like (†) it excludes the solution $\lambda_0 = \ldots = \lambda_p = 0$. Back to Example 1.5, our PLP-solver running on the normalized PLOP only builds the irredundant constraints $\mathcal{Z}^\star_2 \geq 0$, $\mathcal{Z}^\star_3 \geq 0$ and $\mathcal{Z}^\star_4 \geq 0$ associated to the regions of Fig. 1(b).

Note that we must be able to provide a point $\mathring{\boldsymbol{x}}$ in the interior of $\mathcal{P}^\star$ while $\mathcal{P}^\star$ is not already known. Finding such a point is obvious for projection, convex-hull and Minkowski sum. It is feasible because the operators based on PLP are applied on polyhedra with non-empty interior; the treatment of polyhedra with equalities is explained in Example 3 below. For projection, $\mathring{\boldsymbol{x}}$ is obtained from a point $\boldsymbol{x}$ in the interior of the input polyhedron $\mathcal{P}$. Removing the coordinates of variables marked for elimination provides a point $\mathring{\boldsymbol{x}}$ that will be in the interior of the projected polyhedron $\mathcal{P}^\star$.

Example 3. Consider the case of a polyhedron over variables x, x', x'' made of inequalities $\mathcal{P}$ and an equality $E : x'' = f(x, x')$. The computation of the projection $(\mathcal{P} \wedge E)_{/\{x', x''\}}$ is done in two steps: we use equation $x'' = f(x, x')$ to eliminate x'' from $\mathcal{P}$ by substitution. If implicit equalities show up we exploit them in the same way, otherwise we apply the projection via PLP on $\mathcal{P}[x''/f(x, x')]$ to eliminate the remaining variable x'.

6.2 A Normalized PLOP Is Free of Redundancy

The advantage of PLP over Fourier-Motzkin comes from the following theorem:

Theorem 1. *Let* $\widetilde{\mathcal{Z}}^\star \stackrel{def}{=} \min\{\widetilde{\mathcal{Z}}_1^\star, \ldots, \widetilde{\mathcal{Z}}_r^\star\}$ *be the optimal solution of a* normalized parametric minimization problem. *Then each solution* $\widetilde{\mathcal{Z}}_k^\star$ *that is not the constant function* $\boldsymbol{x} \mapsto 1$ *is irredundant with respect to polyhedron* $[\![\widetilde{\mathcal{Z}}^\star \geq 0]\!]$.

Proof. Theorem 1 is a direct consequence of three intermediates results: (i) each region of optimality in a normalized PLOP is a cone pointed in $\mathring{\boldsymbol{x}}$ (Lemma 3); (ii) each piece $\mathcal{Z}_k^\star$ which is not constant, is decreasing on its region of optimality along lines starting at $\mathring{\boldsymbol{x}}$ (Lemma 4); (iii) each piece that crosses 0 on its region produces an irredundant constraint (Lemma 5).

Let us summarize the key facts that are needed for exposing the proof of the lemmata: Projection via PLP leads to a parametric linear minimization problem whose solution is a function $\widetilde{\mathcal{Z}}^\star$ defined by pieces $\{\widetilde{\mathcal{Z}}_1^\star$ on $\mathcal{R}_1, \ldots, \widetilde{\mathcal{Z}}_r^\star$ on $\mathcal{R}_r\}$; each $\mathcal{R}_k$ is the *region of optimality* of $\widetilde{\mathcal{Z}}_k^\star$, meaning that among all the pieces $\widetilde{\mathcal{Z}}_k^\star$ is the minimal one on $\mathcal{R}_k$, *i.e.* $\mathcal{R}_k = \{\boldsymbol{x} \mid \widetilde{\mathcal{Z}}^\star(\boldsymbol{x}) = \widetilde{\mathcal{Z}}_k^\star(\boldsymbol{x})\}$. By construction, $\widetilde{\mathcal{Z}}^\star(\boldsymbol{x})$ is the minimum of $\{\widetilde{\mathcal{Z}}_1^\star(\boldsymbol{x}), \ldots, \widetilde{\mathcal{Z}}_r^\star(\boldsymbol{x})\}$ and $\widetilde{\mathcal{Z}}^\star(\mathring{\boldsymbol{x}}) = \widetilde{\mathcal{Z}}_1^\star(\mathring{\boldsymbol{x}}) = \ldots = \widetilde{\mathcal{Z}}_r^\star(\mathring{\boldsymbol{x}}) = 1$ is enforced by the (‡)-normalization constraint.

This is where λ_0 comes into play: the fact that $\boldsymbol{\lambda} = (1, 0, ..., 0)$ fulfills (‡) and (α), hence leading to the constant function $\mathcal{Z}_{\boldsymbol{\lambda}}^\star = 1$, sets an upper-bound on $\mathcal{Z}^\star$. Therefore, any minimal piece $\widetilde{\mathcal{Z}}_k^\star$, which evaluates to 1 on $\mathring{\boldsymbol{x}}$, can not grow on its region of optimality otherwise it would not be minimal compared to $\mathcal{Z}_{\boldsymbol{\lambda}}^\star = 1$. Thus, $\widetilde{\mathcal{Z}}_k^\star$ is either constant and equal to 1 or it satisfies $\forall \boldsymbol{x} \in \mathring{\mathcal{R}}_k,\ 1 > \mathcal{Z}_k^\star(\boldsymbol{x})$ which entails its decline on the infinite region $\mathcal{R}_k$ as meant by Lemma 4, causing its nullification in $\mathcal{R}_k$, hence its irredundancy (Lemma 5). The constant piece $\mathcal{Z}_{\boldsymbol{\lambda}}^\star = 1$ arises among the solutions of a normalized PLOP when the resulting polyhedron $\mathcal{P}^\star$ is unbounded as illustrated alongside.

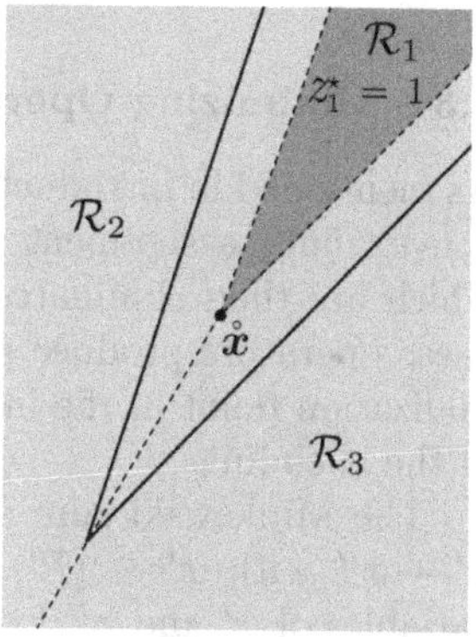

We focus on the proof of Lemma 5 which gives a criterion of irredundancy illustrated on Fig. 1. The proofs of the other lemmata are just computational arguments; they are provided in the appendix of the extended version of this paper [22].

Lemma 3. $\forall \boldsymbol{x} \in \mathbb{Q}^n,\ \boldsymbol{x} \in \mathring{\mathcal{R}}_k \Rightarrow \mathring{\boldsymbol{x}} + \mu(\boldsymbol{x} - \mathring{\boldsymbol{x}}) \in \mathring{\mathcal{R}}_k,\ \forall \mu > 0.$

Lemma 4. *Either* $\widetilde{\mathcal{Z}}_k^\star$ *is the constant function* $\boldsymbol{x} \mapsto 1$, *or it decreases on lines of* $\mathcal{R}_k$ *starting at* $\mathring{\boldsymbol{x}}$, *i.e.* $\forall \boldsymbol{x} \in \mathring{\mathcal{R}}_k,\ \forall \mu > 1,\ \widetilde{\mathcal{Z}}_k^\star(\boldsymbol{x}) > \widetilde{\mathcal{Z}}_k^\star(\mathring{\boldsymbol{x}} + \mu(\boldsymbol{x} - \mathring{\boldsymbol{x}}))$.

Lemma 5. $\left([\![\widetilde{\mathcal{Z}}_k^\star = 0]\!] \cap [\![\mathring{\mathcal{R}}_k]\!]\right) \neq \emptyset \Rightarrow \widetilde{\mathcal{Z}}_k^\star \geq 0$ *is irredundant* w.r.t. $\widetilde{\mathcal{Z}}^\star \geq 0$.

Proof by contradiction. Consider $\widetilde{\mathcal{Z}}_k^\star$, a piece of $\widetilde{\mathcal{Z}}^\star$ such that $[\![\widetilde{\mathcal{Z}}_k^\star = 0]\!] \cap [\![\mathring{\mathcal{R}}_k]\!] \neq \emptyset$. Let us assume that $\widetilde{\mathcal{Z}}_k^\star$ is redundant. Then, by Farkas Lemma 1, $\exists\,(\lambda_j)_{j \neq k} \geq 0,\ \forall \boldsymbol{x} \in \mathbb{Q}^n,\ \sum_{j \neq k} \lambda_j \widetilde{\mathcal{Z}}_j^\star(\boldsymbol{x}) \leq \widetilde{\mathcal{Z}}_k^\star(\boldsymbol{x})$.

Let $\boldsymbol{x}$ be a point of the nonempty set $[\![\widetilde{\mathcal{Z}}_k^\star = 0]\!] \cap [\![\mathring{\mathcal{R}}_k]\!]$. Then $\widetilde{\mathcal{Z}}_k^\star(\boldsymbol{x}) = 0$, as $\boldsymbol{x} \in [\![\widetilde{\mathcal{Z}}_k^\star = 0]\!]$, and the previous Farkas inequality becomes

$$\sum_{j \neq k} \lambda_j \widetilde{\mathcal{Z}}_j^\star(\boldsymbol{x}) \leq 0 \tag{7}$$

Since $\boldsymbol{x} \in \mathring{\mathcal{R}}_k$, then, $\widetilde{\mathcal{Z}}_k^\star(\boldsymbol{x}) < \widetilde{\mathcal{Z}}_j^\star(\boldsymbol{x})$ for $j \neq k$ by definition of $\mathcal{R}_k$ as the region of optimality of $\widetilde{\mathcal{Z}}_k^\star$. More precisely, $0 < \widetilde{\mathcal{Z}}_j^\star(\boldsymbol{x})$ since $\boldsymbol{x} \in [\![\widetilde{\mathcal{Z}}_k^\star = 0]\!]$. Therefore, $0 < \lambda_j \widetilde{\mathcal{Z}}_j^\star(\boldsymbol{x})$ for $j \neq k$ as $\lambda_j \geq 0$. Then, summing up this inequation for all $j \neq k$, we obtain

$$0 < \sum_{j \neq k} \lambda_j \widetilde{\mathcal{Z}}_j^\star(\boldsymbol{x}) \tag{8}$$

(7) and (8) are contradictory, proving thereby that $\widetilde{\mathcal{Z}}_k^\star$ is irredundant. □

6.3 Minimizing Operators Based on Projection via PLP

As mentioned in introduction, several polyhedral operators, e.g. Minkowski sum, convex hull, assignment and linearization, are encoded using extra variables which are then eliminated by projection. If the projection is done by PLP, all these operators produce polyhedra free of redundancy if we can provide a normalization point in the interior of the expected polyhedron. Let us give insights of the encodings.

The Minkowski sum of two polyhedra $\mathcal{P}'$ and $\mathcal{P}''$ is the set of points $\boldsymbol{x} = \boldsymbol{x}' + \boldsymbol{x}''$ with $\boldsymbol{x}' \in [\![\mathcal{P}']\!]$ and $\boldsymbol{x}'' \in [\![\mathcal{P}'']\!]$. It is computed by eliminating the variables of $\boldsymbol{x}'$ and $\boldsymbol{x}''$ from the polyhedron $\mathcal{P}'(\boldsymbol{x}') \wedge \mathcal{P}''(\boldsymbol{x}'') \wedge \{\, \boldsymbol{x} = \boldsymbol{x}' + \boldsymbol{x}'' \,\}$, where $\mathcal{P}'(\boldsymbol{x}')$ (resp. $\mathcal{P}''(\boldsymbol{x}'')$) denotes the set of constraints of $\mathcal{P}'$ (resp. $\mathcal{P}''$) over variables $\boldsymbol{x}'$ (resp. $\boldsymbol{x}''$). We use $\mathring{\boldsymbol{x}} \stackrel{def}{=} \mathring{\boldsymbol{x}}' + \mathring{\boldsymbol{x}}''$ as normalization point where $\mathring{\boldsymbol{x}}'$ (resp. $\mathring{\boldsymbol{x}}''$) is a point lying within the interior of $\mathcal{P}'$ (resp. $\mathcal{P}''$).

The convex-hull of $\mathcal{P}'$ and $\mathcal{P}''$ is the smallest convex polyhedron that includes $\mathcal{P}'$ and $\mathcal{P}''$. It is the set of barycentres of $\boldsymbol{x}' \in [\![\mathcal{P}']\!]$ and $\boldsymbol{x}'' \in [\![\mathcal{P}'']\!]$ which can be formally defined as $\mathcal{P}'(\boldsymbol{x}') \wedge \mathcal{P}''(\boldsymbol{x}'') \wedge \{\boldsymbol{x} = \beta_1 \times \boldsymbol{x}' + \beta_2 \times \boldsymbol{x}'', \beta_1 + \beta_2 = 1, \beta_1 \geq 0, \beta_2 \geq 0\}$. The equation defining $\boldsymbol{x}$ is non-linear but it can be linearized using a simple change of variable [2]. Then, the convex-hull is obtained by elimination of β_1, β_2 and the variables of $\boldsymbol{x}'$ and $\boldsymbol{x}''$ to get a polyhedron over $\boldsymbol{x}$. We can use $\mathring{\boldsymbol{x}}'$ or $\mathring{\boldsymbol{x}}''$ as normalization point.

Assignment and more generally, image by an affine map represented by a matrix $\boldsymbol{M}$ can be encoded as intersection with equalities $\boldsymbol{x}' = \boldsymbol{M}\boldsymbol{x}$, projection of the unprimed variables, and then renaming of the prime variables into unprimed ones; the reverse image is just substitution. We use the image by $\boldsymbol{M}$ of a point $\mathring{\boldsymbol{x}}$ in the interior of the input polyhedron for normalization.

Our linearization operator for computing a polyhedral over-approximation of a conjunctions of linear and polynomial constraints $\bigwedge_i g_i(\boldsymbol{x}) \geq 0$ is also implemented in the VPL via PLP [21]. However, it does not prevent redundancies as we do not know how to provide a normalization point satisfying $\bigwedge_i g_i(\mathring{\boldsymbol{x}}) \geq 0$.

7 Experiments

Benchmarks. We reused the benchmark suite of [23]. It contains polyhedra generated randomly from several characteristics: number of constraints, number of variables and density (ratio of the number of zero coefficients by the number of variables). Constraints are created by picking up a random integer between -100 and 100 as coefficient of each variable. All constraints are attached the same constant bound ≤ 20. These polyhedra have a potatoid shape, as shown on the right-hand side figure.

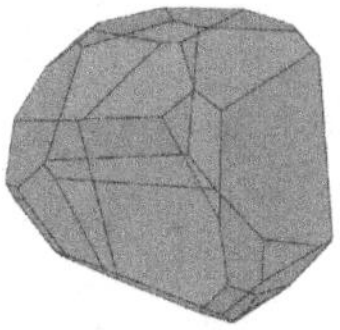

We compare three libraries on projection/minimization problems: NEWPOLKA [16] as representative of the double description framework, VPL [10] based on Fourier-Motzkin elimination, and our implementation based on PLP. As we produce polyhedra in minimized form, we asked NEWPOLKA and VPL to perform a minimization afterwards.

On each problem we measure the execution time, with a timeout fixed at 300 s. In addition to the number of constraints C, the density D and the number of variables V, we consider the effect of the projection ratio P (number of projected variable over dimension). Figure 2 shows the effect of these characteristics on execution time (in seconds). The vertical axis is always displayed in log scale, for readability. Each point is the average execution time for the projection and minimization of 10 polyhedra sharing the same characteristics.

Fourier-Motzkin Elimination in the VPL. As mentioned earlier, Fourier-Motzkin elimination generates many redundant constraints and the challenge of a good implementation is their fast removal. The Fourier-Motzkin elimination implemented in the VPL uses well-known tricks for dynamically removing constraints that can be shown redundant by syntactic arguments [23]. However, as shown by [8, 3.2.3, p. 76], this forbids the use of Kohler's redundancy criterion: when eliminating k variables, a constraint resulting from the combination of $k+1$ constraints is redundant. When syntactic criteria fail to decide the redundancy of a constraint, the VPL calls a LP solver. Hence, polyhedra are minimized after each single-variable elimination.

Projection Ratio. Figure 2(a) gives the time measurements when projecting polyhedra of 15 constraints, 10 variables and a density of 50%, with a projection ratio varying from 10 to 90%. Fourier-Motzkin is very efficient when projecting a small number of variables. Its exponential behavior mainly occurs for high projection ratio, as it eliminates variables one after the other and the number of faces tends to grow at each projection. PLP is not suitable when there is only few variables to project, e.g. in the case of a single assignment. On the contrary, it becomes interesting compared to Fourier-Motzkin elimination when the projection ratio exceeds 50%, *i.e.* when projecting more than half of the variables. This ratio is always reached when computing Minkowski sums or convex hulls by projection (Sect. 6.3). It can also be the case on exits of program blocks where a whole set of local variables must be forgotten. As PLP usefulness grows with a high projection ratio we will focus on the case $P = 75\%$, studying the effect of other characteristics.

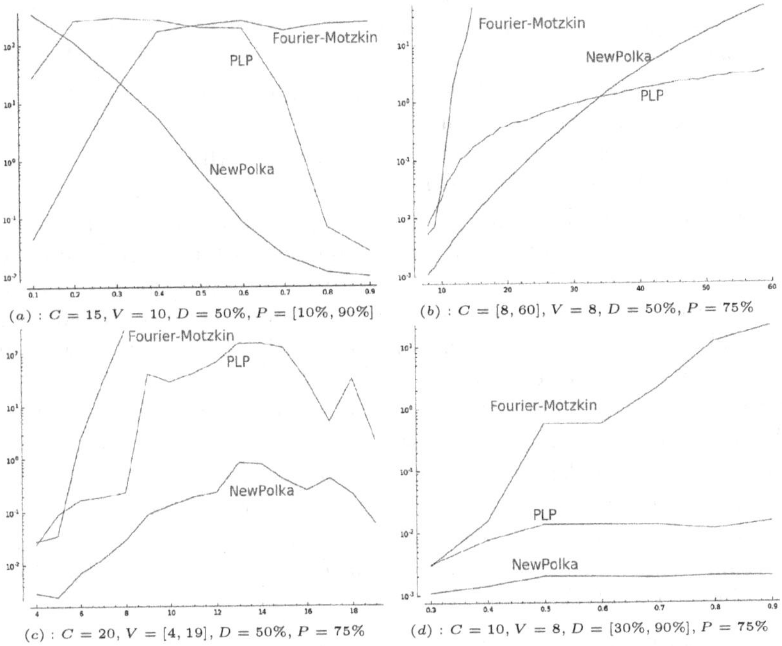

Fig. 2. Execution time in seconds of NewPolka (blue), Fourier-Motzkin (red) and PLP (green) depending on respectively (a) projection ratio, (b) number of constraints, (c) number of variables and (d) density. (Color figure online)

Number of Constraints. Fig. 2(b) shows the time measurements when projecting polyhedra with 8 variables, a density of 50% and a projection ratio of 75% (*i.e.* elimination of 6 variables). The number of constraints varies in $[8, 60]$. While Fourier-Motzkin blows up when reaching 15 constraints, PLP and NewPolka scale better and the curves shows that PLP wins when the number of constraints exceeds 35.

Dimension. The evolution of execution time in terms of dimension is given in Fig. 2(c). With 20 constraints, the exponential behavior of Fourier-Motzkin elimination emerges. PLP and NewPolka show a similar curves with an overhead for PLP on a log scale, *i.e.* a proportionality factor on execution time. It would be interesting to see the effect of dimension beyond 20 variables, which takes considerable time since it requires increasing the number of constraints. Indeed, when the dimension is greater than the number of constraints, polyhedra have a really special shape with very few generators and the comparison would be distorted.

Density. The effect of density on execution time is shown on Fig. 2(d). NewPolka and PLP are little sensitive to density. The case of Fourier-Motzkin can be explained: Elimination of a variable x with FM consists in combining every pair of constraints having an opposite sign for x. The more non-zero coefficients within the constraints, the greater the number of possible combinations.

What can we conclude from these experiments? On small problems our projection is less efficient than that of a double description (DD) library but the shape of the curves of NewPolka and PLP is similar on a logarithmic scale, meaning that there is a proportionality factor between the two algorithms. This is an encouraging result as projection – and the operators encoded as projection – are the Achilles heel of constraints-only representation whereas it is straightforward in DD: the complexity is exponential with FM elimination but linear in the number of generators. On the other hand, the conjunction operator, which, in constraints-only representation, consists in the union of two sets followed by a fast minimization [23], is less efficient in DD because it triggers one step of Chernikova's algorithm per constraint.

8 Conclusion and Future Work

We have shown how usual operations over convex polyhedra (projection, convex hull, Minkowski sums, image by an affine map, linearization) can be formulated as PLOP instances. In short, all costly operations on polyhedra in constraints-only representation can be implemented using PLOP.

This approach was made practical by the combination of an efficient PLP-solver and a normalization constraint ensuring that the solutions of the PLOP are free of redundancies, which avoids costly post-processing minimization. This makes the VPL, a polyhedra library in constraints-only representation, competitive with other libraries in double description, and much faster on problems that have exponential generator representations.

Experiments on Minkowski sum met our expectations but raised an issue for convex-hull: On large problems with the same characteristics, we beat other libraries, but we suffer from an exponential blow-up of region subdivisions when the two polyhedra have many faces in common, which induces a high degree of degeneracy. Our PLP-solver does not have special counter-measures to deal with degeneracy. Proposals exist for tackling primal and dual degeneracies but they come with an extra-cost [18]. Thus, dealing with degeneracy is a trade-off and we need a deeper understanding of the phenomenon before addressing it in our PLP-solver or by a pre-processing for convex-hull.

As future work, our approach can be combined with Cartesian product factorization [13,31]. While the main advantage of factorization is to avoid exponential generator representations, which we also do because we never compute generators, using low dimension factors is likely to speed up parametric linear programming.

Other avenues of research include experiments in the large on static analysis of actual programs, the parallelization of the algorithms (we already use a parallel minimization algorithm) and the increased use of floating-point computations instead of exact rational arithmetic without destroying soundness.

Acknowledgments. The authors would like to thank Alexis Fouilhé, Andy King, Jacob Howe, and Paul Feautrier for their help on the early stages of this work.

References

1. Bastoul, C.: Contributions to high-level program optimization. Habilitation thesis, Université Paris-Sud (2012)
2. Benoy, F., King, A., Mesnard, F.: Computing convex hulls with a linear solver. Theor. Pract. Logic Program. (TPLP) **5**(1–2), 259–271 (2005)
3. Chernikova, N.V.: Algorithm for discovering the set of all the solutions of a linear programming problem. USSR Comput. Math. Math. Phys. **8**(6), 282–293 (1968)
4. Chvatal, V.: Linear Programming. Series of books in the Mathematical Sciences. W.H. Freeman, New York (1983)
5. Cousot, P., Cousot, R.: Abstract interpretation: a unified lattice model for static analysis of programs by construction or approximation of fixpoints. In: ACM Principles of Programming Languages (POPL), pp. 238–252. ACM Press (1977)
6. Cousot, P., Halbwachs, N.: Automatic discovery of linear restraints among variables of a program. In: ACM Principles of Programming Languages (POPL), pp. 84–97. ACM Press (1978)
7. Dantzig, G.B., Thapa, M.N.: Linear Programming 2: Theory and Extensions. Springer Series in Operations Research and Financial Engineering. Springer, New York (2003)
8. Fouilhé, A.: Revisiting the abstract domain of polyhedra: constraints-only representation and formal proof. Ph.D. thesis, Université de Grenoble (2015)
9. Fouilhe, A., Boulmé, S.: A certifying frontend for (sub)polyhedral abstract domains. In: Giannakopoulou, D., Kroening, D. (eds.) VSTTE 2014. LNCS, vol. 8471, pp. 200–215. Springer, Cham (2014). doi:10.1007/978-3-319-12154-3_13
10. Fouilhe, A., Monniaux, D., Périn, M.: Efficient generation of correctness certificates for the abstract domain of polyhedra. In: Logozzo, F., Fähndrich, M. (eds.) SAS 2013. LNCS, vol. 7935, pp. 345–365. Springer, Heidelberg (2013). doi:10.1007/978-3-642-38856-9_19
11. Gal, T., Nedoma, J.: Multiparametric linear programming. Manage. Sci. **18**(7), 406–422 (1972)
12. Halbwachs, N.: Détermination automatique de relations linéaires vérifiées par les variables d'un programme. Ph.D. thesis, Université Scientifique et Médicale de Grenoble (1979). (in french)
13. Halbwachs, N., Merchat, D., Gonnord, L.: Some ways to reduce the space dimension in polyhedra computations. Formal Meth. Syst. Des. **29**(1), 79–95 (2006)

14. Henry, J., Monniaux, D., Moy, M.: PAGAI: a path sensitive static analyser. Electron. Notes Theoret. Comput. Sci. **289**, 15–25 (2012)
15. Howe, J.M., King, A.: Polyhedral analysis using parametric objectives. In: Miné, A., Schmidt, D. (eds.) SAS 2012. LNCS, vol. 7460, pp. 41–57. Springer, Heidelberg (2012). doi:10.1007/978-3-642-33125-1_6
16. Jeannet, B., Miné, A.: APRON: a library of numerical abstract domains for static analysis. In: Bouajjani, A., Maler, O. (eds.) CAV 2009. LNCS, vol. 5643, pp. 661–667. Springer, Heidelberg (2009). doi:10.1007/978-3-642-02658-4_52
17. Jones, C.N., Kerrigan, E.C., Maciejowski, J.M.: On polyhedral projections and parametric programming. J. Optim. Theory Appl. **138**(2), 207–220 (2008)
18. Jones, C.N., Kerrigan, E.C., Maciejowski, J.M.: Lexicographic perturbation for multiparametric linear programming with applications to control. Automatica **43**(10), 1808–1816 (2007)
19. Kohler, D.: Projection of convex polyhedral sets. Ph.D. thesis, University of California, Berkeley (1967)
20. Le Verge, H.: A note on Chernikova's algorithm. Technical report 1662, INRIA (1992)
21. Maréchal, A., Fouilhé, A., King, T., Monniaux, D., Périn, M.: Polyhedral approximation of multivariate polynomials using handelman's theorem. In: Jobstmann, B., Leino, K.R.M. (eds.) VMCAI 2016. LNCS, vol. 9583, pp. 166–184. Springer, Heidelberg (2016). doi:10.1007/978-3-662-49122-5_8
22. Maréchal, A., Monniaux, D., Périn, M.: Scalable minimizing-operators on polyhedra via parametric linear programming. Technical report 4, Verimag, June 2017
23. Maréchal, A., Périn, M.: Efficient elimination of redundancies in polyhedra by Raytracing. In: Bouajjani, A., Monniaux, D. (eds.) VMCAI 2017. LNCS, vol. 10145, pp. 367–385. Springer, Cham (2017). doi:10.1007/978-3-319-52234-0_20
24. McMullen, P.: The maximum numbers of faces of a convex polytope. Mathematika **17**, 179–184 (1970)
25. McMullen, P., Shepard, G.C.: Convex Polytopes and the Upper Bound Conjecture. London Mathematical Society Lecture Note Series, vol. 3. Cambridge University Press, Cambridge (1971)
26. Miné, A.: The octagon abstract domain. High. Order Symbolic Comput. **19**(1), 31–100 (2006)
27. Monniaux, D.: Quantifier elimination by lazy model enumeration. In: Touili, T., Cook, B., Jackson, P. (eds.) CAV 2010. LNCS, vol. 6174, pp. 585–599. Springer, Heidelberg (2010). doi:10.1007/978-3-642-14295-6_51
28. Roberto, B., Hill, P.M., Zaffanella, E.: The Parma polyhedra library: toward a complete set of numerical abstractions for the analysis and verification of hardware and software systems. Sci. Comput. Program. **72**(1–2), 3–21 (2008)
29. Schrijver, A.: Theory of Linear and Integer Programming. Wiley, Hoboken (1999)
30. Simon, A., King, A.: Exploiting sparsity in polyhedral analysis. In: Hankin, C., Siveroni, I. (eds.) SAS 2005. LNCS, vol. 3672, pp. 336–351. Springer, Heidelberg (2005). doi:10.1007/11547662_23
31. Singh, G., Püschel, M., Vechev, M.: Fast polyhedra abstract domain. In: ACM Principles of Programming Languages (POPL), pp. 46–59. ACM Press (2017)
32. Singh, G., Püschel, M., Vechev, M.T.: Making numerical program analysis fast. In: Programming Language Design and Implementation (PLDI), pp. 303–313. ACM Press (2015)

Hyperhierarchy of Semantics - A Formal Framework for Hyperproperties Verification

Isabella Mastroeni and Michele Pasqua(✉)

Dipartimento di Informatica, University of Verona,
Strada le Grazie 15, 37134 Verona, Italy
{isabella.mastroeni,michele.pasqua}@univr.it

Abstract. Hyperproperties are becoming the, de facto, standard for reasoning about systems executions. They differ from classical trace properties since they are represented by *sets of sets* of executions instead of sets of executions. In this paper, we extend and lift the hierarchy of semantics developed in 2002 by P. Cousot in order to cope with verification of hyperproperties. In the standard hierarchy, semantics at different levels of abstraction are related with each other by abstract interpretation. In the same spirit, we propose an *hyper*hierarchy of semantics adding a new, more concrete, hyper level. The semantics defined at this hyper level are suitable for hyperproperties verification. Furthermore, all the semantics in the hyperhierarchy (the standard and the hyper ones) are still related by abstract interpretation.

1 Introduction

Since its origin in 1977, abstract interpretation [8] has been widely used, implicitly or explicitly, to describe and formalize approximate computations in many different areas of computer science, from its very beginning use in formalizing (compile-time) program analysis frameworks to more recent applications in model checking, program verification, comparative semantics, data and SW security, malware detection, code obfuscation, etc. When reasoning about systems executions a key point is the degree of approximation given by the choice of the semantics used to represent computations. In this direction, comparative semantics consists in comparing semantics at different levels of abstraction, always by abstract interpretation [7,18]. The choice of the semantics is a key point, not only for finding the desirable trade-off between precision and decidability of program analysis in terms, for instance, of property verification, but also because not all the semantics are suitable for proving any possible property of interest. This means that the property to verify necessarily affect the semantics we have to choose for modeling the system to analyze. For instance, if we are interested in a property which is not a safety property [2], then we have necessarily to consider a semantics able to approximate the whole computation (not only the past of a computation), as static analysis does. While, when we are interested in safety property then we have to consider a *safety abstraction* of the semantics [13,19]. Analogously, if we have to characterize slices (extraction of executable

F. Ranzato (Ed.): SAS 2017, LNCS 10422, pp. 232–252, 2017.
DOI: 10.1007/978-3-319-66706-5_12

code sub-fragments of a program [21]) of potentially non-terminating programs then we need a semantics able to characterize also what happens after loops [17].

These were only examples, but in general new (classes of) properties of interest may induce the necessity of defining new semantics, i.e., new semantic models for computational systems. In particular, we observed that *hyperproperties*, namely sets of properties, recently gained more and more interest due to their capability to capture program features that cannot be caught by classical properties, namely features that cannot be characterized by a predicate defined on single computations. For instance, information flow properties can be verified only by comparing *sets* of computations, hence they are hyperproperties, and not properties in the standard sense. Hence, what we propose here is a general formal framework for comparing semantics including the so-called *hypersemantics*, modeling programs as sets of sets of computations, since we need such a more concrete observation of systems computations in order to verify, potentially by using approximation, hyperproperties. The framework we propose is indeed an extension of the Cousot hierarchy of semantics [7] enriched with an hyper level, where still all the semantics are compared by abstract interpretation. Moreover, we show that at least two existing program analysis approaches (one recent approach for information flow analysis [3] and standard program static analysis [9]) can be included or compared in our framework.

2 Transition Systems, Semantics and Approximations

In this section, we introduce the hierarchy of semantics (both definition and construction of semantics) proposed by Cousot [7], from which we move towards the hyperlevel. In this way, while providing a formal framework for hypersemantics we can formally prove its relation with the standard semantics framework.

2.1 Trace Semantics of Systems

We reason about semantics of systems independently from systems themselves. Let $\mathcal{S}$ be the set of possible denotations of states of (computational) systems. The *concrete* semantics of a system P is given by the transition system $\langle \Sigma, \Upsilon, \Omega, \tau \rangle$, where $\Sigma \subseteq \mathcal{S}$ is the set of possible states of P, $\Upsilon \subseteq \Sigma$ is the set of *all* initial states of P, $\tau \subseteq \Sigma \times \Sigma$ is the transition relation between states of P, and $\Omega \subseteq \Sigma$ is the set of blocking/final states of P, i.e., those states σ such that $\forall \sigma' \in \Sigma . \langle \sigma, \sigma' \rangle \notin \tau$. For instance, a system could be any program written in a programming language, the state denotations could be any possible mappings from program variables to values and the transition system is given by the operational semantics of the language.

The executions of a system are modeled by sequences of transitions [7]. The set $\mathcal{S}^{\vec{n}} \overset{\text{def}}{=} [0, n) \mapsto \mathcal{S}$, $n \in \mathbb{N}$, is the set of finite sequences $s = s_0 s_1 \dots s_{n-1}$ of length $|s| = n$ over $\mathcal{S}$. The set of finite non-empty sequences is $\mathcal{S}^{\vec{+}} \overset{\text{def}}{=} \bigcup_{0<n<\omega} \mathcal{S}^{\vec{n}}$. The set $\mathcal{S}^{\vec{\omega}} \overset{\text{def}}{=} \mathbb{N} \mapsto \mathcal{S}$ contains infinite sequences $s = s_0 s_1 \dots$ of length $|s| = \omega$ over $\mathcal{S}$. The set of non-empty sequences is $\mathcal{S}^{\vec{\infty}} \overset{\text{def}}{=} \mathcal{S}^{\vec{+}} \cup \mathcal{S}^{\vec{\omega}}$. The empty sequence is ϵ. Given $s, s' \in \mathcal{S}^{\vec{\infty}}$, s' can be appended to s iff $s_{|s|-1} = s'_0$ and their append is $s \frown s' \stackrel{\text{def}}{=} s_0 s_1 \ldots s_{|s|-1} s'_1 s'_2 \ldots s'_{|s'|-1}$ [7]. Given a system P, $\Sigma^{\vec{\infty}} \subseteq \mathcal{S}^{\vec{\infty}}$ is the set of all sequences on the states Σ of P, analogous for $\Sigma^{\vec{+}} \subseteq \mathcal{S}^{\vec{+}}$ and $\Sigma^{\vec{\omega}} \subseteq \mathcal{S}^{\vec{\omega}}$.

An execution (*trace*) of a system P is a sequence of states in Σ where adjacent elements are in τ. $\tau^{\dot{\vec{n}}} \stackrel{\text{def}}{=} \{\sigma \in \Sigma^{\vec{n}} \mid \forall i \in [0, n-1) \,.\, \langle \sigma_i, \sigma_{i+1} \rangle \in \tau\}$ are the finite traces of length n, while the set of finite blocking traces of length n is $\tau^{\vec{n}} \stackrel{\text{def}}{=} \{\sigma \in \Sigma^{\vec{n}} \mid \sigma_{n-1} \in \Omega \wedge \forall i \in [0, n-1) \,.\, \langle \sigma_i, \sigma_{i+1} \rangle \in \tau\}$.

The *maximal finite trace semantics* (set of blocking/terminating executions) is $\tau^{\vec{+}} \stackrel{\text{def}}{=} \bigcup_{0<n<\omega} \tau^{\vec{n}}$. The *infinite trace semantics* (set of non-blocking/non-terminating executions) is $\tau^{\vec{\omega}} \stackrel{\text{def}}{=} \{\sigma \in \Sigma^{\vec{\omega}} \mid \forall i \in \mathbb{N} \,.\, \langle \sigma_i, \sigma_{i+1} \rangle \in \tau\}$. The *maximal trace semantics* is $\tau^{\vec{\infty}} \stackrel{\text{def}}{=} \tau^{\vec{+}} \cup \tau^{\vec{\omega}}$ [7]. In the following, in order to avoid ambiguity, we can make explicit the system, e.g., we can write $\tau^{\vec{\infty}}[P]$ instead of just $\tau^{\vec{\infty}}$ in order to denote the maximal trace semantics of P.

2.2 Fixpoint Semantics Approximation

A semantics $\mathcal{T}$ is said to be *constructive*, i.e., expressible in fixpoint form, if there exists a *fixpoint semantic specification* $\langle F, D, \preccurlyeq \rangle$, where $\langle D, \preccurlyeq, \vee, \bot \rangle$ is a partially ordered set with (partially defined) least upper bound $\vee$ and minimum $\bot$ (usually at least a DCPO[1]), $F : D \to D$ is $\preccurlyeq$-monotone and iteratable[2] and $\mathcal{T} = \mathit{lfp}^{\preccurlyeq}_{\bot} F = F^{\delta}$, where δ is the least ordinal such that $F^{\delta} = F(F^{\delta})$ and F^{δ} is equal to $\bigvee_{n \leq \delta} F^n(\bot)$ [14].

Consider now the semantic specifications $\langle F, D, \preccurlyeq \rangle, \langle \bar{F}, \bar{D}, \bar{\preccurlyeq} \rangle$, and suppose that $\langle D, \preccurlyeq \rangle, \langle \bar{D}, \bar{\preccurlyeq} \rangle$ form a *Galois connection*[3], by means of the functions $\alpha : D \xrightarrow{m} \bar{D}$ (abstraction) and $\gamma : \bar{D} \xrightarrow{m} D$ (concretization), namely α and γ are adjoint functions. When the semantics is expressed in fixpoint form, we can derive an abstract fixpoint semantics by abstraction of a concrete one, or vice versa. The Kleenian fixpoint approximation theorem [7], requires abstraction soundness, i.e., $\alpha \circ F \mathrel{\bar{\preccurlyeq}} \bar{F} \circ \alpha$, guaranteeing fixpoint approximation, i.e., $\alpha(\mathit{lfp}^{\preccurlyeq}_{\bot} F) \mathrel{\bar{\preccurlyeq}} \mathit{lfp}^{\bar{\preccurlyeq}}_{\bar{\bot}} \bar{F}$. The (in the following called *backward*) Kleenian fixpoint transfer theorem [7] requires completeness, i.e., $\alpha \circ F = \bar{F} \circ \alpha$, guaranteeing the fixpoint transfer from concrete to abstract domain, i.e., $\alpha(\mathit{lfp}^{\preccurlyeq}_{\bot} F) = \mathit{lfp}^{\bar{\preccurlyeq}}_{\bar{\bot}} \bar{F}$.

Suppose now we are interested in transferring the fixpoint from an abstract domain to the concrete one[4]. Unfortunately, the completeness requirement observed in the abstract domain (called *backward*), i.e., $\alpha \circ F = \bar{F} \circ \alpha$, is not

---

[1] A *DCPO* is a poset where it exists the least upper bound of every directed subset.

[2] A function F over D is said *iteratable* if the transfinite iterates of F from $\bot$ are well defined. The *transfinite iterates* of F from $\bot$ are $F^0 = \bot$ and $F^{\delta+1} = F(F^{\delta})$ for successor ordinals $\delta + 1$ and $F^{\zeta} = \bigvee_{\delta<\zeta} F^{\delta}$ for limit ordinals ζ.

[3] α, γ form a Galois connection between concrete $\langle D, \preccurlyeq \rangle$ and abstract $\langle \bar{D}, \bar{\preccurlyeq} \rangle$ domains, denoted $\langle D, \preccurlyeq \rangle \underset{\alpha}{\overset{\gamma}{\leftrightarrows}} \langle \bar{D}, \bar{\preccurlyeq} \rangle$, if $\forall c \in D, a \in \bar{D} \,.\, \alpha(c) \mathrel{\bar{\preccurlyeq}} a \Leftrightarrow c \preccurlyeq \gamma(a)$. If $\alpha \circ \gamma = id_{\bar{D}}$ then they form a Galois insertion, denoted $\langle D, \preccurlyeq \rangle \underset{\alpha}{\overset{\gamma}{\leftrightarrows}} \langle \bar{D}, \bar{\preccurlyeq} \rangle$.

[4] This direction does not change anything in the approximation case, since the soundness requirement is equivalent also when we check it on the concrete, i.e., $\alpha \circ F \mathrel{\bar{\preccurlyeq}} \bar{F} \circ \alpha$ iff $F \circ \gamma \preccurlyeq \gamma \circ \bar{F}$.

the same as checking completeness on the concrete domain (called *forward*), i.e., $F \circ \gamma = \gamma \circ \bar{F}$. In order to transfer fixpoints from abstract to concrete we need precisely the latter direction. In this case, we provide the forward version of the Kleenian fixpoint transfer theorem.

Theorem 1 (*Forward* Kleenian fixpoint transfer). *Suppose that $\langle F, D, \preccurlyeq \rangle$ and $\langle \bar{F}, \bar{D}, \bar{\preccurlyeq} \rangle$ are concrete and abstract fixpoint semantics specifications. Let $\gamma : \bar{D} \to D$ be a strict Scott-continuous*[5] *concretization function. If $\gamma \circ \bar{F} = F \circ \gamma$ (forward completeness) then $\gamma(lfp_{\bot}^{\bar{\preccurlyeq}} \bar{F}) = lfp_{\bot}^{\preccurlyeq} F$.*

In the abstract interpretation framework, it is well known that the Kleenian fixpoint approximation trivially hold when $\bar{F}$ is the best correct approximation (bca) of F, i.e., $\bar{F} = \alpha \circ F \circ \gamma$. Hence, we look for a similar characterization in the dual case. In particular, we look for a systematic way to retrieve a concrete semantics which best represents a given abstract function. Exploiting the "duality principle" of abstract interpretation [10] we can obtain the best correct concretization as $F \stackrel{\text{def}}{=} \gamma \circ \bar{F} \circ \alpha$. Then we still trivially have that $\gamma(lfp_{\bot}^{\bar{\succcurlyeq}} \bar{F}) \succcurlyeq lfp_{\bot}^{\succcurlyeq} F$ and $lfp_{\bot}^{\bar{\succcurlyeq}} \bar{F} \mathrel{\bar{\succcurlyeq}} \alpha(lfp_{\bot}^{\succcurlyeq} F)$. Moreover, in a Galois insertion settings, it is always possible to derive a complete (backward and forward) concretisation, called *best complete concretisation*, of a given abstract semantics:

Theorem 2 (Best Complete Concretization). *Let $\langle D, \preccurlyeq \rangle$ and $\langle \bar{D}, \bar{\preccurlyeq} \rangle$ be partially ordered sets such that $\langle D, \preccurlyeq \rangle \underset{\alpha}{\overset{\gamma}{\leftrightarrows}} \langle \bar{D}, \bar{\preccurlyeq} \rangle$. Let $\bar{F} : \bar{D} \xrightarrow{m} \bar{D}$ and $F^{\text{bcc}} = \gamma \circ \bar{F} \circ \alpha$. Then $\bar{D}$ is both backward and forward complete for F^{bcc}.*

Note that $\bar{F}$ is exactly the bca of F^{bcc} in $\bar{D}$, indeed ${F^{\text{bcc}}}^{\text{bca}} = \alpha \circ F^{\text{bcc}} \circ \gamma = \alpha \circ \gamma \circ \bar{F} \circ \alpha \circ \gamma = \bar{F}$. Hence, given an abstract function $\bar{F}$ it is possible to derive a concrete function F, for which $\bar{F}$ is an approximation, such that $\alpha(lfp_{\bot}^{\preccurlyeq} F) = lfp_{\bot}^{\bar{\preccurlyeq}} F^{\sharp}$ and $lfp_{\bot}^{\preccurlyeq} F = \gamma(lfp_{\bot}^{\bar{\preccurlyeq}} \bar{F})$.

2.3 Standard Hierarchy of Semantics

In [7] the author showed that many well-known semantics can be computed as abstract interpretations of the maximal trace semantics, and they can be organized in a hierarchy. For instance, the *relational semantics* τ^{∞} associates an input/output relation with system traces by using the $\bot$ symbol to denote non-termination, while *denotational semantics* $\tau^{\natural}$ gives semantics by considering input/output functions. Each semantics (said to be in *natural style*) have three different abstractions, for instance the *angelic* abstraction, which observes only finite computations, e.g., the *angelic trace semantics* $\tau^{\vec{+}}$ observes only finite traces, while the *angelic relational semantics* τ^{+} and the *angelic denotational semantics* $\tau^{\flat}$ the corresponding relations and functions. In [7] the author consider also several other semantics but, in sake of simplicity, we focus only in the subset of the hierarchy depicted in Fig. 1, on the left. Another useful semantics is *partial trace semantics* (finite prefixes of computations, starting from initial states): $\tau^{\vec{\propto}} = \bigcup_{0<n<\omega} \{\sigma \in \tau^{\vec{n}} \mid \sigma_0 \in \Upsilon\}$ [12].

[5] A function f is said *Scott-continuous* if preserves the least upper bound of directed subsets of X and it is said *strict* if $f(\bot) = \bot$.

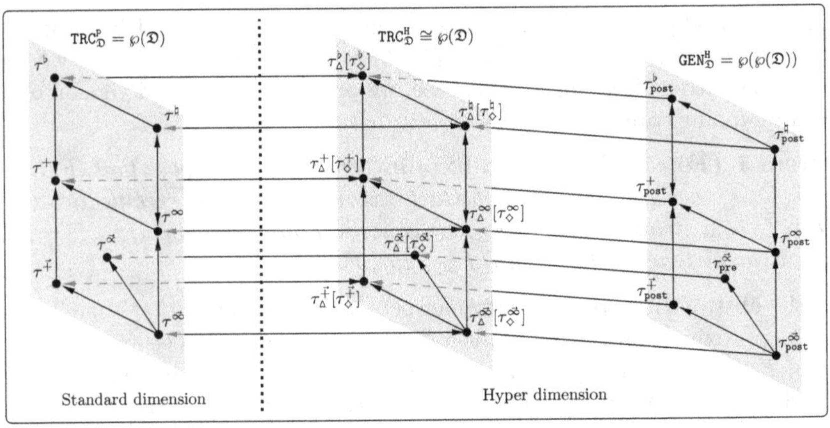

Fig. 1. A part of the standard hierarchy of semantics with its hyper counterparts

Furthermore, these semantics can all be computed by fixpoint of a monotone operator over an ordered domain [7,12]. In this case, it is not always possible to obtain semantics by fixpoint w.r.t. the standard inclusion order ($\subseteq$), also called the approximation order. In fact, in some cases the fixpoint operator is not monotone on the approximation order, and therefore we have to define a computational order forcing monotonicity, and therefore convergence of the fixpoint operator. For instance, the maximal trace semantics of P can be computed as: $\tau^{\vec{\infty}} = \mathit{lfp}^{\sqsubseteq^{\vec{\infty}}}_{\perp^{\vec{\infty}}} F^{\vec{\infty}}$, where $F^{\vec{\infty}} : \wp(\Sigma^{\vec{\infty}}) \rightarrow \wp(\Sigma^{\vec{\infty}})$ is defined as $F^{\vec{\infty}} \stackrel{\text{def}}{=} \lambda X \,.\, \tau^{\vec{1}} \cup (\tau^{\vec{2}} \frown X)$, which is monotone on the computational order $X \sqsubseteq^{\vec{\infty}} Y \stackrel{\text{def}}{=} ((X \cap \Sigma^{\vec{+}}) \subseteq (Y \cap \Sigma^{\vec{+}})) \wedge (X \cap \Sigma^{\vec{\omega}}) \supseteq (Y \cap \Sigma^{\vec{\omega}}))$ (the corresponding lub is $\bigsqcup^{\vec{\infty}} X_i \stackrel{\text{def}}{=} \bigcup (X_i \cap \Sigma^{\vec{+}}) \cup \bigcap (X_i \cap \Sigma^{\vec{\omega}})$ and $\perp^{\vec{\infty}} \stackrel{\text{def}}{=} \Sigma^{\vec{\omega}}$). As far as the partial semantics is concerned, the semantics operator is computed as: $\tau^{\vec{\propto}} = \mathit{lfp}^{\subseteq}_{\varnothing} F^{\vec{\propto}}$, where $F^{\vec{\propto}} : \wp(\Sigma^{\vec{+}}) \rightarrow \wp(\Sigma^{\vec{+}})$ is defined as $F^{\vec{\propto}} \stackrel{\text{def}}{=} \lambda X \,.\, \Upsilon \cup (X \frown \tau^{\vec{2}})$, which is monotone on the standard approximation order ($\subseteq$) [12].

Example 1. Let $P \stackrel{\text{def}}{=} l := 4;\ \textbf{if}\ (h = 1)\ \textbf{then}\ l := 2h\ \textbf{else while}\ (\mathsf{true})\ \textbf{do}\ \{l := 6\}$, and let us denote states as maps between variables to values ($[n, m]$ means $l \mapsto n$, $h \mapsto m$). Maximal trace semantics $\tau^{\vec{\infty}}[\![P]\!]$ and relational semantics $\tau^{\infty}[\![P]\!]$ are:

$$\tau^{\vec{\infty}}[\![P]\!] = \{\, [n,1][4,1][2,1], [4,1][2,1], [2,1], [n,m][4,m][6,m]^{\omega} \mid n \in \mathbb{N}, m \in \mathbb{N} \setminus \{1\}\}$$
$$\tau^{\infty}[\![P]\!] = \{\ \langle [n,1], [2,1]\rangle,\ \langle [4,1][2,1]\rangle,\ \langle [2,1][2,1]\rangle,\ \langle [n,m], \perp\rangle \mid n \in \mathbb{N}, m \in \mathbb{N} \setminus \{1\}\}$$

3 *Hyper*properties

In the security context, there are policies that can be expressed as trace properties, like access control, and others which cannot, like non-interference. In this latter case, it is necessary to specify it as an hyperproperty. Intuitively, a property is defined exclusively in terms of individual executions and, in general, do not specify a relation between different executions of the system. Instead, an hyperproperty specifies the set of *sets of system executions* allowed by the security policy, therefore expressing relations between executions. In [5] it is stated that in order to formalize security policies, it is sufficient to consider hyperproperties. This means that hyperproperties are able to define every possible security policy (this is true for systems modeled as set of states traces).

In this section, we introduce the notion of *hyperproperty* [5], i.e., a set of sets of executions. In the original formulation, systems are modeled by non-empty sets of infinite traces, where terminating executions are modeled by repeating the final state of the trace an infinite number of times [5]. In our work, we will reason about hyperproperties keeping generality, so we are not restricted to only infinite sequences.

Safety Hyperproperties [5]. In the context of trace properties, a particular kind of properties are *safety* ones [2], expressing the fact that "nothing bad happens". These properties are interesting because they depend only on the *history/past* of single executions, meaning that safety properties are dynamically monitorable [2]. Similarly, *safety hyperproperties* (or hypersafety) are the lift to sets of safety properties. This means that, for each set of executions that is not in a safety hyperproperty, there exists a finite prefix set of finite executions (the "bad thing") which cannot be extended for satisfying the property.

Another particular class of hyperproperties are the k-safety hyperproperties (or k-hypersafety). They are safety hyperproperties in which the "bad thing" never involves more than k executions [5]. This means that it is possible to check the violation of a k-hypersafety just observing a set of k executions (note that 1-hypersafeties are exactly safety properties). This is important for verification, in fact, it is possible to reduce the verification of a k-hypersafety on system P to the verification of a safety on the self-composed systems P^k [5]. Furthermore, lots of interesting security policies can be formalized as k-hypersafety; for instance, some definitions of non-interference are 2-hypersafety.

The topic of hyperproperties verification is quite new. Besides the reduction to safety, in [1] the authors introduce a runtime refutation methods for k-safety, based on a three-valued logic. Similarly, [4,15] define hyperlogics, i.e., extensions of temporal logic able to quantify over multiple traces. The use of abstract interpretation in hyperproperties verification is limited to [3], analyzed in Sect. 7.

4 Verifying Hyperproperties

In this section, we deal with hyperproperties *verification*. Here, by verification we mean both *validation*, i.e., checking whether a system fulfills the property, and *confutation*, i.e., checking whether a system does not fulfill the property. It is well known that we cannot always answer to both these problems precisely.

Consider the set of state denotations $\mathcal{S}$ and a set $\mathfrak{D}$ of all possible executions of any system P on states $\mathcal{S}$. The execution of a system could be a sequence (finite or infinite), a pair, etc., of elements in $\mathcal{S}$, depending on how we mean to represent computations. In the following, given a system P, we denote by $[\![P]\!] \subseteq \mathfrak{D}$ a generic semantics of P, parametric on the executions domain $\mathfrak{D}$. For instance, if

$\mathfrak{D} = \mathcal{S}^{\vec{\infty}}$ then we consider the maximal trace semantics of P, i.e., $[\![P]\!] = \tau^{\vec{\infty}}$, while if $\mathfrak{D} = \mathcal{S} \times \mathcal{S}$ then we consider the angelic relational semantics of P, i.e., $[\![P]\!] = \tau^{+}$. Usually, a trace property is modeled as the set of all executions satisfying it. Hence, let $\mathfrak{P} \subseteq \mathfrak{D}$ be such a property, then it is well known that a system P *satisfies* $\mathfrak{P}$, denoted as $P \models \mathfrak{P}$, iff $[\![P]\!] \subseteq \mathfrak{P}$. Hence, by definition, $\mathfrak{P}$ is fulfilled for a system P iff $\mathfrak{P}$ is fulfilled for each one of its executions, i.e., $P \models \mathfrak{P}$ iff $\forall s \in [\![P]\!] \,.\, s \in \mathfrak{P}$ (validation). This is quite useful because in order to disprove that a system fulfills a trace property we just need one counterexample, i.e., $P \not\models \mathfrak{P}$ iff $\exists s \in [\![P]\!] \,.\, s \notin \mathfrak{P}$ (confutation). We denote by $\mathtt{TRC}^{\mathtt{P}}_{\mathfrak{D}}$ the set of all trace properties, i.e., $\wp(\mathfrak{D})$. For instance, trace properties in $\wp(\mathfrak{D})$, for $\mathfrak{D} = \mathcal{S}^{\vec{\infty}}$, are *termination* $\mathtt{Term} \stackrel{\text{def}}{=} \mathcal{S}^{\vec{+}}$ and $\mathtt{Even}^{l} \stackrel{\text{def}}{=} \{s \in \mathcal{S}^{\vec{\infty}} \mid \forall i > 0 \,.\, s_i(l) \text{ even}\}$ (saying that variable l is always even after initialization). Note that, the program in Example 1 satisfies $\mathtt{Even}^{l}$ but not $\mathtt{Term}$, since $\tau^{\vec{\infty}}[P] \subseteq \mathtt{Even}^{l}$, while $\tau^{\vec{\infty}}[P] \not\subseteq \mathtt{Term}$.

For hyperproperties, the satisfiability relation changes from set-inclusion to set-membership [5], namely $P \models \mathfrak{Hp}$ iff $[\![P]\!] \in \mathfrak{Hp}$.

4.1 Hyperproperties Verification

As introduced in Sect. 2, hyperproperties are sets of sets of executions, hence the domain of hyperproperties is $\wp(\wp(\mathfrak{D}))$. We denote by $\mathtt{GEN}^{\mathtt{H}}_{\mathfrak{D}}$ the set of all (generic) hyperproperties, i.e., $\wp(\wp(\mathfrak{D}))$. Similarly to what happens for trace properties, we characterize hyperproperty validation as:

$$P \models \mathfrak{Hp} \in \mathtt{GEN}^{\mathtt{H}}_{\mathfrak{D}} \;\Leftrightarrow\; [\![P]\!] \in \mathfrak{Hp} \;\Leftrightarrow\; \{[\![P]\!]\} \subseteq \mathfrak{Hp}$$

This means that the strongest hyperproperty of a system P is $[\![P]\!]_{\diamond} \stackrel{\text{def}}{=} \{[\![P]\!]\}$ [6], since every hyperproperty of P is implied by, i.e., include, $[\![P]\!]_{\diamond}$. An example of a generic hyperproperty for $\mathfrak{D} = \mathcal{S}^{\vec{\infty}}$ is *generalized non-interference* $\mathtt{GNI} \stackrel{\text{def}}{=} \{X \subseteq \wp(\mathfrak{D}) \mid \forall s, s' \in X \,\exists \bar{s} \in X \,.\, (\bar{s}_{\vdash} =_{\mathtt{H}} s_{\vdash} \wedge \bar{s} \approx_{\mathtt{L}} s')\}$ [5], stating that, for each pair s, s' of executions there exists an interleaving one $\bar{s}$ which agrees with s on private variables ($\mathtt{H}$) in input ($\vdash$) and with s' on public variables ($\mathtt{L}$)[6]. The program in Example 1 do not satisfy $\mathtt{GNI}$, since $\tau^{\vec{\infty}}[P] \notin \mathtt{GNI}$.

At this point, we wonder whether we can use standard semantics for verifying, at least, a subset of hyperproperties. Let us consider the following restriction.

Definition 1 (Trace hyperproperty). *$\mathfrak{tHp} \in \mathtt{GEN}^{\mathtt{H}}_{\mathfrak{D}}$ is called* trace *hyperproperty if $\mathfrak{tHp} = \wp(\bigcup \mathfrak{tHp})$, i.e., if $\langle \mathfrak{tHp}, \subseteq, \cup, \cap, \varnothing, \bigcup \mathfrak{tHp}\rangle$ is a boolean algebra*[7].

We denote with $\mathtt{TRC}^{\mathtt{H}}_{\mathfrak{D}}$ the set of all trace hyperproperties, i.e., $\mathtt{TRC}^{\mathtt{H}}_{\mathfrak{D}}$ is the set $\{\mathfrak{tHp} \in \mathtt{GEN}^{\mathtt{H}}_{\mathfrak{D}} \mid \wp(\bigcup \mathfrak{tHp}) = \mathfrak{tHp}\}$. Hence, we have validation as

$$P \models \mathfrak{tHp} \in \mathtt{TRC}^{\mathtt{H}}_{\mathfrak{D}} \;\Leftrightarrow\; \{\{s\} \mid s \in [\![P]\!]\} \subseteq \mathfrak{tHp} \;\Leftrightarrow\; \forall s \in [\![P]\!] \,.\, \{s\} \in \mathfrak{tHp}$$

---

[6] Note that $=_{\mathtt{H}}$ is an equivalence on states while $\approx_{\mathtt{L}}$ is on traces.

[7] A *boolean algebra* is a complemented (each $x \in X$ has complement $y \in X$: $x \wedge y = \bot$, $x \vee y = \top$) and distributive ($\forall x, y, z \in X \,.\, x \wedge (y \vee y) = (x \vee y) \wedge (x \vee z)$) lattice.

This means that, exactly as it happens for properties, we can check this kind of hyperproperties on single executions: if we find at least one execution not satisfying the hyperproperty, then the whole system does not satisfy it. For example, $\mathtt{Even}^l_{\mathcal{H}} \overset{\text{def}}{=} \wp(\mathtt{Even}^l)$ is the trace hyperproperty equivalent to trace property $\mathtt{Even}^l$.

The hyperproperties which we can verify with standard trace semantics are all and only the trace hyperproperties, as stated by the following theorem.

Theorem 3. *For every hyperproperty* $\mathfrak{Hp}$*:*

$$\mathfrak{Hp} \in \mathtt{TRC}^{\mathtt{H}}_{\mathfrak{D}} \;\Leftrightarrow\; \exists \mathfrak{P} \in \mathtt{TRC}^{\mathtt{P}}_{\mathfrak{D}}\, \forall P \in \mathit{systems}\,.\, (P \models \mathfrak{P} \Leftrightarrow P \models \mathfrak{Hp})$$

Direction ($\Rightarrow$) holds since, by definition, $\mathfrak{Hp} \in \mathtt{TRC}^{\mathtt{H}}_{\mathfrak{D}}$ implies $\mathfrak{Hp} = \wp(\bigcup \mathfrak{Hp})$, and setting $\mathfrak{P} = \bigcup \mathfrak{Hp}$ we have $[\![P]\!] \subseteq \bigcup \mathfrak{Hp} \Leftrightarrow \wp([\![P]\!]) \subseteq \wp(\bigcup \mathfrak{Hp}) \Leftrightarrow [\![P]\!] \in \mathfrak{Hp}$. For the converse ($\Leftarrow$) we give only an intuition. Take, for instance, $\mathfrak{Hp} = \{\{a\}, \{b\}\} \notin \mathtt{TRC}^{\mathtt{H}}_{\mathfrak{D}}$, so $\forall \mathfrak{P} \in \mathtt{TRC}^{\mathtt{P}}_{\mathfrak{D}}\, \exists P \in$ systems such that $P \models \mathfrak{P} \Leftrightarrow P \models \mathfrak{Hp}$ do not hold. Indeed, if $\mathfrak{P} \cap \bigcup \mathfrak{Hp} \supseteq \{a, b\}$ consider $[\![P]\!] = \{a, b\}$, then we have $[\![P]\!] \subseteq \mathfrak{P}$ but $[\![P]\!] \notin \mathfrak{Hp}$. Otherwise, if $\mathfrak{P} \cap \bigcup \mathfrak{Hp} \supseteq \{a\}$ take $[\![P]\!] = \{b\}$, otherwise take $[\![P]\!] = \{a\}$, in any case we can show that $[\![P]\!] \in \mathfrak{Hp}$ but $[\![P]\!] \not\subseteq \mathfrak{P}$.

We can further generalize this restriction, allowing us to preserve the possibility of verifying hyperproperty on trace semantics at least for confutation. It should be clear that, in the general case, we have to compute the whole semantics $[\![P]\!]$ in order to verify (both validate and confute) the hyperproperty $\mathfrak{Hp}$. However, it is worth noting that there is a particular kind of hyperproperties that generalizes hypersafety and whose verification test can be simplified.

Definition 2 (Subset-closed hyperproperty). $\mathfrak{cHp} \in \mathtt{GEN}^{\mathtt{H}}_{\mathfrak{D}}$ *is called a* subset-closed *hyperproperty if* $\mathfrak{cHp}$ *is such that* $X \in \mathfrak{cHp} \Rightarrow (\forall Y \subseteq X\,.\, Y \in \mathfrak{cHp})$.

We denote with $\mathtt{SSC}^{\mathtt{H}}_{\mathfrak{D}}$ the set of all subset-closed hyperproperties, i.e., $\mathtt{SSC}^{\mathtt{H}}_{\mathfrak{D}}$ is the set $\{\mathfrak{cHp} \in \mathtt{GEN}^{\mathtt{H}}_{\mathfrak{D}} \mid X \in \mathfrak{cHp} \Rightarrow (\forall Y \subseteq X\,.\, Y \in \mathfrak{cHp})\}$. Note that all trace hyperproperties are subset-closed but not vice-versa (one example is observational determinism [22]). In particular, a subset-closed hyperproperty $\mathfrak{cHp}$ is also a trace hyperproperty if, in addition, it holds: $X, Y \in \mathfrak{cHp} \Rightarrow X \cup Y \in \mathfrak{cHp}$. It turns out that lots of interesting hyperproperties are subset-closed, e.g., all hypersafety and some hyperliveness [5]. In this case, validation becomes

$$P \models \mathfrak{cHp} \in \mathtt{SSC}^{\mathtt{H}}_{\mathfrak{D}} \;\Leftrightarrow\; \wp([\![P]\!]) \subseteq \mathfrak{cHp} \;\Leftrightarrow\; \forall X \subseteq [\![P]\!]\,.\, X \in \mathfrak{cHp}$$

where $[\![P]\!]_{\Delta} \overset{\text{def}}{=} \wp([\![P]\!])$ is the strongest subset-closed hyperproperty of P. It is clear that this does not change the validation of $\mathfrak{cHp}$, but it may in general simplify the confutation, since we do not need the whole semantics $[\![P]\!]$: it is sufficient to find a $X \subseteq [\![P]\!]$ such that $X \notin \mathfrak{cHp}$ in order to imply $\{[\![P]\!]\} \not\subseteq \mathfrak{cHp}$. A subset-closed hyperproperty for $\mathfrak{D} = \mathcal{S} \times \mathcal{S}_{\perp}$ which is not a trace hyperproperty is *termination insensitive non-interference* $\mathtt{TINI} \overset{\text{def}}{=} \{X \subseteq \wp(\mathfrak{D}) \mid \forall s, s' \in X\,.\, s_{\vdash} =_{\mathtt{L}} s'_{\vdash} \Rightarrow (s_{\dashv} = \perp \vee s'_{\dashv} = \perp \vee s_{\dashv} =_{\mathtt{L}} s'_{\dashv})\}$ [5], stating that, each pair of executions agreeing on public variables ($\mathtt{L}$) in input ($\vdash$), must terminate agreeing on public variables in output ($\dashv$). The program in Example 1, with typing $\Gamma(l) = \mathtt{L}, \Gamma(h) = \mathtt{H}$, satisfies

TINI since all terminating traces provides the same value for l, i.e., $\tau^\infty[P] \in$ TINI. In [5], the authors proved that TINI is 2-hypersafety, hence it is subset-closed, and, conversely, they proved that GNI is not subset-closed.

Finally, we can provide a further characterization of subset-closed hyperproperties as union of trace hyperproperties.

Proposition 1. *Every subset-closed hyperproperty* $\mathfrak{cHp}$ *can be decomposed in a conjunction of trace hyperproperties, namely:*

$$\mathfrak{cHp} = \bigcup_{Y \in \max_\subseteq(\mathfrak{cHp})} \wp(Y) \quad with \quad \max_\subseteq(\mathcal{X}) \stackrel{\text{def}}{=} \left\{ X \in \mathcal{X} \;\middle|\; \begin{array}{l} \forall X' \in \mathcal{X} \,. \\ X \subseteq X' \Rightarrow X = X' \end{array} \right\}$$

where $\max_\subseteq(\mathcal{X})$ *is the set of maximals of* $\subseteq$*-chains in* $\mathcal{X}$.

Clearly, for all Y in $\max_\subseteq(\mathfrak{cHp})$, it holds $\wp(\bigcup \wp(Y)) = \wp(Y)$ so $\wp(Y)$ is a trace hyperproperty. Hence any subset-closed hyperproperty can be characterized as $\mathfrak{cHp} = \bigcup_{i \in \Delta} \mathfrak{tHp}_i$ (for a set $\Delta \subseteq \mathbb{N}$). This implies that, in order to validate $\mathfrak{cHp}$ on standard trace semantics it is sufficient to validate just one of these $\mathfrak{tHp}_i$. In fact, if $P \models \mathfrak{tHp}_i$, i.e., $[\![P]\!] \in \mathfrak{tHp}_i$, then $[\![P]\!] \in \mathfrak{cHp}$ and hence $P \models \mathfrak{cHp}$.

4.2 Hyperproperties Relations and Algebraic Structures

In this section, we show the relations existing among the notions of hyperproperties we have introduced. Moreover, we describe the algebraic structures of hyperproperties domains. In the following, we omit the subscript of properties/hyperproperties domain when it is clear from the context or not relevant.

It is straightforward to note that $\mathtt{TRC}^\mathtt{H} \subsetneq \mathtt{SSC}^\mathtt{H} \subsetneq \mathtt{GEN}^\mathtt{H}$ and that $\mathtt{SSC}^\mathtt{H}$ (and therefore $\mathtt{TRC}^\mathtt{H}$) do not contain $\varnothing$. Indeed the empty set has no members, so it cannot be subset-closed. In addition, the unique singleton subset-closed is $\{\varnothing\}$.

Now let $\rho_\star$ be the function $\lambda\mathcal{X} \,.\, \gamma_\star \circ \alpha_\star(\mathcal{X})$, where $\alpha_\star \stackrel{\text{def}}{=} \lambda X \,.\, \bigcup X$ and $\gamma_\star \stackrel{\text{def}}{=} \lambda X \,.\, \wp(X)$, and let ρ_Δ be the function $\lambda\mathcal{X} \,.\, \{X \mid \exists Y \in \mathcal{X} \,.\, X \subseteq Y\}$. It is easy to note that they are both upper closure operators of $\mathtt{GEN}^\mathtt{H}$ (i.e., monotone operators in $\wp(\wp(\mathfrak{D})) \to \wp(\wp(\mathfrak{D}))$ which are extensive and idempotent)[8].

Proposition 2. $\mathtt{SSC}^\mathtt{H} = \rho_\Delta(\mathtt{GEN}^\mathtt{H})$ *and* $\mathtt{TRC}^\mathtt{H} = \rho_\star(\mathtt{GEN}^\mathtt{H}) = \rho_\star(\mathtt{SSC}^\mathtt{H})$.

Note that $\langle \mathtt{SSC}^\mathtt{H}, \subseteq, \cup, \cap, \{\varnothing\}, \wp(\mathfrak{D})\rangle$ is a complete lattice, where the bottom is $\{\varnothing\}$ because $\varnothing$ is contained in every subset-closed set and the top is $\wp(\mathfrak{D})$ because it is the top of $\mathtt{GEN}^\mathtt{H}$ and it is subset-closed. For the same reasons they are the bottom and the top of the complete lattice $\langle \mathtt{TRC}^\mathtt{H}, \subseteq, \cup, \cap, \{\varnothing\}, \wp(\mathfrak{D})\rangle$, which is the sublattice of $\mathtt{SSC}^\mathtt{H}$ (and $\mathtt{GEN}^\mathtt{H}$) comprising its boolean algebras. Finally, it is straightforward to note that $\mathtt{TRC}^\mathtt{H}$ is isomorphic, through $\langle \alpha_\star, \gamma_\star\rangle$, to $\mathtt{TRC}^\mathtt{P}$. The big picture is depicted by the commutative diagram in Fig. 2. Recall that the approximation order plays the role of implication. So the strongest hyperproperty, i.e., the one which implies any other hyperproperty, is $\varnothing$ for $\mathtt{GEN}^\mathtt{H}$ and

[8] The adjunction $\langle \alpha_\star, \gamma_\star\rangle$ and its link with systems properties were already introduced in [3] (their $\langle \alpha_{\text{hpp}}, \gamma_{\text{hpp}}\rangle$) and even before in [13] (their $\langle \alpha_\Theta, \gamma_\Theta\rangle$).

$\{\varnothing\}$ for $\mathtt{SSC}^{\mathtt{H}}, \mathtt{TRC}^{\mathtt{H}}$. Conversely, the weakest hyperproperty, i.e., the one which is implied by any other one, is $\wp(\mathfrak{D})$ for $\mathtt{GEN}^{\mathtt{H}}, \mathtt{SSC}^{\mathtt{H}}, \mathtt{TRC}^{\mathtt{H}}$. For what concerns $\mathtt{TRC}^{\mathtt{P}}$, it is isomorphic to $\mathtt{TRC}^{\mathtt{H}}$ hence the strongest trace property is $\alpha_\star(\{\varnothing\}) = \varnothing$ and the weakest is $\alpha_\star(\wp(\mathfrak{D})) = \mathfrak{D}$, as expected.

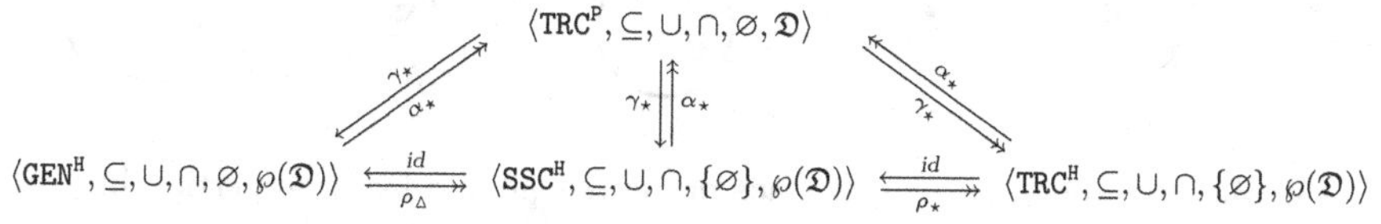

Fig. 2. Relations between hyperproperties

5 Approximating Hyperproperties Verification

In this section, we investigate how we can approximate hyperproperty verification. Let us briefly recall how we can approximate standard property verification. In order to cope with the potential non decidability of trace properties verification, approximation of systems semantics is necessary. In the standard framework of abstract interpretation [8,9] we can compute a sound over-approximation $O \supseteq [\![P]\!]$ of a system semantics allowing sound validation of trace properties (Fig. 3, part [a]). This is obtained by means of an abstraction of the concrete domain, where the abstract semantics plays the role of the over-approximation. Let P be a system, $\hat{A} \subseteq \mathtt{TRC}^{\mathtt{P}}$ an abstract domain, $\mathfrak{P} \in \mathtt{TRC}^{\mathtt{P}}$ a trace property and $[\![P]\!]^\sharp$ an abstract interpretation of $[\![P]\!]$ in $\hat{A}$, i.e., $[\![P]\!] \subseteq \hat{\gamma}([\![P]\!]^\sharp)$, then:

$$\langle \mathtt{TRC}^{\mathtt{P}}, \subseteq \rangle \underset{\hat{\alpha}}{\overset{\hat{\gamma}}{\leftrightarrows}} \langle \hat{A}, \preccurlyeq \rangle \text{ and } \hat{\gamma}([\![P]\!]^\sharp) \subseteq \mathfrak{P} \text{ implies } P \models \mathfrak{P}$$

Recall that, by under-approximation we can improve decidability of the confutation of a property, since if $U \subseteq [\![P]\!]$ and $U \not\subseteq \mathfrak{P}$ then we have that $[\![P]\!] \not\models \mathfrak{P}$. At this point, we can show that trace hyperproperties can be verified in the standard analysis framework based on abstract interpretation.

Proposition 3. *Let P be a system, $\hat{A} \subseteq \mathtt{TRC}^{\mathtt{P}}$ be an abstract domain, $\mathfrak{tHp} \in \mathtt{TRC}^{\mathtt{H}}$ be a trace hyperproperty and $[\![P]\!]^\sharp$ be an abstraction of $[\![P]\!]$ in $\hat{A}$, i.e., $[\![P]\!] \subseteq \hat{\gamma}([\![P]\!]^\sharp)$, then $\langle \mathtt{TRC}^{\mathtt{P}}, \subseteq \rangle \underset{\hat{\alpha}}{\overset{\hat{\gamma}}{\leftrightarrows}} \langle \hat{A}, \preccurlyeq \rangle$ and $\hat{\gamma}([\![P]\!]^\sharp) \subseteq \bigcup \mathfrak{tHp}$ implies $P \models \mathfrak{tHp}$.*

Hence, we can still use standard analysis based on over-approximation for verifying trace hyperproperties. Moreover, when dealing with confutation of properties, also in this case we can use under-approximation in the standard way, since if we have $U \subseteq [\![P]\!]$ and $U \not\subseteq \bigcup \mathfrak{tHp}$ then still we can derive that $P \not\models \mathfrak{tHp}$.

Unfortunately, when we do not have restrictions on hyperproperties, standard trace semantics, in general, does not provide enough information for approximating

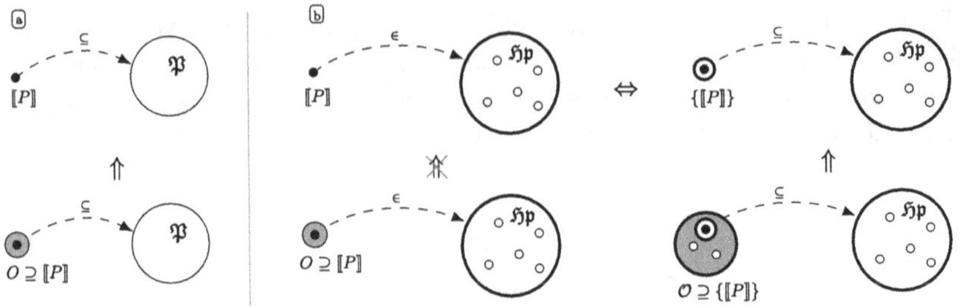

Fig. 3. Over-approximation of trace properties [a] and hyperproperties [b]

verification, since $O \supseteq [\![P]\!] \wedge O \in \mathfrak{Hp} \not\Rightarrow [\![P]\!] \in \mathfrak{Hp}$ (Fig. 3, part [b] on the left). Over-approximations do not work properly because we are approximating on the wrong domain. Indeed, if we move towards $\mathtt{GEN}^{\mathtt{H}}$ (or $\mathtt{SSC}^{\mathtt{H}}$), then $\mathcal{O} \supseteq \{[\![P]\!]\} \wedge \mathcal{O} \subseteq \mathfrak{Hp} \Rightarrow \{[\![P]\!]\} \subseteq \mathfrak{Hp}$, i.e., $[\![P]\!] \in \mathfrak{Hp}$ (Fig. 3, part [b] on the right). The problem is due to the fact that the property is defined on the domain $\mathtt{GEN}^{\mathtt{H}}$, different from the domain $\mathtt{TRC}^{\mathtt{P}}$, where the system semantics is computed.

The idea we propose in the following sections, consists in moving the systems semantics on a more concrete domain, i.e., we build the semantics at the same level of the properties, namely at the *hyper* level. In this way, we can exploit the abstract interpretation framework even for approximating hyperproperties verification. Our goal is to define the system P semantics on the hyper level, i.e., we define the *hyper semantics* $[\![P]\!]_{\mathcal{H}}$ such that $\{[\![P]\!]\} \subseteq [\![P]\!]_{\mathcal{H}}$.

An over-approximation of $[\![P]\!]_{\mathcal{H}}$ clearly leads to a sound verification mechanism for hyperproperties. In fact, let P be a system, $\tilde{\mathcal{A}} \subseteq \mathtt{GEN}^{\mathtt{H}}$ be an abstract domain, $\mathfrak{Hp} \in \mathtt{GEN}^{\mathtt{H}}$ be an hyperproperty, $[\![P]\!]_{\mathcal{H}}$ be a semantics on $\mathtt{GEN}^{\mathtt{H}}$ and $[\![P]\!]^{\sharp}_{\mathcal{H}}$ be an abstract interpretation of $[\![P]\!]_{\mathcal{H}}$ in $\tilde{\mathcal{A}}$, i.e., $[\![P]\!]_{\mathcal{H}} \subseteq \tilde{\gamma}([\![P]\!]^{\sharp}_{\mathcal{H}})$, then:

$$\langle \mathtt{GEN}^{\mathtt{H}}, \subseteq \rangle \underset{\tilde{\alpha}}{\overset{\tilde{\gamma}}{\longleftrightarrow}} \langle \tilde{\mathcal{A}}, \precsim \rangle \text{ and } \tilde{\gamma}([\![P]\!]^{\sharp}_{\mathcal{H}}) \subseteq \mathfrak{Hp} \text{ imply } P \models \mathfrak{Hp}$$

Hence, we build an hyper semantics of the system, and then we can over-approximate it in some abstraction of the hyper domain. This is depicted in Fig. 4, where in [a] we have the standard case and in [b] the hyper case.

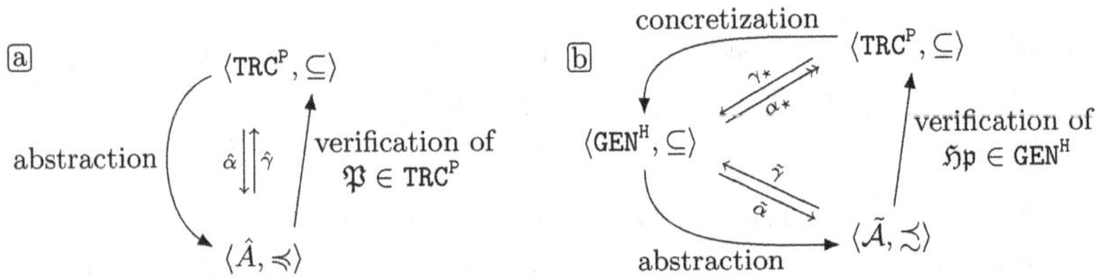

Fig. 4. Verification (abstract interpretation) of properties [a] and hyperproperties [b]

6 Hyperhierarchy of Semantics

In Sect. 2.3 we introduced the hierarchy of semantics proposed in [7], where most well known semantics have been related by Galois insertions. In this section, we aim at extending this hierarchy in order to include an hyper level of semantics suitable for hyperproperties verification. The intuition of lifting the classical hierarchy of semantics to sets of sets was already present in [3], where it was just sketched. Here we analyze the problem in a deeper and comprehensive way. Note that, as observed in Sect. 4.2, we have different notions of hyperproperties, implying different possible approaches for verification. We do not have precisely the same distinction when dealing with systems semantics.

6.1 Defining Hypersemantics

In the following, we indicate with $[\![P]\!]$ a generic standard semantics of the system P, namely an element of the standard hierarchy, as we have done in Sect. 4. So, for instance, $[\![P]\!]$ can stand for $\tau^{\vec{\infty}}[P]$, or it can stand for $\tau^{+}[P]$, etc.

Subset-Closed and Generic Hypersemantics. The first level comprises subset-closed systems semantics. This means that every element of this hierarchy, which is parametric by systems denotations ($\mathfrak{D}$) as in the standard case, is in the set $\mathtt{SSC}^{\mathtt{H}}$. It turns out that, given a system P, its subset-closed hypersemantics is $[\![P]\!]_{\Delta} = \wp([\![P]\!])$, which is indeed its strongest subset-closed hyperproperty. This happens because any semantics have a maximal set of computations, therefore an $\mathtt{SSC}^{\mathtt{H}}$ semantics is in particular a boolean algebra.

The second level comprises generic systems hypersemantics. This means that every element of this hierarchy, which is again parametric on systems denotations ($\mathfrak{D}$), is in $\mathtt{GEN}^{\mathtt{H}}$. It turns out that, given a system P, its generic hypersemantics is $[\![P]\!]_{\diamond} = \{[\![P]\!]\}$, which is indeed its strongest generic hyperproperty.

It is worth nothing that, $[\![P]\!]_{\Delta} \in \mathtt{SSC}^{\mathtt{H}}$ and $[\![P]\!]_{\diamond} \in \mathtt{GEN}^{\mathtt{H}}$ do not give us more information on the executions of P than $[\![P]\!]$, being isomorphic to $[\![P]\!]$. Namely these parallel hierarchies does not provide different observables, but only new verification methods for hyperproperties. In particular, over-approximations of hypersemantics on these more expressive semantic levels, provide verification methods for subset-closed and generic hyperproperties. We cannot verify these hyperproperties within the standard hierarchy of semantics.

Post/Pre Hypersemantics. In the previous sections, we considered only hyper-semantics isomorphic to standard ones. It is clear, that the hyper level is indeed strictly more concrete than the standard level, hence we aim at defining hyper semantics strictly more expressive than standard ones. In particular, we can extends to the hyper levels both the maximal trace semantics and the partial trace semantics and we observe how we can exploit the expressiveness of these semantics when dealing with hyperproperties verification.

The *Post hypersemantics* $\tau^{\vec{\infty}}_{\texttt{post}}$ is defined as:

$$\tau^{\vec{\infty}}_{\texttt{post}} \stackrel{\text{def}}{=} \left\{ \{ \bigcup_{n>0} \tau^{\vec{n}}_{X} \cup \tau^{\vec{\omega}} \} \;\middle|\; X \subseteq \Omega \right\} \qquad \text{where } \tau^{\vec{n}}_{X} \stackrel{\text{def}}{=} \{ \sigma \in \tau^{\vec{n}} \mid \sigma_{n-1} \in X \}$$

The *Pre hypersemantics* $\tau^{\vec{\propto}}_{\texttt{pre}}$ is defined as:

$$\tau^{\vec{\propto}}_{\texttt{pre}} \stackrel{\text{def}}{=} \left\{ \{ \bigcup_{n>0} \tau^{\dot{\vec{n}}}_{X} \} \;\middle|\; X \subseteq \Upsilon \wedge X \neq \varnothing \right\} \qquad \text{where } \tau^{\dot{\vec{n}}}_{X} \stackrel{\text{def}}{=} \{ \sigma \in \tau^{\dot{\vec{n}}} \mid \sigma_0 \in X \}$$

The first collects the sets of maximals (terminating) computations partitioned by all the possible sets of final states, plus the infinite computations of course. This is a backward semantics and intuitively says which initial states we need to take in order to reach some given final states. The second do the opposite, namely it collects the sets of partial (finite) computations partitioned by all the possible sets of initial states. This is a forward semantics and intuitively says which partial computations we obtain starting from some given initial states.

Example 2. As example, consider the transition system with $\Sigma = \{a, b, c, d, e\}$, $\tau = \{\langle a, b\rangle, \langle a, c\rangle, \langle b, d\rangle, \langle c, c\rangle, \langle e, b\rangle, \langle e, e\rangle\}$, $\Upsilon = \{a, e\}$ and $\Omega = \{d\}$. Then

$$\begin{aligned} \tau^{\vec{\infty}} &= \{d, bd, abd\} \cup \{e^n bd\}_{n\geq 1} \cup \{c^\omega, ac^\omega, e^\omega\} \\ \tau^{\vec{\propto}} &= \{a, ab, abd\} \cup \{ac^n\}_{n\geq 1} \cup \{e^n\}_{n\geq 1} \cup \{e^n b\}_{n\geq 1} \cup \{e^n bd\}_{n\geq 1} \end{aligned}$$

The hyper versions are

$$\begin{aligned} \tau^{\vec{\infty}}_{\texttt{post}} &= \{\tau^{\vec{\infty}}, \{c^\omega, ac^\omega, e^\omega\}\} \\ \tau^{\vec{\propto}}_{\texttt{pre}} &= \{\tau^{\vec{\propto}}, \{a, ab, abd\} \cup \{ac^n\}_{n\geq 1}, \{e^n\}_{n\geq 1} \cup \{e^n b\}_{n\geq 1} \cup \{e^n bd\}_{n\geq 1}\} \end{aligned}$$

being $\wp(\Omega) = \{\{d\}, \varnothing\}$ and $\wp(\Upsilon) \setminus \{\varnothing\} = \{\{a, e\}, \{a\}, \{e\}\}$.

These hypersemantics can be used for *partially verifying hyperproperties*, since they provide the semantics parametrically on the subsets of blocking/initial states. Suppose that, instead of checking *whether* a system fulfills an hyperproperty $\mathfrak{H}\mathfrak{p}$, we want to check *when* a system fulfills it. The problem boils down to analyze the intersection $\tau^{\vec{\infty}}_{\texttt{post}} \cap \mathfrak{H}\mathfrak{p}$ [or $\tau^{\vec{\propto}}_{\texttt{pre}} \cap \mathfrak{H}\mathfrak{p}$]. If the intersection is $\varnothing$ then the answer is "never", if the answer is $\tau^{\vec{\infty}}_{\texttt{post}}$ [or $\tau^{\vec{\propto}}_{\texttt{pre}}$] then $P \models \mathfrak{H}\mathfrak{p}$, otherwise we have that for particular final states [initial states] the system satisfies the hyperproperty. Hence we have a form of *partial satisfiability*. This is in practice useful, for example when we want to know under what conditions we can still use an unsafe system.

The Hyperhierarchy. Up to now, we simply reasoned on single semantics. Finally, we can show that the whole hierarchy of standard semantics can be lifted on the hyper levels, preserving all the abstraction relations between semantics. In the standard hierarchy, $\tau^{\vec{\infty}}$ and $\tau^{\vec{+}}$ (and hence all their relational/denotational abstractions) are *backward* semantics in the sense they are suffix-closed [11]. This means that they represents systems executions with complete traces and all their suffixes. Instead, the semantics $\tau^{\vec{\propto}}$ is *forward* in the sense it is prefix-closed [13]. This means that it represents systems executions with all the partial computations starting from initial states (i.e., trace prefixes).

Note that all the semantics in the standard hierarchy are abstractions of $\tau^{\vec{\infty}}$ and, analogously, every hypersemantics is an abstraction of $\tau^{\vec{\infty}}_{\mathtt{post}}$.

Proposition 4. *Let* $\mathfrak{y} \in \{\vec{\infty}, \vec{+}, \vec{\propto}, \infty, +, \natural, \flat\}$*, let* α *be such that* $\tau^{\mathfrak{y}} = \alpha(\tau^{\vec{\infty}})$ *in the standard hierarchy of semantics, and let* $\alpha_{\upharpoonright} \stackrel{\text{def}}{=} \lambda \mathcal{X} \,.\, \{\alpha(X) \mid X \in \mathcal{X}\}$*, then:*

$$\tau^{\mathfrak{y}}_{\mathtt{post}} = \alpha_{\upharpoonright}(\tau^{\vec{\infty}}_{\mathtt{post}}) \text{ and } \alpha \circ \alpha_{\star} = \alpha_{\star} \circ \alpha_{\upharpoonright}$$

The subset-closed ($\triangle$) and generic ($\diamond$) hypersemantics are isomorphic to the standard ones, trough $\langle \alpha_{\star}, \gamma_{\star} \rangle$ and $\langle \alpha_{\star}, \lambda X \,.\, \{X\} \rangle$ respectively. This means that for these hypersemantics the commutativity trivially holds. So, lifting to sets the abstraction function used to go from a semantics to another semantics, in the standard hierarchy, results in an abstraction between the respective hypersemantics at the hyper level. Proposition 4 justifies Fig. 1, where an arrow between semantics means that there is an abstraction relation, while a double arrow means that the semantics are isomorphic. On the left we have the standard hierarchy and on the right the hyper levels. The central level represents subset-closed ($\triangle$) and generic ($\diamond$) hypersemantics, which are isomorphic to standard semantics. This allows us, with the same information, to gain expressiveness in verification. On the right, we have the level of post/pre hypersemantics, namely semantics which contains strictly more information w.r.t. the standard ones and which can be used for partial verification. From these hypersemantics we obtain the standard ones through the abstraction $\langle \alpha_{\star}, \gamma_{\star} \rangle$ and hence, by composition with the isomorphism, also subset-closed ($\triangle$) and generic ($\diamond$) hypersemantics are abstractions of them.

6.2 Computing Hypersemantics

In this section, we show how we can compute the semantics at the hyper levels, similarly to what happens in the standard hierarchy of semantics [7], where each semantics is obtained as fixpoint of a monotone operator.

Computing Hypersemantics by Using bcc *and Additive Lift.* Suppose we are interested in computing the standard semantics at the hyper level. In this case, our aim is simply to emulate the standard semantics computation on the hyper level. This may be considered useful for approximating computation when dealing with hyperproperty verification, as explained in Sect. 5. In this case we have to *transfer* the fixpoint computation from the abstract domain of standard semantics, to the concrete domain of hypersemantics, and we can follow two possible ways: we can use the *best complete concretization* (bcc) of the standard semantic operator, or we can *lift* the operator to sets. Basically, we aim at computing by fixpoint a semantics $\llbracket P \rrbracket_{\mathcal{H}}$ (one of the semantics in Fig. 1, on the central level), namely we want to find a monotone operator $F_{\mathcal{H}} : \wp(\wp(\mathfrak{D})) \to \wp(\wp(\mathfrak{D}))$, such that $\llbracket P \rrbracket_{\mathcal{H}} = \mathit{lfp}\ F_{\mathcal{H}}$, built on top of the standard semantics operator F.

First, consider $F_{\mathcal{H}} \stackrel{\text{def}}{=} F_{\Delta} = \gamma_{\star} \circ F \circ \alpha_{\star}$ (namely we apply Theorem 2 considering F_{Δ} as the best complete concretization of F). Since $\gamma_{\star}$ is a strict Scott-continuous concretization map between $\langle \mathtt{TRC}^{\mathtt{P}}, \subseteq, \cup, \cap, \varnothing, \mathfrak{D} \rangle$ and $\langle \mathtt{SSC}^{\mathtt{H}}, \subseteq, \cup, \cap, \{\varnothing\}, \wp(\mathfrak{D}) \rangle$ and the forward completeness holds by definition, we can apply Theorem 1 and hence $\gamma_{\star}(\mathit{lfp}^{\subseteq}_{\varnothing} F) = \mathit{lfp}^{\subseteq}_{\{\varnothing\}} F_{\Delta}$, i.e., $\gamma_{\star}(\llbracket P \rrbracket) = \wp(\llbracket P \rrbracket) = \llbracket P \rrbracket_{\Delta} = \mathit{lfp}^{\subseteq}_{\{\varnothing\}} F_{\Delta}$. Indeed F_{Δ} is $\subseteq$-monotone and $F^0_{\Delta}(\{\varnothing\}) = \{\varnothing\} \subseteq F^1_{\Delta}(\{\varnothing\}) = \wp(F(\varnothing)) \subseteq F^2_{\Delta}(\{\varnothing\}) = \wp(F^2(\varnothing)) \subseteq \ldots F^n_{\Delta}(\{\varnothing\}) = \wp(F^n(\varnothing))$ since, for every n, $F^n(\varnothing) \subseteq F^{n+1}(\varnothing)$. It should be clear that, with this operator, we move inside elements of $\mathtt{TRC}^{\mathtt{H}}$, which is a strict subset of $\mathtt{SSC}^{\mathtt{H}}$.

The second choice consists in defining $F_{\mathcal{H}}$ as the additive lift of F, i.e., $F_{\mathcal{H}} \stackrel{\text{def}}{=} F_{\diamond} = \lambda \mathcal{X} . \{F(X) \mid X \in \mathcal{X}\}$. Unfortunately, the lift does not guarantee monotonicity. Indeed the iterates of $F_{\diamond}$ from the bottom are: $F^0_{\diamond}(\varnothing) = \varnothing$, $F^1_{\diamond}(\varnothing) = \{\varnothing\}$, $F^2_{\diamond}(\varnothing) = \{F(\varnothing)\}$, $\ldots F^n_{\diamond}(\varnothing) = \{F^{n-1}(\varnothing)\}$. Clearly the iterates do not form an increasing $\subseteq$-chain and so $\langle F_{\diamond}, \mathtt{GEN}^{\mathtt{H}}, \subseteq \rangle$ is not a fixpoint semantics specification. In this case we need to change the computational domain. Let us consider the following computational order $\subseteq_{\star}$:

$$\mathcal{X} \subseteq_{\star} \mathcal{Y} \stackrel{\text{def}}{=} \begin{array}{c} (\mathcal{X} = \varnothing \ \vee (\forall X \in \mathcal{X}\, \exists Y \in \mathcal{Y} . X \subseteq Y)) \wedge \\ (\mathcal{Y} = \varnothing \vee ((\forall Y \in \mathcal{Y}\, \exists X \in \mathcal{X} . Y \subseteq X) \Rightarrow \mathcal{X} = \mathcal{Y})) \end{array} \tag{1}$$

Namely, for each element $X \in \mathcal{X}$ there exists an element of $\mathcal{Y}$ in the $\subseteq$ relation with X (the second conjunction just forces antisymmetry). Furthermore, the equalities with the empty-set add the axiom $\varnothing \subseteq_{\star} \varnothing \subseteq_{\star} \mathcal{X}$, for any $\mathcal{X}$. The bottom is $\varnothing$ and the (partial) least upper bound is $\uplus_{\star}$ defined as:

$$\mathcal{X} \uplus_{\star} \mathcal{Y} \stackrel{\text{def}}{=} \begin{array}{l} \{X \cup Y \mid X \in \mathcal{X} \wedge Y \in \mathcal{Y} \wedge (X \subseteq Y \vee Y \subseteq X)\} \cup \\ \{X \mid X \in \mathcal{X} \wedge (\mathcal{Y} = \varnothing \vee \forall Y \in \mathcal{Y} . (X \nsubseteq Y \wedge Y \nsubseteq X))\} \cup \\ \{Y \mid Y \in \mathcal{Y} \wedge (\mathcal{X} = \varnothing \vee \forall X \in \mathcal{X} . (Y \nsubseteq X \wedge X \nsubseteq Y))\} \end{array} \tag{2}$$

The lub makes the union of the elements of $\mathcal{X}$ and $\mathcal{Y}$ which are in relation $\subseteq$, and adds all the other elements of both sets, as they are. The domain $\langle \mathtt{GEN}^{\mathtt{H}}, \subseteq_{\star}, \uplus_{\star}, \varnothing \rangle$ is a pointed DCPO with (partial) lub and bottom, indeed we have $\varnothing \subseteq_{\star} \mathcal{X}$ for every $\mathcal{X} \in \mathtt{GEN}^{\mathtt{H}}$ and $\mathcal{X} \subseteq_{\star} \mathcal{Y}$ implies $\mathcal{X} \uplus_{\star} \mathcal{Y} = \mathcal{Y}$. Then we have that $\langle F_{\diamond}, \mathtt{GEN}^{\mathtt{H}}, \subseteq_{\star} \rangle$ is a fixpoint semantic specification, since $F_{\diamond}$ is $\subseteq_{\star}$-monotone.

Proposition 5. *If* $\langle F, \mathtt{TRC}^{\mathtt{P}}, \subseteq \rangle$ *and* $\llbracket P \rrbracket = \mathit{lfp}^{\subseteq}_{\varnothing} F = \bigcup_{n>0} F^n(\varnothing)$ *then we have:* $\langle F_{\diamond}, \mathtt{GEN}^{\mathtt{H}}, \subseteq_{\star} \rangle$ *and* $\llbracket P \rrbracket_{\diamond} = \mathit{lfp}^{\subseteq_{\star}}_{\varnothing} F_{\diamond} = \biguplus_{\star\, n>0} F^n_{\diamond}(\varnothing) = \{\llbracket P \rrbracket\}$.

Also in this case we simply compute standard semantics on the hyperlevel, but we do not really exploit the more concrete level at which we are computing the semantics. In other words, as before, we are emulating the standard computation on the generic hypersemantics domain. Indeed, the semantics $\llbracket P \rrbracket_{\diamond}$ is isomorphic to the standard semantics $\llbracket P \rrbracket$.

Computing Post/Pre Hypersemantics. Here, we aim at exploiting the concrete domain on which we are computing by defining new operators moving freely among elements of $\mathtt{GEN}^{\mathtt{H}}$ and not only on elements of $\mathtt{TRC}^{\mathtt{H}}$. We consider only one case for the backward hypersemantics, the most concrete, but the others are similar. We take $\mathfrak{D} = \mathcal{S}^{\vec{\infty}}$, so let

$$F^{\vec{\infty}}_{\mathtt{post}} \stackrel{\text{def}}{=} \lambda \mathcal{X} . \{X \cup \Sigma^{\vec{\omega}} \mid X \subseteq \tau^{\vec{1}}\} \boxast^{\vec{\infty}} \{X \sqcup^{\vec{\infty}} \tau^{\dot{\vec{2}}} \frown X \mid X \in \mathcal{X}\}$$

Then we have that $\tau^{\vec{\infty}}_{\mathtt{post}} = \mathit{lfp}^{\sqsubseteq^{\vec{\infty}}_{\star}}_{\{\Sigma^{\vec{\omega}}\}} F^{\vec{\infty}}_{\mathtt{post}} = \boxast^{\vec{\infty}}_{n>0} {F^{\vec{\infty}}_{\mathtt{post}}}^{n}(\{\Sigma^{\vec{\omega}}\})$. Where $\sqsubseteq^{\vec{\infty}}_{\star}$ is defined as in Eq. 1, substituting $\subseteq$ with $\sqsubseteq^{\vec{\infty}}$ in the definition, the lub $\boxast^{\vec{\infty}}$ is defined as in Eq. 2, substituting $\cup$ with $\sqcup^{\vec{\infty}}$ in the definition and the bottom is $\{\Sigma^{\vec{\omega}}\}$. Analogously, we can do the same for the forward case. Here we have only one case, hence we take $\mathfrak{D} = \mathcal{S}^{\vec{\propto}}$ and we have $\tau^{\vec{\propto}}_{\mathtt{pre}} = \mathit{lfp}^{\subseteq_{\star}}_{\varnothing} F^{\vec{\propto}}_{\mathtt{pre}} = \uplus_{n>0} {F^{\vec{\propto}}_{\mathtt{pre}}}^{n}(\varnothing)$, where

$$F^{\vec{\propto}}_{\mathtt{pre}} \stackrel{\text{def}}{=} \lambda \mathcal{X} . (\wp(\Upsilon) \setminus \{\varnothing\}) \uplus \{X \cup X \frown \tau^{\dot{\vec{2}}} \mid X \in \mathcal{X}\}$$

We can show that the standard operator $F^{\vec{\infty}}$ is the fixpoint transfer (on the abstract domain of standard semantics), by means of the Galois insertion $\langle \alpha_{\star}, \gamma_{\star} \rangle$, of the concrete semantic operator $F^{\vec{\infty}}_{\mathtt{post}}$. Analogously, transferring the operator $F^{\vec{\propto}}_{\mathtt{pre}}$ on the standard semantic domain, we fall back on $F^{\vec{\propto}}$.

Theorem 4. *The following hold:*

1. $\mathit{lfp}^{\sqsubseteq^{\vec{\infty}}}_{\Sigma^{\vec{\omega}}} F^{\vec{\infty}} = \alpha_{\star}(\mathit{lfp}^{\sqsubseteq^{\vec{\infty}}_{\star}}_{\{\Sigma^{\vec{\omega}}\}} F^{\vec{\infty}}_{\mathtt{post}}) = \alpha_{\star}(\tau^{\vec{\infty}}_{\mathtt{post}})$ *and* $F^{\vec{\infty}} \circ \alpha_{\star} = \alpha_{\star} \circ F^{\vec{\infty}}_{\mathtt{post}}$.
2. $\mathit{lfp}^{\subseteq}_{\varnothing} F^{\vec{\propto}} = \alpha_{\star}(\mathit{lfp}^{\subseteq_{\star}}_{\varnothing} F^{\vec{\propto}}_{\mathtt{pre}}) = \alpha_{\star}(\tau^{\vec{\propto}}_{\mathtt{pre}})$ *and* $F^{\vec{\propto}} \circ \alpha_{\star} = \alpha_{\star} \circ F^{\vec{\propto}}_{\mathtt{pre}}$.

7 Concluding: Hypersemantics Around Us

In this work, we have introduced a formal framework for modeling system semantics at the same level of hyperproperties. These more expressive semantics not only allow us to provide weaker forms of satisfiability, as shown in Sect. 6, but provide a promising methodology allowing us to lift static analysis (for hyperproperties) directly at the hyper level. We believe that this approach could provide a deep insight and useful formal tools also for tackling the problem of *analyzing analyzers*, aiming at systematically analyzing static analyses [16].

Finally, we present two verification methods that, explicitly or implicitly, can be generalized in our work. The first is an ad-hoc hypersemantics of programs [3], made for the verification of information flow policies. The second is the classical framework of static analysis for program properties verification [9].

7.1 Hypercollecting Semantics

As observed in the previous sections, there is an hyper hierarchies of semantics that mimic the standard one in more expressive domains. This gain of expressiveness allows us to verify (by over-approximation) *hyper*properties.

To the best of our knowledge, the only work that perform verification by mean of abstract interpretation exploiting the full expressiveness of hyperproperties is [3]. They deal with information flow policies that are k-hypersafety and they focus on the definition of the abstract domains over sets of sets needed for the analysis. They proposed an ad-hoc hypersemantics (termed *hypercollecting semantics*) to show how to apply the abstract interpretation framework. This semantics is computed denotationally starting from the code of the program to analyze (their systems are programs of a toy programming language) and it is used to verify some information flow policies, such as some formulations of non-interference. In order to perform information flow verification, they consider the domain of finite relational traces, namely $\wp(\mathcal{S} \times \mathcal{S})$ (their $\wp(\mathbf{Trc})$), or better its hyper version, namely $\wp(\wp(\mathcal{S}\times\mathcal{S}))$ (their $\wp(\wp(\mathbf{Trc}))$). States are maps from variables to values, i.e., $\mathcal{S} = \mathrm{Var} \to \mathrm{Val}$ (their **States**). Their semantics computes, denotationally, the *angelic relational semantics* $\tau^{+}[P]$, in the Cousot hierarchy. More formally, for every program P, the collecting semantics $\{\!|P|\!\}\mathbf{IniTrc}$ of [3], where **IniTrc** is the set of all possible inputs[9], is $\tau^{+}[P]$ in the standard hierarchy of semantics ([3], Sect. 2). Then they propose the hypercollecting semantics $(\!|\cdot|\!)$ such that $\{\!|P|\!\}X \in (\!|P|\!)\{X\}$ (this implies $\{\tau^{+}[P]\} \subseteq (\!|P|\!)\{\mathbf{IniTrc}\}$).

Proposition 6. $(\!|P|\!)\wp(\mathbf{IniTrc}) = \tau^{+}_{\Delta}[P]$.

Hence, the hypercollecting semantics proposed in [3], starting from $\wp(\mathbf{IniTrc})$[10], is exactly the hyper angelic relational semantics $\tau^{+}_{\Delta}[P]$ in our hyper hierarchy.

Let us consider, now, the computation of the semantics for a program P for the verification of a given property. We can observe that Proposition 6 guarantees the equivalence of these two semantics for property verification only for subset-closed hyper property, while for general hyperproperty the two semantics are not comparable. In particular, let $\mathfrak{cHp} \in \mathtt{SSC}^{\mathtt{H}}$, we can observe that

$$P \models \mathfrak{cHp} \;\Leftrightarrow\; \tau^{+}_{\Delta}[P] \subseteq \mathfrak{cHp} \;\Leftrightarrow\; (\!|P|\!)\wp(\mathbf{IniTrc}) \subseteq \mathfrak{cHp} \;\Leftrightarrow\; (\!|P|\!)\{\mathbf{IniTrc}\} \subseteq \mathfrak{cHp}$$

where the first implication holds for our definition of verification, the second holds by Proposition 6 and the third one holds since the hyperproperty is subset-closed. On the other hand, if we consider a generic hyper property $\mathfrak{Hp} \in \mathtt{GEN}^{\mathtt{H}}$ the last implication does not hold in general. In particular, the hypercollecting semantics is the additive lift of the standard semantics for all commands except the **while**. Indeed, as also the authors underline, when the program contains a loop their semantics adds the sets of traces that exit the loop at each iteration ([3], Sect. 4). For this reason, the hypercollecting semantics is not complete for generic hyperproperties verification.

[9] Precisely is the set of all pairs $\langle\sigma, \sigma\rangle$ where σ is an initial state.
[10] $\wp(\mathbf{IniTrc})$ is the concretization of **IniTrc** to set of sets, i.e., $\wp(\mathbf{IniTrc}) = \gamma_{\star}(\mathbf{IniTrc})$.

Example 3. Let $P \stackrel{\text{def}}{=} \textbf{while}\,(x < 2)\,\textbf{do}\,\{\, x := x + 1 \,\}$, with the unique variable x ranging over the values $\{0, 1, 2\}$. Then $\textbf{IniTrc} = \{\langle 0, 0\rangle, \langle 1, 1\rangle, \langle 2, 2\rangle\}$, where $\langle v, v'\rangle$ is a concise representation of the couple of mapping (i.e., **States**) $\langle x \mapsto v, x \mapsto v'\rangle$. The angelic relational semantics of c is $\tau^{+}[P] = \{\langle 0, 2\rangle, \langle 1, 2\rangle, \langle 2, 2\rangle\}$, which is exactly $\{\!|P|\!\}\textbf{IniTrc}$. The hypercollecting semantics $(\!|P|\!)_{\wp}(\textbf{IniTrc})$ is computed as follow. The least fixpoint of the while is the set of sets of traces:

$$\wp(\textbf{IniTrc}) \cup \left\{ \begin{array}{c} \{\langle 0,1\rangle\}, \{\langle 1,2\rangle\}, \{\langle 0,1\rangle, \langle 1,2\rangle\}, \{\langle 0,1\rangle, \langle 2,2\rangle\}, \{\langle 1,2\rangle, \langle 2,2\rangle\}, \{\langle 0,2\rangle\}, \\ \{\langle 0,1\rangle, \langle 1,2\rangle, \langle 2,2\rangle\}, \{\langle 0,2\rangle, \langle 2,2\rangle\}, \{\langle 0,2\rangle, \langle 1,2\rangle\}, \{\langle 0,2\rangle, \langle 1,2\rangle, \langle 2,2\rangle\} \end{array} \right\}$$

At the while exit we have to keep only the traces making false the guard [3], i.e.,

$$(\!|P|\!)_{\wp}(\textbf{IniTrc}) = \left\{ \begin{array}{c} \varnothing, \{\langle 2,2\rangle\}, \{\langle 1,2\rangle\}, \{\langle 1,2\rangle, \langle 2,2\rangle\}, \{\langle 0,2\rangle\}, \{\langle 0,2\rangle, \langle 2,2\rangle\}, \\ \{\langle 0,2\rangle, \langle 1,2\rangle\}, \{\langle 0,2\rangle, \langle 1,2\rangle, \langle 2,2\rangle\} \end{array} \right\}$$

which is exactly $\wp(\{\!|P|\!\}\textbf{IniTrc}) = \wp(\tau^{+}[P]) = \tau^{+}_{\Delta}[P]$.

7.2 Standard Static Program Analysis

In the literature, standard static program analysis has been modeled as reachability analysis, since the collected values are all the *reachable* values for a variable. Assume that $\langle \Sigma, \Upsilon, \Omega, \tau\rangle$ is the transition system associated to the program P, and $\Psi \subseteq \Upsilon$ is a subset of initial states. Static analysis can be seen as the characterization, potentially approximated, of the set of reachable states from initial Ψ, i.e., $\tau^{\mathrm{r}}(\Psi) = \{\varsigma \mid \exists \sigma \in \tau^{\infty}, i \in \mathbb{N} \,.\, \sigma_0 \in \Psi \wedge \sigma_i = \varsigma\}$, which provides a, potentially approximated, invariant of the program [9]. In order to properly model *flow-sensitive* static analysis, where we look for invariants for each program point, we can simply consider a more concrete definition of state, which is not simply a memory, i.e., an element of $\mathbb{M} = \mathrm{Var} \rightarrow \mathrm{Val}$, but it is a pair associating with each program point a memory [9]. Formally, given a program P, its possible states are $\Sigma_P \stackrel{\text{def}}{=} \mathbb{L}_P \times \mathbb{M}$, where $\mathbb{L}_P$ is the set of program points in P. When we move towards approximation, instead of manipulating states we manipulate sets of states, i.e., elements of $\wp(\Sigma_P)$, for which holds the following

$$\wp(\mathbb{L}_P \times \mathbb{M}) \cong \mathbb{L}_P \rightarrow \wp(\mathbb{M}) = \mathbb{L}_P \rightarrow \wp(\mathrm{Var} \rightarrow \mathrm{Val})$$

Let $\iota : \wp(\Sigma_P) \rightarrow (\mathbb{L}_P \rightarrow \wp(\mathrm{Var} \rightarrow \mathrm{Val}))$ be such an isomorphism, then $\iota(\tau^{\mathrm{r}}(\Psi))$ is a map associating each program point with the set of all "reached" *memories*, in the computations starting from Ψ. In [20] the author shows that this semantics corresponds to the solution of a system of equations generated from the program syntax. Static analysis abstracts this semantics considering the map associating with each variable all the *values* "reached", for each program point, in the computations starting in Ψ. This abstraction is $\alpha_c = \lambda f \,.\, (\lambda l \,.\, \dot{\bigvee} f(l))$, where $\dot{\bigvee}\{g_i\} \stackrel{\text{def}}{=} \lambda x \,.\, \bigcup_i g_i(x)$. So the composition $\alpha_c \circ \iota$ is a function in $\wp(\Sigma_P) \rightarrow (\mathbb{L}_P \rightarrow (\mathrm{Var} \rightarrow \wp(\mathrm{Val}))$. We denote with $\alpha_{\iota,c}$ this composition.

Example 4. Consider a program with two variables, x and y, the memory is the association of a natural value to these variables, i.e., $[x \mapsto v_1, y \mapsto v_2]$, that we denote concisely with $(v_1; v_2)$. A state is an association between a program point and a memory, i.e., $^{\mathbf{i}}m_i$ meaning that with the **i**-th program point is associated the memory m_i. Hence, consider the following transition system: (suppose we have only three program points)

$$\Sigma = \left\{ \begin{array}{l} \overbrace{\langle {}^{\mathbf{1}}(1;2), {}^{\mathbf{2}}(1;3), {}^{\mathbf{3}}(2;3)\rangle}^{a}, \overbrace{\langle {}^{\mathbf{1}}(1;2), {}^{\mathbf{2}}(1;4), {}^{\mathbf{3}}(2;3)\rangle}^{b}, \overbrace{\langle {}^{\mathbf{1}}(1;2), {}^{\mathbf{2}}(1;4), {}^{\mathbf{3}}(3;4)\rangle}^{c} \\ \underbrace{\langle {}^{\mathbf{1}}(2;2), {}^{\mathbf{2}}(2;3), {}^{\mathbf{3}}(3;3)\rangle}_{d}, \underbrace{\langle {}^{\mathbf{1}}(2;2), {}^{\mathbf{2}}(2;4), {}^{\mathbf{3}}(3;3)\rangle}_{e}, \underbrace{\langle {}^{\mathbf{1}}(2;2), {}^{\mathbf{2}}(2;4), {}^{\mathbf{3}}(4;4)\rangle}_{f} \end{array} \right\}$$

$$\Upsilon = \{a, d\} \quad \Omega = \{c, f\} \quad \tau = \{\langle a, b\rangle, \langle b, c\rangle, \langle d, e\rangle, \langle e, f\rangle\}$$

Hence, $\alpha_{\iota,c}(\Sigma) = \langle {}^{\mathbf{1}}(\{1,2\};\{2\}), {}^{\mathbf{2}}(\{1,2\};\{3,4\}), {}^{\mathbf{3}}(\{2,3,4\};\{3,4\})\rangle$.

At this point, we can observe that the semantics of an (abstract) interpreter of a program P is an abstraction of the hypersemantics of P. First of all, note that $\tau^{\mathrm{r}}(\Psi)$ is an abstraction of $\tau^{\vec{\propto}}$, through the function $\lambda X\,.\,\alpha_r(\{\sigma \in X \mid \sigma_0 \in \Psi\})$, where $\alpha_r \overset{\text{def}}{=} \lambda X\,.\,\{\varsigma \mid \exists \sigma \in X, i \in \mathbb{N}\,.\,\sigma_i = \varsigma\}$ [13]. Analogously, we show that the semantics of an abstract interpreter, associating with each possible subset of initial states, the corresponding reachable states, is an abstraction of $\tau^{\vec{\propto}}_{\mathbf{pre}} \subseteq \wp(\Sigma^{\vec{+}}_P)$. As usual, we obtain *abstract* invariants in the abstract domain $\mathcal{A}$ exploiting a Galois insertion $\langle \wp(\mathrm{Val}), \subseteq \rangle \overset{\gamma}{\underset{\alpha}{\leftrightarrows}} \langle \mathcal{A}, \preccurlyeq \rangle$.

Proposition 7. *The semantics of the abstract interpreter w.r.t. abstract domain* $\mathcal{A}$ *is* $\alpha^{\mathcal{A}}_{\iota,c}\!\restriction \circ\, \alpha_r\!\restriction(\tau^{\vec{\propto}}_{\mathbf{pre}})$[11]*, i.e., it is an abstraction of the hypersemantics* $\tau^{\vec{\propto}}_{\mathbf{pre}}$.

Example 5. Consider Example 4. Then $\tau^{\vec{\propto}} = \{a, ab, abc, d, de, def\}$ and $\tau^{\vec{\propto}}_{\mathbf{pre}} = \{\{a, ab, abc\}, \{d, de, def\}, \tau^{\vec{\propto}}\}$. We do not consider any abstraction $\mathcal{A}$, then:

$$\begin{aligned} \alpha_{\iota,c} \circ \alpha_r(\tau^{\vec{\propto}}) &= \alpha_{\iota,c}(\{a,b,c,d,e,f\}) = \langle {}^{\mathbf{1}}(\{1,2\};\{2\}), {}^{\mathbf{2}}(\{1,2\};\{3,4\}), {}^{\mathbf{3}}(\{2,3,4\};\{3,4\})\rangle \\ \alpha_{\iota,c} \circ \alpha_r(\{a, ab, abc\}) &= \alpha_{\iota,c}(\{a,b,c\}) = \langle {}^{\mathbf{1}}(\{1\};\{2\}), {}^{\mathbf{2}}(\{1\};\{3,4\}), {}^{\mathbf{3}}(\{2,3\};\{3,4\})\rangle \\ \alpha_{\iota,c} \circ \alpha_r(\{d, de, def\}) &= \alpha_{\iota,c}(\{d,e,f\}) = \langle {}^{\mathbf{1}}(\{2\};\{2\}), {}^{\mathbf{2}}(\{2\};\{3,4\}), {}^{\mathbf{3}}(\{3,4\};\{3,4\})\rangle \end{aligned}$$

Hence, the set of invariants, depending on the set of initial states, is:

$$\alpha_{\iota,c}\!\restriction \circ\, \alpha_r\!\restriction(\tau^{\vec{\propto}}_{\mathbf{pre}}) = \left\{ \begin{array}{l} \langle {}^{\mathbf{1}}(\{1,2\};\{2\}), {}^{\mathbf{2}}(\{1,2\};\{3,4\}), {}^{\mathbf{3}}(\{2,3,4\};\{3,4\})\rangle, \\ \langle {}^{\mathbf{1}}(\{1\};\{2\}), {}^{\mathbf{2}}(\{1\};\{3,4\}), {}^{\mathbf{3}}(\{2,3\};\{3,4\})\rangle, \\ \langle {}^{\mathbf{1}}(\{2\};\{2\}), {}^{\mathbf{2}}(\{2\};\{3,4\}), {}^{\mathbf{3}}(\{3,4\};\{3,4\})\rangle, \end{array} \right\}$$

References

1. Agrawal, S., Bonakdarpour, B.: Runtime verification of k-safety hyperproperties in HyperLTL. In: IEEE 29th Computer Security Foundations Symposium, CSF 2016, Lisbon, Portugal, 27 June–1 July, 2016, pp. 239–252 (2016). http://dx.doi.org/10.1109/CSF.2016.24
2. Alpern, B., Schneider, F.B.: Defining liveness. Inf. Process. Lett. **21**(4), 181–185 (1985)

[11] $\alpha^{\mathcal{A}}_{\iota,c}$ returns abstract invariants maps, i.e., $\alpha^{\mathcal{A}}_{\iota,c} \in \wp(\Sigma_P) \to (\mathbb{L}_P \to (\mathrm{Var} \to \mathcal{A}))$.

3. Assaf, M., Naumann, D.A., Signoles, J., Totel, E., Tronel, F.: Hypercollecting semantics and its application to static analysis of information flow. In: Proceedings of the 44th ACM SIGPLAN Symposium on Principles of Programming Languages, POPL 2017, Paris, France, 18–20 January 2017, pp. 874–887 (2017). http://dl.acm.org/citation.cfm?id=3009889
4. Clarkson, M.R., Finkbeiner, B., Koleini, M., Micinski, K.K., Rabe, M.N., Sánchez, C.: Temporal logics for hyperproperties. In: Proceedings of the 3rd Conference on Principles of Security and Trust (POST 2014) (2014)
5. Clarkson, M.R., Schneider, F.B.: Hyperproperties. J. Comput. Secur. **18**(6), 1157–1210 (2010). http://dl.acm.org/citation.cfm?id=1891823.1891830
6. Cousot, P.: Abstract interpretation. ACM Comput. Surv. **28**(2), 324–328 (1996). http://doi.acm.org/10.1145/234528.234740
7. Cousot, P.: Constructive design of a hierarchy of semantics of a transition system by abstract interpretation. Theor. Comput. Sci. **277**(1–2), 47–103 (2002)
8. Cousot, P., Cousot, R.: Abstract interpretation: a unified lattice model for static analysis of programs by construction or approximation of fixpoints. In: Proceedings of the 4th ACM SIGACT-SIGPLAN Symposium on Principles of Programming Languages, POPL 1977, pp. 238–252. ACM, New York (1977)
9. Cousot, P., Cousot, R.: Systematic design of program analysis frameworks. In: Proceedings of the 6th ACM SIGACT-SIGPLAN Symposium on Principles of Programming Languages, POPL 1979, NY, USA, pp. 269–282 (1979). http://doi.acm.org/10.1145/567752.567778
10. Cousot, P., Cousot, R.: Abstract interpretation frameworks. J. Log. Comput. **2**(4), 511–547 (1992). http://dx.doi.org/10.1093/logcom/2.4.511
11. Cousot, P., Cousot, R.: A case study in abstract interpretation based program transformation. Electron. Notes Theor. Comput. Sci. **45**, 41–64 (2001). http://www.sciencedirect.com/science/article/pii/S157106610480954X
12. Cousot, P., Cousot, R.: Systematic design of program transformation frameworks by abstract interpretation. In: Proceedings of the 29th ACM SIGPLAN-SIGACT Symposium on Principles of Programming Languages, POPL 2002, NY, USA, pp. 178–190. ACM, New York (2002)
13. Cousot, P., Cousot, R.: An abstract interpretation framework for termination. In: Conference Record of the 39th Annual ACM SIGPLAN-SIGACT Symposium on Principles of Programming Languages, Philadelphia, PA, pp. 245–258. ACM, New York, January 2012
14. Cousot, R., Cousot, P.: Constructive versions of Tarski's fixed point theorems. Pac. J. Math. **82**(1), 43–57 (1979)
15. Finkbeiner, B., Rabe, M.N., Sánchez, C.: Algorithms for model checking HyperLTL and HyperCTL*. In: Kroening, D., Păsăreanu, C.S. (eds.) CAV 2015. LNCS, vol. 9206, pp. 30–48. Springer, Cham (2015). doi:10.1007/978-3-319-21690-4_3
16. Giacobazzi, R., Logozzo, F., Ranzato, F.: Analyzing program analyses. In: Proceedings of the 42nd Annual ACM SIGPLAN-SIGACT Symposium on Principles of Programming Languages, POPL 2015, Mumbai, India, 15–17 January 2015, pp. 261–273 (2015)
17. Giacobazzi, R., Mastroeni, I.: Non-standard semantics for program slicing. High. Order Symbolic Comput. **16**(4), 297–339 (2003)
18. Giacobazzi, R., Mastroeni, I.: Transforming semantics by abstract interpretation. Theor. Comput. Sci. **337**(1–3), 1–50 (2005)
19. Mastroeni, I., Giacobazzi, I.: An abstract interpretation-based model for safety semantics. Int. J. Comput. Math. **88**(4), 665–694 (2011)

20. Miné, A.: Backward under-approximations in numeric abstract domains to automatically infer sufficient program conditions. Sci. Comput. Program. **93**(Part B), 154–182 (2014). Special Issue on Invariant Generation
21. Weiser, M.: Program slicing. IEEE Trans. Softw. Eng. **10**(4), 352–357 (1984)
22. Zdancewic, S., Myers, A.C.: Observational determinism for concurrent program security. In: Proceedings of IEEE Computer Security Foundations Workshop, Pacific Grove, CA, pp. 29–43, June 2003

Thread-Local Semantics and Its Efficient Sequential Abstractions for Race-Free Programs

Suvam Mukherjee[1(✉)], Oded Padon[2], Sharon Shoham[2], Deepak D'Souza[1], and Noam Rinetzky[2]

[1] Indian Institute of Science, Bengaluru, India
suvamm@outlook.com
[2] Tel Aviv University Tel Aviv, Israel

Abstract. Data race free (DRF) programs constitute an important class of concurrent programs. In this paper we provide a framework for designing and proving the correctness of data flow analyses that target this class of programs, and which are in the same spirit as the "sync-CFG" analysis originally proposed in [9]. To achieve this, we first propose a novel concrete semantics for DRF programs called *L-DRF* that is *thread-local* in nature with each thread operating on its own copy of the data state. We show that abstractions of our semantics allow us to reduce the analysis of DRF programs to a *sequential* analysis. This aids in rapidly porting existing sequential analyses to scalable analyses for DRF programs. Next, we parameterize the semantics with a partitioning of the program variables into "regions" which are accessed atomically. Abstractions of the region-parameterized semantics yield more precise analyses for region-race free concurrent programs. We instantiate these abstractions to devise efficient relational analyses for race free programs, which we have implemented in a prototype tool called RATCOP. On the benchmarks, RATCOP was able to prove upto 65% of the assertions, in comparison to 25% proved by a version of the analysis from [9].

1 Introduction

Our aim in this paper is to provide a framework for developing data-flow analyses which specifically target the class of data race free (DRF) concurrent programs. The starting point of this work is the so-called "sync-CFG" style of analysis proposed in [9] for race-free programs. The analysis here essentially runs a sequential analysis on each thread, communicating data-flow facts between threads only via "synchronization edges" that go from a release statement in one thread to a corresponding acquire statement in another thread. The analysis thus runs on the control-flow graphs (CFGs) of the threads augmented with synchronization edges, as shown in the center of Fig. 1, which explains the name for this style of analysis. The analysis computes data flow facts about the value of a variable that are sound *only* at points where that variable is *relevant*, in that it is read or written to at that point. The analysis thus trades unsoundness of facts at irrelevant points for the efficiency gained by restricting interference between threads to points of synchronization alone.

F. Ranzato (Ed.): SAS 2017, LNCS 10422, pp. 253–276, 2017.
DOI: 10.1007/978-3-319-66706-5_13

However, the analysis proposed in [9] suffers from some drawbacks. Firstly, the analysis is intrinsically a "value-set" analysis, which can only keep track of the set of values each variable can assume, and not the relationships *between* variables. Any naive attempt to extend the analysis to a more precise relational one quickly leads to unsoundness. The second issue is to do with the technique for establishing soundness. A convenient way to prove soundness of an analysis is to show that it is a consistent abstraction [7] of a canonical analysis, like the collecting semantics for sequential programs or the interleaving semantics for concurrent programs. However, a sync-CFG style analysis *cannot* be shown to be a consistent abstraction of the standard interleaving semantics, due largely to the unsoundness at irrelevant points. Instead, one needs to use an intricate argument, as done in [9], which essentially shows that in the least fixed point of the analysis, every write to a variable will flow to a read of that variable via a happens-before path (that is guaranteed to exist by the property of race-freedom). Thus, while one can argue soundness of an analysis that abstracts the value-set analysis by showing it to be a consistent abstraction of the value set analysis, to argue soundness of any other proposed sync-CFG style analysis (in particular one that is more precise than the value-set analysis), one would have to resort to a similar involved proof as in [9].

Towards addressing these issues, we propose a framework that facilitates the design of different sync-CFG analyses with varying degrees of precision and efficiency. The foundation of this framework is a thread-local semantics for DRF programs, which can play the role of a "most precise" analysis which other sync-CFG analyses can be shown to be consistent abstractions of. This semantics, which we call *L-DRF*, is similar to the interleaving semantics of concurrent programs [20], but keeps thread-local (or per-thread) copies of the shared state. Intuitively, our semantics works as follows. Apart from its local copy of the shared data state, each thread t also maintains a per-variable version count, which is incremented whenever t updates the variable. The exchange of information between threads is via buffers, associated with release points in the program. When a thread releases a lock, it stores its data state to the corresponding buffer, along with the version counts of the variables. As a result, the buffer of a release point records both the local data state and the variable versions as they were when the release was last executed. When some thread t acquires a lock m, it compares its per-variable version count with those in the buffers pertaining to release points associated with m, and copies over the valuation of a variable to its local state, if it is newer in some buffer (as indicated by a higher version count). Similar to a sync-CFG analysis, the value of a shared variable in the local state of a thread may be *stale*. *L-DRF* leverages the race freedom property to ensure that the value of a variable is correct in a local state at program points where it is *read*. It thus captures the essence of a sync-CFG analysis. The *L-DRF* semantics is also of independent interest, since it can be viewed as an alternative characterization of the behavior of data race free programs.

The analysis induced by the *L-DRF* semantics is shown to be sound for DRF programs. In addition, the analysis is in a sense the most precise sync-CFG analysis one can hope for, since at every point in a thread, the relevant part of the thread-local copy of the shared state is *guaranteed* to arise in some execution of the program.

Using the *L-DRF* semantics as a basis, we now propose several precise and efficient *relational* sync-CFG analyses. The soundness of these analyses all follow immediately, since they can easily be shown to be consistent abstractions of the *L-DRF* analysis. The key idea behind obtaining a sound relational analysis is suggested by the *L-DRF* analysis: at each `acquire` point we apply a *mix* operator on the abstract values, which essentially amounts to forgetting all correlations between the variables.

While these analyses allow maintaining fully-relational properties within thread-local states, communicating information over cross-thread edges loses all correlations due to the *mix* operation. To improve precision further, we refine the *L-DRF* semantics to take into account *data regions*. Technically, we introduce the notion of *region race freedom* and develop the *R-DRF* semantics: the programmer can partition the program variables into "regions" that should be accessed *atomically*. A program is *region race free* if it does not contain conflicting accesses to variables in the same region, that are unordered by the happens-before relation. The classical notion of data race freedom is a special case of region race freedom where each region consists of a single variable, and techniques to determine that a program is race free can be naturally extended to determine region race freedom (see Sect. 6). For region race free programs, *R-DRF*, which refines *L-DRF* by taking into account the atomic nature of accesses that the program makes to variables in the same region, produces executions which are indistinguishable, with respect to reads of the regions, from the ones produced by *L-DRF*. By leveraging the *R-DRF* semantics as a starting point, we obtain more precise sequential analyses that track relational properties *within regions* across threads. This is obtained by refining the granularity of the *mix* operator from single variables to regions.

We have implemented our analyses in a prototype analyzer called RATCOP, and provide a thorough empirical evaluation in Sect. 7. We show that RATCOP attains a precision of up to 65% on a subset of race-free programs from the SV-COMP15 suite. In contrast, an interval based value-set analysis derived from [9] was able to prove only 25% of the assertions. On a separate set of experiments, RATCOP turns out to be nearly 5 orders of magnitude faster than an existing state-of-the-art abstract interpretation based tool [25].

2 Overview

We illustrate the *L-DRF* semantics, and its sequential abstractions, on the simple program in Fig. 1. We assume that all variables are shared and are initialized to 0. The threads access x and y only after acquiring lock m. The program is free from data races.

R-DRF	L-DRF	Value-Set	Thread t₁	Thread t₂	Value-Set	L-DRF	R-DRF
$0=x=y=z$	$0=x=y=z$	$0=x=y=z$			$0=x=y=z$	$0=x=y=z$	$0=x=y=z$
			1: acquire (m);	8: z++;			
$x=y,$ $0 \le y,$ $0 \le z \le 1$	$0 \le x,$ $0 \le y,$ $0 \le z \le 1$	$0 \le x,$ $0 \le y,$ $0 \le z \le 1$			$x=0,$ $y=0,$ $0 \le z \le 1$	$0=x=y,$ $z=1$	$0=x=y,$ $z=1$
			2: x := y;	9: assert (z = 1);			
$x=y,$ $0 \le y,$ $0 \le z \le 1$	$x=y,$ $0 \le y,$ $0 \le z \le 1$	$0 \le x,$ $0 \le y,$ $0 \le z \le 1$			$x=0,$ $y=0,$ $0 \le z \le 1$	$0=x=y,$ $z=1$	$0=x=y,$ $z=1$
			3: x++;	10: acquire (m);			
			4: y++;	11: assert (x = y);	$0 \le x,$ $0 \le y,$ $0 \le z \le 1$	$0 \le x,$ $0 \le y,$ $0 \le z \le 1$	$x=y,$ $0 \le y,$ $0 \le z \le 1$
$x=y,$ $1 \le y,$ $0 \le z \le 1$	$x=y,$ $1 \le y,$ $0 \le z \le 1$	$1 \le x,$ $1 \le y,$ $0 \le z \le 1$			$0 \le x,$ $0 \le y,$ $0 \le z \le 1$	$0 \le x,$ $0 \le y,$ $0 \le z \le 1$	$x=y,$ $0 \le y,$ $0 \le z \le 1$
			5: assert (x = y);	12: release (m); 13:			
$x=y,$ $1 \le y,$ $0 \le z \le 1$	$x=y,$ $1 \le y,$ $0 \le z \le 1$	$1 \le x,$ $1 \le y,$ $0 \le z \le 1$					
			6: release (m); 7:				

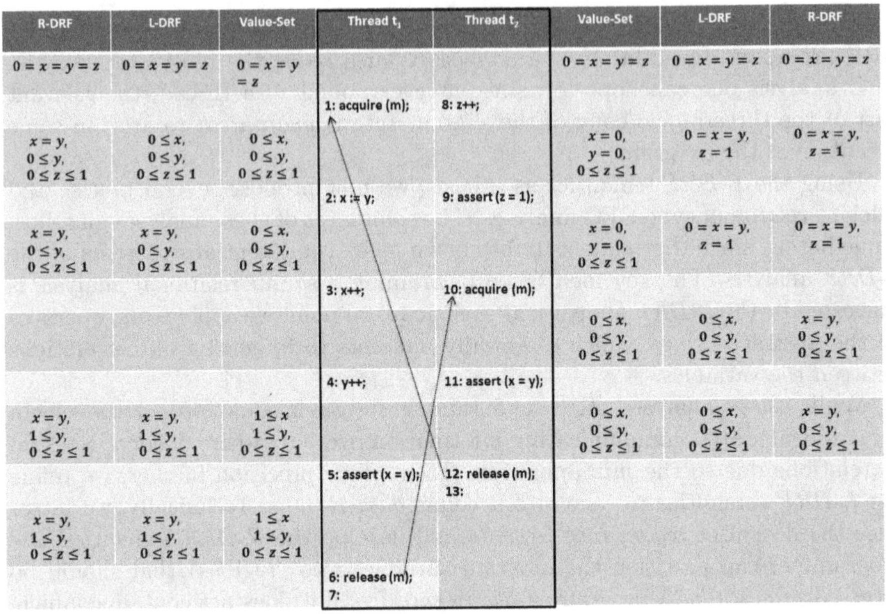

Fig. 1. A simple race free program with two threads t_1 and t_2, with all variables being shared and initialized to 0. The columns L-DRF and R-DRF show the facts computed by polyhedral abstractions of our thread-local semantics and its region-parameterized version, respectively. The Value-Set column shows the facts computed by interval abstractions of the Value-Set analysis of [9]. R-DRF is able to prove all 3 assertions, while L-DRF fails to prove the assertion at line 11. Value-Set only manages to prove the simple assertion at line 9.

A state in the L-DRF semantics keeps track of the following components: a location map pc mapping each thread to the location of the next command to be executed, a lock map μ which maps each lock to the thread holding it, a local environment (variable to value map) Θ for each thread, and a function Λ which maps each buffer (associated with each location following a release command) to an environment. Every release point of each lock m has an associated buffer, where a thread stores a copy of its local environment when it executes the corresponding release instruction. In the environments, each variable x has a version count associated with it which, along any execution π, essentially associates this valuation of x with a unique prior write to it in π. As an example, the "versioned" environment $\langle x \mapsto 1^1, y \mapsto 1^1, z \mapsto 0^0 \rangle$ says that x and y have the value 1 by the 1st writes to x and y, and z has not been written to. An execution is an interleaving of commands from the different threads. Consider an execution where, after a certain number of steps, we have the state $pc(t_1 \mapsto 6, t_2 \mapsto 10), \Theta(t1) = \langle x \mapsto 1^1, y \mapsto 1^1, z \mapsto 0^0 \rangle, \Theta(t2) = \langle x \mapsto 0^0, y \mapsto 0^0, z \mapsto 1^1 \rangle, \mu(m) = t_1, \Lambda = \bot$. The buffers are all empty as no thread has executed a release yet. Note that the values (and versions) of x and y in $\Theta(t_2)$ are *stale*, since it was t_1 which last modified them (similarly for z in $\Theta(t_1)$). Next, t_1 can execute the `release` at line 6, thereby setting $\mu(m) = \_$ and storing its current local state to $\Lambda(7)$. Now t_2 can execute the `acquire` at line 10. The state now becomes $pc(t_1 \mapsto 7, t_2 \mapsto 11)$, $\mu(m) = t_2$, and t_2 now "imports" the most up-to-date values (and versions) of the x and y from $\Lambda(7)$. This results in its local state becoming $\langle x \mapsto 1^1, y \mapsto 1^1, z \mapsto 1^1 \rangle$ (the valuations of x and y are pulled in from the buffer, while the valuation of z in t_2's local state persists). The value of x and y in $\Theta(t_2)$ is no longer stale: *L-DRF* leveraged the race freedom to ensure that the values of x and y are correct when they are read at line 11.

Roughly, we obtain *sequential* abstractions of *L-DRF* via the following steps: (i.) Provide a data abstraction of sets of environments (ii.) Define the state to be a map from locations to these abstract data values (iii.) Draw inter-thread edges by connecting releases and acquires of the same lock (as shown in Fig. 1) (iv.) Define an abstract *mix* operation which soundly approximates the "import" step outlined earlier (v.) Analyze the program as if it was a sequential program, with *inter*-thread join points (the `acquire`'s) using the *mix* operator.

The analysis in [9] is precisely such a sequential abstraction, where the abstract data values are abstractions of *value-sets* (variables mapped to sets of values). Value sets do not track correlations between variables, and only allow coarse abstractions like Intervals [6]. The *mix* operator, in this case, turns out to be the standard join. For Fig. 1, the interval analysis only manages to prove the assertion at line 9.

A more precise relational abstraction of *L-DRF* can be obtained by abstracting the environments as, say, convex polyhedra [8]. As shown in Fig. 1, the resulting analysis is more precise than the interval analysis, being able to prove the assertions at lines 5 and 9. However, in this case, the *mix* must forget the correlations among variables in the incoming states: it essentially treats them as value sets. This is essential for soundness. Thus, even though the `acquire` at line 10 obtains the fact that $x = y$ from the buffer at 7, and the incoming fact from 9 also has $x = y$, it fails to maintain this correlation after the *mix*. Consequently, it fails to prove the assertion at line 11.

Finally, one can exploit the fact that x and y form a data region, that is always accessed atomically by the two threads. The program is thus *region race free*, for this particular region definition. One can parameterize the *L-DRF* semantics with this region definition, to yield the *R-DRF* semantics. The resulting sequential abstraction maintains relational information as in polyhedra based analysis derived from *L-DRF*, but has a more precise *mix* operator which preserves relational facts which hold *within* a region. Since both the incoming facts at line 10 satisfy $x = y$, the *mix* preserves this fact, and the analysis is able to prove the assertion at 11.

Note that in all the three analyses, we are guaranteed to compute sound facts for variables *only* at points where they are accessed. For example, all three analyses claim that x and y are both 0 at line 9, which is clearly wrong. However, x and y are not accessed at this point. We make this trade-off for the soundness guarantee in order to achieve a more efficient analysis. Also note that in

Fig. 1, the inter-thread edges add a spurious loop in the program graph (and, therefore, in the analysis of the program), which prevents us from computing an upper bound for the values of x and y. We show in a later section how we can appropriately abstract the versions to avoid some of these spurious loops.

3 Preliminaries

Mathematical Notations. We use $\rightarrow$ and $\rightharpoonup$ to denote total and partial functions, respectively, and $\perp$ to denote a function which is not defined anywhere. We use $\_$ to denote an irrelevant value which is implicitly existentially quantified. We write $\bar{S}$ to denote a (possibly empty) finite sequence of elements coming from a set S. We denote the *length* of a sequence π by $|\pi|$, and the i-th element of π, for $0 \leq i < |\pi|$, by π_i. We denote the domain of a function ϕ by $\mathrm{dom}(\phi)$ and write $\phi[x \mapsto v]$ to denote the function $\lambda y. if\, y = x\; then\, v\; else\, \phi(y)$. Given a pair of function $\upsilon = \langle \phi, \nu \rangle$, we write $\upsilon\phi$ and $\upsilon\nu$ to denote ϕ and ν, respectively.

Table 1. Program commands

Type	Syntax	Description
Assignment	$x := e$	Assigns the value of expression e to variable $x \in \mathcal{V}$
Assume	$\texttt{assume}(b)$	Blocks the computation if boolean condition b does not hold
Acquire	$\texttt{acquire}(m)$	Acquires lock m, provided it is not *held* by any thread
Release	$\texttt{release}(m)$	Releases lock m, provided the executing thread holds it

3.1 Programming Language and Programs

A multi-threaded program P consists of four finite sets: *threads* $\mathcal{T}$, *control locations* $\mathcal{L}$, program *variables* $\mathcal{V}$ and *locks* (*mutexes*) $\mathcal{M}$. We denote by $\mathbb{V}$ the set of values the program variables can assume. Without loss of generality, we assume in this work that $\mathbb{V}$ is simply the set of integers. Figure 2 lists the semantic domains we use in this paper and the metavariables ranging over them.

Every thread $t \in \mathcal{T}$ has an entry location ent_t and a set of instructions $inst_t \subseteq \mathcal{L} \times cmd \times \mathcal{L}$, which defines the *control flow graph* of t. An instruction $\langle n_s, c, n_t \rangle$ comprises a *source* location n_s, a *command* $c \in cmd$, and a *target* location n_t. The set of program commands, denoted by cmd, is defined in Table 1 (Commands like `fork` and `join` of a bounded number of threads can be simulated using locks.). For generality, we refrain from defining the syntax of the expressions e and boolean conditions b.

We denote the set of commands appearing in program P by $cmd(P)$. We refer to an assignment $x := e$ as a *write-access* to x, and as a *read-access* to every variable that appears in e. Without loss of generality, we assume variables appearing in conditions of `assume()` commands in instructions of some thread t do not appear in any instruction of any other thread $t' \neq t$.

We denote by $\mathcal{L}_t$ the set of locations in instructions of thread t, and require that the sets be disjoint for different threads. For a location $n \in \mathcal{L}\ (= \bigcup_{t\in\mathcal{T}} \mathcal{L}_t)$, we denote by $tid(n)$ the thread t which contains location n, i.e., $n \in \mathcal{L}_t$. We forbid different instructions from having the same source and target locations, and further expect instructions pertaining to assignments, `acquire`() and `release`() commands to have unique source and target locations. Let $\mathcal{L}_t^{rel}$ be the set of program locations in the body of thread t following a `release`() command. We refer to $\mathcal{L}_t^{rel}$ as t's *post-release points* and denote the set of *release points* in a program by $\mathcal{L}^{rel} = \bigcup_{t\in\mathcal{T}} \mathcal{L}_t^{rel}$. Similarly, we define t's *pre-acquire points*, denoted by $\mathcal{L}_t^{acq}$, and denote a program's *acquire points* by $\mathcal{L}^{acq} = \bigcup_{t\in\mathcal{T}} \mathcal{L}_t^{acq}$. We denote the sets of post-release and pre-acquire points pertaining to operations on lock m by $\mathcal{L}_m^{rel}$ and $\mathcal{L}_m^{acq}$, respectively.

3.2 Standard Interleaving Semantics

Let us fix a program $P = (\mathcal{T}, \mathcal{L}, \mathcal{V}, \mathcal{M})$ for the rest of this paper. We define the standard interleaving semantics of a program using a labeled transition system $\langle \mathcal{S}, s_{ent}, TR^{\mathsf{s}} \rangle$, where $\mathcal{S}$ is the set of *states*, $s_{ent} \in \mathcal{S}$ is the *initial state*, and $TR^{\mathsf{s}} \subseteq \mathcal{S} \times \mathcal{T} \times \mathcal{S}$ is a transition relation, as defined below.

$t \in \mathcal{T}$	Thread identifiers	$pc \in PC \equiv \mathcal{T} \to \mathcal{L}$	Program counters
$n \in \mathcal{L}$	Program locations	$\mu \in LM \equiv \mathcal{M} \rightharpoonup \mathcal{T}$	Lock map
$x, y \in \mathcal{V}$	Variable identifiers	$\phi \in Env \equiv \mathcal{V} \to \mathbb{V}$	Environments
$l \in \mathcal{M}$	Lock identifiers	$\nu \in \mathcal{V}V \equiv \mathcal{V} \to \mathbb{N}$	Variable versions
$r \in R$	Region identifiers	$\upsilon \in VE \equiv Env \times \mathcal{V}V$	Versioned environments
$v \in \mathbb{V}$	Values		

$$s = \langle pc, \mu, \phi \rangle \in \mathcal{S} \equiv PC \times LM \times Env \qquad \text{Standard States}$$
$$\sigma = \langle pc, \mu, \Theta, \Lambda \rangle \in \Sigma \equiv PC \times LM \times (\mathcal{T} \to VE) \times (\mathcal{L} \to VE) \quad \text{Thread-Local States}$$

Fig. 2. Semantic domains.

States. A *state* $s \in \mathcal{S}$ is a tuple $\langle pc, \mu, \phi \rangle$, where $pc \in PC \stackrel{\text{def}}{=} \mathcal{T} \to \mathcal{L}$ records the *program counter* (or location) of every thread, $\mu \in LM \stackrel{\text{def}}{=} \mathcal{M} \rightharpoonup \mathcal{T}$ is a *lock map* which associates every lock to the thread that holds it (if such a thread exists), and $\phi \in Env \stackrel{\text{def}}{=} \mathcal{V} \to \mathbb{V}$ is an *environment*, mapping variables to their values.

Initial State. We refer to the state $s_{ent} = \langle \lambda t.\ ent_t, \bot, \lambda x.\ 0 \rangle$ where every thread is at its entry program location, no thread holds a lock, and all the variables are initialized to zero as the *initial state*.

Transition Relation. The transition relation $TR_P^{\mathsf{s}} \subseteq \mathcal{S} \times \mathcal{T} \times \mathcal{S}$ captures the interleaving semantics of a program P. A transition $\tau = \langle s, t, s' \rangle$, also denoted by $\tau = s \to_t s'$, says that thread t can execute a command which transforms (the *source*) state s to (the *target*) state s'. As such, the transition relation is the set of all possible transitions generated by its commands, i.e. $TR_P^{\mathsf{s}} = \bigcup_{c\in cmd(P)} TR_c^{\mathsf{s}}$.

In these transitions, one thread executes a command, and changes its program counter accordingly, while all other threads remain stationary. Due to space constraints, we omit the formal definitions of $TR^{\mathbf{s}}_{c}$, which is standard, and only provide a brief informal description. An assignment $x := e$ command updates the value of the variables according to the expression e. An `assume`(b) command generates transitions only from states in which the boolean interpretation of the condition b is *True*. An `acquire`(m) command executed by thread t sets $\mu(m) = t$, provided the lock m is not held by any other thread, A `release`(m) command executed by thread t sets $\mu(m) = \_$, provided t holds m. A thread attempting to release a lock that it does not own gets stuck.[1]

Notations. For a transition $\tau = \langle pc, \mu, \phi\rangle \rightarrow_t \langle pc', \mu', \phi'\rangle \in TR^{\mathbf{s}}_{P}$, we denote by $t(\tau) = t$ the thread that *executes* the transition, and by $c(\tau)$ the (unique) command $c \in cmd(P)$, such that $\langle pc(t), c, pc'(t)\rangle \in inst_t$, which it executes. We denote by $n(\tau) = pc(t)$ and $n'(\tau) = pc'(t)$, the source and target locations of the executed instruction respectively.

Executions. An execution π of a concurrent program P is a finite sequence of transitions coming from its transition relation, such that s_{ent} is the source of transition π_0 and the source state of every transition π_i, for $0 < i < |\pi|$, is the target state of transition π_{i-1}.

By abuse of notation, we also write executions as sequences of states interleaved with thread identifiers: $\pi = s_0 \xrightarrow{t_1} s_1 \xrightarrow{t_2} \dots \xrightarrow{t_n} s_n$.

Collecting Semantics. The collecting semantics of a program P according to the standard semantics is the set of reachable states starting from the initial state s_{ent}:

$$[\![P]\!]^{\mathbf{s}} = LFP\ \lambda X. \{s_{ent}\} \cup \{s' \mid s \rightarrow_t s' \wedge s \in X \wedge t \in T\}$$

3.3 Data Races and the Happens-Before Relation

We say that two commands *conflict* on a variable x, if they both access x, and at least one access is a write. A program contains a *data race* when two concurrent threads may execute conflicting commands, and the threads use no explicit mechanism to prevent their accesses from being simultaneous [29]. A program which has no data races is said to be *data race free*. A standard way to formalize the notion of *data race freedom* (DRF), is to use the *happens before* [19] relation induced by executions. An execution is *racy* if it contains a pair of transitions executing conflicting commands which are not ordered according to the happens-before relation. A program which has no racy execution is said to be *data race free*.

For a given execution, the happens-before relation is defined as the reflexive and transitive closure of the *program-order* and *synchronizes-with* relations, formalized below.

[1] The decision to block a thread releasing a lock it does not own was made to simplify the semantics. Our results hold even if this action aborts the program.

Definition 1 (Program order). *Let π be an execution of P. Transition π_i is related to the transition π_j according to the* program-order *relation in π, denoted by $\pi_i \xrightarrow{po}_\pi \pi_j$, if $j = \min\{k \mid i < k < |\pi| \wedge t(\pi_k) = t(\pi_i)\}$, i.e., π_i and π_j are successive executions of commands by the same thread.*[2]

Definition 2 (Synchronize-with). *Let π be an execution of P. Transition π_i is related to the transition π_j according to* synchronizes-with *relation in π, denoted by $\pi_i \xrightarrow{sw}_\pi \pi_j$, if $c(\pi_i) = \texttt{release}(m)$ for some lock m, and $j = \min\{k \mid i < k < |\pi| \wedge c(\pi_k) = \texttt{acquire}(m)\ \}$, i.e., π_i and π_j are successive release and acquire commands of the same lock in the execution.*

Definition 3 (Happens before). *The* happens-before *relation pertaining to an execution π of P, denoted by $\cdot \xrightarrow{hb}_\pi \cdot$, is the reflexive and transitive closure of the union of the program-order and synchronizes-with relations induced by the execution π.*

Note that transitions executed by the same thread are always related according to the happens-before relation.

Definition 4 (Data Race). *Let π be an execution of P. Transitions π_i and π_j constitute a racing pair, or a data-race, if the following conditions are satisfied: (i) $c(\pi_i)$ and $c(\pi_j)$ both access the variable x, with at least one of the accesses being a write to x, and (ii)neither $\pi_i \xrightarrow{hb}_\pi \pi_j$ nor $\pi_j \xrightarrow{hb}_\pi \pi_i$ holds.*

4 Thread-Local Semantics for Data-Race Free Programs (*L-DRF*)

In this section, we define a new thread-local semantics for datarace free concurrent programs, which we refer to as *L-DRF* semantics. The new semantics, like the standard one defined in Sect. 3, is based on the interleaving of transitions made by different threads, and the use of a lock map to coordinate the use of locks. However, unlike the standard semantics, where the threads share access to a single *global* environment, in the *L-DRF* semantics, every thread has its own *local* environment which it uses to evaluate conditions and perform assignments.

Threads exchange information through *release buffers*: every post-release point $n \in \mathcal{L}_t^{rel}$ of a thread t is associated with a *buffer*, $\Lambda(n)$, which records a snapshot of t's local environment the last time t ended up at the program point n. Recall that this happens right after t executes the instruction $\langle n_s, \texttt{release}(\texttt{m}), n\rangle \in inst_t$. When a thread t acquires a lock $\texttt{m}$, it updates its local environment using the snapshots stored in the buffers pertaining to the release of $\texttt{m}$. To ensure that t updates its environment such that the value of every variable is up-to-date, every thread maintains its own *version map* $\nu : \mathcal{V} \to \mathbb{N}$,

[2] Strictly speaking, the various relations we define are between indices $\{0, \ldots, |\pi| - 1\}$ of an execution, and not transitions, so we should have written, e.g., $i \xrightarrow{po}_\pi j$ instead of $\pi_i \xrightarrow{po}_\pi \pi_j$. We use the rather informal latter notation, for readability.

which associates a counter to each variable. A thread increments $\nu(x)$ whenever it writes to x. Along any execution, the version $\nu(x)$, for $x \in \mathcal{V}$, in the version map ν of thread t, associates a unique prior write with this particular valuation of x. It also reflects the total number of write accesses made (by any thread) to x to obtain the value of x stored in the map. A thread stores both its local environment and ν in the buffer after releasing a lock m. When a thread subsequently acquires lock m, it copies from the release buffers at $\mathcal{L}_m^{rel}$ the most up-to-date (according to the version numbers) value of every variable. We prove that for data race free programs, there can be only one such value. As in Sect. 3.2, we define *L-DRF* in terms of a labeled transition system $(\Sigma, \sigma_{ent}, TR_P)$.

States. A *state* $\sigma \in \Sigma$ of the *L-DRF* semantics is a tuple $\langle pc, \mu, \Theta, \Lambda \rangle$. Here, pc and μ have the same role as in the standard semantics, i.e., they record the program counter of every thread and the ownership of locks, respectively. A versioned environment $\upsilon = \langle \phi, \nu \rangle \in VE = Env \times (\mathcal{V} \to \mathbb{N})$ is a pair comprising an environment ϕ and a version map ν. The local environment map $\Theta : \mathcal{T} \to VE$ maps every thread to its versioned environment and $\Lambda : \mathcal{L}^{rel} \to VE$ records the snapshots of versioned environments stored in buffers.

Initial State. The initial state is $\sigma_{ent} = \langle \lambda t.\, ent_t, \bot, \lambda t.\, \upsilon_{ent}, \bot \rangle$, where $\upsilon_{ent} = \langle \lambda x.0, \lambda x.0 \rangle$ is the initial versioned environment. In σ_{ent}, every thread is at its entry program location, no thread holds a lock, in all the versioned environments all the variables and variable versions are initialized to zero, and all the release buffers are empty.

Transition Relation. The transition relation $TR_P \subseteq \Sigma \times \mathcal{T} \times \Sigma$ captures the interleaving nature of the *L-DRF* semantics of P. A transition $\tau = \langle \sigma, t, \sigma' \rangle$, also denoted by $\tau = \sigma \Rightarrow_t \sigma'$, says that thread t can execute a command which transforms state $\sigma \in \Sigma$ to state $\sigma' \in \Sigma$. We define the transition system which captures the *L-DRF* semantics of a program P by defining the transitions generated by every command in P.

Assignments and Assume Commands. We define the meaning of assignments and `assume`() commands (as functions from versioned environments to sets of versioned environments) by executing the standard interpretation over the environment component of a versioned environment. In addition, assignments increment the version of a variable being assigned to. Formally,

$$[\![x := e]\!] : VE \to \wp(VE) = \lambda \langle \phi, \nu \rangle . \{ \langle \phi[x \mapsto v], \nu[x \mapsto \nu(x)+1] \rangle \mid v \in [\![e]\!]\phi \}$$
$$[\![\texttt{assume}(b)]\!] : VE \to \wp(VE) = \lambda \langle \phi, \nu \rangle . \{ \langle \phi, \nu \rangle \mid [\![b]\!]\phi \}$$

where $[\![e]\!]\phi$, $[\![b]\!]\phi$ denote the value of the (possibly non-deterministic) expression e and the Boolean expression b, respectively, in ϕ. The set of transitions TR_c generated by an `assume`() or an assignment command c is given by:

$$TR_c = \{ \langle pc, \mu, \Theta, \Lambda \rangle \Rightarrow_t \langle pc[t \mapsto n'], \mu, \Theta[t \mapsto \upsilon'], \Lambda \rangle \mid \langle pc(t), c, n' \rangle \in inst_t \wedge \upsilon' \in [\![c]\!](\Theta(t)) \}$$

Note that each thread t only accesses and modifies its *own* local versioned environment.

Acquire commands. An $\texttt{acquire}(m)$ command executed by a thread t has the same effect on the lock map component in *L-DRF* as in the standard semantics. (See Sect. 3.2.) In addition, it updates $\Theta(t)$ based on the contents of the *relevant* release buffers. The release buffers relevant to a thread when it acquires m are the ones at $\mathcal{L}_m^{rel}$. We write $\mathcal{G}(\bar{n})$ as a synonym for $\mathcal{L}_m^{acq}$, for any post-release point $\bar{n} \in \mathcal{L}_m^{rel}$. The auxiliary function *updEnv* is used to update the value of each $x \in \mathcal{V}$ (along with its version) in $\Theta(t)$, by taking its value from a snapshot stored at a relevant buffer which has the highest version of x, if the latter version is higher than $\Theta(t)\nu(x)$. If the version of x is highest in $\Theta(t)\nu(x)$, then t simply retains this value. Finding the most up-to-date snapshot for x (or determining that $\Theta(t)\nu(x)$ is the highest) is the role of the auxiliary function $take_x$. It takes as input $\Theta(t)$, as well as the versioned environments of the relevant release buffers, and returns the versioned environments for which the version associated with x is the highest. We separately prove that, along any execution, if there is a state in the *L-DRF* semantics σ with two component versioned environments (in thread local states or buffers) υ_1 and υ_2 such that $\upsilon_1\nu(x) = \upsilon_2\nu(x)$, then $\upsilon_1\phi(x) = \upsilon_2\phi(x)$. The set of transitions pertaining to an acquire command $c = \texttt{acquire}(m)$ is

$$\begin{aligned} TR_c = \{\langle pc, \mu, \Theta, \Lambda\rangle \Rightarrow_t \langle pc[t \mapsto n''], \mu[m \mapsto t], \Theta[t \mapsto \upsilon], \Lambda\rangle \mid \\ \langle pc(t), c, n''\rangle \in inst_t \wedge \mu(m) = \_ \wedge \upsilon \in updEnv(\Theta(t), \Lambda)\} \end{aligned}$$

where $updEnv : (VE \times (\mathcal{L}^{rel} \rightarrow VE)) \rightarrow \wp(VE)$ given by

$$updEnv(\upsilon, \Lambda) = \{\upsilon'' \mid \textstyle\bigwedge_{x\in\mathcal{V}} \exists \upsilon_x \in take_x(Y) : \upsilon''\phi(x) = \upsilon_x\phi(x) \wedge \upsilon''\nu(x) = \upsilon_x\nu(x)\}$$

with

$$Y = \{\upsilon\} \cup \{\Lambda(\bar{n}) \mid \bar{n} \in \mathcal{L}_m^{rel} \bigwedge pc(t) \in \mathcal{G}(\bar{n})\}$$

and

$$take_x \stackrel{\text{def}}{=} \lambda Y \in \wp(VE). \{\langle\phi, \nu\rangle \in Y \mid \nu(x) = \max\{\nu''(x) \mid \langle\phi'', \nu''\rangle \in Y\}\} .$$

For example, in Fig. 1, when the program counters are $pc(t_1 \mapsto 7, t_2 \mapsto 10)$, and t_2 executes the $\texttt{acquire}()$, $take_x\, (\Theta(t_2) \cup \Lambda(7) \cup \Lambda(13)) = \Lambda(7)$. Similarly, $take_y$ also returns $\Lambda(7)$. However, $take_z$ returns $\Theta(t_2)$, since this contains the highest version of z. Thus, $updEnv\, (\Theta(t_2), \Lambda(7), \Lambda(12))$ returns the versioned environment $\langle x \mapsto 1^1, y \mapsto 1^1, z \mapsto 1^1\rangle$.

Release commands A $\texttt{release}(m)$ command executed by a thread t has the same effect on the lock map component of the state in the *L-DRF* semantics that it has in the standard semantics. (See Sect. 3.2.) In addition, it stores $\Theta(t)$ in the buffer associated with the post-release point pertaining to the executed $\texttt{release}(m)$ instruction. The set of transitions pertaining to a release command $c = \texttt{release}(m)$ is

$$\begin{aligned} TR_c = \{\langle pc, \mu, \Theta, \Lambda\rangle \Rightarrow_t \langle pc[t \mapsto n'], \mu[m \mapsto \_], \Theta, \Lambda[n' \mapsto \Theta(t)]\rangle \mid \\ \langle pc(t), c, n'\rangle \in inst_t \wedge \mu(m) = t\} \end{aligned}$$

Program transition relation. The transition relation TR_P of a program P according to the *L-DRF* semantics, is the set of all possible transitions generated by its commands, and is defined as $TR_P = \bigcup_{c \in cmd(P)} TR_c$.

Collecting Semantics. The collecting semantics of a program P according to the *L-DRF* semantics is the set of reachable states starting from the initial state σ_{ent}:

$$[\![P]\!] = LFP\ \lambda X. \{\sigma_{ent}\} \cup \{\sigma' \mid \sigma \Rightarrow_t \sigma' \in TR_P \wedge \sigma \in X \wedge t \in \mathcal{T}\}$$

4.1 Soundness and Completeness of *L-DRF* Semantics

For the class of data race free programs, the thread local semantics *L-DRF* is sound and complete with respect to the standard interleaving semantics (Sect. 3). To formalize the above claim, we define a function which extracts a state in the interleaving semantics from a state in the *L-DRF* semantics.

Definition 5 (Extraction Function χ).

$$\chi : \Sigma \to \mathcal{S} = \lambda \langle pc, \mu, \Theta, \Lambda \rangle . \left\langle pc, \mu, \lambda x.\Theta \left(\underset{t \in \mathcal{T}}{argmax}\, \Theta\,(t)\, \nu(x) \right) \phi(x) \right\rangle$$

The function χ preserves the values of the program counters and the lock map, while it takes the value of every variable x from the thread which has the maximal version count for x in its local environment. χ is well-defined for *admissible* states where, if $\Theta(t)\nu(x) = \Theta(t')\nu(x)$, then $\Theta(t)\phi(x) = \Theta(t')\phi(x)$. We denote the set of admissible states by $\tilde{\Sigma}$. The *L-DRF* semantics only produces admissible states, as formalized by the following lemma:

Lemma 6. *Let $\sigma_{ent} \to_{t_1} \dots \to_{t_N} \sigma_N$ be an execution of P in the L-DRF semantics. Then, for any σ_i, with two component versioned environments (in thread local states or buffers) υ_1 and υ_2 such that $\upsilon_1\nu(x) = \upsilon_2\nu(x)$, we have $\upsilon_1\phi(x) = \upsilon_2\phi(x)$.*

The function χ can be extended to executions in the *L-DRF* semantics by applying it to each state in the execution. The following theorems state our soundness and completeness results:

Theorem 7. ***Soundness.*** *For any trace $\pi = s_0 \to_{t_1} \dots \to_{t_n} s_n$ of P in the standard interleaving semantics, there exists a trace $\hat{\pi} = \sigma_0 \to_{t_1} \dots \to_{t_n} \sigma_n$ in the L-DRF semantics such that $\chi(\hat{\pi}) = \pi$. Moreover, for any transition π_i, if $c(\pi_i)$ involves a read of variable $x \in \mathcal{V}$, then $s_{i-1}\phi(x) = \sigma_{i-1}\Theta(t_i)\phi(x)$. In other words, in $\hat{\pi}$, the valuation of a variable x in the local environment of a thread t coincides with the corresponding valuation in the standard semantics only at points where t reads x.*

Theorem 8. ***Completeness.*** *For any trace $\hat{\pi}$ of P in the L-DRF semantics, $\chi(\hat{\pi})$ is a trace of the standard interleaving semantics.*

The proofs of all the claims are available in [26].

Remark 9. Till now we assumed that buffers associated with every post-release point in $\mathcal{L}_m^{rel}$ are relevant to each pre-acquire point in $\mathcal{L}_m^{acq}$, i.e., $\forall \bar{n} \in \mathcal{L}_m^{rel} : \mathcal{G}(\bar{n}) = \mathcal{L}_m^{acq}$. However, if no (standard) execution of a program contains a transition τ_i (with the target location being $\bar{n}$) which synchronizes-with a transition τ_j (with source location n), then Theorem 7 (as well as Theorem 8) holds even if we remove n from $\mathcal{G}(\bar{n})$. This is true because in race-free programs, conflicting accesses are ordered by the happens-before relation. Thus, if the most up-to-date value of a variable accessed by t was written by another thread t', then in between these accesses there must be a (sequence of) synchronization operations starting at a lock released by t' and ending at a lock acquired by t. This refinement of the set $\mathcal{G}$ based on the above observation can be used to improve the precision of the analyses derived from *L-DRF*, as it reduces the set of possible release points an acquire can observe.

5 Sequential Abstractions for Data-Race Free Programs

In this section, we show how to employ standard *sequential* analyses to compute over-approximations of the *L-DRF* semantics. Thanks to Theorems 7 and 8, the obtained results can be used to derive sound facts about the (concurrent) behavior of data race free programs in the *standard* semantics. In particular, this also allows us to establish the soundness of the *sync*-CFG analysis [9] by casting it as an abstract interpretation of the *L-DRF* semantics.

Technically, the analyses are derived by two (successive) abstraction steps: First, we abstract the *L-DRF* semantics using a thread-local cartesian abstraction which ignores version numbers and forgets the correlation between the local states of the different threads. This results in cartesian states where every program point is associated with a set of (thread-local) environments. Note that the form of these cartesian states is precisely the one obtained when computing the collecting semantics of sequential programs. Thus, they can be further abstracted using any sequential abstraction, in particular relational ones. This allows maintaining correlations between variables at all points except synchronization points (acquires and releases of locks). Note that we make the initial decision to abstract away the versions for simplicity, and we refine this abstraction later in Remark 11.

Thread-Local Cartesian Abstract Domain. The abstract domain is a complete lattice over *cartesian states*, functions mapping program locations to sets of environments, ordered by pointwise inclusions. We denote the set of cartesian states by $\mathcal{A}_\times$ and range over it using $a_\times$, and define the least upper bound operator $\sqcup_\times$ in the standard way.

$$\mathcal{D}_\times \equiv \langle \mathcal{A}_\times, \sqsubseteq_\times \rangle \quad \text{where } \mathcal{A}_\times \equiv \mathcal{L} \to \wp(Env) \quad \text{and} \quad a_\times \sqsubseteq_\times a'_\times \iff \forall n \in \mathcal{L}.\, a_\times(n) \subseteq a'_\times(n)$$

The abstraction function $\alpha_\times$ maps a set of *L-DRF* states $C \subseteq \Sigma$ to a *cartesian state* $a_\times \in \mathcal{A}_\times$. The abstract value $\alpha_\times(C)(n)$ contains the collection of t's environments (where $t = \mathit{tid}(n)$)) coming from any state $\sigma \in C$ where t is at location n. In addition, if n is a post-release point, $\alpha_\times(C)(n)$ also contains the contents of the buffer $\Lambda(n)$ for each state $\sigma \in C$. As a first cut, we abstract away the versions entirely. The concretization function $\gamma_\times$ maps a cartesian state $a_\times$ to a set of (admissible) *L-DRF* states C in which the local state of a thread t, at program point $n \in \mathcal{L}_t$, comes from $a_\times(n)$, and the contents of the release buffer pertaining to the post-release location $n \in \mathcal{L}^{rel}$ also comes from $a_\times(n)$.

$$
\begin{aligned}
&\alpha_\times : \wp(\Sigma) \rightarrow \mathcal{A}_\times, \\
&\quad \text{where } \alpha_\times(C) = \lambda n \in \mathcal{L}.\, \{\phi \mid \langle pc, \mu, \Theta, \Lambda\rangle \in C \wedge pc(t) = n \wedge \langle \phi, \nu\rangle = \Theta(\mathit{tid}(n))\} \cup \\
&\qquad\qquad\qquad\qquad\qquad\quad \{\phi \mid \langle pc, \mu, \Theta, \Lambda\rangle \in C \wedge n \in \mathcal{L}^{rel} \wedge \langle \phi, \nu\rangle = \Lambda(n)\}
\end{aligned}
$$

$$
\begin{aligned}
&\gamma_\times : \mathcal{A}_\times \rightarrow \wp(\Sigma), \\
&\quad \text{where } \gamma_\times(a_\times) = \left\{ \langle pc, \mu, \Theta, \Lambda\rangle \in \tilde{\Sigma} \;\middle|\; \begin{array}{l} pc \in PC \wedge \mu \in LM \wedge \\ \forall t \in \mathcal{T}.\, \Theta(t) = \langle \phi, \lambda x.\_\rangle \wedge \phi \in a_\times(pc(t)) \wedge \\ \forall n \in \mathcal{L}^{rel}.\, \Lambda(n) = \langle \phi, \lambda x.\_\rangle \wedge \phi \in a_\times(n)\} \end{array} \right\}
\end{aligned}
$$

Abstract Transitions. The abstract cartesian semantics is defined using a transition relation, $TR^\times \subseteq \mathcal{A}_\times \times \mathcal{T} \times \mathcal{A}_\times$.

Assignments and assume commands. As we have already abstracted away the version numbers, we define the meaning of assignments and assume() commands c using their interpretation according to the standard semantics, denoted by $[\![c]\!]_{\mathbf{s}}$. Hence, the set of transitions coming from an assume() or an assignment command c is:

$$
TR^\times_c = \left\{ a_\times \Rightarrow^\times_t a_\times \left[n' \mapsto a_\times(n') \cup \bigcup_{\phi \in a_\times(n)} [\![c]\!]_{\mathbf{s}}(\phi) \right] \;\middle|\; \langle n, c, n'\rangle \in \mathit{inst}_t \right\}
$$

Acquire Commands. With the omission of any information pertaining to ownership of locks, an acquire command executed at program location n is only required to over-approximate the effect of updating the environment of a thread based on the contents of relevant buffers. To do so, we define an abstract *mix* operation which mixes together different environments at the granularity of single variables. The set of transitions pertaining to an acquire command $c = \mathtt{acquire}(m)$ is

$$
\begin{aligned}
TR^\times_c &= \{a_\times \Rightarrow^\times_t a_\times[n'' \mapsto E_{mix}] \mid \langle n, c, n''\rangle \in \mathit{inst}_t\} \text{ , where} \\
E_{mix} &= \mathit{mix}(a_\times(n'') \cup \bigcup \{a_\times(\bar{n}) \mid \bar{n} \in \mathcal{L}^{rel}_m \wedge n \in \mathcal{G}(\bar{n})\}) \quad \text{, and} \\
\mathit{mix} &: \wp(\mathit{Env}) \rightarrow \wp(\mathit{Env}) \equiv \lambda B_\times.\{\phi'' \mid \forall x \in \mathcal{V}, \exists \phi \in B_\times : \phi''(x) = \phi(x)\}
\end{aligned}
$$

In other words, the *mix* takes a cartesian product of the input states. Note that as a result of abstracting away the version numbers, a thread cannot determine the most up-to-date value of a variable, and thus conservatively picks any possible value found either in its own local environment or in a relevant release buffer.

Release Commands. Interestingly, the effect of release commands in the cartesian semantics is the same as `skip`: This is because the abstraction neither tracks ownership of locks nor explicitly manipulates the contents of buffers. Hence, the set of transitions pertaining to a release command $c = \mathtt{release}(m)$ is

$$TR_c^{\times} = \{a_{\times} \Rightarrow_t^{\times} a_{\times}[n' \mapsto a_{\times}(n') \cup a_{\times}(n)] \mid \langle n, c, n' \rangle\rangle \in inst_t\}$$

Collecting semantics. The collecting semantics of a program P, according to the thread-local cartesian semantics, is the cartesian state obtained as the least fixpoint of the abstract transformer obtained from $TR^{\times} = \bigcup_{c \in cmd(P)} TR_c^{\times}$ starting from $a_{\times}^{ent} = \alpha_{\times}(\{\sigma_{ent}\})$, the cartesian state corresponding to the initial state of the semantics:

$$\begin{aligned}\llbracket P \rrbracket_{\times} &= LFP\ \lambda a_{\times}.\, a_{\times}^{ent} \sqcup_{\times} \left(\bigsqcup\nolimits_{\times} \{a'_{\times} \mid a_{\times} \Rightarrow_t^{\times} a'_{\times} \in TR^{\times} \wedge t \in \mathcal{T}\} \right) \text{ , where}\\ a_{\times}^{ent} &= \alpha_{\times}(\{\sigma_{ent}\})\end{aligned}$$

Theorem 10 (Soundness of Sequential Abstractions). $\gamma_{\times}(\llbracket P \rrbracket_{\times}) \supseteq \llbracket P \rrbracket$.

Sequential Analyses. Note that the collecting semantics of P, according to the thread-local cartesian abstraction, can be viewed as the collecting semantics of a sequential program P' obtained by adding to P's CFG edges from post-release points $\bar{n}$ to pre-acquire points n in $n \in \mathcal{G}(\bar{n})$, and where a special *mix* operator is used to combine information at the acquire points. Further, note that we abstract the environment of buffers and their corresponding release location into a single entity, which is the standard over-approximation of the set of environments at a given program location. Hence, the concurrent analysis of P can be reduced to a *sequential analysis* of P', provided a sound over-approximation of the *mix* operator is given.

Soundness of the Value-Set analysis. The analysis in [9] is obtained by abstracting the thread-local cartesian states using the value set abstraction on the environments domain. Note that in the value set domain, where every variable is associated with (an over approximation of) the set of its possible values, the mix operator reduces to a join operator.

Remark 11. We can improve upon the sequential abstraction presented earlier by not forgetting the versions entirely. We augment $\mathcal{A}_{\times}$ with a set S of "recency" information based on the versions as follows:

$$S = \lambda C.\{\bar{t} \mid \exists \sigma \in C, x \in \mathcal{V} : \left(\operatorname*{argmax}_{t \in \mathcal{T}} \sigma\Theta(t)\nu(x) \right) = \bar{t}\}$$

In other words, S soundly approximates the set of threads which contain the most up-to-date value of some variable $x \in \mathcal{V}$. This additional information can now be used to improve the precision of *mix*. We show in the experiments that the abstract domain, when equipped with this set of thread-identifiers, results in a significant gain in precision (primarily because it helps avoid spurious read-write loops between post-release and pre-acquire points, like the one in Fig. 1).

6 Improved Analysis for Region Race Free Programs

In this section we introduce a refined notion of data race freedom, based on *data regions*, and derive from it a more precise abstract analysis capable of transferring *some* relational information between threads at synchronization points.

Essentially, regions are a user defined partitioning of the set of shared variables. We call each partition a *region* r, and denote the set of regions as R and the region of a variable x by $r(x)$. The semantics precisely tracks correlations between variables *within* regions *across* inter-thread communication, while abstracting away the correlations between variables across regions. With suitable abstractions, the tracked correlations can improve the precision of the analysis for programs which conform to the notion of race freedom defined below. We note that [9, 22] do not permit relational analyses.

Region Race Freedom. We define a new notion of race freedom, parameterized on the set of regions R, which we call *region race freedom* (abbreviated as *R-DRF*). *R-DRF* refines the standard notion of data race freedom by ensuring that variables residing in the same region are manipulated atomically across threads.

A *region-level data race* occurs when two concurrent threads access variables from the same region r (not necessarily the same variable), with at least one access being a write, and the accesses are devoid of any ordering constraints.

Definition 12 (Region-level races). *Let P be a program and let R be a region partitioning of P. An execution π of P, in the standard interleaving semantics, has a* region-level race *if there exists $0 \leq i < j < |\pi|$, such that $c(\pi_i)$ and $c(\pi_j)$ both access variables in region $r \in R$, at least one access is a write, and it is not the case that $\pi_i \xrightarrow{hb}_\pi \pi_j$.*

Remark 13. The problem of checking for region races can be reduced to the problem of checking for dataraces as follows. We introduce a fresh variable $\mathtt{X}_r$ for each region $r \in R$. We now transform the input program P to a program P' with the following addition: We precede every assignment statement $\mathtt{x} := \mathtt{e}$, where r_w is the region which is written to, and $r_1, \ldots, r_n$ are the regions read, with a sequence of instructions $\mathtt{X}_{r_w} := \mathtt{X}_{r_1}; \ldots \mathtt{X}_{r_w} := \mathtt{X}_{r_n};$. Statements of the form $\mathtt{assume}(b)$ do not need to be changed because b may refer only to thread-private variables. Note that these modifications do not alter the semantics of the original program (for each trace of P there is a corresponding trace in P', and vice versa). We now check for data races on the variables $\mathtt{X}_r$'s.

The *R-DRF* Semantics. The *R-DRF* semantics is obtained via a simple change to the *L-DRF* semantics, a write-access to a variable x leads to incrementing the version of every variable that resides in x's region:

$$[\![x := e]\!] : VE \to \wp(VE) = \lambda \langle \phi, \nu \rangle . \{ \langle \phi[x \mapsto v], \nu[y \mapsto \nu(y) + 1 \mid r(x) = r(y)] \rangle \mid v \in [\![e]\!]\phi \}$$

It is easy to see that Theorems 7 and 8 hold if we consider the *R-DRF* semantics instead of the *L-DRF* semantics, provided the program is region race free with respect to the given region specification. Hence, we can analyze such programs using abstractions of *R-DRF* and obtain sound results with respect to the standard interleaving semantics (Sect. 3).

Thread-Local Abstractions of the *R-DRF* Semantics. The cartesian abstractions defined in Sect. 5 can be extended to accommodate regions in a natural way. The only difference lies in the definition of the *mix* operation, which now operates over *regions*, rather than variables:

$$mix : \wp(Env) \to \wp(Env) \stackrel{\text{def}}{=} \lambda B_{\times}.\{\phi' \mid \forall r \in R, \exists \phi \in B_{\times} : \forall x \in \mathcal{V}.\, r(x) = r \implies \phi'(x) = \phi(x)\}$$

where the function *rg* maps a variable to its region. Mixing environments at the granularity of regions is permitted because the *R-DRF* semantics ensures that all the variables in the same region have the same version. Thus, their most up-to-date values reside in either the thread's local environment or in one of the release buffers. As before, we can obtain an effective analysis using any sequential abstraction, provided that the abstract domain supports the (more precise) region based mix operator.

7 Implementation and Evaluation

RATCOP: Relational Analysis Tool for COncurrent Programs. In this section, we perform a thorough empirical evaluation of our analyses using a prototype analyzer which we have developed, called RATCOP[3], for the analysis of race-free concurrent Java programs. RATCOP comprises around 4000 lines of Java code, and implements a variety of relational analyses based on the theoretical underpinnings described in earlier sections of this paper. Through command line arguments, each analysis can be made to use any one of the following three numerical abstract domains provided by the Apron library [17]: Convex Polyhedra (with support for strict inequalities), Octagons and Intervals. RATCOP also makes use of the Soot [30] analysis framework. The tool reuses the code for fixed point computation and the graph data structures in the implementation of [9].

The tool takes as input a Java program with assertions marked at appropriate program points. We first checked all the programs in our benchmarks for dataraces and region races using Chord [27]. For detecting region races, we have implemented the translation scheme outlined in Remark 11 in Sect. 6. RATCOP

[3] The project artifacts are available at https://bitbucket.org/suvam/ratcop.

then performs the necessary static analysis on the program until a fixpoint is reached. Subsequently, the tool automatically tries to prove the assertions using the inferred facts (which translates to checking whether the inferred fact at a program point implies the assertion condition): if it fails to prove an assertion, it dumps the corresponding inferred fact in a log file for manual inspection.

As benchmarks, we use a subset of concurrent programs from the SV-COMP 2015 suite [2]. We ported the programs to Java and introduced locks appropriately to remove races. We also use a program from [23]. While these programs are not too large, they have challenging invariants to prove, and provide a good test for the precision of the various analyses. We ran the tool in a virtual machine with 16GB RAM and 4 cores. The virtual machine, in turn, ran on a machine with 32GB RAM and a quad-core Intel i7 processor. We evaluate 5 analyses on the benchmarks, with the following abstract domains: (i) **A1:** Without regions and thread identifiers[4]. (ii) **A2:** With regions, but with no thread identifiers. (iii) **A3:** Without regions, but with thread identifiers. (iv) **A4:** With regions and thread identifiers. The analyses **A1:** - **A4:** all employ the Octagon numerical abstract domain. And finally, (v) **A5:** The value-set analysis of [9], which uses the Interval domain. In terms of the precision of the abstract domains, the analyses form the following partial order: **A5** $\prec$ **A1** $\prec$ **A3** $\prec$ **A4** and **A5** $\prec$ **A1** $\prec$ **A2** $\prec$ **A4**. We use **A5** as the baseline.

Porting Sequential Analyses to Concurrent Analyses. For the sequential commands, we perform a lightweight parsing of statements and simply re-use the built-in transformers of Apron. The only operator we need to define afresh is the abstract *mix*. Since Apron exposes functions to perform each of the constituent steps, implementing the abstract *mix* is straight forward as well.

Precision and Efficiency. Figure 2 summarizes the results of the experiments (Table 2). While all the analyses failed to prove the assertions in `reorder_2`, **A2** and **A4** were able to prove them when they used convex polyhedra instead of octagons. Since none of the analyses track arrays precisely, all of them failed to prove the original assertion in `sigma` (which involves checking a property involving the sum of the array elements). However, **A3** and **A4** correctly detect a potential array out-of-bounds violation in the program. The improved precision is due to the fact that **A3** and **A4** track thread identifiers in the abstract state, which avoids spurious read-write cycles in the analysis of `sigma`. The program `twostage_3` has an actual bug, and the assertions are expected to fail. This program provides a "sanity check" of the soundness of the analyses. Programs marked with * contain assertions which we have altered completely and/or weakened. In these cases, the original assertion was either expected to fail or was too precise (possibly requiring a disjunctive domain in order to prove it). In `qw2004`, for example, we prove assertions of the form $x = y$. **A2** and **A4** perform well in this case, since we can specify a region containing x and y, which precisely

[4] By thread-identifiers we are referring to the abstraction of the versions outlined in Remark 11.

Table 2. Summary of the experiments. Superscript ^{B} indicates that the program has an actual bug. (C) indicates the use of Convex Polyhedra as abstract data domain. * indicates a program where we have altered/weakened the original assertion.

Program	LOC	Threads	Asserts	A1		A2		A3		A4		A5	
				✓	Time (ms)	✓	Time (ms)	✓	Time (ms)	✓	Time (ms)	✓	Time (ms)
reorder_2	106	5	2	0(C)	77	2(C)	43	0(C)	71	2(C)	37	0	25
sigma^{B}*	118	5	5	0	132	0	138	4	48	4	50	0	506
sssc12	98	3	4	4	6	4	90	4	82	4	86	2	28
unverif	82	3	2	0	115	0	121	0	84	0	86	0	46
spin2003	65	3	2	2	6	2	9	2	10	2	10	2	8
simpleLoop	74	3	2	2	56	2	61	2	57	2	64	0	27
simpleLoop5	84	4	1	0	40	0	50	0	31	0	37	0	20
doubleLock_p3	64	3	1	1	11	1	24	1	16	1	19	1	9
fib_Bench	82	3	2	0	138	0	118	0	129	0	102	0	56
fib_Bench_Longer	82	3	2	0	95	0	103	0	123	0	91	0	35
indexer	119	2	2	2	1522	2	1637	2	1750	2	1733	2	719
twostage_3^{B}	93	2	2	0	61	0	48	0	57	0	28	0	59
singleton_with_uninit	59	2	1	1	31	1	29	1	14	1	10	1	28
stack	85	2	2	0	151	0	175	0	127	0	129	0	71
stack_longer	85	1	2	0	1163	0	669	0	1082	0	1186	0	597
stack_longest	85	2	2	0	1732	0	1679	0	1873	0	2068	0	920
sync01 *	65	2	2	2	7	2	25	2	37	2	33	2	10
qw2004 *	90	2	4	0	1401	4	1890	0	1478	4	1913	0	698
[23] Fig. 3.11	89	2	2	0	49	2	46	0	54	2	36	0	19
Total	1625	3 (Avg)	42	14	361 (Avg)	22	366 (Avg)	18	374 (Avg)	26	406 (Avg)	10	204 (Avg)

track their correlation across threads. The imprecision in the remaining cases are mostly due to the program requiring *disjunctive* domains to discharge the assertions, or the presence of spurious write-write cycles which weakens the inferred facts.

Of the total 40 "valid" assertions (excluding the two in `twostage_3`), **A4** is the most precise, being able to prove 65% of them. It is followed by **A2** (55%), **A3** (45%), **A1** (35%) and, lastly, **A5** (25%). Thus, the new analyses derived from *L-DRF* and *R-DRF* perform significantly better than the value-set analysis of [9]. Moreover, this total order respects the partial ordering between the analyses defined earlier.

With respect to the running times, the maximum time taken, across all the programs, is around 2 s, by **A4**. **A5** turns out to be the fastest in general, due to its lightweight abstract domain. **A2** and **A4** are typically slower that **A1** and **A3** respectively. The slowdown can be attributed to the additional tracking of regions by the former analyses.

Comparing with a current abstract interpretation based tool. We also compared the efficiency of RATCOP with that of Batman, a tool implementing the previous state-of-the-art analyses based on abstract interpretation [24,25] (a discussion on the precision of our analyses against those in [24] is presented in Sect. 8).

The basic structure of the benchmark programs for this experiment is as follows: each program defines a set of shared variables. A `main` thread then partitions the set of shared variables, and creates threads which access and modify variables in a unique partition. Thus, the set of memory locations accessed by any two threads is disjoint. In our experiments, each thread simply performed a sequence of writes to a specific set of shared variables. In some sense, these programs represent a "best-case" scenario because there are no interferences between threads. Unlike RATCOP, the Batman tool, in its current form, only supports a small toy language and does not provide the means to automatically check assertions. Thus, for the purposes of this experiment, we only compare the time required to reach a fixpoint in the two tools. We compare **A3** against Batman running with the Octagon domain and the BddApron library [16] (Bm-oct).

#Threads	A3 Time (ms)	Bm-oct Time (ms)
2	61	7706
3	86	82545
4	138	507663
5	194	2906585
6	261	13095977
7	368	53239574

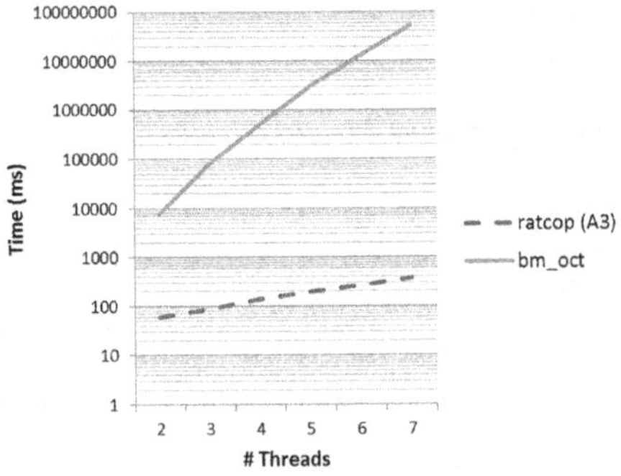

Fig. 3. Running times of RATCOP (**A3**) and Batman (Bm-oct) on loosely coupled threads. The number of shared variables is fixed at 6. The graph on the right shows the running times on a log scale.

The running times of the two analyses are given in Fig. 3. In the benchmarks, with increasing number of threads, RATCOP was upto 5 orders of magnitude faster than Bm-oct. The rate of increase in running time was almost linear for RATCOP, while it was almost exponential for Bm-oct. Unlike RATCOP, the analyses in [24,25] compute sound facts at *every* program point, which contributes to the slowdown.

8 Related Work and Discussion

In this paper, we presented a framework for developing data-flow analyses for data race free shared-memory concurrent programs, with a statically fixed number of threads, and with variables having primitive data types. There is a rich literature on concurrent dataflow analyses and [28] provides a detailed survey of some of them. We compare some of the relevant ones in this section. [5] automatically lifts a given sequential analysis to a sound analysis for concurrent programs, using a datarace detector. Here, data-flow facts are not communicated across threads, and this can lose a lot of precision. The work in [4,22] allows a greater degree of inter-thread communication. However, unlike our semantics, they are unable to infer relational properties between variables. The methods described in [9,10,15] present concurrent dataflow algorithms by building specialized concurrent flow graphs. However, the class of analyses they address are restricted – [10] handles properties expressible as Quantified Regular Expressions, [15] handles reaching definitions, while [9] only handles value-set analyses.

In [24], an abstract interpretation formulation of the rely-guarantee proof technique [18,31] is presented in the form of a precise semantics. The semantics in [24] involves a nested fixed-point computation, compared to our single fixed-point formulation. The analysis aims to be sound at *all* program points (e.g., in Fig. 1 the value of y at line 9 in t_2), due to which many more interferences will have to be propagated than we do, leading to a less efficient analysis. Moreover, for certain programs, our abstract analyses are more precise. Figure 4 shows a program which is race free, even though the conflicting accesses to x in lines 2 and 12 are not protected by a common lock. The "lock invariants" in [24] would consider these accesses as potentially racy, and would allow the read at line 12 to observe the write at line 2, thereby being unable to prove the assertion. However, our analyses would ensure that the read only observes the write at line 11, and is able to prove the assertion. [13] presents an operational semantics for concurrent programs, parameterized by a relation. It makes additional assumptions about code regions which are unsynchronized (allowing only read-only shared variables and local variables in such regions). Moreover, it too computes sound facts at every point, resulting in less efficient abstractions.

A traditional approach to analyzing concurrent programs involves *resource invariants* associated with every lock (e.g. [14]). This approach depends on a *locking policy* where a thread only accesses global data if it holds a protecting lock. In contrast, our approach does not require a particular locking policy (e.g., see Fig. 4), and is based on a parameterized notion of data-race-freedom, which allows to encode locking policies as a particular case. Thus, our new semantics provides greater flexibility to analysis writers, at the cost of assuming data-race-freedom.

Our notion of region races is inspired by the notion of high-level data races [1]. The concept of splitting the state space into regions was earlier used in [21], which

```
1  acquire(m)
2  x := 1
3  y := 1
4  release(m)
```

(a) Thread 1

```
6  while p ≠ 1 do {
7     acquire(m)
8     p := y
9     release(m)
10 }
11 x := 2
12 p := x
13 assert (p ≠ 1)
```

(b) Thread 2

Fig. 4. Example demonstrating that a program can be DRF, even when a read from a global variable is not directly guarded by any lock.

used these regions to perform shape analysis for concurrent programs. However, that algorithm still performs a full interleaving analysis which results in poor scalability. The notion of variable packing [3] is similar to our notion of data regions. However, variable packs constitute a purely *syntactic* grouping of variables, while regions are semantic in nature. A syntactic block may not access all variables in a semantic region, which would result in a region partitioning more refined than what the programmer has in mind, which would result in decreased precision. In contrast to our approach, the techniques in [11,12] provide an approach to verifying properties of concurrent programs using *data flow* graphs, rather than use control flow graphs like we do.

As future work, we would like to evaluate the performance of our tool when equipped with disjunctive relational domains. In this paper, we do not consider dynamically allocated memory, and extending the *L-DRF* semantics to account for the heap memory is interesting future work. Abstractions of such a semantics could potentially yield efficient shape analyses for race free concurrent programs.

Acknowledgments. We would like to thank the anonymous reviewers for their insightful and helpful comments. This research was supported by the European Research Council under the European Union's Seventh Framework Programme (FP7/2007-2013)/ERC grant agreement n° [321174], by Len Blavatnik and the Blavatnik Family foundation, and by the Blavatnik Interdisciplinary Cyber Research Center, Tel Aviv University.

References

1. Artho, C., Havelund, K., Biere, A.: High-level data races. In: New Technologies for Information Systems, Proceedings of the 3rd International Workshop on New Developments in Digital Libraries, NDDL 2003, pp. 82–93 (2003)
2. Beyer, D.: Software verification and verifiable witnesses. In: Baier, C., Tinelli, C. (eds.) TACAS 2015. LNCS, vol. 9035, pp. 401–416. Springer, Heidelberg (2015). doi:10.1007/978-3-662-46681-0_31
3. Blanchet, B., Cousot, P., Cousot, R., Feret, J., Mauborgne, L., Miné, A., Monniaux, D., Rival, X.: A static analyzer for large safety-critical software. CoRR, abs/cs/0701193 (2007)
4. Carre, J.-L., Hymans, C.: From single-thread to multithreaded: an efficient static analysis algorithm. CoRR, abs/0910.5833 (2009)
5. Chugh, R., Voung, J.W., Jhala, R., Lerner, A.: Dataflow analysis for concurrent programs using datarace detection. In: Proceedings of the ACM SIGPLAN 2008 Conference on Programming Language Design and Implementation, Tucson, AZ, USA, 7–13 June 2008, pp. 316–326 (2008)
6. Cousot, P., Cousot, R.: Static determination of dynamic properties of programs. In: Proceedings of the 2nd International Symposium on Programming, Paris, France. Dunod (1976)
7. Cousot, P., Cousot, R.: Abstract interpretation: a unified lattice model for static analysis of programs by construction or approximation of fixpoints. In: Proceedings of the 4th ACM SIGACT-SIGPLAN Symposium on Principles of Programming Languages, pp. 238–252. ACM (1977)

8. Cousot, P., Halbwachs, N.: Automatic discovery of linear restraints among variables of a program. In: Proceedings of the 5th ACM SIGACT-SIGPLAN symposium on Principles of Programming Languages, pp. 84–96. ACM (1978)
9. De, A., D'Souza, D., Nasre, R.: Dataflow analysis for datarace-free programs. In: Barthe, G. (ed.) ESOP 2011. LNCS, vol. 6602, pp. 196–215. Springer, Heidelberg (2011). doi:10.1007/978-3-642-19718-5_11
10. Dwyer, M.B., Clarke, L.A.: Data flow analysis for verifying properties of concurrent programs. In: Proceedings of the Second ACM SIGSOFT Symposium on Foundations of Software Engineering, SIGSOFT 1994, New Orleans, Louisiana, USA, 6–9 December 1994, pp. 62–75 (1994)
11. Farzan, A., Kincaid, Z.: Verification of parameterized concurrent programs by modular reasoning about data and control. In: Proceedings of the 39th ACM SIGPLAN-SIGACT Symposium on Principles of Programming Languages, pp. 297–308 (2012)
12. Farzan, A., Kincaid, Z., Podelski, A.: Inductive data flow graphs. In: The 40th Annual ACM SIGPLAN-SIGACT Symposium on Principles of Programming Languages, pp. 129–142 (2013)
13. Ferreira, R., Feng, X., Shao, Z.: Parameterized memory models and concurrent separation logic. In: Gordon, A.D. (ed.) ESOP 2010. LNCS, vol. 6012, pp. 267–286. Springer, Heidelberg (2010). doi:10.1007/978-3-642-11957-6_15
14. Gotsman, A., Berdine, J., Cook, B., Sagiv, M.: Thread-modular shape analysis. In: Proceedings of the ACM SIGPLAN 2007 Conference on Programming Language Design and Implementation, pp. 266–277 (2007)
15. Grunwald, D., Srinivasan, H.: Data flow equations for explicitly parallel programs. In: Proceedings of the Fourth ACM SIGPLAN Symposium on Principles & Practice of Parallel Programming (PPOPP), pp. 159–168 (1993)
16. Jeannet, B.: Some experience on the software engineering of abstract interpretation tools. Electron. Notes Theor. Comput. Sci. **267**(2), 29–42 (2010)
17. Jeannet, B., Miné, A.: APRON: a library of numerical abstract domains for static analysis. In: Bouajjani, A., Maler, O. (eds.) CAV 2009. LNCS, vol. 5643, pp. 661–667. Springer, Heidelberg (2009). doi:10.1007/978-3-642-02658-4_52
18. Jones, C.B.: Developing methods for computer programs including a notion of interference. Ph.D. thesis, University of Oxford, UK (1981)
19. Lamport, L.: Time, clocks, and the ordering of events in a distributed system. Commun. ACM **21**, 558–565 (1978)
20. Lamport, L.: How to make a multiprocessor computer that correctly executes multiprocess progranm. IEEE Trans. Comput. **9**, 690–691 (1979)
21. Manevich, R., Lev-Ami, T., Sagiv, M., Ramalingam, G., Berdine, J.: Heap decomposition for concurrent shape analysis. In: Alpuente, M., Vidal, G. (eds.) SAS 2008. LNCS, vol. 5079, pp. 363–377. Springer, Heidelberg (2008). doi:10.1007/978-3-540-69166-2_24
22. Miné, A.: Static analysis of run-time errors in embedded real-time parallel C programs. Log. Methods Comput. Sci. **8**(1), 1–63 (2012)
23. Miné, A.: Static analysis by abstract interpretation of concurrent programs. Ph.D. thesis, Ecole Normale Supérieure de Paris-ENS Paris (2013)
24. Miné, A.: Relational thread-modular static value analysis by abstract interpretation. In: McMillan, K.L., Rival, X. (eds.) VMCAI 2014. LNCS, vol. 8318, pp. 39–58. Springer, Heidelberg (2014). doi:10.1007/978-3-642-54013-4_3
25. Monat, R., Miné, A.: Precise thread-modular abstract interpretation of concurrent programs using relational interference abstractions. In: Bouajjani, A., Monniaux, D. (eds.) VMCAI 2017. LNCS, vol. 10145, pp. 386–404. Springer, Cham (2017). doi:10.1007/978-3-319-52234-0_21

26. Mukherjee, S., Padon, O., Shoham, S., D'Souza, D., Rinetzky, N.: Thread-local semantics and its efficient sequential abstractions for race-free programs. http://www.csa.iisc.ernet.in/TR/2016/3/sasTechReport.pdf
27. Naik, M.: Chord: a program analysis platform for Java. http://www.cis.upenn.edu/~mhnaik/chord.html. Accessed 27 Mar 2017
28. Rinard, M.: Analysis of multithreaded programs. In: Cousot, P. (ed.) SAS 2001. LNCS, vol. 2126, pp. 1–19. Springer, Heidelberg (2001). doi:10.1007/3-540-47764-0_1
29. Savage, S., Burrows, M., Nelson, G., Sobalvarro, P., Anderson, T.E.: Eraser: a dynamic data race detector for multi-threaded programs. In: Proceedings of the Sixteenth ACM Symposium on Operating System Principles, SOSP, pp. 27–37 (1997)
30. Vallée-Rai, R., Co, P., Gagnon, E., Hendren, L., Lam, P., Sundaresan, V.: Soot-a Java bytecode optimization framework. In: Proceedings of the 1999 conference of the Centre for Advanced Studies on Collaborative research, p. 13. IBM Press (1999)
31. Qiwen, X., de Roever, W.-P., He, J.: The rely-guarantee method for verifying shared variable concurrent programs. Form. Asp. Comput. **9**, 149–174 (1997)

Quantitative Static Analysis of Communication Protocols Using Abstract Markov Chains

Abdelraouf Ouadjaout(✉) and Antoine Miné

Sorbonne Universités, UPMC, LIP6, Paris, France
{abdelraouf.ouadjaout,antoine.mine}@lip6.fr

Abstract. In this paper we present a static analysis of communication protocols for inferring parametric bounds of performance metrics. Our analysis is formalized within the theory of abstract interpretation and soundly takes all possible executions into account. We model the concrete executions as Markov chains and we introduce a novel notion of *Abstract Markov Chains* that provides a finite and symbolic representation to over-approximate the (possibly unbounded) set of concrete behaviors. Our analysis operates in two steps. The first step is a classic abstract interpretation of the source code, using stock numerical abstract domains and a specific automata domain, in order to extract the abstract Markov chain of the program. The second step extracts from this chain particular invariants about the stationary distribution and computes its symbolic bounds using a parametric Fourier-Motzkin elimination algorithm. We present a prototype implementation of the analysis and we discuss some preliminary experiments on a number of communication protocols.

1 Introduction

The analysis of probabilistic programs represents a challenging problem. The difficulty comes from the fact that execution traces are characterized by probability distributions that are affected by the behavior of the program, resulting in very complex forms of stochastic processes. In addition, in such particular context, programmers are interested in quantitative properties not supported by conventional semantics analysis, such as the inference of expected values of performance metrics or the probability of reaching bug states. In this work, we focus on the analysis of communication protocols and we aim at assessing their performance formally.

Stationary Distribution. Generally, the quantification of performance metrics for such systems is based on computing the stationary distribution of the associated random process. It gives the proportion of time spent in every reachable state of the system by considering all possible executions. This information is fundamental to compute the expected value of most common performance metrics. For instance, the throughput represents the average number of transmitted

This work is partially supported by the European Research Council under Consolidator Grant Agreement 681393 – MOPSA.

F. Ranzato (Ed.): SAS 2017, LNCS 10422, pp. 277–298, 2017.
DOI: 10.1007/978-3-319-66706-5_14

```
int n = 0, a = 0;
while(1) {
  data = sense();
  //Uniform backoff
  sleep(uniform(1, B));
  //Transmission with ack
  if (unicast(data)) a++;
  n++;
  //Save energy
  sleep(S);
}
```

(a)

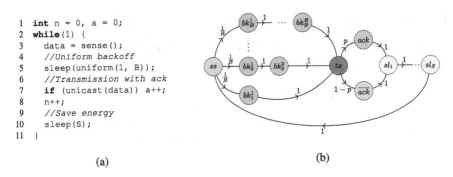

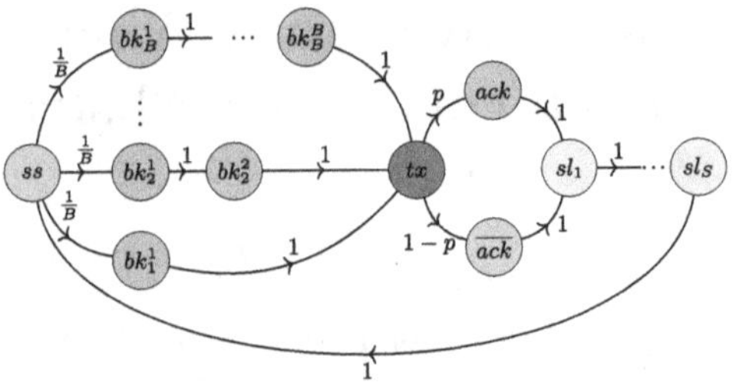

(b)

Fig. 1. (a) Backoff-based transmission. (b) Associated discrete time Markov chain.

packets per time unit. By identifying the program locations where packets are transmitted and by computing the value of the stationary distribution at these locations, we obtain therefore the proportion of packets sent in one time unit. Similarly, many other metrics are based on this distribution, such as the duty cycle (proportion of time where the transceiver is activated) or the goodput (the proportion of successfully transmitted data).

To our knowledge, no existing approach can obtain such information (*i*) *automatically* by analyzing the source code, (*ii*) *soundly* by considering all executions in possibly infinite systems and (*iii*) *symbolically* by expressing the distribution in terms of the protocol parameters. Indeed, while most proposed solutions focus on computing probabilities of program assertions [4,26] or expectation invariants [1,5], only PRISM [16], thanks to its extension PARAM [14], can compute stationary distributions of parametric Markov chains, but is limited to finite state systems with parametric transition probabilities only, while we also support systems where the number of states is a (possibly unbounded) parameter.

Example 1. We illustrate our motivation with a simple wireless protocol shown in Fig. 1(a). This example illustrates a basic embedded application in which a set of sensing devices transmit periodically their readings to a remote central station. To derive the goodput Γ of a sensor, we model the protocol as a discrete time Markov chain as shown in Fig. 1(b). The program begins by acquiring the sensor measurements by calling the function `sense`. This operation corresponds to the state ss in which the chain remains one time tick. To avoid collisions when sending the data, a random backoff is performed using a uniform distribution on the range $[1, B]$, where B is a parameter of the protocol. This is modeled as a fork from state ss to B backoff levels. Each transition is labeled with probability $\frac{1}{B}$ and the chain remains i ticks at level i. An important random aspect of the system is the lossy nature of the wireless links, which is modeled as a Bernoulli distribution with parameter p. This means that at each call of the function `unicast` at state tx, the packet is transmitted and acknowledged with probability p, or lost with probability $1-p$. Finally, before transmitting the next reading, the program executes the `sleep` statement to save energy for a duration determined by parameter S, which is modeled with the transitions $sl_1 \xrightarrow{1} \ldots \xrightarrow{1} sl_S$.

The goodput Γ of the protocol is the proportion of time spent in state *ack*, which can be obtained by computing the stationary distribution $\boldsymbol{\pi}$ of the chain. To do so, we first construct the stochastic matrix P where its entries correspond to the probabilities of the chain's transitions. After that, we compute the vector $\boldsymbol{\pi}$ as the eigenvector of the stochastic matrix P associated to the eigenvalue 1. Since the structure and the size of the matrix depend on the parameters B and S, existing solutions can not derive automatically the stationary distribution symbolically in terms of B, S and p. □

Contributions. We propose a solution for this problem based on two main contributions:

1. First, we introduce a novel notion of *Abstract Markov Chains* that approximates a family of discrete time Markov chains. These abstract chains are inferred automatically by analyzing the source code of the program. Thanks to a novel widening algorithm, these chains are guaranteed to have a finite size while covering all possible probabilistic traces of the program.
2. Our second contribution is a result for extracting *distribution invariants* from an abstract Markov chain in the form of a system of parametric linear inequalities for bounding the concrete stationary distribution. Using a parametric-version of the Fourier-Motzkin elimination algorithm, we can infer symbolic and guaranteed bounds of the property of interest.

Example 2. By applying our analysis on the previous example, we can infer that:

$$\frac{B^2(p-1) - B(p-3) + 2(p-1)}{3B^2 + 2BS + B + 4} \leq \Gamma \leq \frac{(B^2 - B + 2)\,p}{3B^2 + 2BS + B + 4} \tag{1}$$

System designers can use this invariant to find appropriate parameter values that ensure certain performance constraints. For instance, assume that we know that the deployment zone is characterized by a link quality varying in $[0.7, 0.9]$ and we want to figure out which parameter configuration guarantees that Γ always fit within $[1, 5]$ packets/s (with the assumption that a time tick is 1ms). Using (1), we can show that the instance $\langle B \mapsto 4, S \mapsto 308\rangle$ produces a chain that always verifies these constraints. □

Limitations. Our approach is still in a preliminary development phase and presents some limitations. The analysis supports only discrete probability distributions, such as Bernoulli and discrete uniform distributions. Secondly, we limit the description herein to a simple C-like language and we do not support yet the analysis of real-world implementations. Finally, we do not consider pure non-deterministic statements.

Outline. The remaining of the paper is organized as follows. We present in Sect. 2 the concrete semantics of the analysis. Section 3 introduces the domain of Abstract Markov Chains and we detail in Sect. 4 the method to extract the stationary distribution invariants from an abstract chain and how we can infer symbolic bounds of the property of interest. The results of the preliminary experiments are presented in Sect. 5. We discuss the related work in Sect. 6 and we conclude the paper in Sect. 7.

2 Concrete Semantics

We consider communication protocols that can be represented as (possibly infinite) discrete time Markov chains, since it is one of the most widespread stochastic models for performance evaluation used by the networking community. For describing these protocols, we use a simplified probabilistic language having the following C-like syntax:

$$
\begin{array}{rll}
\mathit{Stmt} ::= & x = e; & \llparenthesis x \in \mathcal{V}, e \in \mathit{Exp} \rrparenthesis \\
| & \texttt{if}(e \bowtie 0)\{s_1\}\{s_2\} & \llparenthesis s_1, s_2 \in \mathit{Stmt}, \bowtie \in \{=, \neq, \leq, <, \geq, >\} \rrparenthesis \\
| & \texttt{while}(e \bowtie 0)\{s\} & \\
| & x = \texttt{uniform}_l(e_1, e_2) & \llparenthesis e_1, e_2 \in \mathit{Exp}, l \in \mathcal{L} \rrparenthesis \\
| & x = \texttt{bernoulli}_l() & \\
| & \texttt{ticks}_l(e) &
\end{array}
$$

where $\mathcal{V}$ is the set of program variables, $\mathcal{L}$ is the set of program locations and Exp is the set of (non-probabilistic) numeric expressions the syntax of which is classic and omitted here. In addition to the common statements of assignments, `if` conditionals and `while` loops, we consider the following additional markovian statements. The function $\texttt{uniform}_l(e_1, e_2)$ draws a random integer value from a discrete uniform distribution over the interval $[e_1, e_2]$, while the function $\texttt{bernoulli}_l()$ returns a boolean value according to a Bernoulli distribution with parameter p_l. Finally, the function $\texttt{ticks}_l(e)$ models the fact that the program will spend e ticks in the current control location, which results in triggering a transition in the Markov chain of the program. Each of these functions is annotated with the call site location l. Using these primitive functions, we can define any markovian behavior. Since we are interested in communication protocols, we defined a number of auxiliary functions based on these primitives, such as the functions `unicast()` and `sleep()` presented previously.

2.1 Markovian Traces

We develop a particular stochastic semantics that is isomorphic to a discrete time Markov chain. At the bottom level of this semantics, we have the notion of random events Ξ representing the outcomes of the probability distributions generated during program execution. We can distinguish between two types of random events. The events b_l and $\overline{b}_l$ denote the two outcomes of a statement $\texttt{bernoulli}_l()$. Also, the outcomes of the statement $\texttt{uniform}_l(e_1, e_2)$ are given by the set $\{u_l^{i,a,b} \mid i \in [a, b]\}$, where a and b are the evaluation in the current execution environment of e_1 and e_2 respectively.

Naively, we can consider a Markov chain as a classic automaton over the alphabet Ξ recognizing the probabilistic traces of the program as sequences of random events. However, Markov chains are not just a set of probabilistic traces, but embed a notion of time that is fundamental. Indeed, transitions in a Markov chain occur solely when at least one time tick has elapsed, since a state of the chain can not have a null sojourn time. As we consider that only the `ticks`(e) statement advances time, some of the program transitions become non-observable at the time scale of the chain. This leads to a *two-level trace semantics* making the distinction between observable and non-observable transitions, which has been introduced by Radhia Cousot in her thesis [9, Sect. 2.5.4]. We give here a definition of these two types of traces adapted to our settings:

Definition 1 (Scenarios). *A sequence of non-observable transitions is called a scenario and is defined as $\omega \in \Omega \triangleq \Xi^*$ expressing sequences of random events that occur between two observable states. In the sequel, we denote by ε the empty scenario word.*

Definition 2 (Markovian traces). *The observable markovian traces are the set $\mathcal{T}_\Sigma^\Omega \triangleq \{\sigma_0 \xrightarrow{\omega_1} \sigma_1 \xrightarrow{\omega_2} \cdots \mid \sigma_i \in \Sigma \wedge \omega_i \in \Omega\}$ of transitions among observable states labeled with scenarios. An observable state is a tuple $(l, \rho, \nu) \in \Sigma \triangleq \mathcal{L} \times \mathcal{E} \times \mathbb{N}$ where (i) $l \in \mathcal{L}$ is a program location, (ii) $\rho \in \mathcal{E} \triangleq \mathcal{V} \to \mathbb{Z}$ is a program environment and (iii) $\nu \in \mathbb{N}$ is a sojourn time representing the number of ticks spent in that state.*

This notion of markovian traces is a set-based representation of Markov chains that fits well within the framework of abstract interpretation. It allows a fluent extension of the classical trace semantics for supporting the particular stochastic and temporal features of discrete time Markov chains. In the following paragraph, we define this semantics domain and we present the most important transfer functions.

2.2 Semantics Domain

The concrete semantics domain of our analysis is defined as $\mathcal{D} \triangleq \wp(\mathcal{T}_\Sigma^\Omega \times \mathcal{E} \times \Omega)$. An element $(\tau, \rho, \omega) \in \mathcal{T}_\Sigma^\Omega \times \mathcal{E} \times \Omega$ encodes the set of traces reaching a given program location and is composed of three parts: (i) the observable trace $\tau \in \mathcal{T}_\Sigma^\Omega$ containing the past markovian transitions before the current time tick, (ii) the current memory environment $\rho \in \mathcal{E}$, and (iii) the partial scenario $\omega \in \Omega$ of non-observable random events that occurred between the last tick and the current execution moment.

To obtain the set of all traces of a program P, we proceed by induction on its abstract syntax tree using a set of concrete transfer functions $\mathbf{S}[\![.]\!] \in \mathcal{D} \to \mathcal{D}$. We give in Fig. 2 a summary of these functions. We assume given (in a standard way) the function $\mathbf{E}[\![e]\!] \in \wp(\mathcal{E}) \to \wp(\mathcal{E})$ that provides the possible evaluations

$$\begin{array}{ll}
\mathbf{S}[\![x = e]\!]R & = \{(\tau, \rho[x \mapsto v], \omega) \mid (\tau, \rho, \omega) \in R \wedge v \in \mathbf{E}[\![e]\!]\{\rho\}\} \\
\mathbf{S}[\![\mathtt{if}(e \bowtie 0)\{s_1\}\{s_2\}]\!]R & = (\mathbf{S}[\![s_1]\!] \circ \mathbf{S}[\![(e \bowtie 0)]\!]R) \cup (\mathbf{S}[\![s_2]\!] \circ \mathbf{S}[\![(e \not\bowtie 0)]\!]R) \\
\mathbf{S}[\![\mathtt{while}(e \bowtie 0)\{s\}]\!]R & = \mathbf{S}[\![(e \not\bowtie 0)]\!](\mathtt{lfp}\,\lambda X.\, R \cup \mathbf{S}[\![s]\!] \circ \mathbf{S}[\![(e \bowtie 0)]\!]X) \\
\mathbf{S}[\![(e \bowtie 0)]\!]R & = \{(\tau, \rho, \omega) \in R \mid \exists v \in \mathbf{E}[\![e]\!]\{\rho\} : v \bowtie 0\} \\
\mathbf{S}[\![\mathtt{ticks}_l(e)]\!]R & = \{(\tau \xrightarrow{\omega} (l, \rho, \nu), \rho, \varepsilon) \mid (\tau, \rho, \omega) \in R \wedge \nu \in \mathbf{E}[\![e]\!]\{\rho\}\} \\
\mathbf{S}[\![x = \mathtt{bernoulli}_l()]\!]R & = \{(\tau, \rho[x \mapsto b], \omega.\xi) \mid (\tau, \rho, \omega) \in R \wedge (b, \xi) \in \{(1, b_l), (0, \overline{b}_l)\}\} \\
\mathbf{S}[\![x = \mathtt{uniform}_l(e_1, e_2)]\!]R & = \{(\tau, \rho[x \mapsto i], \omega.u_l^{i,a,b}) \mid (\tau, \rho, \omega) \in R \wedge a \in \mathbf{E}[\![e_1]\!]\{\rho\} \wedge \\
& \qquad b \in \mathbf{E}[\![e_2]\!]\{\rho\} \wedge i \in [a, b]\}
\end{array}$$

Fig. 2. Concrete transfer functions.

of an expression in a set of environments. Non-probabilistic statements have a standard definition. The assignment statement updates the current memory environment by mapping the left-hand variable to the evaluation of the expression. For the `if` assignment, we filter the current environments depending on the evaluation of the condition, and we analyze each branch independently before merging the results. Also, a loop statement is formalized as a fixpoint on the sequences of body evaluation with a filter to extract the iterations violating the loop condition.

The semantics of the statement $x = \mathtt{bernoulli}_l()$ is to fork the current partial scenarios ω depending on the result of the function. We append the event b_l in the true case, or the event $\overline{b}_l$ in the false case and we update the variable x with the returned value in the current memory environment. For the statement $x = \mathtt{uniform}_l(e_1, e_2)$, we also fork the partial scenarios and update the variable x accordingly, but the difference is that the number of branches depends on the evaluations of e_1 and e_2 in the current memory environment. More precisely, the number of forks corresponds to the number of integer points between the values of e_1 and e_2. Note that, for these two statements, the markovian traces part is not modified since they are tick-less. This is not the case for the $\mathtt{ticks}_l(e)$ statement that appends the markovian traces with a new transition to a state where the sojourn time is equal to the evaluation of the expression e. The label of this new transition is simply the computed partial scenario, which is reset to the empty word ε since we keep track of events traces only between two `ticks` statements.

2.3 Stationary Distribution

After collecting the set $T \subseteq \mathcal{T}_\Sigma^\Omega$ of all possible markovian traces, we want to compute the *stationary distribution* of the associated Markov chain, which reflects the proportion of time spent in every observable state. To do that, we have first to construct a particular transition matrix $\mathbf{P}$, that differs slightly from the classic stochastic matrix of discrete time Markov chains since states in our model embed different values of sojourn time:

$$\mathbf{P}_{(l,\rho,\nu),(l',\rho',\nu')} \triangleq \frac{\nu'}{\nu} \sum_{(l,\rho,\nu) \xrightarrow{\omega} (l',\rho',\nu') \in T} \Pr(\omega) \tag{2}$$

where (l, ρ, ν) and (l', ρ', ν') are two reachable states in the traces T. The function $\Pr \in \Omega \rightarrow [0,1]$ gives the probability of the scenarios and is computed as follows:

$$\begin{cases} \Pr(\varepsilon) \triangleq 1, \Pr(b_l) \triangleq p_l, \Pr(\overline{b}_l) \triangleq 1 - p_l, \Pr(u_l^{i,a,b}) \triangleq \frac{1}{b-a+1} \\ \Pr(\omega\xi) \triangleq \Pr(\omega)\Pr(\xi) \end{cases} \tag{3}$$

Finally, as for the classic matrix, the stationary distribution of the chain represents the eigenvector $\boldsymbol{\pi}$ of $\mathbf{P}$ associated to the eigenvalue 1, which is obtained by solving the system $\boldsymbol{\pi} = \boldsymbol{\pi}\mathbf{P}$ with the additional normalization constraint $\sum_{(l,\rho,\nu)} \boldsymbol{\pi}_{(l,\rho,\nu)} = 1$. Since the size of $\mathbf{P}$ depends on the size of the reachable states space, $\boldsymbol{\pi}$ can not be computed automatically in general. In the following, we propose a computable abstraction of Markov chains to over-approximate the traces T. Afterwards, we show how we can infer guaranteed bounds of $\boldsymbol{\pi}$ using information provided by our abstract chain.

3 Abstract Semantics

In order to analyze a program statically, we need a computable abstraction of the concrete semantics domain $\mathcal{D}$. The basic idea is to first partition the set of observable program states $\mathcal{L} \times \mathcal{E} \times \mathbb{N}$ with respect to the program locations, resulting into the intermediate abstraction $\mathcal{L} \times \wp(\mathcal{E} \times \mathbb{N})$. For each location, the set of associated environments is then abstracted with a stock numerical domain $\mathfrak{E}^\sharp$, by considering the sojourn time as a program variable ν. We obtain the abstract states domain $\Sigma^\sharp \triangleq \mathcal{L} \times \mathfrak{E}^\sharp$. As a consequence of this partitioning, observable states at the same program location will be merged. Therefore, we obtain a special structure in which observable abstract states are connected through possibly multiple scenarios coming from the merged concrete states.

Example 3. We illustrate this fact in Fig. 3(a) depicting a more complex probabilistic modeling of the previous `sense()` function using a bounded geometric

```
void* sense() {
  warmup(); //~ticks(1);
  int count = 0, success = 0;
  do {
    if (check()) //~bernoulli()
      success = 1;
    else
      count++;
  } while (count < 10 && !success);
  if (success)
    return doDetection(); //~ticks(4)
  else
    return doAbsence(); //~ticks(2)
}
```

(a)

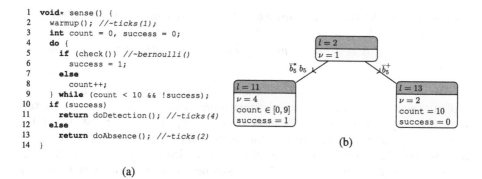

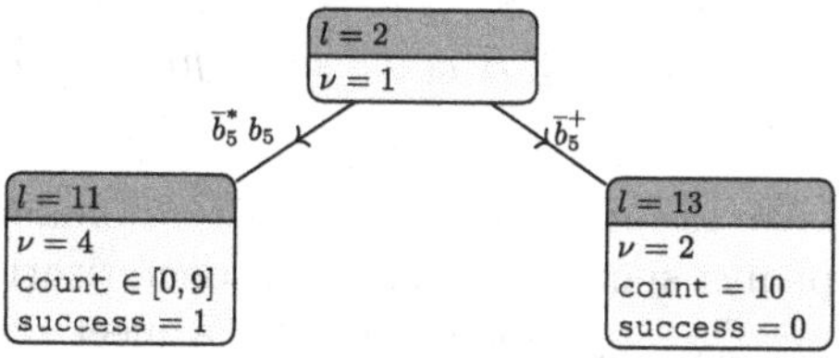

(b)

Fig. 3. (a) A simple probabilistic model for the `sense()` function. (b) An abstraction of observable traces represented as a hierarchical automaton.

distribution that works as follows. We start by warming up the sensing device during one tick. After that, we check whether the sensor detects some external activity (high temperature, sound noise, etc.) and we perform this check for at most 10 times. We assume that these external activities follow a Bernoulli distribution. At the end, we perform some processing during 4 ticks in case of detection and 2 ticks in case of non-detection.

We can see in Fig. 3(b) that between the observable program locations 2 and 11 many scenarios are possible, which are abstracted with the regular expression $\overline{b}_5^* \, b_5$ that encodes the pattern of having a number of Bernoulli failure outcomes at line 5 before a successful one. However, between lines 2 and 13, we can have only a sequence of failures, which is expressed as $\overline{b}_5^+$. □

The presence of these multi-words transitions leads to a *hierarchical automata* structure organized in two levels. On the one hand, one automata structure is used to encode the transitions between observable abstract states. On the other hand, and for each observable transition, another automata structure is used to encode the regular expressions of scenarios connecting the endpoints of the transition. In other words, we abstract markovian traces with an automaton, the transitions of which have also an automata structure representing a set of scenarios. For modularity reasons, we present however a single generic automata domain to represent regular languages over any abstract alphabet. Afterwards, we instantiate two automata-based domains for abstracting events words and markovian traces.

3.1 Abstract Automata

Le Gall et al. proposed a lattice automata domain [17] to represent words over an abstract alphabet having a lattice structure. We extend this domain to support also abstraction at the state level by merging states into abstract states, which is important to approximate markovian traces. To do so, we define a functor domain $\mathscr{A}(\mathfrak{A}^\sharp, \mathfrak{S}^\sharp)$ parameterized by an abstract alphabet domain $\mathfrak{A}^\sharp$ and an abstract state domain $\mathfrak{S}^\sharp$:

Definition 3 (Abstract automata). *An abstract automaton* $A \in \mathscr{A}(\mathfrak{A}^\sharp, \mathfrak{S}^\sharp)$ *is a tuple* $A = (S, s_0^\sharp, F, \Delta)$*, where* $S \subseteq \mathfrak{S}^\sharp$ *is the set of states,* $s_0^\sharp \in S$ *is the initial state,* $F \subseteq S$ *is the set of final states and* $\Delta \subseteq S \times \mathfrak{A}^\sharp \times S$ *is the transition relation.*

We assume that the parameter domain $\mathfrak{A}^\sharp$ is an abstraction of some concrete alphabet symbols $\mathcal{A}$, having a concretization function $\gamma_{\mathfrak{A}} \in \mathfrak{A}^\sharp \to \wp(\mathcal{A})$, a partial order $\sqsubseteq_{\mathfrak{A}}$, a join operator $\sqcup_{\mathfrak{A}}$, a meet operator $\sqcap_{\mathfrak{A}}$, a least element $\bot_{\mathfrak{A}}$ and a widening operator $\triangledown_{\mathfrak{A}}$. The second parameter domain $\mathfrak{S}^\sharp$ is assumed to be an abstraction of some concrete states $\mathcal{S}$ equipped with a concretization function $\gamma_{\mathfrak{S}} \in \mathfrak{S}^\sharp \to \wp(\mathcal{S})$, a partial order $\sqsubseteq_{\mathfrak{S}}$, a join operator $\sqcup_{\mathfrak{S}}$, a least element $\bot_{\mathfrak{S}}$ and a widening operator $\triangledown_{\mathfrak{S}}$.

Let us define some important operators for the $\mathscr{A}$ functor domain. In the following, we denote by $A = (S, s_0^\sharp, F, \Delta)$, $A_1 = (S_1, s_{0_1}^\sharp, F_1, \Delta_1)$ and

$A_2 = (S_2, s^\sharp_{0_2}, F_2, \Delta_2)$ three instances of $\mathscr{A}\left(\mathfrak{A}^\sharp, \mathfrak{S}^\sharp\right)$. We also define the auxiliary functions $\mathbf{L} \in \mathscr{A}\left(\mathfrak{A}^\sharp, \mathfrak{S}^\sharp\right) \to \wp\left(\mathfrak{A}^{\sharp\star}\right)$ and $\mathbf{T} \in \mathscr{A}(\mathfrak{A}^\sharp, \mathfrak{S}^\sharp) \to \wp\left(\mathcal{T}^{\mathfrak{A}^\sharp}_{\mathfrak{S}^\sharp}\right)$ giving respectively the set of accepted abstract words and abstract traces.

Definition 4 (Concretization). *The sets of concrete words and traces abstracted by an abstract automaton A are given by:*

$$\begin{cases} \gamma^{\mathbf{L}}_{\mathscr{A}}(A) = \{a_1 a_2 \cdots \mid \exists a^\sharp_1 a^\sharp_2 \cdots \in \mathbf{L}(A), \forall i : a_i \in \gamma_{\mathfrak{A}}(a^\sharp_i)\} \\ \gamma^{\mathbf{T}}_{\mathscr{A}}(A) = \{s_1 \xrightarrow{a_1} \cdots \mid \exists s^\sharp_1 \xrightarrow{a^\sharp_1} \cdots \in \mathbf{T}(A), \forall i : s_i \in \gamma_{\mathfrak{S}}(s^\sharp_i) \wedge a_i \in \gamma_{\mathfrak{A}}(a^\sharp_i)\} \end{cases} \tag{4}$$

Order. To compare two abstract automata, we define the following simulation relation that extends the classical simulation concept found in transition systems by considering the abstraction in the alphabet and states:

Definition 5 (Simulation relation). *A binary relation $\mathcal{R} \subseteq \mathfrak{S}^\sharp \times \mathfrak{S}^\sharp$ is a simulation between A_1 and A_2 iff $\forall(s^\sharp_1, s^\sharp_2) \in \mathcal{R}$ we have $s^\sharp_1 \sqsubseteq_{\mathfrak{S}} s^\sharp_2$ and:*

$$\forall s^\sharp_1 \xrightarrow{a^\sharp_1} q^\sharp_1 \in \Delta_1, \exists s^\sharp_2 \xrightarrow{a^\sharp_2} q^\sharp_2 \in \Delta_2 : a^\sharp_1 \sqsubseteq_{\mathfrak{A}} a^\sharp_2 \wedge q^\sharp_1 \mathcal{R} q^\sharp_2 \tag{5}$$

We denote $\preccurlyeq$ the smallest simulation relation between A_1 and A_2 verifying $s^\sharp_{0_1} \preccurlyeq s^\sharp_{0_2}$.

Using this notion we define the partial order relation $\sqsubseteq_{\mathscr{A}}$ as:

$$A_1 \sqsubseteq_{\mathscr{A}} A_2 \Leftrightarrow \forall(s^\sharp_1, s^\sharp_2) \in \preccurlyeq : s^\sharp_1 \in F_1 \Rightarrow s^\sharp_2 \in F_2 \tag{6}$$

which means that A_2 should simulate and accept every accepted trace in A_1.

Join. To compute the union of two abstract automata A_1 and A_2, we need to extend the simulation-based traversal in a way to include traces contained in one automaton only, which is formalized with the following concept of *product relation*. The intuition behind it is depicted in Fig. 4 in which we consider transitions decorated with an illustrative regular language over an alphabet $\{b, \overline{b}\}$. In Fig. 4(a), the input transitions $s^\sharp_1 \xrightarrow{b^\star\overline{b}} q^\sharp_1$ and $s^\sharp_2 \xrightarrow{\overline{b}b^\star} q^\sharp_2$ are combined into a single product transition that accepts the merged alphabet symbol $b^\star\overline{b} + \overline{b}b^\star$. While proceeding similarly for all cases preserves the soundness of the operator, we can gain in precision by separating singular transitions as shown in Fig. 4(b).

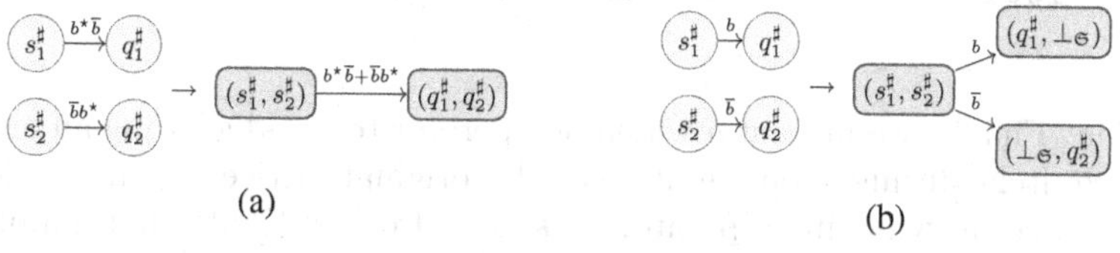

Fig. 4. Cases of construction of a product transition.

In this case, no intersection exists between the transitions $s_1^\sharp \xrightarrow{b} q_1^\sharp$ and $s_2^\sharp \xrightarrow{\overline{b}} q_2^\sharp$. This means that the automata A_1 and A_2 can not perform a simultaneous transition at $s_1^\sharp$ and $s_2^\sharp$, which is expressed as two singular transitions to $(q_1^\sharp, \bot_{\mathfrak{S}})$ and $(\bot_{\mathfrak{S}}, q_2^\sharp)$.

Note that comparing alphabet symbols is not the only means to detect singular transitions. Indeed, in some situations, destination states $q_1^\sharp$ and $q_2^\sharp$ should be kept separated in order for the analysis to preserve some of its precision. To illustrate this point, let us consider the computation of the goodput of a protocol. In order to obtain a precise quantification of this metric, it is necessary to avoid merging states encapsulating different situations of packet transmission status (reception, loss). To do so, we assume that the abstract states domain $\mathfrak{A}^\sharp$ is provided with some equivalence relation $\equiv_{\mathfrak{S}}$ that partitions the states into a finite set of equivalence classes depending on the property of interest. Using this information, we define our product relation as follows:

Definition 6 (Product relation). *A binary relation $\mathcal{R} \subseteq \mathfrak{S} \times \mathfrak{S}$ is a product of A_1 and A_2 iff $\forall (s_1^\sharp, s_2^\sharp) \in \mathcal{R}$ we have $s_1^\sharp \equiv_{\mathfrak{S}} s_2^\sharp$ and:*

$$\begin{cases} q_1^\sharp \mathcal{R} q_2^\sharp \;\; \text{if } \exists s_1^\sharp \xrightarrow{a_1^\sharp} q_1^\sharp \in \Delta_1, \exists s_2^\sharp \xrightarrow{a_2^\sharp} q_2^\sharp \in \Delta_2 : a_1^\sharp \sqcap_{\mathfrak{A}} a_2^\sharp \neq \bot_{\mathfrak{A}} \wedge q_1^\sharp \equiv_{\mathfrak{S}} q_2 \\ q_1^\sharp \mathcal{R} \bot_{\mathfrak{S}} \;\; \text{if } \exists s_1^\sharp \xrightarrow{a_1^\sharp} q_1^\sharp \in \Delta_1, \forall s_2^\sharp \xrightarrow{a_2^\sharp} q_2^\sharp \in \Delta_2 : q_1^\sharp \not\equiv_{\mathfrak{S}} q_2^\sharp \vee a_1^\sharp \sqcap_{\mathfrak{A}} a_2^\sharp = \bot_{\mathfrak{A}} \\ \bot_{\mathfrak{S}} \mathcal{R} q_2^\sharp \;\; \text{if } \exists s_2^\sharp \xrightarrow{a_2^\sharp} q_2^\sharp \in \Delta_2, \forall s_1^\sharp \xrightarrow{a_1^\sharp} q_1^\sharp \in \Delta_1 : q_1^\sharp \not\equiv_{\mathfrak{S}} q_2^\sharp \vee a_1^\sharp \sqcap_{\mathfrak{A}} a_2^\sharp = \bot_{\mathfrak{A}} \end{cases} \tag{7}$$

with the convention that $s^\sharp \equiv_{\mathfrak{S}} \bot_{\mathfrak{S}}, \forall s^\sharp \in \mathfrak{S}^\sharp$. The smallest product relation containing $(s_{0_1}^\sharp, s_{0_2}^\sharp)$ is denoted $\bowtie$.

Consequently, to derive the join automaton A, we simply map product state $s_1^\sharp \bowtie s_2^\sharp$ to $s_1^\sharp \sqcup_{\mathfrak{S}} s_2^\sharp$. The final states are the subset of these images where at least $s_1^\sharp$ or $s_2^\sharp$ is final.

Append. We introduce also the append operator $\odot_\phi \in \mathscr{A}(\mathfrak{A}^\sharp, \mathfrak{S}^\sharp) \times \mathfrak{A}^\sharp \rightarrow \mathscr{A}(\mathfrak{A}^\sharp, \mathfrak{S}^\sharp)$ that extends an abstract automaton with a set of new leave transitions labeled with a given abstract alphabet symbol. From every final state $s_i^\sharp \in F$, a new edge is created to a new final state, computed as the image of $s_i^\sharp$ through the transfer function $\phi \in \mathfrak{S}^\sharp \rightarrow \mathfrak{S}^\sharp$ that annotates the operator $\odot_\phi$. This operator can be formulated as follows:

$$A \odot_\phi a^\sharp \triangleq \texttt{let}\, F' = \{\phi(s^\sharp) \mid s^\sharp \in F\} \,\texttt{in}\, (S \cup F', s_0^\sharp, F', \Delta \cup \{s^\sharp \xrightarrow{a^\sharp} \phi(s^\sharp) \mid s^\sharp \in F\}) \tag{8}$$

Widening. Finally, we present a widening operator to avoid growing an automaton indefinitely during loop iterations. The original lattice automata domain [17] proposed a widening operator, inspired from [11,29], that employs a bisimulation-based minimization to merge similar states by comparing their

Input : Two automata A_1 and A_2
$A = (S, s_0^\sharp, F, \Delta) \leftarrow A_1$;
⟨ Find the increment transitions ⟩
$\delta \leftarrow \texttt{increments}(A, A_2)$;
repeat
  $(s_1^\sharp, s_2^\sharp \xrightarrow{a_3^\sharp} q_2^\sharp) \leftarrow \texttt{head}(\delta)$;
  $q_\equiv^\sharp \leftarrow q_2^\sharp$;
  ⟨ Search in A for better candidates ⟩
  $Q_\equiv \leftarrow \{s^\sharp \in S \mid s^\sharp \equiv_\mathfrak{S} q_2^\sharp\}$;
  if $Q_\equiv \neq \varnothing$ **then**
    $q_\equiv \leftarrow \texttt{head} \circ \texttt{sort}(\mathcal{I}_{q_2^\sharp}^{A,A_2}, Q_\equiv)$;
  end
  $S' \leftarrow S \cup \{q_\equiv^\sharp\}$;
  $F' \leftarrow F \cup (q_\equiv^\sharp \in F_2)?\{q_\equiv^\sharp\} : \varnothing$;
  $\Delta' \leftarrow \Delta \cup \{s_1^\sharp \xrightarrow{a_1^\sharp \nabla_\mathfrak{A} a_2^\sharp} q_\equiv^\sharp \mid s_1^\sharp \xrightarrow{a_1^\sharp} q_\equiv^\sharp \in \Delta \vee a_1^\sharp = a_2^\sharp\}$;
  $A \leftarrow (S', s_0^\sharp, F', \Delta')$;
  $\delta \leftarrow \texttt{increments}(A, A_2)$;
until $\delta \neq \varnothing$;

(a)

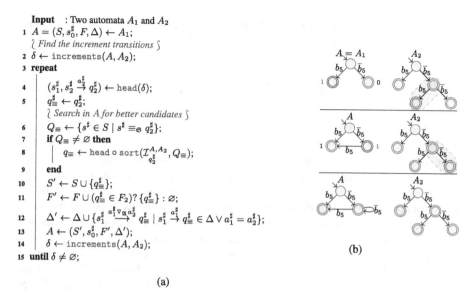

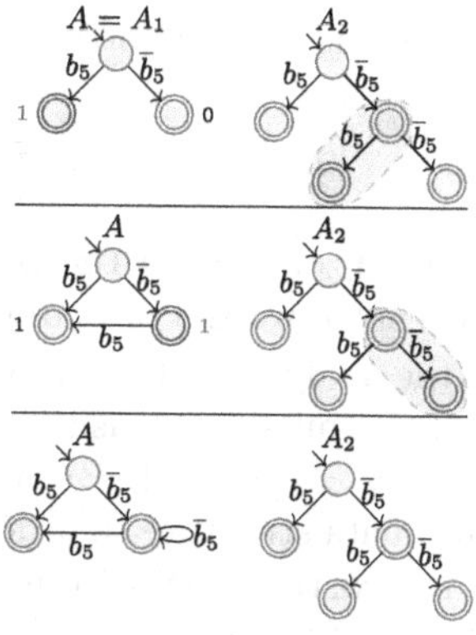

(b)

Fig. 5. (a) Structural widening algorithm. (b) Result of $(b_5 + \bar{b}_5) \nabla_\mathscr{A} (b_5 + \bar{b}_5(b_5 + \bar{b}_5)^?)$.

transitions at some given depth. However, it assumes that the abstract alphabet domain is provided with an equivalence relation that partitions the symbols into a finite set of equivalence classes. We believe that it is more meaningful to perform this partitioning on the abstract states as explained earlier for the computation of the product relation. Therefore, we employ a different approach inspired from graph widening [18,28,30]. Basically, we compare the result of successive loop iterations and we try to detect the increment transitions to extrapolate them by creating cycles. However, existing graph widening is limited to finite alphabets and may not ensure the convergence on ascending chains, so we propose an extension to alleviate these shortcomings.

The proposed algorithm is executed in two phases. Firstly, we perform a *structural widening* to extrapolate the language recognized by the input automata and we ignore for the moment the abstract states. We show in Fig. 5(a) the main steps of this widening. Assume that A_1 and A_2 are the results of two successive iterations. Without loss of generality, we assume that $A_1 \sqsubseteq_\mathscr{A} A_2$. First, we compare A_1 and A_2 in order to extract the increment transitions using the following function:

$$\texttt{increments}(A_1, A_2) = \{(s_1^\sharp, s_2^\sharp \xrightarrow{a_3^\sharp} q_2^\sharp) \mid s_1^\sharp \asymp s_2^\sharp \wedge s_1^\sharp, s_2^\sharp \neq \bot_\mathfrak{S} \wedge \\ \exists s_2^\sharp \xrightarrow{a_3^\sharp} q_2^\sharp \in \Delta_2, \forall s_1^\sharp \xrightarrow{a_1^\sharp} q_1^\sharp : q_1^\sharp \not\equiv_\mathfrak{S} q_2^\sharp \vee a_2^\sharp \not\sqsubseteq_\mathfrak{A} a_1^\sharp\}$$

Basically, an increment $(s_1^\sharp, s_2^\sharp \xrightarrow{a^\sharp} q_2^\sharp)$ means that A_1 at state $s_1^\sharp$ can not recognize the symbol $a^\sharp$ while A_2 recognizes it through a move from $s_2^\sharp$ to $q_2^\sharp$. Now, we need to extrapolate A_1 in order to recover this difference, which is done by adding the missing word suffix $a_2^\sharp$ while trying not to grow A_1 in size.

The basic idea is to sort states in A_1 depending on how they compare to the missing state $q_2^\sharp$. The comparison is performed with the following *similarity index* expressing the proportion of common partial traces that a state shares with $q_2^\sharp$:

$$\mathcal{I}_{q_2^\sharp}^{A_1,A_2}(q_1^\sharp) = \left| \{a_1^\sharp \dots a_n^\sharp \in \overleftrightarrow{\mathbf{L}}_{A_2,k}(q_2^\sharp) \mid \exists {a^\sharp}'_1 \dots {a^\sharp}'_n \in \overleftrightarrow{\mathbf{L}}_{A_1,k}(q_1^\sharp), \forall i : a_i^\sharp \sqsubseteq_{\mathfrak{A}} {a^\sharp}'_i\} \right|$$

where $\overleftrightarrow{\mathbf{L}}_{A,k}(s^\sharp)$ is the set of words, of length less than k, starting from $s^\sharp$ (reachable words) or ending at $s^\sharp$ (co-reachable words), where k is a parameter of the analysis. After selecting the state $q_{\equiv}^\sharp$ with the highest similarity index, we add the missing transitions after widening the alphabet symbol if a transition already exists in A. By iterating over all increment transitions, we obtain an automata structure that does not grow indefinitely since we add new states only if no existing one is equivalent. By assuming that the number of equivalence classes of $\equiv_{\mathfrak{S}}$ is finite, the widening ensures termination.

After the structural widening, we inspect the states of the resulting automaton to extrapolate them if necessary. We simply compute the simulation relation $\preccurlyeq$ between A_2 and the widened automaton A, and we replace every state $s^\sharp \in S$ with $s^\sharp \nabla_{\mathfrak{S}} (s_1^\sharp \sqcup_{\mathfrak{S}} s_2^\sharp \sqcup_{\mathfrak{S}} \dots)$ where $s_i^\sharp \preccurlyeq s^\sharp, \forall i$.

Example 4. We show in Fig. 5(a) the result of applying this structural widening on the `do-while` loop of the previous `sense()` function of Fig. 3(a). The first two iterations of the loop produce the regular expressions $b_5 + \overline{b}_5$ and $b_5 + \overline{b}_5(b_5 + \overline{b}_5)$ respectively. The widening algorithm starts by detecting the leaf increment transition b_5 and computes the different distances to select an adequate equivalent state. By adding the new transition, we obtain the regular expression $b_5 + \overline{b}_5 b_5$. The next increment transition is labeled with the event $\overline{b}_5$ and its addition to the widened automaton produces a loop which results in the final regular expression $\overline{b}_5^* b_5$. □

3.2 Abstract Scenarios

Using the functor domain $\mathscr{A}$, we instantiate an abstract scenario domain for approximating words of random events. Two considerations are important to take into account. First, the length of the these words may depend on some variables of the program. It is clear that ignoring these relations may lead to imprecise computations of the stationary distribution. Consequently, we enrich the domain with an abstract Parikh vector [25] to count the number of occurrences of random event within accepted words. By using a relational numerical domain, such as octagons [21] or polyhedra [7], we preserve some relationships between the number of events and program variables.

The second consideration is related to the uniform distribution. As shown previously in the concrete transfer function in Fig. 2, the number of outcomes depends on the bounds provided as argument to the function `uniform`. Since these arguments are evaluated in the running environment, we can have an infinite number of outcomes at a given control location when considering all possible executions.

We perform a simplifying abstraction of the random events Ξ in order to obtain a finite size alphabet and avoid the explosion of the uniform distribution outcomes. Assume that we are analyzing the statement $x = \texttt{uniform}_l(e_1, e_2)$ in abstract environment $\rho^\sharp$. Several abstractions are possible. In this work, we choose to partition the outcomes into a fixed number U of abstract outcomes, where U is a parameter of the analysis. The first $U-1$ partitions represent the individual outcomes $\{\min(e_1+i-1, e_2) \mid i \in [1, U-1]\}$, to which we associate the abstract events $\{\mathbf{u}_l^i \mid i \in [1, U-1]\}$. For the remaining outcomes, we merge them into a single abstract event $\mathbf{u}_l^\star$.

Formally, we obtain a simple finite set of abstract events $\Xi^\sharp$ defined as $\Xi^\sharp \triangleq \{\mathbf{b}_l, \overline{\mathbf{b}}_l \mid b_l \in \Xi\} \cup \{\mathbf{u}_l^i, \mathbf{u}_l^\star \mid u_l^- \in \Xi \wedge 1 \le i \le U-1\}$. For the Parikh vector, we associate to every abstract event $\xi^\sharp \in \Xi^\sharp$ a counter variable $\kappa_{\xi^\sharp} \in \mathbb{N}$ that will be incremented whenever the event $\xi^\sharp$ occurs.

Therefore, we define the domain of abstract scenarios as $\Omega^\sharp \triangleq \mathscr{A}(\wp(\Xi^\sharp), \Sigma^\sharp)$ where $\Sigma^\sharp$ is our previous mapping $\mathcal{L} \to \mathfrak{E}^\sharp$ from program locations to the stock numeric abstract domain. Let us now describe how probabilistic statements affect an abstract scenario. For the $\texttt{bernoulli}_l()$ statement, we create two new transitions labeled with the abstract events $\mathbf{b}_l$ and $\overline{\mathbf{b}}_l$ respectively and we update the Parikh vector accordingly:

$$
\begin{aligned}
&\mathbf{S}[\![x = \texttt{bernoulli}_l()]\!]_\Omega^\sharp \omega^\sharp \triangleq \\
&\quad \texttt{let}\, \phi_0(-, \rho^\sharp) = (l, \mathbf{S}[\![\kappa_{\overline{\mathbf{b}}_l}\texttt{++}]\!]_\mathfrak{E}^\sharp \circ \mathbf{S}[\![x = 0]\!]_\mathfrak{E}^\sharp \rho^\sharp) \\
&\quad \texttt{and}\, \phi_1(-, \rho^\sharp) = (l, \mathbf{S}[\![\kappa_{\mathbf{b}_l}\texttt{++}]\!]_\mathfrak{E}^\sharp \circ \mathbf{S}[\![x = 1]\!]_\mathfrak{E}^\sharp \rho^\sharp) \\
&\quad \texttt{in}\, \left(\omega^\sharp \odot_{\phi_0} \{\overline{\mathbf{b}}_l\}\right) \sqcup_\mathscr{A} \left(\omega^\sharp \odot_{\phi_1} \{\mathbf{b}_l\}\right)
\end{aligned}
$$

Similarly, we give the following abstract transfer function for the $\texttt{uniform}_l(e_1, e_2)$ statement that generates U new transitions with appropriate state updates:

$$
\begin{aligned}
&\mathbf{S}[\![x = \texttt{uniform}_l(e_1, e_2)]\!]_\Omega^\sharp \omega^\sharp \triangleq \\
&\quad \texttt{let}\, \phi(i) = \lambda\,(-, \rho^\sharp).\, (l, \mathbf{S}[\![\kappa_{\mathbf{u}_l^i}\texttt{++}]\!]_\mathfrak{E}^\sharp \circ \mathbf{S}[\![(x \le e_2)]\!]_\mathfrak{E}^\sharp \circ \mathbf{S}[\![x = e_1 + i - 1]\!]_\mathfrak{E}^\sharp \rho^\sharp) \\
&\quad \texttt{and}\, \phi^\star = \lambda\,(-, \rho^\sharp).\, (l, \mathbf{S}[\![\kappa_{\mathbf{u}_l^\star}\texttt{++}]\!]_\mathfrak{E}^\sharp \circ \mathbf{S}[\![(e_1 + U \le x \le e_2)]\!]_\mathfrak{E}^\sharp \circ \mathbf{S}[\![x = \top]\!]_\mathfrak{E}^\sharp \rho^\sharp) \\
&\quad \texttt{in}\, \Big(\bigsqcup_{1 \le i \le U-1} \omega^\sharp \odot_{\phi(i)} \{\mathbf{u}_l^i\}\Big) \sqcup_\mathscr{A} \left(\omega^\sharp \odot_{\phi^\star} \{\mathbf{u}_l^\star\}\right)
\end{aligned}
$$

3.3 Abstract Markov Chains

The product $\mathcal{D}^\sharp \triangleq \mathcal{T}^\sharp \times \Omega^\sharp$ defines the domain of Abstract Markov Chains. It is composed of two parts. The first one is an abstraction of the markovian traces and is defined as the instance $\mathcal{T}^\sharp \triangleq \mathscr{A}(\Omega^\sharp, \Sigma^\sharp)$. This automaton is used to approximate the set of past observable traces reaching a given program location. The second part is an abstraction of the current partial scenarios starting from the last `ticks` statement. Since the states of an abstract scenario automaton already embed an abstraction of the program environments, we also employ this part to encode the current environments.

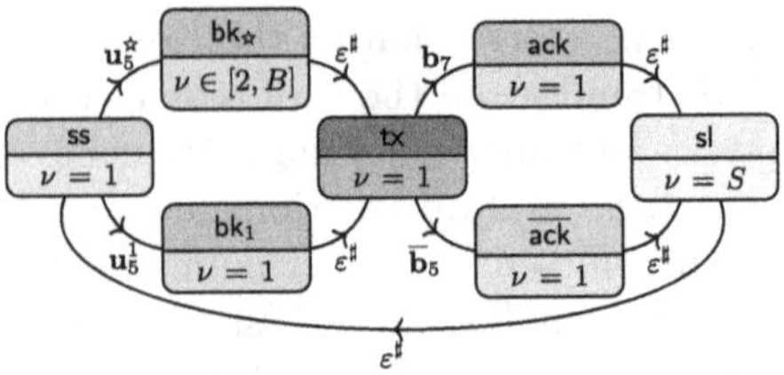

Fig. 6. Abstract Markov chain of the motivating example.

The concretization function gives the set of concrete markovian traces and partial scenarios encoded by an abstract Markov chain, and employs the previous trace and word concretizations (see Definition 4) as follows:

$$\gamma(\tau^\sharp, \omega^\sharp) = \{(\tau, \rho, \omega) \mid \tau \in \gamma_{\mathscr{A}}^{\mathbf{T}}(\tau^\sharp) \wedge \exists (l_1, \rho_1^\sharp) \xrightarrow{\xi_1^\sharp} \dots \xrightarrow{\xi_{n-1}^\sharp} (l_n, \rho_n^\sharp) \in \mathbf{T}(\omega^\sharp) : \\ \rho \in \gamma_{\mathfrak{E}}(\rho_n^\sharp) \wedge \omega \in \gamma_{\mathscr{A}}^{\mathbf{L}}(\xi_1^\sharp \dots \xi_{n-1}^\sharp)\}$$

Let us define now the abstract transfer function for the $\texttt{ticks}_l(e)$ statement since it is the only one that modifies the structure of the abstract Markov chain. It indicates that a new observable state has been encountered and that the pending scenarios are no longer partial and should be used to label the new transition, as shown by the following:

$$\mathbf{S}[\![x = \texttt{ticks}_l(e)]\!]^\sharp(\tau^\sharp, \omega^\sharp) \triangleq \texttt{let}\, \phi(-, \rho^\sharp) = (l, \mathbf{S}[\![\nu = e]\!]_{\mathfrak{E}}^\sharp \rho^\sharp)\, \texttt{in}\, (\tau^\sharp \odot_\phi \omega^\sharp, \varepsilon^\sharp)$$

where $\varepsilon^\sharp$ is the empty scenario word where all Parikh counters are reset to 0. The remaining statements are passed to the underlying $\Omega^\sharp$ and $\mathfrak{E}^\sharp$ domains and affect only the partial scenarios part. We can show that the following soundness condition is preserved:

$$\left(\mathbf{S}[\![s]\!] \circ \gamma\right)(\tau^\sharp, \omega^\sharp) \subseteq \left(\gamma \circ \mathbf{S}[\![s]\!]^\sharp\right)(\tau^\sharp, \omega^\sharp), \forall s \in \mathit{Stmt}, \forall (\tau^\sharp, \omega^\sharp) \in \mathcal{D}^\sharp \quad (9)$$

Example 5. The abstract markovian traces of our motivating example are depicted in Fig. 6 as an abstract automaton corresponding to the result of the analysis with $U = 2$. For the sake of clarity, we give to each abstract state a unique identifier and we show the inferred invariants about the sojourn time variable ν. The program locations and the remaining environment invariants are not represented. □

4 Stationary Distribution

In this section, we present a method for extracting safe bounds of the stationary distribution using information embedded in an abstract Markov chain. We do so by deriving a *distribution invariant* that establishes a set of parametric linear inequalities over the abstract states. Using the Fourier-Motzkin elimination algorithm, we can find guaranteed bounds of time proportion spent in a given abstract state.

We begin with some preliminary definitions. Let $T^\sharp = (S, s_0^\sharp, F, \Delta)$ be the markovian traces part of the program's abstract Markov chain over-approximating a set $T \subseteq \mathcal{T}_\Sigma^\Omega$ of concrete markovian traces. For each statement $\texttt{uniform}_l(e_1, e_2)$, we denote by $\overleftarrow{\text{ue}_l} = e_1$ and $\overrightarrow{\text{ue}_l} = e_2$ the bounds expressions of the distribution. Also, we define the functions $\hat{\mathbf{max}}[\![e]\!], \hat{\mathbf{min}}[\![e]\!] \in \Sigma^\sharp \to Exp \cup \{\infty\}$ giving respectively the evaluation of the maximal and minimal values of an expression e in a given abstract state, which is generally provided for free by the underlying numerical domain. In the case of relational domains, the returned bounds can be symbolic. For the sake of simplicity, we write $\hat{\mathbf{min}}_\star[\![e]\!]$ and $\hat{\mathbf{max}}_\star[\![e]\!]$ to denote respectively the minimal and maximal evaluations over the set of all reachable abstract states. The following definition gives a means to compute the probability of given abstract scenario.

Definition 7. *Let $\omega^\sharp \in \Omega^\sharp$ be an abstract scenario. Its probability is given by:*

$$\begin{cases} \hat{\Pr}(\varepsilon^\sharp) = 1, \hat{\Pr}(\mathbf{b}_l) = p_l, \hat{\Pr}(\overline{\mathbf{b}}_l) = 1 - p_l, \\ \hat{\Pr}(\mathbf{u}_l^i) = \frac{1}{\hat{\mathbf{min}}_\star[\![\overrightarrow{\text{ue}_l}]\!] - \hat{\mathbf{max}}_\star[\![\overleftarrow{\text{ue}_l}]\!] + 1}, \hat{\Pr}(\mathbf{u}_l^\star) = \frac{\hat{\mathbf{max}}_\star[\![\overrightarrow{\text{ue}_l}]\!] - \hat{\mathbf{min}}_\star[\![\overleftarrow{\text{ue}_l}]\!] + 2 - U}{\hat{\mathbf{min}}_\star[\![\overrightarrow{\text{ue}_l}]\!] - \hat{\mathbf{max}}_\star[\![\overleftarrow{\text{ue}_l}]\!] + 1} \\ \hat{\Pr}(\omega^\sharp \xi^\sharp) = \hat{\Pr}(\omega^\sharp)\hat{\Pr}(\xi^\sharp), \hat{\Pr}(\omega_1^\sharp + \omega_2^\sharp) = \hat{\Pr}(\omega_1^\sharp) + \hat{\Pr}(\omega_2^\sharp) \end{cases} \tag{10}$$

By combining the sojourn and probability invariants embedded in the abstract chain, we construct an abstract transition matrix that characterizes completely the stochastic properties of the program inside one finite data structure:

Definition 8 (Abstract transition matrix). *The abstract transition matrix $\hat{\mathbf{P}}$ is a square matrix of size $|S|$ where the entry for every abstract states $\sigma_i^\sharp, \sigma_j^\sharp \in S$ is defined as:*

$$\hat{\mathbf{P}}_{\sigma_i^\sharp, \sigma_j^\sharp} \triangleq \frac{\hat{\mathbf{max}}[\![\nu]\!](\sigma_j^\sharp)}{\hat{\mathbf{min}}[\![\nu]\!](\sigma_i^\sharp)} \sum_{\sigma_i^\sharp \xrightarrow{\omega^\sharp} \sigma_j^\sharp \in \Delta} \hat{\Pr}(\omega^\sharp) \tag{11}$$

Example 6. Consider our previous motivating example and its abstract chain represented in Fig. 6. Let $S = \langle \mathsf{ss}, \mathsf{bk}_1, \mathsf{bk}_\star, \mathsf{tx}, \mathsf{ack}, \overline{\mathsf{ack}}, \mathsf{sl} \rangle$ be the vector of abstract states. To obtain the matrix $\hat{\mathbf{P}}$, we iterate over all the transitions of the abstract chain. Consider for example the case of the transition $\mathsf{ss} \xrightarrow{\mathbf{u}_5^\star} \mathsf{bk}_\star$. First, we apply (10) to compute the transitions probabilities $\hat{\Pr}(\mathbf{u}_5^\star) = \frac{B-1}{B}$. Afterwards, we extract the sojourn time bounds $\hat{\mathbf{max}}[\![\nu]\!](\mathsf{bk}_\star) = B$ and $\hat{\mathbf{min}}[\![\nu]\!](\mathsf{ss}) = 1$ from the embedded numeric environments. Finally, we apply (11) to obtain the matrix cell $\hat{\mathbf{P}}_{\mathsf{ss},\mathsf{bk}_\star} = \frac{B(B-1)}{B} = B - 1$. By iterating the same process for all transitions we obtain:

$$\hat{\mathbf{P}} = \begin{pmatrix} 0 & 0 & 0 & 0 & 0 & 0 & \frac{1}{S} \\ \frac{1}{B} & 0 & 0 & 0 & 0 & 0 & 0 \\ B-1 & 0 & 0 & 0 & 0 & 0 & 0 \\ 0 & 1 & \frac{1}{2} & 0 & 0 & 0 & 0 \\ 0 & 0 & 0 & 1-p & 0 & 0 & 0 \\ 0 & 0 & 0 & p & 0 & 0 & 0 \\ 0 & 0 & 0 & 0 & S & S & 0 \end{pmatrix}$$

□

The vector $\hat{\boldsymbol{\pi}}$ containing the proportion of time spent in every abstract state is called the *abstract stationary distribution*. It is defined as:

$$\hat{\boldsymbol{\pi}}_{\sigma^\sharp} \triangleq \sum_{\sigma \in \gamma_\Sigma(\sigma^\sharp)} \boldsymbol{\pi}_\sigma, \forall \sigma^\sharp \in S \tag{12}$$

where $\boldsymbol{\pi}$ is the concrete stationary distribution described in Sect. 2.3. It is important to note that since spurious concrete states $\sigma \in \gamma_\Sigma(\sigma^\sharp)$ have a null concrete stationary probability $\boldsymbol{\pi}_\sigma$, the abstract stationary probability $\hat{\boldsymbol{\pi}}_{\sigma^\sharp}$ represents the exact sum of the stationary probabilities of the real concrete states abstracted by $\sigma^\sharp$. Therefore, any lower and/or upper bounds that can be found about $\hat{\boldsymbol{\pi}}_{\sigma^\sharp}$ are also valid for the concrete states abstracted by $\sigma^\sharp$. To compute such bounds, we use $\hat{\mathbf{P}}$ with the following result:

Theorem 1 (Distribution invariant). $\hat{\boldsymbol{\pi}} \leq \hat{\boldsymbol{\pi}}\hat{\mathbf{P}}$.

This theorem allows us to establish a system of parametric linear inequalities where the unknowns are the entries of the vector $\hat{\boldsymbol{\pi}}$. By adding the normalization condition $\sum_{\sigma^\sharp \in S} \hat{\boldsymbol{\pi}}_{\sigma^\sharp} = 1$, we can use this system to find safe bounds of the property of interest. Without loss of generality, assume that the time proportion of this property is associated to the stationary probability of some state $s^\sharp$. To compute a safe range of $\hat{\boldsymbol{\pi}}_{s^\sharp}$, we just have to perform a projection of the linear system $\hat{\boldsymbol{\pi}} \leq \hat{\boldsymbol{\pi}}\hat{\mathbf{P}}$ that keeps only $\hat{\boldsymbol{\pi}}_{s^\sharp}$ and removes the other unknowns while preserving all constraints.

To do so, we have implemented a parametric Fourier-Motzkin projection algorithm [13,27] that returns parametric solutions to such problems. It eliminates the unnecessary unknowns sequentially and builds a decision tree that gives the system solutions depending on adequate parameters conditions. The general idea of the algorithm is the following. Assume that we are at the step of eliminating the unknown $\hat{\boldsymbol{\pi}}_{s_i^\sharp}$. We iterate over all leaves of the current decision tree $\{\langle C, I\rangle\}$, where I is a set of linear inequalities on the remaining unknowns and C is the condition on the parameters for obtaining the solution I. We examine the coefficients $\{a_{i,j}\}$ of $\hat{\boldsymbol{\pi}}_{s_i^\sharp}$ in I and we partition the inequalities depending on the sign of these coefficients. When the sign can not be determined, we create new branches within the decision tree to eliminate this ambiguity and we append the appropriate sign condition ($a_{i,j} > 0$, $a_{i,j} < 0$ and $a_{i,j} = 0$) to the branch condition C. At the end, we obtain a set of new leaves where all coefficients of $\hat{\boldsymbol{\pi}}_{s_i^\sharp}$ have known signs. At this point, we can transform I into a new system of inequalities by combining every couple of inequalities having opposite coefficient signs in a way to eliminate $\hat{\pi}_{s_i^\sharp}$, and we keep the inequalities where the coefficient is null. After eliminating all untargeted unknowns, we obtain a set of bounding inequalities of $\hat{\pi}_{s^\sharp}$ annotated by some parameters conditions.

Two important points should be noted. Firstly, this algorithm may not scale well for complex problems because the size of the decision tree can grow considerably in the presence of too many parametric coefficients.[1] To improve the efficiency of the algorithm, we can reduce the precision of these linear parametric inequalities by using more abstract representations such as the domain of *interval linear inequalities* [6]. The second point is related to the soundness of the result. In our current implementation, we rely on an underlying symbolic environment to determine the sign of coefficients, which prevents us from ensuring the soundness of floating points operations during these computations. Nevertheless, we believe that we can inspire from *guaranteed linear programming* [24] to strengthen the resolution process and overcome this problem.

5 Experiments

The proposed approach has been implemented in a prototype analyzer called MARCHAL (*MARkov CHains AnaLyzer*) using the OCaml language, the CIL frontend [23] and the Apron library [15]. Also, we implemented the parametric Fourier-Motzkin elimination algorithm in Mathematica. For our benchmarks, we compare MARCHAL to PRISM on three commonly used backoff mechanisms and we compute for each case the expected value of the throughput. The first backoff mechanism is the motivating example shown in Fig. 1 in which a single backoff is performed before transmitting every packet. In the second backoff mechanism, the sender tries to enhance the transmission reliability by performing an unbounded number of backoffs until receiving an acknowledgment from the destination. Finally, the third case study employs a bounded number of backoffs in which the number of successive attempts is limited by a parameter N. For all these cases, the backoff window is chosen uniformly from $[1, B]$ and the sleep period after the transmission transaction is determined by a parameter S.

The benchmarks consist in two categories of experiments in order to highlight the differences between MARCHAL and PRISM. For the first category, we fix the parameters to some small values and we configure MARCHAL to perform a complete partitioning of the uniform distribution. In this case, both tools are able to obtain the exact stationary distributions within a small delay, as summarized in Table 1(a), with an advantage of PRISM in many cases. In the second category, we extend the parameters space by considering three sub-cases: (i) the parameters have fixed large value, (ii) the parameters are not fixed but are bounded in some intervals, and finally (iii) the parameters are unbounded. To cover these cases in finite time, MARCHAL applies an approximate partitioning

[1] That being said, this algorithm has shown to be more effective than built-in functions of many off-the-shelf symbolic environments, such as Sage and Mathematica, that did not return solutions for most benchmarks.

Table 1. Analysis time in seconds with (a) complete and (b) approximate partitioning.

Protocol	PRISM	MARCHAL Box	MARCHAL Octagon	MARCHAL Polyhedra
Single backoff				
$B = 2, S = 100$	2.96	1.92	2.57	1.94
$B = 4, S = 100$	2.94	2.19	4.54	2.65
Unbounded backoffs				
$B = 2, S = 100$	5.06	3.38	10.69	4.75
$B = 4, S = 100$	5.44	7.98	42.98	15.89
Bounded backoffs				
$B = 2, S = 100, N = 2$	4.12	8.96	28.59	14.52
$B = 4, S = 100, N = 2$	6.37	22.64	100.6	45.70

(a)

Protocol	PRISM	MARCHAL Box		MARCHAL Octagon		MARCHAL Polyhedra	
		$U = 2$	$U = 4$	$U = 2$	$U = 4$	$U = 2$	$U = 4$
Single backoff							
$B = 20, S = 1000$	13.75	1.87	2.16	2.64	4.73	2.03	2.78
$B \in [2, 20], S \in [100, 1000]$	674.80	1.77	2.31	2.40	4.39	2.30	3.07
$B \geq 2, S \geq 100$	∞	1.7	1.84	2.57	4.10	2.11	2.69
Unbounded backoffs							
$B = 20, S = 1000$	45.11	5.12	10.28	12.81	44.10	6.87	17.72
$B \in [2, 20], S \in [100, 1000]$	∞	6.91	33.99	10.43	105.75	33.88	86.30
$B \geq 2, S \geq 100$	∞	2.87	4.95	39.09	102.44	35.0	83.20
Bounded backoffs							
$B = 20, S = 1000, N = 7$	50.24	7.01	17.58	43.33	173.10	17.64	61.84
$B \in [2, 20], S \in [100, 1000], N \in [1, 7]$	∞	16.82	57.77	120.34	338.45	110.31	252.79
$B \geq 2, S \geq 100, N \geq 1$	∞	6.49	16.51	75.79	251.78	55.32	150.66

(b)

(into $U = 2$ and $U = 4$ partitions) and therefore can infer approximate and safe bounds of the throughput. However, PRISM can obtain only precise results and therefore can not provide an answer in most cases within a timeout of 30mn. The analysis times of this category of experiments are summarized in Table 1(b).

Let us now discuss the precision of the proposed approach. To evaluate it, we first compute the distance between the maximal and minimal bounds of the throughput over a large sample of parameters values, which results in a discrete set of observations of the maximal error of the analysis. From the resulting set of values, we compute the empirical distribution that gives the fraction of observations having a given maximal error. After that, we compute the cumulative distribution function for a better visualization of the variation of the error for the parameters sample.

We depict in Figs. 7, 8 and 9 the obtained results when setting $U = 4$. We can notice that the analysis with the octagon and polyhedra domains returned always the same precision level. Also, all domains give the same precision for the case of fixed parameters values. This is justified by the fact that the choice of the numerical domain affects the form of the sojourn time invariants used to compute the abstract transition matrix. In the studied programs, all invariants

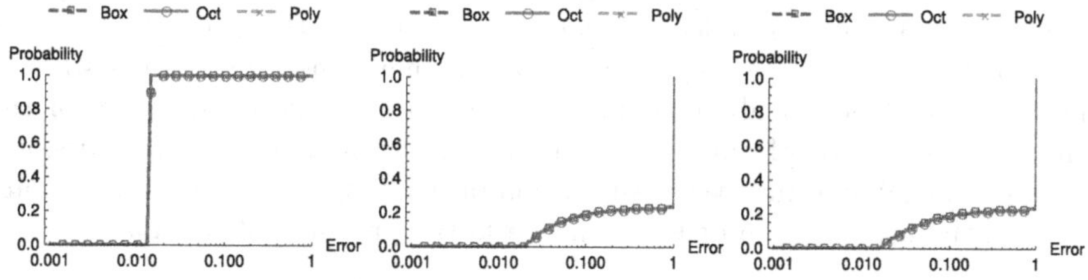

(a) Single backoff (b) Unbounded backoffs (c) Bounded backoffs

Fig. 7. Error distribution for the case $B = 20, S = 10^3$ with $U = 4$.

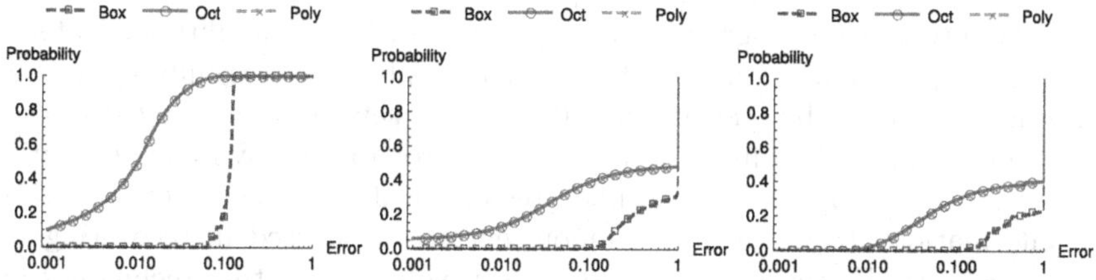

(a) Single backoff (b) Unbounded backoffs (c) Bounded backoffs

Fig. 8. Error distribution for the case $B \in [2, 20], S \in [10^2, 10^3]$ with $U = 4$.

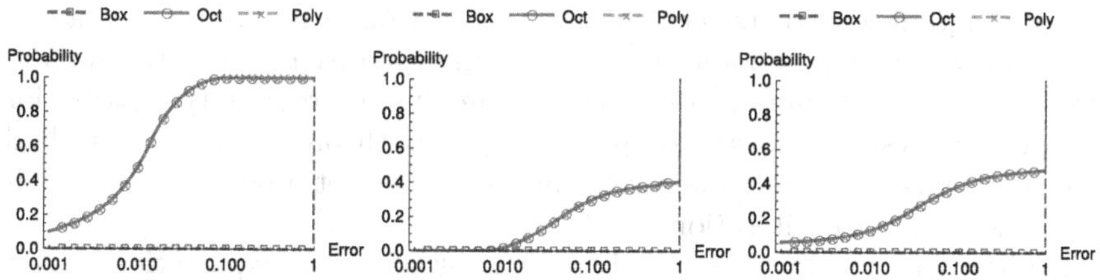

(a) Single backoff (b) Unbounded backoffs (c) Bounded backoffs

Fig. 9. Error distribution for the case $B \geq 2, S \geq 10^2$ with $U = 4$.

have an octagonal form, so there is no need to infer more precise invariants. For the particular case of fixed parameters values, these invariants are just numeric intervals, which justifies that all domains offered the same precision level.

Additionally, we notice that the precision of the analysis for the unbounded and bounded backoff mechanisms is lower than the single backoff case, which is principally due to the partitioning of the uniform distribution that was too coarse in these cases. In practice, we were able to improve the precision of the inferred bounds by increasing the partition parameter U, but at the cost of analysis time. It is clear that more adequate partitioning techniques are necessary to obtain more precise results. Another source of precision loss is related to the current construction of the abstract transition matrix. We can see in (11) that the entries of the matrix reflect numeric constraints of the sojourn time over individual states only. However, some programs may constrain also the sojourn time over a sequence of abstract states, which is the case for example of the bounded backoff protocol that imposes a limit on the number of retransmissions. Since a retransmission involves a succession of many states, some invarants are ignored in the construction of $\hat{\mathbf{P}}$ which affects the precision of the analysis.

6 Related Work

The analysis of probabilistic programs has gained great interest over the last years. Many techniques have been proposed for extracting automatically quantiative properties from programs with varying precision/scalability tradeoffs.

PRISM [16] is a famous model checker that has been successfully applied for analyzing many probabilistic systems. It supports several interesting stochastic models, but is limited to finite state systems. Probabilistic symbolic execution [12,26] is another approach that annotates classical symbolic execution states with information about the past random events to be used in recovering the path probability. However, in most solutions, volume counting techniques are required, which limit their scalability.

Monniaux [22] and Di Pierro et al. [10] were the first propositions to extend abstract interpretation to probabilistic programs. Later, several works were proposed in the same direction [2,3,19], but they lack the ability to analyze some classical program constructs such as loops. In [8], Cousot et al. proposed a more general framework for probabilistic abstract interpretation that introduces the concept of *law abstraction* as a means to approximate probability distributions on program states. This formalism provides general theoretic guidelines to build sound probabilistic abstract interpretations, but does not provide practical solutions for widening loop iterations.

Another family of approaches is based on a weakest pre-expectation calculus introduced by McIver et al. [20] in order to infer *quantitative invariants* expressed as expectations of some program expressions. Chakarov et al. [4] extended this work in order to infer bounds of the probability of program assertions using the theory of Martingales. In [5], Chakarov et al. proposed another pre-expectation based analysis using abstract interpretation for discovering expectation invariants through the abstract domain of polyhedra with an appropriate widening operator. More recently, Barthe et al. [1] described a symbolic execution method that uses Doob's decomposition in order to infer Martingale expressions that help in deriving post-loop expectation of program variables.

7 Conclusion

We have presented a novel approach for obtaining guaranteed bounds of performance metrics of communication protocols. The method is based on the framework of abstract interpretation and proposes an Abstract Markov Chains domain for approximating the probabilistic semantics of programs. We have also explained how to exploit the information encapsulated within this domain in order to infer a sound approximation of the stationary distribution of the protocol, which is the key ingredient for computing a large range of performance metrics such as the throughput and the energy consumption. A prototype of the analysis have been presented along with some preliminary results. Many problems are still open to enhance the proposed approach. To enhance precision, we believe that is important to consider (*i*) developing more adequate partitioning of the `uniform` distribution and (*ii*) inferring multi-state sojourn time invariants. Finally, we have presented the analysis of a single process and we are interested in extending it to networked concurrent programs.

References

1. Barthe, G., Espitau, T., Ferrer Fioriti, L., Hsu, J.: Synthesizing probabilistic invariants via Doob's decomposition. In: CAV 2016. LNCS, vol. 9779, pp. 43–61. Springer, Cham (2016)
2. Bouissou, O., Goubault, E., Goubault-Larrecq, J., Putot, S.: A generalization of p-boxes to affine arithmetic. Computing **94**(2), 189–201 (2012)
3. Bouissou, O., Goubault, E., Putot, S., Chakarov, A., Sankaranarayanan, S.: Uncertainty propagation using probabilistic affine forms and concentration of measure inequalities. In: Chechik, M., Raskin, J.-F. (eds.) TACAS 2016. LNCS, vol. 9636, pp. 225–243. Springer, Heidelberg (2016). doi:10.1007/978-3-662-49674-9_13
4. Chakarov, A., Sankaranarayanan, S.: Probabilistic program analysis with martingales. In: Sharygina, N., Veith, H. (eds.) CAV 2013. LNCS, vol. 8044, pp. 511–526. Springer, Heidelberg (2013). doi:10.1007/978-3-642-39799-8_34
5. Chakarov, A., Sankaranarayanan, S.: Expectation invariants for probabilistic program loops as fixed points. In: Müller-Olm, M., Seidl, H. (eds.) SAS 2014. LNCS, vol. 8723, pp. 85–100. Springer, Cham (2014). doi:10.1007/978-3-319-10936-7_6
6. Chen, L., Miné, A., Wang, J., Cousot, P.: An abstract domain to discover interval linear equalities. In: Barthe, G., Hermenegildo, M. (eds.) VMCAI 2010. LNCS, vol. 5944, pp. 112–128. Springer, Heidelberg (2010). doi:10.1007/978-3-642-11319-2_11
7. Cousot, P., Halbwachs, N.: Automatic discovery of linear restraints among variables of a program. In: POPL 1978, pp. 84–97. ACM, New York (1978)
8. Cousot, P., Monerau, M.: Probabilistic abstract interpretation. In: Seidl, H. (ed.) ESOP 2012. LNCS, vol. 7211, pp. 169–193. Springer, Heidelberg (2012). doi:10.1007/978-3-642-28869-2_9
9. Cousot, R.: Fondements des Méthodes de Preuve d'invariance et de fatalité de Programmes Parallèles. Thèse d'État ès sciences mathématiques, Institut National Polytechnique de Lorraine, Nancy, France (1985)
10. Di Pierro, A., Wiklicky, H.: Concurrent constraint programming: towards probabilistic abstract interpretation. In: PPDP 2000, pp. 127–138. ACM, New York (2000)
11. Feret, J.: Abstract interpretation-based static analysis of mobile ambients. In: Cousot, P. (ed.) SAS 2001. LNCS, vol. 2126, pp. 412–430. Springer, Heidelberg (2001). doi:10.1007/3-540-47764-0_24
12. Geldenhuys, J., Dwyer, M.B., Visser, W.: Probabilistic symbolic execution. In: ISSTA 2012, pp. 166–176. ACM, New York (2012)

13. Grïßlinger, A.: Extending the polyhedron model to inequality systems with non-linear parameters using quantifier elimination. Master thesis, University of Passau (2003)
14. Hahn, E., Hermanns, H., Zhang, L.: Probabilistic reachability for parametric markov models. Int. J. Softw. Tools Technol. Transf. **13**(1), 3–19 (2011)
15. Jeannet, B., Miné, A.: APRON: a library of numerical abstract domains for static analysis. In: Bouajjani, A., Maler, O. (eds.) CAV 2009. LNCS, vol. 5643, pp. 661–667. Springer, Heidelberg (2009). doi:10.1007/978-3-642-02658-4_52
16. Kwiatkowska, M., Norman, G., Parker, D.: PRISM 4.0: verification of probabilistic real-time systems. In: Gopalakrishnan, G., Qadeer, S. (eds.) CAV 2011. LNCS, vol. 6806, pp. 585–591. Springer, Heidelberg (2011). doi:10.1007/978-3-642-22110-1_47
17. Gall, T., Jeannet, B.: Lattice automata: a representation for languages on infinite alphabets, and some applications to verification. In: Nielson, H.R., Filé, G. (eds.) SAS 2007. LNCS, vol. 4634, pp. 52–68. Springer, Heidelberg (2007). doi:10.1007/978-3-540-74061-2_4
18. Lesens, D., Halbwachs, N., Raymond, P.: Automatic verification of parameterized networks of processes. Theor. Comput. Sci. **256**(1–2), 113–144 (2001)
19. Mardziel, P., Magill, S., Hicks, M., Srivatsa, M.: Dynamic enforcement of knowledge-based security policies. In: CSF 2011, pp. 114–128 (2011)
20. McIver, A., Morgan, C.: Abstraction, Refinement And Proof For Probabilistic Systems. Monographs in Computer Science. Springer, New York (2004)
21. Miné, A.: The octagon abstract domain. Higher-Order Symbolic Comput. **19**(1), 31–100 (2006)
22. Monniaux, D.: Abstract interpretation of probabilistic semantics. In: Palsberg, J. (ed.) SAS 2000. LNCS, vol. 1824, pp. 322–339. Springer, Heidelberg (2000). doi:10.1007/978-3-540-45099-3_17
23. Necula, G.C., McPeak, S., Rahul, S.P., Weimer, W.: CIL: intermediate language and tools for analysis and transformation of C programs. In: Horspool, R.N. (ed.) CC 2002. LNCS, vol. 2304, pp. 213–228. Springer, Heidelberg (2002). doi:10.1007/3-540-45937-5_16
24. Neumaier, A., Shcherbina, O.: Safe bounds in linear and mixed-integer linear programming. Math. Program. **99**(2), 283–296 (2004)
25. Parikh, R.: On context-free languages. J. ACM **13**(4), 570–581 (1966)
26. Sankaranarayanan, S., Chakarov, A., Gulwani, S.: Static analysis for probabilistic programs: Inferring whole program properties from finitely many paths. In: PLDI 2013, pp. 447–458. ACM, New York (2013)
27. Suriana, P.: Fourier-Motzkin with non-linear symbolic constant coefficients. Master thesis, Massachusetts Institute of Technology (2016)
28. Van Hentenryck, P., Cortesi, A., Le Charlier, B.: Type analysis of Prolog using type graphs. J. Logic Program. **22**(3), 179–209 (1995)
29. Venet, A.: Automatic analysis of pointer aliasing for untyped programs. Sci. Comput. Program. **35**(2), 223–248 (1999)
30. Villemot, S.: Automates finis et intérpretation abstraite: application à l'analyse statique de protocoles de communication. Rapport de DEA, École normale supérieure (2002)

Portability Analysis for Weak Memory Models PORTHOS: One *Tool* for all *Models*

Hernán Ponce-de-León[1(✉)], Florian Furbach[2], Keijo Heljanko[3], and Roland Meyer[4]

[1] fortiss GmbH, München, Germany
ponce@fortiss.org
[2] TU Kaiserslautern, Kaiserslautern, Germany
furbach@cs.uni-kl.de
[3] Aalto University and HIIT, Espoo, Finland
keijo.heljanko@aalto.fi
[4] TU Braunschweig, Braunschweig, Germany
roland.meyer@tu-braunschweig.de

Abstract. We present PORTHOS, the first tool that discovers porting bugs in performance-critical code. PORTHOS takes as input a program and the memory models of the source architecture for which the program has been developed and the target model to which it is ported. If the code is not portable, PORTHOS finds a bug in the form of an unexpected execution — an execution that is consistent with the target but inconsistent with the source memory model. Technically, PORTHOS implements a bounded model checking method that reduces the portability analysis problem to satisfiability modulo theories (SMT). There are two main problems in the reduction that we present novel and efficient solutions for. First, the formulation of the portability problem contains a quantifier alternation (consistent + inconsistent). We introduce a formula that encodes both in a single existential query. Second, the supported memory models (e.g., Power) contain recursive definitions. We compute the required least fixed point semantics for recursion (a problem that was left open in [48]) efficiently in SMT. Finally we present the first experimental analysis of portability from TSO to Power.

1 Introduction

Porting code from one architecture to another is a routine task in system development. Given that no functionality has to be added, porting is rarely considered interesting from a programming point of view. At the same time, porting is non-trivial as the hardware influences both the semantics and the compilation of the code in subtle ways. The unfortunate combination of being routine and yet subtle makes porting prone to mistakes. This is particularly true for performance-critical code that interacts closely with the execution environment.

This work was carried out when Hernán Ponce-de-León and Roland Meyer were at Aalto University.

F. Ranzato (Ed.): SAS 2017, LNCS 10422, pp. 299–320, 2017.
DOI: 10.1007/978-3-319-66706-5_15

Such code often has data races and thus exposes the programmer to the details of the underlying hardware. When the architecture is changed, the code may have to be adapted to the primitives of the target hardware.

We tackle the problem of porting performance-critical code among hardware architectures. Our contribution is the new (and to the best of our knowledge first) tool PORTHOS to fight porting bugs. The tool takes as input a piece of code, a model of the source architecture for which the code has been developed, and a model of the target architecture to which the code is to be ported. PORTHOS automatically checks whether every behaviour of the code on the target architecture is also allowed on the source platform. This guarantees that correctness of the program in terms of safety properties (in particular properties like mutual exclusion) carries over to the targeted hardware, and the program remains correct after porting.

Portability requires an analysis method that is hardware-architecture-aware in the sense that a description of the memory models of source and target platforms has to be part of the input. A language for memory models, called CAT [4], has been developed only recently. In CAT, memory models are defined in terms of relations between memory operations of a program. There are some base relations (program order, reads from, coherence) that are common to all memory models. A memory model may define further so-called derived relations by restricting and composing base relations. The memory model specifies axioms in the form of acyclicity and irreflexivity constraints over relations. An execution is consistent if it satisfies all axioms. Our work builds on the CAT language.

There are three problems that make portability different from most common verification tasks.

(i) We have to deal with user-defined memory models. These models may define derived relations as least fixed points.
(ii) The formulation of portability involves an alternation (consistent + inconsistent) of quantifiers.
(iii) High-level code may be compiled into different low-level code depending on the architecture (see, e.g., Fig. 1).

Concerning the first problem, we implement in SMT the operations that CAT defines on relations. Notably, we propose an encoding for derived relations that are defined as least fixed points. Such least fixed points are prominently used in the Power memory model [8] and their computation was identified as a key problem in [48]. To quote the authors *[...] the proper fixpoint construction [...] is much more expensive than a fixed unrolling.* We show that, with our encoding, this is not the case. A naive approach would implement the Kleene iteration in SAT by introducing copies of the variables for each iteration step, resulting in a very large encoding. We show how to employ SAT + integer difference logic [19] to compactly encode the Kleene iteration process. Notably, every bounded model checking technique reasoning about complex memory models defined in CAT (e.g., Power) will face the problem of dealing with recursive definitions and can make use of our technique to solve it efficiently.

The second problem is to encode the quantifier alternation underlying the definition of portability. A porting bug is an execution that is consistent with the target but inconsistent with the source memory model. We capture this alternation with a single existential query. Consistency is specified in terms of acyclicity (and irreflexivity) of relations. Hence, an execution is inconsistent if a derived relation of the (source) memory model contains a cycle (or is not irreflexive). The naive idea would be to model cyclicity by unsatisfiability. Instead, we reduce cyclicity to satisfiability by introducing auxiliary variables that guess the cycle.

The reader may criticise our definition of portability: one could claim that all that matters is whether safety is preserved, even if the executions differ. To be precise, a state-based notion of portability requires that every state computable under the target architecture is already computable on the source platform. We study state portability and come up with two results.

(a) Algorithmically, state portability is beyond SAT.
(b) Empirically, there is little difference between state portability and our notion.

The third problem is that the same high-level program is compiled to different assembly programs depending on the source and the target architectures. Even the number of registers and the semantics of the synchronisation primitives provided by those architectures usually differ. Consider the program from Fig. 1, written in C++11 and compiled to x86 and Power. The observation is this. Even if the assembly programs differ, one can map every assembly memory access to the corresponding read or write operation in the high-level code. In the example, clearly "`MOV [y],$1`" and "`stw r1,y`" correspond to "`y.store(memory_order_relaxed, 1)`". This allows us to relate low-level and high-level executions and to compare executions of both assembly programs by checking if they map to the same high-level execution. With this observation, our analysis can be extended by translating an input program into two corresponding assembly programs and making explicit the relation among the low-level and high-level executions. While this relation among executions is not studied in the present paper, details of how to construct it and how to incorporate it into our approach can be found in [38].

In summary, we make the following contributions.

1. We present the first SMT-based implementation of a core subset of CAT which can handle recursive definitions efficiently.
2. We formulate the portability problem based on the CAT language.
3. We develop a bounded analysis for portability. Despite the apparent alternation of quantifiers, our SMT encoding is a satisfiability query of polynomial size and optimal in the complexity sense.
4. We compare our notion of portability to a state-based notion and show that the latter does not afford a polynomial SAT encoding.
5. We present experiments showing that *(i)* in a large majority of cases both notions of portability coincide, and *(ii)* mutual exclusion algorithms are often not portable, particularly we perform the first analysis from TSO to Power.

2 Portability Analysis on an Example

Consider program **IRIW** in Fig. 1, written in C++11 and using the atomic operator `memory_order_relaxed` which provides no guarantees on how memory accesses are ordered. When porting, the program is compiled to two different architectures. The corresponding low-level programs behave differently on x86 and on IBM's Power. On TSO, the memory model implemented by x86, each thread has a store buffer of pending writes. A thread can see its own writes before they become visible to other threads (by reading them from its buffer), but once a write hits the memory it becomes visible to all other threads simultaneously: TSO is a multi-copy-atomic model [18]. Power on the other hand does not guarantee that writes become visible to all threads at the same point in time. Think of each thread as having its own copy of the memory. With these two architectures in mind, consider the execution in Fig. 1. Thread t_2 reads $x = 1, y = 0$ and thread t_3 reads $x = 0, y = 1$, indicated by the solid edges *rfe* and *rf*. Since under TSO every execution has a unique global view of all operations, no interleaving allows both threads to read the above values of the variables. Under Power, this is possible. Our goal is to automatically detect such differences when porting a program from one architecture to another, here from TSO to Power.

Our tool PORTHOS applies to various architectures, and we not only have a *language for programs* but also a *language for memory models*. The semantics of a program on a memory model is defined axiomatically, following two steps [8,48].

thread t_0 `y.store(memory_order_relaxed, 1)`	**thread** t_1 `x.store(memory_order_relaxed, 1)`
thread t_2 $r_1 =$ `x.load(memory_order_relaxed);` $r_2 =$ `y.load(memory_order_relaxed)`	**thread** t_3 $r_1 =$ `y.load(memory_order_relaxed);` $r_2 =$ `x.load(memory_order_relaxed)`

x86 ASSEMBLY

thread t_0	thread t_1	thread t_2	thread t_3
`MOV [y],$1`	`MOV [x],$1`	`MOV EAX,[x]`	`MOV EAX,[y]`
		`MOV EAX,[y]`	`MOV EAX,[x]`

POWER ASSEMBLY

thread t_0	thread t_1	thread t_2	thread t_3
`li r1,1`	`li r1,1`	`lwz r1,x`	`lwz r1,y`
`stw r1,y`	`stw r1,x`	`lwz r3,y`	`lwz r3,x`

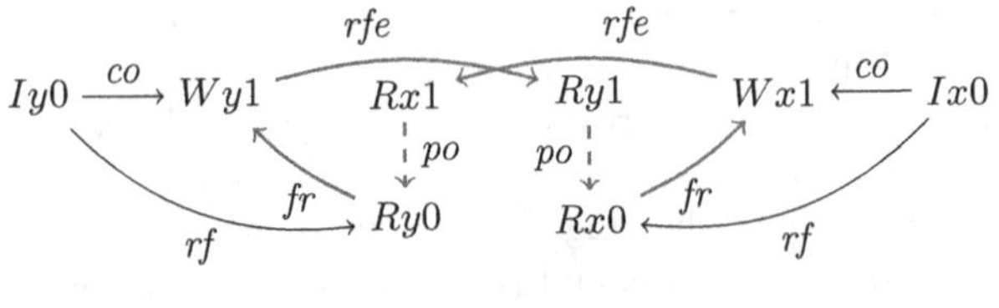

Fig. 1. Portability of program **IRIW** from TSO to Power.

Consistent$_{TSO}$

❶ $acyclic((po \cap sloc) \cup rf \cup fr \cup co)$
❷ $acyclic(rfe \cup co \cup fr \cup (po \setminus (\mathbb{W} \times \mathbb{R})) \cup mfence)$

$fr := rf^{-1}; co$
$rfe := rf \setminus sthd$

Fig. 2. TSO.

We first associate with the program (and independent of the memory model) a set of executions which are candidates for the semantics. An execution is a graph (Fig. 1) whose nodes (events) are program instructions and whose edges are basic dependencies: the program order *po*, the reads-from relation *rf* (giving the write that a load reads from), and the coherence order *co* (stating the order in which writes take effect). The memory model then defines which executions are consistent and thus form the semantics of the program on that model.

We describe memory models in the recently proposed language CAT [4]. Besides the base relations, a model may define so-called derived relations. The consistency requirements are stated in terms of acyclicity and irreflexivity axioms over these (base and derived) relations. The CAT formalisation of TSO is given in Fig. 2. It forbids executions forming a cycle over $rfe \cup fr \cup (po \setminus (\mathbb{W} \times \mathbb{R}))$. The red edges in Fig. 1 yield such a cycle; the execution is not consistent with TSO. Power further relaxes the program order (Fig. 6), the relations denoted by the dotted lines are no longer considered for cycles and thus the execution is consistent. Hence, **IRIW** has executions consistent with Power but not with TSO and is therefore not portable.

Our contribution is a bounded analysis for portability implemented in the PORTHOS tool (http://github.com/hernanponcedeleon/PORTHOS). First, the program is unrolled up to a user-specified bound. Within this bound, PORTHOS is guaranteed to find all portability bugs. It will neither see bugs beyond the bound nor will it be able to prove a cyclic program portable. The unrolled program, together with the CAT models, is transformed into an SMT formula where satisfying assignments correspond to bugs.

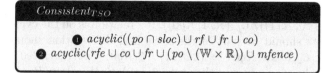

A bug is an execution consistent with the target memory model $\mathcal{M}_T$ but inconsistent with the source $\mathcal{M}_S$. We express this combination of consistency and inconsistency with only one existential quantification. The key observation is that the derived relations, which may differ in $\mathcal{M}_T$ and $\mathcal{M}_S$, are fully defined by the execution. Hence, by guessing an execution we also obtain the derived relations (there is nothing more to guess). Checking consistency for $\mathcal{M}_T$ is then an acyclicity (or irreflexivity) constraint on the derived relations that immediately yields an SMT query. Inconsistency for $\mathcal{M}_S$ requires cyclicity. The trick is to explicitly guess the cycle. We introduce Boolean variables for every event and every edge that could be part of the cycle. In Fig. 1, if $Rx1$ is on the cycle, indicated by the variable $\mathtt{C}(Rx1)$ being set, then there should be one incoming and one outgoing edge also in the cycle. Besides the incoming edge shown in the graph, $Rx1$ could read from the initial value $Ix0$. Since there are two possible incoming edges but only one outgoing edge, we obtain $\mathtt{C}(Rx1) \Rightarrow ((\mathtt{C}_{rfe}(Wx1, Rx1) \vee \mathtt{C}_{rf}(Ix0, Rx1)) \wedge \mathtt{C}_{po}(Rx1, Ry0))$. If a relation is on the cycle, then also both end-points should be part of the cycle and the relation should belong to the execution: $\mathtt{C}_{po}(Rx1, Ry0) \Rightarrow (\mathtt{C}(Rx1) \wedge \mathtt{C}(Ry0) \wedge \mathtt{po}(Rx1, Ry0))$. Finally, at least one event has to be part of the cycle: $\mathtt{C}(Ix0) \vee \mathtt{C}(Wx1) \vee \mathtt{C}(Rx1) \vee \mathtt{C}(Rx0) \vee \mathtt{C}(Iy0) \vee \mathtt{C}(Wy1) \vee \mathtt{C}(Ry1) \vee \mathtt{C}(Ry0)$. The execution in Fig. 1 contains the relations marked in red and forms a cycle which violates Axiom ❷ in TSO. The execution respects the axioms of Power (Fig. 6), showing the existence of a portability bug in **IRIW** from TSO to Power.

The other challenge is to capture relations that are defined recursively. The Kleene iteration process [43] starts with the empty relation and repeatedly adds pairs of events according to the recursive definitions. We encode this into (quantifier-free) integer difference logic [19]. For every recursive relation $\mathtt{r}$ and every pair of events (e_1, e_2), we introduce an integer variable $\Phi^{\mathtt{r}}_{e_1,e_2}$ representing the iteration step in which the pair entered the value of $\mathtt{r}$. A Kleene iteration then corresponds to a total ordering on these integer variables. Crucially, we only have one Boolean variable $\mathtt{r}(e_1, e_2)$ per pair rather than one per iteration step. We illustrate the encoding on a simplified version of the preserved program order for Power defined as *ppo* := *ii* ∪ *ic* (cf. Fig. 6 for the full definition). The relation is derived from the mutually recursive relations *ii* := *dd* ∪ *ic* and *ic* := *cd* ∪ *ii*, where *dd* and *cd* represent data and control dependencies. Call $Rx1$ and $Ry0$ respectively e_1 and e_2. The encoding is

$$\mathtt{ii}(e_1, e_2) \Leftrightarrow (\mathtt{dd}(e_1, e_2) \wedge (\Phi^{\mathtt{ii}}_{e_1,e_2} > \Phi^{\mathtt{dd}}_{e_1,e_2})) \vee (\mathtt{ic}(e_1, e_2) \wedge (\Phi^{\mathtt{ii}}_{e_1,e_2} > \Phi^{\mathtt{ic}}_{e_1,e_2}))$$

$$\mathtt{ic}(e_1, e_2) \Leftrightarrow (\mathtt{cd}(e_1, e_2) \wedge (\Phi^{\mathtt{ic}}_{e_1,e_2} > \Phi^{\mathtt{cd}}_{e_1,e_2})) \vee (\mathtt{ii}(e_1, e_2) \wedge (\Phi^{\mathtt{ic}}_{e_1,e_2} > \Phi^{\mathtt{ii}}_{e_1,e_2})).$$

The pair (e_1, e_2) that belongs to relation *dd* in step $\Phi^{\mathtt{dd}}_{e_1,e_2}$ of the Kleene iteration can be added to relation *ii* at a later step $\Phi^{\mathtt{ii}}_{e_1,e_2} > \Phi^{\mathtt{dd}}_{e_1,e_2}$. As *ii* := *dd* ∪ *ic*, the disjunction allows us to also add the elements of *ic* to *ii*. Since *dd* and *cd* are empty for **IRIW**, the relations *ii* and *ic* have to be identical. Identical non-empty relations will not yield a solution: the integer variables cannot satisfy $(\Phi^{\mathtt{ii}}_{e_1,e_2} > \Phi^{\mathtt{ic}}_{e_1,e_2})$ and $(\Phi^{\mathtt{ic}}_{e_1,e_2} > \Phi^{\mathtt{ii}}_{e_1,e_2})$ at the same time. Hence, the only satisfying assignment is the one where both *ii* and *ic* are the empty relation, which implies that *ppo* is empty. This is consistent with the preserved program order of Power for **IRIW**.

3 Programs and Memory Models

We introduce our language for programs and the core of the language CAT. The presentation follows [4,48] and we refer the reader to those works for details.

Programs. Our language for shared memory concurrent programs is given in Fig. 3. Programs consist of a finite number of threads from a while-language. The threads operate on assembly level, which means they explicitly read from the shared memory into registers, write from registers into memory, and support local computations on the registers. The language has various fence instructions (sync, lwsync, and isync on Power and mfence on x86) that enforce ordering and visibility constraints among instructions. We refrain from explicitly defining the expressions and predicates used in assignments and conditionals. They will depend on the data domain. For our analysis, we only require the domain to admit an SMT encoding in a logic which has its satisfiability problem in NP. For the rest of the paper we will assume that programs are acyclic: any while statement is removed by unrolling the program to a depth specified by the user. Since verification is generally undecidable for while-programs [39], this under-approximation is necessary for cyclic programs.

$$
\begin{aligned}
\langle prog\rangle &::= \texttt{program}\ \langle thrd\rangle^{*}\\
\langle thrd\rangle &::= \texttt{thread}\ \langle tid\rangle\ \langle inst\rangle\\
\langle inst\rangle &::= \langle atom\rangle \mid \langle inst\rangle;\langle inst\rangle\\
&\mid \texttt{while}\ \langle pred\rangle\ \langle inst\rangle\\
&\mid \texttt{if}\ \langle pred\rangle\ \texttt{then}\ \langle inst\rangle\\
&\qquad\qquad \texttt{else}\ \langle inst\rangle\\
\langle atom\rangle &::= \langle reg\rangle \leftarrow \langle exp\rangle \mid \langle reg\rangle \leftarrow \langle loc\rangle\\
&\mid \langle loc\rangle := \langle reg\rangle \mid \langle mfence\rangle\\
&\mid \langle sync\rangle \mid \langle lwsync\rangle \mid \langle isync\rangle
\end{aligned}
$$

Fig. 3. Programming language.

$$
\begin{aligned}
\langle MCM\rangle &::= \langle assert\rangle \mid \langle rel\rangle \mid \langle MCM\rangle \wedge \langle MCM\rangle\\
\langle assert\rangle &::= acyclic(\langle r\rangle) \mid irreflexive(\langle r\rangle)\\
\langle r\rangle &::= \langle b\rangle \mid \langle r\rangle \cup \langle r\rangle \mid \langle r\rangle \cap \langle r\rangle \mid \langle r\rangle \setminus \langle r\rangle\\
&\mid \langle r\rangle^{-1} \mid \langle r\rangle^{+} \mid \langle r\rangle^{*} \mid \langle r\rangle;\langle r\rangle\\
\langle b\rangle &::= po \mid rf \mid co \mid ad \mid dd \mid cd \mid sthd \mid sloc\\
&\mid mfence \mid sync \mid lwsync \mid isync\\
&\mid id(\langle set\rangle) \mid \langle set\rangle \times \langle set\rangle \mid \langle name\rangle\\
\langle set\rangle &::= \mathbb{E} \mid \mathbb{W} \mid \mathbb{R}\\
\langle rel\rangle &::= \langle name\rangle := \langle r\rangle
\end{aligned}
$$

Fig. 4. Core of CAT [4].

Executions. The semantics of a program is given in terms of *executions*, partial orders where the events represent occurrences of the instructions and the ordering edges represent dependencies. The definition is given in Fig. 5. An execution consists of a set $\mathbb{X}$ of executed events and so-called *base* and *induced relations* satisfying the Axioms ❸-⓲. Base relations *rf* and *co* and the set $\mathbb{X}$ define an execution (they are the ones to be guessed). Induced relations can be extracted directly from the source code of the program. The axioms in Fig. 5 are common to all memory models and natively implemented by our tool. To state them, let $\mathbb{E}$ represents memory events coming from program instructions accessing the memory. Memory accesses are either reads or writes $\mathbb{E} := \mathbb{R} \cup \mathbb{W}$. By $\mathbb{R}_l$ and $\mathbb{W}_l$ we refer respectively to the reads and writes that access location l. The events of thread t form the set $\mathbb{E}_t$. Relations *sthd* and *sloc* are equivalences relating events belonging to the same thread ❸ and accessing the same location ❹. Relations *po*, *ad*, *dd* and *cd* represent program order and address/data/control dependencies. Axiom ❺ states that the *program order po* is an intra-thread relation which ❻ forms a total order when projected to events in the same thread (predicate $total(r, A)$ holds if r is a total order on the set A). *Address dependencies* are either read-to-read or read-to-write ❼, *data dependencies* are read-to-write ❽, and *control dependencies* originate from reads ❾. Fence relations are architecture specific and relate only events in program order ❿-⓭. Axiom ⓮, which

$sloc, sthd \subseteq \mathbb{E} \times \mathbb{E}$ same location, same thread
$po, ad, dd, cd \subseteq \mathbb{E} \times \mathbb{E}$ program order, address/data/control dependency
$mfence \subseteq \mathbb{E} \times \mathbb{E}$ fences in x86
$sync, lwsync, isync \subseteq \mathbb{E} \times \mathbb{E}$ fences in Power

(3) $equiv(sthd, \mathbb{E})$ (4) $equiv(sloc, \mathbb{M})$ (5) $po \subseteq sthd$ (6) $total(po, \mathbb{E}_t)$
(7) $ad \subseteq (\mathbb{R} \times \mathbb{M}) \cap po$ (8) $dd \subseteq (\mathbb{R} \times \mathbb{W}) \cap po$ (9) $cd \subseteq (\mathbb{R} \times \mathbb{E}) \cap po$
(10) $sync \subseteq po$ (11) $lwsync \subseteq po$ (12) $isync \subseteq po$ (13) $mfence \subseteq po$

$\mathbb{X} \subseteq \mathbb{E}$ executed events $rf, co \subseteq \mathbb{E} \times \mathbb{E}$ reads-from, coherence order

(14) $path$ (15) $rf \subseteq (\mathbb{W} \times \mathbb{R}) \cap sloc$ (16) $rf; rf^{-1} = id(\mathbb{E})$
(17) $co \subseteq ((\mathbb{W} \times \mathbb{W}) \cap sloc) \setminus id(\mathbb{E})$ (18) $total(co, \mathbb{W}_l)$

Fig. 5. Executions; adapted from [48].

we do not make explicit, requires the executed events $\mathbb{X}$ to form a path in the threads' control flow. By Axioms (15) and (16), the *reads-from relation rf* gives for each read a unique write to the same location from which the read obtains its value. Here, $r_1; r_2 := \{(x, y) \mid \exists z : (x, z) \in r_1 \text{ and } (z, y) \in r_2\}$ is the composition of the relations r_1 and r_2. We write $r^{-1} := \{(y, x) \mid (x, y) \in r\}$ for the inverse of relation r. Finally, $id(A)$ is the identity relation on A. By Axioms (17) and (18), the *coherence relation co* relates writes to the same location, and it forms a total order for each location. We will assume the existence of an initial write event for each location which assigns value 0 to the location. This event is first in the coherence order.

Memory Consistency Models. We give in Fig. 4 a core subset of the CAT language for memory consistency models (MCMs). A *memory model* is a constraint system over so-called *derived relations*. Derived relations are built from the base and induced relations in an execution, hand-defined relations that refer to the different sets of events, and named relations that we will explain in a moment. The assertions are acyclicity and irreflexivity constraints over derived relations. CAT also supports recursive definitions of relations. We assume a set $\langle name \rangle$ of relation names (different from the predefined relations) and require that each name used in the memory model has associated a defining equation $\langle name \rangle := \langle r \rangle$. Notably, $\langle r \rangle$ may again contain relation names, making the system of defining equations recursive. The actual relations that are denoted by the names are defined to be the least solution to this system of equations. We can compute the least solution with a standard Kleene iteration [43] starting from the empty relations and iterating until the least fixed point is reached.

In Sect. 6 we study portability to Power; we use its formalization [8] in the core of CAT as given in Fig. 6. Power is a highly relaxed memory model that supports program-order relaxations depending on address and data dependencies, that is

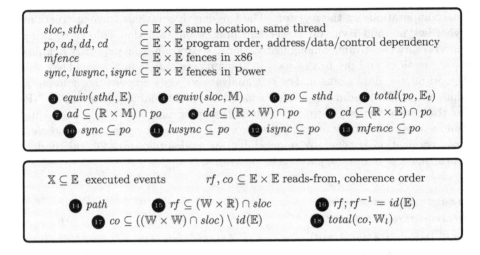

Consistent$_{Power}$

❶ $acyclic((po \cap sloc) \cup rf \cup fr \cup co)$ ⓳ $acyclic(hb)$
⓴ $irreflexive(fre; prop; hb^*)$ ㉑ $acyclic(co \cup prop)$

Preserved Program Order

$dp := ad \cup dd \quad rdw := (po \cap sloc) \cap (fre; rfe) \quad detour := (po \cap sloc) \cap (coe; rfe)$

$ii_0 := dp \cup rdw \cup rfi \quad ci_0 := cd\text{-}isync \cup detour$

$ic_0 := \emptyset \quad cc_0 := dp \cup (po \cap sloc) \cup cd \cup (ad; po)$

$ii := ii_0 \cup ci \cup (ic; ci) \cup (ii; ii) \quad ci := ci_0 \cup (ci; ii) \cup (cc; ci)$

$ic := ic_0 \cup ii \cup cc \cup (ic; cc) \cup (ii; ic) \quad cc := cc_0 \cup ci \cup (ci; ic) \cup (cc; cc)$

$ppo := ((\mathbb{R} \times \mathbb{R}) \cap ii) \cup ((\mathbb{R} \times \mathbb{W}) \cap ic)$

Fences

$fence := sync \cup (lwsync \setminus (\mathbb{W} \times \mathbb{R}))$

Thin Air

$hb := ppo \cup fence \cup rfe$

Propagation

$prop\text{-}base := (fence \cup (rfe; fence)); hb^*$

$prop := ((\mathbb{W} \times \mathbb{W}) \cap prop\text{-}base) \cup (com^*; prop\text{-}base^*; sync; hb^*)$

Fig. 6. Power [8].

not multi-copy atomic, and that has a complex set of fence instructions. The axioms defining Power are uniproc ❶ and the constraints ⓳ to ㉑. The model relies on the recursively defined relations *ii*, *ci*, *ic*, and *cc*.

4 Portability Analysis

Let $cons_{\mathcal{M}}(P)$ be the set of executions of program P consistent with $\mathcal{M}$. Given a program P and two MCMs $\mathcal{M}_S$ and $\mathcal{M}_T$, our goal is to find an execution X which is consistent with the target ($X \in cons_{\mathcal{M}_T}(P)$) but not with the source ($X \notin cons_{\mathcal{M}_S}(P)$). In such a case P is not portable from $\mathcal{M}_S$ to $\mathcal{M}_T$.

Definition 1 (Portability). *Let $\mathcal{M}_S$, $\mathcal{M}_T$ be two MCMs. A program P is* portable from $\mathcal{M}_S$ to $\mathcal{M}_T$ *if $cons_{\mathcal{M}_T}(P) \subseteq cons_{\mathcal{M}_S}(P)$.*

Our method finds non-portable executions as satisfying assignments to an SMT formula. Recall that an execution is uniquely represented by the set $\mathbb{X}$ and the relations *rf* and *co*, which need to be guessed by the solver. All other relations are derived from these guesses, the source code of the program, and the MCMs in question. Therefore, we also have to encode the derived relations of the two MCMs defined in the language of Fig. 4. As the last part, we encode the assertions expressed in the language of Fig. 4 on these relations in such a way that the guessed execution is allowed by $\mathcal{M}_T$ (all the assertions stated for $\mathcal{M}_T$ hold) while the same execution is not allowed by $\mathcal{M}_S$ (at least one of the axioms of $\mathcal{M}_S$ is violated). The full SMT formula is of the form $\phi_{CF} \wedge \phi_{DF} \wedge \phi_{\mathcal{M}_T} \wedge \phi_{\neg\mathcal{M}_S}$.

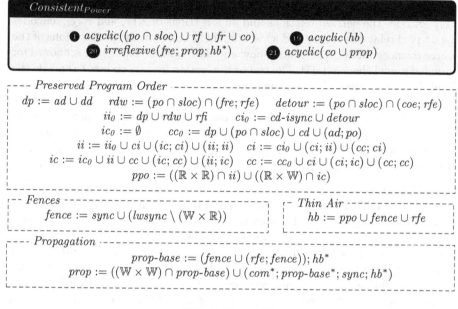

Here, ϕ_{CF} and ϕ_{DF} encode the control flow and data flow of the executions, $\phi_{\mathcal{M}_T}$ encodes the derived relations and all assertions of $\mathcal{M}_T$, and $\phi_{\neg\mathcal{M}_S}$ encodes the derived relations of $\mathcal{M}_S$ and a violation of at least one of the assertions of the source memory model. The control-flow and data-flow encodings are standard for bounded model checking [17]. The rest of the section focuses on how to encode the derived relations needed for representing both MCMs, how to encode assertions for the target memory model and how to encode an assertion violation in the source memory model. The encoding for assertions in the target memory model and the encoding for most of the relations is similar to [6], the most notable difference being that they do not discuss how to handle mutually recursively defined relations while we do so in an efficient way.

Encoding Derived Relations. For any pair of events $e_1, e_2 \in \mathbb{E}$ and relation $r \subseteq \mathbb{E} \times \mathbb{E}$ we use a Boolean variable $\mathtt{r}(e_1, e_2)$ representing the fact that $e_1 \xrightarrow{r} e_2$ holds. We similarly use fresh Boolean variables to represent the derived relations, using the encoding to force their values as follows. For the union (resp. intersection) of two relations, at least one of them (resp. both of them) should hold; set difference requires that the first relation holds and the second one does not; for the composition of relations we iterate over a third event and check if it belongs to the range of the first relation and the domain of the second. Computing a reverse relation requires reversing the events. We define the transitive closure of r recursively where the base case tc_0 holds if events are related according to r and the recursive case uses a relation composition. This is computed with the iterative squaring technique using the relation composition. Finally reflexive and transitive closure checks if the events are the same or are related by r^+. The encodings are summarized below.

$$\mathtt{r}_1 \cup \mathtt{r}_2(e_1,e_2) \Leftrightarrow \mathtt{r}_1(e_1,e_2) \vee \mathtt{r}_2(e_1,e_2) \qquad \mathtt{r}_1 \cap \mathtt{r}_2(e_1,e_2) \Leftrightarrow \mathtt{r}_1(e_1,e_2) \wedge \mathtt{r}_2(e_1,e_2)$$
$$\mathtt{r}_1 \backslash \mathtt{r}_2(e_1,e_2) \Leftrightarrow \mathtt{r}_1(e_1,e_2) \wedge \neg \mathtt{r}_2(e_1,e_2) \qquad \mathtt{r}^{-1}(e_1,e_2) \Leftrightarrow \mathtt{r}(e_2,e_1)$$
$$\mathtt{r}_1 ; \mathtt{r}_2(e_1,e_2) \Leftrightarrow \bigvee_{e_3 \in \mathbb{E}} \mathtt{r}_1(e_1,e_3) \wedge \mathtt{r}_2(e_3,e_2) \qquad \mathtt{r}^*(e_1,e_2) \Leftrightarrow \mathtt{r}^+(e_1,e_2) \vee (e_1 = e_2)$$

$$\begin{aligned} \mathtt{r}^+(e_1,e_2) &\Leftrightarrow \mathtt{tc}_{\lceil \log |\mathbb{E}| \rceil}(e_1,e_2), \textit{ where} \\ \mathtt{tc}_0(e_1,e_2) &\Leftrightarrow \mathtt{r}(e_1,e_2), \textit{ and} \\ \mathtt{tc}_{i+1}(e_1,e_2) &\Leftrightarrow \mathtt{r}(e_1,e_2) \vee \mathtt{tc}_i ; \mathtt{tc}_i(e_1,e_2). \end{aligned}$$

Recall that some of the relations (e.g., *ii* and *ic* of Power) can be defined mutually recursively, and that we are using the least fixed point (smallest solution) semantics for cyclic definitions. A classical algorithm for solving such equations is the Kleene fixpoint iteration. The iteration starts from the empty relations as initial approximation and on each round computes a new approximation until the (least) fixed point is reached. Such an iterative algorithm can be easily encoded into SAT. The problem of such an encoding is the potentially large number of iterations needed, and thus the resulting formula size can grow to be very large. A more clever way to encode this is an approach that has been already used in earlier work on encoding mutually recursive monotone equation systems with nested least and greatest fixpoints [30]. The encoding of this paper uses an extension of SAT with integer difference logic (IDL), a logic that is still NP complete. A SAT encoding is also possible but incurs an overhead in the encoding size: if the SMT encoding is of size $O(n)$, the SAT encoding is of size $O(n \log n)$ [30]. We chose IDL since our experiments showed the encoding to be the most time consuming of the tasks.

Here, the basic idea is to guess a certificate that contains the iteration number in which a pair would be added to the relation in the Kleene iteration. For this we use additional integer variables and enforce that they locally follow the propagations made by the fixed point iteration algorithm. Thus, for any pair of events $e_1, e_2 \in \mathbb{E}$ and relation $r \subseteq \mathbb{E} \times \mathbb{E}$ we introduce an integer variable $\Phi^{\mathtt{r}}_{e_1,e_2}$ representing the round in which $\mathtt{r}(e_1, e_2)$ would be set by the Kleene iteration algorithm. Using these new variables we guess the execution of the Kleene fixed point iteration algorithm, and then locally check that every guess that was made is also a valid propagation of the fixed point iteration algorithm. To give an example, consider a definition where $r_1 := r_2 \cup r_3$ and $r_2 := r_1 \cup r_4$. The encoding is as follows

$$\begin{aligned}
\mathtt{r}_1(e_1, e_2) &\Leftrightarrow (\mathtt{r}_2(e_1, e_2) \wedge (\Phi^{\mathtt{r}_1}_{e_1,e_2} > \Phi^{\mathtt{r}_2}_{e_1,e_2})) \vee (\mathtt{r}_3(e_1, e_2) \wedge (\Phi^{\mathtt{r}_1}_{e_1,e_2} > \Phi^{\mathtt{r}_3}_{e_1,e_2}))\\
\mathtt{r}_2(e_1, e_2) &\Leftrightarrow (\mathtt{r}_1(e_1, e_2) \wedge (\Phi^{\mathtt{r}_2}_{e_1,e_2} > \Phi^{\mathtt{r}_1}_{e_1,e_2})) \vee (\mathtt{r}_4(e_1, e_2) \wedge (\Phi^{\mathtt{r}_2}_{e_1,e_2} > \Phi^{\mathtt{r}_4}_{e_1,e_2})).
\end{aligned}$$

A pair (e_1, e_2) is added to r_1 by the Kleene iteration in step $\Phi^{\mathtt{r}_1}_{e_1,e_2}$. It comes from either r_2 or r_3. If it came from r_2 then it is of course also in r_2 and it was added to r_2 in an earlier iteration $\Phi^{\mathtt{r}_2}_{e_1,e_2}$ and thus $(\Phi^{\mathtt{r}_1}_{e_1,e_2} > \Phi^{\mathtt{r}_2}_{e_1,e_2})$. It is similar if it came from r_3. The only satisfying assignment for the encoding is one where both r_1 and r_2 are the union of r_3 and r_4.

Encoding Target MCM Assertions. For the target architecture we need to encode all acyclicity and irreflexivity assertions of the memory model. For handling acyclicity we again use non-Boolean variables in our SMT encoding for compactness reasons. One can encode that a relation is acyclic by adding a numerical variable $\Psi_e \in \mathbb{N}$ for each event e in the relation we want to be acyclic. Then acyclicity of relation r is encoded as $\mathit{acyclic}(r) \Leftrightarrow \bigwedge_{e_1,e_2 \in \mathbb{E}} (\mathtt{r}(e_1, e_2) \Rightarrow (\Psi_{e_1} < \Psi_{e_2}))$. Notice that we can impose a total order with all $\Psi_{e_1} < \Psi_{e_2}$ constraints iff there is no cycle. Our encoding is the same as the SAT + IDL encoding in [28] where more discussion of SAT modulo acyclicity can be found. The irreflexive constraint is simply encoded as: $\mathit{irreflexive}(r) \Leftrightarrow \bigwedge_{e \in \mathbb{E}} \neg \mathtt{r}(e, e)$.

Encoding Source MCM Assertions. For the source architecture we have to encode that one of the derived relations does not fulfill its assertions. On the top level this can be encoded as a simple disjunction over all the assertions of the source memory model, forcing at least one of the irreflexivity or acyclicity constraints to be violated.

For the irreflexivity violation, we can reuse the same encoding as for the target memory model simply as $\neg\mathit{irreflexive}(r)$. What remains to be encoded is $\mathit{cyclic}(r)$, which requires the relation r to be cyclic. Here, we give an encoding that uses only Boolean variables. We add Boolean variables $\mathtt{C}(e)$ and $\mathtt{C}_\mathtt{r}(e_1, e_2)$, which guess the edges and nodes constituting the cycle. We ensure that for every event in the cycle, there should be at least one incoming edge and at least one outgoing edge that are also in the cycle:

$$c_n = \bigwedge_{e_1 \in \mathbb{E}} (\mathtt{C}(e_1) \Rightarrow (\bigvee_{e_2 \xrightarrow{r} e_1} \mathtt{C}_\mathtt{r}(e_2, e_1) \wedge \bigvee_{e_1 \xrightarrow{r} e_2)} \mathtt{C}_\mathtt{r}(e_1, e_2))).$$

If an edge is guessed to be in a cycle, the edge must belong to relation r, and both events must also be guessed to be on the cycle:

$$c_e = \bigwedge_{e_1, e_2 \in \mathbb{E}} (\mathtt{C}_\mathtt{r}(e_1, e_2) \Rightarrow (\mathtt{r}(e_1, e_2) \wedge \mathtt{C}(e_1) \wedge \mathtt{C}(e_2))).$$

A cycle exists, if these formulas hold and there is an event in the cycle:

$$\mathit{cyclic}(r) \Leftrightarrow (c_e \wedge c_n \wedge \bigvee_{e \in \mathbb{E}} \mathtt{C}(e)).$$

5 State Portability

Portability from $\mathcal{M}_S$ to $\mathcal{M}_T$ requires that there are no new executions in $\mathcal{M}_T$ that did not occur in $\mathcal{M}_S$. One motivation to check portability is to make sure that safety properties of $\mathcal{M}_S$ carry over to $\mathcal{M}_T$. Safety properties only depend on the values that can be computed, not on the actual executions. Therefore, we now study a more liberal notion of so-called *state portability*: $\mathcal{M}_T$ may admit new executions as long as they do not compute new states. Admitting more executions means we require less synchronization (fences) to consider a ported program correct, and thus state portability promises more efficient code. This notion has been used in [31].

The main finding in this section is negative: a polynomial encoding of state portability to SAT does not exist (unless the polynomial hierarchy collapses). Phrased differently, state portability does not admit an efficient bounded analysis (like our method for portability). Fortunately, our experiments indicate that new executions often compute new states. This means portability is not only a sufficient condition for state portability but, in practice, the two are equivalent. Combined with the better algorithmics of portability, we do not see a good motivation to move to state portability. Proofs of all stated results can be found in [38]. We remind the reader that we restrict our input to acyclic programs (that can be obtained from while-programs with bounded unrolling); for while-programs, verification tasks are generally undecidable [39].

A state is a function that assigns a value to each location and register. An execution X computes the state $\mathit{state}(X)$ defined as follows: a location receives the value of the last write event (according to co) accessing it; for a register, its value depends on the last event in po that writes to it. The relationship between the notions is as in Lemma 1.

Definition 2 (State Portability). *Let $\mathcal{M}_S$, $\mathcal{M}_T$ be MCMs. Program P is* state portable from $\mathcal{M}_S$ to $\mathcal{M}_T$ *if $state(cons_{\mathcal{M}_T}(P)) \subseteq state(cons_{\mathcal{M}_S}(P))$.*

Lemma 1. *(1) Portability implies state portability. (2) State portability does not imply portability.*

For Lemma 1.(2), consider a variant of **IRIW** (Fig. 1) where all written values are 0. The program is trivially state portable from Power to TSO, but like **IRIW**, not portable.

We turn to the hardness argumentation. To check state portability, every $\mathcal{M}_T$-computable state seems to need a formula checking whether some $\mathcal{M}_S$-consistent execution computes it. The result would be an exponential blow-up or a quantified Boolean formula, which is not practical. But can this exponential blow-up or quantification be avoided by some clever encoding trick? The answer is no! Theorem 1 shows that state portability is in a higher class of the polynomial hierarchy than portability. It is indeed harder to check than portability.

The polynomial hierarchy [42] contains complexity classes between NP and PSPACE. Each class is represented by the problem of checking validity of a Boolean formula with a fixed number of quantifier alternations. We need here the classes co-NP $= \Pi_1^P \subseteq \Pi_2^P$. The *tautology problem* (validity of a closed Boolean formula with a universal quantifier $\forall x_1 \dots x_n : \psi$) is a Π_1^P-complete problem. The higher class Π_2^P allows for a second quantifier: validity of a formula $(\forall x_1 \dots x_n \exists y_1 \dots y_n : \psi)$ is a Π_2^P-complete problem. Theorem 1 refers to a class of common memory models that we define in a moment. Moreover, we assume that the given pair of memory models $\mathcal{M}_S$ and $\mathcal{M}_T$ is *non-trivial* in the sense that $cons_{\mathcal{M}_T}(P) \subseteq cons_{\mathcal{M}_S}(P)$ fails for some program, and similar for state portability.

Theorem 1. *Let $\mathcal{M}_S, \mathcal{M}_T$ be a non-trivial pair of common MCMs. (1) Portability from $\mathcal{M}_S$ to $\mathcal{M}_T$ is Π_1^P-complete. (2) State portability is Π_2^P-complete.*

By Theorem 1.(2), state portability cannot be solved efficiently. The first part says that our portability analysis is optimal. We focus on this lower bound to give a taste of the argumentation: given a non-trivial pair of memory models, we know there is a program that is not portable. Crucially, we do not know the program but give a construction that works for any program. The proof of Theorem 1.(2) is along similar lines but more involved.

Definition 3. *We call an MCM* common[1] *if*

(i) the inverse operator is only used in the definition of fr,
(ii) the constructs sthd, sloc, and $\langle set\rangle \times \langle set\rangle$ are only used to restrict (in a conjunction) other relations,
(iii) it satisfies uniproc (Axiom ❶), and
(iv) every program is portable from this MCM to SC.

[1] Notice that all memory models considered in [8] and in this paper are common ones.

We explain the definition. When formulating an MCM, one typically forbids well-chosen cycles of base relations (and *fr*). To this end, derived relations are introduced that capture the paths of interest, and acyclicity constraints are imposed on the derived relations. The operators inverse and $\langle set\rangle \times \langle set\rangle$ may do the opposite, they add relations that do not correspond to paths of base relations (and *fr*). Besides stating what is common in MCMs, Properties *(i)* and *(ii)* help us compose programs (cf. next paragraph). Uniproc is a fundamental property without which an MCM is hard to program. Since the purpose of an MCM is to capture SC relaxations, we can assume MCMs to be weaker than SC. Properties *(iii)* and *(iv)* guarantee that the program P_ψ given below is portable between any common MCMs.

The crucial property of common MCMs is the following. For every pair of events e_1, e_2 in a derived relation, (1) there are (potentially several) sequences of base relations (and *fr*) that connect e_1 and e_2, and (2) the derived relation only depends on these sequences. The property ensures that if we append a program P' to a location-disjoint program P, any executions composed from consistent executions of P and P' is also consistent.

It remains to prove Π_1^P-hardness of portability by constructing a program that is portable iff a formula ψ is a tautology. We first introduce the program P_ψ that generates some assignment and checks if it satisfies the Boolean formula $\psi(x_1 \ldots x_m)$ (over the variables $x_1 \ldots x_m$). The program $P_\psi := t_1 \parallel t_2$ consists of the two threads t_1 and t_2 defined below. Note that we cannot directly write a constant i to a location, so we first assign i to register $r_{c,i}$.

thread t_1	*thread* t_2
$r_{c,0} \leftarrow 0;\ r_{c,1} \leftarrow 1;\ r_{c,2} \leftarrow 2$	$r_{c,1} \leftarrow 1;$
$x_1 := r_{c,0} \ldots x_m := r_{c,0};$	$x_1 := r_{c,1} \ldots x_m := r_{c,1};$
$r_1 \leftarrow x_1 \ldots r_m \leftarrow x_m;$	
if $\psi(r_1 \ldots r_m)$ **then**	
$\quad y := r_{c,2};$	
else $y := r_{c,1};$	

We reduce checking whether $\forall x_1 \ldots x_m : \psi(x_1 \ldots x_m)$ holds to portability of a program $P_{\forall\psi}$. The idea for $P_{\forall\psi}$ is this. First P_ψ is run, it guesses and evaluates an assignment for ψ. If ψ is not satisfied ($y = 1$), then some non-portable program P_{np} is executed. The program $P_{\forall\psi}$ is portable iff the non-portable part is never executed. This is the case iff ψ is satisfied by all assignments.

Let $\mathcal{M}_S$, $\mathcal{M}_T$ be common and non-trivial. By non-triviality, there is a program $P_{np} = t'_1 \parallel \cdots \parallel t'_k$ that is not portable from $\mathcal{M}_S$ to $\mathcal{M}_T$. We can assume P_{np} has no registers or locations in common with P_ψ. Program $P_{\forall\psi}$ prepends P_ψ to the first two threads of P_{np}. Once $y = 1$, P_{np} starts running. Formally, let t_1 and t_2 be the threads in P_ψ and let $t_i := skip$ for $3 \leq i \leq k$. We define $P_{\forall\psi} := t''_1 \parallel \cdots \parallel t''_k$ with $t''_i := t_i;\ r \leftarrow y;$ **if**$(r = 1)$ **then** t'_i.

We show that $P_{\forall\psi}$ is portable iff ψ is satisfied for every assignment.

6 Experiments

The encoding from Sect. 4 has been implemented in a tool called PORTHOS. We evaluate PORTHOS on benchmark programs and a wide range of well-known MCMs. For SC, TSO, PSO, RMO and Alpha (henceforth called traditional architectures) we use the formalizations from [3]; for Power the one in Fig. 6. We divide our results into three categories: portability of mutual exclusion algorithms, empirical comparison between portability and state portability, and performance of the tool.

Portability of Mutual Exclusion Algorithms. Most of the tools that are MCM-aware [8,35,45,48,49] accept only litmus tests as inputs. PORTHOS, however, can analyze cyclic programs with control flow branching and merging by unrolling them into acyclic form. In order to show the broad applicability of our method, we tested portability of several mutual exclusion algorithms: Lamport's bakery [32], Burns' protocol [15], Dekker's [23], Lamport's fast mutex [33], Peterson's [37] and Szymanski's [44]. The benchmarks also include previously known fenced versions for TSO taken from [12] (marked as x86) and new versions we introduced using Power fences (marked as POWER). The loops were unrolled once in all the experiments to obtain an acyclic program, and the discussion in what follows is for the portability analysis of this acyclic program.

While these algorithms have been proven correct for SC, it is well known that they do not guarantee mutual exclusion when ported to weaker architectures. The effects of relaxing the program order have been widely studied; there are techniques that even place fences automatically to guarantee portability, but

Table 1. (Left) Bounded portability analysis of mutual exclusion algorithms: portable (✔), non-portable (✗). **(Right)** Portability vs. State Portability on litmus tests.

Benchmark	SC-TSO	SC-Power	TSO-Power
BAKERY	✗	✗	✗
BAKERY x86	✔	✗	✗
BAKERY POWER	✔	✔	✔
BURNS	✗	✗	✗
BURNS x86	✔	✗	✗
BURNS POWER	✔	✔	✔
DEKKER	✗	✗	✗
DEKKER x86	✔	✗	✗
DEKKER POWER	✔	✔	✔
LAMPORT	✗	✗	✗
LAMPORT x86	✔	✗	✗
LAMPORT POWER	✔	✔	✔
PETERSON	✗	✗	✗
PETERSON x86	✔	✗	✗
PETERSON POWER	✔	✔	✔
SZYMANSKI	✗	✗	✗
SZYMANSKI x86	✔	✗	✗
SZYMANSKI POWER	✔	✔	✔

				Deadness	
	✗✗	✔✔	✗✔	✔✔	✗✔
SC-TSO	27	898	75	933	40
SC-PSO	27	777	196	836	137
SC-RMO	27	737	236	780	193
SC-Alpha	27	846	127	887	86
TSO-PSO	0	833	67	883	27
TSO-RMO	0	760	240	798	202
TSO-Alpha	0	877	133	912	88
PSO-RMO	0	831	169	844	156
PSO-Alpha	0	968	32	973	27
RMO-Alpha	0	999	1	999	1
Alpha-RMO	0	856	144	864	136
	0.98%	85.29 %	13.73 %	88.26 %	10.73 %
SC-Power	1477	898	52	936	14
TSO-Power	917	1132	378	1166	344
PSO-Power	502	1880	45	1892	33
RMO-Power	40	2227	160	2239	148
Alpha-Power	0	2427	0	2427	0
	24.20%	70.57%	5.23%	71.35%	4.45%

they assume SC as the source architecture [5,12]. In Table 1 (left) we do not only confirm that fenceless versions of the benchmarks are not portable from SC to TSO and fenced versions of them are, we also show that those fences are not enough to guarantee mutual exclusion when porting from TSO to Power. We have used PORTHOS to find portability bugs when porting from TSO to Power and manually added fences to forbid such executions (see benchmarks marked as POWER). To the best of our knowledge these are the first results about portability of mutual exclusion algorithms from memory models weaker than SC to the Power architecture.

Portability vs. State Portability. We empirically compare both notions of portability by using PORTHOS (which implements portability) and the HERD7 tool (http://diy.inria.fr/herd) which reasons about state reachability. HERD7 systematically constructs all consistent executions of the program and exhaustively enumerates all possible computable states. Such enumeration can be very expensive for programs with lots of computable states, e.g., for programs with a very large level of concurrency. Since HERD7 only allows to reason about one memory model at a time, for each test we run the tool twice (once for each MCM) and compare the set of computable states. The program is not state portable if the target MCM generates computable states that are not computable states of the source MCM.

Our experiments contain two test suites: TS_1 contains 1000 randomly generated litmus tests in x86 assembly (to test traditional architectures) and TS_2 contains 2427 litmus tests in Power assembly taken from [36]. Each test contains between 2 and 4 threads and between 4 and 20 instructions. Table 1 (right) reports the number of non-portable (w.r.t. both definitions) litmus tests (✗✗), the number of portable and state portable litmus tests (✔✔) and the number of litmus tests that are not portable but are still state portable (✗✔). In the last case the new executions allowed by the target memory model do not result in new computable states of the program. We show that in many cases both notions of portability coincide. On traditional architectures, TS_1 contains very few non state portable tests (0.98%). Here, a non portable program is state portable in only 13.73% of the cases. For TS_2 from traditional architectures to Power, the number of non state portable litmus tests rises to 24.20%, while only in 5.24% of the cases the two notions of portability do not match because the new executions do not result in a new computable state for the program.

In order to remove some executions that do not lead to new computable states, PORTHOS optionally supports the use of syntactic deadness which has

(22) $domain(cd) \subseteq range(rf)$ (23) $imm(co); imm(co); imm(co^{-1}) \subseteq rf^?; (po; (rf^{-1})^?)^?$	$imm(r) := r \setminus (r; r^+)$

Fig. 7. Syntactic deadness [48].

been recently proposed in [48]. Dead executions are either consistent or lead to not computable states. Formally an execution X is dead if $X \notin cons_{\mathcal{M}}(P)$ implies that $state(X) \neq state(Y)$ for all $Y \in cons_{\mathcal{M}}(P)$. Instead of looking for any execution which is not consistent for the source architecture, we want to restrict the search to non-consistent and dead executions of $\mathcal{M}_S$. This is equivalent to checking state portability. As shown by Wickerson et al. [48], dead executions can be approximated with constraints (22) and (23) given in Fig. 7 where $r^?$ is the reflexive closure of r. These constraints can be easily encoded into SAT. Our tool has an implementation which rules out quite a few executions not computing new states. The last two columns of Table 1 (right) show that by restricting the search to (syntactic) dead executions, the ratio of litmus tests the tool reports as non portable, but are actually state portable (due to syntactic dead executions that are not semantically dead) is reduced to 10.73% for traditional architectures and to 4.44% for Power.

The experiments above show that in most of the cases both notions of portability coincide, especially when using dead executions or porting to Power. To test state portability, our method can be complemented with an extra query to check if the final state of the counter-example execution is also reachable in the source model by another execution. As shown in Sect. 5, the price to obtain such a result is to go one level higher in the polynomial hierarchy which affects the performance. However, once an execution is found that disproves portability, one could check if the execution implies non state portability with a single existential query.

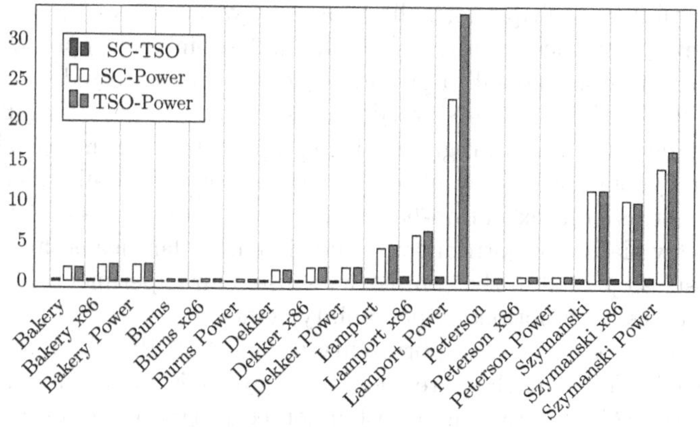

Fig. 8. Solving times (in secs.) for portability of mutual exclusion algorithms.

Performance. We evaluate the solving times of our tool on the mutual exclusion benchmarks as shown in Fig. 8. Our prototype encoding implementation is done in Python; the encoding times have a minimum of 13 seconds and a maximum of 3030 seconds. The encodings involving Power are usually more time consuming than traditional models since Power has both transitive closures and least fixed points in its encoding. For the mutual exclusion algorithms, the solving times are actually much lower than the encoding times of our prototype implementation. We expect that the encoding times could be vastly improved by a careful C/C++ implementation of the encoding.

We acknowledge that for small litmus test, the running times of HERD7 outperform our prototype implementation. However, as soon as the programs become bigger, HERD7 does not perform as well as PORTHOS. We believe this is due to the use of efficient search techniques in the SMT solver. In contrast, the number of executions HERD7 has to enumerate explicitly grows exponentially with the test size.

7 Related Work

Semantics and verification under weak memory models have been the subject of study at least since 2007. Initially, the behavior of x86 and TSO has been clarified [13,41], then the Power architecture has been addressed [36,40], now ARM is being tackled [26]. The study also looks beyond hardware, in particular C++11 received considerable attention [10,11]. Research in semantics goes hand in hand with the development of verification methods. They come in two flavors: program logics [46,47] and algorithmic approaches [1,2,6,8,9,12,14,20,21]. Notably, each of these methods and tools is designed for a specific memory model and hence is not directly able to handle porting tasks.

The problem of verifying consistency under weak memory models has been extensively studied. Multiple formalisations and variations of the problem and their complexity have been analyzed [16,24,25]. A prominent approach is testing where an execution is (partially) given and consistency is tested for a specified model [27,29]. In this line we showed that state portability (formulated as a bounded analysis for cyclic programs) is Π_2^p-complete. This means there is no hope for a polynomial encoding into SAT (unless the polynomial hierarchy collapses). In contrast, our execution-based notion of portability is co-NP complete (we look for a violation to portability), which in particular means that our portability analysis is optimal in the complexity sense. Our experiments show that in most of the cases both notions of portability coincide.

A problem less general than portability is solved in [12] where non-portable traces from SC to TSO are characterized. The problem is reduced to state reachability under the SC semantics in an instrumented program and a minimal number of fences is synthesized to enforce portability. One step further, one can enforce portability not only to TSO, but also to weaker memory models [22]. The OFFENCE tool [7] does this, but can only analyze litmus test and is limited to restoring SC. Checking the existence of critical cycles (i.e. portability bugs) on complex programs has been tackled in [5], where such cycles are broken by automatically introducing fences. The cost of different types of fences is considered and the task is encoded as an optimization problem. The MUSKETEER tool analyzes C programs and has shown to scale up to programs with thousands of lines of code, but the implementation is also restricted to the case were the source model is SC. Fence insertion can also be used to guarantee safety properties (rather than restoring SC behaviors). The FENDER and DFENCE tools [31,34] can verify real-world C code, but they are restricted to TSO, PSO, and RMO.

8 Conclusion and Outlook

We introduce the first method that tests portability between any two axiomatic memory models defined in the CAT language. The method reduces portability analysis to satisfiability of an SMT formula in SAT + integer difference logic. We propose efficient solutions for two crucial tasks: reasoning about two user-defined MCMs at the same time and encoding mutually recursively defined relations (needed for Power) into SMT. The latter technique can be re-used by any bounded model checking technique reasoning about complex memory models such as Power.

Our complexity analysis and experimental results both suggest that our definition of portability is preferable over the state-based notion of portability. The complexity results show that checking for state-based portability cannot be done with a single SMT solver query, unlike the approach to portability analysis suggested in this paper. We also show that our method is not restricted to litmus tests and present an automated tool-based portability analysis of mutual exclusions algorithms from several axiomatic memory models to Power.

Acknowledgements. We thank John Wickerson for his explanations about dead executions, Luc Maranget for several discussions about CAT models, and Egor Derevenetc for providing help with the mutual exclusion benchmarks. This work has been partially developed under contracting of Liebherr Aerospace Lindenberg GmbH and supported by the Academy of Finland project 277522. Florian Furbach was supported by the DFG project R2M2: Robustness against Relaxed Memory Models.

References

1. Abdulla, P.A., Aronis, S., Atig, M.F., Jonsson, B., Leonardsson, C., Sagonas, K.: Stateless Model Checking for TSO and PSO. In: Baier, C., Tinelli, C. (eds.) TACAS 2015. LNCS, vol. 9035, pp. 353–367. Springer, Heidelberg (2015). doi:10.1007/978-3-662-46681-0_28
2. Abdulla, P.A., Atig, M.F., Jonsson, B., Leonardsson, C.: Stateless model checking for POWER. In: Chaudhuri, S., Farzan, A. (eds.) CAV 2016. LNCS, vol. 9780, pp. 134–156. Springer, Cham (2016). doi:10.1007/978-3-319-41540-6_8
3. Alglave, J.: A Shared Memory Poetics. Thèse de doctorat, L'université Paris Denis Diderot (2010)
4. Alglave, J., Cousot, P., Maranget, L.: Syntax and semantics of the weak consistency model specification language CAT. CoRR (2016). abs/1608.07531
5. Alglave, J., Kroening, D., Nimal, V., Poetzl, D.: Don't sit on the fence—a static analysis approach to automatic fence insertion. In: CAV, LNCS, vol. 8559, pp. 508–524. Springer, Vienna (2014)

6. Alglave, J., Kroening, D., Tautschnig, M.: Partial orders for efficient bounded model checking of concurrent software. In: CAV, LNCS, vol. 8044, pp. 141–157. Springer, Saint Petersburg (2013)
7. Alglave, J., Maranget, L.: Stability in weak memory models. In: Gopalakrishnan, G., Qadeer, S. (eds.) CAV 2011. LNCS, vol. 6806, pp. 50–66. Springer, Heidelberg (2011). doi:10.1007/978-3-642-22110-1_6
8. Alglave, J., Maranget, L., Tautschnig, M.: Herding cats: Modelling, simulation, testing, and data mining for weak memory. ACM Trans. Program. Lang. Syst. **36**(2), 7:1–7:74 (2014)
9. Atig, M.F., Bouajjani, A., Burckhardt, S., Musuvathi, M.: On the verification problem for weak memory models. In: POPL, pp. 7–18. ACM, Madrid (2010)
10. Batty, M., Donaldson, A.F., Wickerson, J.: Overhauling SC atomics in C11 and OpenCL. In: POPL, pp. 634–648. ACM, St. Petersburg (2016)
11. Batty, M., Owens, S., Sarkar, S., Sewell, P., Weber, T.: Mathematizing C++ concurrency. In: POPL, pp. 55–66. ACM, Austin (2011)
12. Bouajjani, A., Derevenetc, E., Meyer, R.: Checking and enforcing robustness against TSO. In: Felleisen, M., Gardner, P. (eds.) ESOP 2013. LNCS, vol. 7792, pp. 533–553. Springer, Heidelberg (2013). doi:10.1007/978-3-642-37036-6_29
13. Burckhardt, S., Alur, R., Martin, M.M.K.: CheckFence: checking consistency of concurrent data types on relaxed memory models. In: PLDI, pp. 12–21. ACM, San Diego (2007)
14. Burckhardt, S., Musuvathi, M.: Effective program verification for relaxed memory models. In: Gupta, A., Malik, S. (eds.) CAV 2008. LNCS, vol. 5123, pp. 107–120. Springer, Heidelberg (2008). doi:10.1007/978-3-540-70545-1_12
15. Burns, J.E., Lynch, N.A.: Bounds on shared memory for mutual exclusion. Inf. Comput. **107**(2), 171–184 (1993)
16. Cantin, J.F., Lipasti, M.H., Smith, J.E.: The complexity of verifying memory coherence and consistency. IEEE Trans. Parallel Distrib. Syst. **16**(7), 663–671 (2005)
17. Collavizza, H., Rueher, M.: Exploration of the capabilities of constraint programming for software verification. In: Hermanns, H., Palsberg, J. (eds.) TACAS 2006. LNCS, vol. 3920, pp. 182–196. Springer, Heidelberg (2006). doi:10.1007/11691372_12
18. Collier, W.W.: Reasoning About Parallel Architectures. Prentice Hall, Upper Saddle River (1992)
19. Cotton, S., Asarin, E., Maler, O., Niebert, P.: Some progress in satisfiability checking for difference logic. In: Lakhnech, Y., Yovine, S. (eds.) FORMATS/FTRTFT -2004. LNCS, vol. 3253, pp. 263–276. Springer, Heidelberg (2004). doi:10.1007/978-3-540-30206-3_19
20. Dan, A.M., Meshman, Y., Vechev, M., Yahav, E.: Predicate abstraction for relaxed memory models. In: Logozzo, F., Fähndrich, M. (eds.) SAS 2013. LNCS, vol. 7935, pp. 84–104. Springer, Heidelberg (2013). doi:10.1007/978-3-642-38856-9_7
21. Dan, A.M., Yuri, M., Yahav, M.T., Eran, Y.: Effective abstractions for verification under relaxed memory models. In: D 'Souza, D., Lal, A., Larsen, K.G. (eds.) VMCAI 2015. LNCS, vol. 8931, pp. 449–466. Springer, Heidelberg (2015). doi:10.1007/978-3-662-46081-8_25
22. Derevenetc, E., Meyer, R.: Robustness against power is PSpace-complete. In: Esparza, J., Fraigniaud, P., Husfeldt, T., Koutsoupias, E. (eds.) ICALP 2014. LNCS, vol. 8573, pp. 158–170. Springer, Heidelberg (2014). doi:10.1007/978-3-662-43951-7_14
23. Dijkstra, E.W.: Cooperating sequential processes. In: The Origin of Concurrent Programming, pp. 65–138. Springer, New York (2002)

24. Enea, C., Farzan, A.: On atomicity in presence of non-atomic writes. In: Chechik, M., Raskin, J.-F. (eds.) TACAS 2016. LNCS, vol. 9636, pp. 497–514. Springer, Heidelberg (2016). doi:10.1007/978-3-662-49674-9_29
25. Farzan, A., Madhusudan, P.: Monitoring atomicity in concurrent programs. In: Gupta, A., Malik, S. (eds.) CAV 2008. LNCS, vol. 5123, pp. 52–65. Springer, Heidelberg (2008). doi:10.1007/978-3-540-70545-1_8
26. Flur, S., Gray, K.E., Pulte, C., Sarkar, S., Sezgin, A., Maranget, L., Deacon, W., Sewell, P.: Modelling the ARMv8 architecture, operationally: concurrency and ISA. In: POPL, pp. 608–621. ACM, St. Petersburg (2016)
27. Furbach, F., Meyer, R., Schneider, K., Senftleben, M.: Memory-model-aware testing: a unified complexity analysis. ACM Trans. Embedded Comput. Syst. **14**(4), 63 (2015)
28. Gebser, M., Janhunen, T., Rintanen, J.: SAT modulo graphs: Acyclicity. In: Fermé, E., Leite, J. (eds.) JELIA 2014. LNCS (LNAI), vol. 8761, pp. 137–151. Springer, Cham (2014). doi:10.1007/978-3-319-11558-0_10
29. Gibbons, P.B., Korach, E.: Testing shared memories. SIAM J. Comput. **26**, 1208–1244 (1997)
30. Heljanko, K., Keinänen, M., Lange, M., Niemelä, I.: Solving parity games by a reduction to SAT. J. Comput. Syst. Sci. **78**(2), 430–440 (2012)
31. Kuperstein, M., Vechev, M.T., Yahav, E.: Automatic inference of memory fences. SIGACT News **43**(2), 108–123 (2012)
32. Lamport, L.: A new solution of Dijkstra's concurrent programming problem. Commun. ACM **17**(8), 453–455 (1974)
33. Lamport, L.: A fast mutual exclusion algorithm. ACM Trans. Comput. Syst. **5**(1), 1–11 (1987)
34. Liu, F., Nedev, N., Prisadnikov, N., Vechev, M.T., Yahav, E.: Dynamic synthesis for relaxed memory models. In: PLDI, pp. 429–440. ACM, Beijing (2012)
35. Mador-Haim, S., Alur, R., Martin, M.M.K.: Generating litmus tests for contrasting memory consistency models. In: Touili, T., Cook, B., Jackson, P. (eds.) CAV 2010. LNCS, vol. 6174, pp. 273–287. Springer, Heidelberg (2010). doi:10.1007/978-3-642-14295-6_26
36. Mador-Haim, S., Maranget, L., Sarkar, S., Memarian, K., Alglave, J., Owens, S., Alur, R., Martin, M.M.K., Sewell, P., Williams, D.: An axiomatic memory model for POWER multiprocessors. In: Madhusudan, P., Seshia, S.A. (eds.) CAV 2012. LNCS, vol. 7358, pp. 495–512. Springer, Heidelberg (2012). doi:10.1007/978-3-642-31424-7_36
37. Peterson, G.L.: Myths about the mutual exclusion problem. Inf. Process. Lett. **12**(3), 115–116 (1981)
38. Ponce de León, H., Furbach, F., Heljanko, K., Meyer, R.: Portability analysis for axiomatic memory models. PORTHOS: One tool for all models. CoRR (2017). abs/1702.06704
39. Rice, H.G.: Classes of recursively enumerable sets and their decision problems. Trans. Am. Math. Soc. **74**(2), 358–366 (1953)
40. Sarkar, S., Sewell, P., Alglave, J., Maranget, L., Williams, D.: Understanding POWER multiprocessors. In: PLDI, pp. 175–186. ACM, San Jose (2011)
41. Sarkar, S., Sewell, P., Nardelli, F.Z., Owens, S., Ridge, T., Braibant, T., Myreen, M.O, Alglave, J.: The semantics of x86-CC multiprocessor machine code. In: POPL, pp. 379–391. ACM, Savannah (2009)
42. Stockmeyer, L.J.: The polynomial-time hierarchy. Theor. Comput. Sci. **3**(1), 1–22 (1976)

43. Stoltenberg-Hansen, V., Griffor, E.R., Lindstrom, I.: Mathematical Theory of Domains. Cambridge Tracts in Theoretical Computer Science. Cambridge University Press, Cambridge (1994)
44. Szymanski, B.K.: A simple solution to Lamport's concurrent programming problem with linear wait. In: ICS, pp. 621–626. ACM, Saint Malo (1988)
45. Torlak, E., Vaziri, M., Dolby, J.: MemSAT: Checking axiomatic specifications of memory models. In: PLDI, pp. 341–350. ACM, Toronto (2010)
46. Turon, A., Vafeiadis, V., Dreyer, D.: GPS: Navigating weak memory with ghosts, protocols, and separation. In: OOPSLA, pp. 691–707. ACM, Portland (2014)
47. Vafeiadis, V., Narayan, C.: Relaxed separation logic: A program logic for C11 concurrency. In: OOPSLA, pp. 867–884. ACM, Indianapolis (2013)
48. Wickerson, J., Batty, M., Sorensen, T., Constantinides, G.A.: Automatically comparing memory consistency models. In: POPL, pp. 190–204. ACM, Paris (2017)
49. Yang, Y., Gopalakrishnan, G., Lindstrom, G., Slind, K.: Nemos: A framework for axiomatic and executable specifications of memory consistency models. IEEE Computer Society, In: IPDPS (2004)

Template Polyhedra with a Twist

Sriram Sankaranarayanan[1(✉)] and Mohamed Amin Ben Sassi[2]

[1] University of Colorado, Boulder, CO, USA
srirams@colorado.edu
[2] Mediterranean Institute of Technology (MedTech), Tunis, Tunisia
mohamed.bensassi@medtech.tn

Abstract. In this paper, we draw upon connections between bilinear programming and the process of computing (post) fixed points in abstract interpretation. It is well-known that the data flow constraints for numerical domains are expressed in terms of bilinear constraints. Algorithms such as policy and strategy iteration have been proposed for the special case of bilinear constraints that arise from template numerical domains. In particular, policy iteration improves upon a known post-fixed point by alternating between solving for an improved post-fixed point against finding certificates that are used to prove the new fixed point.

In this paper, we draw upon these connections to formulate a policy iteration scheme that changes the template on the fly in order to prove a target reachability property of interest. We show how the change to the template naturally fits inside a policy iteration scheme, and thus propose a policy iteration scheme that updates the template matrices associated with each program location. We demonstrate that the approach is effective over a set of benchmark instances, wherein starting from a simple predefined choice of templates, the approach is able to infer appropriate template directions to prove a property of interest. We also note some key theoretical questions regarding the convergence of the policy iteration scheme with template updates, that remain open at this time.

1 Introduction

In this paper, we study policy iterations for computing inductive invariants of programs using template abstract domains, and present an approach that modifies templates on the fly. In a template abstract domain, we fix the left-hand side expressions of the invariant properties of interest and use abstract interpretation to compute valid right-hand side constants so that the resulting inequalities form an inductive invariant. As such, template domains such as intervals [15], octagons [30,31], octahedra [11], pentagons [28], linear templates [36], and quadratic templates [2] have been well studied as effective numerical domains for proving safety of runtime assertions in software [5,6,18,24,29,39]. Template domains have given rise to specialized approaches such as policy iteration [13,20] for improving post-fixed points, and strategy iteration for computing the least fixed point [21,22].

F. Ranzato (Ed.): SAS 2017, LNCS 10422, pp. 321–341, 2017.
DOI: 10.1007/978-3-319-66706-5_16

Policy iteration starts from a known post-fixed point, and alternates between finding a "policy" that certifies the current solution versus finding the best solution under the current "policy". This approach was originally proposed by Costan et al. for the interval domain [13] and generalized to arbitrary templates subsequently [20]. Extensions have been proposed for quadratic templates [2]. On the other hand, strategy iteration approach works in a bottom up fashion starting from the bottom of the lattice and exploiting the "monotonicity" property in the dataflow equations for the template domain [21]. Specifically, the system of data flow equations are linearized around the current solution, and a fixed point of the linearized system is obtained as the next solution.

Our approach here exploits a connection between policy iteration approach and classic bilinear optimization problems. In fact, policy iteration is a variant of the popular alternating coordinate descent that has been used widely in the control systems and optimization communities [23]. Using this connection, we notice that the alternation between solutions and multipliers can be extended to update the templates on the fly, as the iteration proceeds. Significantly, the update to the templates can be made *property-directed* in a simple manner. By combining these observations, we arrive at a policy iteration approach that can start from initial, user-defined templates and update them on the fly. However policy iteration is not guaranteed to converge to a globally optimal solution, which would correspond to the least fixed point solution in the abstract domain. In practice, the technique gets stuck in a local minimum, yielding a suboptimal solution. A result by Helton and Merino on more general biconvex programs suggests that the alternating minimization almost never converges to a local minimum (technically a solution satisfying the KKT conditions) [27]. Adjé et al. demonstrate an approach that computes an optimal solution for systems which are nonexpansive [3]. However, the general applicability of this result is unclear. To circumvent this issue, we work in a property directed fashion, wherein the goal of the approach is to find a suitably strong invariant that is sufficient to prove a property of interest. Such a property can be established with a solution that is not necessarily a least fixed point.

An implementation of the approach and evaluation over a set of small benchmarks shows that the approach of updating the policies on the fly is an effective solution to inferring appropriate templates in a property directed manner.

1.1 Related Work

Colón et al. were the first to discover the connection between linear invariant synthesis problems and bilinear constraints through the use of Farkas lemma in linear programming [12]. These constraints were solved using specialized quantifier elimination techniques, but restricted to small problems [40]. Sankaranarayanan et al. explored the use of heuristic approaches to solve bilinear constraints [35]. These approaches were generalized by Cousot, as instances of *Lagrangian relaxations* [14]. Additionally, Cousot's work uses numerical optimization tools to prove total correctness properties of programs. His approach relies on formulating the constraints as Linear or Bilinear Matrix inequalities (LMI/BMI).

However, the use of numerical solvers requires rigorous symbolic verification of the results. Recent experiences reveal surprising pitfalls, including erroneous invariants obtained, even when the error tolerances are quite low [33,38]. In fact, one of the advantages of policy iterations lies in the use of exact arithmetic LP solvers to avoid floating point errors. Other approaches to solving the resulting constraints have restricted the multiplier variables to finite domains, enabling linear arithmetic solvers [26].

Template polyhedra and their generalization to support functions have proven useful for constructing reachable sets of linear and nonlinear hybrid systems [8,19,25,34]. The problem of inferring template directions has also been studied in this context. Many heuristics were proposed by Sankaranarayanan et al. in their paper on linear templates, including the use of expressions found in programs, "increasing" / "decreasing" expressions, and preconditions of already added template expressions [36]. However, none of these are guaranteed to be relevant to the property. Adjé et al. use the idea of Lyapunov-like functions to effectively infer templates that are shown to be effective in proving bounds on variables [1].

The idea of updating templates on the fly was previously proposed by Ben Sassi et al. for analyzing the largest invariant region of a dynamical system [37]. The approach searches for a polytope whose facets are transverse to the flow, failing which, the facet directions are adjusted and tested again. The approach to adjusting facets is based on a local sensitivity analysis to obtain the invariant region around an equilibrium (which facilitates basin of attraction analysis for dynamical systems). Compared to the present work, the differences include the treatment of multiple program locations and transitions, the use of policy iteration, and a property-directed approach that seeks to prove a property rather than find a largest invariant region.

Abraham et al. propose effective heuristics to guide the choice of directions for constructing reachable sets of linear hybrid systems [9]. Recently, Bogomolov et al. propose a counter-example guided approach for inferring facets of template polyhedra for hybrid systems reachability analysis [7]. The key differences include: (a) we are interested in computing a single polyhedron per location whereas flowpipe construction approaches use a disjunction of polytopes, and (b) we seek to compute time-unbounded invariants, whereas flowpipes are typically time bounded. Another interesting approach by Amato et al. uses principal component analysis (PCA) over concrete states reached by execution traces to design templates [4].

2 Motivating Example

Consider a simple system over two real-valued variables $(x_1, x_2) \in \mathbb{R}^2$, initialized to $(x_1, x_2) \in [-1, 1] \times [-1, 1]$. The system executes the following action

$$\textbf{if } (x_1, x_2) \in [-8, 8]^2 \textbf{ then } \left[\begin{pmatrix} x_1 \\ x_2 \end{pmatrix} := M \begin{pmatrix} x_1 \\ x_2 \end{pmatrix}\right] \textbf{ else } \left[\begin{pmatrix} x_1 \\ x_2 \end{pmatrix} := \begin{pmatrix} x_1 \\ x_2 \end{pmatrix}\right]$$

wherein $M = \begin{pmatrix} 0.92 & 0.18 \\ 0.18 & 0.92 \end{pmatrix}$. Our goal is to prove that the set $U : \{(x_1, x_2) \mid x_2 - x_1 \geq 2.1\}$ is never reached by any execution of the system. In order to prove the property using a template domain, the user specifies a template matrix [20,36]:

$$T : \begin{pmatrix} 1 & 0 \\ -1 & 0 \\ 0 & 1 \\ 0 & -1 \end{pmatrix}, \quad \begin{matrix} (* \ 1x_1 + 0x_2 \ *) \\ (* \ -1x_1 + 0x_2 \ *) \\ (* \ 0x_1 + 1x_2 \ *) \\ (* \ 0x_1 - 1x_2 \ *) \end{matrix}$$

wherein the rows represent the expressions $x_1, -x_1, x_2, -x_2$, respectively. The template domain analysis seeks to find an invariant of the form $T\boldsymbol{x} \leq \mathbf{c}$ by discovering the unknown constants $\mathbf{c}$ that represent the RHS of the template. For the example shown above, the best possible invariant is obtained as $\mathbf{c} : \left(8.8 \ 8.8 \ 8.8 \ 8.8\right)^T$, yielding the range $[-8.8, 8.8] \times [-8.8, 8.8]$ for (x_1, x_2). In fact, given our instance on using the template T, this is the best invariant possible (see Fig. 1(a) to verify this).

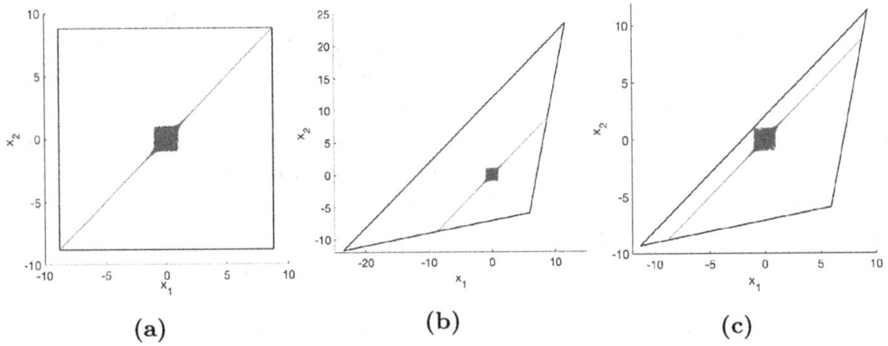

Fig. 1. Invariants synthesized for the three steps of the policy iteration with property directed template modification. The simulation traces are shown in red. Note: each figure is drawn to a different scale. (Color figure online)

For this example, the policy iterative scheme presented in this paper is successful in choosing a new template:

$$\hat{T} : \begin{pmatrix} -1 & 1 \\ 1 & -0.1957 \\ 0.1957 & -1 \\ -1 & 1 \end{pmatrix}, \quad \begin{matrix} (* \ -x_1 + x_2 \ *) \\ (* \ x_1 - 0.1957x_2 \ *) \\ (* \ 0.1957x_1 - x_2 \ *) \\ (* \ -x_1 + x_2 \ *) \end{matrix}$$

Along with this policy, we compute a tighter invariant shown in Fig. 1(c), that establishes the invariant $x_2 - x_1 \leq 2$, and thus proving U unreachable. We note that (a) the choice of templates is directed by the property, and (b) unlike the original policy iteration approach proposed by Gaubert et al. [20], this approach does not guarantee that the iterates are strictly descending. In fact, the iterates obtained are often incomparable.

3 Preliminaries

Let $\mathbb{R}$ denote the set of real numbers and $\mathbb{R}_+ : \mathbb{R} \cup \pm\infty$ denote the extended reals with infinity. We first define the transition system model used throughout this paper. Let X be a set of real-valued variables and $\Pi[X]$ represent a language of assertions over these variables, drawn from a suitable fragment of the first order logic over the reals. For any assertion $\varphi \in \Pi[X]$, we denote its corresponding set of models by $[\![\varphi]\!]$. For convenience, the set of variables X are arranged as a column vector, written as $\boldsymbol{x}$.

Definition 1 (Transition System). *A (numerical)* transition system *is a tuple* $\langle X, \mathcal{L}, \mathcal{T}, \mathcal{I}, \ell_0, \Theta \rangle$, *wherein*

1. $X : \{x_1, \ldots, x_n\}$ *represents a set of* real-valued *program variables,*
2. $\mathcal{L} : \{\ell_1, \ldots, \ell_m\}$ *represents a set of program locations,*
3. $\mathcal{T} : \{\tau_1, \ldots, \tau_k\}$ *represents a set of transitions, wherein each transition* τ_i *is a tuple* $\langle \ell_i, m_i, \psi_i, g_i \rangle$, *wherein*
   (a) $\ell_i, m_i \in \mathcal{L}$ *are the pre and the post locations, respectively.*
   (b) $\psi_i \in \Pi[X]$, *an assertion over* X, *represents the guard of the transition.*
   (c) $g_i : \mathbb{R}^n \to \mathbb{R}^n$, *an update function, represents the (simultaneous) assignment:* $(x_1, \ldots, x_n) := g_i(x_1, \ldots, x_n)$.
4. ℓ_0 *is the initial location, and* $\Theta \in \Pi[X]$ *is an assertion over* X *representing the initial valuations of the program variables.*

A state of the transition system is a tuple $\langle \ell, \boldsymbol{x} \rangle$ wherein $\ell \in L$ is the control location and $\boldsymbol{x} \in \mathbb{R}^n$ represents a set of valuations for the program variable. Given a transition system, its executions are a finite/infinite sequence of states:

$$(\ell_0, \boldsymbol{x}_0) \xrightarrow{\tau_1} (\ell_1, \boldsymbol{x}_1) \xrightarrow{\tau_2} \cdots \xrightarrow{\tau_i} (\ell_i, \boldsymbol{x}_i) \cdots,$$

such that: (a) ℓ_0 is the initial location and $\boldsymbol{x}_0 \in [\![\Theta]\!]$; (b) ℓ_{i-1}, ℓ_i are the pre/post locations (respectively) of the transition τ_i for all $i \geq 1$; (c) $\boldsymbol{x}_{i-1} \in [\![\psi_i]\!]$ for all $i \geq 1$ wherein ψ_i is the guard corresponding to the transition τ_i; and (d) $\boldsymbol{x}_i = g_i(\boldsymbol{x}_{i-1})$ for all $i \geq 1$, wherein g_i is the update function for τ_i.

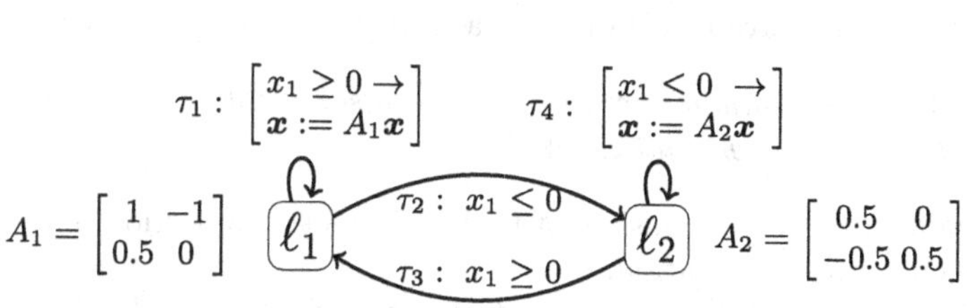

Fig. 2. Example of a transition system with two variables x_1, x_2, two locations ℓ_1, ℓ_2 and four transitions shown as arrows.

Example 1. Figure 2 shows an example of a transition system with $X : \{x_1, x_2\}$, $\mathcal{L} : \{\ell_1, \ell_2\}$ and $\mathcal{T} : \{\tau_1, \tau_2, \tau_3, \tau_4\}$. The guards and updates of the transitions are as shown in Fig. 2. The identity update $\boldsymbol{x} := \boldsymbol{x}$ is not shown, however. The initial location is ℓ_1 and the initial condition on $\boldsymbol{x}$ is $(x_1, x_2) \in [0.5, 1.5] \times [0.5, 1]$.

A state $(\ell, \boldsymbol{x})$ is reachable if there is an execution that reaches the state.

For this paper, we study *linear transition systems.* A linear expression is of the form $e : \boldsymbol{a}^T \boldsymbol{x}$ for vector $\boldsymbol{a} \in \mathbb{R}^n$. A linear inequality is of the form $\boldsymbol{a}^T \boldsymbol{x} \leq b$ and a linear assertion is a finite conjunction of linear inequalities $(\boldsymbol{a}_1^T \boldsymbol{x} \leq b_1 \ \wedge \ \cdots \ \wedge \ \boldsymbol{a}_k^T \boldsymbol{x} \leq b_k)$ conveniently written in matrix form as $A\boldsymbol{x} \leq \boldsymbol{b}$.

Definition 2 (Linear Transition Systems). *A linear transition system (LTS) is a transition system with the following restrictions:*

1. *The initial conditions and transition guards are all linear assertions over* X
2. *The update function for each transition is an affine function:* $g_i(\boldsymbol{x}) : U_i \boldsymbol{x} + \boldsymbol{v_i}$.

Throughout this paper, we will tackle linear transition systems. An error specification is written as $\langle \ell, \psi \rangle$ for a location ℓ and a linear assertion ψ. The goal is to prove that no reachable state for location ℓ satisfies ψ. I.e, all reachable states $\boldsymbol{x}$ at location ℓ satisfy $\boldsymbol{x} \not\in [\![\psi]\!]$. To prove a given specification, we use an *inductive invariant.*

Definition 3 (Inductive Invariant Map). *An inductive invariant map* $\eta : \mathcal{L} \to \Pi[X]$ *maps each location* $\ell \in \mathcal{L}$ *to an assertion* $\eta(\ell)$ *such that the following conditions hold:*

- Initial Condition: *At the initial location* ℓ_0, *the entailment* $\Theta \models \eta(\ell_0)$ *holds.*
- Consecution Condition: *For each transition* $\tau : \langle \ell_1, \ell_2, \psi_i, g_i \rangle$, *the following consecution condition holds:*

$$\eta(\ell_1) \ \wedge \ \psi_i \ \wedge \ \boldsymbol{x}' = g_i(\boldsymbol{x}) \ \models \ \eta(\ell_2)[\boldsymbol{x}'] \,.$$

The condition states that starting from any state $\boldsymbol{x} \in [\![\eta(\ell_1)]\!]$, *a single step of the transition* τ, *if enabled, yields a state* $\boldsymbol{x}' \in [\![\eta(\ell_2)]\!]$.

Let η be an inductive assertion map and $\langle \ell, \psi \rangle$ be an error specification.

Theorem 1. *If the conjunction* $\eta(\ell) \ \wedge \ \psi$ *is unsatisfiable, then for every reachable state* $(\ell, \boldsymbol{x})$, *it follows that* $\boldsymbol{x} \not\in [\![\psi]\!]$.

The problem therefore consists of finding inductive assertion maps that can prove a given error specification.

Abstract interpretation provides a framework for systematically computing inductive assertions using a pre-specified lattice of assertions called an *abstract domain* [16, 17]. The key insight lies in characterizing inductive assertion maps as post-fixed points of a monotone operator over sets of states.

An abstract domain is defined by a lattice $\mathcal{A} : \langle A, \sqsubseteq, \sqcup, \sqcap, \bot, \top \rangle$ with inclusion $\sqsubseteq$, join operator $\sqcup$, meet operator $\sqcap$, a bottom element $\bot$ and top element $\top$.

Each element $a \in A$ represents a corresponding set of states (technically, an element of the concrete domain) through the concretization function $\gamma(a)$, and likewise, for every set of states S (element of the concrete domain), we define a corresponding abstraction $\alpha(S)$.

The theory of abstract interpretation defines a set of operations including the abstract post condition $b : \widehat{post}(a, \tau)$, that given $a \in A$ and transition τ results in an abstract element $b \in A$ such that $\gamma(b)$ over approximates the reachable states obtained by starting from some state in $\gamma(a)$ and applying the transition τ. Other useful abstract domain operations include $\sqcup$ for merging sets of states, $\sqcap$ for handling conditional branches, $\bot$ for the empty set of states, $\top$ for the universal set of states, $\sqsubseteq$ to test containment between abstract elements and a special operation called widening ∇ that enforces termination. We will omit a detailed presentation of abstract interpretation from this paper. The interested reader may obtain these from standard references [16,17,32].

3.1 Template Domains

The rest of this paper will focus on the abstract domain of template polyhedra [36]. Let $\mathcal{S} : \langle \mathcal{L}, X, \mathcal{T}, \ell_0, \Theta \rangle$ be a linear transition system. Let $\boldsymbol{x}$ represent the system variables in X as a vector and $n = |X|$.

A template associates each location $\ell \in \mathcal{L}$ with a $m_\ell \times n$ matrix T_ℓ. We drop the subscript ℓ from the template matrix if the location ℓ is clear from the context. A $m \times n$ template T defines a lattice $\mathcal{A}(T)$:

$$\mathcal{A}(T) : \{\boldsymbol{c} \in \mathbb{R}_+^m\}, \text{ wherein, } \gamma(\boldsymbol{c}) : \ T\boldsymbol{x} \leq \boldsymbol{c}\,.$$

In other words, each element of the template abstract domain is a possible valuation $\boldsymbol{c}$ to the RHS of inequalities $T\boldsymbol{x} \leq \boldsymbol{c}$. Note that the entries in $\boldsymbol{c}$ can include $\pm\infty$. Naturally, we define the linear inequality $e \leq \infty$ to be synonymous with *true* and $e \leq -\infty$ is synonymous with *false*.

Given an assertion φ over $\boldsymbol{x}$, its abstraction $\boldsymbol{c} : \alpha(\varphi)$ is computed as a vector whose i^{th} entry $\boldsymbol{c}_i$ is the solution to the optimization problem:

$$\boldsymbol{c}_i : \ \max \ T_i\boldsymbol{x} \text{ s.t. } \varphi(\boldsymbol{x})\,.$$

Since the abstraction is often computed for linear assertions φ, this is a linear programming (LP) problem.

For each template element, its *canonical representative* $\mathsf{can}(\boldsymbol{c})$ is defined as the instantiation $\boldsymbol{d}$, whose i^{th} entry $\boldsymbol{d}_i$ is the solution to the following LP:

$$\boldsymbol{d}_i : \ \max \ T_i\boldsymbol{x} \text{ s.t. } T\boldsymbol{x} \leq \boldsymbol{c}\,.$$

Note that the solution to an unbounded problem is taken to be $+\infty$ and an infeasible problem to be $-\infty$. Note that the template polyhedron defined by $T\boldsymbol{x} \leq \boldsymbol{c}$ is identical to the polyhedron $T\boldsymbol{x} \leq \mathsf{can}(\boldsymbol{c})$. A template element $\boldsymbol{c}$ is *canonical* in $\mathcal{A}(T)$ if and only $\boldsymbol{c} = \mathsf{can}(\boldsymbol{c})$.

The inclusion operator $\sqsubseteq$ in $\mathcal{A}(T)$ is defined as

$$\boldsymbol{c}_1 \sqsubseteq \boldsymbol{c}_2 \text{ iff } \mathsf{can}(\boldsymbol{c}_1) \leq \mathsf{can}(\boldsymbol{c}_2)\,,$$

wherein $\leq$ operation over vectors compares elements entrywise. The join operator $\boldsymbol{c}_1 \sqcup \boldsymbol{c}_2$ is simply the entrywise maximum $\max(\boldsymbol{c}_1, \boldsymbol{c}_2)$. Likewise, the meet operator is the canonical entry wise minimum.

Let T_ℓ be the template associated with location ℓ and T_m with location m. The abstract post with respect to a transition $\langle \ell, m, \varphi : A\boldsymbol{x} \leq \boldsymbol{b}, g : U\boldsymbol{x} + \boldsymbol{v} \rangle$ is an operator $\widehat{post} : \mathcal{A}(T_\ell) \times \mathcal{T} \rightarrow \mathcal{A}(T_m)$. Given $\boldsymbol{c} \in \mathcal{A}(T_\ell)$, the result $\boldsymbol{d} : \widehat{post}(\boldsymbol{c}, \tau)$ is a vector wherein $\boldsymbol{d}_i$ is given as the solution to the following LP:

$$\boldsymbol{d}_i : \begin{pmatrix} \max T_{m,i}\boldsymbol{x} & \\ \text{s.t. } T_\ell \boldsymbol{y} & \leq \boldsymbol{c} \\ \quad A\boldsymbol{y} & \leq \boldsymbol{b} \\ \quad \boldsymbol{x} & = U\boldsymbol{y} + \boldsymbol{v} \end{pmatrix}$$

Widening and narrowing operators for the template domain are defined by extensions of the standard interval widening operator [36].

The template domain is a convenient numerical abstract domain that uses linear programming solvers as a primitive for implementing the domain operations. However, a common critique of the template approach is that it requires users to specify the template T. In practice, users default to popular choices such as *intervals*, *octagons* and *pentagons* which avoid repeated calls to LP solvers by using special properties of the constraints in these templates. We proceed by assuming that an initial template has been specified for each location using one of the schemes outlined above. Our approach can change this template as part of the solution scheme.

4 Bilinear Constraints and Policy Iteration

In this section, we consider the data flow equations for template abstract domain, connecting them to a class of nonconvex optimization problems called *bilinear optimization problem* (BOP). We present the *policy iteration* approach, proposed by Gaubert et al. as a technique for solving such bilinear inequalities that alternates between solving linear programs [20]. Once again we fix a linear transition system $\mathcal{S}$ and assume for simplicity that each location ℓ is labeled with the same $m \times n$ matrix T. The approach can be easily extended to the case where the template matrices differ between locations.

We will make use of Farkas' lemma, a standard result in linear programming. Let $\varphi :\ A\boldsymbol{x} \leq \boldsymbol{b}$ be a linear assertion with $m \times n$ matrix A and $m \times 1$ vector $\boldsymbol{b}$, $\psi :\ \boldsymbol{c}^T\boldsymbol{x} \leq d$ be a given linear inequality.

Theorem 2 (Farkas Lemma). *If φ is satisfiable, then $\varphi \models \psi$ iff there exists nonnegative multipliers $\boldsymbol{\lambda} \in \mathbb{R}^m$ such that*

$$A^T\boldsymbol{\lambda} = \boldsymbol{c} \ \wedge \ \boldsymbol{b}^T\boldsymbol{\lambda} \leq d \ \wedge \ \boldsymbol{\lambda} \geq 0\,.$$

Furthermore, φ is unsatisfiable if and only if there exists multipliers $\boldsymbol{\lambda} \in \mathbb{R}^m$ such that

$$A^T\boldsymbol{\lambda} = \mathbf{0} \ \wedge \ \boldsymbol{b}^T\boldsymbol{\lambda} \le -1 \ \wedge \ \boldsymbol{\lambda} \ge 0 .$$

The constraints can be seen as encoding the entailment $\varphi \models \mathbf{0}^T\boldsymbol{x} \le -1$.

Note that Farkas lemma handles the entailment of a single linear inequality. However, for a polyhedron $C\boldsymbol{x} \le \boldsymbol{d}$, we may encode the entailment $A\boldsymbol{x} \le \boldsymbol{b} \models C\boldsymbol{x} \le \boldsymbol{d}$ as a series of single inequality entailments: $A\boldsymbol{x} \le \boldsymbol{b} \models C_j\boldsymbol{x} \le \boldsymbol{d}_j$ for each row j of $C, \boldsymbol{d}$. The resulting constraints can be collectively written as:

$$A^T\Lambda = C, \ \Lambda^T\boldsymbol{b} \le \boldsymbol{d}, \ \Lambda \ge 0 .$$

All equalities and inequalities between matrices are interpreted entrywise. Here Λ is a matrix with as many rows as A and as many columns as the number of rows in C. The jth column of Λ contains the multipliers corresponding to the inequality $C_j\boldsymbol{x} \le \boldsymbol{d}_j$. This notation will be used throughout the rest of the paper.

Using Farkas' lemma, we may now derive a system of constraints corresponding to the *data flow equations* for the template domain. Let T be a $m \times n$ template matrix. We associate each location ℓ with an unknown vector $\boldsymbol{c}(\ell) \in \mathcal{A}(T)$ such that the assertion map $\eta(\ell) : \ T\boldsymbol{x} \le \boldsymbol{c}(\ell)$ is inductive.

We wish to encode the constraints for initiation:

$$\Theta \models T\boldsymbol{x} \le \boldsymbol{c}(\ell_0) , \qquad (1)$$

and for each transition $\tau : \langle \ell, m, \varphi, g \rangle$, we wish to model consecution:

$$T\boldsymbol{x} \le \boldsymbol{c}(\ell) \ \wedge \ \varphi \ \wedge \ \boldsymbol{x}' = g(\boldsymbol{x}) \ \models \ T\boldsymbol{x}' \le \boldsymbol{c}(m) . \qquad (2)$$

Initiation: Let $\Theta : A_0\boldsymbol{x} \le \boldsymbol{b}_0$ be the assertion for the initial condition. Using Farkas' lemma for the entailment in Eq. (1), we obtain the condition:

$$A_0^T\Lambda_0 = T \ \wedge \ \Lambda_0^T\boldsymbol{b}_0 \le \boldsymbol{c}(\ell_0) \ \wedge \ \Lambda_0 \ge 0 . \qquad (3)$$

Here Λ_0 is a $k \times m$ matrix wherein k is the number of rows in A_0 and m is the number of rows in T. We write $\Lambda_0 \ge 0$ to indicate that all entries in Λ_0 are non-negative.

Consecution: Let τ be a transition with guard $A_\tau\boldsymbol{x} \le \boldsymbol{b}_\tau$ and update $g(\boldsymbol{x}) : U_\tau\boldsymbol{x} + \boldsymbol{v}_\tau$. The consecution condition in Eq. (2) can be rewritten through substitution of $\boldsymbol{x}'$ and arranged as follows:

$$\begin{array}{r|l} \Lambda_\tau \rightarrow & \quad T\boldsymbol{x} \le \boldsymbol{c}(\ell) \\ \Gamma_\tau \rightarrow & \ A_\tau\boldsymbol{x} \le \boldsymbol{b}_\tau \\ \hline \models & T U_\tau\boldsymbol{x} \le \boldsymbol{c}(m) - T\boldsymbol{v}_\tau \end{array}$$

$$
\begin{array}{rl}
\textbf{TemplateVars}: & \boldsymbol{c}(\ell),\ \ell \in \mathcal{L} \\
\textbf{BilinearMults}: & \Lambda_\tau,\ \tau \in \mathcal{T} \\
\textbf{LinearMults}: & \Lambda_0, \Gamma_\tau,\ \tau \in \mathcal{T} \\
\hline
\textbf{Constraints}: & A_0^T \Lambda_0 = T_{\ell_0} \qquad \text{(* Initiation *)} \\
& \Lambda_0^T \boldsymbol{b}_0 \leq \boldsymbol{c}(\ell_0) \\
& T_l^T \Lambda_\tau + A_\tau^T \Gamma_\tau = T_m U_\tau \qquad \text{(* Consecution } \tau : \langle l, m, \varphi, g\rangle \text{ *)} \\
& \Lambda_\tau^T \boldsymbol{c}(\ell) + \Gamma_\tau^T \boldsymbol{b}_\tau \leq \boldsymbol{c}(m) - T_m \boldsymbol{v}_\tau \\
& \Lambda_0, \Lambda_\tau, \Gamma_\tau \geq 0 \qquad \text{(* Nonnegative multipliers *)} \\
\hline
\end{array}
$$

Fig. 3. Bilinear system of constraints at a glance. The constraints are generalized to allow for possibly different templates T_ℓ at each location.

The notation above shows the constraints and the associated dual multipliers with each block of constraints. Furthermore, we have substituted $\boldsymbol{x}' = U_\tau \boldsymbol{x} + \boldsymbol{v}_\tau$. This is dualized using Farkas' lemma to yield the following constraints:

$$
\begin{array}{c}
T^T \Lambda_\tau + A_\tau^T \Gamma_\tau = T U_\tau \\
\Lambda_\tau^T \boldsymbol{c}(\ell) + \Gamma_\tau^T \boldsymbol{b}_\tau \leq \boldsymbol{c}(m) - T \boldsymbol{v}_\tau \\
\Lambda_\tau, \Gamma_\tau \geq 0
\end{array}
\tag{4}
$$

Note that Eq. (3) for the initiation yields a system of linear constraints involving $\boldsymbol{c}(\ell_0)$ and unknown multipliers in Λ_0. However, the consecution constraints in Eq. (4) for each transition τ involve the product $\Lambda_\tau^T \boldsymbol{c}(\ell)$ both of which are unknown. This makes the constraints for consecution fall into a special class called *bilinear constraints*. I.e., for a fixed Λ_τ these constraints are linear in the remaining variables $\boldsymbol{c}(\ell), \Gamma_\tau$. Similarly, for fixed values of $\boldsymbol{c}(\ell)$, these constraints are linear in the variables $\Lambda_\tau, \Gamma_\tau$. Figure 3 summarizes the constraints obtained at a glance.

Connection with Min-policies: The original "min-policy" approach of Costan et al. [13] considers data flow equations of the form:

$$
\boldsymbol{c} \geq \min(\boldsymbol{a}_{i,1}^T \boldsymbol{c}, \ldots, \boldsymbol{a}_{i,k}^T \boldsymbol{c}),\ i = 1, \ldots, M,\ k = 1, \ldots, N. \tag{5}
$$

We will demonstrate that the equations shown in Fig. 3 can be equivalently expressed in this form. For simplicity, we consider the case for a single location ℓ with template T and unknown template RHS variables $\boldsymbol{c}$. All transitions are assumed to be self-loops around this location. From Eq. (4), a given solution $\boldsymbol{c}$ satisfies the consecution for transition τ iff there exist $\Lambda_\tau, \Gamma_\tau$ such that

$$
\boldsymbol{c} \ \geq\ \Lambda_\tau^T \boldsymbol{c} + \Gamma_\tau^T \boldsymbol{b}_\tau + T \boldsymbol{v}_\tau \tag{6}
$$

$$
T^T \Lambda_\tau + A_\tau^T \Gamma_\tau \ =\ T U_\tau \tag{7}
$$

$$
\Lambda_\tau, \Gamma_\tau \ \geq 0 \tag{8}
$$

Let us define a polyhedron $P(\Lambda_\tau, \Gamma_\tau)$ defined by collecting the constraints in lines (7) and (8) above. We may rewrite the constraints equivalently as:

$$
\boldsymbol{c} \ \geq \min_{(\Lambda_\tau, \Gamma_\tau) \in P} \left(\Lambda_\tau^T \boldsymbol{c} + \Gamma_\tau^T \boldsymbol{b}_\tau + T \boldsymbol{v}_\tau \right) \tag{9}
$$

Note that P is a polyhedron. Let us assume that it is defined by N vertices:

$$(\Lambda_1, \Gamma_1), \ldots, (\Lambda_N, \Gamma_N).$$

The min in Eq. (9) can be equivalently written as a minimization over the finite set of vertices of P:

$$\boldsymbol{c} \geq \min_{j=1}^{N} \left(\Lambda_j^T \boldsymbol{c} + \Gamma_j^T \boldsymbol{b}_\tau + T \boldsymbol{v}_\tau \right) \tag{10}$$

We note that this form arises from the specific structure of the data flow equations for the template abstract domain. In particular, not all bilinear constraints satisfy this property.

4.1 Policy Iteration

We now describe policy iteration as an alternation between solving for unknown $\boldsymbol{c}(\ell)$ for each $\ell \in \mathcal{L}$ and solving for the unknown bilinear multipliers Λ_τ. Policy iteration starts from a known sound solution $\boldsymbol{c}^0(\ell)$ and successively improves the solution to obtain better solutions (smaller in the lattice) until no further improvements can be obtained. The initial solution may be obtained by using Kleene iteration with widening. For simplicity, we will assume that $\boldsymbol{c}^0(\ell) \neq \bot$, for each $\ell \in \mathcal{L}$. If this were the case, then the location ℓ is unreachable, and can be removed from the system.

The overall scheme alternates between (I) *solving for the unknown multipliers* $\Lambda_\tau, \Gamma_\tau, \Lambda_0$ given a fixed value of $\boldsymbol{c}$, and (II) *solving for the unknown template RHS* $\boldsymbol{c}(\ell)$ given $\Lambda_\tau, \Gamma_\tau$ and Λ_0. Since Γ_τ and Λ_0 are not involved in any bilinear term, we do not fix them to specific values when solving for $\boldsymbol{c}(\ell)$.

Solving for Multipliers: Given the values for the current solution $\boldsymbol{c}^{(i)}(\ell)$ at each location, we simply plug in these values and solve the system in Fig. 3.

Lemma 1. *The constraints shown in Fig. 3 become linear if we replace $\boldsymbol{c}(\ell)$ at each location by fixed (constant) values.*

The remaining constraints are linear over Λ_0, Λ_τ and Γ_τ for each transition τ, and can be thus solved using a LP solver. The following lemma guarantees that the constraints will always yield a feasible solution provided the values $\boldsymbol{c}^{(i)}$ are a valid post-fixed point.

Lemma 2. *If the solution $\boldsymbol{c}^{(i)}(\ell)$ for each $\ell \in \mathcal{L}$ is a post-fixed point, the constraints in the Fig. 3 are feasible for the remaining multipliers, when $\boldsymbol{c}(\ell)$ is replaced by $\boldsymbol{c}^{(i)}(\ell)$.*

Let $\Lambda_\tau^{(i)}$ be the resulting values of the bilinear multipliers returned by the LP solver when we replace $\boldsymbol{c} : \boldsymbol{c}^{(i)}$. These are also called policies [20].

Solving for Template RHS: Next, let us assume that the variables Λ_τ for each transition are set to constants $\Lambda_\tau^{(i)}$.

Lemma 3. *If we set Λ_τ for each τ to constants $\Lambda_\tau^{(i)}$ for the constraints in Fig. 3, the resulting problem is linear over $\mathbf{c}(\ell)$ for each $\ell \in \mathcal{L}$ and the linear multipliers Γ_τ, Λ_0.*

Once we set Λ_τ to specific values, the resulting system is once again a linear program. Let us call this problem $\mathcal{C}_i$.

Lemma 4. *The LP $\mathcal{C}_i$ is always feasible.*

To see this, we note that $\mathbf{c}(\ell) = \mathbf{c}^{(i)}$ is already a solution to this LP due to how the values of $\Lambda_\tau^{(i)}$ were obtained in the first place. We call the resulting values $\mathbf{c}^{(i+1)}(\ell)$.

The overall policy iteration scheme alternates between solving for $\mathbf{c}(\ell)$ and solving for Λ_τ variables. Gaubert et al. show that the number of policies needed is finite (but large), and thus the process is guaranteed to yield a stable solution such that $\mathbf{c}^{(i+1)}(\ell) = \mathbf{c}^{(i)}(\ell)$.

5 Policies with Template Update

In this section, we extend policy iteration process to achieve two goals simultaneously: (a) be goal-directed towards a specific property and (b) allow the template T at each location to be updated.

Let (ℓ, ψ) be a error specification at location ℓ that we wish to prove unreachable. Our goal is to compute an inductive assertion map η such that at location ℓ, the conjunction $\eta(\ell) \wedge \psi$ is unsatisfiable. Once again, we will first assume for the sake of exposition that the same template matrix T is used at each location.

Using Farkas' lemma, the invariant $T\boldsymbol{x} \leq \mathbf{c}(\ell)$ proves the unreachability of the error specification $\psi : P\boldsymbol{x} \leq \boldsymbol{q}$ iff there exist multipliers $\boldsymbol{\lambda}_s, \boldsymbol{\gamma}_s \geq 0$ s.t.

$$T^{\mathsf{T}}\boldsymbol{\lambda}_s + P^T\boldsymbol{\gamma}_s = \mathbf{0},\ \ \underbrace{\mathbf{c}(\ell)^T\boldsymbol{\lambda}_s + \boldsymbol{q}^T\boldsymbol{\gamma}_s \leq -1}_{I},\ \ \boldsymbol{\lambda}_s, \boldsymbol{\gamma}_s \geq 0\,. \tag{11}$$

However, if the invariant fails to prove the property, we will be unable to find suitable multipliers $\boldsymbol{\lambda}_s, \boldsymbol{\gamma}_s \geq 0$. Since, our procedure will involve intermediate solutions that do not satisfy the property, we will consider the following optimization-based formulation by moving the inequality labeled "I" in (11) to the objective, as follows:

$$\begin{array}{ll} \min \mathbf{c}(\ell)^T\boldsymbol{\lambda}_s + \boldsymbol{q}^T\boldsymbol{\gamma}_s & \\ \text{s.t.} \quad T^T\boldsymbol{\lambda}_s + P^T\boldsymbol{\gamma}_s = \mathbf{0} & \\ \qquad\qquad\quad \mathbf{1}^T\boldsymbol{\lambda}_s = 1 \ (\text{* normalization constraint *}) & \\ \qquad\qquad\quad \boldsymbol{\lambda}_s, \boldsymbol{\gamma}_s \geq 0 & \end{array} \tag{12}$$

Note that we have added a *normalization constraint* requiring that the sum of the multipliers $\boldsymbol{\lambda}_s$ equal 1. Without such a constraint, the problem always has a trivial solution 0 by setting all the multipliers $(\boldsymbol{\lambda}_s, \boldsymbol{\gamma}_s)$ to 0, which is undesirable for the policy iteration scheme to be discussed subsequently.

Lemma 5. *Suppose $T_i = -P_j$ for row i of matrix T, row j of matrix P, and $\mathbf{c}(\ell)_i < \infty$ then the optimization problem in Eq. (12) is feasible.*

Furthermore, its objective value is strictly negative iff $T\boldsymbol{x} \leq \mathbf{c}(\ell)$ proves the specification $(\ell, \psi : P\boldsymbol{x} \leq \boldsymbol{q})$.

Proof. Given that $T_i = -P_j$, we then choose $\boldsymbol{\lambda}_s(i) = 1$ and the rest of entries to zero. Likewise, $\boldsymbol{\gamma}_s(j) = 1$ and the remaining entries of $\boldsymbol{\gamma}_s$ are set to 0. We can now verify that this will satisfy the constraints, thus providing a feasible solution.

Note that if we find a solution $(\boldsymbol{\lambda}_s, \boldsymbol{\gamma}_s)$ such that the objective value is $\epsilon < 0$, then $(\frac{\boldsymbol{\lambda}_s}{|\epsilon|}, \frac{\boldsymbol{\gamma}_s}{|\epsilon|})$ satisfy the constraints in Eq. (11). The rest follows from Farkas' lemma.

Thus, we will use the optimization formulation as an objective function that measures how "far away" the current solution at ℓ is from proving the property of interest.

5.1 Updating Templates

Next, we allow the template T to change at each step to a new template $T + \Delta$, wherein Δ is the unknown change in the template. In doing so, we update the constraints to introduce an unknown change Δ. However, allowing arbitrary changes to the template will not work since choosing $\Delta = -T$ immediately makes the template trivial, and not useful for our purposes. Therefore, we specify upper and lower limits to the change in the template. These limits can be set using different strategies that we will explore in the experimental evaluation section. Let L be the lower limit and U be the upper limit so that $L \leq \Delta \leq U$. As a technical condition, we require $0 \in [L, U]$, i.e., the option to keep T unchanged is allowed.

Vars :	$\mathbf{c}(\ell),\ \ell \in \mathcal{L}$	(* Template RHS *)
	$\Delta_\ell,\ \ell \in \mathcal{L}$	(* Template update *)
	$\Lambda_\tau,\ \tau \in \mathcal{T}$	(* Bilinear mult.*)
	$\boldsymbol{\lambda}_s$	(* Error Spec.*)
	$\Lambda_0, \Gamma_\tau,\ \tau \in \mathcal{T}$	(* Linear Mults. *)
	$\boldsymbol{\gamma}_s$	(* Error Spec.*)
min :	$\boldsymbol{\lambda}_s^T \mathbf{c}(\ell) + \boldsymbol{\gamma}_s^T \boldsymbol{q}$	
s.t.	$A_0^T \Lambda_0 = T_{\ell_0} + \Delta_{\ell_0}$	(* Initiation *)
	$\Lambda_0^T \boldsymbol{b}_0 \leq \mathbf{c}(\ell_0)$	
	$(T_l + \Delta_l)^T \Lambda_\tau + A_\tau^T \Gamma_\tau = (T_m + \Delta_m) U_\tau$	(* Consecution $\tau : \langle l, m, \varphi, g\rangle$ *)
	$\Lambda_\tau^T \mathbf{c}(\ell) + \Gamma_\tau^T \boldsymbol{b}_\tau \leq \mathbf{c}(m) - (T_m + \Delta_m)\boldsymbol{v}_\tau$	
	$(T_\ell + \Delta_\ell)^T \boldsymbol{\lambda}_s + P^T \boldsymbol{\gamma}_s = 0$	(* Error spec. $\psi : P\boldsymbol{x} \leq \boldsymbol{q}$ *)
	$\Lambda_0, \Lambda_\tau, \boldsymbol{\lambda}_s, \Gamma_\tau, \boldsymbol{\gamma}_s \geq 0$	(* Nonnegative multipliers *)
	$L_l \leq \Delta_l \leq U_l$	(* Limits on template change *)

Fig. 4. Bilinear system of constraints with objective function and template update variables Δ_l.

Figure 4 shows the bilinear optimization problem

$$\mathcal{B}\left((\mathbf{c}(\ell), \Delta_\ell), (\Lambda_\tau, \boldsymbol{\lambda}_s)\right),$$

obtained when the change in the template variables is also considered. We note that the variables involved in the bilinear terms are once again separated into two sets, represented in different colors for convenience.

5.2 Template Updates and Policy Iteration

We now update the policy iteration process to consider the change in templates, as shown in Fig. 4. Let $\mathbf{c}^{(0)}$ be an initial value such that $T\boldsymbol{x} \leq \mathbf{c}^{(0)}(\ell)$ is inductive. The initial update $\Delta_\ell^{(0)} = 0$ for each location ℓ.

Multiplier Update: At each iteration i, the multiplier update uses $\mathbf{c}^{(i)}, \Delta^{(i)}$ to obtain values of $\Lambda_\tau^{(i)}, \boldsymbol{\lambda}_s^{(i)}$. Formally, we consider the problem

$$\mathcal{M}_i : \mathcal{B}\left((\mathbf{c}^{(i)}(\ell), \Delta_\ell^{(i)}), (\Lambda_\tau, \boldsymbol{\lambda}_s)\right)$$

Lemma 6. *1. $\mathcal{M}_i$ is a linear program over unknown multipliers $\Lambda_\tau, \boldsymbol{\lambda}_s, \Gamma_\tau, \gamma_s, \Lambda_0$.*
2. It is feasible iff the map $\eta^{(i)}$ formed by the assertions $(T_\ell + \Delta_\ell^{(i)})\boldsymbol{x} \leq \mathbf{c}^{(i)}(\ell)$ for $\ell \in \mathcal{L}$, is an inductive assertion map.
3. The value of the objective function cannot increase, i.e., for $i > 1$,

$$\mathbf{c}^{(i)}(\ell)^T \boldsymbol{\lambda}_s^{(i)} + \boldsymbol{q}^T \gamma_s^{(i)} \leq \mathbf{c}^{(i)}(\ell)^T \boldsymbol{\lambda}_s^{(i-1)} + \boldsymbol{q}^T \gamma_s^{(i-1)}.$$

4. The value of the objective is negative iff $\eta^{(i)}$ proves the specification (ℓ, ψ).

The result of multiplier update yields values for the variables $(\Lambda_\tau, \boldsymbol{\lambda}_s)$: $(\Lambda_\tau^{(i)}, \boldsymbol{\lambda}_s^{(i)})$.

Template Update: Given the current values $(\Lambda_\tau^{(i)}, \boldsymbol{\lambda}_s^{(i)})$ for the multipliers, we derive new values $\mathbf{c}^{(i+1)}(\ell), \Delta_\ell^{(i+1)}$ for the template variables by solving the problem

$$\mathcal{C}_{i+1} : \mathcal{B}\left((\mathbf{c}(\ell), \Delta_\ell), (\Lambda_\tau^{(i)}, \boldsymbol{\lambda}_s^{(i)})\right).$$

Lemma 7. *1. $\mathcal{C}_{i+1}$ is a linear program over the unknown template variables $\mathbf{c}(\ell), \Delta_\ell$ and unknown linear multipliers $\Gamma_\tau, \gamma_s, \Lambda_0$.*
2. It is always feasible provided $0 \in [L_\ell, U_\ell]$ at each location.
3. The assertion map $\eta^{(i+1)}$ formed by the solution

$$(T_\ell + \Delta_\ell^{(i+1)})\boldsymbol{x} \leq \mathbf{c}^{(i+1)}(\ell) \text{ for } \ell \in \mathcal{L},$$

is inductive.

4. *The value of the objective function cannot increase, i.e., for* $i \geq 0$,

$$\mathbf{c}^{(i+1)}(\ell)^T \boldsymbol{\lambda}_s^{(i)} + \boldsymbol{q}^T \boldsymbol{\gamma}_s^{(i+1)} \leq \mathbf{c}^{(i)}(\ell)^T \boldsymbol{\lambda}_s^{(i)} + \boldsymbol{q}^T \boldsymbol{\gamma}_s^{(i)} .$$

5. *The value of the objective function* $\mathbf{c}^{(i+1)}(\ell)^T \boldsymbol{\lambda}_s^{(i)} + \boldsymbol{q}^T \boldsymbol{\gamma}_s^{(i+1)}$ *is negative iff the* $\eta^{(i+1)}$ *proves the property.*

The overall scheme alternates between updating the multipliers and the template variables, until no more changes can occur. We also observe that starting from a valid inductive invariant, the solutions obtained during the policy iteration continue to remain inductive or post-fixed points. However, they are post-fixed points over the lattice $\mathcal{A}(T_\ell + \Delta_\ell^{(i)},\ \ell \in \mathcal{L})$, which is different from the original lattice. As observed already in the motivating example (Sect. 2), these invariants can be mutually incomparable. However, we show that at each step, the value of the objective function measuring progress towards proving the specification cannot increase.

5.3 Discussion

We now focus on issues such as convergence and the complexity of each step.

Convergence: In general, the known results about the convergence of alternating minimization schemes for bilinear optimization problems indicate that the process *seldom* converges to a global optimal value [27]. Often, these iterations get "stuck" in a local *saddle point*, from which no further progress is possible. Nevertheless, our goal here is not to converge to a global optimum but to a *good enough* solution whose objective function value is strictly negative, thus proving the property of interest.

By allowing template updates to the process, it is no longer clear that the process will necessarily converge (even if it converges to a saddle point) in finitely many steps. It is entirely possible that the value of the objective function remains unchanged but the process produces a new template $T_\ell + \Delta_\ell^{(i)}$ at each step. Depending on how the limits to the template change L_ℓ, U_ℓ are specified, this process may produce a fresh new template at each step.

Nevertheless, we note that the lack of convergence does not pose a serious hurdle to an application of template update to policy iteration. It is possible to iterate while each step provides at least $\epsilon > 0$ decrease in the value of the objective function, and stop otherwise.

Complexity: At each step, we solve a linear programming problem. For a transition system with n variables, $|\mathcal{L}|$ locations, $|\mathcal{T}|$ transitions, k template rows at each step, the size of each LP in terms of number of variables + constraints is $\mathcal{O}\left(|\mathcal{L}|kn + |\mathcal{T}|k^2\right)$. Although this is polynomial, the process can be prohibitively expensive for large programs. In our future work, we wish to exploit the block structure of these constraints in order to allow us to solve the LPs using standard approaches such as Benders or Danzig-Wolfe decomposition techniques [10].

Collecting Invariants: Finally, we note that each step yields an invariant map $\eta^{(i)}$ that is not necessarily comparable to the invariant obtained in the next step $\eta^{(i+1)}$. However, we note that the finite conjunction

$$\eta^{(0)} \wedge \cdots \wedge \eta^{(N)},$$

over all the iterations of this process can be a stronger invariant than each of them. This is already demonstrated by the motivating example in Sect. 2.

6 Experimental Evaluation

We present a preliminary experimental evaluation of the ideas presented thus far using a prototype implementation.

Prototype Implementation: A prototype implementation was developed in Python, using the exact arithmetic LP solver QSOptEx. The QSOptEx solver provides a fast and convenient interface to an optimized Simplex implementation in exact arithmetic. Our implementation allows the specification of a transition system and supports a few additional features on top of those presented in the paper including location invariants. We also support the option to specify different templates at various program locations. During the template update, our approach considers independent updates to the template at each location.

Specifying Template Changes: We consider a simple approach to specifying the limits L_ℓ, U_ℓ to the change in template at each location ℓ. First, the option for $\Delta_\ell = 0$ must be allowed, secondly, $\Delta_\ell = -T$ must be disallowed. For each $T_\ell(i,j) = 0$, we specify corresponding limits $L_\ell(i,j) = -z$ and $U_\ell(i,j) = z$ for a fixed constant $z > 0$ (taken as 1000 in our experiments). For $T_\ell(i,j) \neq 0$, we allow Δ to range between $\frac{1}{2}T_\ell(i,j)$ and $2T_\ell(i,j)$ in our experiments.

Benchmark Examples: We consider a small set of benchmark examples that are illustrative of applications that we encounter in the verification of discrete-time affine hybrid systems. Table 1 briefly describes each benchmark example.

Experimental Comparison: Table 2 shows the comparison between abstract interpretation using Kleene iteration, policy iteration without template update

Table 1. Description of the benchmarks used and the sizes in terms of (# variables, # locations, # transitions)

ID	Size	Remark
1	(4, 2, 2)	Switched linear system with 4 state variables
2	(2, 2, 4)	Example in Fig. 2
3	(2, 1, 1)	Linear System with 1 location and transition
4	(2, 1, 1)	Motivating example from Sect. 2
5	(3, 1, 4)	Adjé et al. [1]
6	(2, 35, 169)	Grid-based piecewise linearization of Van Der Pol oscillator

Table 2. Experimental results including a comparison between policy iteration without template update and with template updated (shaded rows). All experiments were run on a Macbook Air laptop with 1.8 GHz Intel processor, 8 GB RAM running OSX10.12. All timings are in seconds. **Legend: T. Upd:** Template updated at each iteration? **Proved?**: whether the property was proved, if not, the objective value is reported, |BOP|: size of the bilinear problem (# bilinear template variables, # bilinear mult. variables, # linear mult. variables), # Iter: # policy iterations - A (*) next to this number indicates that the iteration was stopped due to 5 consecutive steps with same objective value.

id	Initial template	Kleene		Policy iteration				
	Type, $\|T\|$	Time	Proved?	T. Upd.	|BOP|	Time	# Iter	Proved
1	Pentagon, 26	0.37	N (0.2)	N	(52, 1176, 1249)	0.5	2	N(0.2)
				Y	(240, 1176, 1249)	18.2	5(*)	N(0.2)
2	Octagon, 8	0.15	N(0.2)	N	(16, 264, 353)	0.1	2	N(0.2)
				Y	(48, 264, 353)	0.4	6	Y
3	Octagon, 8	0.04	N(0.5)	N	(8, 72, 161)	0.02	1	N(0.5)
				Y	(24, 72, 161)	0.05	2	Y
4	Interval, 4	0.02	N(15.5)	N	(4, 20, 33)	0.01	1	N(15.5)
				Y	(12, 20, 33)	0.02	2	Y
5	Pentagon, 10	1.5	N(2.83)	N	(10, 410, 681)	0.3	2	Y
				Y	(40, 410, 681)	0.3	2	Y
6	Interval, 4	2.5	N(0.75)	N	(140, 836, 2033)	1.5	5(*)	N(0.75)
				Y	(168, 836, 2033)	2.9	5(*)	N(0.75)

and with template update for the 6 benchmarks. The table reports the objective value of the initial solution obtained after the Kleene iteration using widening/narrowing terminates. A non-negative value of the objective function indicates the failure to prove the property. Overall, we see that policy iteration with template update is *effective* in these benchmarks in proving properties in 4 out of the 6 cases, whereas without template update we prove the property in just 1 out of 6. It is interesting that whenever the approaches manage to reduce the objective value of the initial solution, they end up proving the property. Further experiments are needed to clarify whether this represents an artifact of the benchmarks chosen.

Figure 5 shows the sequence of iterates at the two locations for the transition system shown in Fig. 2 corresponding to benchmark number 2. The goal is to establish the unreachability of $x_2 \geq 0.8$ at location ℓ_2. The final invariant for ℓ_2 is shown in green, proving the specification.

Thus, we provide preliminary evidence that the bilinear approach is effective in cases where Kleene or policy iteration fail. At the same time, we notice that the size of the bilinear problem, though polynomial in the original transition system and template size, is often large with thousands of variables. However, the problems are sparse with each constraint involving just a tiny fraction of these variables.

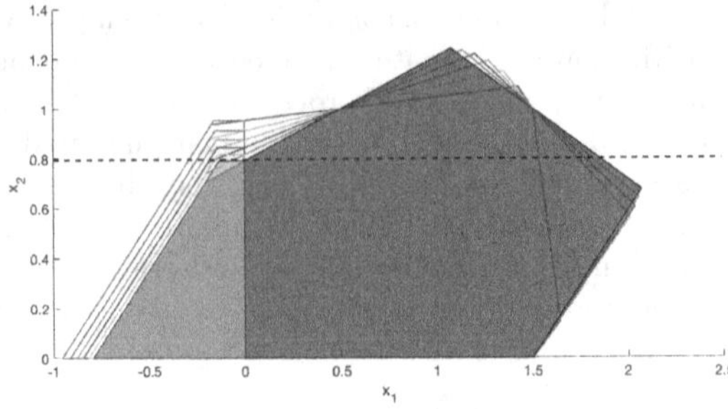

Fig. 5. Sequence of iterates for benchmark id 2 culminating in the final invariants shown shaded in blue and green. The property $x_2 \geq 0.8$ is shown unreachable at the green location by the final iterate. (Color figure online)

This points out the need for simplification techniques and approaches to solving bilinear problems that exploit this sparsity to make the approach more efficient.

7 Conclusions

To conclude, we exploit the connection between template domains and bilinear constraints. In doing so, we show that policy iteration allows the template directions to be updated on the fly in a property directed fashion. We present preliminary evidence that such an approach can be effective, though many challenges remain. Our future work will focus on techniques to make progress when the policy iteration is stuck in a local saddle point, *without sacrificing the soundness of the approach.* In this context, we are investigating strategy iteration approaches that can incorporate the template update process [22]. Our previous work on invariant set computation for polynomial differential equations mentioned earlier, already contains clues to such an approach [37]. As mentioned earlier, exploiting the sparsity of constraints to provide a more scalable solver is also another fruitful future direction.

Acknowledgments. The authors gratefully acknowledge the anonymous reviewers for their valuable comments and suggestions. This work was funded in part by NSF under award numbers SHF 1527075. All opinions expressed are those of the authors, and not necessarily of the NSF.

References

1. Adjé, A., Garoche, P.-L.: Automatic synthesis of piecewise linear quadratic invariants for programs. In: D'Souza, D., Lal, A., Larsen, K.G. (eds.) VMCAI 2015. LNCS, vol. 8931, pp. 99–116. Springer, Heidelberg (2015). doi:10.1007/978-3-662-46081-8_6
2. Adjé, A., Gaubert, S., Goubault, E.: Coupling policy iteration with semi-definite relaxation to compute accurate numerical invariants in static analysis. Log. Methods Comput. Sci. **8**(1), 1–32 (2012)

3. Adjé, A., Gaubert, S., Goubault, E.: Computing the smallest fixed point of order-preserving nonexpansive mappings arising in positive stochastic games and static analysis of programs. J. Math. Anal. Appl. **410**(1), 227–240 (2014)
4. Amato, G., Parton, M., Scozzari, F.: Deriving numerical abstract domains via principal component analysis. In: Cousot, R., Martel, M. (eds.) SAS 2010. LNCS, vol. 6337, pp. 134–150. Springer, Heidelberg (2010). doi:10.1007/978-3-642-15769-1_9
5. Blanchet, B., Cousot, P., Cousot, R., Feret, J., Mauborgne, L., Miné, A., Monniaux, D., Rival, X.: A static analyzer for large safety-critical software. In: Programming Language Design and Implementation, pp. 196–207. ACM Press (2003)
6. Blanchet, B., Cousot, P., Cousot, R., Feret, J., Mauborgne, L., Miné, A., Monniaux, D., Rival, X.: Design and implementation of a special-purpose static program analyzer for safety-critical real-time embedded software. In: Mogensen, T.Æ., Schmidt, D.A., Sudborough, I.H. (eds.) The Essence of Computation. LNCS, vol. 2566, pp. 85–108. Springer, Heidelberg (2002). doi:10.1007/3-540-36377-7_5
7. Bogomolov, S., Frehse, G., Giacobbe, M., Henzinger, T.A.: Counterexample-guided refinement of template polyhedra. In: Legay, A., Margaria, T. (eds.) TACAS 2017. LNCS, vol. 10205, pp. 589–606. Springer, Heidelberg (2017). doi:10.1007/978-3-662-54577-5_34
8. Chen, X., Abraham, E., Sankaranarayanan, S.: Taylor model flowpipe construction for non-linear hybrid systems. In: Real Time Systems Symposium (RTSS), pp. 183–192. IEEE Press (2012)
9. Chen, X., Ábrahám, E.: Choice of directions for the approximation of reachable sets for hybrid systems. In: Moreno-Díaz, R., Pichler, F., Quesada-Arencibia, A. (eds.) EUROCAST 2011. LNCS, vol. 6927, pp. 535–542. Springer, Heidelberg (2012). doi:10.1007/978-3-642-27549-4_69
10. Chvátal, V.: Linear Programming. Freeman, New York (1983)
11. Clariso, R., Cortadella, J.: The octahedron abstract domain. Sci. Comput. Program. **64**(1), 115–139 (2007)
12. Colón, M.A., Sankaranarayanan, S., Sipma, H.B.: Linear invariant generation using non-linear constraint solving. In: Hunt, W.A., Somenzi, F. (eds.) CAV 2003. LNCS, vol. 2725, pp. 420–432. Springer, Heidelberg (2003). doi:10.1007/978-3-540-45069-6_39
13. Costan, A., Gaubert, S., Goubault, E., Martel, M., Putot, S.: A Policy Iteration Algorithm for Computing Fixed Points in Static Analysis of Programs. In: Etessami, K., Rajamani, S.K. (eds.) CAV 2005. LNCS, vol. 3576, pp. 462–475. Springer, Heidelberg (2005). doi:10.1007/11513988_46
14. Cousot, P.: Proving program invariance and termination by parametric abstraction, lagrangian relaxation and semidefinite programming. In: Cousot, R. (ed.) VMCAI 2005. LNCS, vol. 3385, pp. 1–24. Springer, Heidelberg (2005). doi:10.1007/978-3-540-30579-8_1
15. Cousot, P., Cousot, R.: Static determination of dynamic properties of programs. In: Proceedings of ISOP 1976, pp. 106–130. Dunod, Paris (1976)
16. Cousot, P., Cousot, R.: Comparing the Galois connection and widening/narrowing approaches to abstract interpretation. In: Bruynooghe, M., Wirsing, M. (eds.) PLILP 1992. LNCS, vol. 631, pp. 269–295. Springer, Heidelberg (1992). doi:10.1007/3-540-55844-6_142
17. Cousot, P., Cousot, R.: Abstract Interpretation: A unified lattice model for static analysis of programs by construction or approximation of fixpoints. In: ACM Principles of Programming Languages, pp. 238–252 (1977)

18. Delmas, D., Souyris, J.: Astrée: from research to industry. In: Nielson, H.R., Filé, G. (eds.) SAS 2007. LNCS, vol. 4634, pp. 437–451. Springer, Heidelberg (2007). doi:10.1007/978-3-540-74061-2_27
19. Frehse, G., Guernic, C., Donzé, A., Cotton, S., Ray, R., Lebeltel, O., Ripado, R., Girard, A., Dang, T., Maler, O.: SpaceEx: scalable verification of hybrid systems. In: Gopalakrishnan, G., Qadeer, S. (eds.) CAV 2011. LNCS, vol. 6806, pp. 379–395. Springer, Heidelberg (2011). doi:10.1007/978-3-642-22110-1_30
20. Gaubert, S., Goubault, E., Taly, A., Zennou, S.: Static analysis by policy iteration on relational domains. In: Nicola, R. (ed.) ESOP 2007. LNCS, vol. 4421, pp. 237–252. Springer, Heidelberg (2007). doi:10.1007/978-3-540-71316-6_17
21. Gawlitza, T., Seidl, H.: Precise fixpoint computation through strategy iteration. In: Nicola, R. (ed.) ESOP 2007. LNCS, vol. 4421, pp. 300–315. Springer, Heidelberg (2007). doi:10.1007/978-3-540-71316-6_21
22. Gawlitza, T.M., Seidl, H.: Solving systems of rational equations through strategy iteration. ACM Trans. Program. Lang. Syst. **33**(3), 11:1–11:48 (2011)
23. Ghaoui, L.E., Balakrishnan, V.: Synthesis of fixed-structure controllers via numerical optimization. In: Proceedings of the 33rd Conference on Decision and Control (CDC). IEEE (1994)
24. Goubault, E., Putot, S., Baufreton, P., Gassino, J.: Static analysis of the accuracy in control systems: principles and experiments. In: Leue, S., Merino, P. (eds.) FMICS 2007. LNCS, vol. 4916, pp. 3–20. Springer, Heidelberg (2008). doi:10.1007/978-3-540-79707-4_3
25. Guernic, C.L., Girard, A.: Reachability analysis of linear systems using support functions. Nonlinear Anal. Hybrid Syst. **4**(2), 250–262 (2010)
26. Gulwani, S., Srivastava, S., Venkatesan, R.: Program analysis as constraint solving. In: PLDI. pp. 281–292. ACM (2008)
27. Helton, J., Merino, O.: Coordinate optimization for bi-convex matrix inequalities. In: IEEE Conference on Decision and Control (CDC), pp. 3609–3613 (1997)
28. Logozzo, F., Fähndrich, M.: Pentagons: a weakly relational abstract domain for the efficient validation of array accesses. In: Symposium on Applied Computing, SAC 2008, NY, USA, pp. 184–188. ACM, New York (2008)
29. Mathworks Inc.: PolySpace design verifier. http://www.mathworks.com/products/polyspace/. Accessed Apr 2017
30. Miné, A.: A new numerical abstract domain based on difference-bound matrices. In: Danvy, O., Filinski, A. (eds.) PADO 2001. LNCS, vol. 2053, pp. 155–172. Springer, Heidelberg (2001). doi:10.1007/3-540-44978-7_10
31. Miné, A.: The octagon abstract domain. In: AST 2001 in WCRE 2001, pp. 310–319. IEEE, IEEE CS Press, October 2001
32. Nielson, F., Nielson, H.R., Hankin, C.: Principles of Program Analysis. Springer, Heidelberg (1999)
33. Roux, P., Voronin, Y.-L., Sankaranarayanan, S.: Validating numerical semidefinite programming solvers for polynomial invariants. In: Rival, X. (ed.) SAS 2016. LNCS, vol. 9837, pp. 424–446. Springer, Heidelberg (2016). doi:10.1007/978-3-662-53413-7_21
34. Sankaranarayanan, S., Dang, T., Ivančić, F.: Symbolic model checking of hybrid systems using template polyhedra. In: Ramakrishnan, C.R., Rehof, J. (eds.) TACAS 2008. LNCS, vol. 4963, pp. 188–202. Springer, Heidelberg (2008). doi:10.1007/978-3-540-78800-3_14
35. Sankaranarayanan, S., Sipma, H.B., Manna, Z.: Constraint-based linear-relations analysis. In: Giacobazzi, R. (ed.) SAS 2004. LNCS, vol. 3148, pp. 53–68. Springer, Heidelberg (2004). doi:10.1007/978-3-540-27864-1_7

36. Sankaranarayanan, S., Sipma, H.B., Manna, Z.: Scalable analysis of linear systems using mathematical programming. In: Cousot, R. (ed.) VMCAI 2005. LNCS, vol. 3385, pp. 25–41. Springer, Heidelberg (2005). doi:10.1007/978-3-540-30579-8_2
37. Sassi, M.A.B., Girard, A., Sankaranarayanan, S.: Iterative computation of polyhedral invariants sets for polynomial dynamical systems. In: IEEE Conference on Decision and Control (CDC), pp. 6348–6353. IEEE Press (2014)
38. Sassi, M.A.B., Sankaranarayanan, S., Chen, X., Ábraham, E.: Linear relaxations of polynomial positivity for polynomial Lyapunov function synthesis. IMA J. Math. Control Inf. **33**, 723–756 (2016)
39. Venet, A., Brat, G.P.: Precise and efficient static array bound checking for large embedded C programs. In: PLDI, pp. 231–242. ACM (2004)
40. Weispfenning, V.: Quantifier elimination for real algebra–the quadratic case and beyond. Appl. Algebr. Error-Correct. Codes (AAECC) **8**, 85–101 (1997)

A New Abstraction Framework for Affine Transformers

Tushar Sharma[1(✉)] and Thomas Reps[1,2]

[1] University of Wisconsin, Madison, WI, USA
tsharma@cs.wisc.edu
[2] GrammaTech, Inc., Ithaca, NY, USA

Abstract. This paper addresses the problem of abstracting a set of affine transformers $\overrightarrow{v}' = \overrightarrow{v} \cdot C + \overrightarrow{d}$, where $\overrightarrow{v}$ and $\overrightarrow{v}'$ represent the pre-state and post-state, respectively. We introduce a framework to harness any base abstract domain $\mathcal{B}$ in an abstract domain of affine transformations. Abstract domains are usually used to define constraints on the variables of a program. In this paper, however, abstract domain $\mathcal{B}$ is re-purposed to constrain the elements of C and $\overrightarrow{d}$—thereby defining a set of affine transformers on program states. This framework facilitates intra- and interprocedural analyses to obtain function and loop summaries, as well as to prove program assertions.

1 Introduction

Most critical applications, such as airplane and rocket controllers, need correctness guarantees. Usually these correctness guarantees can be described as safety properties in the form of assertions. Verifying an assertion amounts to showing that the assertion holds true for all possible runs of an application. Proving an assertion is, in general, an undecidable problem. Nevertheless, there exist static-analysis techniques that are able to verify automatically some kinds of program assertions. One such technique is abstract interpretation [3], which soundly abstracts the concrete executions of the program to elements in an abstract domain, and checks the correctness guarantees using the abstraction.

In this paper, we provide analysis techniques to abstract the behavior of the program as a set of affine transformations over bit-vectors. An affine transformer is a relation on states, defined by $\overrightarrow{v}' = \overrightarrow{v} \cdot C + \overrightarrow{d}$, where $\overrightarrow{v}'$ and $\overrightarrow{v}$ are row vectors that represent the post-transformation state and the pre-transformation

Supported, in part, by a gift from Rajiv and Ritu Batra; DARPA MUSE award FA8750-14-2-0270 and DARPA STAC award FA8750-15-C-0082; and by the UW-Madison Office of the Vice Chancellor for Research and Graduate Education with funding from the Wisconsin Alumni Research Foundation. Any opinions, findings, and conclusions or recommendations expressed in this publication are those of the authors, and do not necessarily reflect the views of the sponsoring agencies.

T. Reps has an ownership interest in GrammaTech, Inc., which has licensed elements of the technology discussed in this publication.

F. Ranzato (Ed.): SAS 2017, LNCS 10422, pp. 342–363, 2017.
DOI: 10.1007/978-3-319-66706-5_17

state, respectively. C is the linear component of the transformation and $\overrightarrow{d}$ is a constant vector. For example, $[x' \; y'] = [x \; y] \begin{bmatrix} 1 & 0 \\ 2 & 0 \end{bmatrix} + [10 \; 0]$ denotes the affine transformation $(x' = x + 2y + 10 \wedge y' = 0)$ over variables $\{x, y\}$. We denote an affine transformation by $C : \overrightarrow{d}$. The paper is based on the following observation:

Observation 1. *Abstract domains are usually used to define constraints on the variables of a program. However, they can be re-purposed to constrain the elements of* $C : \overrightarrow{d}$ *—thereby defining a set of affine transformers on program states.*

The Need for Abstraction over Affine Transformers. Abstractions of affine transformers can be used to obtain affine-relation invariants at each program point in the program [12]. An affine relation is a linear-equality constraint between numeric-valued variables of the form $\sum_{i=1}^{n} a_i v_i + b = 0$. For a given set of variables $\{v_i\}$, affine-relation analysis (ARA) identifies affine relations that are invariants of a program. The results of ARA can be used to determine a more precise abstract value for a variable via *semantic reduction* [4], or detect the relationship between program variables and loop-counter variables.

Furthermore, when the abstract-domain elements are abstractions of affine transformers, abstract interpretation can be used to provide useful function summaries or loop summaries [2,18]. In principle, summaries can be computed offline for large libraries of code so that client static analyses can use them to provide verification results more efficiently.

Previous work [6] compared two abstract domains for affine-relation analysis over bitvectors: (i) an affine-closed abstraction of relations over program variables (AG), and (ii) an affine-closed abstraction of affine transformers over program variables (MOS). Müller-Olm and Seidl [13] introduced the MOS domain, whose elements are the affine-closed sets of affine transformers. An MOS element can be represented by a set of square matrices. Each matrix T is an affine transformer of the form $T = \left[\begin{array}{c|c} 1 & \overrightarrow{d} \\ \hline 0 & C \end{array}\right]$, which represents the state transformation $\overrightarrow{v}' := \overrightarrow{v} \cdot C + \overrightarrow{d}$, or, equivalently, $[1|\overrightarrow{v}'] := [1|\overrightarrow{v}]\, T$. In [6], the authors observe that the MOS domain can encode two-vocabulary relations that are not affine-closed even though the affine transformers themselves are affine closed. (See Sect. 2.5 for an example.) Thus, moving the abstraction from affine relations over program variables to affine relations over affine transformations possibly offers some advantages because it allows some non-affine-closed sets to be representable.

While the MOS domain is useful for finding affine-relation invariants in a program, the join operation used at confluence points can lose precision in many cases, leading to imprecise function summaries. Furthermore, the analysis does not scale well as the number of variables in the vocabulary increases. In other words, it has one baked-in performance-versus-precision aspect.

Problem Statement. Our goal is to generalize the ideas used in the MOS domain—in particular, to have an abstraction of *sets of affine transformers*—but to provide a way for a client of the abstract domain to have some control over the performance/precision trade-off. Toward this end, we define a new family of numerical abstract domains, denoted by ATA[$\mathcal{B}$]. (ATA stands for Affine-Transformers Abstraction.) Following Observation 1, ATA[$\mathcal{B}$] is parameterized by a base numerical abstract domain $\mathcal{B}$, and allows one to represent a set of affine transformers (or, alternatively, certain disjunctions of transition formulas).

Summary of the Approach. Let the $(k+k^2)$-tuple $(d_1, d_2, \ldots, d_k, c_{11}, c_{12}, \ldots, c_{1k}, c_{21}, c_{22}, \ldots, c_{kk})$ denote the affine transformation $\bigwedge_{j=1}^{k} \left(v'_j = \sum_{i=1}^{k} (c_{ij} v_i) + d_j \right)$, also written as "$C : \overrightarrow{d}$." The key idea is that we will use $(k + k^2)$ symbolic constants to represent the $(k+k^2)$ coefficients in a transformation of the form $C : \overrightarrow{d}$, and use a base abstract domain $\mathcal{B}$—provided by a client of the framework—to represent *sets* of possible values for these symbolic constants. In particular, $\mathcal{B}$ is an abstract domain for which, for all $b \in \mathcal{B}$, $\gamma(b)$ is a set of $(k + k^2)$-tuples—each tuple of which provides values for $\{d_i\} \cup \{c_{ij}\}$, and can thus be interpreted as an affine transformation $C : \overrightarrow{d}$.

With this approach, a given $b \in \mathcal{B}$ represents the disjunction $\bigvee\{(C : \overrightarrow{d}) \in \gamma(b)\}$. When $\mathcal{B}$ is a non-relational domain, each $b \in \mathcal{B}$ constrains the values of $\{d_i\} \cup \{c_{ij}\}$ *independently.* When $\mathcal{B}$ is a relational domain, each $b \in \mathcal{B}$ can impose *intra-component* constraints on the allowed tuples $(d_1, d_2, \ldots, d_k, c_{11}, c_{12}, \ldots, c_{1k}, c_{21}, c_{22}, \ldots, c_{kk})$.

ATA[$\mathcal{B}$] generalizes the MOS domain, in the sense that the MOS domain is exactly ATA[AG], where AG is a relational abstract domain that captures affine equalities of the form $\sum_i a_i k_i = b$, where $a_i, b \in Z_{2^w}$ and $\mathbb{Z}_{2^w}$ is the set of w-bit bitvectors [6,9] (see Sect. 2.4). For instance, an element in ATA[AG] can capture the set of affine transformers "$x' = k_1 * x + k_1 * y + k_2$, where k_1 is odd, k_2 is even, and k_1 is the coefficient of both x and y." On the other hand, an element in the abstract domain ATA[$\mathcal{I}_{\mathbb{Z}_{2^w}}^{(k+k^2)}$], where $\mathcal{I}_{\mathbb{Z}_{2^w}}^{(k+k^2)}$ is the abstract domain of $(k+k^2)$-tuples of intervals over bitvectors, can capture a set of affine transformers such as $x' = k_3 * x + k_4 * y + k_5$, where $k_3 \in [0, 1]$, $k_4 \in [2, 2]$, and $k_5 \in [0, 10]$.

This paper addresses a wide variety of issues that arise in defining the ATA[$\mathcal{B}$] framework, including describing the abstract-domain operations of ATA[$\mathcal{B}$] in terms of the abstract-domain operations available in the base domain $\mathcal{B}$.

Contributions. The overall contribution of our work is the framework ATA[$\mathcal{B}$], for which we present

- methods to perform basic abstract-domain operations, such as equality and join.
- a method to perform abstract composition, which is needed to perform abstract interpretation.

– a faster method to perform abstract composition when the base domain is non-relational.

Section 2 introduces the terminology used in the paper; and presents some needed background material. Section 3 demonstrates the framework with the help of an example. Section 4 formally introduces the parameterized abstract domain ATA[$\mathcal{B}$]. Section 5 provides discussion and related work. Proofs are given in Appendices A and B of [19].

2 Preliminaries

All numeric values in this paper are integers in $\mathbb{Z}_{2^w}$ for some bit width w. That is, values are w-bit machine integers with the standard operations for machine addition and multiplication. Addition and multiplication in $\mathbb{Z}_{2^w}$ form a ring, not a field, so some facets of standard linear algebra do not apply.

Throughout the paper, k is the size of the *vocabulary* $V = \{v_1, v_2, .., v_k\}$— i.e., the variable-set under analysis. We use $\overrightarrow{v}$ to denote the vector $[v_1 v_2 .. v_k]$ of variables in vocabulary V. A *two-vocabulary* relation $R[V; V']$ is a transition relation between values of variables in the *pre-state* vocabulary V and values of variables in the *post-state* vocabulary V'. For instance, a transition relation $R[V; V']$ in the concrete collecting semantics is a subset of $\mathbb{Z}_{2^w}^k \times \mathbb{Z}_{2^w}^k$ (which is isomorphic to $\mathbb{Z}_{2^w}^{2k}$).

Matrix addition and multiplication are defined as usual, forming a matrix ring. We denote the transpose of a matrix M by M^t. A *one-vocabulary matrix* is a matrix with $k+1$ columns. A *two-vocabulary matrix* is a matrix with $2k+1$ columns. In each case, the "+1" is related to the fact that we capture affine rather than linear relations. I_n denotes the $n \times n$ identity matrix. Given a matrix C, we use $C[i, j]$ to refer to the entry at the i-th column and j-th row of C. Given a vector $\overrightarrow{d}$, we use $\overrightarrow{d}[j]$ to refer to the j-th entry in $\overrightarrow{d}$.

2.1 Affine Programs

$$
\begin{array}{rcl}
\langle \mathit{Block} \rangle & :: & l : ((\langle \mathit{Stmt} \rangle\ ;)^*\ \langle \mathit{Next} \rangle \\
\langle \mathit{Next} \rangle & :: & \textbf{jump}\ l; \\
 & | & \textbf{jump}\ \langle \mathit{Cond} \rangle\ ?\ l_1 : l_2 \\
\langle \mathit{Cond} \rangle & :: & ?\ |\ \langle \mathit{Expr} \rangle\ \mathit{Op}\ \langle \mathit{Expr} \rangle \\
\langle \mathit{Op} \rangle & :: & = | \neq | \geqslant | \leqslant \\
\langle \mathit{Expr} \rangle & :: & c_0 + \sum_{i=1}^{k} c_i * v_i \\
\langle \mathit{Stmt} \rangle & :: & v_j := \langle \mathit{Expr} \rangle \\
 & | & v_j := ?
\end{array}
$$

We borrow the notion of affine programs from [13]. We restrict our affine programs to consist of a single procedure. The statements are restricted to either affine assignments or non-deterministic assignments. The control-flow instruction consists of either an unconditional jump statement, or a conditional jump with an affine equality, an affine disequality, an affine inequality, or unknown guard condition.

2.2 Abstract-Domain Operations

The two important steps in abstract interpretation (AI) are:

1. Abstraction: The abstraction of the program is constructed using the abstract domain and abstract semantics.
2. Fixpoint analysis: Fixpoint iteration is performed on the abstraction of the program to identify invariants.

For the purpose of our analysis, the program is abstracted to a control-flow graph, where each edge in the graph is labeled with an abstract transformer. An abstract transformer is a *two-vocabulary* transition relation $R[V; V']$. Concrete states described by an abstract transformer are represented by row vectors of length $2k$. A (two-vocabulary) concrete state is sometimes called an *assignment* to the variables of the pre-state and the post-state vocabulary.

Table 1. Abstract-domain operations.

Type	Operation	Description	Type	Operation	Description
$\mathcal{A}$	$\bot$	*Bottom element*	$\mathcal{A}$	$\alpha(v_j := ?)$	*Abstraction for nondeterministic assignments*
bool	$(a_1 == a_2)$	*Equality*			
$\mathcal{A}$	$(a_1 \sqcup a_2)$	*Join*	$\mathcal{A}$	$\alpha(v_j := c_0 + \sum_{i=1}^{k} c_{ij} * v_i)$	*Abstraction for affine assignments*
$\mathcal{A}$	$(a_1 \nabla a_2)$	*Widen*			
$\mathcal{A}$	*Id*	*Identity element*	$\mathcal{A}$	$(a_1 \circ a_2)$	*Composition*

Table 1 lists the abstract-domain operations needed to generate the program abstraction and perform fixpoint analysis on it. Bottom, equality, and join are standard abstract-domain operations. The *widen* operation is needed for domains with infinite ascending chains to ensure termination. The two operations of the form $\alpha(Stmt)$ perform abstraction on an assignment statement *Stmt* to generate an abstract transformer. *Id* is the identity element; which represents the identity transformation ($\bigwedge_{i=1}^{k} v_i' = v_i$). Finally, the abstract-composition operation $a_1 \circ a_2$ returns a sound overapproximation of the composition of the abstract transformation a_1 with the abstract transformation a_2.

2.3 The Müller-Olm/Seidl Domain

An element in the Müller-Olm/Seidl domain (MOS) is an affine-closed set of affine transformers, as detailed in [13]. An MOS element is represented by a set of $(k+1)$-by-$(k+1)$ matrices. Each matrix T is a one-vocabulary transformer of the form $T = \left[\begin{array}{c|c} 1 & b \\ \hline 0 & M \end{array}\right]$, which represents the state transformation $\overrightarrow{v}' := \overrightarrow{v} \cdot M + b$, or, equivalently, $[1|\overrightarrow{v}'] := [1|\overrightarrow{v}]\, T$.

An MOS element $\mathcal{M}$, consisting of a set of matrices, represents the affine span of the set, denoted by $\langle\mathcal{M}\rangle$. $\langle\mathcal{M}\rangle$ is defined as follows: $\langle\mathcal{M}\rangle \stackrel{\text{def}}{=} \left\{T \,\middle|\, \exists \overrightarrow{u} \in \mathbb{Z}_{2^w}^{|\mathcal{M}|} : T = \sum_{M \in \mathcal{M}} u_M M \wedge T_{1,1} = 1\right\}$. The meaning of $\mathcal{M}$ is the union of the graphs of the affine transformers in $\langle\mathcal{M}\rangle$. Thus, $\gamma_{\text{MOS}}(\mathcal{M}) \stackrel{\text{def}}{=} \left\{(\overrightarrow{v}, \overrightarrow{v}') \,\middle|\, \overrightarrow{v}, \overrightarrow{v}' \in \mathbb{Z}_{2^w}^k \wedge \exists T \in \langle\mathcal{M}\rangle \colon [1|v]\, T = [1|v']\right\}$.

Example 1. If $w = 4$, the MOS element $\mathcal{M} = \left\{ \left[\begin{array}{c|cc} 1 & 0 & 0 \\ \hline 0 & 1 & 0 \\ 0 & 0 & 0 \end{array}\right], \left[\begin{array}{c|cc} 1 & 0 & 2 \\ \hline 0 & 1 & 0 \\ 0 & 0 & 0 \end{array}\right] \right\}$ represents the affine span $\langle\mathcal{M}\rangle = \left\{ \left[\begin{array}{c|cc} 1 & 0 & 0 \\ \hline 0 & 1 & 0 \\ 0 & 0 & 0 \end{array}\right], \left[\begin{array}{c|cc} 1 & 0 & 2 \\ \hline 0 & 1 & 0 \\ 0 & 0 & 0 \end{array}\right], \left[\begin{array}{c|cc} 1 & 0 & 4 \\ \hline 0 & 1 & 0 \\ 0 & 0 & 0 \end{array}\right], \ldots, \left[\begin{array}{c|cc} 1 & 0 & 12 \\ \hline 0 & 1 & 0 \\ 0 & 0 & 0 \end{array}\right], \left[\begin{array}{c|cc} 1 & 0 & 14 \\ \hline 0 & 1 & 0 \\ 0 & 0 & 0 \end{array}\right] \right\}$, which corresponds to the transition relation in which $v_1' = v_1$, v_2 can have any value, and v_2' can have any even value. □

Table 2 gives the abstract-domain operations for the MOS domain. The bottom element of the MOS domain is the empty set $\varnothing$, and the MOS element that represents the identity relation is the singleton set $\{I\}$. The equality check can be done by checking if the span of the matrices in the two values is equal. [6] provides an normal form for the MOS domain, which can be used to reduce the equality check to *syntactic* equality checks on the matrices in M_1 and M_2. The widening operation is not needed for MOS because it is a finite-height lattice. The abstraction operation for the affine-assignment statement $\alpha(v_j := d_0 + \sum_{i=1}^{k} c_{ij} * v_i)$ gives back an MOS-element with a single matrix where every variable $v \in V - \{v_j\}$

Table 2. Abstract-domain operations for the MOS-domain.

Type	Operation	Description
$\mathcal{A}$	$\bot_{\text{MOS}}$	$\varnothing$
bool	$(M_1 == M_2)$	$\langle M_1\rangle == \langle M_2\rangle$
$\mathcal{A}$	$(M_1 \sqcup M_2)$	$M_1 \cup M_2$
$\mathcal{A}$	$(a_1 \nabla a_2)$	*Not applicable*
$\mathcal{A}$	$\alpha(v_j := d_0 + \sum_{i=1}^{k} c_{ij} * v_i)$	$\left\{ \left[\begin{array}{c|ccc} 1 & 0 & d_0 & 0 \\ \hline 0 & I_{j-1} & [c_{1j}, c_{2j}, \ldots c_{(j-1)j}]^t & 0 \\ 0 & 0 & c_{jj} & 0 \\ 0 & 0 & [c_{(j+1)j}, c_{(j+2)j}, \ldots c_{kj}]^t & I_{k-j} \end{array}\right] \right\}$
$\mathcal{A}$	$\alpha(v_j := ?)$	$\left\{ \left[\begin{array}{c|ccc} 1 & 0 & 0 & 0 \\ \hline 0 & I_{j-1} & 0 & 0 \\ 0 & 0 & 0 & 0 \\ 0 & 0 & 0 & I_{k-j} \end{array}\right], \left[\begin{array}{c|ccc} 1 & 0 & 1 & 0 \\ \hline 0 & I_{j-1} & 0 & 0 \\ 0 & 0 & 0 & 0 \\ 0 & 0 & 0 & I_{k-j} \end{array}\right] \right\}$
$\mathcal{A}$	Id	$\{I_{k+1}\}$
$\mathcal{A}$	$(M_1 \circ M_2)$	$\{A_2 A_1 \mid A_i \in M_i\}$

is left unchanged, and the variable v_j is transformed to reflect the assignment by updating the corresponding column in the matrix with the assignment coefficients. The abstraction operation for the non-deterministic assignment statement $\alpha(v_j := ?)$ gives back an MOS-element containing two matrices. Similar to the abstraction for affine assignment operation, every variable $v \in V - v_j$ is left unchanged in both the matrices. v_j is set to 0 in the first and 1 in the second matrix. The affine-closed set of these two matrices ensures that v_j is assigned to non-deterministically. The abstract-composition operation performs multiplication for each pair of the matrices in M_1 and M_2.

2.4 The Affine-Generator Domain

An element in the Affine Generator domain ($\mathrm{AG}[\overrightarrow{v}; \overrightarrow{v}']$) is a two-vocabulary matrix whose rows are the affine generators of a two-vocabulary relation over variables $\overrightarrow{v}$. An $\mathrm{AG}[\overrightarrow{v}; \overrightarrow{v}']$ element is an r-by-$(2k+1)$ matrix G, with $0 < r \leq 2k+1$. The concretization of an $\mathrm{AG}[\overrightarrow{v}; \overrightarrow{v}']$ element is

$$\gamma_{\mathrm{AG}}(G) \stackrel{\mathrm{def}}{=} \{(\overrightarrow{v}, \overrightarrow{v}') \mid \overrightarrow{v}, \overrightarrow{v}' \in \mathbb{Z}_{2^w}^k \wedge [1|v\ v'] \in \mathrm{row}\, G\}.$$

The *row space* of a matrix G is defined by $\mathrm{row}\, G \stackrel{\mathrm{def}}{=} \left\{ r \,\middle|\, \exists \overrightarrow{u} : \overrightarrow{u} G = r \right\}$.

The $\mathrm{AG}[\overrightarrow{v}; \overrightarrow{v}']$ domain captures all two-vocabulary affine spaces, and treats them as relations between pre-states and post-states.

The bottom element of the AG domain is the empty matrix, and the $\mathrm{AG}[\overrightarrow{v}; \overrightarrow{v}']$ element that represents the identity relation is the matrix $\begin{array}{c} \begin{array}{ccc} 1 & \overrightarrow{v} & \overrightarrow{v}' \end{array} \\ \left[\begin{array}{c|cc} 1 & 0 & 0 \\ \hline 1 & I & I \end{array}\right] \end{array}$.

The $\mathrm{AG}[\{v_1, v_2\}; \{v_1', v_2'\}]$ element $\begin{array}{c} \begin{array}{ccccc} 1 & v_1 & v_2 & v_1' & v_2' \end{array} \\ \left[\begin{array}{c|cccc} 1 & 0 & 0 & 0 & 0 \\ \hline 1 & 1 & 0 & 1 & 0 \\ 1 & 0 & 1 & 0 & 0 \\ 1 & 0 & 0 & 0 & 2 \end{array}\right] \end{array}$ represents the transition relation in which $v_1' = v_1$, v_2 can have any value, and v_2' can have any even value.

To compute the join of two AG elements, stack the two matrices vertically and get the canonical form of the result [6, Sect. 2.1].

2.5 Relating MOS and AG

There are two ways to relate the MOS and AG domains. One way is to use them as abstractions of two-vocabulary relations and provide (approximate) inter-conversion methods. The other is to use a variant of the AG domain to represent the elements of the MOS domain exactly.

Comparison of MOS and AG Elements as Abstraction of Two-Vocabulary Relations. As shown in [6, Sect. 4.1], the MOS and AG domains are incomparable: some relations are expressible in each domain that are not expressible in the other. Intuitively, the central difference is that MOS is a domain of sets of *functions*, while AG is a domain of *relations*.

AG can capture 1-vocabulary guards on both the pre-state and post-state vocabularies, while MOS can capture 1-vocabulary guards only on its post-state vocabulary.

Example 2. For example, when $k = 1$, the AG element for "assume $x = 2$" is $\overset{\begin{matrix}1 & x & x'\end{matrix}}{\left[\begin{array}{c|cc}1 & 2 & 2\end{array}\right]}$, i.e., "$x = 2 \wedge x' = 2$". In contrast, there is no MOS element that represents $x = 2 \wedge x' = 2$. The smallest MOS element that over-approximates "assume $x = 2$" is the identity transformer $\left\{\left[\begin{array}{c|c}1 & 0 \\ \hline 0 & 1\end{array}\right]\right\}$. □

On the other hand, the MOS-domain can encode two-vocabulary relations that are not affine-closed.

Example 3. One example is the matrix basis $M = \left\{\left[\begin{array}{c|cc}1 & 0 & 0 \\ \hline 0 & 1 & 1 \\ 0 & 0 & 0\end{array}\right], \left[\begin{array}{c|cc}1 & 0 & 0 \\ \hline 0 & 0 & 0 \\ 0 & 1 & 1\end{array}\right]\right\}$. The set that M encodes is

$$\begin{aligned}
\gamma_{\mathrm{MOS}}(M) &= \left\{ \left[x\ y\ x'\ y'\right] \;\middle|\; \begin{array}{c}\exists u_0, u_1 : \left[1 | x\ y\right] \left[\begin{array}{c|cc}1 & 0 & 0 \\ \hline 0 & u_0 & u_0 \\ 0 & u_1 & u_1\end{array}\right] = \left[1 | x'\ y'\right] \\ \wedge\ u_0 + u_1 = 1\end{array} \right\} \\
&= \left\{ \left[x\ y\ x'\ y'\right] \;\middle|\; \exists u_0 : x' = y' = u_0 x + (1 - u_0) y \right\} \qquad (1) \\
&= \left\{ \left[x\ y\ x'\ y'\right] \;\middle|\; \exists u_0 : x' = y' = x + (1 - u_0)(y - x) \right\} \\
&= \left\{ \left[x\ y\ x'\ y'\right] \;\middle|\; \exists p : x' = y' = x + p(y - x) \right\}
\end{aligned}$$

Affine spaces are closed under affine combinations of their elements. Thus, $\gamma_{\mathrm{MOS}}(M)$ is not an affine space because some affine combinations of its elements are not in $\gamma_{\mathrm{MOS}}(M)$. For instance, let $a = \left[1\ {-1}\ 1\ 1\right]$, $b = \left[2\ {-2}\ 6\ 6\right]$, and $c = \left[0\ 0\ {-4}\ {-4}\right]$. By Eq. (1), we have $a \in \gamma_{\mathrm{MOS}}(M)$ when $p = 0$ in Eq. (1), $b \in \gamma_{\mathrm{MOS}}(M)$ when $p = -1$, and $c \notin \gamma_{\mathrm{MOS}}(M)$ (the equation "$-4 = 0 + p(0-0)$" has no solution for p). Moreover, $2a - b = c$, so c is an affine combination of a and b. Thus, $\gamma_{\mathrm{MOS}}(M)$ is not closed under affine combinations of its elements, and so $\gamma_{\mathrm{MOS}}(M)$ is not an affine space. □

Soundly converting an MOS element M to an overapproximating AG element is equivalent to stating two-vocabulary affine constraints satisfied by M [6, Sect. 4.2]).

Reformulation of MOS Elements as AG Elements. An MOS element $M = \{M_1, M_2, ..., M_n\}$ represents the set of $(k+1) \times (k+1)$ matrices in the affine closure of the matrices in M. Each matrix can be thought of as a $(k + 1) \times (k+1)$ vector, and hence M can be represented by an AG element of size $n \times ((k+1) \times (k+1))$.

Example 4. Table 3 shows the two ways MOS and AG elements can be related. Column 1 shows the MOS element M from Example 3, which represents the set of matrices in the affine closure of the two $(k+1) \times (k+1)$ matrices, with $k = 2$. The second column gives the AG element A_1 (a matrix with $2k+1$ columns) representing the affine-closed space over $\{x, y, x', y'\}$ satisfied by M.

Consequently, $\gamma_{\mathrm{AG}}(A_1) \supseteq \gamma_{\mathrm{MOS}}(M)$. Column 3 shows the two matrices of M as the $2 \times ((k+1) \times (k+1))$ AG element A_2. Because A_2 is just a reformulation of M, $\gamma_{\mathrm{AG}}(A_2) = \gamma_{\mathrm{MOS}}(M)$. □

3 Overview

In this section, we motivate and illustrate the ATA[$\mathcal{B}$] framework, with the help of several examples. The first two examples illustrate the following principle, which restates Observation 1 more formally:

Observation 2. *Each affine transformation $C : \overrightarrow{d}$ in a set of affine transformations involves $(k+1)^2$ coefficients $\in \mathbb{Z}_{2^w}$: $(1, d_1, d_2, \ldots, d_k, 0, c_{11}, c_{12}, \ldots, 0, c_{21}, \ldots c_{kk})$.*[1] *Thus, we may use any abstract domain whose elements concretize to subsets of $\mathbb{Z}_{2^w}^{(k+1)^2}$ as a method for representing a set of affine transformers.* □

Example 5. The AG element A_2 in column 3 of Table 3 illustrates how an AG element with $(k+1)^2$ columns represents the same set of affine transformers as the MOS element M shown in column 1. For instance, the first row of A_2 represents the first matrix in M. □

Example 6. Consider the element $E = ([1,1], [0,10], [0,0], [0,0], [1,1], [2,3], [0,0], [0,0], [1,1])$ of $\mathcal{I}^9_{\mathbb{Z}_{2^w}}$. E can be depicted more mnemonically as the following matrix:

$$\begin{array}{c} \begin{array}{ccc} 1 & x & y \end{array} \\ \left[\begin{array}{c|cc} [1,1] & [0,10] & [0,0] \\ \hline [0,0] & [1,1] & [2,3] \\ [0,0] & [0,0] & [1,1] \end{array}\right] \end{array}$$

where every element in E is an interval ($\mathcal{I}_{\mathbb{Z}_{2^w}}$). E represents the point set $\{(x', y', x, y) : \exists i_1, i_2 \in \mathbb{Z}_{2^w} : x' = x + i_1 \wedge y' = i_2 x + y \wedge 0 \leqslant i_1 \leqslant 10 \wedge 2 \leqslant i_2 \leqslant 3\}$. □

Examples 5 and 6 both exploit Observation 2, but use different abstract domains. Example 5 uses the AG domain with $(k+1)^2$ columns, whereas

Table 3. Example demonstrating two ways of relating MOS and AG.

MOS element (M)	Overapproximating AG element (A_1)	Reformulation as abstraction over affine transformers (A_2)
$\left\{ \begin{array}{c} 1\ x\ y \\ \left[\begin{array}{c\|cc} 1 & 0 & 0 \\ \hline 0 & 1 & 1 \\ 0 & 0 & 0 \end{array}\right] \end{array}, \begin{array}{c} 1\ x\ y \\ \left[\begin{array}{c\|cc} 1 & 0 & 0 \\ \hline 0 & 0 & 0 \\ 0 & 1 & 1 \end{array}\right] \end{array} \right\}$	$\begin{array}{c} 1\ x\ y\ x'\ y' \\ \left[\begin{array}{c\|cccc} 1 & 0 & 0 & 0 & 0 \\ 1 & 0 & 0 & 1 & 1 \end{array}\right] \end{array}$	$\begin{array}{c} 1\ a_{01}\ a_{02}\ a_{10}\ a_{11}\ a_{12}\ a_{20}\ a_{21}\ a_{22} \\ \left[\begin{array}{c\|cccccccc} 1 & 0 & 0 & 0 & 1 & 1 & 0 & 0 & 0 \\ 1 & 0 & 0 & 0 & 0 & 0 & 0 & 1 & 1 \end{array}\right] \end{array}$

[1] k of the coefficients are always 0, and one coefficient is always 1 (i.e., the first column is always $(1|\ 0\ 0\ \ldots\ 0)^t$). For this reason, we really need only $k + k^2$ elements, but we will sometimes refer to $(k+1)^2$ elements for brevity.

Example 6 uses the domain $\mathcal{I}_{\mathbb{Z}_{2^w}}^{(k+1)^2}$. In particular, an abstract-domain element in our framework ATA[$\mathcal{B}$] is a set of affine transformations $\overrightarrow{v}' = \overrightarrow{v} \cdot C + \overrightarrow{d}$, such that the allowed coefficients in the matrix C and the vector $\overrightarrow{d}$ are abstracted by a base abstract domain $\mathcal{B}$.

The remainder of this section shows how different instantiations of Observation 2 allow different properties of a program to be recovered.

Example 7. In this example, the variable r of function f is initialized to 0 and conditionally incremented by $2x$ inside a loop with 10 iterations.

```
ENT: int f(int x) {
L0:    int i = 0, r = 0;
L1:    while(i <= 10) {
L2:       if(*)
L3:          r = r + 2*x;
L4:       i = i + 1;
       }
L5:    return r;
     }
```

The exact function summary for function f, denoted by S_f, is $(\exists k. r' = 2kx \wedge 0 \leqslant k \leqslant 10)$. Note that S_f expresses two important properties of the function: (i) the return value r' is an even multiple of x, and (ii) the multiplicative factor is contained in an interval. □

$\mathcal{B}$ = AG with $(k+1)^2$ columns: Fig. 1(a) shows the abstract transformers generated with the MOS domain.[2] Each matrix of the form $\begin{bmatrix} 1 & d_1 & d_2 & d_3 \\ \hline 0 & c_{11} & c_{12} & c_{13} \\ 0 & c_{21} & c_{22} & c_{23} \\ 0 & c_{31} & c_{32} & c_{33} \end{bmatrix}$ represents the state transformation $(x' = d_1 + c_{11}x + c_{21}i + c_{31}r) \wedge (i' = d_2 + c_{12}x + c_{22}i + c_{32}r) \wedge (r' = d_3 + c_{13}x + c_{23}i + c_{33}r)$.

For instance, the abstract transformer for $L3 \rightarrow L4$ is an MOS-domain element with a single matrix that represents the affine transformation: $(x' = x) \wedge (i' = i) \wedge (r' = 2x + r)$. The edges absent from Fig. 1(a), e.g., $L1 \rightarrow L2$, have the identity MOS-domain element.

Edge	Transformer
$L0 \rightarrow L1$	$\left\{ \begin{bmatrix} 1 & 0 & 0 & 0 \\ \hline 0 & 1 & 0 & 0 \\ 0 & 0 & 0 & 0 \\ 0 & 0 & 0 & 0 \end{bmatrix} \right\}$
$L3 \rightarrow L4$	$\left\{ \begin{bmatrix} 1 & 0 & 0 & 0 \\ \hline 0 & 1 & 0 & 2 \\ 0 & 0 & 1 & 0 \\ 0 & 0 & 0 & 1 \end{bmatrix} \right\}$
$L4 \rightarrow L1$	$\left\{ \begin{bmatrix} 1 & 0 & 1 & 0 \\ \hline 0 & 1 & 0 & 0 \\ 0 & 0 & 1 & 0 \\ 0 & 0 & 0 & 1 \end{bmatrix} \right\}$

(a)

Iteration	Node L1
(i)	$\left\{ \begin{bmatrix} 1 & 0 & 0 & 0 \\ \hline 0 & 1 & 0 & 0 \\ 0 & 0 & 0 & 0 \\ 0 & 0 & 0 & 0 \end{bmatrix} \right\}$
(ii)	$\left\{ \begin{bmatrix} 1 & 0 & 0 & 0 \\ \hline 0 & 1 & 0 & 0 \\ 0 & 0 & 0 & 0 \\ 0 & 0 & 0 & 0 \end{bmatrix}, \begin{bmatrix} 1 & 0 & 1 & 0 \\ \hline 0 & 1 & 0 & 2 \\ 0 & 0 & 0 & 0 \\ 0 & 0 & 0 & 0 \end{bmatrix} \right\}$
(iii)	$\left\{ \begin{bmatrix} 1 & 0 & 0 & 0 \\ \hline 0 & 1 & 0 & 0 \\ 0 & 0 & 0 & 0 \\ 0 & 0 & 0 & 0 \end{bmatrix}, \begin{bmatrix} 1 & 0 & 1 & 0 \\ \hline 0 & 1 & 0 & 2 \\ 0 & 0 & 0 & 0 \\ 0 & 0 & 0 & 0 \end{bmatrix}, \begin{bmatrix} 1 & 0 & 2 & 0 \\ \hline 0 & 1 & 0 & 4 \\ 0 & 0 & 0 & 0 \\ 0 & 0 & 0 & 0 \end{bmatrix} \right\}$

(b)

Fig. 1. Abstract transformers and snapshots in the fixpoint analysis with the MOS domain for Example 7.

[2] We will continue to refer to the MOS domain directly, rather than "the instantiation of Observation 2 with an AG element containing $(k+1)^2$ columns" (à la Example 5).

To obtain function summaries, an iterative fixed-point computation needs to be performed. An abstract-domain element a is a *summary* at some program point L, if it describes a two-vocabulary transition relation that overapproximates the (compound) transition relation from the beginning of the function to program point L. Figure 1(b) provides the iteration results for the summary at the program point $L1$. After iteration (i), the result represents $(x' = x) \wedge (i' = 0) \wedge (r' = 0)$. After iteration (ii), it adds the affine transformer $(x' = x) \wedge (i' = 1) \wedge (r' = 2x)$ to the summary. Quiescence is discovered on the third iteration because the affine-closure of the three matrices is the same as the affine-closure of the two matrices after the second iteration. As a result, the function summary that MOS learns, denoted by S_{MOS}, is $\exists k.r' = 2kx$, which is an overapproximation of the exact function summary S_f. Imprecision occurs because the MOS-domain is not able to represent inequality guards. Hence, the summary captures the evenness property, but not the bounds property.

$\underline{\mathcal{B} = \mathcal{I}_{\mathbb{Z}_{2^w}}^{(k+1)^2}}$: By using different $\mathcal{B}$s, an analyzer will be able to recover different properties of a program. Now consider what happens when the program above is analyzed with ATA[$\mathcal{B}$] instantiated with the non-relational base domain of environments of intervals ($\mathcal{I}_{\mathbb{Z}_{2^w}}^{(k+1)^2}$). The identity transformation for the abstract domain ATA[$\mathcal{I}_{\mathbb{Z}_{2^w}}^{(k+1)^2}$] is $\left[\begin{array}{c|ccc} 1 & [0,0] & [0,0] & [0,0] \\ \hline 0 & [1,1] & [0,0] & [0,0] \\ 0 & [0,0] & [1,1] & [0,0] \\ 0 & [0,0] & [0,0] & [1,1] \end{array}\right]$. The bottom element for the abstract domain ATA[$\mathcal{I}_{\mathbb{Z}_{2^w}}^{(k+1)^2}$], denoted by $\bot_{\text{ATA}[\mathcal{I}_{\mathbb{Z}_{2^w}}^{(k+1)^2}]}$ is $\left[\begin{array}{c|ccc} 1 & \bot_{\mathcal{I}_{\mathbb{Z}_{2^w}}} & \bot_{\mathcal{I}_{\mathbb{Z}_{2^w}}} & \bot_{\mathcal{I}_{\mathbb{Z}_{2^w}}} \\ \hline 0 & \bot_{\mathcal{I}_{\mathbb{Z}_{2^w}}} & \bot_{\mathcal{I}_{\mathbb{Z}_{2^w}}} & \bot_{\mathcal{I}_{\mathbb{Z}_{2^w}}} \\ 0 & \bot_{\mathcal{I}_{\mathbb{Z}_{2^w}}} & \bot_{\mathcal{I}_{\mathbb{Z}_{2^w}}} & \bot_{\mathcal{I}_{\mathbb{Z}_{2^w}}} \\ 0 & \bot_{\mathcal{I}_{\mathbb{Z}_{2^w}}} & \bot_{\mathcal{I}_{\mathbb{Z}_{2^w}}} & \bot_{\mathcal{I}_{\mathbb{Z}_{2^w}}} \end{array}\right]$.[3]

Figure 2 shows the abstract transformers and the fixpoint analysis for the node $L1$ with the ATA[$\mathcal{I}_{\mathbb{Z}_{2^w}}^{(k+1)^2}$] domain. One advantage of using intervals as the base domain is that they can express inequalities. For instance, the abstract transformer for the edge $L1 \rightarrow L2$ specifies the transformation $(x' = x) \wedge (0 \leqslant i' \leqslant 10) \wedge (r' = r)$. Consequently, the function summary that ATA[$\mathcal{I}_{\mathbb{Z}_{2^w}}^{(k+1)^2}$] learns, denoted by $S_{\text{ATA}[\mathcal{I}_{\mathbb{Z}_{2^w}}^{(k+1)^2}]}$, is $r' = [0, 20]x$. This summary captures the bounds property, but not the evenness property. Notice that, $S_f = S_{\text{ATA}[\mathcal{I}_{\mathbb{Z}_{2^w}}^{(k+1)^2}]} \wedge S_{\text{MOS}}$.

Consider the instantiation of the ATA framework with strided-intervals over bitvectors [14], denoted by $\mathcal{SI}_{\mathbb{Z}_{2^w}}^{(k+1)^2}$. A strided interval represents a set of the form $\{l, l+s, l+2s, ..., l+(n-1)s\}$. Here, l is the beginning of the interval, s

---

[3] The abstract domain $\mathcal{I}_{\mathbb{Z}_{2^w}}^{(k+1)^2}$ is the product domain of $(k+1)^2$ interval domains, that is, $\mathcal{I}_{\mathbb{Z}_{2^w}}^{(k+1)^2} = \mathcal{I}_{\mathbb{Z}_{2^w}} \times \mathcal{I}_{\mathbb{Z}_{2^w}} \times \ldots \times \mathcal{I}_{\mathbb{Z}_{2^w}}$. $\mathcal{I}_{\mathbb{Z}_{2^w}}^{(k+1)^2}$ uses smash product to maintain a canonical representation for $\bot_{\text{ATA}[\mathcal{I}_{\mathbb{Z}_{2^w}}^{(k+1)^2}]}$. Thus, if any of the coefficients in an abstract-domain element $b \in \text{ATA}[\mathcal{I}_{\mathbb{Z}_{2^w}}^{(k+1)^2}]$ is $\bot_{\mathcal{I}_{\mathbb{Z}_{2^w}}}$, then b is smashed to $\bot_{\text{ATA}[\mathcal{I}_{\mathbb{Z}_{2^w}}^{(k+1)^2}]}$.

Edge	Transformer
$L0 \to L1$	$\left[\begin{array}{cccc} 1 & [0,0] & [0,0] & [0,0] \\ \hline 0 & [1,1] & [0,0] & [0,0] \\ 0 & [0,0] & [0,0] & [0,0] \\ 0 & [0,0] & [0,0] & [0,0] \end{array}\right]$
$L1 \to L2$	$\left[\begin{array}{cccc} 1 & [0,0] & [0,10] & [0,0] \\ \hline 0 & [1,1] & [0,0] & [0,0] \\ 0 & [0,0] & [0,0] & [0,0] \\ 0 & [0,0] & [0,0] & [1,1] \end{array}\right]$
$L3 \to L4$	$\left[\begin{array}{cccc} 1 & [0,0] & [0,0] & [0,0] \\ \hline 0 & [1,1] & [0,0] & [2,2] \\ 0 & [0,0] & [1,1] & [0,0] \\ 0 & [0,0] & [0,0] & [1,1] \end{array}\right]$
$L4 \to L1$	$\left[\begin{array}{cccc} 1 & [0,0] & [1,1] & [0,0] \\ \hline 0 & [1,1] & [0,0] & [0,0] \\ 0 & [0,0] & [1,1] & [0,0] \\ 0 & [0,0] & [0,0] & [1,1] \end{array}\right]$

(a)

Iteration	Node L1
(i)	$\left[\begin{array}{cccc} 1 & [0,0] & [0,0] & [0,0] \\ \hline 0 & [1,1] & [0,0] & [0,0] \\ 0 & [0,0] & [0,0] & [0,0] \\ 0 & [0,0] & [0,0] & [0,0] \end{array}\right]$
(ii)	$\left[\begin{array}{cccc} 1 & [0,0] & [0,1] & [0,0] \\ \hline 0 & [1,1] & [0,0] & [0,2] \\ 0 & [0,0] & [0,0] & [0,0] \\ 0 & [0,0] & [0,0] & [0,0] \end{array}\right]$
...	...
(xi)	$\left[\begin{array}{cccc} 1 & [0,0] & [0,10] & [0,0] \\ \hline 0 & [1,1] & [0,0] & [0,20] \\ 0 & [0,0] & [0,0] & [0,0] \\ 0 & [0,0] & [0,0] & [0,0] \end{array}\right]$

(b)

Fig. 2. Abstract transformers and fixpoint analysis with the ATA$[\mathcal{I}_{\mathbb{Z}_{2^w}}^{(k+1)^2}]$ domain for Example 7.

is the stride, and n is the interval size. Consequently, ATA$[\mathcal{SI}_{\mathbb{Z}_{2^w}}^{(k+1)^2}]$ learns the function summary $\exists k.r' = kx \wedge k = 2[0, 10]$, which captures both the evenness property and the bounds property. Note that a traditional (non-ATA-framework) analysis based on the strided-interval domain alone would not be able to capture the desired summary because the strided-interval domain is non-relational.

Widening Concerns. In principle, abstract domains $\mathcal{I}_{\mathbb{Z}_{2^w}}^{(k+1)^2}$ and $\mathcal{SI}_{\mathbb{Z}_{2^w}}^{(k+1)^2}$ do not need widening operations because the lattice height is finite. However, the height is exponential in the bitwidth w of the program variables, and thus in practice we need widening operations to speed-up the fixpoint iteration. In the presence of widening, neither ATA$[\mathcal{I}_{\mathbb{Z}_{2^w}}^{(k+1)^2}]$ nor ATA$[\mathcal{SI}_{\mathbb{Z}_{2^w}}^{(k+1)^2}]$ will be able to capture the bounds property for Example 7, because they are missing relational information between the loop counter i and the variable r. However, the reduced product of ATA$[\mathcal{I}_{\mathbb{Z}_{2^w}}^{(k+1)^2}]$ (or ATA$[\mathcal{SI}_{\mathbb{Z}_{2^w}}^{(k+1)^2}]$) and MOS can learn the exact function summary.

4 Affine-Transformer-Abstraction Framework

In this section, we formally introduce the Affine-Transformer-Abstraction framework (ATA) and describe abstract-domain operations for the framework. We also discuss some specific instantiations.

ATA$[\mathcal{B}]$ *Definition.* Let C be a k-by-k matrix: $[c_{ij}]$, where each c_{ij} is a symbolic constant for the entry at i-th row and j-th column. Let $\overrightarrow{d}$ be a k-vector, $[d_i]$, where each d_i is a symbolic constant for the i-th entry in the vector. As mentioned in Sect. 1, an affine transformer, denoted by $C : \overrightarrow{d}$, describes the relation $\overrightarrow{v}' =$

$\overrightarrow{v} \cdot C + \overrightarrow{d}$, where $\overrightarrow{v}'$ and $\overrightarrow{v}$ are row vectors of size k that represent the post-transformation state and the pre-transformation state, respectively, on program variables.

Given a base abstract domain $\mathcal{B}$, the ATA framework generates a corresponding abstract domain ATA[$\mathcal{B}$] whose elements represent a transition relation between the pre-state and the post-state program vocabulary. Each element $a \in$ ATA[$\mathcal{B}$] is represented using an element $base(a) \in \mathcal{B}$, such that:

$$\gamma(a) = \{(\overrightarrow{v}, \overrightarrow{v}') | \ \exists(C : \overrightarrow{d}) \in \gamma(base(a)) : \overrightarrow{v}' = \overrightarrow{v} \cdot C + \overrightarrow{d}\}.$$

4.1 Abstract-Domain Operations for ATA[$\mathcal{B}$]

In this subsection, we provide all the abstract-domain operations for ATA[$\mathcal{B}$], with the exception of abstract composition, which is discussed in Sect. 4.2.

In the ATA[$\mathcal{B}$] framework, the symbolic constants in the base domain $\mathcal{B}$ are denoted by $symbols(C\colon \overrightarrow{d})$, where $symbols(C\colon \overrightarrow{d}) = (d_1, d_2, \ldots, d_n, c_{11}, c_{12}, \ldots, c_{1k}, c_{21}, c_{22}, \ldots, c_{2k}, \ldots, c_{kk})$ is the tuple of $k+k^2$ symbolic constants in the affine transformation. Table 4 lists the abstract-domain interface for the base abstract domain $\mathcal{B}$ needed to implement these operations for ATA[$\mathcal{B}$]. The first five operations in the interface are standard abstract-domain operations. $havoc(b_1, S)$ takes an element b_1 and a subset $S \subseteq symbols(C\colon \overrightarrow{d})$ of symbolic constants, and returns an element without any constraints on the symbolic constants in S. The last operation in Table 4 defines an abstraction for a concrete affine transformer ct. A concrete affine transformer is a mapping from the symbolic constants in the affine transformer to bitvectors of size w. We represent concrete state ct with the $(k+1) \times (k+1)$ matrix: $\left[\begin{array}{c|cccc} 1 & ct(d_1) & ct(d_2) & \ldots & ct(d_k) \\ \hline 0 & ct(c_{11}) & ct(c_{12}) & \ldots & ct(c_{1k}) \\ 0 & ct(c_{21}) & ct(c_{22}) & \ldots & ct(c_{2k}) \\ \ldots & \ldots & \ldots & \ldots & \ldots \\ 0 & ct(c_{k1}) & ct(c_{k2}) & \ldots & ct(c_{kk}) \end{array}\right]$, where $ct(s)$ denotes the concrete value in $\mathbb{Z}_{2^w}$ of symbol s in the concrete state ct.

Table 4. Base abstract-domain operations.

Type	Operation	Description
$\mathcal{B}$	$\perp$	*Bottom element*
$\mathcal{B}$	$\top$	*Top element*
bool	$(b_1 == b_2)$	*Equality*
$\mathcal{B}$	$(b_1 \sqcup b_2)$	*Join*
$\mathcal{B}$	$(b_1 \nabla b_2)$	*Widen*
$\mathcal{B}$	$havoc(b_1, S)$	*Remove all constraints on symbolic constants in S*
$\mathcal{B}$	$\alpha(ct)$	*Abstraction for the concrete affine transformer ct, Where* $ct \in symbols(C : \overrightarrow{d}) \to \mathbb{Z}_{2^w}$

Table 5 gives the abstract-domain operations for ATA[$\mathcal{B}$] in terms of the base abstract-domain operations in $\mathcal{B}$. The first operation is the $\perp$ element, which is simply defined as $\perp_{\mathcal{B}}$, the bottom element in the base domain. Similarly, equality, join, and widen operations are defined as the equality, join, and widen operations in the base domain. The equality operation is not the exact equality operation; that is, $(a_1 \widetilde{==} a_2)$ can return false, even if $\gamma(a_1) = \gamma(a_2)$. However, the equality operation is sound; that is, when $(a_1 \widetilde{==} a_2)$ returns true, then $\gamma(a_1) = \gamma(a_2)$. The $\tilde{\sqcup}$ operation for the ATA[$\mathcal{B}$] is a quasi-join operation [7]. In other words, the least upper bound does not necessarily exist for ATA[$\mathcal{B}$], but a sound upper-bound operation $\tilde{\sqcup}$ is available.

The abstraction operation for the affine-assignment statement $\alpha(v_j := d_0 + \sum_{i=1}^{k} c_{ij} * v_i)$ gives back an ATA[$\mathcal{B}$]-element with a single transformer where every variable $v \in V - \{v_j\}$ is left unchanged and the variable v_j is transformed to reflect the assignment by updating the coefficients of the corresponding column. The abstraction operation for the non-deterministic assignment statement $\alpha(v_j := ?)$ gives back an ATA[$\mathcal{B}$]-element, such that every variable $v \in V - \{v_j\}$ is left unchanged but the symbolic constant corresponding to the coefficients in the column j of the affine transformation can be any value. This operation is carried out by performing *havoc* on the identity transformation with respect to the set $\{d_j, c_{1j}, c_{2j}, ..., c_{kj}\}$ of symbolic constants. The identity transformation *Id* is obtained by abstracting the concrete affine transformer *ct* that represents the identity transformer. We provide proofs of soundness for these abstract-domain operations in [19, Appendix A].

4.2 Abstract Composition

We have shown that all the abstract-domain operations for ATA[$\mathcal{B}$] can be implemented in terms of abstract-domain operations in $\mathcal{B}$, with the exception of

Table 5. Abstract-domain operations for the ATA[$\mathcal{B}$]-domain.

Type	Operation	Description
$\mathcal{A}$	$\perp$	$\perp_{\mathcal{B}}$
bool	$(a_1 \widetilde{==} a_2)$	$(base(a_1) == base(a_2))$
$\mathcal{A}$	$(a_1 \tilde{\sqcup} a_2)$	$(base(a_1) \sqcup base(a_2))$
$\mathcal{A}$	$(a_1 \nabla a_2)$	$(base(a_1) \nabla base(a_2))$
$\mathcal{A}$	$\alpha(v_j := d_j + \sum_{i=1}^{k} c_{ij} * v_i)$	$\alpha\left(\left[\begin{array}{c\|cccc} 1 & 0 & d_j & 0 \\ \hline 0 & I_{j-1} & [c_{1j}, c_{2j}, \ldots c_{(j-1)j}]^t & 0 \\ 0 & 0 & c_{jj} & 0 \\ 0 & 0 & [c_{(j+1)j}, c_{(j+2)j}, \ldots c_{kj}]^t & I_{k-j} \end{array}\right]\right)$
$\mathcal{A}$	$\alpha(v_j := ?)$	$havoc(\alpha(I_{k+1}), \{d_j, c_{1j}, c_{2j}, ..., c_{kj}\})$
$\mathcal{A}$	Id	$\alpha(I_{k+1})$

abstract composition. Let us consider the composition of two abstract values $a, a' \in \text{ATA}[\mathcal{B}]$, representing the two-vocabulary relations $R[\overrightarrow{v}; \overrightarrow{v}'] = \gamma(a)$ and $R'[\overrightarrow{v}'; \overrightarrow{v}''] = \gamma(a')$. An abstract operation $\circ^{\sharp}$ is a sound abstract-composition operation if, for all $a'' = a' \circ^{\sharp} a$, $\gamma(a'') \supseteq \{ (\overrightarrow{v}; \overrightarrow{v}'') | \exists \overrightarrow{v}'. R[\overrightarrow{v}; \overrightarrow{v}'] \wedge R'[\overrightarrow{v}'; \overrightarrow{v}''] \}$. This condition translates to:

$$\begin{aligned}\gamma(base(a'')) \supseteq \{(\overrightarrow{v}, \overrightarrow{v}'') \mid \exists (C : \overrightarrow{d}) \in \gamma(base(a)), (C' : \overrightarrow{d}') \in \gamma(base(a')), \\ (C'' : \overrightarrow{d}''): (\overrightarrow{v}'' = \overrightarrow{v} \cdot C'' + \overrightarrow{d}'') \wedge (C'' = C \cdot C') \\ \wedge (\overrightarrow{d}'' = \overrightarrow{d} \cdot C' + \overrightarrow{d}')\}\end{aligned} \tag{2}$$

The presence of the quadratic components $C \cdot C'$ and $\overrightarrow{d} \cdot C'$ makes the implementation of abstract composition non-trivial. One extremely expensive method to implement abstract composition is to enumerate the set of all concrete transformers $(C : \overrightarrow{d}) \in \gamma(base(a))$ and $(C' : \overrightarrow{d}') \in \gamma(base(a'))$, perform matrix multiplication for each pair of concrete transformers, and perform join over all pairs of them. This approach is impractical because the set of all concrete transformers in an abstract value can be very large.

First, we provide a general method to implement abstract composition. Then, we provide methods for abstract composition when the base domain $\mathcal{B}$ has certain properties, like non-relationality and weak convexity. The latter methods are faster, but are only applicable to certain classes of base abstract domains.

General Case. We present a general method to perform abstract composition by reducing it to the symbolic-abstraction problem. The *symbolic abstraction* of a formula φ in logic $\mathbb{L}$, denoted by $\widehat{\alpha}(\varphi)$, is the best value in $\mathcal{B}$ that over-approximates the set of all concrete affine transformers $(C : \overrightarrow{d})$ that satisfy φ [15,22]. For all $b \in \mathcal{B}$, the *symbolic concretization* of $\mathcal{B}$, denoted by $\widehat{\gamma}(b)$, maps b to a formula $\widehat{\gamma}(b) \in \mathbb{L}$ such that b and $\widehat{\gamma}(b)$ represent the same set of concrete affine transformers (i.e., $\gamma(b) = [\![\widehat{\gamma}(b)]\!]$). We expect the base domain $\mathcal{B}$ to provide the $\widehat{\gamma}$ operation. In our framework, there are slightly different variants of $\widehat{\alpha}$ and $\widehat{\gamma}$ according to which vocabulary of symbolic constants are involved. For instance, we use $\widehat{\gamma}'$ to denote symbolic concretization in terms of the primed symbolic constants $symbols(C' : \overrightarrow{d}')$. Similarly, $\widehat{\alpha}''$ denotes symbolic abstraction in terms of the double-primed symbolic constants $symbols(C'' : \overrightarrow{d}'')$. The function *dropPrimes* shifts the vocabulary of symbolic constants by removing the primes from the symbolic constants that an abstract value represents.

We use $\mathbb{L} = QF\_BV$, i.e., quantifier-free bit-vector logic, to express abstract composition symbolically as follows:

$$\begin{aligned}base(a'') = dropPrimes(\widehat{\alpha}''(\varphi)), \text{ where} \\ \varphi = (C'' = C \cdot C') \wedge (\overrightarrow{d}'' = \overrightarrow{d} \cdot C' + \overrightarrow{d}') \\ \wedge \widehat{\gamma}(base(a)) \wedge \widehat{\gamma}'(base(a')).\end{aligned} \tag{3}$$

(Note that $\widehat{\gamma}(base(a))$ and $\widehat{\gamma}'(base(a'))$ are formulas over $symbols(C : \overrightarrow{d})$ and $symbols(C' : \overrightarrow{d}')$ respectively). Past literature [6,15,22] provides various algorithms to implement symbolic abstraction. Symbolic-abstraction methods are usually slow because they make repeated calls to an SMT solver. Specifically, the symbolic-abstraction algorithms in [15,22] require $\mathcal{O}(h'')$ calls to SMT, where h'' is the height of the abstract-domain element—i.e., $base(a'')$ in the lattice $\mathcal{B}$.

Algorithm 1 is a variant of the symbolic-abstraction algorithm from [15]. Algorithm 1 needs a method to enumerate a generator set gs for each $b \in \mathcal{B}$. Such a set can easily be obtained from the generator representation of $\mathcal{B}$. For instance, each row in an AG element is an affine transformer, and a generator set for the AG element is the set of all rows in the AG matrix: the affine combination of the rows generate the concrete affine transformers that the AG element (see Sect. 2.4) represents. Note that the generator set for an abstract value b is usually much smaller than the set of all affine transformers in b. For the AG domain, the generating set is worst-case polynomial size, whereas the set of all affine transformers is worst-case exponential in the number of variables k.

In Algorithm 1, line 3 initializes the value $lower$ to the product of each pair of abstract transformers. The product $t \times t'$, where $t = \left[\begin{array}{c|c} 1 & \overrightarrow{d} \\ \hline 0 & C \end{array}\right]$ and $t' = \left[\begin{array}{c|c} 1 & \overrightarrow{d}' \\ \hline 0 & C' \end{array}\right]$ is $\left[\begin{array}{c|c} 1 & \overrightarrow{d} \cdot C' + \overrightarrow{d}' \\ \hline 0 & C \cdot C' \end{array}\right]$. Because $lower$ is initialized to $\{t \times t' \mid t \in gs_1, t' \in gs_2\}$ rather than $\bot$, the number of SMT calls in the symbolic abstraction is significantly reduced, compared to the algorithm from [15]. The function $GetModel$, used at line 5, returns the model $M \in symbols(C'' : \overrightarrow{d}'') \to \mathbb{Z}_{2^w}$ satisfying the formula $(\varphi \wedge \neg\widehat{\gamma}(lower))$ given to the SMT solver at line 4. Thus, the model M is a concrete affine transformer in a''. The representation function β, used at line 6, maps a singleton model M to the least value in $\mathcal{B}$ that overapproximates $\{M\}$ [15]. While the SMT call at line 4 is satisfiable, the loop keeps improving the value of $lower$ by adding the satisfying model M to $lower$ via the representation function β and the join operation. When line 4 is unsatisfiable, the loop terminates and returns $lower$. This method is sound because the unsatisfiable call proves that $\varphi \Rightarrow \widehat{\gamma}(lower)$. The loop terminates when the height of the base domain $\mathcal{B}$ is finite.

Algorithm 1. Abstract Composition via Symbolic Abstraction

1: $gs_1 \leftarrow \{t_1, t_2, ..., t_{l_1}\}$ ▷ where $base(a) = \bigsqcup_{i=0}^{l_1} t_i$
2: $gs_2 \leftarrow \{t'_1, t'_2, ..., t'_{l_2}\}$ ▷ where $base(a') = \bigsqcup_{i=0}^{l_2} t'_i$
3: $lower \leftarrow \{t \times t' \mid t \in gs_1, t' \in gs_2\}$
4: **while** $r \leftarrow SMTCall(\varphi \wedge \neg\widehat{\gamma}(lower))$ *is Sat* **do**
5: $\quad M \leftarrow GetModel(r)$
6: $\quad lower \leftarrow lower \sqcup \beta(M)$
7: **return** $lower$

Non-relational Base Domains. In this section, we present a method to implement abstract composition for ATA[$\mathcal{B}$], when $\mathcal{B}$ is non-relational. We focus on the non-relational case separately because it allows us to implement a sound abstract-composition operation efficiently.

Foundation Domain. Each element in the non-relational domain $\mathcal{B}$ is a mapping from symbols S to a subset of Z_{2^w}. We introduce the concept of a *foundation domain*, denoted by $\mathcal{F}_{\mathcal{B}}$, to represent the abstractions of subsets of Z_{2^w} in the base abstract-domain elements. We can define a non-relational base domain in terms of the foundation domain as follows: $\mathcal{B} \stackrel{def}{=} S \rightarrow \mathcal{F}_{\mathcal{B}}$. For instance, the non-relational domain of intervals $\mathcal{I}_{\mathbb{Z}_{2^w}}^{(k+1)^2}$ can be represented by $S \rightarrow \mathcal{I}_{\mathbb{Z}_{2^w}}$, where $\mathcal{I}_{\mathbb{Z}_{2^w}}$ represents the interval lattice over $\mathbb{Z}_{2^w}$, and S is a set of $(k+1)^2$ symbolic constants that represent the coefficients of an affine transformer.

A foundation domain $\mathcal{F}$ is a lattice whose elements concretize to subsets of Z_{2^w}. Table 6 present the foundation-domain operations for $\mathcal{F}$. Bottom, equality, join, widen, and $\alpha(bv)$ are standard abstract-domain operations. The abstract addition and multiplication operations provide a sound reinterpretation of the collecting semantics of concrete addition and multiplication. For instance, with the interval foundation domain, $[0,7] +^\sharp [-3,17] = [-3,24]$ and $[0,6] \times^\sharp [-3,3] = [-18,18]$.

Table 6. Foundation-domain operations.

Type	Operation	Description	Type	Operation	Description
$\mathcal{F}$	$\bot$	*Empty set*	$\mathcal{F}$	$\alpha(bv)$	*Abstraction for the bitvector value* $bv \in Z_{2^w}$
bool	$(f_1 == f_2)$	*Equality*			
$\mathcal{F}$	$(f_1 \sqcup f_2)$	*Join*	$\mathcal{F}$	$(f_1 +^\sharp f_2)$	*Abstract addition*
$\mathcal{F}$	$(f_1 \nabla f_2)$	*Widen*	$\mathcal{F}$	$(f_1 \times^\sharp f_2)$	*Abstract multiplication*

Abstract composition for a non-relational domain is defined as follows:

$$\begin{aligned} a' \circ_{\mathrm{NR}} a = \Big\{ (\overrightarrow{v}, \overrightarrow{v}') \mid \exists (C : \overrightarrow{d}) : (\overrightarrow{v}' = \overrightarrow{v} \cdot C + \overrightarrow{d}) \wedge b \in (symbols(C : \overrightarrow{d}) \rightarrow \mathcal{F}) \quad (4) \\ \wedge \Big(\bigwedge_{1 \leqslant i,j \leqslant k} (\ b[c_{ij}] = \underset{1 \leqslant l \leqslant k}{\Sigma^\sharp} (base(a)[c_{il}] \times^\sharp base(a')[c_{lj}]) \Big) \\ \wedge \Big(\bigwedge_{1 \leqslant j \leqslant k} b[d_j] = \underset{1 \leqslant l \leqslant k}{\Sigma^\sharp} (base(a)[d_l] \times^\sharp base(a')[c_{lj}]) +^\sharp base(a')[d_j] \Big) \Big\}. \end{aligned}$$

The term $b[s]$, where $b \in \mathcal{B}$ and $s \in symbols(C : \overrightarrow{d})$, refers to the element in the foundation domain $f \in \mathcal{F}_{\mathcal{B}}$, that corresponds to the symbol s. $\Sigma^\sharp_{1 \leqslant l \leqslant k}$ is calculated by abstractly adding the k terms indexed by l. Abstract composition for a non-relational domain uses abstract addition and abstract multiplication to soundly overapproximate the quadratic terms occurring in Eq. (2). We provide a proof of the soundness for $a' \circ_{\text{NR}} a$ in [19, Appendix B.1]. The abstract-composition operation requires $\mathcal{O}(k^3)$ abstract-addition operations and $\mathcal{O}(k^3)$ abstract-multiplication operations.

Examples of foundation domains. We now present a few foundation domains that allow to construct the non-relational small-set, interval [2], and strided-interval [14] base domains.

Small sets. $\mathcal{F}_{SS_n} \stackrel{def}{=} \{\top\} \cup \{S | S \subseteq \mathbb{Z}_{2^w} \wedge |S| \leqslant n\}$. The join operation is defined by: $(f_1 \sqcup f_2) = \begin{cases} f_1 \cup f_2 & \textit{if } |f_1 \cup f_s| \leqslant n \\ \top & \textit{otherwise} \end{cases}$ n denotes the maximum cardinality allowed in the non-top elements of $\mathcal{F}_{SS_n}$. Other abstract operators, including abstract addition and multiplication, are implemented in a similar manner.

Intervals. $\mathcal{F}_{\mathcal{I}_{\mathbb{Z}_{2^w}}} \stackrel{def}{=} \{\bot\} \cup \{[a, b] |\ a, b \in \mathbb{Z}_{2^w}, a \leqslant b\}$. Most abstract operations are straightforward (See [2] for details). The abstract-addition and abstract-multiplication operations need to be careful about overflows to preserve soundness. For instance,

$$[a_1, b_1] +^\sharp [a_2, b_2] = \begin{cases} [a_1 + a_2, b_1 + b_2] & \textit{if neither } a_1 + a_2 \textit{ nor } b_1 + b_2 \\ & \textit{overflows} \\ [min, max] & \textit{otherwise} \end{cases}$$

Strided Interval. $\mathcal{F}_{S\mathcal{I}_{\mathbb{Z}_{2^w}}} \stackrel{def}{=} \{\bot\} \cup \{s[a, b] \mid a, b, s \in \mathbb{Z}_{2^w}, a \leqslant b\}$, where $\gamma(s[a, b]) = \{i \mid a \leqslant i \leqslant b, i \equiv a (mod\ s)\}$. (See [14,17] for the details of the abstract-domain operations.)

Affine-Closed Base Domain. We discuss the special case when the base domain $\mathcal{B}$ is affine-closed, i.e., $\mathcal{B} = \text{AG}$. The abstract composition is defined as:

$$a' \circ_{\text{AG}} a = a'', \textit{ where } base(a'') = \langle \{t_i \times t'_j | \ 1 \leqslant i \leqslant l, 1 \leqslant j \leqslant l'\} \rangle \wedge \quad (5)$$
$$base(a) = \langle \{t_1, t_2, ... t_l\} \rangle \wedge base(a') = \langle \{t'_1, t'_2, ... t'_{l'}\} \rangle$$

Lemma 5.1 in [13] asserts that the above abstract composition method is sound by linearity of affine-closed abstractions. The abstract composition has time complexity $\mathcal{O}(hh'k^3)$, h (respectively h') is the height of the abstract-domain element $base(a)$ (or $base(a')$) in the AG lattice. Because the height of the AG lattice with $(k+1)^2$ columns is $\mathcal{O}(k^2)$, the time complexity for the abstract composition operation translates to $\mathcal{O}(k^7)$. Algorithm 1 essentially implements Eq. (5), but makes an extra *SMT* call to ensure that the result is sound. Because Eq. (5) is sound by linearity for the AG domain, the very first *SMT* call in the while-loop condition at line 4 in Algorithm 1 will be unsatisfiable.

Weakly-Convex Base Domain. We present methods to perform abstract composition when the base domain $\mathcal{B}$ satisfies a property we call *weak convexity*. Base domain $\mathcal{B}$ is *weakly convex* iff

- The abstraction of a single concrete affine transformer is exact: $\gamma(\alpha(t_i)) = \{t_i\}$.
- All abstract-domain elements $b \in \mathcal{B}$ are contained in a convex space over rationals: For any set of concrete affine transformers $\{t_0, t_1, ..., t_l\}$, such that $b = \bigsqcup_{i=0}^{l} t_i$, and any $t \in \gamma(b)$:
  $\exists \lambda_1, \lambda_2, \ldots, \lambda_l \in \mathbb{Q}.(0 \leqslant \lambda_1, \lambda_2, ..., \lambda_l \leqslant 1) \wedge \sum_{i=0}^{l} \lambda_i = 1 \wedge\, cast_{\mathbb{Q}}(t) = \sum_{i=0}^{l} \lambda_i\, cast_{\mathbb{Q}}(t_i)$.
  The $cast_{\mathbb{Q}}$ function is used to specify the convexity property by moving the point space from bitvectors to rationals. For instance, the expression $\Sigma_{i=0}^{l} \lambda_i . cast_{\mathbb{Q}}(t_i)$ specifies the convex combination of the concrete affine transformers m_i in the rational space $cast_{\mathbb{Q}}^{(k+k^2)}$.

Any convex abstract domain over rationals, such as polyhedra [5] or octagons [10], can be used to create a weakly-convex domain over bitvectors [20,21]. Abstract composition for weakly-convex base domains is defined as follows:

$$a' \circ_{\mathrm{WC}} a = a'', \text{ where } base(a'') = \quad (6)$$

$$\begin{cases} \{t_i \times t'_j \mid 1 \leqslant i \leqslant l, 1 \leqslant j \leqslant l'\} & \textit{if there are no overflows in any matrix multiplication } t_i \times t'_j \\ \top_{\mathcal{B}} & \textit{otherwise} \end{cases}$$

$$\text{where } base(a) = \{t_1, t_2, ..., t_l\} \text{ and } base(a') = \{t'_1, t'_2, ..., t'_{l'}\}.$$

The intuition is that the weak-convexity properties are preserved under matrix multiplication in the absence of overflows. This principle is similar to the linearity argument used to show that abstract composition is sound when the base domain is affine-closed. (See above for more details.) We provide a proof of the soundness for $a' \circ_{\mathrm{WC}} a$ in [19, Appendix B.2]. Similar to the affine-closed case, abstract composition has time complexity $\mathcal{O}(H^2 k^3)$, where H is the height of the $\mathcal{B}$ lattice.

5 Discussion and Related Work

The abstract-domain elements in our framework abstract two-vocabulary relationships arising between the pre-transformation state and post-transformation state. For the sake of simplicity, we assumed that the variable sets in the pre-transformation and post-transformation state are the same, and an affine transformer is represented by a $(k+1) \times (k+1)$ matrix, where k is the number of variables in the pre-transformation state. However, this requirement is not mandatory. We can easily adapt our abstract-domain operations to work on $(k+1) \times (k'+1)$ matrices where k' is the number of variables in the post-transformation state.

The abstract-domain elements in our framework are not necessarily closed under intersection. Consider the two abstract values a_1 and a_2 for the vocabulary $V = \{v_1\}$. Let a_1 represent the affine transformation $v_1' = 0$ and a_2 represent the identity affine transformation $v_1' = v_1$. Thus, $a_1 = \alpha(\left[\begin{smallmatrix}1 & 0\\ 0 & 0\end{smallmatrix}\right])$, and $a_2 = \alpha(\left[\begin{smallmatrix}1 & 0\\ 0 & 1\end{smallmatrix}\right])$. The intersection of $\gamma(a_1)$ and $\gamma(a_2)$ is the point $p = (v_1' = 0, v_1 = 0)$. There does not exist an abstract value in ATA[$\mathcal{B}$], that can exactly represent the point p, because any abstract value containing p must contain at least one affine transformer of the form $v_1' = v_1 \cdot c$, and thus must contain all points of the form $(v_1' = t \cdot c, v_1 = t)$, where $t \in \mathcal{Z}_{2^w}$. As a consequence, there does not exist a Galois connection between ATA[$\mathcal{B}$] and the concrete domain $\mathcal{C}$ of all two-vocabulary relations $R[V; V']$, which implies that there does not exist a best abstraction for a set of concrete points. For instance, consider the abstraction of the guard statement $S_G = \{v_1 \leqslant 10\}$, with the ATA[$\mathcal{I}_{\mathbb{Z}_{2^w}}^{(k+1)^2}$] domain. Consider $a_3 = \left[\begin{smallmatrix}1 & [0,10]\\ 0 & [0,0]\end{smallmatrix}\right]$ and $a_4 = \left[\begin{smallmatrix}1 & [0,0]\\ 0 & [1,1]\end{smallmatrix}\right]$. a_3 specifies the guard constraint $0 \leqslant v_1' \leqslant 10$, while a_4 is the identity transformation $v_1' = v_1$. Note that these abstract values are incomparable and can be used to represent the abstract transformer for S_G. Furthermore, $a_3 \sqcap a_4$ does not exist. Thus, an analysis has to settle for either a_3 or a_4. (In Sect. 3, we used an abstract transformer similar to a_3 for the guard in the while statement in Example 7. Using an identity transfer for the guard statement would not have been useful to capture the desired bounds constraint.)

The ATA constructor preserves finiteness; that is, if the base domain $\mathcal{B}$ is finite, then the domain ATA[$\mathcal{B}$] is finite as well.

It is also possible to use the ATA constructor to infer affine transformations over rationals or reals. In these cases, the symbolic-composition methods for weakly-convex base domains (see Sect. 4.2) will carry over to affine transformations over rationals or reals for convex base domains (e.g., polyhedra) with only slight modifications. For instance. abstract composition for convex base domains over rationals or reals is defined as follows:

$$a' \circ a = a'', \textit{ where } base(a'') = \{t_i \times t_j' |\ 1 \leqslant i \leqslant l, 1 \leqslant j \leqslant l'\}$$
$$\text{where } base(a) = \{t_1, t_2, ..., t_l\} \textit{ and } base(a') = \{t_1', t_2', ..., t_{l'}'\}.$$

Chen et al. [1] devised the *interval-polyhedra* domain which can express constraints of the form $\Sigma_k [a_k, b_k] x_k \leqslant c$ over rationals. Interval polyhedra are more expressive than classic convex polyhedra, and thus can express certain non-convex properties. Abstract-domain operations for interval polyhedra are constructed by linear programming and interval Fourier-Motzkin elimination. The domain has similarities to the ATA[$\mathcal{I}_{\mathbb{Z}_{2^w}}^{(k+1)^2}$] domain because the coefficients in the abstract values are intervals.

Miné [11] introduced *weakly relational domains*, which are a parameterized family of relational domains, parameterized by a non-relational base abstract domain. They can express constraints of the form $(v_j - v_i) \in \mathcal{F}$, where $\mathcal{F}$ is an abstraction over $\mathcal{P}(\mathbb{Z})$. Similar to ATA[$\mathcal{B}$], Miné's framework requires the base non-relational domain to provide abstract-addition and abstract-unary-minus operations. These operations are used to propagate information between constraints via a closure operation that is similar to finding shortest paths.

Sankaranarayanan et al. [16] introduced a domain based on template constraint matrices (TCMs) that is less powerful than polyhedra, but more general than intervals and octagons. Their analysis discovers linear-inequality invariants using polyhedra with a predefined fixed shape. The predefined shape is given by the client in the form of a template matrix. Our approach is similar because an affine transformer with symbolic constants can be seen as a template. However, the approaches differ because Sankaranarayanan et al. use an LP solver to find values for template parameters, whereas we use operations and values from an abstract domain to find and represent a set of allowed values for template parameters.

An abstract-domain element in ATA[$\mathcal{B}$] can be seen as an abstraction over sets of functions: $\mathbb{Z}_{2^w}^k \rightarrow \mathbb{Z}_{2^w}^k$. Jeannet et al. [8] provide a theoretical treatment of the relational abstraction of functions. They describing existing and new methods of abstracting functions of signature: $D_1 \rightarrow D_2$, resulting in a family of relational abstract domains. ATA[$\mathcal{B}$] is not captured by their framework of functional abstractions.

References

1. Chen, L., Miné, A., Wang, J., Cousot, P.: Interval polyhedra: an abstract domain to infer interval linear relationships. In: Palsberg, J., Su, Z. (eds.) SAS 2009. LNCS, vol. 5673, pp. 309–325. Springer, Heidelberg (2009). doi:10.1007/978-3-642-03237-0_21
2. Cousot, P., Cousot, R.: Static determination of dynamic properties of programs. In: Proceedings of 2nd International Symposium on Programming, Paris, April 1976
3. Cousot, P., Cousot, R.: Abstract interpretation: a unified lattice model for static analysis of programs by construction of approximation of fixed points. In: POPL, pp. 238–252 (1977)
4. Cousot, P., Cousot, R.: Systematic design of program analysis frameworks. In: POPL (1979)
5. Cousot, P., Halbwachs, N.: Automatic discovery of linear constraints among variables of a program. In: POPL (1978)
6. Elder, M., Lim, J., Sharma, T., Andersen, T., Reps, T.: Abstract domains of affine relations. In: TOPLAS (2014)
7. Gange, G., Navas, J.A., Schachte, P., Søndergaard, H., Stuckey, P.J.: Abstract interpretation over non-lattice abstract domains. In: Logozzo, F., Fähndrich, M. (eds.) SAS 2013. LNCS, vol. 7935, pp. 6–24. Springer, Heidelberg (2013). doi:10.1007/978-3-642-38856-9_3
8. Jeannet, B., Gopan, D., Reps, T.: A relational abstraction for functions. In: Hankin, C., Siveroni, I. (eds.) SAS 2005. LNCS, vol. 3672, pp. 186–202. Springer, Heidelberg (2005). doi:10.1007/11547662_14
9. King, A., Søndergaard, H.: Automatic abstraction for congruences. In: Barthe, G., Hermenegildo, M. (eds.) VMCAI 2010. LNCS, vol. 5944, pp. 197–213. Springer, Heidelberg (2010). doi:10.1007/978-3-642-11319-2_16

10. Miné, A.: The octagon abstract domain. In: WCRE (2001)
11. Miné, A.: A few graph-based relational numerical abstract domains. In: Hermenegildo, M.V., Puebla, G. (eds.) SAS 2002. LNCS, vol. 2477, pp. 117–132. Springer, Heidelberg (2002). doi:10.1007/3-540-45789-5_11
12. Müller-Olm, M., Seidl, H.: Precise interprocedural analysis through linear algebra. In: POPL (2004)
13. Müller-Olm, M., Seidl, H.: Analysis of modular arithmetic. TOPLAS **29**(5) (2007). Article No. 29
14. Reps, T., Balakrishnan, G., Lim, J.: Intermediate-representation recovery from low-level code. In: Proceedings of the 2006 ACM SIGPLAN Symposium on Partial Evaluation and Semantics-based Program Manipulation (2006)
15. Reps, T., Sagiv, M., Yorsh, G.: Symbolic implementation of the best transformer. In: Steffen, B., Levi, G. (eds.) VMCAI 2004. LNCS, vol. 2937, pp. 252–266. Springer, Heidelberg (2004). doi:10.1007/978-3-540-24622-0_21
16. Sankaranarayanan, S., Sipma, H.B., Manna, Z.: Scalable analysis of linear systems using mathematical programming. In: Cousot, R. (ed.) VMCAI 2005. LNCS, vol. 3385, pp. 25–41. Springer, Heidelberg (2005). doi:10.1007/978-3-540-30579-8_2
17. Sen, R., Srikant, Y.: Executable analysis using abstract interpretation with circular linear progressions. In: MEMOCODE (2007)
18. Sharir, M., Pnueli, A.: Two approaches to interprocedural data flow analysis. In: Program Flow Analysis Theory and Applications. Prentice-Hall, Englewood Cliffs (1981)
19. Sharma, T., Reps, T.: A new abstraction framework for affine transformers. Technical report UW-TR-1846r1:SR17, Computer Science Department, University of Wisconsin, Madison, WI, May 2017. Revised July 2017
20. Sharma, T., Reps, T.: Sound bit-precise numerical domains. In: Bouajjani, A., Monniaux, D. (eds.) VMCAI 2017. LNCS, vol. 10145, pp. 500–520. Springer, Cham (2017). doi:10.1007/978-3-319-52234-0_27
21. Simon, A., King, A.: Taming the wrapping of integer arithmetic. In: Nielson, H.R., Filé, G. (eds.) SAS 2007. LNCS, vol. 4634, pp. 121–136. Springer, Heidelberg (2007). doi:10.1007/978-3-540-74061-2_8
22. Thakur, A., Elder, M., Reps, T.: Bilateral algorithms for symbolic abstraction. In: Miné, A., Schmidt, D. (eds.) SAS 2012. LNCS, vol. 7460, pp. 111–128. Springer, Heidelberg (2012). doi:10.1007/978-3-642-33125-1_10

Synthesizing Imperative Programs from Examples Guided by Static Analysis

Sunbeom So and Hakjoo Oh(✉)

Korea University, Seoul, South Korea
{sunbeom_so,hakjoo_oh}@korea.ac.kr

Abstract. We present a novel algorithm for efficiently synthesizing imperative programs from examples. Given a set of input-output examples and a partial program, our algorithm generates a complete program that is consistent with every example. Our algorithm is based on enumerative synthesis, which explores all candidate programs in increasing size until it finds a solution. This algorithm, however, is too slow to be used in practice. Our key idea to accelerate the speed is to perform static analysis alongside the enumerative search, in order to "statically" identify and safely prune out partial programs that eventually fail to be a solution. We have implemented our algorithm in a tool, SIMPL, and evaluated it on 30 introductory programming problems gathered from online forums. The results show that our static analysis approach improves the speed of enumerative synthesis by 25x on average.

1 Introduction

In this paper, we show that semantic-based static analysis (à la abstract interpretation) can be effectively used to speed up enumerative program synthesis. While static analysis has played key roles in program bug-finding, verification, and optimization, its application to program synthesis remains to be seen. Static type systems have been used for synthesizing functional programs [8,9,24,26], but type-directed synthesis is not generally applicable to languages with, for instance, dynamic or unsafe type systems. This paper explores an alternative, static-analysis-guided program synthesis.

We focus on the problem of synthesizing imperative programs, where type-based techniques are not useful. The inputs of our algorithm are a partial program with constraints on variables and constants, and input-output examples that specify a resulting program's behavior. The output is a complete program whose behavior matches all of the given input-output examples.

The key novelty of our algorithm is to combine enumerative program synthesis and static analysis. It basically enumerates every possible candidate program in increasing size until it finds a solution. This algorithm, however, is too slow to be used due to the huge search space of programs. Our key idea to accelerate the speed is to perform static analysis, in order to "statically" identify and safely prune out partial programs that eventually fail to be a solution. More specifically, we prune partial programs whose over-approximated results do not

F. Ranzato (Ed.): SAS 2017, LNCS 10422, pp. 364–381, 2017.
DOI: 10.1007/978-3-319-66706-5_18

satisfy expected behaviors defined by input-output examples. We formalize our pruning technique and its safety property.

The experimental results show that our static-analysis-guided algorithm is remarkably effective to synthesize imperative programs. We have implemented the algorithm in a tool, SIMPL, and evaluated its performance on 30 introductory programming tasks manipulating integers and arrays of integers. The benchmarks are gathered from online forums and include problems non-trivial for beginner-level programmers. With our pruning technique, SIMPL is fast enough to solve each problem in 6.6 s on average. Without it, however, the baseline algorithm, which already adopts well-known optimization techniques, takes 165.5 s (25x slowdown) on average.

Contributions. We summarize our contributions below:

- We present a new algorithm for synthesizing imperative programs from examples. The key idea is to combine enumerative program synthesis with static analysis, which greatly accelerates the speed while guaranteeing to find a solution.
- We prove the effectiveness of our algorithm on 30 introductory programming problems gathered from online forums, including non-trivial ones for beginner-level students. The results show that our algorithm quickly solves the problems, in 6.6 s on average.
- We make our tool, SIMPL, and benchmark problems publicly available, so that readers can use our tool and reproduce the experimental results:

http://prl.korea.ac.kr/simpl

2 Motivating Examples

In this section, we showcase SIMPL with four programming problems. To use SIMPL, users need to provide (1) a set of input-output examples, (2) a partial program, and (3) resources that SIMPL can use. The resources consist of a set of integers, a set of integer-type variables, and a set of array-type variables. The job of SIMPL is to complete the partial program w.r.t. the input-output examples, using only the given resources.

Problem 1 (Reversing integer). Consider the problem of writing the function `reverse` that reverses a given natural number. For example, given 12, the function should return 21. Suppose a partial program is given as

```
reverse (n) { r := 0; while (?) { ? }; return r; }
```

where **?** denotes holes that need to be completed. Suppose further SIMPL is provided with input-output examples $\{1 \mapsto 1, 12 \mapsto 21, 123 \mapsto 321\}$, integers $\{0, 1, 10\}$, and integer variables $\{\mathtt{n}, \mathtt{r}, \mathtt{x}\}$, where $a \mapsto b$ indicates a single example with input a and output b.

```
reverse(n){
  r := 0;
  while (n > 0){
    x := n % 10;
    r := r * 10;
    r := r + x;
    n := n / 10;
  };
  return r;
}
```

(a) Problem1 (# 16)

```
count(n,a){

  while (n > 0){
    t := n % 10;
    a[t] := a[t] + 1;
    n := n / 10;
  };
  return a;

}
```

(b) Problem 2 (# 30)

```
sum(n){
  r := 0;
  while (n > 0){
    t := n;
    while (t > 0){
      r := r + t;
      t := t - 1;
    };
    n := n - 1;
  };
  return r;
}
```

(c) Problem 3 (# 14)

```
abssum(a, len){
  r := 0;
  i := 0;
  while (i < len){
    if (a[i] < 0)
      {r := r - a[i];}
    else
      {r := r + a[i];}
    i := i + 1;
  };
  return r;
}
```

(d) Problem 4 (# 29)

Fig. 1. Synthesized results by SIMPL (in the boxes). #n denotes the number in Table 1.

Given these components, SIMPL produces the solution in Fig. 1(a) in 2.5 s. Note that SIMPL finds out the integer '1' is unnecessary and the final program does not contain it.

Problem 2 (Counting). The next problem is to write a function that counts the number of each digit in an integer. The program takes an integer and an array as inputs, where each element of the array is initially 0. As output, the program returns that array but now each array element at index i stores the number of is that occur in the given integer. For example, when a tuple $(220, \langle 0,0,0\rangle)$ is given, the function should output $\langle 1,0,2\rangle$; 0 occurs once, 1 does not occur, and 2 occurs twice in '220'. Suppose the partial program is given as

```
count (n,a) { while(?){?}; return a;}
```

with examples $\{(11, \langle 0,0\rangle) \mapsto \langle 0,2\rangle, (220, \langle 0,0,0\rangle) \mapsto \langle 1,0,2\rangle\}$, integers $\{0,1,10\}$, integer variables {`i`,`n`,`t`}, and an array variable {`a`}.

For this problem, SIMPL produces the program in Fig. 1(b) in 0.2 s. Note that `i` is not used though it is given as a usable resource.

Problem 3 (Sum of sum). The third problem is to compute $1 + (1+2) + ... + (1 + 2 + ... + n)$ for a given integer n. Suppose the partial program

```
sum(n){ r := 0; while(?){?}; return r;}
```

is given with examples $\{1 \mapsto 1, 2 \mapsto 4, 3 \mapsto 10, 4 \mapsto 20\}$, integers $\{0, 1\}$, and integer-type variables $\{\texttt{n}, \texttt{t}, \texttt{r}\}$.

Then, SIMPL produces the program in Fig. 1(c) in 37.6 s. Note that SIMPL newly introduced the inner loop, which is absent in the partial program.

Problem 4 (Absolute sum). The last problem is to sum the absolute values of all the elements in a given array. We provide the partial program:

```
abssum(a, len){ r := 0; i := 0;
  while(i < len){ if(?){?} else{?}; i:=i+1;};
return r;}
```

where the goal is to complete the condition and bodies of the if-then-else statement. Additionally, given a set of input-output examples $\{(\langle -1, -2\rangle, 2) \mapsto 3, (\langle 2, 3, -4\rangle, 3) \mapsto 9\}$, an integer $\{0\}$, integer variables $\{\texttt{r}, \texttt{i}\}$, and an array variable $\{\texttt{a}\}$, SIMPL produces the program in Fig. 1(d) in 12.1 s.

Finally, we emphasize the following points regarding usage scenarios of SIMPL:

- SIMPL requires only a few input-output examples. In experiments (Table 1), it was enough to provide 2–4 input-output examples for each programming task. These examples are simple enough to conceive.
- Resources can be over-estimated if uncertain (Problem 1, Problem 2). The unnecessary resources will be ignored by SIMPL.

3 Problem Definition

Language. We designed an imperative language that is small yet expressive enough to deal with various introductory programming problems. The syntax of the language is defined by the grammar in Fig. 2.

A l-value (l) is a variable (x) or an array reference ($x[y]$). An arithmetic expression (a) is an integer constant (n), an l-value (l), or a binary operation ($\oplus$). A boolean expression (b) is a boolean constant ($true, false$), a binary relation ($\prec$), a negation ($\neg$), or a logical conjunction ($\wedge$) and disjunction ($\vee$). Commands

$$\begin{array}{l}
\oplus ::= + \mid - \mid * \mid / \mid \%, \quad \prec ::= \; = \mid > \mid < \\
l ::= x \mid x[y], \quad a ::= n \mid l \mid l_1 \oplus l_2 \mid l \oplus n \mid \Diamond \\
b ::= \mathit{true} \mid \mathit{false} \mid l_1 \prec l_2 \mid l \prec n \mid b_1 \wedge b_2 \mid b_1 \vee b_2 \mid \neg b \mid \triangle \\
c ::= l := a \mid \mathit{skip} \mid c_1; c_2 \mid \mathit{if}\; b\; c_1\; c_2 \mid \mathit{while}\; b\; c \mid \square
\end{array}$$

Fig. 2. Language

$$\begin{aligned}
\mathcal{A}[\![n]\!](m) &= n \\
\mathcal{A}[\![x]\!](m) &= m(x) \\
\mathcal{A}[\![x[y]]\!](m) &= m(x)_{m(y)} \\
\mathcal{A}[\![l_1 \oplus l_2]\!](m) &= \mathcal{A}[\![l_1]\!](m) \oplus \mathcal{A}[\![l_2]\!](m) \\
\mathcal{A}[\![l \oplus n]\!](m) &= \mathcal{A}[\![l]\!](m) \oplus n \\
\mathcal{B}[\![\mathit{true}]\!](m) &= \mathit{true} \\
\mathcal{B}[\![\mathit{false}]\!](m) &= \mathit{false} \\
\mathcal{B}[\![l_1 \prec l_2]\!](m) &= \mathcal{A}[\![l_1]\!](m) \prec \mathcal{A}[\![l_2]\!](m) \\
\mathcal{B}[\![l \prec n]\!](m) &= \mathcal{A}[\![l]\!](m) \prec n \\
\mathcal{B}[\![b_1 \wedge b_2]\!](m) &= \mathcal{B}[\![b_1]\!](m) \wedge \mathcal{B}[\![b_2]\!](m) \\
\mathcal{B}[\![b_1 \vee b_2]\!](m) &= \mathcal{B}[\![b_1]\!](m) \vee \mathcal{B}[\![b_2]\!](m) \\
\mathcal{B}[\![\neg b]\!](m) &= \neg \mathcal{B}[\![b]\!](m)
\end{aligned}$$

$$\begin{aligned}
\mathcal{C}[\![x := a]\!](m) &= m[x \mapsto \mathcal{A}[\![a]\!](m)] \\
\mathcal{C}[\![x[y] := a]\!](m) &= m[x \mapsto m(x)_{m(y)}^{\mathcal{A}[\![a]\!](m)}] \\
\mathcal{C}[\![\mathit{skip}]\!](m) &= m \\
\mathcal{C}[\![c_1; c_2]\!](m) &= (\mathcal{C}[\![c_2]\!] \circ \mathcal{C}[\![c_1]\!])(m) \\
\mathcal{C}[\![\mathit{if}\ b\ c_1\ c_2]\!](m) &= \mathsf{cond}(\mathcal{B}[\![b]\!], \mathcal{C}[\![c_1]\!], \mathcal{C}[\![c_2]\!])(m) \\
\mathcal{C}[\![\mathit{while}\ b\ c]\!](m) &= (\mathsf{fix}\ F)(m) \\
\text{where } F(g) &= \mathsf{cond}(\mathcal{B}[\![b]\!], g \circ \mathcal{C}[\![c]\!], \lambda x.x) \\
\mathsf{cond}(p, f, g)(m) &= \begin{cases} f(m) \text{ if } p(m) = \mathit{true} \\ g(m) \text{ if } p(m) = \mathit{false} \end{cases}
\end{aligned}$$

Fig. 3. Semantics of the language

include assignment ($l := a$), skip (skip), sequence ($c_1; c_2$), conditional statement ($\mathit{if}\ b\ c_1\ c_2$), and while-loop ($\mathit{while}\ b\ c$).

A program $P = (x, c, y)$ is a command with input and output variables, where x is the input variable, c is the command, and y is the output variable. The input and output variables x and y can be either of integer or array types. For presentation brevity, we assume that the program takes a single input, but our implementation supports multiple input variables as well.

An unusual feature of the language is that it allows to write incomplete programs. Whenever uncertain, any arithmetic expressions, boolean expressions, and commands can be left out with holes ($\Diamond, \triangle, \Box$). The goal of our synthesis algorithm is to automatically complete such partial programs.

The semantics of the language is defined for programs without holes. Let $\mathbb{X}$ be the set of program variables, which is partitioned into integer and array types, i.e., $\mathbb{X} = \mathbb{X}_i \uplus \mathbb{X}_a$. A memory state

$$m \in \mathbb{M} = \mathbb{X} \to \mathbb{V}, \quad v \in \mathbb{V} = \mathbb{Z} + \mathbb{Z}^*$$

is a partial function from variables to values ($\mathbb{V}$). A value is either an integer or an array of integers. An array $a \in \mathbb{Z}^*$ is a sequence of integers. For instance, we write $\langle 1, 2, 3 \rangle$ for the array of integers 1, 2, and 3. We write $|a|$, a_i, and a_i^k for the length of a, the element at index i, and the array $a_0 \ldots a_{i-1} k a_{i+1} \cdots a_{|a|-1}$, respectively.

The semantics of the language is defined by the functions:

$$\mathcal{A}[\![a]\!] : \mathbb{M} \to \mathbb{V}, \quad \mathcal{B}[\![b]\!] : \mathbb{M} \to \mathbb{B}, \quad \mathcal{C}[\![c]\!] : \mathbb{M} \to \mathbb{M}$$

where $\mathcal{A}[\![a]\!]$, $\mathcal{B}[\![b]\!]$, and $\mathcal{C}[\![c]\!]$ denote the semantics of arithmetic expressions, boolean expressions, and commands, respectively. Figure 3 presents the denotational semantics, where fix is a fixed point operator. Note that the semantics for holes is undefined.

Synthesis Problem. A synthesis task is defined by the five components:

$$((x, c_0, y), \mathcal{E}, \Gamma, \mathbb{X}_i, \mathbb{X}_a)$$

where (x, c_0, y) is an initial incomplete program with holes, and $\mathcal{E} \subseteq \mathbb{V} \times \mathbb{V}$ is a set of input-output examples. The resource components to be used are given as a triplet, where Γ is a set of integers, $\mathbb{X}_i$ is a set of integer-type variables, and $\mathbb{X}_a$ is a set of array-type variables.[1] The goal of our synthesis algorithm is to produce a complete command c without holes such that

- c uses constants and variables in Γ and $\mathbb{X}_i \cup \mathbb{X}_a$, and
- c is consistent with every input-output example:

$$\forall (v_i, v_o) \in \mathcal{E}.\ \big(\mathcal{C}[\![c]\!]([x \mapsto v_i])\big)(y) = v_o.$$

4 Synthesis Algorithm

In this section, we present our synthesis algorithm that combines enumerative search with static analysis. We formalize the synthesis problem as a state search problem (Sect. 4.1) and presents a basic enumerative search algorithm (Sect. 4.2). Section 4.3 presents our pruning with static analysis.

4.1 Synthesis as State-Search

We first reduce the synthesis task to a state-search problem. Consider a synthesis task $((x, c_0, y), \mathcal{E}, \Gamma, \mathbb{X}_i, \mathbb{X}_a)$. The corresponding search problem is defined by the transition system

$$(S, \rightsquigarrow, s_0, F)$$

where S is a set of states, $(\rightsquigarrow) \subseteq S \times S$ is a transition relation, $s_0 \in S$ is an initial state, and $F \subseteq S$ is a set of solution states.

- **States:** A state $s \in S$ is a command possibly with holes, which is defined by the grammar in Sect. 3.
- **Initial state:** An initial state s_0 is an initial partial command c_0.
- **Transition relation:** Transition relation $(\rightsquigarrow) \subseteq S \times S$ determines a next state that is immediately reachable from a current state. The relation is defined as a set of inference rules in Fig. 4. Intuitively, a hole can be replaced by an arbitrary expression (or command) of the same type. Given a state s, we write $\mathsf{next}(s)$ for the set of all immediate next states from s, i.e., $\mathsf{next}(s) = \{s' \mid s \rightsquigarrow s'\}$.

Example 1. Given $\Gamma = \{1\}$, $\mathbb{X}_i = \{x\}$ and $\mathbb{X}_a = \emptyset$, consider a state $s = (\square; r := 1; r := \lozenge)$. Then, $\mathsf{next}(s) = \{(x := \lozenge; r := 1; r := \lozenge), (\mathit{skip}; r := 1; r := \lozenge), (\square; \square; r := 1; r := \lozenge), (\mathit{if}\ \triangle\ \square\ \square; r := 1; r := \lozenge), (\mathit{while}\ \triangle\ \square; r := 1; r := \lozenge), (\square; r := 1; r := 1;), (\square; r := 1; r := x), (\square; r := 1; r := x + x), (\square; r := 1; r := x - x), (\square; r := 1; r := x * x), (\square; r := 1; r := x/x), (\square; r := 1; r := x\%x), (\square; r := 1; r := x + 1), (\square; r := 1; r := x - 1), (\square; r := 1; r := x * 1), (\square; r := 1; r := x/1), (\square; r := 1; r := x\%1)\}$.

[1] Resource variables may not exactly coincide with program variables (e.g., Problem 2 in Sect. 2). However, for legibility, we abuse the notation between them.

$$\frac{a \rightsquigarrow_a a'}{l := a \rightsquigarrow l := a'} \quad \frac{c_1 \rightsquigarrow c_1'}{c_1; c_2 \rightsquigarrow c_1'; c_2} \quad \frac{c_2 \rightsquigarrow c_2'}{c_1; c_2 \rightsquigarrow c_1; c_2'}$$

$$\frac{b \rightsquigarrow_b b'}{\mathit{if}\ b\ c_1\ c_2 \rightsquigarrow \mathit{if}\ b'\ c_1\ c_2} \quad \frac{c_1 \rightsquigarrow c_1'}{\mathit{if}\ b\ c_1\ c_2 \rightsquigarrow \mathit{if}\ b\ c_1'\ c_2} \quad \frac{c_2 \rightsquigarrow c_2'}{\mathit{if}\ b\ c_1\ c_2 \rightsquigarrow \mathit{if}\ b\ c_1\ c_2'}$$

$$\frac{b \rightsquigarrow_b b'}{\mathit{while}\ b\ c \rightsquigarrow \mathit{while}\ b'\ c} \quad \frac{c \rightsquigarrow c'}{\mathit{while}\ b\ c \rightsquigarrow \mathit{while}\ b\ c'}$$

$$\frac{b_1 \rightsquigarrow_b b_1'}{b_1 \wedge b_2 \rightsquigarrow_b b_1' \wedge b_2} \quad \frac{b_2 \rightsquigarrow_b b_2'}{b_1 \wedge b_2 \rightsquigarrow_b b_1 \wedge b_2'} \quad \frac{b_1 \rightsquigarrow_b b_1'}{b_1 \vee b_2 \rightsquigarrow_b b_1' \vee b_2} \quad \frac{b_2 \rightsquigarrow_b b_2'}{b_1 \vee b_2 \rightsquigarrow_b b_1 \vee b_2'} \quad \frac{b \rightsquigarrow_b b'}{\neg b \rightsquigarrow_b \neg b'}$$

$$\overline{\Box \rightsquigarrow l := \Diamond} \quad \overline{\Box \rightsquigarrow \mathit{skip}} \quad \overline{\Box \rightsquigarrow \Box; \Box} \quad \overline{\Box \rightsquigarrow \mathit{if}\ \triangle\ \Box\ \Box} \quad \overline{\Box \rightsquigarrow \mathit{while}\ \triangle\ \Box}$$

$$\overline{\triangle \rightsquigarrow_b \mathit{true}} \quad \overline{\triangle \rightsquigarrow_b \mathit{false}} \quad \overline{\triangle \rightsquigarrow_b l_1 \prec l_2} \quad \overline{\triangle \rightsquigarrow_b l \prec n}$$

$$\overline{\triangle \rightsquigarrow_b \triangle \wedge \triangle} \quad \overline{\triangle \rightsquigarrow_b \triangle \vee \triangle} \quad \overline{\triangle \rightsquigarrow_b \neg \triangle}$$

$$\overline{\Diamond \rightsquigarrow_a n} \quad \overline{\Diamond \rightsquigarrow_a l} \quad \overline{\Diamond \rightsquigarrow_a l_1 \oplus l_2} \quad \overline{\Diamond \rightsquigarrow_a l \oplus n}$$

Fig. 4. Transition relation ($n \in \Gamma$, $l \in \mathbb{X}_i \cup \{x[y] \mid x \in \mathbb{X}_a \wedge y \in \mathbb{X}_i\}$)

We write $s \not\rightsquigarrow$ for terminal states, i.e., states with no holes.

- **Solution states:** A state s is a solution iff s is a terminal state and it is consistent with all input-output examples:

$$\mathsf{solution}(s) \iff s \not\rightsquigarrow \wedge \forall (v_i, v_o) \in \mathcal{E}.\ \big(\mathcal{C}[\![s]\!]([x \mapsto v_i])\big)(y) = v_o.$$

4.2 Baseline Search Algorithm

Algorithm 1 shows the basic architecture of our enumerative search algorithm. The algorithm initializes the workset W with s_0 (line 1). Then, it picks a state s with the smallest size and removes the state from the workset (line 3). We compute a size of a state using a heuristic cost model $\mathcal{M}_c : c \to \mathbb{Z}$ which is inductively defined as follows:

$$\begin{aligned}
\mathcal{M}_c(l := a) &= \mathit{cost}_1 + \mathcal{M}_a(a) \\
\mathcal{M}_c(\mathit{skip}) &= \mathit{cost}_2 \\
\mathcal{M}_c(c_1; c_2) &= \mathit{cost}_3 + \mathcal{M}_c(c_1) + \mathcal{M}_c(c_2) \\
\mathcal{M}_c(\mathit{while}\ b\ c) &= \mathit{cost}_4 + \mathcal{M}_b(b) + \mathcal{M}_c(c) \\
\mathcal{M}_c(\mathit{if}\ b\ c_1\ c_2) &= \mathit{cost}_5 + \mathcal{M}_b(b) + \mathcal{M}_c(c_1) + \mathcal{M}_c(c_2) \\
\mathcal{M}_c(\Box) &= \mathit{cost}_6
\end{aligned}$$

where integer constants from cost_1 to cost_6 represent costs related to each command. After computing the sizes of all the states in the workset W, we pick the smallest state since the smaller ones are likely to generalize behavior better

Algorithm 1. Synthesis Algorithm

Input: A synthesis problem $((x, c_0, y), \mathcal{E}, \Gamma, \mathbb{X}_i, \mathbb{X}_a)$
Output: A complete program consistent with $\mathcal{E}$

1: $W \leftarrow \{s_0\}$ where $s_0 = c_0$
2: **repeat**
3:     Pick the smallest state s from W
4:     **if** s is a terminal state **then**
5:         **if** $\mathsf{solution}(s)$ **then return** (x, s, y)
6:     **else**
7:         **if** $\neg\mathsf{prune}(s)$ **then** $W \leftarrow W \cup \mathsf{next}(s)$
8: **until** $W = \emptyset$

while avoiding overfitting for the given examples. Therefore, our current implementation prefers programs without holes to programs with holes (i.e., $cost_6 > cost_1, ..., cost_5$). Likewise, the cost models for arithmetic expressions ($\mathcal{M}_a : a \to \mathbb{Z}$) and boolean expressions ($\mathcal{M}_b : b \to \mathbb{Z}$) are also defined to prefer expressions without holes to expressions with holes.

If s is a solution state, the algorithm terminates and s is returned (line 5). For a non-terminal state, the algorithm attempts to prune the state by invoking the function prune (line 7). If pruning fails, the next states of s are added into the workset and the loop repeats. The details of our pruning technique is described in Sect. 4.3. At the moment, assume prune always fails.

The baseline algorithm implicitly performs well-known optimization techniques; it normalizes states in order to avoid exploring syntactically different but semantically the same ones. For instance, suppose we are exploring the state $(r := 0; r := x * 0; \square)$. We normalize it to $(r := 0; \square)$ and add it to the workset only when the resulting state has not been processed before. To do so, we first maintain previously explored states and never reconsider them. Secondly, we use four code optimization techniques: constant propagation, copy propagation, dead code elimination, and expression simplification [1]. For example, starting from $(r := 0; r := x * 0; \square)$, we simplify the expression $(x * 0)$ and obtain $(r := 0; r := 0; \square)$. Then, we apply dead code elimination to remove the first assignment $(r := 0; \square)$. Lastly, we also reorder variables in a fixed order. For example, when we assume alphabetical order, $(x := b + a)$ is rewritten as $(x := a + b)$. These normalization techniques significantly improve the speed of enumerative search.

In addition, the algorithm considers terminating programs only. Our language has unrestricted loops, so the basic algorithm may synthesize non-terminating programs. To exclude them from the search space, we use syntactic heuristics to detect potentially non-terminating loops. The heuristics are: (1) we only allow boolean expressions of the form $x < y$ (or $x > n$) in loop conditions, (2) the last statement of the loop body must increase (or decrease) the induction variable x, and (3) x and y are not defined elsewhere in the loop. If the states belong

```
example1(n){
  r := 0;
  while (n > 0){
    r := n + 1;
    n := ◊;
  };
  return r;
}
```

(a)

```
example2(n) {
  r := 0;
  while (n > 0){
         □;
    r := x * 10;
    n := n / 10;
  };
  return r;
}
```

(b)

Fig. 5. States that are pruned away

to one of the three cases, we prune the states. For example, we prune the state $(r := 0; \textit{while}\ (x > 0)\{x := \Diamond; \Box; x := x - 1\})$ since the induction variable x will be defined at the beginning of the loop body (i.e., the state violated the third rule).

4.3 Pruning with Static Analysis

Now we present the main contribution of this paper, pruning with static analysis. Static analysis allows to safely identify states that eventually fail to be a solution. We first define the notion of failure states.

Definition 1. *A state s is a failure state, denoted* $\mathsf{fail}(s)$*, iff every terminal state s' reachable from s is not a solution, i.e.,*

$$\mathsf{fail}(s) \iff ((s \rightsquigarrow^* s') \wedge s' \not\rightsquigarrow \implies \neg\mathsf{solution}(s')).$$

Our goal is to detect as many failure states as possible. We observed two typical cases of failure states that often show up during the baseline search algorithm.

Example 2. Consider the program in Fig. 5(a) and input-output example $(1, 1)$. When the program is executed with $n = 1$, no matter how the hole $(\Diamond)$ gets instantiated, the output value r is no less than 2 at the return statement. Therefore, the program cannot but fail to satisfy the example $(1, 1)$.

Example 3. Consider the program in Fig. 5(b) and input-output example $(1, 1)$. Here, we do not know the exact values of x and r, but we know that $10 * x = 1$ must hold at the end of the program. However, there exists no such integer x, and we conclude the partial program is a failure state.

Static Analysis. We designed a static analysis that aims to effectively identify these two types of failure states. To do so, our analysis combines numeric and symbolic analyses; the numeric analysis is designed to detect the cases of Example 2 and the symbolic analysis for the cases of Example 3. The abstract domain of the analysis is defined as follows:

$$\widehat{m} \in \widehat{\mathbb{M}} = \mathbb{X} \to \widehat{\mathbb{V}}, \quad \widehat{v} \in \widehat{\mathbb{V}} = \mathbb{I} \times \mathbb{S}$$

$$\begin{aligned}
\widehat{\mathcal{A}}[\![n]\!](\widehat{m}) &= ([n,n],n)\\
\widehat{\mathcal{A}}[\![l]\!](\widehat{m}) &= \widehat{m}(x)\ (l = x \text{ or } x[y])\\
\widehat{\mathcal{A}}[\![l_1 \oplus l_2]\!](\widehat{m}) &= \widehat{\mathcal{A}}[\![l_1]\!](\widehat{m})\ \widehat{\oplus}\ \widehat{\mathcal{A}}[\![l_2]\!](\widehat{m})\\
\widehat{\mathcal{A}}[\![l \oplus n]\!](\widehat{m}) &= \widehat{\mathcal{A}}[\![l_1]\!](\widehat{m})\ \widehat{\oplus}\ n\\
\widehat{\mathcal{A}}[\![\Diamond]\!](\widehat{m}) &= ([-\infty,+\infty],\top)\\
\widehat{\mathcal{B}}[\![true]\!](\widehat{m}) &= \widehat{true}\\
\widehat{\mathcal{B}}[\![false]\!](\widehat{m}) &= \widehat{false}\\
\widehat{\mathcal{B}}[\![l_1 \prec l_2]\!](\widehat{m}) &= \widehat{\mathcal{A}}[\![l_1]\!](\widehat{m})\ \widehat{\prec}\ \widehat{\mathcal{A}}[\![l_2]\!](\widehat{m})\\
\widehat{\mathcal{B}}[\![l \prec n]\!](\widehat{m}) &= \widehat{\mathcal{A}}[\![l]\!](\widehat{m})\ \widehat{\prec}\ n\\
\widehat{\mathcal{B}}[\![b_1 \wedge b_2]\!](\widehat{m}) &= \widehat{\mathcal{B}}[\![b_1]\!](\widehat{m})\ \widehat{\wedge}\ \widehat{\mathcal{B}}[\![b_2]\!](\widehat{m})\\
\widehat{\mathcal{B}}[\![b_1 \vee b_2]\!](\widehat{m}) &= \widehat{\mathcal{B}}[\![b_1]\!](\widehat{m})\ \widehat{\vee}\ \widehat{\mathcal{B}}[\![b_2]\!](\widehat{m})\\
\widehat{\mathcal{B}}[\![\neg b]\!](\widehat{m}) &= \widehat{\neg}\widehat{\mathcal{B}}[\![b]\!](\widehat{m})\\
\widehat{\mathcal{B}}[\![\triangle]\!](\widehat{m}) &= \top
\end{aligned}$$

$$\begin{aligned}
\widehat{\mathcal{C}}[\![x := \Diamond]\!](\widehat{m}) &= \widehat{m}[x \mapsto ([-\infty,+\infty],\beta_x)]\\
\widehat{\mathcal{C}}[\![x[y] := \Diamond]\!](\widehat{m}) &= \widehat{m}[x \mapsto ([-\infty,+\infty],\top)]\\
\widehat{\mathcal{C}}[\![x := a]\!](\widehat{m}) &= \widehat{m}[x \mapsto \widehat{\mathcal{A}}[\![a]\!](\widehat{m})]\\
\widehat{\mathcal{C}}[\![x[y] := a]\!](\widehat{m}) &= \widehat{m}[x \mapsto \widehat{\mathcal{A}}[\![a]\!](\widehat{m}) \sqcup \widehat{m}(x)]\\
\widehat{\mathcal{C}}[\![skip]\!](\widehat{m}) &= \widehat{m}\\
\widehat{\mathcal{C}}[\![c_1;c_2]\!](\widehat{m}) &= (\widehat{\mathcal{C}}[\![c_2]\!] \circ \widehat{\mathcal{C}}[\![c_1]\!])(\widehat{m})\\
\widehat{\mathcal{C}}[\![if\ b\ c_1\ c_2]\!](\widehat{m}) &= \widehat{\mathsf{cond}}(\widehat{\mathcal{B}}[\![b]\!],\widehat{\mathcal{C}}[\![c_1]\!],\widehat{\mathcal{C}}[\![c_2]\!])(\widehat{m})\\
\widehat{\mathcal{C}}[\![while\ b\ c]\!](\widehat{m}) &= (\mathsf{fix}\ \widehat{F})(\widehat{m})\\
\text{where } \widehat{F}(g) &= \widehat{\mathsf{cond}}(\widehat{\mathcal{B}}[\![b]\!], g \circ \widehat{\mathcal{C}}[\![c]\!], \lambda x.x)\\
\widehat{\mathcal{C}}[\![\square]\!](\widehat{m})(x) &= \begin{cases} ([-\infty,+\infty],\beta_x) & x \in \mathbb{X}_i\\ ([-\infty,+\infty],\top) & x \in \mathbb{X}_a \end{cases}\\
\widehat{\mathsf{cond}}(p,f,g)(\widehat{m}) &= \begin{cases} \bot & \text{if } p(\widehat{m}) = \bot\\ f(\widehat{m}') & \text{if } p(\widehat{m}) = \widehat{true}\\ g(\widehat{m}') & \text{if } p(\widehat{m}) = \widehat{false}\\ f(\widehat{m}') \sqcup g(\widehat{m}') & \text{if } p(\widehat{m}) = \top \end{cases}\\
\text{where } \widehat{m}' &= \bigsqcup\{\widehat{m}'' \sqsubseteq_{\widehat{\mathbb{M}}} \widehat{m} \mid \widehat{m}'' \models p\}
\end{aligned}$$

Fig. 6. Abstract semantics

An abstract memory state $\widehat{m}$ maps variables to abstract values ($\widehat{\mathbb{V}}$). An abstract value is a pair of intervals ($\mathbb{I}$) and symbolic values ($\mathbb{S}$). The domain of intervals is standard [6]:

$$\mathbb{I} = (\{\bot\} \cup \{[l,u] \mid l,u \in \mathbb{Z} \cup \{-\infty,+\infty\} \wedge l \le u\}, \sqsubseteq_{\mathbb{I}}).$$

For symbolic analysis, we define the following flat domain:

$$\mathbb{S} = (\mathsf{SE}_\bot^\top, \sqsubseteq_{\mathbb{S}}) \quad where \quad \mathsf{SE} ::= \ n \mid \beta_x\ (x \in \mathbb{X}_i) \mid \mathsf{SE} \oplus \mathsf{SE}$$

A symbolic expression $se \in \mathsf{SE}$ is an integer (n), a symbol (β_x), or a binary operation with symbolic expressions. We introduce symbols one for each integer-type variable in the program. The symbolic domain is flat and has the partial order: $s_1 \sqsubseteq_{\mathbb{S}} s_2 \iff (s_1 = \bot) \vee (s_1 = s_2) \vee (s_2 = \top)$. We define the abstraction function $\alpha : \mathbb{V} \to \widehat{\mathbb{V}}$ that transforms concrete values to abstract values:

$$\begin{aligned}
\alpha(n) &= ([n,n],n)\\
\alpha(n_1 \ldots n_k) &= ([\min\{n_1,\ldots,n_k\}, \max\{n_1,\ldots,n_k\}],\top).
\end{aligned}$$

The abstract semantics is defined in Fig. 6 by the functions:

$$\widehat{\mathcal{A}}[\![a]\!] : \widehat{\mathbb{M}} \to \widehat{\mathbb{V}}, \quad \widehat{\mathcal{B}}[\![b]\!] : \widehat{\mathbb{M}} \to \widehat{\mathbb{B}}, \quad \widehat{\mathcal{C}}[\![c]\!] : \widehat{\mathbb{M}} \to \widehat{\mathbb{M}}$$

where $\widehat{\mathbb{B}} = \{\widehat{true}, \widehat{false}\}_\bot^\top$ is the abstract boolean lattice.

Intuitively, the abstract semantics over-approximates the concrete semantics of *all* terminal states that are reachable from the current state. This is done by defining the sound semantics for holes: $\widehat{\mathcal{A}}[\![\Diamond]\!](\widehat{m})$, $\widehat{\mathcal{B}}[\![\triangle]\!](\widehat{m})$, and $\widehat{\mathcal{C}}[\![\square]\!](\widehat{m})$.

An exception is that integer variables get assigned symbols, rather than $\top$, in order to generate symbolic constraints on integer variables.

In our analysis, array elements are abstracted into a single element. Hence, the definitions of $\widehat{\mathcal{A}}[\![x[y]]\!]$ and $\widehat{\mathcal{C}}[\![x[y] := a]\!]$ do not involve y. Because an abstract array cell may represent multiple concrete cells, arrays are weakly updated by joining ($\sqcup$) old and new values. For example, given a memory state $\widehat{m} = [x \mapsto ([5,5], \top), ...]$, $\widehat{\mathcal{C}}[\![x[y] := 1]\!](\widehat{m})$ evaluates to $[x \mapsto ([1,5], \top), ...]$.

For while-loops, the analysis performs a sound fixed point computation. If the computation does not reach a fixed point after a fixed number of iterations, we apply widening for infinite interval domain, in order to guarantee the termination of the analysis. We use the standard widening operator in [6]. The function $\widehat{\mathsf{fix}}$ and $\widehat{\mathsf{cond}}$ in Fig. 6 denote a post-fixed point operator and a sound abstraction of cond, respectively.

Pruning. Next we describe how we do pruning with the static analysis. Suppose we are given examples $\mathcal{E} \subseteq \mathbb{V} \times \mathbb{V}$ and a state s with input (x) and output (y) variables. For each example $(v_i, v_o) \in \mathcal{E}$, we first run the static analysis with the input $\alpha(v_i)$ and obtain the analysis result (itv_s, se_s) :

$$(itv_s, se_s) = \big(\widehat{\mathcal{C}}[\![s]\!]([x \mapsto \alpha(v_i)])\big)(y).$$

We only consider the case when $itv_s = [l_s, u_s]$ (when $itv_s = \bot$, the program is semantically ill-formed and therefore we just prune out the state). Then, we obtain the interval abstraction $[l_o, u_o]$ of the output v_o, i.e., $([l_o, u_o], -) = \alpha(v_o)$, and generate the constraints $C^s_{(v_i,v_o)}$:

$$C^s_{(v_i,v_o)} = (l_s \leq l_o \wedge u_o \leq u_s) \wedge (se_s \in \mathsf{SE} \implies l_o \leq se_s \leq u_o).$$

The first (resp., second) conjunct means that the interval (resp., symbolic) analysis result must over-approximate the output example. We prune out a state s iff $C^s_{(v_i,v_o)}$ is unsatisfiable for some example $(v_i, v_o) \in \mathcal{E}$:

Definition 2. *The predicate* prune *is defined as follows:*

$$\mathsf{prune}(s) \iff C^s_{(v_i,v_o)} \textit{ is unsatisfiable for some } (v_i, v_o) \in \mathcal{E}.$$

The unsatisfiability can be easily checked, for instance, with an off-the-shelf SMT solver. Examples 4 and 5 show how the above pruning works.

Example 4. Consider the Example 2 again, where $(1,1) \in \mathcal{E}$. Let s be the state in Fig. 5(a). If we run the analysis with the input $\alpha(1)$, we get

$$([2, +\infty], \top) = \big(\widehat{\mathcal{C}}[\![s]\!]([n \mapsto \alpha(1)])\big)(r).$$

To see why, each time the loop-body is executed, the interval value of n becomes $[-\infty, +\infty]$, and the interval value of r is stabilized at $[2, +\infty]$ after the third execution of the loop-body. Also, the resulting symbolic value of r is $\top$, because if we join the first loop-body execution result 2 and the second loop-body execution result $\beta_n + 1$, the resulting value becomes $\top$ and stabilized as $\top$ thereafter. As a result, we get the constraint

$$C^s_{(v_i,v_o)} = (2 \leq 1 \wedge 1 \leq +\infty)$$

since $(itv_s, se_s) = ([2, +\infty], \top)$, $[l_o, u_o] = [1, 1]$, and $\top \notin \mathsf{SE}$. The constraint is unsatisfiable since $2 \leq 1$ is never true. Hence, we prune out the state s.

Example 5. Consider the Example 3 again, where $(1, 1) \in \mathcal{E}$. Let s be the state in Fig. 5(b). If we run the analysis with the input $\alpha(1)$, we get

$$([-\infty, +\infty], \beta_x * 10) = \big(\widehat{\mathcal{C}}[\![s]\!]([n \mapsto \alpha(1)])\big)(r)$$

since, by the semantic computations of the command hole ($\square$), interval values of the variables become $[-\infty, +\infty]$ and symbolic value of r is fixed at $\beta_x * 10$. As a result, we get the constraint

$$C^s_{(v_i,v_o)} = (-\infty \leq 1 \wedge 1 \leq +\infty) \wedge (\beta_x * 10 \in \mathsf{SE} \implies 1 \leq \beta_x * 10 \leq 1)$$

where $(itv_s, se_s) = ([-\infty, +\infty], \beta_x * 10)$ and $[l_o, u_o] = [1, 1]$. This constraint is unsatisfiable since $\beta_x * 10$ is in SE (i.e., $\beta_x * 10 \in \mathsf{SE}$), but no β_x exists such that $1 \leq \beta_x * 10 \leq 1$ holds. Therefore, we prune out the state s.

The following theorem states that our pruning is safe:

Theorem 1 (Safety). $\forall s \in S.\ \mathsf{prune}(s) \implies \mathsf{fail}(s)$.

That is, we prune out a state only when it is a failure state, which formally guarantees that the search algorithm with our pruning finds a solution if and only if the baseline algorithm (Sect. 4.2) does so.

5 Evaluation

To evaluate our synthesis algorithm, we gathered 30 introductory level problems from several online forums[2] (Table 1). All of the benchmark problems we used are publicly available with our tool SIMPL[3]. The problems consist of various tasks of manipulating integers and arrays of integers. Some problems are non-trivial for novice programmers to solve; the problems require the novices to come up with various control structures such as nested loops and combinations of loops and conditional statements.

[2] E.g., http://www.codeforwin.in.

[3] http://prl.korea.ac.kr/simpl.

For all but three problems (#23, #24, #29), we used partial programs similar to those in Fig. 1(a)–(c), which consist of initialization statements followed by a single loop with empty condition and body: e.g.,

```
problem (n) { r := 0; while (?) { ? }; return r; }
```

That is, in most cases, the synthesis goal is to complete the loop condition and body. For the other problems (#23, #24, #29), we used partial programs similar to the one in Fig. 1(d), where the job is to complete the condition and body of conditional statements. For instance, for problem #23, we used the following template on the left-hand side. The synthesized program is given on the right-hand side.

```
problem23 (arr, len) {              problem23 (arr, len) {
  i := 0;                             i := 0;
  m := arr[i];                        m := arr[i];
  while (i < len) {                   while (i < len) {
    if (?) { ? };                       if (arr[i]>m) {m:=arr[i]};
    i=i+1;                              i=i+1;
  };                                  };
  return m;                           return m;
}                                   }
```

For each benchmark, we report the number of integer-type variables (the column 'IVars'), array-type variables (the column 'AVars'), integer constants (the column 'Ints'), and input-output examples (the column 'Exs') provided, respectively. To show practicality of SIMPL, we gave over-estimated resources ('IVars', 'AVars', 'Ints') for some benchmarks, provided small number (2–4) of input-output examples, and configured the examples to be easy even for the beginners to come up with, as shown in Sect. 2. All of the experiments were conducted on MacBook Pro with Intel Core i7 and 16 GB of memory.

Table 1 shows the performance of our algorithm. The column 'Enum' shows the running time of enumerative search without state normalization. In that case, the average runtime was longer than 616 s, and three of the benchmarks timed out (>1 h). The column 'Base' reports the performance of our baseline algorithm with normalization. It shows that normalizing states succeeds to solve all benchmark problems and improves the speed by more than 3.7 times on average, although it degrades the speed for some cases due to normalization runtime overhead.

On top of 'Base', we applied our static-analysis-guided pruning technique (the column 'Ours'). The results show that our pruning technique is remarkably effective. It reduces the average time to 6.6 s, improving the speed of 'Base' by 25 times and the speed of 'Enum' by more than 93 times. We manually checked that all of the synthesized solutions are correct. We also found that all the solutions are quite intuitive and instructive as demonstrated in Sect. 2.

Table 1. Performance of SIMPL. ⊥ denotes timeout (>1 h). Assume ⊥ as 3,600 s for the average of 'Enum'.

	No	Description	Vars		Ints	Exs	Time (sec)		
			IVars	AVars			Enum	Base	Ours
Integer	1	Given n, return $n!$.	2	0	2	4	0.0	0.0	0.0
	2	Given n, return $n!!$.	3	0	3	4	0.0	0.0	0.0
	3	Given n, return $\sum_{i=1}^{n} i$.	3	0	2	4	0.1	0.0	0.0
	4	Given n, return $\sum_{i=1}^{n} i^2$.	4	0	2	3	122.4	18.1	0.3
	5	Given n, return $\prod_{i=1}^{n} i^2$.	4	0	2	3	102.9	13.6	0.2
	6	Given a and n, return a^n.	4	0	2	4	0.7	0.1	0.1
	7	Given n and m, return $\sum_{i=n}^{m} i$.	3	0	2	3	0.2	0.0	0.0
	8	Given n and m, return $\prod_{i=n}^{m} i$.	3	0	2	3	0.2	0.0	0.1
	9	Count the digits of an integer.	3	0	3	3	0.0	0.0	0.0
	10	Sum the digits of an integer.	3	0	3	4	5.2	2.2	1.3
	11	Find the product of each digit of an integer.	3	0	3	3	0.7	2.3	0.3
	12	Count the number of binary digit of an integer.	2	0	3	3	0.0	0.0	0.0
	13	Find the nth Fibonacci number.	3	0	3	4	98.7	13.9	2.6
	14	Given n, return $\sum_{i=1}^{n}(\sum_{m=1}^{i} m)$).	3	0	2	4	⊥	324.9	37.6
	15	Given n, return $\prod_{i=1}^{n}(\prod_{m=1}^{i} m)$).	3	0	2	4	⊥	316.6	86.9
	16	Reverse a given integer.	3	0	3	3	⊥	367.3	2.5
Array	17	Find the sum of all elements of an array.	3	1	2	2	8.1	3.6	0.9
	18	Find the product of all elements of an array.	3	1	2	2	7.6	3.9	0.9
	19	Sum two arrays of same length into one array.	3	2	2	2	44.6	29.9	0.2
	20	Multiply two arrays of same length into one array.	3	2	2	2	47.4	26.4	0.3
	21	Cube each element of an array.	3	1	1	2	1283.3	716.1	13.0
	22	Manipulate each element of an array into fourth power.	3	1	1	2	1265.8	715.5	13.0
	23	Find a maximum element.	3	1	2	2	0.9	0.7	0.4
	24	Find a minimum element.	3	1	2	2	0.8	0.3	0.1
	25	Add 1 to each element.	2	1	1	3	0.3	0.0	0.0
	26	Find the sum of square of each element.	3	1	2	2	2700.0	186.2	11.5
	27	Find the product of square of each element.	3	1	1	2	1709.8	1040.3	12.6
	28	Sum the products of matching elements of two arrays.	3	2	1	3	20.5	38.7	1.5
	29	Sum the absolute values of each element.	2	1	1	2	45.0	50.5	12.1
	30	Count the number of each element.	3	1	3	2	238.9	1094.1	0.2
		Average					> 616.8	165.5	6.6

6 Related Work

In this section, we broadly survey recent approaches in program synthesis. Most importantly, our work is different from existing program synthesis techniques in that we combine enumerative program synthesis with semantic-based static analysis.

Program Synthesis Techniques. We compare our algorithm with three most prevalent synthesis approaches: enumerative synthesis, version space algebra (VSA), and solver-aided method.

Enumerative synthesis has been widely used to synthesize recursive functional programs [2,8,9,24,26], API-completion [7,12,13,22,25], tree-structured data transformation [33], and regular expressions [21]. ESCHER [2] uses a heuristic goal-directed search to synthesize functional programs. Unlike ours, their algorithm finds smaller programs that partially satisfy given examples, and combines partial solutions with if-then-else statements. Although effective for recursive programs, it may cause overfitting in our case. In [7–9,12,13,22,24–26], type systems are used to exclude ill-typed programs from search space (i.e., type-directed synthesis). However, type-based pruning is not applicable to ours because enumerated terms are all well-typed. This is also the case for regular expression synthesis [21]. In λ^2 [8], deduction is also used in order to reject partial programs that are logically inconsistent with input-output examples. Feser et al. [8] designed a set of deduction rules for higher-order components such as `map` and `fold`. However, the deduction approach is not applicable to ours; it is completely nontrivial to design useful deduction rules for programming constructs such as while-loop and conditional. ALPHAREGEX [21] performs over- and under approximations on partial regular expressions to prune them when further search cannot produce any solutions. But those pruning techniques are specialized for regular expression synthesis. HADES [33] uses SMT solvers and decision tree learning to perform path transformations, but again it is not appropriate for imperative program synthesis. To sum up, we cannot use existing pruning techniques and in this paper we show that using static value analysis is a promising alternative for synthesizing imperative programs.

Many program synthesis approaches using version space algebra (VSA) have been proposed for string manipulation [10,17,23,27,32], number transformation [28], extracting data [4,20], and data filtering [31]. VSA is a kind of divide-and-conquer search strategy where a solution program is constructed by combining the solutions to sub-problems (e.g., some portions of the examples) in a top-down way. In contrast, we do not look for a sub-solution for each of the sub-problems, but instead in a bottom-up way, we find a total solution that satisfies all the examples at once.

Solver-aided methods have also been used many times to synthesize recursive functions [18], dynamic programming implementations [15], loop-free programs for bit-vector applications [11], and low-level missing details for programmers [29]. They use counter-example guided inductive synthesis (CEGIS) which iteratively refines the target concept from the counter-examples provided by SMT/SAT solver until the solution is verified by the solver. We use solvers to check the satisfiability of the symbolic constraints generated by the static analysis, not to refine the search space based on the counter-examples.

Additionally, DeepCoder [3] uses deep learning to guide search in program synthesis. In DeepCoder, a probabilistic distribution is learned to predict the presence or absence of each function in domain-specific languages. For example, given an input-output list $[-17, -3, 4, 11] \mapsto [-12, -68]$, DeepCoder learns that a list-filtering function is likely to be involved in the resulting program, since the number of elements in the input list is reduced. This idea of learning to rank programs is orthogonal to our approach. In [16], model checking was applied to guide genetic algorithm. Katz and Peled used model checking in computing fitness function, which computes fitness score of each candidate. Essentially, however, the genetic algorithm does not guarantee finding a solution unlike enumerative synthesis approach.

Imperative Program Synthesis. There has been little work on imperative program synthesis. In 2003, Lau et al. [19] proposed an approach to learning programs in a subset of imperative Python using version space algebra. However, the system requires a value trace for each program point as input (i.e., programming by demonstration), which is unrealistic to be used. In 2005, Colón [5] presented a schema-guided synthesis of imperative programs from pre- and post condition that compute polynomial functions where the programs can only be generated from a collection of available schemas, which has an inherent disadvantage of incompleteness. In 2006, Ireland et al. [14] proposed an approach to constructing imperative programs from logical assertions by leveraging theorem proving technique. We believe that it is a good direction to use theorem proving techniques with lightweight logical specifications as inputs for future work in order to synthesize more complicated programs. In 2010, Srivastava et al. [30], the most recent work on imperative program synthesis to the best of our knowledge, presented a view that treats a synthesis problem as verification problem. The researchers showed that they can synthesize complex tasks such as sorting and dynamic programming. Although inspiring, their system's ability is limited to underlying program verifiers that solve given synthesis conditions, thus more efficient verifiers need to be developed first in order to deal with more complicated synthesis tasks.

7 Conclusion

In this paper, we have shown that combining enumerative synthesis with static analysis is a promising way of synthesizing imperative programs. The enumerative search allows us to find the smallest possible, therefore general, program while the semantic-based static analysis dramatically accelerates the search in a safe way. We demonstrated the effectiveness on 30 introductory programming problems gathered from online forums.

Acknowledgements. We appreciate the anonymous reviewers for their helpful comments. This work was supported by Institute for Information & communications Technology Promotion (IITP) grant funded by the Korea government (MSIP) (No. 2017-0-00184, Self-Learning Cyber Immune Technology Development) This research was also supported by Basic Science Research Program through the National Research Foundation of Korea (NRF) funded by the Ministry of Science, ICT & Future Planning (NRF-2016R1C1B2014062).

References

1. Aho, A.V., Sethi, R., Ullman, J.D.: Compilers: Principles, Techniques, and Tools. Addison-Wesley Longman Publishing Co. Inc., Boston (1986)
2. Albarghouthi, A., Gulwani, S., Kincaid, Z.: Recursive program synthesis. In: Sharygina, N., Veith, H. (eds.) CAV 2013. LNCS, vol. 8044, pp. 934–950. Springer, Heidelberg (2013). doi:10.1007/978-3-642-39799-8_67
3. Balog, M., Gaunt, A.L., Brockschmidt, M., Nowozin, S., Tarlow, D.: Deepcoder: learning to write programs. In: ICLR (2017)
4. Barowy, D.W., Gulwani, S., Hart, T., Zorn, B.: Flashrelate: extracting relational data from semi-structured spreadsheets using examples. In: PLDI (2015)
5. Colón, M.A.: Schema-guided synthesis of imperative programs by constraint solving. In: Etalle, S. (ed.) LOPSTR 2004. LNCS, vol. 3573, pp. 166–181. Springer, Heidelberg (2005). doi:10.1007/11506676_11
6. Cousot, P., Cousot, R.: Abstract interpretation: a unified lattice model for static analysis of programs by construction or approximation of fixpoints. In: POPL (1977)
7. Feng, Y., Martins, R., Wang, Y., Dillig, I., Reps, T.W.: Component-based synthesis for complex APIs. In: POPL (2017)
8. Feser, J.K., Chaudhuri, S., Dillig, I.: Synthesizing data structure transformations from input-output examples. In: PLDI (2015)
9. Frankle, J., Osera, P.-M., Walker, D., Zdancewic, S.: Example-directed synthesis: a type-theoretic interpretation. In: POPL (2016)
10. Gulwani, S.: Automating string processing in spreadsheets using input-output examples. In: POPL (2011)
11. Gulwani, S., Jha, S., Tiwari, A., Venkatesan, R.: Synthesis of loop-free programs. In: PLDI (2011)
12. Gvero, T., Kuncak, V., Kuraj, I., Piskac, R.: Complete completion using types and weights. In: PLDI (2013)
13. Gvero, T., Kuncak, V., Piskac, R.: Interactive synthesis of code snippets. In: Gopalakrishnan, G., Qadeer, S. (eds.) CAV 2011. LNCS, vol. 6806, pp. 418–423. Springer, Heidelberg (2011). doi:10.1007/978-3-642-22110-1_33
14. Ireland, A., Stark, J.: Combining proof plans with partial order planning for imperative program synthesis. Autom. Softw. Eng. **13**(1), 65–105 (2006)
15. Itzhaky, S., Singh, R., Solar-Lezama, A., Yessenov, K., Lu, Y., Leiserson, C., Chowdhury, R.: Deriving divide-and-conquer dynamic programming algorithms using solver-aided transformations. In: OOPSLA (2016)
16. Katz, G., Peled, D.: Synthesizing, correcting and improving code, using model checking-based genetic programming. In: Bertacco, V., Legay, A. (eds.) HVC 2013. LNCS, vol. 8244, pp. 246–261. Springer, Cham (2013). doi:10.1007/978-3-319-03077-7_17
17. Kini, D., Gulwani, S.: Flashnormalize: programming by examples for text normalization. In: IJCAI (2015)
18. Kneuss, E., Kuraj, I., Kuncak, V., Suter, P.: Synthesis modulo recursive functions. In: OOPSLA (2013)
19. Lau, T., Domingos, P., Weld, D.S.: Learning programs from traces using version space algebra. In: K-CAP (2003)
20. Le, V., Gulwani, S.: Flashextract: a framework for data extraction by examples. In: PLDI (2014)

21. Lee, M., So, S., Oh, H.: Synthesizing regular expressions from examples for introductory automata assignments. In: GPCE (2016)
22. Mandelin, D., Xu, L., Bodík, R., Kimelman, D.: Jungloid mining: helping to navigate the API jungle. In: PLDI (2005)
23. Manshadi, M., Gildea, D., Allen, J.: Integrating programming by example and natural language programming. In: AAAI (2013)
24. Osera, P.-M., Zdancewic, S.: Type-and-example-directed program synthesis. In: PLDI (2015)
25. Perelman, D., Gulwani, S., Ball, T., Grossman, D.: Type-directed completion of partial expressions. In: PLDI (2012)
26. Polikarpova, N., Kuraj, I., Solar-Lezama, A.: Program synthesis from polymorphic refinement types. In: PLDI (2016)
27. Raza, M., Gulwani, S., Milic-Frayling, N.: Compositional program synthesis from natural language and examples. In: IJCAI (2015)
28. Singh, R., Gulwani, S.: Synthesizing number transformations from input-output examples. In: Madhusudan, P., Seshia, S.A. (eds.) CAV 2012. LNCS, vol. 7358, pp. 634–651. Springer, Heidelberg (2012). doi:10.1007/978-3-642-31424-7_44
29. Solar-Lezama, A.: Program synthesis by sketching. Ph.D. thesis, Berkeley, CA, USA (2008)
30. Srivastava, S., Gulwani, S., Foster, J.S.: From program verification to program synthesis. In: POPL (2010)
31. Wang, X., Gulwani, S., Singh, R.: FIDEX: filtering spreadsheet data using examples. In: OOPSLA (2016)
32. Wu, B., Knoblock, C.A.: An iterative approach to synthesize data transformation programs. In: IJCAI (2015)
33. Yaghmazadeh, N., Klinger, C., Dillig, I., Chaudhuri, S.: Synthesizing transformations on hierarchically structured data. In: PLDI (2016)

A Gradual Interpretation of Union Types

Matías Toro(✉) and Éric Tanter

PLEIAD Laboratory, Computer Science Department (DCC),
University of Chile, Santiago, Chile
{mtoro,etanter}@dcc.uchile.cl

Abstract. Union types allow to capture the possibility of a term to be of several possibly unrelated types. Traditional static approaches to union types are untagged and tagged unions, which present dual advantages in their use. Inspired by recent work on using abstract interpretation to understand gradual typing, we present a novel design for union types, called gradual union types. Gradual union types combine the advantages of tagged and untagged union types, backed by dynamic checks. Seen as a gradual typing discipline, gradual union types are restricted imprecise types that denote a finite number of static types. We apply the Abstracting Gradual Typing (AGT) methodology of Garcia et al. to derive the static and dynamic semantics of a language that supports both gradual unions and the traditional, totally-unknown type. We uncover that gradual unions interact with the unknown type in a way that mandates a stratified approach to AGT, relying on a composition of two distinct abstract interpretations in order to retain optimality. Thanks to the abstract interpretation framework, the resulting language is type safe and satisfies the refined criteria for gradual languages. We also show how to compile such a language to a threesome cast calculus, and prove that the compilation preserves the semantics and properties of the language.

1 Introduction

Gradual typing originated as an approach to smoothly combine static and dynamic type checking within the same programming language [29]. Over the years, gradual typing has been applied to languages with more advanced features, such as objects [26], polymorphism [2], and type inference [13] among others. Gradual typing has also been developed beyond the original static/dynamic typing dualistic view to accommodate the integration of static typing disciplines of different strengths, such as information-flow typing [10], effects [3], and logical refinements [21].

Recently, Garcia et al. [14] identified that the general framework of Abstract Interpretation (AI) [9] can be applied, *at the type level*, to lay down solid foundations of gradual typing in its various forms, thereby justifying several design

M. Toro—Funded by CONICYT-PCHA/Doctorado Nacional/2015-21150510.
É. Tanter—Partially funded by FONDECYT Project 1150017.

F. Ranzato (Ed.): SAS 2017, LNCS 10422, pp. 382–404, 2017.
DOI: 10.1007/978-3-319-66706-5_19

decisions and criteria that were originally discovered and refined by trial-and-error. In essence, the Abstracting Gradual Typing approach (AGT for short) conceives of gradual types as abstracting (in the AI sense) a set of possible static types. Exploiting an underlying Galois connection, one can systematically derive a gradually-typed language that is crisply connected to the original static discipline, and satisfies a number of essential criteria for such languages [30].

Stepping back, AGT reinforces an even broader interpretation of gradual typing: that of soundly dealing with *imprecision* at the type level. Indeed, one can see dynamically-typed languages as languages with highly-imprecise static type information, and the original gradually-typed languages as allowing to reason about partial type information. For instance, consider a function f of gradual type $\mathsf{Int} \rightarrow ?$; this type is imprecise in that it does not provide any information about the values returned by f, but it does specify precisely that f is a function, which furthermore expects an integer argument. Therefore, the gradual language can statically reject $f + 1$ or $f(\mathsf{true})$, accept $f(1)$, and optimistically accept $f(1) + 2$ subject to a *dynamic check* that the value of $f(1)$ is indeed an integer. Similarly, integrating a simply-typed language with gradual support for effects [3] can be viewed as dealing with imprecision of effect information.

Inspired by this focus on imprecision, we observe that standard static type systems have long been proposed to deal with a basic form of imprecision: the possibility for a value to be of several, possibly-unrelated types. In the literature, two approaches have been developed to safely, and fully statically, deal with the possibility of an expression to have possibly different types: *disjoint (or tagged) union types*, such as sum types $T_1 + T_2$ and variant types, and *untagged union types*, usually noted $T_1 \vee T_2$ [23]. Both forms of union types have complementary pros and cons when viewed from a pragmatic angle.

The understanding of both gradual types and union types as different ways to deal with imprecision at the type level suggests a novel, *gradual* interpretation of union types. Following the abstract interpretation of gradual types put forth in AGT, a *gradual union* $T_1 \oplus T_2$ is a gradual type that abstracts both T_1 and T_2. Seen in this light, a gradual union is a gradual type that is more precise than the prototypical, fully-unknown, gradual type ?, which abstracts any possible type. Starting from this insight, systematically applying the AGT methodology yields a novel point in the design space of both union types and gradual types.

Adding gradual unions to a simply-typed language relaxes the typing discipline, but does not allow full dynamic type checking. To achieve this, one needs to include both the unknown type ? and gradual unions. A second contribution of this paper is to uncover that combining these two gradual type constructors in the same language demands a stratified approach to AGT, in which the semantics of gradual types comes from the *composition* of two distinct abstract interpretations.

Contributions. This article makes the following specific contributions:

- **A novel design of union types** that combines benefits of both tagged and untagged unions, with added static flexibility backed by runtime checks. Compared to a standard gradually-typed language with only the totally-unknown

type ?, the resulting design is stricter, allowing more blatantly wrong programs to be statically rejected.
- **A first example of a stratified approach to AGT.** To derive the static semantics of a gradual language, AGT requires a Galois connection between gradual types and sets of static types, which then guides the lifting of functions and predicates on static types to their gradual counterparts [14]. We observe that applying AGT directly to introduce both the unknown type and gradual unions breaks optimality of the abstraction, thereby weakening the meaning of type information, both statically and dynamically. To address this, we develop a *stratified* approach that allows us to recover optimality. More specifically, we first apply AGT to support only the unknown type, and lift this Galois connection and derived liftings to their powerset counterpart. We then apply AGT once more with another Galois connection to introduce support for gradual unions, which allows us to define liftings based on the previously-defined powerset liftings. We prove that the composed abstraction is optimal. We conjecture that this technique might prove helpful in integrating other gradualization efforts.
- **The formalization and meta-theory of the proposed language**, including type safety and the gradual guarantees of Siek et al. [30]; these results follow directly, by construction, from relying on the AGT methodology.
- **A compilation scheme to an internal language with threesomes**, a space-efficient representation for casts [28]. We prove the correctness of the compilation with respect to the reference semantics derived by AGT using logical relations; this is the first case of formally relating the reference dynamic semantics obtained by AGT with a cast insertion translation.

Structure. Section 2 briefly reviews tagged and untagged unions, highlighting their pros and cons, and then informally introduces gradual unions, comparing them with standard gradual types and with the other kinds of unions, including those supported by several recent languages such as Flow and TypeScript, among others. Section 3 describes the static semantics of GTFL$^{\oplus}$, a language with both gradual unions and the unknown type, using the Abstracting Gradual Typing methodology. Section 4 describes the runtime semantics of the language by translation to a threesome cast calculus, and gives the formal properties of the language. Section 5 discusses related work and Sect. 6 concludes.

Complete definitions, as well as the proofs of all the results stated in the paper, can be found in the companion technical report [33]. A prototype implementation is available online, showing interactive typing and reduction derivations for arbitrary source programs: http://pleiad.cl/gradual-unions/.

2 Background and Motivation

We first briefly review standard tagged and untagged union types [23], highlighting the tradeoffs associated with each approach, and then introduce gradual union types as a novel point in the design space. We compare gradual unions to other approaches to union types, including practical languages with unions supported by runtime type tests. Finally, we compare gradual unions with the standard gradual types introduced by Siek and Taha [29].

2.1 Tagged Unions

Tagged unions, also called *disjoint* union types, denote values of possibly different types. The "disjointness" of the union comes from the fact that elements must be explicitly *tagged* so that it is clear to which type an element belongs. Tagging allows type-safe disambiguation through a case analysis construct.

The simplest form of tagged unions are binary *sum types*, noted $T_1 + T_2$, with injection forms inl and inr, and a disambiguation case expression. For instance, inl 10 :: Int + Bool injects the integer 10 into the sum type Int + Bool. The tag inl denotes the *left* part of the sum. Similarly, inr true :: Int + Bool injects true to the right of the sum. Note that the ascription :: is necessary to maintain a simple syntax-directed type system; different techniques can be used to alleviate notation for programmers [23].

Given a value of type Int + Bool, one cannot use it directly. For instance, λx : Int + Bool.$x + 1$ is not well typed. To use a tagged value, one must first disambiguate through an explicit case analysis, considering each tag explicitly, *e.g.* λx : Int + Bool.case x of inl $x \Rightarrow x + 1$ | inr $x \Rightarrow$ if x then 1 else 0.

Note that Int + Bool is different from Bool + Int because the injection tag is relative to the *position* in the sum type. Sums can be generalized to *variants*, which are n-ary sums with custom labels instead of the positional inl and inr tags. In the case of variants, a type-case construct similar to case forces programmers to consider all possible alternatives, thereby statically ensuring the absence of runtime type errors.

To deal with with values of statically-unknown types, several proposals add a type Dynamic whose values are pairs of a plain value and a type tag [1,16]. The type Dynamic is therefore akin to an infinite tagged union, where tags are types. Disambiguation through case analysis therefore requires a default branch to handle unconsidered alternatives generally.

This general approach also explains how several languages support union types without needing any explicit tagging operation. For instance, in safe dynamic languages, all values are readily tagged with their *class* (either in the sense of Harper [15], *e.g.* Int, Bool, Function, or, for class-based object-oriented languages, their actual class). This allows disambiguation of unions through runtime type testing (either via a type-case analysis or casts that can fail). This approach is exploited in several retrofitted type systems such as TypeScript [8], Flow [11] and Typed Racket [31,32]. Explicit disambiguation of unions can also be supported through pattern matching, as in ℂDuce [5] and Dotty [25].

2.2 Untagged Unions

An untagged union, noted $T_1 \vee T_2$, denotes the union of the values of type T_1 and of type T_2, without any tagging mechanism to support disambiguation. In this set-theoretic interpretation [4,12,22], $\mathsf{Int} \vee \mathsf{Int}$ is the same type as Int; and a value of type T_1 is a value of type $T_1 \vee T_2$, without any injection construct.

Untagged unions can be used to allow the branches of conditionals to have unrelated types: for instance, the function $\lambda x : \mathsf{Bool}.\mathsf{if}\ x\ \mathsf{then}\ 1\ \mathsf{else}\ \mathsf{false}$ can be considered well-typed at $\mathsf{Bool} \rightarrow \mathsf{Int} \vee \mathsf{Bool}$. This is the approach followed by the ℂDuce programming language [5], for instance.

Automatically introducing imprecision through untagged unions can however lead to unwanted programs being accepted. An alternative approach is for the typing rule for conditional expressions to require both branches to be of the same type, and to expect the programmer to use an explicit type *ascription* to specify that imprecision is desired; *e.g.* $\lambda x : \mathsf{Bool}.\mathsf{if}\ x\ \mathsf{then}\ (1 :: \mathsf{Int} \vee \mathsf{Bool})\ \mathsf{else}\ \mathsf{false}$. Note that the ascription does *not* imply any runtime tagging; it is a purely static artifact. Also, because of the set-theoretic interpretation of types, it is sufficient to ascribe imprecision in one of the two branches.

Untagged unions have no projection construct either; the only safe operations on a value of type $T_1 \vee T_2$ are those that are supported by *both* T_1 and T_2. Note that this makes untagged union restrictive to *use*; for instance, nothing useful can be done with a value of type $\mathsf{Int} \vee \mathsf{Bool}$. For instance, $\lambda x : \mathsf{Int} \vee \mathsf{Bool}.x + 1$ is not well-typed, because x could be a boolean value; and there is no disambiguation expression like case to handle each alternative separately.

This does not mean that untagged unions are useless; for instance, if the language has records, then it is safe to access fields that are common to both types. As noted by Pierce [23], untagged unions have traditionally been much more frequent in program analysis than in programming languages, where they were mostly used in type systems for semi-structured data [6,18], before being generalized in ℂDuce. Finally, note that the C language supports *unsafe* untagged unions, allowing programmers to use operations that are supported by *either* T_1 or T_2, at their own risk!

2.3 Gradual Unions

Tagged and untagged unions are the only safe approaches to *statically* deal with imprecision: either explicitly tag the imprecision so as to be able to safely discriminate later on, or assume the loss of precision and restrict what can be done with imprecisely-typed values. Tagged unions have the benefit of allowing programmers to fully use values, but only after explicit case-based disambiguations. Untagged unions have the benefit of requiring neither explicit injection nor projection, but only allow restricted usage of values.

If we are willing to accept some form of dynamic checking errors, however, we can combine the benefits of both tagged and untagged unions by viewing a union type as a kind of *gradual* type: $T_1 \oplus T_2$ is a gradual type that represents both T_1 and T_2. A gradual union supports the same kind of optimistic static checking that standard gradual typing provides.

For instance, $f \triangleq \lambda x : \mathsf{Int} \oplus \mathsf{Bool}.x + 1$ is (optimistically) well typed, because x might possibly be an Int, without any explicit projection or case analysis. The expressions $f\ 1$ and $f\ \mathsf{true}$ are also well-typed because injection to a gradual union is implicit. The expression $f\ 1$ evaluates to 2, as expected. But because x might in fact be a Bool, a runtime check is implicitly introduced before applying the + operator: hence the expression f true produces a runtime cast error.

As a gradual type, a gradual union allows clearly incorrect programs to be rejected statically. For instance, changing the body of f to $x\ 1$ is statically rejected, because x cannot possibly be a function. Similarly, f "hola" is statically rejected, because f only tolerates integer or boolean arguments.

Note that compared to untagged unions, the use of a value with a gradual union type $T_1 \oplus T_2$ is accepted if the operations make sense for *either* T_1 *or* T_2 (and not both). This is just like untagged unions in C, but backed by runtime checks to ensure type safety. Injecting values into a gradual union type can be done implicitly as when applying g in the example above, or using an ascription, *e.g.* $g \triangleq \lambda x$: Bool.if x then (1::Int $\oplus$ Bool) else (false::Int $\oplus$ Bool) has type Bool $\rightarrow$ Int $\oplus$ Bool.[1]

2.4 Comparing Unions

We summarize the characteristics of each form of union types as follows:

	injection	projection	use
Tagged unions			
sums	explicit	explicit	full
type tests/casts	implicit	explicit	full
Untagged unions	none	none	restricted
Gradual unions	implicit	implicit	full

To illustrate the convenience of gradual unions compared to alternative approaches, consider the following simple program:

```
let x: Bool ⊕ Int ⊕ String = 10
(λx: Int ⊕ Bool. x+1) x
```

The program introduces a variable x that can be one of three types, and initializes it to the number 10. It then passes it as argument to a lambda that expects either an Int or a Bool, and adds 1 to it. This program is well-typed, and returns 11. If x is initialized with a string, the program fails at runtime before the application of the function; if it is initialized with a boolean, the runtime error occurs before the addition.

This example would not be well-typed with untagged unions. This is because the intersection of Int and Bool and String is empty. If all three types have a common method, say `toString`, then the body of the lambda can only safely invoke `x.toString()`.

Turning to tagged unions, using standard sum types, the equivalent program would be fairly cumbersome to write because all injections and projections have to be manually introduced by the programmer, and deal with exact positions:

[1] Similarly to untagged unions, one could design a language whose conditional expression implicitly introduces imprecision, without the need for any ascription (Sect. 2.2); we do not further consider this possible design and use ascriptions explicitly.

```
let x: Bool + (Int + String) = inr inl 10
let x2: Int + Bool = case x of
  | inl y => inr y
  | inr y => case y of
             | inl z => inl z
             | inr z => throw new Error("not␣an␣Int␣or␣Bool")
(λx: Int + Bool. case x of
                 | inl y => y + 1
                 | inr y => throw new Error("not␣an␣Int")) x2
```

Note the need for an explicit intermediate step (x2) to safely go from the ternary union to the binary union.

The same program can also be written using implicitly-tagged unions with type-test disambiguation. As expected, the code is more lightweight than with sums thanks to implicit injection. For instance, in Flow:

```
1 const x: boolean | number | string = 10
2 const foo = (x: number | boolean ): number => {
3     if(typeof x =="number") return x + 1
4     else throw new Error("not␣a␣number")
5 }
6 if(typeof x =="boolean"|| typeof x =="number") foo(x)
7 else throw new Error("not␣a␣boolean␣or␣number")
```

Note that projections must be realized manually via `typeof` (lines 3, 4, 6 and 7).

Evolving precision. The advantage of gradual unions does not only lie in the simplicity and compactness of the program definition. It also lies in its robustness in the face of precision-related changes. For instance, suppose that as the software matures, the programmer is now convinced that `x` will always be initialized with a number and that the function can simply only accept numbers. With sums, the program is so fragile that it would need to be modified at every injection and projection point to account for this change in precision. The Flow version would still run as is, but would feature a lot of dead code. Further decreasing precision would require adding checks at various projection points. With gradual unions, *it is enough to adjust the type annotations*—the rest of the program is unchanged!

The fact that the static-to-dynamic spectrum is navigated solely through the precision of type annotations, without requiring further modification of the program, is a key asset of gradual typing in general. The gradual guarantee of Siek et al. [30] further characterizes the relation between the static and dynamic semantics of programs that only differ in the precision of their type annotations, and will be discussed further when addressing the meta-theory of GTFL$^{\oplus}$.

Higher-order types. Finally, a major limitation of projections from unions using explicit type tests is that they do not support higher-order types. For instance, because one cannot decide whether an arbitrary function (*e.g.* of tag/class Function) always behave as a function of a particular type, programmers have to manually wrap functions with pre-post type checks.

Consider, in Flow or TypeScript, two functions of the following types:

```
f: (number | boolean) => (number | boolean)
g: ((number | string) => (boolean | string)) => string
```

To safely support the application `g(f)`, one needs to explicitly wrap `f` as follows:

```
const wrapper = (x: number | string): string | boolean =>{
    if (typeof x ==="number") {
        const result = f(x)
        if (typeof result ==="boolean") return result
        else throw new Error("not␣a␣boolean")
    } else throw new Error("not␣a␣number")
}
```

and then pass the wrapped function as argument: `g(wrapper)`.

Conversely, with gradual unions, one can simply write:

```
let f: (Int ⊕ Bool) -> (Int ⊕ Bool) = ...
let g: ((Int ⊕ String) -> (Bool ⊕ String)) -> String = ...
g(f)
```

for the exact same behavior; all the necessary checks and wrappers are handled under the hood.

2.5 Gradual Unions vs. Standard Gradual Types

Gradual typing has always been formulated in terms of an unknown type, frequently written ?, which denotes any possible type [29]. Furthermore, when structural types are supported, gradual types can be more precise than the fully-unknown type: for instance $\mathsf{Int} \rightarrow ?$ denotes all function types from Int to possibly any type.

To illustrate the key difference between gradual unions and standard gradual types, consider a function h that always returns either an Int or a Bool. Starting from a simple typing discipline, with standard gradual types, the most precise type one can give to h is $\mathsf{Bool} \rightarrow ?$. However, this type allows for too much flexibility that was not intended: because h true has type ?, it can subsequently be used in any context, even (h true) 1, which is clearly always going to fail since h never returns a function. The problem comes form the fact that the gradual type used for the codomain of h, ?, is too imprecise—yet it is the only available type to denote both Int and Bool. Hence, the programmer cannot express a more restricted form of flexibility. Gradual unions address this need. For instance, recalling function g from Sect. 2.3 above, (g true) 1 is statically rejected.

Gradual union types are a novel way to relax a static typing discipline in a restricted manner. While the discussion above insists on the advantages of this restricted flexibility, it necessarily presents drawbacks as well. In particular, a language with only gradual unions cannot fully embed the untyped lambda calculus. In order to get the best of both worlds, one needs a language that supports both the fully-unknown gradual type ? in addition to gradual unions. This way, programmers can navigate the full static-to-dynamic spectrum, with more interesting intermediate points offered by gradual unions. In the rest of this paper, we design and formalize such a language.

3 GTFL$^{\oplus}$: Static Semantics

We now formalize GTFL$^{\oplus}$, a gradual language with both gradual unions and the unknown type. As hinted previously, we follow the Abstracting Gradual Typing (AGT) methodology [14] to derive the static semantics of GTFL$^{\oplus}$:

1. We start from a language with a fully static typing discipline, STFL.
2. We define the syntax of gradual types, and give them meaning via a concretization function and its corresponding most precise abstraction, forming a Galois connection. Crucially, in this step we realize that the two forms of gradual types must be handled in a stratified manner in order to ensure optimality.
3. We derive the static semantics of the gradual language by lifting type predicates and type functions used in the static type system through the Galois connection.

The most novel part of our development are steps 2 and 3, which showcase how to compose Galois connections related to different gradual type constructors. We address the dynamic semantics of GTFL$^{\oplus}$ to Sect. 4.

3.1 The Static Language: STFL

Our starting point is a simply-typed functional language with booleans and integers, called STFL [14]. A term can be a lambda abstraction, a boolean, a number, a variable, an application, an addition, a conditional, or an ascription. The typing rules are standard—omitted for space reasons, available in [33]—save for the fact that their presentation follows some simple conventions, helpful for gradualization [14]: the type of each sub-expression is kept opaque, the type relations (=) are made explicit as side conditions, and partial type functions (*dom*, *cod*, *equate*) are used explicitly instead of relying on matching metavariables. The dynamic semantics and type safety of STFL are completely standard.

3.2 Defining Gradual Types Separately

GTFL$^{\oplus}$ supports both the unknown type ? and gradual unions with $\oplus$. In this section, we look at both gradual type constructors separately in order to precisely define their meaning. Recall that following AGT, the *meaning* of a gradual type is the set of static types that it possibly represents, defined by a concretization function γ. Given such a meaning, the AGT methodology directs us to define a sound and optimal abstraction function α, hence forming a Galois connection [14], which is then used to lift static type predicates and type functions to operate on gradual types. We study both gradual type constructors in turn.

Let us first recall from [14] the Galois connection for gradual types made up with the (nullary constructor) ?, here denoted GTYPE.

$$G \in \text{GTYPE}$$
$$G ::= \; ? \mid \mathsf{Bool} \mid \mathsf{Int} \mid G \rightarrow G$$

The meaning of these gradual types is standard, and defined through concretization by Garcia et al. [14] as follows:

Definition 1 (GType Concretization). $\gamma_? : \text{GTYPE} \rightarrow \mathcal{P}(\text{TYPE})$

$$\gamma_?(\mathsf{Int}) = \{\, \mathsf{Int} \,\} \qquad \gamma_?(\mathsf{Bool}) = \{\, \mathsf{Bool} \,\} \qquad \gamma_?(?) = \text{TYPE}$$

$$\gamma_?(G_1 \rightarrow G_2) = \{\, T_1 \rightarrow T_2 \mid T_1 \in \gamma_?(G_1) \wedge T_2 \in \gamma_?(G_2) \,\}$$

Note in particular that the meaning of the fully unknown type ? is the set of all types. Similarly, the meaning of the imprecise type $\mathsf{Int} \rightarrow ?$ is the set of all function types $\mathsf{Int} \rightarrow T$, for any $T \in \text{TYPE}$.

Concretization naturally induces the notion of *precision* among gradual types, which reflects the amount of static information of a gradual type [14].

Definition 2 (GType Precision). *G_1 is less imprecise than G_2, notation $G_1 \sqsubseteq G_2$, if and only if $\gamma_?(G_1) \subseteq \gamma_?(G_2)$.*

The following abstraction $\alpha_?$ naturally forms a Galois connection with $\gamma_?$:[2]

Definition 3 (GType Abstraction). $\alpha_? : \mathcal{P}(\text{TYPE}) \rightharpoonup \text{GTYPE}$

$$\alpha_?(\{\, T \,\}) = T \qquad \alpha_?(T_1 \rightarrow T_2) = \alpha_?(T_1) \rightarrow \alpha_?(T_2) \qquad \alpha_?(\emptyset) = \textit{undefined}$$

$$\alpha_?(T) = ? \; \textit{otherwise}$$

The abstraction retains as much precision as possible (*e.g.* singletons, function type constructor) and degrades to the unknown type otherwise. Note that $\alpha_?$ is undefined for the empty set [14].

Importantly, $\gamma_?$ and $\alpha_?$ form a Galois connection:

Proposition 1 ($\alpha_?$ is Sound and Optimal). *If T is not empty, then*

$$(a)\; T \subseteq \gamma_?(\alpha_?(T)). \qquad (b)\; T \subseteq \gamma_?(G) \Rightarrow \alpha_?(T) \sqsubseteq G.$$

Soundness (a) means that α always produces a gradual type whose concretization overapproximates the information in the original set. Optimality (b) means that α is the best sound approximation function: it produces the most precise gradual type that abstracts a given set.

---

[2] We use the hat notation X to refer to a set of elements X (*e.g.* T is a set of static types, and T is a set of sets of static types).

Let us now consider a Galois connection for the novel gradual type constructor introduced in this work, gradual unions. We use STYPE to denote gradual types made up only of gradual unions, *i.e.* without ?.

$$S \in \text{STYPE}$$
$$S ::= S \oplus S \mid \mathsf{Bool} \mid \mathsf{Int} \mid S \rightarrow S$$

Note that this syntax admits n-ary unions recursively through $S \oplus S$. We consider gradual unions to be *syntactically* equivalent up to associativity of $\oplus$, *i.e.* $S_1 \oplus (S_2 \oplus S_3) \equiv (S_1 \oplus S_2) \oplus S_3$. Gradual unions represent the *finite* set of types represented (recursively) by each constituent:

Definition 4 (SType Concretization). $\gamma_{\oplus} : \text{STYPE} \rightarrow \mathcal{P}_{fin}(\text{TYPE})$

$$\gamma_{\oplus}(\mathsf{Int}) = \{\,\mathsf{Int}\,\} \qquad \gamma_{\oplus}(\mathsf{Bool}) = \{\,\mathsf{Bool}\,\} \qquad \gamma_{\oplus}(S_1 \oplus S_2) = \gamma_{\oplus}(S_1) \cup \gamma_{\oplus}(S_2)$$

$$\gamma_{\oplus}(S_1 \rightarrow S_2) = \{\, T_1 \rightarrow T_2 \mid T_1 \in \gamma_{\oplus}(S_1) \wedge T_2 \in \gamma_{\oplus}(S_2)\,\}$$

For instance $\gamma_{\oplus}(\mathsf{Int} \oplus \mathsf{Bool} \oplus (\mathsf{Int} \rightarrow \mathsf{Bool})) = \{\,\mathsf{Int}, \mathsf{Bool}, \mathsf{Int} \rightarrow \mathsf{Bool}\,\}$. Because gradual unions only produce finite sets of static types, the corresponding abstraction also only needs to be defined on finite sets, and therefore can produce the gradual union with all the elements, noted $\oplus T$:

Definition 5 (SType Abstraction). $\alpha_{\oplus} : \mathcal{P}_{fin}(\text{TYPE}) \rightharpoonup \text{STYPE}$

$$\alpha_{\oplus}(T) = \oplus T \qquad if\, T \neq \emptyset$$

Here again, $\langle \gamma_{\oplus}, \alpha_{\oplus} \rangle$ forms a Galois connection.

3.3 Combining Gradual Types: Take 1

Now that we have defined the meaning of gradual types formed with the unknown type ?, as well as the meaning of gradual types formed with gradual unions $\oplus$, we turn to defining the meaning of gradual types in GTFL$^{\oplus}$, which combine both constructors, denoted UTYPE:

$$U \in \text{UTYPE}$$
$$U ::= \;?\; \mid U \oplus U \mid \mathsf{Bool} \mid \mathsf{Int} \mid U \rightarrow U \quad \text{(gradual types)}$$

A first seemingly natural approach is to define the concretization function for UTYPE by combining both concretization functions for GTYPE and STYPE:

Definition 6 (UType Concretization, Take 1). $\gamma : \text{UTYPE} \rightarrow \mathcal{P}(\text{TYPE})$

$$\gamma(\mathsf{Int}) = \{\,\mathsf{Int}\,\} \qquad \gamma(\mathsf{Bool}) = \{\,\mathsf{Bool}\,\} \qquad \gamma(U_1 \oplus U_2) = \gamma(U_1) \cup \gamma(U_2)$$

$$\gamma(?) = \text{TYPE} \qquad \gamma(U_1 \rightarrow U_2) = \{\, T_1 \rightarrow T_2 \mid T_1 \in \gamma(U_1) \wedge T_2 \in \gamma(U_2)\,\}$$

While this definition seems sensible, it does not accommodate a corresponding optimal abstraction. Indeed, the abstraction functions for GType and SType conflict with each other: how should we abstract a set of different types?

For a set of base types, say $\{\,\mathsf{Int}, \mathsf{Bool}\,\}$, we can either abstract to ? or to $\mathsf{Int} \oplus \mathsf{Bool}$; the latter being optimal, while the former is not. In fact, to preserve optimality, we ought to defer to the unknown type only for heterogeneous *infinite* sets. Even if we would adjust the definition of the combined abstraction to make such a distinction, it would not be optimal. To see why, consider the type $(? \to \mathsf{Int}) \oplus (\mathsf{Int} \to ?)$, whose concretization is:

$$\begin{aligned}\gamma((? \to \mathsf{Int}) \oplus (\mathsf{Int} \to ?)) &= \gamma(? \to \mathsf{Int}) \cup \gamma(\mathsf{Int} \to ?)\\ &= \{\, T \to \mathsf{Int} \mid T \in \textsc{Type}\,\} \cup \{\, \mathsf{Int} \to T \mid T \in \textsc{Type}\,\}\\ &= \{\, \mathsf{Int} \to \mathsf{Int}, \mathsf{Bool} \to \mathsf{Int}, \mathsf{Int} \to \mathsf{Bool}, \ldots\,\}\\ &\triangleq T\end{aligned}$$

By taking the union of both sets, we "forget" a specificity of the original gradual type—namely that it only represents functions that necessarily have Int either as domain or as codomain. For instance, $\mathsf{Bool} \to \mathsf{Bool}$ is *not* present in the resulting set T. However, the abstraction function that we obtain by directly combining the two abstractions we have seen above is unable to recover an optimal gradual type: because T is infinite and only contains arrow types, the best the abstraction can do is to keep the arrow constructor, and then separately abstracts the domain and codomain types (just like $\alpha_?$). As a result:

$$\alpha(T) = ? \to ?$$

While this abstraction is sound, it is not optimal: there exists a more precise gradual type that represents T, the type $(? \to \mathsf{Int}) \oplus (\mathsf{Int} \to ?)$ we started with.

Losing optimality directly affects the programmer's experience. For instance, in the type system, this means that the gain of precision that gradual unions are supposed to provide (recall Sect. 2.5) is lost; similarly, type annotations would not be strictly enforced at runtime.

3.4 Combining Gradual Types: Take Two

In order to define a proper Galois connection to give meaning to the gradual types of GTFL$^{\oplus}$, we introduce a *stratified*, sketched in Fig. 1:

- **Step 1.** We start from the Galois connection between GType and $\mathcal{P}(\textsc{Type})$, named *classic interpretation* hereafter, which interprets the unknown type. We already described this Galois connection in Sect. 3.2.
- **Step 2.** We lift this connection to operate on finite sets of gradual types, with the standard collecting semantics, forming a new Galois connection between $\mathcal{P}_{fin}(\textsc{GType})$ and $\mathcal{P}_{fin}(\mathcal{P}(\textsc{Type}))$, named the *classic set interpretation*.

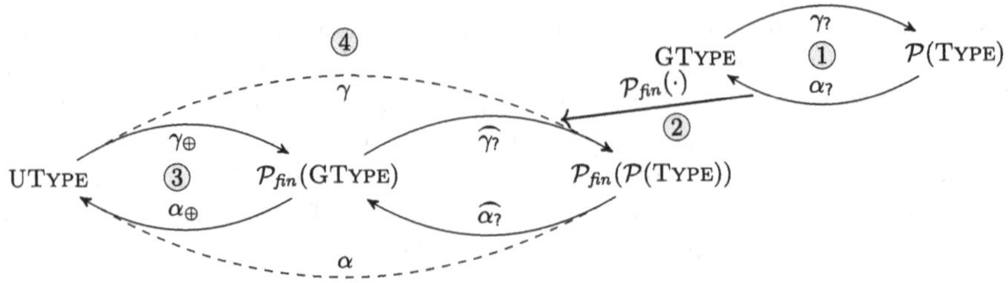

Fig. 1. Stratified interpretation of UTYPE.

- **Step 3.** We introduce a Galois connection between UTYPE and $\mathcal{P}_{fin}(\text{GTYPE})$, named *union interpretation*, which adds support for gradual unions among gradual types that include the unknown type.
- **Step 4.** We combine the classic set interpretation and the union interpretation. This combination gives a *stratified interpretation* of $\text{GTFL}^\oplus$ gradual types, UTYPE, in terms of finite sets of (possibly-infinite) sets of static types.

As we show, the stratified interpretation is itself a proper Galois connection, and we can subsequently use it to lift the static (and dynamic) semantics of STFL in order to define the semantics of $\text{GTFL}^\oplus$.

Step 2. Lifting the Classic Interpretation. Recall that $\langle \gamma_?, \alpha_? \rangle$ from Definitions 1 and 3 form a Galois connection between GTYPE and $\mathcal{P}(\text{TYPE})$ [14]. Our first step is to lift this connection to operate on sets of gradual types with the unknown type, *i.e.* to relate $\mathcal{P}_{fin}(\text{GTYPE})$ and $\mathcal{P}_{fin}(\mathcal{P}(\text{TYPE}))$. The *powerset lifting* of $\gamma_?$, denoted $\gamma_?$, is simply the piecewise application of $\gamma_?$:

Definition 7 ($\mathcal{P}_{fin}$(GType) Concretization). $\gamma_? : \mathcal{P}_{fin}(\text{GTYPE}) \rightarrow \mathcal{P}_{fin}(\mathcal{P}(\text{TYPE}))$

$$\gamma_?(G) = \{\, \gamma_?(G) \mid G \in G \,\}$$

Similarly, the powerset lifting of the abstraction function $\alpha_?$, denoted $\alpha_?$, is the union of the piecewise application of $\alpha_?$:

Definition 8 ($\mathcal{P}_{fin}$(GType) Abstraction). $\alpha_? : \mathcal{P}_{fin}(\mathcal{P}(\text{TYPE})) \rightharpoonup \mathcal{P}_{fin}(\text{GTYPE})$

$$\alpha_?(\emptyset) = \mathit{undefined} \qquad \alpha_?(T) = \bigcup_{T \in T} \alpha_?(T)$$

As expected, $\langle \gamma_?, \alpha_? \rangle$ is a proper Galois connection.

Proposition 2 ($\alpha_?$ is Sound and Optimal). *If T is not empty, then*

$$(a)\ T \subseteq \gamma_?(\alpha_?(T)). \qquad (b)\ T \subseteq \gamma_?(G) \Rightarrow \alpha_?(T) \sqsubseteq G.$$

Step 3. Introducing the union interpretation. We define a Galois connection between UTYPE and $\mathcal{P}_{fin}$(GTYPE) by naturally extending the definition of the connection between STYPE and $\mathcal{P}_{fin}$(TYPE) from Definitions 4 and 5, so that it now operates over types in UTYPE instead of only types in STYPE.

Definition 9 (UType Concretization). $\gamma_{\oplus} : \text{UTYPE} \rightarrow \mathcal{P}_{fin}(\text{GTYPE})$

$$\gamma_{\oplus}(\mathsf{Int}) = \{\,\mathsf{Int}\,\} \qquad \gamma_{\oplus}(\mathsf{Bool}) = \{\,\mathsf{Bool}\,\} \qquad \gamma_{\oplus}(?) = \{\,?\,\}$$

$$\gamma_{\oplus}(U_1 \rightarrow U_2) = \{\, T_1 \rightarrow T_2 \mid T_1 \in \gamma_{\oplus}(U_1) \wedge T_2 \in \gamma_{\oplus}(U_2)\,\}$$

$$\gamma_{\oplus}(U_1 \oplus U_2) = \gamma_{\oplus}(U_1) \cup \gamma_{\oplus}(U_2)$$

Compared to Definition 4, the only additional case to consider is that the unknown type ? can now occur: it is handled like other nullary type constructors, by concretizing to a singleton.

The abstraction is direct from Definition 5.

Definition 10 (UType Abstraction). $\alpha_{\oplus} : \mathcal{P}_{fin}(\text{GTYPE}) \rightharpoonup \text{UTYPE}$

$$\alpha_{\oplus}(G) = \oplus G \qquad if\, G \neq \emptyset$$

where $\oplus G$ denotes the gradual union of all the types in the set T.

Again, $\langle \gamma_{\oplus}, \alpha_{\oplus} \rangle$ is a Galois connection.

Proposition 3 ($\alpha_{\oplus}$ is Sound and Optimal). *If G is not empty, then*

$$(a)\ G \subseteq \gamma_{\oplus}(\alpha_{\oplus}(G)). \qquad (b)\ G \subseteq \gamma_{\oplus}(U) \Rightarrow \alpha_{\oplus}(G) \sqsubseteq U.$$

Step 4. Composing the Connections. We can now compose the two Galois connections in order to define a stratified interpretation for UTYPE in terms of sets of sets of static types.

Definition 11 (Concretization). $\gamma : \text{UTYPE} \rightarrow \mathcal{P}_{fin}(\mathcal{P}(\text{TYPE}))$, $\gamma = \gamma_{?} \circ \gamma_{\oplus}$

Definition 12 (Abstraction). $\alpha : \mathcal{P}_{fin}(\mathcal{P}(\text{TYPE})) \rightharpoonup \text{UTYPE}$, $\alpha = \alpha_{\oplus} \circ \alpha_{?}$

Because the composition of two Galois connection is a Galois connection, the stratified interpretation $\langle \gamma, \alpha \rangle$ is a Galois connection.

Proposition 4 (α is Sound and Optimal). *If T is not empty, then*

$$(a)\ T \subseteq \gamma(\alpha(T)). \qquad (b)\ T \subseteq \gamma(U) \Rightarrow \alpha(T) \sqsubseteq U.$$

The notion of precision for gradual types used above is similarly induced by concretization, *i.e.* $U_1 \sqsubseteq U_2 \iff \gamma(U_1) \subseteq \gamma(U_2)$. Note that these definitions use containment over sets of sets, defined as $T_1 \subseteq T_2 \iff \forall T_1 \in T_1, \exists T_2 \in T_2, T_1 \subseteq T_2$. Precision can equivalently be defined in terms of the lifted classic abstraction, *i.e.* $U_1 \sqsubseteq U_2 \iff \gamma_{\oplus}(U_1) \sqsubseteq_{?} \gamma_{\oplus}(U_2)$, where $G_1 \sqsubseteq_{?} G_2 \iff \gamma_{?}(G_1) \subseteq \gamma_{?}(G_2)$.

$$(U\text{app})\frac{\Gamma \vdash \widetilde{t}_1 : U_1 \quad \Gamma \vdash \widetilde{t}_2 : U_2 \quad U_2 \sim \widetilde{dom}(U_1)}{\Gamma \vdash \widetilde{t}_1\ \widetilde{t}_2 : \widetilde{cod}(U_1)} \qquad (U+)\frac{\Gamma \vdash \widetilde{t}_1 : U_1 \quad \Gamma \vdash \widetilde{t}_2 : U_2 \quad U_1 \sim \mathsf{Int} \quad U_2 \sim \mathsf{Int}}{\Gamma \vdash \widetilde{t}_1 + \widetilde{t}_2 : \mathsf{Int}}$$

$$(U{::})\frac{\Gamma \vdash \widetilde{t} : U \quad U \sim U_1}{\Gamma \vdash (\widetilde{t} :: U_1) : U_1} \qquad (U\text{if})\frac{\Gamma \vdash \widetilde{t}_1 : U_1 \quad \Gamma \vdash \widetilde{t}_2 : U_2 \quad U_1 \sim \mathsf{Bool} \quad \Gamma \vdash \widetilde{t}_3 : U_3}{\Gamma \vdash \mathsf{if}\ \widetilde{t}_1\ \mathsf{then}\ \widetilde{t}_2\ \mathsf{else}\ \widetilde{t}_3 : U_2 \sqcap U_3}$$

Fig. 2. GTFL$^{\oplus}$: selected typing rules

Illustration. Let us come back to the example of Sect. 3.3 that motivated the need for a stratified interpretation of UTYPE.

$$\begin{aligned}\gamma((? \to \mathsf{Int}) \oplus (\mathsf{Int} \to ?)) &= \{\gamma_?(? \to \mathsf{Int}), \gamma_?(\mathsf{Int} \to ?)\}\\ &= \{\{T \to \mathsf{Int} \mid T \in \text{TYPE}\}, \{\mathsf{Int} \to T \mid T \in \text{TYPE}\}\}\end{aligned}$$

we can now recover exactly the same gradual type

$$\begin{aligned}&\alpha(\{\{T \to \mathsf{Int} \mid T \in \text{TYPE}\}, \{\mathsf{Int} \to T \mid T \in \text{TYPE}\}\})\\ &= \alpha_{\oplus}(\alpha_?(\{T \to \mathsf{Int} \mid T \in \text{TYPE}\}) \cup \alpha_?(\{\mathsf{Int} \to T \mid T \in \text{TYPE}\}))\\ &= \alpha_{\oplus}(? \to \mathsf{Int}, \mathsf{Int} \to ?) = (? \to \mathsf{Int}) \oplus (\mathsf{Int} \to ?)\end{aligned}$$

3.5 Static Semantics of GTFL$^{\oplus}$

The syntax of GTFL$^{\oplus}$ is the same as that of STFL, save for the introduction of gradual types U. Consequently, terms t are lifted to gradual terms $\widetilde{t} \in$ UTERM, *i.e.* terms with gradual type annotations.

The type system of GTFL$^{\oplus}$ is presented in Fig. 2. The typing rules present no surprise with respect to the gradual language with ? presented by Garcia et al. [14]. This is because the novelty of gradual unions is encapsulated in gradual type predicates and functions, such as $\sim$, $\sqcap$, $\widetilde{dom}$, etc.

The essential idea of using abstract interpretation to define a gradual language is that the Galois connection that defines gradual types specifies how to lift both type predicates and functions to obtain their consistent counterpart.[3] For instance, the consistent lifting of a predicate over static types is the *existential* lifting of the predicate through the Galois connection. In other words, for a given binary predicate $P \in \text{TYPE}^2$, its consistent lifting $\widetilde{P} \in \text{GTYPE}^2$ is defined as: $\widetilde{P}(U_1, U_2) \iff \exists T_1 \in \gamma(U_1), \exists T_2 \in \gamma(U_2), P(T_1, T_2)$. Similarly for functions: a lifted function is the abstraction of the application of the static function to all the possible static types denoted by the involved gradual types. Formally, $\widetilde{f} = \alpha \circ f \circ \gamma$, where f is the pointwise application of f to all elements.

[3] The AI framework provides us with *definitions* for consistent predicates and functions; we will provide some equivalent algorithmic *characterizations*.

Lifting for Stratified Interpretation. We need to adapt these definitions from AGT to our stratified setting; indeed, our Galois connection relates gradual types with sets *of sets* of static types, rather than just sets of static types.

We can base our liftings of predicates and types on inclusion and pointwise application that are extended to sets of sets.

Definition 13 (Predicate Lifting). $\widetilde{P}(U_1, U_2) \iff \exists T_1 \in \gamma(U_1), T_2 \in \gamma(U_2), P(T_1, T_2)$ *where* $\in$ *is the existential lifting of* $\in$ *to powersets:* $T \in T \iff \exists T \in T, T \in T$

Equivalently: $\widetilde{P}(U_1, U_2) \iff \exists T_1 \in \gamma(U_1), \exists T_2 \in \gamma(U_2), \exists T_1 \in T_1, \exists T_2 \in T_2, P(T_1, T_2)$

The lifting of a predicate can also be defined in terms of each of the composed interpretations:

Proposition 5. $\widetilde{P}(U_1, U_2) \iff \exists G_1 \in \gamma_{\oplus}(U_1), \exists G_2 \in \gamma_{\oplus}(U_2), \widetilde{P_?}(G_1, G_2)$ *where* $\widetilde{P_?}$ *is the predicate* P *lifted with* $\gamma_?$.

The lifting of a type function f uses the pointwise application of f to all elements of each subset of a powerset, which we note f.

Definition 14 (Function Lifting). $\widetilde{f} = \alpha \circ f \circ \gamma$

Again, we can define the lifting using the separate abstractions: $\widetilde{f} = \alpha_{\oplus} \circ \widetilde{f}_? \circ \gamma_{\oplus}$

Example Liftings. Let us look at the lifting of a type predicate and a type function. We start with *consistency*, $\sim$, which corresponds to the lifting of type equality: two gradual types are consistent if some static types in their concretization are equal.

Definition 15 (Consistency). $U_1 \sim U_2$ *if and only if* $\exists T_1 \in \gamma(U_1), \exists T_1 \in T_1, \exists T_2 \in \gamma(U_2), \exists T_2 \in T_2, T_1 = T_2$.

This definition is equivalent to the following inductive definition:

Proposition 6.

$$\frac{U \sim U_1}{U \sim U_1 \oplus U_2} \qquad \frac{U \sim U_2}{U \sim U_1 \oplus U_2} \qquad \frac{U_1 \sim U}{U_1 \oplus U_2 \sim U} \qquad \frac{U_2 \sim U}{U_1 \oplus U_2 \sim U}$$

$$\frac{}{U \sim U} \qquad \frac{}{? \sim U} \qquad \frac{}{U \sim ?} \qquad \frac{U_{21} \sim U_{11} \quad U_{12} \sim U_{22}}{U_{11} \to U_{12} \sim U_{21} \to U_{22}}$$

Let us now consider the (precision) meet of gradual types, which corresponds to the lifting of the *equate* function used in the typing rule for conditionals. Its algorithmic definition is:

Definition 16 (Gradual Meet). *Let* $\sqcap : \text{UTYPE} \rightharpoonup \text{UTYPE}$ *be defined as:*

1. $U \sqcap U = U$
2. $? \sqcap U = U \sqcap ? = U$
3. $U \sqcap (U_1 \oplus U_2) = (U_1 \oplus U_2) \sqcap U = \begin{cases} U \sqcap U_1 & if\, U \sqcap U_2 \text{ } is\, undefined \\ U \sqcap U_2 & if\, U \sqcap U_1\, is\, undefined \\ (U \sqcap U_1) \oplus (U \sqcap U_2) & otherwise \end{cases}.$
4. $(U_{11} \rightarrow U_{12}) \sqcap (U_{21} \rightarrow U_{22}) = (U_{11} \sqcap U_{21}) \rightarrow (U_{12} \sqcap U_{22})$
5. $U_1 \sqcap U_2$ *is undefined otherwise.*

This algorithmic definition coincides with the lifting of equate:

Proposition 7. $\sqcap = \alpha \circ equate \circ \gamma$

4 GTFL$^\oplus$: Dynamic Semantics and Properties

Following the tradition [29], we now give the dynamic semantics of GTFL$^\oplus$ programs by a cast insertion translation to an internal language with explicit casts. We first describe the internal language GTFL$^\oplus_\Rightarrow$, which is adapted from the (blameless) threesome calculus of Siek et al. [28], and then present a cast insertion translation from GTFL$^\oplus$ to GTFL$^\oplus_\Rightarrow$.

Intermediate Language. GTFL$^\oplus_\Rightarrow$ is an adaptation of the original threesome calculus without blame [28]. A threesome $\langle T_2 \overset{T_3}{\Longleftarrow} T_1 \rangle$ is a cast composed of three types: the source type T_1, the target type T_2, and the middle type T_3. Initially, the middle type of a threesome is the greatest lower bound (in terms of precision), or meet, of the source and target types. The key benefit of threesomes is that two threesomes can be merged into a single threesome by taking the meet of their middle types, hence avoiding space issues [17].

The syntax of GTFL$^\oplus_\Rightarrow$ is a simple extension of that of GTFL$^\oplus$, with cast expressions $\langle U_2 \overset{U_3}{\Longleftarrow} U_1 \rangle t$ and casted values $\langle U_2 \overset{U_3}{\Longleftarrow} U_1 \rangle u$, where u denotes the simple values of GTFL$^\oplus$. For space reasons we only present a representative selection of typing rules in Fig. 3. In the typing rule for cast expressions (IT$\langle\rangle$), the consistency premises are required for a threesome to be well-formed (this is always the case by construction). The other typing rules are basically those of GTFL$^\oplus$, except that type consistency is replaced with type equality; this is because uses of consistency will be guarded by the insertion of casts. For instance, Fig. 3 shows rule (ITapp): while the GTFL$^\oplus$ typing rule (Uapp, Fig. 2) uses the premise $U_2 \sim \widetilde{dom}(U_1)$, the new rule requires the type of t_2 to exactly be $\widetilde{dom}(U_1)$.

Figure 4 presents the dynamic semantics of GTFL$^\oplus_\Rightarrow$, which are similar to [28]. Two threesomes that coincide on their source/target types are combined by meeting their middle types. If the meet is undefined then the term steps to **error**. Otherwise both casts are merged to a new cast where the middle type is now the meet between the middle types. Note that casts are introduced using the following metafunction, which avoids producing useless threesomes:

$$\langle\!\langle U_2 \overset{U_3}{\Longleftarrow} U_1 \rangle\!\rangle t = t \text{ if } U_1 = U_2 = U_3\,; \text{ and } \langle U_2 \overset{U_3}{\Longleftarrow} U_1 \rangle t \text{ otherwise}$$

$$(\text{IT}\langle\rangle)\frac{\Gamma \vdash_{\widetilde{}} t : U_1 \quad U_1 \sim U_2 \quad U_1 \sim U_3 \quad U_3 \sim U_2}{\Gamma \vdash_{\widetilde{}} \langle U_2 \overset{U_3}{\Leftarrow} U_1\rangle t : U_2} \qquad (\text{ITapp})\frac{\Gamma \vdash_{\widetilde{}} t_1 : U_1 \quad \Gamma \vdash_{\widetilde{}} t_2 : \widetilde{dom}(U_1)}{\Gamma \vdash_{\widetilde{}} t_1\, t_2 : \widetilde{cod}(U_1)}$$

Fig. 3. GTFL$^{\oplus}_{\Rightarrow}$: selected typing rules

$$u ::= \mathsf{true} \mid \mathsf{false} \mid n \mid \lambda x.t \qquad v ::= u \mid \langle U \overset{U}{\Leftarrow} U\rangle u \quad \text{(values)}$$

$$f ::= \square + t \mid v + \square \mid \square\, t \mid v\, \square \mid \langle U \overset{U}{\Leftarrow} U\rangle \square \mid \mathsf{if}\ \square\ \mathsf{then}\ t\ \mathsf{else}\ t \quad \text{(frames)}$$

$$\boxed{t \longrightarrow t} \qquad \frac{n_3 = rval(v_1)\ [\![+]\!]\ rval(v_2)}{v_1 + v_2 \longrightarrow n_3} \qquad (\lambda x.t)\ v \longrightarrow [v/x]t$$

$$\mathsf{if}\ v\ \mathsf{then}\ t_1\ \mathsf{else}\ t_2 \longrightarrow \begin{cases} t_2 \text{ if } rval(v) = \mathsf{true} \\ t_3 \text{ if } rval(v) = \mathsf{false} \end{cases}$$

$$\langle U_{21} \to U_{22} \overset{U_3}{\Leftarrow} U_{11} \to U_{12}\rangle u\ v \longrightarrow \langle\!\langle U_{22} \overset{icod(U_3)}{\Longleftarrow} U_{12}\rangle\!\rangle (u\ \langle\!\langle U_{11} \overset{idom(U_3)}{\Longleftarrow} U_{21}\rangle\!\rangle v)$$

$$\langle U_3 \overset{U_{32}}{\Leftarrow} U_2\rangle\langle U_2 \overset{U_{21}}{\Leftarrow} U_1\rangle v \longrightarrow \begin{cases} \langle\!\langle U_3 \overset{U_{32} \sqcap U_{21}}{\Longleftarrow} U_1\rangle\!\rangle v \\ \mathbf{error} \text{ if } U_{32} \sqcap U_{21} \text{ is undefined} \end{cases}$$

$$\boxed{t \longmapsto t} \qquad \frac{t_1 \longrightarrow t_2}{t_1 \longmapsto t_2} \qquad \frac{t_1 \longmapsto t_2}{f[t_1] \longmapsto f[t_2]} \qquad \frac{}{f[\mathbf{error}] \longmapsto \mathbf{error}}$$

Fig. 4. GTFL$^{\oplus}_{\Rightarrow}$: dynamic semantics of GTFL$^{\oplus}_{\Rightarrow}$

Cast Insertion. A GTFL$^{\oplus}$ program is elaborated through a type-driven cast insertion translation. The key idea of the transformation is to insert casts in places where consistency is used to justify the typing derivation. For instance, if $\widetilde{t} : \mathsf{Int} \oplus \mathsf{Bool}$ is used where Int is required, the translation inserts a cast $\langle \mathsf{Int} \Leftarrow \mathsf{Int} \oplus \mathsf{Bool}\rangle t$, where t is the recursive translation of $\widetilde{t}$. This cast plays the role of the implicit projection from the gradual union type. Dually, when a term of type Int is used where a gradual union is expected, the translation adds a cast that performs the implicit injection to the gradual union, *e.g.* $\langle \mathsf{Int} \oplus \mathsf{Bool} \Leftarrow \mathsf{Int}\rangle 10$. Note that a value with a cast that loses precision is like a tagged value in tagged union type systems; the difference again is that the "tag" is inserted implicitly.

The translation judgment has the form $\Gamma \vdash \widetilde{t} \Rightarrow t : U$: under type environment Γ, GTFL$^{\oplus}$ term $\widetilde{t}$ of type U, is translated to GTFL$^{\oplus}_{\Rightarrow}$ term t. The translation rules given in Fig. 5 are standard. Cast insertion rules use twosomes to ease readability; a twosome $\langle U_2 \Leftarrow U_1\rangle t$ is equal to $\langle\!\langle U_2 \overset{U_1 \sqcap U_2}{\Longleftarrow} U_1\rangle\!\rangle t$: the initial middle type is the meet of both ends [28].

$$(\text{Capp})\frac{\Gamma \vdash \widetilde{t_1} \Rightarrow t_1' : U_1 \quad \Gamma \vdash \widetilde{t_2} \Rightarrow t_2' : U_2 \quad U_2 \sim \widetilde{dom}(U_1)}{\Gamma \vdash \widetilde{t_1}\, \widetilde{t_2} \Rightarrow \langle \widetilde{dom}(U_1) \rightarrow \widetilde{cod}(U_1) \Leftarrow U_1 \rangle t_1' \, \langle \widetilde{dom}(U_1) \Leftarrow U_2 \rangle t_2' : \widetilde{cod}(U_1)}$$

$$(\text{C+})\frac{\Gamma \vdash \widetilde{t_1} \Rightarrow t_1' : U_1 \quad \Gamma \vdash \widetilde{t_2} \Rightarrow t_2' : U_2 \quad U_1 \sim \mathsf{Int} \quad U_2 \sim \mathsf{Int}}{\Gamma \vdash \widetilde{t_1} + \widetilde{t_2} \Rightarrow \langle \mathsf{Int} \Leftarrow U_1 \rangle t_1' + \langle \mathsf{Int} \Leftarrow U_2 \rangle t_2' : \mathsf{Int}}$$

$$(\text{C::})\frac{\Gamma \vdash \widetilde{t} \Rightarrow t' : U \quad U \sim U_1}{\Gamma \vdash (\widetilde{t} :: U_1) \Rightarrow \langle U_1 \Leftarrow U \rangle t' : U_1}$$

$$(\text{Cif})\frac{\Gamma \vdash \widetilde{t_1} \Rightarrow t_1' : U_1 \quad U_1 \sim \mathsf{Bool} \quad \Gamma \vdash \widetilde{t_2} \Rightarrow t_2' : U_2 \quad \Gamma \vdash \widetilde{t_3} \Rightarrow t_3' : U_3}{\begin{array}{l}\Gamma \vdash \mathsf{if}\ \widetilde{t_1}\ \mathsf{then}\ \widetilde{t_2}\ \mathsf{else}\ \widetilde{t_3} \Rightarrow \\ \quad \mathsf{if}\ \langle \mathsf{Bool} \Leftarrow U_1 \rangle t_1'\ \mathsf{then}\ \langle U_2 \sqcap U_3 \Leftarrow U_2 \rangle t_2'\ \mathsf{else}\ \langle U_2 \sqcap U_3 \Leftarrow U_3 \rangle t_3' : U_2 \sqcap U_3\end{array}}$$

Fig. 5. Cast insertion: from GTFL$^{\oplus}$ to GTFL$^{\oplus}_{\Rightarrow}$ (selected rules)

Properties of GTFL$^{\oplus}$. GTFL$^{\oplus}$ satisfies a number of properties. First GTFL$^{\oplus}$ satisfies a standard type safety property:

Proposition 8 (Type safety). *Suppose that* $\cdot \vdash \widetilde{t} \Rightarrow t : U$*, then either:* t *is a value* v*;* $t \longmapsto$ **error***; or* $t \longmapsto t'$ *for some* t' *such that* $\cdot \vdash_{\widetilde{\imath}} t' : U$

Second, the gradual type system is a conservative extension of the static type system; *i.e.* both systems coincide on fully-annotated terms.

Proposition 9 (Equivalence for fully-annotated terms). *For any* $t \in$ TERM, $. \vdash_S t : T$ *if and only if* $. \vdash t : T$

Precision on terms, noted $\widetilde{t_1} \sqsubseteq \widetilde{t_2}$, is the natural lifting of type precision to terms. The gradual type system satisfies the static gradual guarantee of Siek et al. [30], *i.e.* losing precision preserves typeability: if a program is well-typed, then a less precise version of it also type checks, at a less precise type.

Proposition 10 (Static gradual guarantee). *If* $. \vdash \widetilde{t_1} : U_1$ *and* $\widetilde{t_1} \sqsubseteq \widetilde{t_2}$*, then* $. \vdash \widetilde{t_2} : U_2$*, for some* U_2 *such that* $U_1 \sqsubseteq U_2$*.*

Similarly, losing precision preserves reduceability: a program that runs without error continues to do so if it is annotated with less precise types.

Proposition 11 (Dynamic gradual guarantee). *Suppose* $\cdot \vdash \widetilde{t_1} \Rightarrow t_1 : U_1$*,* $\cdot \vdash \widetilde{t_2} \Rightarrow t_2 : U_2$*, and* $t_1 \sqsubseteq t_1'$*. If* $t_1 \longmapsto t_2$ *then* $t_1' \longmapsto t_2'$ *where* $t_2 \sqsubseteq t_2'$*.*

A technical novelty of our work is that we establish all the above properties following a route that differs from prior work. Usually, one establishes type safety of the gradual language by first proving type safety of the internal language and then proving that the cast insertion translation preserves typing [29]. With this approach, the gradual guarantees must then be established separately [30].

Our approach exploits the AGT methodology: we first systematically derive the *direct* runtime semantics of GTFL$^{\oplus}$ (*i.e.* which do *not* rely on a cast insertion translation). We then prove safety and the gradual guarantees, which in fact directly follow from the abstract interpretation framework [14]. Then, we prove that the compilation to threesome combined with the semantics of the internal language together are equivalent to the dynamic semantics derived with AGT. This correctness argument proceeds using logical relations.

5 Related Work

In Sect. 2, we have compared gradual unions to both tagged and untagged unions from the standard type system literature [23], highlighting their key characteristics and differences. Gradual unions are unique in admitting runtime errors, with the benefits of more flexible programming patterns. We have also compared gradual unions to retrofitted type systems for dynamic languages with support for unions. Note that in Flow, Typescript, ℂDuce and Typed Racket, a function that expects an argument of type $A + B$ can accept arguments of type A, B, or $A + B$, but neither of type $A + B + C$ nor $A + D$. In contrast, in GTFL$^{\oplus}$, as long as two gradual union types have at least one *compatible* type in their denotation, then they are compatible. So, a function that expects an argument of type $A \oplus B$ accepts arguments of types such as $A \oplus B \oplus C$ and $A \oplus D$.

Flow-sensitive typing approaches such as occurrence typing [20] support more precise type assignments based on the result of some (type) predicate check. Such techniques can avoid the insertion of unnecessary casts [24]. However, in general, the combination of gradual types with type tests raises questions regarding the dynamic gradual guarantee [30], which have not yet been answered.

Interestingly, languages with set-theoretic (untagged) unions usually also consider intersection types, with distributivity relations such as $(T_1 \vee T_2) \rightarrow T_3 \equiv (T_1 \rightarrow T_3) \wedge (T_2 \rightarrow T_3)$. This law states that if a function accepts a value that is *either* of type T_1 *or* of type T_2, then it behaves as *both* a function of type $T_1 \rightarrow T_3$ *and* a function of type $T_2 \rightarrow T_3$. Gradual unions encompass both interpretations, without having to resort to a notion of intersection types: $(T_1 \oplus T_2) \rightarrow T_3 \equiv (T_1 \rightarrow T_3) \oplus (T_2 \rightarrow T_3)$, because both types have the same interpretation, *i.e.* they represent the same concrete set of static types. This simplicity is a consequence of the optimistic interpretation with dynamic checks that is characteristic of gradual typing. (Note that it resonates with the fact that type precision is covariant in both positive and negative positions.)

Siek and Tobin-Hochstadt studied the interaction between gradual typing and union types [27]. While seemingly related, the focus of their work is very different: the addition of the unknown type to a language with *static* union types. Additionally, they only support the union of types with different type constructors, so for instance the union of two function types is not supported.

Similarly, in parallel with this work, Castagna and Lanvin developed a theory for gradual set-theoretic types, supporting union, intersection and the unknown type [7]. Their system can express constructs similar to gradual unions by using a combination of unions and intersection with the unknown type, *e.g.* $\mathsf{Int} \oplus \mathsf{Bool}$ is equivalent to $(\mathsf{Int} \mid \mathsf{Bool})\&?$. They also exploit AGT to derive the static semantics, although the more expressive setting with static unions and intersections makes the design of the Galois connection much more challenging. Our design is minimalist, providing a novel form of union types to languages that do not initially support such set-theoretic types. They mention compilation to threesomes and proving the gradual guarantees as future work.

Jafery and Dunfield [19] present a gradual language that features two types of (datasort) refinement sums, for either exhaustive or non-exhaustive matches. Non-exhaustive matches are backed by dynamic checks in case of an unsuccessful match. Elements with a sum type must be explicitly injected; the sum constructors are neither commutative nor associative. Also, they do not discuss the interaction with the fully-unknown type.

6 Conclusion

Inspired by the interpretation of gradual types as a general approach to deal with imprecision at the type level, and recognizing that unions types are a form of imprecision, we proposed the novel notion of *gradual union types*. Gradual unions are a new design for dealing with the possibility for expressions to have different, unrelated types. Accepting the possibility of runtime cast errors, gradual unions combine and extend the convenience of both tagged and untagged union types. We have presented the meta-theory of gradual union types and their interaction with the traditional unknown type, using the AGT methodology. We have described a compilation semantics to a threesome calculus, and established its desired properties through logical relations. The combination of both gradual type constructors forced us to explore a stratified approach to AGT, whereby each gradual type constructor is interpreted separately and then carefully composed in order to ensure optimality of the resulting abstraction. This compositional approach to designing a gradual language is novel. We hope that it helps understanding how to combine different gradualization efforts that have been developed independently, and may not be fully orthogonal.

Acknowledgments. We thank Gabriel Scherer, Ronald Garcia and the anonymous reviewers for their detailed comments and suggestions.

References

1. Abadi, M., Cardelli, L., Pierce, B., Plotkin, G.: Dynamic typing in a statically typed language. ACM Trans. Program. Lang. Syst. **13**(2), 237–268 (1991)
2. Ahmed, A., Findler, R.B., Siek, J., Wadler, P.: Blame for all. In: POPL 2011 (2011)
3. Bañados Schwerter, F., Garcia, R., Tanter, É.: A theory of gradual effect systems. In: ICFP 2014 (2014)

4. Barbanera, F., Dezani-Ciancaglini, M., De'Liguoro, H.: Intersection and union types: syntax and semantics. Inf. Comput. **119**, 202–230 (1995)
5. Benzaken, V., Castagna, G., Frisch, A.: CDuce: an XML-centric general purpose language. In: ICFP 2003 (2003)
6. Buneman, P., Pierce, B.: Union types for semistructured data. In: Connor, R., Mendelzon, A. (eds.) DBPL 1999. LNCS, vol. 1949, pp. 184–207. Springer, Heidelberg (2000). doi:10.1007/3-540-44543-9_12
7. Castagna, G., Lanvin, V.: Gradual typing with union and intersection types. In: ICFP 2017 (2017)
8. Microsoft Corporation: Typescript language specification. https://www.typescriptlang.org/. Accessed June 2017
9. Cousot, P., Cousot, R.: Abstract interpretation: a unified lattice model for static analysis of programs by construction or approximation of fixpoints. In: POPL 1977 (1977)
10. Disney, T., Flanagan, C.: Gradual information flow typing. In: STOP 2011 (2011)
11. Facebook: Flow: a static type checker for JavaScript. https://flow.org/. Accessed June 2017
12. Frisch, A., Castagna, G., Benzaken, V.: Semantic subtyping. In: LICS 2002 (2002)
13. Garcia, R., Cimini, M.: Principal type schemes for gradual programs. In: POPL 2015 (2015)
14. Garcia, R., Clark, A.M., Tanter, É.: Abstracting gradual typing. In: POPL 2016 (2016)
15. Harper, P.R.: Practical Foundations for Programming Languages. Cambridge University Press, Cambridge (2012)
16. Henglein, F.: Dynamic typing: syntax and proof theory. Sci. Comput. Program. **22**(3), 197–230 (1994)
17. Herman, D., Tomb, A., Flanagan, C.: Space-efficient gradual typing. In: Trends in Functional Programming (2007)
18. Hosoya, H., Vouillon, J., Pierce, B.C.: Regular expression types for XML. In: ICFP 2000 (2000)
19. Jafery, K.A., Dunfield, J.: Sums of uncertainty: refinements go gradual. In: POPL 2017 (2017)
20. Kent, A.M., Kempe, D., Tobin-Hochstadt, S.: Occurrence typing modulo theories. In: PLDI 2016 (2016)
21. Lehmann, N., Tanter, É.: Gradual refinement types. In: POPL 2017 (2017)
22. Pierce, B.C.: Programming with intersection types, union types, and polymorphism. Technical report CMU-CS-91-106 (1991)
23. Pierce, B.C.: Types and Programming Languages. MIT Press, Cambridge (2002)
24. Rastogi, A., Chaudhuri, A., Hosmer, B.: The ins and outs of gradual type inference. In: POPL 2012 (2012)
25. Rompf, T., Amin, N.: Type soundness for dependent object types (DOT). In: OOPSLA 2016 (2016)
26. Siek, J., Taha, W.: Gradual typing for objects. In: Ernst, E. (ed.) ECOOP 2007. LNCS, vol. 4609, pp. 2–27. Springer, Heidelberg (2007). doi:10.1007/978-3-540-73589-2_2
27. Siek, J., Tobin-Hochstadt, S.: The recursive union of some gradual types. In: Wadler Festschrift (2016)
28. Siek, J., Wadler, P.: Threesomes, with and without blame. In: POPL 2010 (2010)
29. Siek, J.G., Taha, W.: Gradual typing for functional languages. In: Scheme and Functional Programming Workshop (2006)

30. Siek, J.G., Vitousek, M.M., Cimini, M., Boyland, J.T.: Refined criteria for gradual typing. In: SNAPL 2015 (2015)
31. Tobin-Hochstadt, S., Felleisen, M.: The design and implementation of typed scheme. In: POPL 2008 (2008)
32. Tobin-Hochstadt, S., Felleisen, M.: Logical types for untyped languages. In: ICFP 2010 (2010)
33. Toro, M., Tanter, É.: Gradual union types–complete definition and proofs. Technical report TR/DCC-2017-1, University of Chile, June 2017

Modular Demand-Driven Analysis of Semantic Difference for Program Versions

Anna Trostanetski[1(✉)], Orna Grumberg[1(✉)], and Daniel Kroening[2(✉)]

[1] Technion – Israel Institute of Technology, Haifa, Israel
{annat,orna}@cs.technion.ac.il
[2] University of Oxford, Oxford, UK
kroening@cs.ox.ac.uk

Abstract. In this work we present a *modular* and *demand-driven* analysis of the semantic difference between program versions. Our analysis characterizes initial states for which final states in the program versions differ. It also characterizes states for which the final states are identical. Such characterizations are useful for regression verification, for revealing security vulnerabilities and for identifying changes in the program's functionality.

Syntactic changes in program versions are often small and local and may apply to procedures that are deep in the call graph. Our approach analyses only those parts of the programs that are affected by the changes. Moreover, the analysis is *modular*, processing a single pair of procedures at a time. Called procedures are not inlined. Rather, their previously computed summaries and *difference summaries* are used. For efficiency, procedure summaries and difference summaries can be *abstracted* and may be *refined* on demand.

We have compared our method to well established tools and observed speedups of one order of magnitude and more. Furthermore, in many cases our tool proves equivalence or finds differences while the others fail to do so.

1 Introduction

In this work we present a modular and demand-driven algorithm for computing the semantic difference between two closely-related, syntactically similar imperative programs. The need to identify semantic difference often arises when a new (patched) program version is built on top of an old one. The difference between the versions can be used for:

- Regression testing, which checks whether the new version introduces security bugs or errors. The old version is considered to be a correct, "golden model" for the new, less-tested version [30].
- Revealing security vulnerabilities that were eliminated by the new version [11]. This information can be used to produce attacks against the old version.

Supported by the ERC project 280053 (CPROVER), the H2020 FET OPEN 712689 SC^2 and the Prof. A. Pazy Research Foundation.

F. Ranzato (Ed.): SAS 2017, LNCS 10422, pp. 405–427, 2017.
DOI: 10.1007/978-3-319-66706-5_20

- More generally, identifying and characterizing changes in the program's functionality [24].

Semantic difference has been widely studied, and a wide range of techniques have been suggested [11,14–16,20,23–26]. We aim at enhancing the scalability and precision of existing techniques by exploiting the modular structure of programs and avoiding unnecessary analysis.

We consider two program versions, consisting of (matched) procedure calls, arranged in call graphs. Some of the matched procedures are known to be syntactically different while the others are identical. Often, the changes between versions are small and limited to procedures deep inside the call graph (Fig. 1). In such cases, it would be helpful to know how these changes affect the program as a whole, without analysing the full program. To achieve this, we first compute a *difference summary* between syntactically different procedures p_1, p_2 (*modified* procedures). Next, we analyse the procedures that call them, using the difference summary for p_1, p_2 computed before. No inlining of called procedures is applied. We also avoid analysing procedures that are not affected by the modified procedures. As a result, the required work may be significantly smaller than analysing the full program.

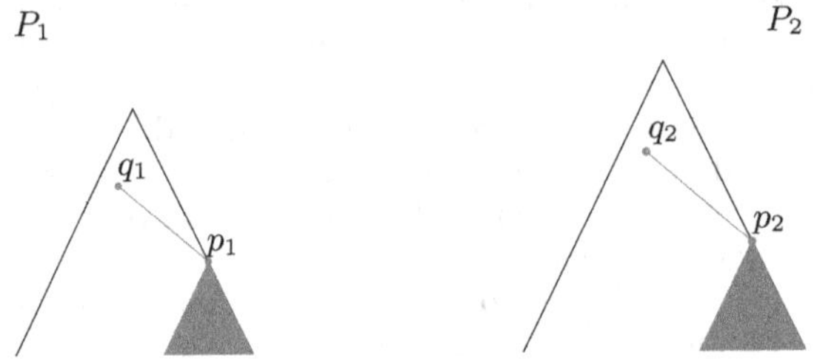

Fig. 1. Call graphs of two program versions P_1, P_2, where their syntactic differences are local to the procedures p_1, p_2, and the bodies of procedures q_1, q_2 are identical

Our work is therefore particularly beneficial when applied to programs that are syntactically similar. While applicable to programs that are very different from each other, our technique would yield less savings in those cases.

Our approach is guided by the following ideas. First, the analysis is *modular*. That is, it is applied to one pair of procedures at a time, thus it is confined to small parts of the program. Called procedures are not inlined. Rather, their previously computed summaries and difference summary are used. We note that any block of code can be treated as a procedure, not only those defined as procedures by the programmer. It is beneficial to choose the smallest possible blocks that were modified between versions, and identify them as "procedures".

Second, the analysis is restricted to only those pairs of procedures whose difference affects the behavior of the full programs.

Third, we provide both under- and over-approximations of the input-output differences between procedures, which can be strengthened on demand.

Finally, procedures need not be fully analysed. Unanalysed parts are *abstracted* and replaced with uninterpreted functions. The abstracted parts are *refined* upon demand if calling procedures need a more precise summary of the called procedures for their own summary.

Our analysis is not guaranteed to terminate. Yet it is an *anytime analysis.* That is, its partial results are meaningful. Furthermore, the longer it runs, the more precise its results are.

In our analysis we do not assume that loops are bounded. We are able to prove equivalence or provide an under- and over-approximation of the difference for unbounded behaviors of the programs. We are also able to handle recursive procedures.

We implemented our method and applied it to computing the semantic difference between program versions. We compared it to well established tools and observed speedups of one order of magnitude and more. Furthermore, in many cases our tool proves equivalence or finds differences while the others failed to do so.

Our Approach in Detail

We now describe our method in more detail. Our analysis starts by choosing a pair of matched procedures p_1 in program P_1 and p_2 in program P_2 that are syntactically different.

The basic block of our analysis is a (partial) *procedure summary* sum_{p_i} with $i \in \{1, 2\}$ for each procedure p_i. The summary is obtained using symbolic execution. It includes *path summarizations* (R_π, T_π) for a subset of the finite paths π of p_i, where R_π is the reachability condition for π to be traversed and T_π is the state transformation mapping initial states to final states when π is executed.

Next, we compute a (partial) *difference summary* $(C(p_1, p_2), U(p_1, p_2))$ for p_1, p_2, where $C(p_1, p_2)$ is a set of initial states for which p_1 and p_2 terminate with different final states. $U(p_1, p_2)$ is a set of initial states for which p_1 and p_2 terminate with identical final states. Both sets are under-approximations. However, the complement of $U(p_1, p_2)$, denoted $\neg U(p_1, p_2)$, also provides an over-approximation of the set of initial states for which the procedures are different.

Note that procedure summaries and difference summaries are both partial. This is because their computation in full is usually infeasible. More importantly, their full summaries are often unnecessary for computing the difference summary between programs P_1, P_2.

If $U(p_1, p_2) \equiv \mathit{true}$ we can conclude that no differences are propagated from p_1, p_2 to their callers. Their callers will not be further analysed then. Otherwise, we can proceed to analysing pairs of procedures q_1, q_2 that include calls to p_1, p_2, respectively. As mentioned before, for building their procedure summaries and difference summary, we use the already computed summaries of p_1, p_2. For the sake of modularity, we develop a new notion of *modular symbolic execution.* We formalize the definitions of symbolic execution and modular symbolic execution, and show the connections between the two.

The analysis terminates when we can fully identify the initial states of P_1, P_2 for which the programs agree/disagree on their final states. Alternatively, we can stop when a predefined threshold is reached. In this case the sets $C(p_1, p_2)$ and $U(p_1, p_2)$ of initial states are guaranteed to represent disagreement and agreement, respectively.

Side results of our analysis are the difference summaries computed for matched procedures in P_1, P_2, that can be reused if the procedures are called by other programs.

The main contributions of this work are:

- We present a modular and demand-driven algorithm for computing semantic difference between closely related programs.
- Our algorithm is unique in that it provides both under- and over-approximations of the differences between program versions.
- We introduce abstraction-refinement into the analysis process so that a trade-off between the amount of computation and the obtained precision will be manageable.
- We develop a new notion of modular symbolic execution.

2 Preliminaries

We start by defining some basic notions of programs and procedures.

Definition 1. *Let P be a program, containing the set of procedures $\Pi = \{p_1, \ldots, p_n\}$. The* ***call graph*** *for P is a directed graph with Π as nodes, and there exists an edge from p_i to p_j if and only if procedure p_i calls procedure p_j.*

The procedure p_1 is a special procedure in the program's call graph that acts as an entry point of the program; it is also referred to as the main procedure in the program P, denoted $main_P$.

Next we formalize the notions of variables and states of procedures.

- The ***visible variables*** of a procedure p are the variables that represent the arguments to the procedure and its return values, denoted V_p^v.
- The ***hidden variables*** of a procedure p are the local variables used by the procedure, denoted V_p^h.
- The ***variables*** of a procedure p are both its visible and hidden variables, denoted V_p ($V_p = V_p^v \cup V_p^h$).
- A ***state*** σ_p is a valuation of the procedure's variables, $\sigma_p = \{v \mapsto c | v \in V_p, c \in D_v\}$, where D_v is the (possibly infinite) domain of variable v.
- A ***visible state*** is the projection of a state to the visible variables.

Without loss of generality we assume that programs have no global variables, since those could be passed as arguments and return values along the entire program. We also assume, without loss of generality, that all program inputs are given to the main procedure at the beginning. The programs we analyze are deterministic, meaning that given a visible state of the main procedure at the beginning of an execution (an ***initial state***), the execution of the program (finite or infinite) is fixed, and for a finite execution the visible state at the end of the execution is fixed (called ***final state***). The same applies to individual procedures as well.

In our work, a program is represented by its *call graph*, and each procedure p is represented by its control flow graph CFG_p (also known as a flow program in [10]), defined below.

Definition 2. *Let p be a procedure with variables V_p. The* ***Control Flow Graph (CFG)*** *for p is a directed graph CFG_p, in which the nodes represent instructions in p and the edges represent possible flow of control from one instruction to its successor(s) in the procedure code. Instructions include:*

- *Assignment: $x = e$, where x is a variable in V_p and e is an expression over V_p. An assignment node has one outgoing edge.*
- *Procedure call: $g(Y)$, where $Y \subseteq V_p$ and the values of variables in Y are assigned to the visible variables of procedure g.*[1] *The variables in Y are assigned with the values of the visible variables of g at the end of the execution of g. A call node has one outgoing edge, to the instruction in p following the return of procedure g.*
- *Test: $B(V_p)$, where $B(V_p)$ is a Boolean expression over V_p; a test node has two outgoing edges, one marked with T, and the other with F.*

A CFG contains one node with no incoming edges, called the entry node, *and one node with no outgoing edges, called the* exit node.

Definition 3. *Given CFG_p of procedure p, a* ***path*** *$\pi = l_1, l_2, \ldots$ is a sequence of nodes (finite or infinite) in the graph CFG_p, such that:*

1. *For all i there exists an edge from l_i to l_{i+1} in CFG_p.*
2. *l_1 is the entry node of p.*

The path π is ***maximal*** *if it is either infinite or it is finite and ends in the exit node of p.*

We assume that each procedure performs a transformation on the values of the visible variables, and has no additional side-effects. Procedure p ***terminates*** on a visible state σ_p^v if the path traversed in p from σ_p^v is finite and maximal. A program terminates on a visible state σ_{main}^v if its main procedure terminates.

The following semantic characteristics are associated with finite paths, similarly to the definitions for flow programs in [10]. The characteristics are given (for a path in a procedure p) in terms of quantifier-free First-Order Logic (FOL), defined over the set V_p^v of visible variables.

Definition 4. *Let π be a finite path in procedure p.*

---

[1] We assume that $Y = \{y_1, \ldots, y_n\}$ and $V_g^v = \{v_1, \ldots, v_n\}$, y_i is assigned to v_i at the entry node, and v_i is assigned to y_i at the exit node.

- *The* ***Reachability Condition*** *of* π, *denoted* $R_\pi(V_p^v)$, *is a condition on the visible states at the beginning of* π, *which guarantees that the control will traverse* π.
- *The* ***State Transformation*** *of* π, *denoted* $T_\pi(V_p^v)$, *describes the final state of* π, *obtained if control traverses* π *starting with some valuation* σ_p^v *of* V_p^v.

$T_\pi(V_p^v)$ is given by $|V_p^v|$ expressions over V_p^v, one for each variable x in V_p^v. The expression for x describes the effect of the path on x in terms of the values of V_p^v at the beginning of π. Let $T_\pi(V_p^v) = (f_1, \ldots, f_{|V_p^v|})$ and $T_{\pi'}(V_p^v) = (f'_1, \ldots, f'_{|V_p^v|})$ be two state transformations. Then, $T_\pi(V_p^v) = T_{\pi'}(V_p^v)$ if and only if, for every $1 \leq i \leq |V_p^v|$, $f_i = f'_i$.

```
1 void p1(int& x) {
2   if (x < 0) {
3     x = -1;
4     return;
5   }
6   if (x >= 2)
7     return;
8   while (x == 2)
9     x = 2;
10  x = 3;
11 }
```

```
1 void p2(int& x) {
2   if (x < 0) {
3     x = -1;
4     return;
5   }
6   if (x > 4)
7     return;
8   while (x == 2)
9     x = 2;
10  x = 3;
11 }
```

Fig. 2. Examples of procedure versions

Example 1. Consider procedure p1 in Fig. 2. Its only visible variable is x, used as both input and output. Consider the paths that correspond to the following line numbers: $\alpha = (2, 3, 4)$ and $\beta = (2, 6, 7)$. Then,

$$R_\alpha(x) = x < 0 \qquad R_\beta(x) = ((\neg(x < 0)) \wedge x \geq 2) \equiv x \geq 2$$
$$T_\alpha(x) = (-1) \qquad T_\beta(x) = (x)$$

A path π is called ***feasible*** if R_π is satisfiable, meaning that there exists an input that traverses the path π. Note that, in p1 from Fig. 2, the path $(2, 6, 8, 9)$ is not feasible.

2.1 Symbolic Execution

Symbolic execution [7,17] (path-based) is an alternative representation of a procedure execution that aims at systematically traversing the entire path space of a given procedure. All visible variables are assigned with symbolic values in place of concrete ones. Then every path is explored individually (in some heuristic order), checking for its feasibility using a constraint solver. During the execution, a symbolic state T and symbolic path constraint R are maintained. The symbolic state maps procedure variables to symbolic expressions (and is naturally extended to map expressions over procedure variables), and the path constraint is a quantifier-free FOL formula over symbolic values.

Given a finite path $\pi = l_1, \ldots, l_n$, we use symbolic execution to compute the reachability condition $R_\pi(V_p^v)$ and state transformation $T_\pi(V_p^v)$. The computation is performed in stages, where for every $1 \leq i \leq n+1$, $R_\pi^i(V_p)$ and $T_\pi^i(V_p)$ are the path condition and state transformation for path $l_1, \ldots, l_{i-1}$, respectively. Initialization:

- For every $x \in V_p$, $T_\pi^1(V_p)[x] = x$.
- $R_\pi^1(V_p) = true$.

Assume $R_\pi^i(V_p)$ and $T_\pi^i(V_p)$ are already defined. $R_\pi^{i+1}(V_p)$ and $T_\pi^{i+1}(V_p)$ are then defined according to the instruction at node i:

- Assignment $x = e$: $R_\pi^{i+1}(V_p) := R_\pi^i(V_p)$, $T_\pi^{i+1}(V_p)[x] := e[V_p \leftarrow T_\pi^i(V_p)]$ and $\forall y \neq x$, $T_\pi^{i+1}(V_p)[y] := T_\pi^i(V_p)[y]$
- Procedure call $g(Y)$: The procedure g is in-lined with the necessary renaming and symbolic execution continues along a path in g, returning to p when (if) g terminates.[2]
- Test $B(V_p)$: $T_\pi^{i+1}(V_p) := T_\pi^i(V_p)$, and

$$R_\pi^{i+1}(V_p) := \begin{cases} R_\pi^i(V_p) \wedge B[V_p \leftarrow T_\pi^i(V_p)] & \text{if the edge } l_i \rightarrow l_{i+1} \text{ is marked T} \\ R_\pi^i(V_p) \wedge \neg B[V_p \leftarrow T_\pi^i(V_p)] & \text{otherwise} \end{cases}$$

As a result, when we reach the last node l_n of a finite path π we get[3]:

$$R_\pi(V_p^v) = R_\pi^{n+1}(V_p)$$
$$T_\pi(V_p^v) = T_\pi^{n+1}(V_p) \downarrow_{V_p^v}$$

As symbolic execution explores the program one path at a time, we start by summarizing single paths, and then extend to procedures.

Definition 5. *Given a finite maximal path π in p, a* ***Path Summary*** *(also known as a partition-effect pair in [25]) is the pair $(R_\pi(V_p^v), T_\pi(V_p^v))$.*

Definition 6. *A* ***Procedure Summary*** *(also known as a symbolic summary in [25]), for a procedure p, is a set of path summaries*

$$sum_p \subseteq \{(R_\pi(V_p^v), T_\pi(V_p^v)) | \pi \text{ is a finite maximal path in } CFG_p\}.$$

---

[2] Current values of Y are assigned to the visible variables of g, and assigned back at termination of g.

[3] Since we assume that all inputs are given through visible variables, and therefore no hidden variable is used before it is initialized, V_p^h will not appear in $R_\pi^{n+1}(V_p)$ and $T_\pi^{n+1}(V_p) \downarrow_{V_p^v}$.

Note that for a given CFG the reachability conditions of any pair of different maximal paths are disjoint, meaning that for every initial state at most one finite maximal path is traversed in the CFG. Thus, a procedure summary partitions the set of initial states into disjoint finite paths, and describes the effect of the procedure p on each path separately. This observation will be useful when procedure summaries are used to compute difference summaries between procedures.

Unfortunately, it is not always possible to cover all paths in symbolic execution due to the path explosion problem (even if all feasible paths are finite, their number may be very large or even infinite). Therefore we allow for a given summary sum_p not to cover all possible paths, meaning $\bigvee_{(r,t)\in sum_p} r$ may not be valid ($\bigvee_{(r,t)\in sum_p} r \not\equiv true$).

Definition 7. *Given a procedure summary sum_p, the **Uncovered Part** of sum_p is $\neg \bigvee_{(r,t)\in sum_p} r$.*

For all inputs that satisfy the uncovered part of the summary nothing is promised: the procedure p might not terminate on such inputs, or terminate with unknown outputs. A summary for which the uncovered part is unsatisfiable ($\bigvee_{(r,t)\in sum_p} r \equiv true$) is called a **full** summary. Note that a full summary only exists for procedures that halt on every input.

Example 2. We return to $p1$ from Fig. 2. Any subset of the set $\{(x < 0, -1), (x \geq 0 \wedge x \geq 2, x), (x \geq 0 \wedge x < 2, 3)\}$ is a summary for p_1. For the summary

$$sum_{p_1} = \{(x < 0, -1), (x \geq 0 \wedge x \geq 2, x)\},$$

the uncovered part is characterized by $x \geq 0 \wedge x < 2$.

2.2 Equivalence

We modify the notions of equivalence from [13] to characterize the set of visible states under which procedures are equivalent, even if they might not be equivalent for every initial state. Let p_1 and p_2 be two procedures with visible variables $V^v_{p_1}$ and $V^v_{p_2}$, respectively. Since their sets of visible variables might be different, we take the union $V^v_{p_1} \cup V^v_{p_2}$ as their set of visible variables V^v_p. Any valuation of this set can be viewed as a visible state of both procedures.

Definition 8. *State-Equivalences*
Let σ^v_p be a visible state for p_1 and p_2.

- *p_1 and p_2 are* **partially equivalent** *for σ^v_p if and only if the following holds: If p_1 and p_2 both terminate on σ^v_p, then they terminate with the same final state.*
- *p_1 and p_2* **mutually terminate** *for σ^v_p if and only if the following holds: p_1 terminates on σ^v_p if and only if p_2 terminates on σ^v_p.*
- *p_1 and p_2 are* **fully equivalent** *for σ^v_p if and only if p_1 and p_2 are partially equivalent for σ^v_p and mutually terminate for σ^v_p.*

3 Modular Symbolic Execution

A major component of our analysis is the modular symbolic execution, which analyses one procedure at a time while avoiding inlining of called procedures. This prevents unnecessary execution of previously explored paths in called procedures. Assume procedure p calls procedure g. Also assume that a procedure summary for g is given by: $sum_g = \{(r^1, t^1), \ldots, (r^n, t^n)\}$.

Modular symbolic execution is defined as symbolic execution for assignment and test instructions (see Sect. 2.1). For procedure call instruction $g(Y)$ (where $Y \subseteq V_p$) it is defined as follows. For given $R^i_\pi(V_p)$ and $T^i_\pi(V_p)$[4]:

$$R^{i+1}_\pi = R^i_\pi \wedge (\bigvee_{(r,t)\in sum_g} r(T^i_\pi[Y])) \tag{1}$$

$$\forall x \notin Y.\ T^{i+1}_\pi[x] = T^i_\pi[x] \tag{2}$$

$$\forall y_j \in Y.\ T^{i+1}_\pi[y_j] = ITE(r^1(T^i_\pi[Y]), t^1_j(T^i_\pi[Y]), ITE(r^2(T^i_\pi[Y]), t^2_j(T^i_\pi[Y]), ITE(\ldots, ITE(r^n(T^i_\pi[Y]), t^n_j(T^i_\pi[Y]), UK)\ldots))),$$

where:

- $ITE(b, e_1, e_2)$ is an expression that returns e_1 if the condition b holds and returns e_2, otherwise. It is similar to the conditional operator (?:) in some programming languages.
- t^k_j refers to the jth element (for y_j) of the path transformation t^k.
- UK represents the value that is given if no path condition from sum_g is satisfied. That it, UK is returned when an unexplored path is traversed. Note, however, that since we added $(\bigvee_{(r,t)\in sum_g} r(T^i_\pi[Y])$ to the path condition R^i_π, a path that satisfies R^{i+1}_π will never return UK. Thus, UK is just a place holder.

Modular symbolic execution, as defined here, restricts the analysis of procedure p to paths along which g is called with inputs traversing paths in g that have already been analyzed. For other paths, the reachability condition will be unsatisfiable. In Sect. 6.1 we define an abstraction, which replaces unexplored paths by uninterpreted functions. Thus, the analysis of p may include unexplored (abstracted) paths of g. If the analysis reveals that the unexplored paths are essential in order to determine difference or similarity on the level of p, then refinement is applied by symbolically analysing more of g's paths.

We prove in [29] the connection between modular symbolic execution and regular symbolic execution on the in-lined version of the program. Intuitively, as long as the paths taken in called procedures are covered by the summaries of the called procedures, the following holds: Assume that a path π in p includes a call to procedure g. Then π corresponds to a set of paths in the in-lined version, each of which executing a different path in g, more formally:

[4] We use $r(T^i_\pi[Y])$ to indicate that every $v_k \in V^v_g$ is replaced by the expression $T^i_\pi[y_k]$.

- For every path π^{in} in the in-lined version of p there is a corresponding path π in p such that:
  - $R_{\pi^{in}} \rightarrow R_{\pi}$
  - $R_{\pi^{in}} \rightarrow T_{\pi^{in}} = T_{\pi}$
- For every path π in p, there are paths $\pi_1^{in}, \ldots, \pi_n^{in}$ in the in-lined version of p such that:
  - $R_{\pi} \leftrightarrow \bigvee_{i=1}^{n} R_{\pi_i^{in}}$
  - $\forall i \in [n].\ R_{\pi_i^{in}} \rightarrow T_{\pi_i^{in}} = T_{\pi}$

4 Difference Summary

Throughout the rest of the paper, we refer to a syntactically different pair of procedures as ***modified***, and to a semantically different pair of procedures (not fully equivalent for every state) as ***affected***. Note that a modified procedure is not necessarily affected. Further, an affected procedure is not necessarily modified, but must call (transitively) a modified and affected procedure.

Our main goal is, given two program versions, to evaluate the difference and similarity between them. For that purpose we define the notion of difference summary, in an attempt to capture the semantic difference and similarity between the programs. A difference summary is defined for procedures and extends to programs, by computing the difference summary for the main procedures in the programs.

We start by defining the notion of full difference summary, which precisely captures the difference and similarity between the behaviors of two given procedures. In this section we give all definitions in terms of sets of states that might be infinite.

Definition 9. *A* ***Full Difference Summary*** *for two procedures p_1 and p_2 is a triplet*

$$\Delta Full_{p_1,p_2} = (ch_{p_1,p_2}, unch_{p_1,p_2}, termin\_ch_{p_1,p_2})$$

where,

- *ch_{p_1,p_2} is the set of visible states for which both procedures terminate with different final states.*
- *$unch_{p_1,p_2}$ is the set of visible states for which both procedures either terminate with the same final states, or both do not terminate.*
- *$termin\_ch_{p_1,p_2}$ is the set of visible states for which exactly one procedure terminates.*

Note that $ch_{p_1,p_2} \cup unch_{p_1,p_2} \cup termin\_ch_{p_1,p_2}$ covers the entire visible state space. The three sets are related to the state equivalence notions of Definition 8 as follows.

- ch_{p_1,p_2} is the set of the visible states that violate partial equivalence. It only captures differences between terminating paths.
- $termin\_ch_{p_1,p_2}$ is the set of visible states that violate mutual termination.

- $unch_{p_1,p_2}$ is the set of visible states for which the procedures are fully equivalent.

Example 3. Consider the procedures in Fig. 2. The full difference summary for this pair of procedures is:

$$ch_{p_1,p_2} = \{\{x \mapsto 4\}\}$$
$$unch_{p_1,p_2} = \{\{x \mapsto c\} \mid c \neq 2 \wedge c \neq 4\}$$
$$termin\_ch_{p_1,p_2} = \{\{x \mapsto 2\}\}$$

For input 2 the old version $p1$ does not change x, while the new version $p2$ reaches an infinite loop, and therefore 2 is in $termin\_ch_{p_1,p_2}$. For input 3, although the paths taken in the two versions are different, the final value of x is the same (3), and therefore 3 is in $unch_{p_1,p_2}$. For input 4, $p1$ does not change x, while $p2$ changes x to 3, and therefore 4 is in ch_{p_1,p_2}.

The full difference summary and any of its three components are generally incomputable, since they require halting information. We therefore suggest to under-approximate the desired sets. In the next section we present an algorithm that computes under-approximated sets and can also strengthen them. The strengthening extends the sets with additional states, thus bringing the computed summary "closer" to the full difference summary.

Definition 10. *Given two procedures p_1, p_2, their **Difference Summary***

$$\Delta_{p_1,p_2} = (C(p_1, p_2), U(p_1, p_2))$$

consists of two sets of states where

- $C(p_1, p_2) \subseteq ch_{p_1,p_2}$.
- $U(p_1, p_2) \subseteq unch_{p_1,p_2}$.

A difference summary gives us both an under-approximation and an over-approximation of the difference between procedures, given by $C(p_1, p_2)$ and $\neg U(p_1, p_2)$[5], respectively.

The algorithm presented in the next section is based on the notion of path difference, presented below. Recall that for a given path π, its path summary is the pair (R_π, T_π) (see Definition 5).

Definition 11. *Let p_1 and p_2 be two procedures with the same visible variables $V_{p_1}^v = V_{p_2}^v = V_p^v$, and let π_1 and π_2 be finite paths in CFG_{p_1} and CFG_{p_2}, respectively. Then the **Path Difference** of π_1 and π_2 is a triplet $(d, T_{\pi_1}, T_{\pi_2})$, where d is defined as follows:*

$$d(V_p^v) \leftrightarrow (R_{\pi_1}(V_p^v) \wedge R_{\pi_2}(V_p^v) \wedge \neg(T_{\pi_1}(V_p^v) = T_{\pi_2}(V_p^v))).$$

---

[5] We use $\neg$ for set complement with respect to the state space.

We call d the *condition* of the path difference. Note that d implies the reachability conditions of both paths, meaning that for any visible state σ that satisfies d, path π_1 is traversed from σ in CFG_{p_1} and path π_2 is traversed from σ in CFG_{p_2}. Moreover, when starting from σ, the final state of π_1 will be different from the final state of π_2 (at least for one of the variables in V_p^v). If d is satisfiable we say that π_1 and π_2 ***show difference***.

5 Computing Difference Summaries

5.1 Call Graph Traversal

Assume we are given two program versions, each consisting of one *main* procedure and many other procedures that call each other. Assume also a *matching* function, which associates procedures in one program with procedures in the other, based on names (added and removed procedures are matched to the empty procedure). Our objective is to efficiently compute difference summaries for matching procedures in the programs. We are particularly interested in the difference of their main procedures. This goal will be achieved gradually, where precision of the resulting summaries increases, as computation proceeds. In this section we replace the sets of states describing difference summaries by their characteristic functions, in the form of FOL formulas.

As mentioned before, any block of code can be treated as a procedure, not only those defined as procedures by the programmer.

Our main algorithm DiffSummarize, presented in Algorithm 1, provides an overview of our method. The algorithm does not assume that the call graph is cycle-free, and therefore is suitable for recursive programs as well.

For each pair of matched procedures, the algorithm computes a Difference summary Diff$[(p_1, p_2)]$, which is a pair of $C(p_1, p_2)$ and $U(p_1, p_2)$. Sum is a mapping from all procedures to their current summary.

The algorithm computes a set *workSet*, which includes all pairs of procedures for which Diff should be computed. The set *workSet* is initialized with all modified procedures, and all their callers (lines 3–8), as those are the only procedures suspected to be affected. We initially trivially under-approximate Diff for the procedures in *workSet* by (*false*, *false*) (line10). We can also safely conclude that all other procedures are not affected (line 14).

Next we analyse all pairs of procedures in *workSet* (lines 17–31), where the order is chosen heuristically. Given procedures p_1 and p_2, if they are syntactically identical, and all called procedures have already been proven to be unaffected (line19) – we can conclude that p_1, p_2 are also unaffected. Otherwise, we compute sum_{p_1} and sum_{p_2} by running ModularSymbolicExecution (presented in Sect. 3) on the code of each procedure separately, up to a certain bound (chosen heuristically).

Since it is possible to visit a pair of procedures p_1, p_2 multiple times we keep the computed summaries in Sum$[p_1]$ and Sum$[p_2]$, and re-use them when re-analyzing the procedures to avoid recomputing path summaries of paths that have already been visited. We then call algorithm ConstructProcDiffSum (explained in Sect. 5.2) for computing a difference summary for p_1 and p_2.

Each time a difference summary changes (line 27), we need to re-analyse all its callers to check how this newly learned information propagates (line 29).

Algorithm DiffSummarize is modular. It handles each pair of procedures separately, without ever considering the full program and without inlining called procedures.

As mentioned before, Algorithm DiffSummarize is not guaranteed to terminate. Yet it is an *anytime algorithm.* That is, its partial results are meaningful. Furthermore, the longer it runs, the more precise its results are.

Algorithm 1. DiffSummarize(P_1, P_2)

Input: Two program versions P_1, P_2
Output: Difference Summary and a set of Path Difference Summaries for each pair of matching procedures, including $main_{P_1}, main_{P_2}$

1: $match$ = ComputeProcedureMatching(P_1, P_2)
2: FoundDiff[(p_1, p_2)] = $\emptyset$, for each $(p_1, p_2) \in match$
3: $workSet := \emptyset$
4: $newWorkSet := \{(p_1, p_2) \in match$: p_1 different syntactically from $p_2\}$
5: **while** $newWorkSet \neq workSet$ **do**
6: $workSet := newWorkSet$
7: $newWorkSet := workSet \cup \{(q_1, q_2) \in match : \exists (p_1, p_2) \in workSet$ s.t. q_1 calls p_1 or q_2 calls $p_2\}$
8: **end while**
9: **for** each $(p_1, p_2) \in workSet$ **do**
10: Diff[(p_1, p_2)] := (*false*, *false*)
11: Sum[p_1]:=$\emptyset$, Sum[p_2]:=$\emptyset$
12: **end for**
13: **for** each $(p_1, p_2) \in match \setminus workSet$ **do**
14: Diff[(p_1, p_2)] := (*false*, *true*)
15: Sum[p_1]:=$\emptyset$, Sum[p_2]:=$\emptyset$
16: **end for**
17: **while** $workSet \neq \emptyset$ **do**
18: (p_1, p_2) := chooseNext($workSet$) ▷ heuristic order
19: **if** p_1, p_2 are syntactically identical and for all $(g_1, g_2) \in match$ s.t. p_1 calls g_1 or p_2 calls g_2, Diff[(g_1, g_2)]=(*,*true*) **then**
20: newDiff := (*false*,*true*)
21: **else**
22: Sum[p_1] := ModularSymbolicExecution(p_1,Sum)
23: Sum[p_2] := ModularSymbolicExecution(p_2,Sum)
24: (newDiff,newFoundDiff) :=ConstProcDiffSum(Sum[p_1],Sum[p_2],Diff[(p_1, p_2)])
25: FoundDiff[(p_1, p_2)]:=FoundDiff[(p_1, p_2)] $\cup$ newFoundDiff
26: **end if**
27: **if** Diff[(p_1, p_2)] $\neq$ newDiff **then**
28: Diff[(p_1, p_2)] := newDiff
29: $workSet := workSet \cup \{(q_1, q_2) \in match$: q_1 calls p_1 or q_2 calls $p_2\}$
30: **end if**
31: **end while**
32: **return** (Diff, FoundDiff)

5.2 Computing the Difference Summaries for a Pair of Procedures

Algorithm ConstProcDiffSum (presented in Algorithm 2) accepts as input procedure summaries sum_{p_1}, sum_{p_2} and also the current difference summary of p_1, p_2. It returns an updated difference summary Δ_{p_1,p_2}. In addition, it returns

Algorithm 2. ConstProcDiffSum(sum_{p_1}, sum_{p_2}, oldDiff)

Input: Procedure summaries sum_{p_1}, sum_{p_2} of procedures p_1, p_2, respectively, and oldDiff, previously computed Δ_{p_1,p_2}
Output: updated Δ_{p_1,p_2}, $found\_diff_{p_1,p_2}$

1: $(C(p_1,p_2), U(p_1,p_2))$:= oldDiff
2: $found\_diff_{p_1,p_2} = \emptyset$
3: **for** each (r_1, t_1) in sum_{p_1} **do**
4:     **for** each (r_2, t_2) in sum_{p_2} **do**
5:         $diffCond := r_1 \wedge r_2 \wedge t_1 \neq t_2$
6:         **if** $diffCond$ is SAT **then**
7:             $C(p_1,p_2) := C(p_1,p_2) \vee diffCond$
8:             $found\_diff_{p_1,p_2} := found\_diff_{p_1,p_2} \cup \{(diffCond, t_1, t_2)\}$
9:         **end if**
10:         $eqCond := r_1 \wedge r_2 \wedge t_1 = t_2$
11:         **if** $eqCond$ is SAT **then**
12:             $U(p_1,p_2) := U(p_1,p_2) \vee eqCond$
13:         **end if**
14:     **end for**
15: **end for**
16: **return** $((C(p_1,p_2), U(p_1,p_2)), found\_diff_{p_1,p_2})$

the set $found\_diff_{p_1,p_2}$ of path differences, for every pair of paths in the two procedure summaries, which *shows difference.*

The construction of *diffCond* in line 5 ensures that $(diffCond, t_1, t_2)$ is a valid path difference. We add *diffCond* to $C(p_1, p_2)$ (line 7), and $(diffCond, t_1, t_2)$ to $found\_diff_{p_1,p_2}$ (line 8). Thus, we not only know under which conditions the procedures show difference, but also maintain the difference itself (by means of t_1 and t_2).

The construction of *eqCond* in line 10 ensures that for all states that satisfy it the final states of both procedures are identical, as required by the definition of $U(p_1, p_2)$. The satisfiability checks in lines 6, 11 are an optimization that ensures we do not complicate the computed formulas unnecessarily with unsatisfiable formulas.

We avoid recomputing previously computed path differences. For simplicity, we do not show it in the algorithm.

6 Abstraction and Refinement

6.1 Abstraction

In Sect. 3 we show how to define symbolic execution modularly. There, we restrict ourselves to procedure calls with previously analyzed inputs. However, full analysis of each procedure is usually not feasible and often not needed for difference analysis at the program level. In this section we show how partial analysis can be used better.

We abstract the unexplored behaviors of the called procedures by means of uninterpreted functions [18]. A demand-driven refinement is applied to the abstraction when greater precision is needed.

We modify the definition of *Modular symbolic execution* for procedure call instruction $g(Y)$ in the following manner:

- First, we now allow the symbolic execution of p to consider paths along which p calls g with inputs for which g traverses an unexplored path. To do so, we change the definition from Eq. (1) to $R_\pi^{i+1} = R_\pi^i$.
- Second, to deal with the lack of knowledge of the output of g, we introduce a set of uninterpreted functions $UF_g = \{UF_g^j | 1 \leq j \leq |V_g^v|\}$[6]. The uninterpreted function $UF_g^j(T_\pi^i[Y])$ replaces UK in $T_\pi^{i+1}[y_j]$ (Eq. (2)), where $y_j \in Y$ is the j-th parameter to g.

We can now improve the precision of $S_{i+1}[y_j]$ if we exploit not only the summaries of g_1 and g_2 but also their difference summaries. In particular, we can use the fact that $U(g_1, g_2)$ characterizes the inputs for which g_1 and g_2 behave the same. We thus introduce three sets of uninterpreted functions: $UF_{g_1}, UF_{g_2}, UF_{g_1,g_2}$.

We now revisit Eq. (2) of the modular symbolic execution for procedure call $g_1(Y)$, where we replace UK in $T_\pi^{i+1}[y_j]$ with

$$ITE(U(g_1, g_2)(T_\pi^i[Y]), UF_{g_1,g_2}^j(T_\pi^i[Y]), UF_{g_1}^j(T_\pi^i[Y])).$$

Similarly, for a procedure call $g_2(Y)$ we replace UK with

$$ITE(U(g_1, g_2)(T_\pi^i[Y]), UF_{g_1,g_2}^j(T_\pi^i[Y]), UF_{g_2}^j(T_\pi^i[Y])).$$

The set UF_{g_1,g_2} includes common uninterpreted functions, representing our knowledge of equivalence between g_1 and g_2 when called with inputs $T_\pi^i[Y]$, even though their behavior in this case is unknown. In some cases this could be enough to prove the equivalence of the calling procedures p_1, p_2. The sets UF_{g_1} and UF_{g_2} are separate uninterpreted functions, which give us no additional information on the differences or similarities of g_1, g_2.

Example 4. Consider again procedures $p1$, $p2$ in Fig. 2. Let their procedure summaries be

$$sum_{p_1}(x) = \{(x < 0, -1), (x \geq 2, x)\}$$
$$sum_{p_2}(x) = \{(x < 0, -1), (x > 4, x)\}$$

and their difference summary be $\Delta_{p_1,p_2} = (\mathit{false}, x < 2 \vee x > 4)$. When symbolic execution of a procedure g reaches a procedure call $p1(a)$, where a is a variable of the calling procedure g, we will perform:

$$\begin{aligned}
R_\pi^{i+1} &= R_\pi^i \\
\forall y_j \neq a.\ T_\pi^{i+1}[y_j] &= T_\pi^i[y_j] \\
T_\pi^{i+1}[a] &= ITE(T_\pi^i[a] < 0, -1, ITE(T_\pi^i[a] \geq 2, T_\pi^i[a], \\
&\quad ITE(T_\pi^i[a] < 2 \vee T_\pi^i[a] > 4, UF_{p1,p2}^x(T_\pi^i[a]), UF_{p1}^x(T_\pi^i[a])))).
\end{aligned}$$

[6] An obvious optimization is to use the previous symbolic state for visible variables of p that are only used by g as inputs but are not changed in g. However, for simplicity of discussion we will not go into those details.

6.2 Refinement

Using the described abstraction, the computed R_π, T_π may contain symbols of uninterpreted functions, and therefore so could *diffCond*= $r_1 \wedge r_2 \wedge t_1 \neq t_2$ and *eqCond* $= r_1 \wedge r_2 \wedge t_1 = t_2$ (lines 5, 10 in Algorithm ConstProcDiffSum). As a result, $C(p_1, p_2)$ and $U(p_1, p_2)$ may include constraints that are *spurious*, that is, constraints that do not represent real differences or similarities between p_1 and p_2. This could occur due to the abstraction introduced by the uninterpreted functions. Thus, before adding *diffCond* to $C(p_1, p_2)$ or *eqCond* to $U(p_1, p_2)$, we need to check whether it is *spurious*. To address spuriousness, we may then need to apply *refinement* by further analysing unexplored parts of the procedures. This includes procedures that are known to be identical in both versions, since their behavior may affect the reachability or the final states, as demonstrated by the example below.

```
void f1(int& x) {
  if (x == 5) {
    abs(x);
    if (x == 0) {
      x = 0;
      return;
    }
  }
}
```

```
void f2(int& x) {
  if (x == 5) {
    abs(x);
    if (x == 0) {
      x = 1;
      return;
    }
  }
}
```

```
void abs(int& x) {
  if (x >= 1)
    return;
  else
    x = -x;
}
```

Fig. 3. Procedure versions in need of refinement

Example 5. To conclude that the procedures in Fig. 3 are equivalent, we need to know that $abs(5)$ cannot be zero. Therefore, we need to analyse abs, even though it was not changed or affected.

We use the technique introduced in [4]: Let φ be a formula we wish to add to either $C(p_1, p_2)$ or $U(p_1, p_2)$ ($\varphi \in \{diffCond, eqCond\}$) such that φ includes symbols of uninterpreted functions. Before being added, it should be checked for spuriousness.

For every $k \in \{1, 2\}$, assume procedure p_k calls procedure $g_k(Y_k)$ at location l_{i_k} on the single path π' from p_k, described by φ. For every $k \in \{1, 2\}$ apply symbolic execution up to a certain limit on g_k with the pre-condition

$$\varphi \wedge \neg \left(\bigvee_{(r,t) \in sum_{g_k}} r\left(T_{\pi'}^{i_k-1}[Y_k]\right) \right) \wedge V_g^v = T_{\pi'}^{i_k-1}[Y_k].$$

When the reachability checks are performed with this precondition, only new paths reachable from this call in p_k are explored. For every such new path π, add (R_π, T_π) to sum_{g_k}, replace the old sum_{g_k} with the new sum_{g_k} in φ and check for satisfiability again. As a result, we either find a real difference or similarity, or eliminate all the spurious path differences that involve the explored path π in g_k. The refinement suggested above can be extended in a straightforward manner to any number of function calls along a path.

Example 6. Consider again the procedures in Fig. 3. Assume that the current summaries of $\text{abs}_1 = \text{abs}_2 = \text{abs}$ are empty, but it is known that both versions are identical (unmodified syntactically). We get (using symbolic execution and Algorithm 2) the *diffCond* for p_1 and p_2:

$$\begin{aligned} \mathit{diffCond} &= \Big[x = 5 \wedge \Big(\mathit{ITE}\,(\mathit{true}, \mathit{UF}_{abs_1,abs_2}(x), \mathit{UF}_{abs_1}(x)) = 0\Big) \\ &\quad \wedge x = 5 \wedge \Big(\mathit{ITE}\,(\mathit{true}, \mathit{UF}_{abs_1,abs_2}(x), \mathit{UF}_{abs_2}(x)) = 0\Big) \wedge 0 \neq 1\Big] \\ &\equiv \Big[x = 5 \wedge \mathit{UF}_{abs_1,abs_2}(x) = 0\Big] \end{aligned}$$

Next we use $x = 5$ as a pre-condition, and perform symbolic execution, updating the summary for abs: $(x \geq 1, x)$. Now *diffCond* is:

$$\begin{aligned} &\Big[x = 5 \wedge \Big(\mathit{ITE}\Big(x \geq 1, x, \mathit{ITE}(\mathit{true}, \mathit{UF}_{abs_1,abs_2}(x), \mathit{UF}_{abs_1}(x))\Big) = 0\Big) \\ &\wedge x = 5 \wedge \Big(\mathit{ITE}\Big(x \geq 1, x, \mathit{ITE}\,(\mathit{true}, \mathit{UF}_{abs_1,abs_2}(x), \mathit{UF}_{abs_2}(x))\Big) = 0\Big) \wedge 0 \neq 1\Big] \\ &\equiv \Big[x = 5 \wedge \Big(\mathit{ITE}\Big(x \geq 1, x, \mathit{UF}_{abs_1,abs_2}(x)\Big) = 0\Big)\Big] \equiv x = 5 \wedge x = 0 \end{aligned}$$

which is now unsatisfiable. We thus managed to eliminate a spurious difference without computing the full summary of *abs*.

Once a difference summary is computed, we can choose whether to refine the difference by exploring more paths in the individual procedures; or, if *diffCond* or *eqCond* contains uninterpreted functions, to explore in a demand driven manner the procedures summarized by the uninterpreted functions; or continue the analysis in a calling procedure, where possibly the unknown parts of the current procedures will not be reachable. In Sect. 8 we describe the results on our benchmarks in two extreme modes: running refinement always immediately when needed (ModDiffRef), and always delaying the refinement (ModDiff).

7 Related Work

A formal definition of equivalence between programs is given in [13]. We extend these definitions to obtain a finer-grained characterization of the differences.

We extend the path-wise symbolic summaries and deltas given in [25], and show how to use them in modular symbolic execution, while abstracting unknown parts.

The SymDiff [20] tool and the Regression Verification Tool (RVT) [14] both check for partial equivalence between pairs of procedures in a program, while abstracting procedure calls (after transforming loops into recursive calls). Unlike our tool, both SymDiff and RVT are only capable of proving equivalences, not disproving them. In [16], a work that has similar ideas to ours, conditional equivalence is used to characterize differences with SymDiff. The algorithm presented in [16] is able to deal with loops and recursion; however, the algorithm is not fully implemented in SymDiff. Our tool is capable of dealing soundly with loops, and as our experiments show, is often able to produce full difference summaries for programs with unbounded loops. We also provide a finer-grained result, by characterizing the inputs for which there are (no) semantic differences.

Both SymDiff and RVT lack refinement, which often causes them to fail at proving equivalence, as shown by our experiments in Sect. 8. Both tools are, however, capable of proving equivalence between programs (using, among others, invariants and proof rules) that cannot be handled by our method. Our techniques can be seen as an orthogonal improvement. SymDiff also has a mode that infers common invariants, as descried in [21], but it failed to infer the required invariants for our examples.

Under-constrained symbolic execution, meaning symbolic execution of a procedure that is not the entry point of the program is presented in [27,28], where it is used to improve scalability while using the old version as a golden model. The algorithm presented in [27,28] does not provide any guarantees on its result, and it does not attempt to propagate found differences to inputs of the programs. By contrast, our algorithm does not stop after analysing only the syntactically modified procedures, but continues to their calling procedures. On the other hand, procedures that do not call modified procedures (transitively) are immediately marked as equivalent. Thus, we avoid unnecessary work. In [27], the new program version is checked, while assuming that the old version is correct. We do not use such assumptions, as we are interested in all differences: new bugs, bug fixes, and functional differences such as new features.

In [5,26] summaries and symbolic execution are also used to compute differences. The technique there leverages a light-weight static analysis to help guide symbolic execution only to potentially differing paths. In [6], symbolic execution is applied simultaneously on both versions, with the purpose of guiding symbolic execution to changed paths. Both techniques, however, lack modularity and abstractions. A possible direction for new research would be to integrate our approach with one of the two.

Our approach is similar to the compositional symbolic execution presented in [4,12], that is applied to single programs. However, the analysis in [4,12] is top-down while ours works bottom-up, starting from syntactically different procedures, proceeding to calling procedures only as long as they are affected by the difference of previously analyzed procedures. The analysis stops as soon as unaffected procedures are reached.

Our algorithm is unique in that it provides both an under- and over-approximations of the differences, while all the described methods have no guarantees or only provide one of the two.

8 Experimental Results

We implemented the algorithm presented in Sect. 5 with the abstractions from Sect. 6 on top of the CProver framework (version 787889a), which also forms the foundation of the verification tools CBMC [8], SatAbs [9], Impact [22] and Wolverine [19]. The implementation is available online [2]. Since we analyse programs at the level of an intermediate language (goto-language, the intermediate language used in the CProver framework), we can support any language that can be translated to this language (currently Java and C). We report results for two variants of our tool – without refinement (ModDiff for Modular Demand-driven Difference), and with refinement (ModDiffRef). The unwinding limit is set to 5 in both variants.

SymDiff and RVT: We compared our results to two well established tools, SymDiff and RVT. For SymDiff, we used the *smack* [3] tool to translate the C programs into the Boogie language, and then passed the generated Boogie files to the latest available online version of SymDiff.

8.1 Benchmarks and Results

We analysed 28 C benchmarks, where each benchmark includes a pair of syntactically similar versions. Our benchmarks are available online [1]. Our benchmarks were chosen to demonstrate some of the benefits of our technique, as explained below. A total of 16 benchmarks are semantically equivalent (Table 1), while some benchmarks contain semantically different procedures. When using refinement, our algorithm was able to prove all equivalences between programs but not between all procedures (although some were actually equivalent). RVT's refinement is limited to loop unrolling, and its summaries are limited as well. Thus, it cannot prove equivalence of ancestors of recursive procedures or loops that are semantically different. Also, if it fails to prove equivalence of semantically equivalent recursive procedures or loops, it cannot succeed in proving equivalence of their ancestors. As previously mentioned, RVT can sometimes prove equivalence when our tool cannot. The latest available version of SymDiff failed to prove most examples, possibly also for lack of refinement.

8.2 Analysis

We now explain in detail the benefit of our method on specific benchmarks. The *LoopUnrch* benchmarks illustrate the advantages of summaries. Our tool analyses foo1 and foo2 from Fig. 4c, finds a condition under which those procedures are different (for example inputs $-1, 1$), and a condition under which they are

Table 1. Experimental results. Numbers are time in seconds, F indicates a failure to prove equivalence in (a), and that the difference summary of main was not full (some differences were not found) in (b).

Benchmark	ModDiff	ModDiffRef	RVT	SymDiff
Const	0.545s	0.541s	4.06s	14.562s
Add	0.213s	0.2s	3.85s	14.549s
Sub	0.258s	0.308s	5.01s	F
Comp	0.841s	0.539s	5.19s	F
LoopSub	0.847s	1.179s	F	F
UnchLoop	F	2.838s	F	F
LoopMult2	1.666s	1.689s	F	F
LoopMult5	F	3.88s	F	F
LoopMult10	F	9.543s	F	F
LoopMult15	F	21.55s	F	F
LoopMult20	F	49.031s	F	F
LoopUnrch2	0.9s	0.941s	F	F
LoopUnrch5	1.131s	1.126s	F	F
LoopUnrch10	1.147s	1.168s	F	F
LoopUnrch15	1.132s	1.191s	F	F
LoopUnrch20	1.157s	1.215s	F	F

(a) Semantically equivalent

Benchmark	ModDiff	MDDiffRef
LoopSub	1.187s	2.426s
UnchLoop	F	8.053s
LoopMult2	3.01s	3.451s
LoopMult5	F	5.914s
LoopMult10	F	10.614s
LoopMult15	F	14.024s
LoopMult20	F	25.795s
LoopUnrch2	2.157s	2.338s
LoopUnrch5	2.609s	3.216s
LoopUnrch10	2.658s	3.481s
LoopUnrch15	2.835s	3.446s
LoopUnrch20	3.185s	3.342s

(b) Semantically different

equivalent ($a \geq 0$). In all versions of this benchmark, foo1 and foo2 are called with positive (increasing) values of a (and b), and hence the loop is never performed. We are able to prove equivalence efficiently in all versions, both with and without refinement.

The *LoopMult* benchmarks illustrate the advantages of refinement. Our tool analyses foo1 and foo2 from Fig. 4a, finds a condition under which those procedures are different (for example inputs $1, -1$), and a condition under which they are equivalent. We also summarise all behaviors that correspond to unwinding of the loop 5 times. This unwinding is sufficient when the procedures are calls with inputs $2, 2$ (benchmark *LoopMult2*, the first main from Fig. 4b), and therefore both MD-Diff and MD-DiffRef are able to prove equivalence quickly. This unwinding is, however, not sufficient for benchmark *LoopMult5* (the second main from Fig. 4b). Thus, MD-Diff is not able to prove equivalence (the summary of foo1/2 does not cover the necessary paths), while MD-DiffRef analyses the missing paths (where $5 \leq a < 7 \wedge b = 5$), and is able to prove equivalence. As the index of the *LoopMult* benchmark increases, the length of the required paths and their number increases, and the analysis takes more time, accordingly, but only necessary paths are explored.

The remaining 12 benchmarks are not equivalent, and our algorithm is able to find inputs for which they differ (presented in Table 1). Since both SymDiff and RVT are only capable of proving equivalences, not disproving them, we did not compare to those tools.

```
int foo1(int a, int b) {
  int c=0;
  for (int i=1; i<=b; ++i)
    c+=a;
  return c;
}

int foo2(int a, int b) {
  int c=0;
  for (int i=1; i<=a; ++i)
    c+=b;
  return c;
}
```

(a) procedures foo1 and foo2 in LoopMult benchmarks

```
int main(int x,
      char*argv[]) {
  //LoopMult2
  return foo(2,2);
}

int main(int x,
      char*argv[]) {
  //LoopMult5
  if (x>=5 && x<7)
    return foo(x,5);
  return 0;
}
```

(b) main functions of LoopMult2 and LoopMult5

```
int foo1(int a, int b) {
  int c=0;
  if (a<0) {
    for (int i=1;
        i<=b;++i)
      c+=a;
  }
  return c;
}

int foo2(int a, int b) {
  int c=0;
  if (a<0) {
    for (int i=1;
        i<=a;++i)
      c+=b;
  }
  return c;
}
```

(c) procedures foo1 and foo2 in LoopUnrch benchmarks

Fig. 4. LoopMult and LoopUnrch benchmarks

9 Conclusion

We developed a modular and demand-driven method for finding semantic differences and similarities between program versions. It is able to soundly analyse programs with loops and guide the analysis towards "interesting" paths. Our method is based on (partially abstracted) procedure summarizations, which can be refined on demand. Our experimental results demonstrate the advantage of our approach due to these features.

References

1. ModDiff benchmarks. https://github.com/AnnaTrost/ModDiff/tree/master/benchmarks
2. ModDiff tool. https://github.com/AnnaTrost/ModDiff
3. SMACK software verifier and verification toolchain. https://github.com/smackers/smack
4. Anand, S., Godefroid, P., Tillmann, N.: Demand-driven compositional symbolic execution. In: Ramakrishnan, C.R., Rehof, J. (eds.) TACAS 2008. LNCS, vol. 4963, pp. 367–381. Springer, Heidelberg (2008). doi:10.1007/978-3-540-78800-3_28
5. Backes, J., Person, S., Rungta, N., Tkachuk, O.: Regression verification using impact summaries. In: Bartocci, E., Ramakrishnan, C.R. (eds.) SPIN 2013. LNCS, vol. 7976, pp. 99–116. Springer, Heidelberg (2013). doi:10.1007/978-3-642-39176-7_7
6. Cadar, C., Palikareva, H.: Shadow symbolic execution for better testing of evolving software. In: Companion Proceedings of the 36th International Conference on Software Engineering, pp. 432–435. ACM (2014)
7. Cadar, C., Sen, K.: Symbolic execution for software testing: three decades later. Commun. ACM **56**(2), 82–90 (2013)

8. Clarke, E., Kroening, D., Lerda, F.: A tool for checking ANSI-C programs. In: Jensen, K., Podelski, A. (eds.) TACAS 2004. LNCS, vol. 2988, pp. 168–176. Springer, Heidelberg (2004). doi:10.1007/978-3-540-24730-2_15
9. Clarke, E., Kroening, D., Sharygina, N., Yorav, K.: SATABS: SAT-based predicate abstraction for ANSI-C. In: Halbwachs, N., Zuck, L.D. (eds.) TACAS 2005. LNCS, vol. 3440, pp. 570–574. Springer, Heidelberg (2005). doi:10.1007/978-3-540-31980-1_40
10. Francez, N.: Program Verification. Addison-Wesley Longman, Boston (1992)
11. Gao, D., Reiter, M.K., Song, D.: BinHunt: automatically finding semantic differences in binary programs. In: Chen, L., Ryan, M.D., Wang, G. (eds.) ICICS 2008. LNCS, vol. 5308, pp. 238–255. Springer, Heidelberg (2008). doi:10.1007/978-3-540-88625-9_16
12. Godefroid, P.: Compositional dynamic test generation. In: ACM SigPlan Notices, vol. 42, pp. 47–54. ACM (2007)
13. Godlin, B., Strichman, O.: Inference rules for proving the equivalence of recursive procedures. Acta Informatica **45**(6), 403–439 (2008)
14. Godlin, B., Strichman, O.: Regression verification. In: Proceedings of the 46th Annual Design Automation Conference, pp. 466–471. ACM (2009)
15. Godlin, B., Strichman, O.: Regression verification: proving the equivalence of similar programs. Softw. Test. Verif. Reliab. **23**(3), 241–258 (2013)
16. Kawaguchi, M., Lahiri, S.K., Rebelo, H.: Conditional equivalence. Technical report, MSR-TR-2010-119 (2010)
17. King, J.C.: Symbolic execution and program testing. Commun. ACM **19**(7), 385–394 (1976)
18. Kroening, D., Strichman, O.: Equality logic and uninterpreted functions. Decision Procedures. Texts in Theoretical Computer Science (An Eatcs Series), pp. 59–80. Springer, Heidelberg (2008). doi:10.1007/978-3-540-74105-3_3
19. Kroening, D., Weissenbacher, G.: Interpolation-based software verification with WOLVERINE. In: Gopalakrishnan, G., Qadeer, S. (eds.) CAV 2011. LNCS, vol. 6806, pp. 573–578. Springer, Heidelberg (2011). doi:10.1007/978-3-642-22110-1_45
20. Lahiri, S.K., Hawblitzel, C., Kawaguchi, M., Rebêlo, H.: SYMDIFF: a language-agnostic semantic Diff tool for imperative programs. In: Madhusudan, P., Seshia, S.A. (eds.) CAV 2012. LNCS, vol. 7358, pp. 712–717. Springer, Heidelberg (2012). doi:10.1007/978-3-642-31424-7_54
21. Lahiri, S.K., McMillan, K.L., Sharma, R., Hawblitzel, C.: Differential assertion checking. In: Proceedings of the 2013 9th Joint Meeting on Foundations of Software Engineering, pp. 345–355. ACM (2013)
22. McMillan, K.L.: Lazy abstraction with interpolants. In: Ball, T., Jones, R.B. (eds.) CAV 2006. LNCS, vol. 4144, pp. 123–136. Springer, Heidelberg (2006). doi:10.1007/11817963_14
23. Partush, N., Yahav, E.: Abstract semantic differencing for numerical programs. In: Logozzo, F., Fähndrich, M. (eds.) SAS 2013. LNCS, vol. 7935, pp. 238–258. Springer, Heidelberg (2013). doi:10.1007/978-3-642-38856-9_14
24. Partush, N., Yahav, E.: Abstract semantic differencing via speculative correlation. In: ACM SIGPLAN Notices, vol. 49, pp. 811–828. ACM (2014)
25. Person, S., Dwyer, M.B., Elbaum, S., Pasareanu, C.S.: Differential symbolic execution. In: Foundations of Software Engineering, pp. 226–237. ACM (2008)
26. Person, S., Yang, G., Rungta, N., Khurshid, S.: Directed incremental symbolic execution. In: ACM SIGPLAN Notices, vol. 46, pp. 504–515. ACM (2011)
27. Ramos, D.A., Engler, D.: Under-constrained symbolic execution: correctness checking for real code. In: 24th USENIX Security Symposium, pp. 49–64 (2015)

28. Ramos, D.A., Engler, D.R.: Practical, low-effort equivalence verification of real code. In: Gopalakrishnan, G., Qadeer, S. (eds.) CAV 2011. LNCS, vol. 6806, pp. 669–685. Springer, Heidelberg (2011). doi:10.1007/978-3-642-22110-1_55
29. Trostanetski, A., Grumberg, O., Kroening, D.: Modular demand-driven analysis of semantic difference for program versions. Technical report, CS-2017-02. http://www.cs.technion.ac.il/users/wwwb/cgi-bin/tr-info.cgi/2017/CS/CS-2017-02
30. Wong, W.E., Horgan, J.R., London, S., Agrawal, H.: A study of effective regression testing in practice. In: The Eighth International Symposium on Software Reliability Engineering, Proceedings, pp. 264–274. IEEE (1997)

Verifying Array Manipulating Programs by Tiling

Supratik Chakraborty[1], Ashutosh Gupta[2], and Divyesh Unadkat[1,3(✉)]

[1] Indian Institute of Technology Bombay, Mumbai, India
supratik@cse.iitb.ac.in
[2] Tata Institute of Fundamental Research, Mumbai, India
agupta@tifr.res.in
[3] TCS Research, Pune, India
divyesh.unadkat@tcs.com

Abstract. Formally verifying properties of programs that manipulate arrays in loops is computationally challenging. In this paper, we focus on a useful class of such programs, and present a novel property-driven verification method that first infers array access patterns in loops using simple heuristics, and then uses this information to compositionally prove universally quantified assertions about arrays. Specifically, we identify *tiles* of array access patterns in a loop, and use the tiling information to reduce the problem of checking a quantified assertion at the end of a loop to an inductive argument that checks only a slice of the assertion for a single iteration of the loop body. We show that this method can be extended to programs with sequentially composed loops and nested loops as well. We have implemented our method in a tool called TILER. Initial experiments show that TILER outperforms several state-of-the-art tools on a suite of interesting benchmarks.

1 Introduction

Arrays are widely used in programs written in imperative languages. They are typically used to store large amounts of data in a region of memory that the programmer views as contiguous, and which she can access randomly by specifying an index (or offset). Sequential programs that process data stored in arrays commonly use looping constructs to iterate over the range of array indices of interest and access the corresponding array elements. The ease with which data can be accessed by specifying an index is often exploited by programmers to access or modify array elements at indices that change in complex ways within a loop. While this renders programming easier, it also makes automatic reasoning about such array manipulating programs significantly harder. Specifically, the pattern of array accesses within loops can vary widely from program to program, and may not be easy to predict. Furthermore, since the access patterns often span large regions of the array that depend on program parameters, the array indices of interest cannot be bounded by statically estimated small constants. Hence, reasoning about arrays by treating each array element as a scalar

F. Ranzato (Ed.): SAS 2017, LNCS 10422, pp. 428–449, 2017.
DOI: 10.1007/978-3-319-66706-5_21

is not a practical option for analyzing such programs. This motivates us to ask if we can automatically infer program-dependent patterns of array accesses within loops, and use these patterns to simplify automatic verification of programs that manipulate arrays in loops.

A commonly used approach for proving properties of sequential programs with loops is to construct an inductive argument with an appropriate loop invariant. This involves three key steps: (i) showing that the invariant holds before entering the loop for the first time, (ii) establishing that if the invariant holds before entering the loop at any time, then it continues to hold after one more iteration of the loop, and (iii) proving that the invariant implies the desired property when the loop terminates. Steps (i) and (ii) allow us to inductively infer that the invariant holds before every iteration of the loop; the addition of step (iii) suffices to show that the desired property holds after the loop terminates. A significant body of research in automated program verification is concerned with finding invariants that allow the above inductive argument to be applied efficiently for various classes of programs.

For programs with loops manipulating arrays, the property of interest at the end of a loop is often a universally quantified statement over array elements. Examples of such properties include $\forall i\,\big((0 \leq i < N) \rightarrow (A[i] \geq minVal) \wedge (A[i] \leq A[i+1])\big)$, $\forall i\ ((0 \leq i < N) \wedge (i\,mod\,2 = 0) \rightarrow (A[i] = i))$ and the like. In such cases, a single iteration of the loop typically only ensures that the desired property holds over a small part of the array. Effectively, each loop iteration incrementally contributes to the overall property, and the contributions of successive loop iterations compose to establish the universally quantified property. This suggests the following approach for proving universally quantified assertions about arrays.

- We first *identify the region of the array where the contribution of a generic loop iteration is localized.* Informally, we call such a region a *tile* of the array. Note that depending on the program, the set of array indices representing a tile may not include all indices updated in the corresponding loop iteration. Identifying the right tile for a given loop can be challenging in general; we discuss more about this later.
- Next, we *carve out a "slice" of the quantified property that is relevant to the tile identified above.* Informally, we want this slice to represent the contribution of a generic loop iteration to the overall property. The inductive step of our approach checks if a generic iteration of the loop indeed ensures this slice of the property.
- Finally, we check that *the tiles cover the entire range of array indices of interest, and successive loop iterations do not interfere with each other's contributions.* In other words, once a loop iteration ensures that the slice of the property corresponding to its tile holds, subsequent loop iterations must not nullify this slice of the property. Formalizing these "range covering" and "non-interference" properties allows us to show that the contributions of different loop iterations compose to yield the overall quantified property at the end of the loop.

The remainder of the paper describes a technique and a tool that uses the above ideas to prove quantified assertions in a useful class of array manipulating programs. We focus on assertions expressed as universally quantified formulas on arrays, where the quantification is over array indices. Specifically, suppose I denotes a sequence of integer-valued array index, A denotes an array and $\mathcal{V}$ denotes a sequence of scalar variables used in the program. We consider assertions of the form $\forall I\, (\Phi(I) \implies \Psi(A, \mathcal{V}, I))$, where $\Phi(I)$ is a quantifier-free formula in the theory of arithmetic over integers, and $\Psi(A, \mathcal{V}, I)$ is a quantifier-free formula in the combined theory of arrays and arithmetic over integers. Informally, such an assertion states that for array indices satisfying condition $\Phi(I)$ (viz. even indices or indices greater than a parameter N), the corresponding array elements satisfy the property $\Psi(A, \mathcal{V}, I)$. The formal syntax of our assertions is explained in Sect. 3. In our experience, assertions of this form suffice to express a large class of interesting properties of array manipulating programs.

Although the general problem of identifying tiles in programs with array manipulating loops is hard, we have developed some heuristics to automate tile identification in a useful class of programs. To understand the generic idea behind our tiling heuristic, suppose the program under consideration has a single loop, and suppose the quantified property is asserted at the end of the loop. We introduce a fresh counter variable that is incremented in each loop iteration. We then use existing arithmetic invariant generation techniques, viz. [1,2], to identify a relation between the indices of array elements that are accessed and/or updated in a loop iteration, and the corresponding value of the loop counter. This information is eventually used to define a tile of the array for the loop under consideration.

In a more general scenario, the program under verification may have a sequence of loops, and the quantified property may be asserted at the end of the last loop. In such cases, we introduce a fresh counter variable for each loop, and repeat the above process to identify a tile corresponding to each loop. For our tiling-based technique to work, we also need invariants, or *mid-conditions*, between successive loops in the program. Since identifying precise invariants is uncomputable in general, we work with *candidate invariants* reported by existing off-the-shelf annotation/candidate-invariant generators. Specifically, in our implementation, we use the dynamic analysis tool DAIKON [2] that informs us of *candidate invariants* that are likely (but not proven) to hold between loops. Our algorithm then checks to see if the candidate invariants reported after every loop can indeed be proved using the tiling-based technique. Only those candidates that can be proved in this way are subsequently used to compose the tiling-based reasoning across consecutive loops. Finally, tiling can be applied to programs with nested loops as well. While the basic heuristic for identifying tiles remains the same in this case, the inductive argument needs to be carefully constructed when reasoning about nested loops. We discuss this in detail later in the paper.

We have implemented the above technique in a tool called TILER. Our tool takes as input a C function with one or more loops manipulating arrays. It also accepts a universally quantified assertion about arrays at the end of the function. TILER automatically generates a tiling of the arrays for each loop in the C function and tries to prove the assertion, as described above. We have applied TILER to a suite of 60 benchmarks comprised of programs that manipulate arrays in different ways. For most benchmarks where the specified assertion holds, TILER was able to prove the assertion reasonably quickly. In contrast, two state-of-the-art tools for reasoning about arrays faced difficulties and timed out on most of these benchmarks. For benchmarks where the specified assertion does not hold, TILER relies on bounded model checking to determine if an assertion violation can be detected within a few unwindings of the loops. There are of course corner cases where TILER remains inconclusive about the satisfaction of the assertion. Overall, our initial experiments suggest tiling-based compositional reasoning can be very effective for proving assertions in a useful class of array manipulating programs.

The primary contributions of the paper can be summarized as follows.

- We introduce the concept of *tiling* for reasoning about quantified assertions in programs manipulating arrays in loops.
- We present a tiling-based practical algorithm for verifying a class of array manipulating programs.
- We describe a tool that outperforms several state-of-the-art tools for reasoning about arrays on a suite of benchmarks. Our tool performs particularly well on benchmarks where the quantified assertion holds.

2 Motivating Example

Figure 1(a) shows a C function snippet adapted from an industrial battery controller. This example came to our attention after a proprietary industry-strength static analysis tool failed to prove the quantified assertion at the end of the function. Note that the function updates an array `volArray` whose size is given by `COUNT`. In general, `COUNT` can be large, viz. 100000. The universally quantified assertion at the end of the "for" loop requires that every element of `volArray` be either zero or at least as large as `MIN`. It is not hard to convince oneself through informal reasoning that the assertion indeed holds. The difficulty lies in proving it automatically. Indeed, neither BOOSTER [3] nor VAPHOR [4], which can reason about arrays with parameterized bounds, are able to prove this assertion within 15 min on a desktop machine. Bounded model checking tools like CBMC [5] and SMACK+CORRAL [6] are able to prove this assertion for arrays with small values of `COUNT`. For large arrays, viz. `COUNT = 100000`, these tools cannot prove the assertion within 15 min on a desktop machine. This is not surprising since a bounded model checker must unwind the loop in the function a large number of times if `COUNT` is large.

Let us now illustrate how tiling-based reasoning works in this example. We introduce a fresh auxiliary variable (say `j`) to denote the index used to update an element of `volArray`. Using arithmetic invariant generation techniques, viz. INVGEN [1], we can now learn that for all array accesses in the ith

```
void BatteryController() {
 int COUNT,MIN,i;
 int volArray[COUNT];

 if(COUNT%4 != 0) return;

 for(i=1;i<=COUNT/4;i++) {

  if(5 >= MIN)
   volArray[i*4-4] = 5;
  else
   volArray[i*4-4] = 0;
  if(7 >= MIN)
   volArray[i*4-3] = 7;
  else
   volArray[i*4-3] = 0;
  if(3 >= MIN)
   volArray[i*4-2] = 3;
  else
   volArray[i*4-2] = 0;
  if(1 >= MIN)
   volArray[i*4-1] = 1;
  else
   volArray[i*4-1] = 0;
 }
}
```

$\forall \mathtt{j}.(0 \leqslant \mathtt{j} < \mathtt{COUNT} \Rightarrow \mathtt{volArray}[j] \geqslant \mathtt{MIN} \vee \mathtt{volArray}[j] = 0)$

(a)

```
1 void BatteryControllerInst() {
2   int COUNT,MIN,i,j;
3   int volArray[COUNT];
4
5   if(COUNT%4 != 0) return;
6
7   assume(i>=1 && i<=COUNT/4);
8   assume(4*i-4<=j && j<4*i);
9
10  if(5 >= MIN)
11    volArray[i*4-4] = 5;
12  else
13    volArray[i*4-4] = 0;
14  if(7 >= MIN)
15    volArray[i*4-3] = 7;
16  else
17    volArray[i*4-3] = 0;
18  if(3 >= MIN)
19    volArray[i*4-2] = 3;
20  else
21    volArray[i*4-2] = 0;
22  if(1 >= MIN)
23    volArray[i*4-1] = 1;
24  else
25    volArray[i*4-1] = 0;
26  assert(volArray[j]>=MIN||volArray[j]==0);
27 }
```

(b)

Fig. 1. Motivating example `period-4`

loop iteration, the value of the index lies between $4 * \mathtt{i} - 4$ and $4 * \mathtt{i}$. Therefore, we choose $[4 * \mathtt{i} - 4, 4 * \mathtt{i})$ as the tile corresponding to the ith iteration of the loop.

In order to successfully apply the tiling-based reasoning, we must ensure that our tiles satisfy certain properties.

- *Covers range:* This ensures that every tile contains only valid array indices, and that no array index of interest in the quantified assertion is left unaccounted for in the tiles. In our example, array indices range from 0 to $\mathtt{COUNT}-1$, while the loop (and hence, tile) counter `i` ranges from 1 to $\mathtt{COUNT}/4$. Since the ith tile comprises of the array indices $4i-4, 4i-3, 4i-2$ and $4i-1$, both the above requirements are met.
- *Sliced property holds for tile:* The sliced property in this case says that the elements of `volArray` corresponding to indices within a tile have values that are either 0 or at least `MIN`. To prove that this holds after an iteration of the loop, we first obtain a loop-free program containing a single generic iteration of the loop, and check that the elements of `volArray` corresponding to the ith tile satisfy the sliced property after the execution of the ith loop iteration. The transformed program is shown in Fig. 1(b). Note that this program has a fresh variable j. The assume statements at lines 7–8 say that i is within the expected range and that j is an index in the ith tile. Since this program is loop-free, we can use a bounded model checker like CBMC [5] to prove the assertion in the transformed program.

- *Non-interference across tiles:* To show this, we assume that the sliced property holds for the i'-th tile, where $0 \le i' < i$, before the ith loop iteration starts. This can be done by adding the following three *extra assumptions* after lines 7 and 8 in Fig. 1(b): (i) $\texttt{assume(1} <= \texttt{i}' < \texttt{i)}$, (ii) $\texttt{assume(4} * \texttt{i}' - 4 <= \texttt{j}' < 4 * \texttt{i}')$, and (iii) $\texttt{assume(volArray[j}'] >= \texttt{MIN} \,||\, \texttt{volArray[j}'] == 0)$. We then assert at the end of the loop body that the sliced property for the i'-th tile continues to hold even after the ith iteration. This can be done by replacing the assertion in line 26 of Fig. 1(b) by $\texttt{assert(volArray[j}'] >= \texttt{MIN} \,||\, \texttt{volArray[j}'] == 0)$. As before, since the program in Fig. 1(b) is loop-free, this assertion can be easily checked using a bounded model checker like CBMC.

Once all the above checks have succeeded, we can conclude that the quantified assertion holds in the original program after the loop terminates. Note the careful orchestration of inductive reasoning to prove the sliced property, and compositional reasoning to aggregate the slices of the property to give the original quantified assertion. Our tiling-based tool proves the assertion in this example in less than a second.

3 Preliminaries

For purposes of this paper, an array-manipulating program P is a tuple $(\mathcal{V}, \mathcal{L}, \mathcal{A}, \mathsf{PB})$, where $\mathcal{V}$ is a set of scalar variables, $\mathcal{L} \subseteq \mathcal{V}$ is a set of scalar loop counter variables, $\mathcal{A}$ is a set of array variables, and PB is the program body generated by the following grammar.

$$
\begin{aligned}
\mathsf{PB} &::= \mathsf{St}\\
\mathsf{St} &::= v := \mathsf{E} \mid A[\mathsf{E}] := \mathsf{E} \mid \textbf{assume}(\mathsf{BoolE}) \mid \textbf{if}(\mathsf{BoolE})\ \textbf{then}\ \mathsf{St}\ \textbf{else}\ \mathsf{St} \mid\\
&\qquad \textbf{for}\ (\ell := 0; \ell < \mathsf{E}; \ell := \ell{+}1)\ \{\mathsf{St}\} \mid \mathsf{St}\ ;\ \mathsf{St}\\
\mathsf{E} &::= \mathsf{E}\ \text{op}\ \mathsf{E} \mid A[\mathsf{E}] \mid v \mid \ell \mid \mathsf{c}\\
\mathsf{BoolE} &::= \mathsf{E}\ \text{relop}\ \mathsf{E} \mid \mathsf{BoolE}\ \text{AND}\ \mathsf{BoolE} \mid \text{NOT}\ \mathsf{BoolE} \mid \mathsf{BoolE}\ \text{OR}\ \mathsf{BoolE}
\end{aligned}
$$

Here, we assume that $A \in \mathcal{A}$, $v \in \mathcal{V} \backslash \mathcal{L}$, $\ell \in \mathcal{L}$ and $\mathsf{c} \in \mathbb{Z}$. We also assume that "op" (resp. "relop") is one of a set of arithmetic (resp. relational) operators. We wish to highlight the following features of programs generated by this grammar:

- There are no unstructured jumps, like those effected by `goto` or `break` statements in C-like languages. The effect of a `break` statement inside a loop in a C-like language can always be modeled by setting a flag, and by conditioning the execution of subsequent statements in the loop body on this flag being not set, and by using this flag to determine whether to exit the loop. The effect of a `break` statement in a conditional branch can also be similarly modeled. Therefore, we can mimic the behaviour of `break` statements in our programs.
- We can have sequences of possibly nested loops, with non-looping program fragments between loops. Furthermore, the body of a loop and the corresponding *loop head*, i.e. control location where the loop is entered, are easily identifiable.

- Every loop is associated with a scalar loop counter variable that is set to 0 when the loop is entered, and incremented after every iteration of the loop. We assume that each loop has a unique counter variable.
- The only assignments to loop counter variables happen when a loop is entered for the first time and at the end of an iteration of the corresponding loop body. Other assignment statements in the program cannot assign to loop counter variables. Loop counter variables can however be freely used in expressions throughout the program.
- The restriction on the usage of loop counter variables simplifies the analysis and presentation, while still allowing a large class of programs to be effectively analyzed. Specifically, whenever the count of iterations of a loop can be expressed in a closed form in terms of constants and variables not updated in the loop, we can mimic its behaviour using our restricted loops. As a generic example, suppose we are told that the loop $\mathtt{for(i := exp1; Cond; i := exp2)\{LoopBody\}}$ iterates $\mathtt{exp3}$ times, where $\mathtt{exp3}$ is an arithmetic expression in terms of constants and variables not updated in the loop. The behaviour of this loop can be mimicked using the following restricted loop, where $\mathtt{l}$ and $\mathtt{flag}$ are fresh variables not present in the original program: $\mathtt{for(l := 0; l < exp3; l := l + 1)\{if(l = 0)\{i := exp1\}; if(Cond)}$ $\mathtt{\{LoopBody; i := exp2\}\}}$.

  To see a specific example of this transformation, suppose the program under verification has the loop: $\mathtt{for(i := 2 * M; i >= 0; i := i - 2)\{LoopBody\}}$, where $\mathtt{M}$ and $\mathtt{i}$ are variables not updated in $\mathtt{LoopBody}$. Clearly, this loop iterates $(M+1)$ times. Therefore, it can be modeled in our restricted language as: $\mathtt{for(l := 0; l < M + 1; l := l + 1)\{if(l = 0)\{i := 2 * M\}; if(i >= 0)\{Loop}$ $\mathtt{Body; i := i - 2\}\}}$.

For clarity of exposition, we abuse notation and use $\mathcal{V}$ and $\mathcal{A}$ to also denote a sequence of scalar and array variables, when there is no confusion. A verification problem for an array manipulating program is a Hoare triple $\{\mathsf{PreCond}\}\ \mathsf{P}\ \{\mathsf{PostCond}\}$, where each of $\mathsf{PreCond}$ and $\mathsf{PostCond}$ are quantified formulae of the form $\forall I\ (\Phi(I) \implies \Psi(\mathcal{A}, \mathcal{V}, I))$. Here, I is assumed to be a sequence of array index variables, Φ is a quantifier-free formula in the theory of arithmetic over integers, and Ψ is a quantifier-free formula in the combined theory of arrays and arithmetic over integers. The formula $\Phi(I)$ identifies the relevant indices of the array where the property $\Psi(\mathcal{A}, \mathcal{V}, I)$ must hold. This allows us to express a large class of useful pre- and post-conditions, including sortedness, which can be expressed as $\forall j\ (0 \leq j < N) \rightarrow (A[j] \leq A[j+1])$.

Let AtomSt denote the set of atomic statements in a program generated by the above grammar. These are statements of the form $v := \mathsf{E}$, $A[\mathsf{E}] := \mathsf{E}$ or **assume**(E). It is common to represent such a program by a *control flow graph* $G = (N, E, \mu)$, where N denotes the set of control locations of the program, $E \subseteq N \times N \times \{\mathbf{tt}, \mathbf{ff}, \mathsf{U}\}$ represents the flow of control, and $\mu : N \rightarrow \mathsf{AtomSt} \cup \mathsf{BoolE}$ annotates every node in N with either an assignment statement, an assume statement or a Boolean condition.

We assume there are two distinguished vertices called Start and End in N, that represent the entry and exit points of control flow for the program. An edge (n_1, n_2, L) represents flow of control from n_1 to n_2 without any other intervening node. The edge is labeled **tt** or **ff** if $\mu(n_1)$ is a Boolean condition, and it is labeled U otherwise. If $\mu(n_1)$ is a Boolean condition, there are two outgoing edges labeled **tt** and **ff** respectively, from n_1. Control flows from n_1 to n_2 along (n_1, n_2, L) only if $\mu(n_1)$ evaluates to L. If $\mu(n_1)$ is an assume or assignment statement, there is a single outgoing edge from n_1, and it is labeled U. Henceforth, we use CFG to refer to a control flow graph.

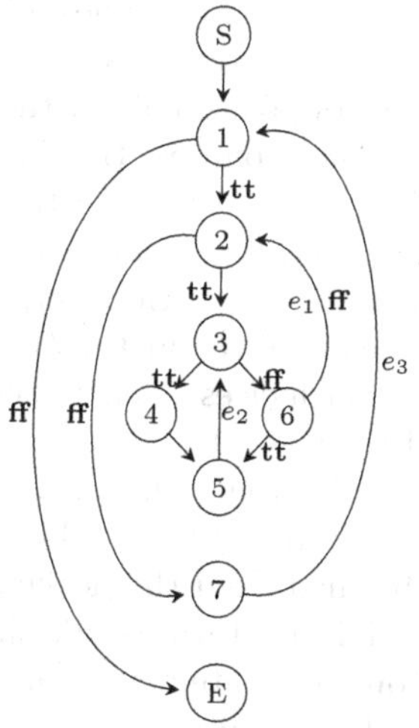

Fig. 2. A CFG

A CFG may have cycles in general. A *back-edge* in a CFG is an edge from a node (control location) within the body of a loop to the node representing the corresponding loop head. Clearly, removing all back-edges from a CFG renders it acyclic. The target nodes of back-edges, i.e. nodes corresponding to loop heads, are also called *cut-points* of the CFG. Every acyclic sub-graph of a CFG that starts from a cut-point or Start and ends at another cut-point or End, and that does not pass through any other cut-points in between and also does not include any back-edge, is called a *segment*. For example, consider the CFG shown in Fig. 2. For clarity, edges labeled U are shown unlabeled in the figure. The cut-points in this CFG are nodes 1, 2 and 3, the back-edges are e_1, e_2 and e_3, and the segments are $S \to 1$, $1 \to 2$, $2 \to 3$, $3 \to \{4, 6\} \to 5$, $2 \to 7$ and $1 \to E$. Note that every segment is an acyclic sub-graph of the CFG with a unique source node and a unique sink node.

4 A Theory of Tiles

In this section, we present a theory of tiles for proving universally quantified properties of arrays in programs that manipulate arrays within loops.

4.1 Tiling in a Simple Setting

Consider a program P as defined in the previous section that accesses elements of an array A in a loop L. Suppose P has a single non-nested loop L with loop counter ℓ and loop exit condition $(\ell < \mathcal{E}_\ell)$, where $\mathcal{E}_\ell$ is an arithmetic expression involving only constants and variables not updated in L. Thus, the loop iterates $\mathcal{E}_\ell$ times, with the value of ℓ initialized to 0 at the beginning of the first iteration, and incremented at the end of each iteration. Each access of an element of A in the loop is either a *read access* or a *write access*. For example, in the program shown in Fig. 3, the loop L (lines 2–11) has three read accesses of A (at lines 5, 6, 7), and three write accesses of A (at lines 3, 6, 7). In order to check an assertion about the array at the end of the loop (see, for example, line 12 of Fig. 3), we wish to tile the array based on how its elements are updated in different iterations of the loop, reason about the effect of each loop iteration on the corresponding tile, and then compose the tile-wise reasoning to prove/disprove the overall assertion. Note that the idea of tiling an array based on access patterns in a loop is not new, and has been used earlier in the context of parallelizing and optimizing compilers [7,8]. However, its use in the context of verification has been limited [9]. To explore the idea better, we need to formalize the notion of *tiles*.

```
1. void ArrayUpdate(int A[], int n) {
2.   for (int l:=0; l < n; l:=l+1) { // loop L
3.     if ((l = 0) OR (l = n-1)) {A[l] := THRESH;}
4.     else {
5.       if (A[l] < THRESH) {
6.         A[l+1] := A[l] + 1;
7.         A[l] := A[l-1];
8.       } // end if
9.     } // end else
11.  } // end for
12.  // assert(forall i in 0..n-1, A[i] >= THRESH);
13. }
```

Fig. 3. Program with interesting tiling

Let $\mathsf{Indices}_A$ denote the range of indices of the array A. We assume that this is available to us; in practice, this can be obtained from the declaration of A if it is statically declared, or from the statement that dynamically allocates the array A. Let Pre and Post denote the pre- and post-conditions, respectively, for the loop L under consideration. Recall from Sect. 3 that both Pre and Post have the form $\forall j\ (\Phi(j) \implies \Psi(\mathsf{A}, \mathcal{V}, j))$, where $\mathcal{V}$ denotes the set of scalar variables in the program. To keep the discussion simple, we consider Post to be of this specific form for the time being, while ignoring the form of Pre. We show later how the specific form of Pre can be used to simplify the analysis further. For purposes of simplicity, we also assume that the array A is one-dimensional; our ideas generalize easily to multi-dimensional arrays, as shown later. Let Inv be a (possibly weak) loop invariant for loop L. Clearly, if $\mathsf{Pre} \implies \mathsf{Inv}$ and $\mathsf{Inv} \wedge \neg(\ell < \mathcal{E}_\mathsf{L}) \implies \mathsf{Post}$, then we are already done, and no tiling is necessary. The situation becomes interesting when Inv is not strong enough to ensure that $\mathsf{Inv} \wedge \neg(\ell < \mathcal{E}_\mathsf{L}) \implies \mathsf{Post}$. We encounter several such cases in our benchmark suite, and it is here that our method adds value to existing verification flows.

A *tiling* of A with respect to L, Inv and Post is a binary predicate $\mathsf{Tile}_{\mathsf{L},\mathsf{Inv},\mathsf{Post}} : \mathbb{N} \times \mathsf{Indices}_\mathsf{A} \rightarrow \{\mathtt{tt}, \mathtt{ff}\}$ such that conditions T1 through T3 listed below hold. Note that these conditions were discussed informally in Sect. 2 in the context of our motivating example. For ease of notation, we use Tile instead of $\mathsf{Tile}_{\mathsf{L},\mathsf{Inv},\mathsf{Post}}$ below, when L, Inv and Post are clear from the context. We also use "ℓ^{th} tile" to refer to all array indices in the set $\{j \mid (j \in \mathsf{Indices}_\mathsf{A}) \wedge \mathsf{Tile}(\ell, j)\}$.

(T1) *Covers range:* Every array index of interest must be present in some tile, and every tile contains array indices in $\mathsf{Indices}_\mathsf{A}$. Thus, the formula $\eta_1 \wedge \eta_2$ must be valid, where $\eta_1 \equiv \forall j((j \in \mathsf{Indices}_\mathsf{A}) \wedge \Phi(j) \implies \exists \ell\,((0 \leq \ell < \mathcal{E}_\ell) \wedge \mathsf{Tile}(\ell, j)))$, and $\eta_2 \equiv \forall \ell\ ((0 \leq \ell < \mathcal{E}_\ell) \wedge \mathsf{Tile}(\ell, j) \implies (j \in \mathsf{Indices}_\mathsf{A}))$.

(T2) *Sliced post-condition holds inductively:* We define the sliced post-condition for the ℓth tile as $\mathsf{Post}_{\mathsf{Tile}(\ell,\cdot)} \triangleq \forall j\,(\mathsf{Tile}(\ell, j) \wedge \Phi(j) \implies \Psi(\mathsf{A}, \mathcal{V}, j))$. Thus, $\mathsf{Post}_{\mathsf{Tile}(\ell,\cdot)}$ asserts that $\Psi(\mathsf{A}, \mathcal{V}, j)$ holds for all relevant j in the ℓth tile. We now require that if the (possibly weak) loop invariant Inv and the sliced post-condition for the ℓ'-th tile for all $\ell' \in \{0, \ldots \ell - 1\}$ hold prior to executing the ℓth loop iteration, then the sliced post condition for the ℓ-th tile and Inv must also hold after executing the ℓth loop iteration.

Formally, if $\mathsf{L_{body}}$ denotes the body of the loop L, the Hoare triple given by $\{\mathsf{Inv} \wedge \bigwedge_{\ell':0 \le \ell' < \ell} \mathsf{Post_{Tile(\ell',\cdot)}}\}\ \mathsf{L_{body}}\ \{\mathsf{Inv} \wedge \mathsf{Post_{Tile(\ell,\cdot)}}\}$ must be valid for all $\ell \in \{0, \ldots \mathcal{E}_\ell - 1\}$.

(T3) *Non-interference across tiles:* For every pair of iterations ℓ, ℓ' of the loop L such that $\ell' < \ell$, the later iteration (ℓ) must not falsify the sliced post condition $\mathsf{Post_{Tile(\ell',\cdot)}}$ rendered true by the earlier iteration (ℓ').

Formally, the Hoare triple $\{\mathsf{Inv} \wedge (0 \le \ell' < \ell) \wedge \mathsf{Post_{Tile(\ell',\cdot)}}\}\mathsf{L_{body}}$ $\{\mathsf{Post_{Tile(\ell',\cdot)}}\}$ must be valid for all $\ell \in \{0, \ldots \mathcal{E}_\ell - 1\}$.

Note that while tiling depends on L, Inv and Post in general, the pattern of array accesses in a loop often suggests a natural tiling of array indices that suffices to prove multiple assertions Post using reasonably weak loop invariants Inv. The motivating example in Sect. 2 illustrated this simplification. The example in Fig. 3 admits the tiling predicate $\mathsf{Tile}(\ell, j) \equiv (j = \ell)$ based on inspection of array access patterns in the loop. Note that in this example, the ℓth iteration of the loop can update both $\mathsf{A}[\ell]$ and $\mathsf{A}[\ell + 1]$. However, as we show later, a simple reasoning reveals that the right tiling choice here is $(j = \ell)$, and not $(\ell \le j \le \ell + 1)$.

Theorem 1. *Suppose* $\mathsf{Tile_{L,Inv,Post}} : \mathbb{N} \times \mathsf{Indices_A} \rightarrow \{\mathbf{tt}, \mathbf{ff}\}$ *satisfies conditions T1 through T3. If* $\mathsf{Pre} \implies \mathsf{Inv}$ *also holds and the loop* L *iterates at least once, then the Hoare triple* $\{\mathsf{Pre}\}\ \mathsf{L}\ \{\mathsf{Post}\}$ *holds.*

Proof sketch: The proof proceeds by induction on the values of the loop counter ℓ. The inductive claim is that at the end of the ℓth iteration of the loop, the post-condition $\bigwedge_{\ell':0 \le \ell' \le \ell} \mathsf{Post_{Tile(\ell',\cdot)}}$ holds. The base case is easily seen to be true from condition T2 and from the fact that $\mathsf{Pre} \implies \mathsf{Inv}$. Condition T3 and the fact that ℓ is incremented at the end of each loop iteration ensure that once we have proved $\mathsf{Post_{Tile(\ell,\cdot)}}$ at the end of the ℓth iteration, it cannot be falsified in any subsequent iteration of the loop. Condition T2 now ensures that the sliced post-condition can be inductively proven for the ℓth tile. By condition T1, we also have $\bigwedge_{0 \le \ell < \mathcal{E}_\ell} \mathsf{Post_{Tile(\ell,\cdot)}} \equiv \mathsf{Post}$. Since the loop L iterates with ℓ increasing from 0 to $\mathcal{E}_\ell - 1$, it follows that Post indeed holds if Inv holds before the start of the first iteration. This is the compositional step in our approach. Putting all the parts together, we obtain a proof of $\{\mathsf{Pre}\}\ \mathsf{L}\ \{\mathsf{Post}\}$. □

A few observations about the conditions are worth noting. First, note that there is an alternation of quantifiers in the check for T1. Fortunately, state-of-the-art SMT solvers like Z3 [10] are powerful enough to check this condition efficiently for tiles expressed as Boolean combinations of linear inequalities on ℓ and $\mathcal{V}$, as is the case for the examples in our benchmark suite. We anticipate that with further advances in reasoning about quantifiers, the check for condition T1 will not be a performance-limiting step.

The checks for T2 and T3 require proving Hoare triples with post-conditions that have a conjunct of the form $\mathsf{Post_{Tile(\ell,\cdot)}}$. From the definition of a sliced post-condition, we know that $\mathsf{Post}_{\mathsf{Tile}(\ell,\cdot)}$ is a universally quantified formula. Additionally, the pre-condition for T2 has a conjunct of the form $\bigwedge_{\ell':0\leq\ell'<\ell}\mathsf{Post}_{\mathsf{Tile}(\ell',\cdot)}$, which is akin to a universally quantified formula. Therefore T2 and T3 can be checked using Hoare logic-based reasoning tools that permit quantified pre- and post-conditions, viz. [11,12]. Unfortunately, the degree of automation and scalability available with such tools is limited today. To circumvent this problem, we propose to use stronger Hoare triple checks that logically imply T2 and T3, but do not have quantified formulas in their pre- and post-conditions. Since the program, and hence $\mathsf{L}_{\mathsf{body}}$, is assumed not to have nested loops, state-of-the-art bounded model checking tools that work with quantifier-free pre- and post-conditions, viz. CBMC, can be used to check these stronger conditions. Specifically, we propose the following pragmatic replacements of T2 and T3.

(T2*) Let $\mathsf{RdAcc}_{\mathsf{L}}(\ell)$ denote the set of array index expressions corresponding to read accesses of A in the ℓth iteration of the loop L. For example, in Fig. 3, $\mathsf{RdAcc}_{\mathsf{L}}(\ell) = \{\ell, \ell-1\}$. Clearly, if $\mathsf{L}_{\mathsf{body}}$ is loop-free, $\mathsf{RdAcc}_{\mathsf{L}}(\ell)$ is a finite set of expressions. Suppose $|\mathsf{RdAcc}_{\mathsf{L}}(\ell)| = k$ and let $e_1, \ldots e_k$ denote the expressions in $\mathsf{RdAcc}_{\mathsf{L}}(\ell)$. Define $\zeta(\ell)$ to be the formula $\bigwedge_{e_k\in\mathsf{RdAcc}_{\mathsf{L}}(\ell)}\big(((0\leq\ell_k<\ell<\mathcal{E}_\ell)\wedge\mathsf{Tile}(\ell_k,e_k)\wedge\Phi(e_k)) \Rightarrow \Psi(\mathsf{A},\mathcal{V},e_k)\big)$, where ℓ_k are fresh variables not used in the program. Informally, $\zeta(\ell)$ states that if $\mathsf{A}[e_k]$ is read in the ℓth iteration of L and if e_k belongs to the ℓ_k-th ($\ell_k < \ell$) tile, then $\Phi(e_k) \implies \Psi(\mathsf{A},\mathcal{V},e_k)$ holds.

We now require the following Hoare triple to be valid, where j is a fresh free variable not used in the program.
$\{\mathsf{Inv}\wedge(0\leq\ell<\mathcal{E}_\ell)\wedge\zeta(\ell)\wedge\mathsf{Tile}(\ell,j)\wedge\Phi(j)\}\ \mathsf{L}_{\mathsf{body}}\{\mathsf{Inv}\wedge\Psi(\mathsf{A},\mathcal{V},j)\}$.

(T3*) Let j' and ℓ' be fresh free variables that are not used in the program. We require the following Hoare triple to be valid:
$\{\mathsf{Inv}\wedge(0\leq\ell'<\ell<\mathcal{E}_\ell)\wedge\mathsf{Tile}(\ell',j')\wedge\Phi(j')\wedge\Psi(\mathsf{A},\mathcal{V},j')\}\ \mathsf{L}_{\mathsf{body}}\ \{\Psi(\mathsf{A},\mathcal{V},j')\}$

Lemma 1. *The Hoare triple in T2* implies that in T2. Similarly, the Hoare triple in T3* implies that in T3.*

The proof follows from the observation that a counterexample for validity of the Hoare triple in T2 or T3 can be used to construct a counterexample for validity of the triple in T2* or T3* respectively.

Observe that T2* and T3* require checking Hoare triples with quantifier-free formulas in the pre- and post-conditions. This makes it possible to use assertion checking tools that work with quantifier-free formulas in pre- and post-conditions. Furthermore, since $\mathsf{L}_{\mathsf{body}}$ is assumed to be loop-free, these checks can also be discharged using state-of-the-art bounded model checkers, viz. CBMC. The scalability and high degree of automation provided by tools like CBMC make conditions T1, T2* and T3* more attractive to use.

4.2 Tiling in More General Settings

The above discussion was restricted to a single uni-dimensional array accessed within a single non-nested loop in a program P. We now relax these restrictions and show that the same technique continues to work with some adaptations.

We consider the case where P is a sequential composition of possibly nested loops. To analyze such programs, we identify all segments in the CFG of P. Let CutPts be the set of cut-points of the CFG. Recall from Sect. 3 that a segment is a sub-DAG of the CFG between a source node in $\mathsf{CutPts} \cup \{\mathsf{Start}\}$ and a sink node in $\mathsf{CutPts} \cup \{\mathsf{End}\}$. Thus, a segment s corresponds to a loop-free fragment of P. Let ℓ_s denote the loop counter variable corresponding to the innermost loop in which s appears. We assign $\perp$ to ℓ_s if s lies outside all loops in P. Let $\mathsf{OuterLoopCtrs}_s$ denote the set of loop counter variables of all outer loops (excluding the innermost one) that enclose (or nest) s. The syntactic restrictions of programs described in Sect. 3 ensure that ℓ_s and $\mathsf{OuterLoopCtrs}_s$ are uniquely defined for every segment s.

Suppose we are given (possibly weak) invariants at every cut-point in P, where Inv_c denotes the invariant at cut-point c. We assume the invariants are of the usual form $\forall I\ (\Phi(I) \implies \Psi(\mathcal{A}, \mathcal{V}, I))$, where I is a sequence of quantified array index variables, and $\mathcal{A}$ and $\mathcal{V}$ are sequences of array and scalar variables respectively. Let $\mathcal{A}_s$ be a sequence of arrays that are updated in the segment s between cut-points c_1 and c_2, and for which $\ell_s \neq \perp$. We define a tiling predicate $\mathsf{Tile}_{s,\mathsf{Inv}_{c_1},\mathsf{Inv}_{c_2}} : \mathbb{N} \times \mathsf{Indices}_{\mathcal{A}_s} \to \{\mathbf{tt}, \mathbf{ff}\}$, where $\mathsf{Indices}_{\mathcal{A}_s} = \prod_{\mathsf{A}' \in \mathcal{A}_s} \mathsf{Indices}_{\mathsf{A}'}$ plays a role similar to that of $\mathsf{Indices}_{\mathsf{A}}$ in Sect. 4.1 (where a single array A was considered). The predicate $\mathsf{Tile}_{s,\mathsf{Inv}_{c_1},\mathsf{Inv}_{c_2}}$ relates values of the loop counter ℓ_s of the innermost loop containing s to the index expressions that define the updates of arrays in $\mathcal{A}_s$ in the program segment s. The entire analysis done in Sect. 4.1 for a simple loop L can now be re-played for segment s, with Inv_{c_1} playing the role of Inv, Inv_{c_2} playing the role of Post, $\mathcal{V} \cup \mathsf{OuterLoopCtrs}_s$ playing the role of $\mathcal{V}$, and ℓ_s playing the role of ℓ. If the segment s is not enclosed in any loop, i.e. $\ell_s = \perp$, we need not define any tiling predicate for this segment. This obviates the need for conditions T1 and T3, and checking T2 simplifies to checking the validity of the Hoare triple $\{\mathsf{Inv}_{c_1}\}\ s\ \{\mathsf{Inv}_{c_2}\}$. In general, Inv_{c_1} and Inv_{c_2} may be universally quantified formulas. In such cases, the technique used to simplify condition T2 to T2* in Sect. 4.1 can be applied to obtain a stronger condition, say T2**, that does not involve any tile, and requires checking a Hoare triple with quantifier-free pre- and post-conditions. If the condition checks for all segments as described above succeed, it follows from Theorem 1 and Lemma 1 that we have a proof of $\{\mathsf{Pre}\}\ \mathsf{P}\ \{\mathsf{Post}\}$.

Recall that in Sect. 4.1, we ignored the specific form of the pre-condition Pre. As defined in Sect. 3, Pre has the same form as that of the post-condition and invariants at cut-points considered above. Therefore, the above technique works if we treat Pre as $\mathsf{Inv}_{\mathsf{Start}}$ and Post as $\mathsf{Inv}_{\mathsf{End}}$.

The extension to multi-dimensional arrays is straightforward. Instead of using one index variable j for accessing arrays, we now allow a tuple of index variables $(j_1, j_2, \ldots j_r)$ for accessing arrays. Each such variable j_l takes values from its own domain, say $\mathsf{Indices}_{\mathsf{A}_l}$. The entire discussion about tiles above continues to hold, including the validity of Theorem 1, if we replace every occurrence of an array index variable j by a sequence of variables $j_1, \ldots j_r$ and every occurrence of $\mathsf{Indices}_{\mathsf{A}}$ by $\mathsf{Indices}_{\mathsf{A}_1} \times \mathsf{Indices}_{\mathsf{A}_2} \ldots \times \mathsf{Indices}_{\mathsf{A}_r}$.

5 Verification by Tiling

The discussion in the previous section suggests a three-phase algorithm, presented as Algorithm 1, for verifying quantified properties of arrays in programs with sequences of possibly nested loops manipulating arrays. In the first phase of the algorithm, we use bounded model checking with small pre-determined loop unrollings to check for assertion violations. If this fails, we construct the CFG of the input program P, topologically sort its cut-points and initialize the sets of candidate invariants at each cut-point to ∅.

Algorithm 1. TiledVerify(P : program, Pre: pre-condn, Post: post-condn)

Let G be the CFG for program $\mathsf{P} = (\mathcal{A}, \mathcal{V}, \mathcal{L}, \mathsf{PB})$, as defined in Section 3.

▷ `Check for shallow counterexample and initialization`

Do bounded model checking with pre-determined small loop unrollings;
if counterexample found **then return** "Post condition violated!";
CutPts := set of cut-points in G;
Remove all back-edges from G and topologically sort CutPts; ▷ Let $\sqsubseteq$ be the sorted order
for each c in CutPts **do**
  CandInv[c] := ∅; ▷ Set of candidate invariants at c
CandInv[Start] := Pre; CandInv[End] := Post; ▷ Fixed invariants at Start and End

▷ `Candidate invariant generation`

for each segment s from c_1 to c_2, where $c_1, c_2 \in$ CutPts ∪ {Start, End} and $c_1 \sqsubseteq c_2$ **do**
  if (s lies within a loop) **then**
    ℓ[s] := loop counter of innermost nested loop containing s;
    OuterLoopCtrs[s] := loop counters of all other outer loops containing s;
  else ▷ s not in any loop
    ℓ[s] := ⊥; OuterLoopCtrs[s] := ∅;
  ScalarVars[s] := $\mathcal{V}$ ∪ OuterLoopCtr[s];
  CandInv[c_2] := CandInv[c_2] ∪ findHeuristicCandidateInvariants($s, c_2, \ell[s]$, ScalarVars[s], $\mathcal{A}$);

▷ `Tiling and verification`

for each segment s from c_1 to c_2 **do**
  if (s lies within a loop) **then**
    CandTile[s] := findHeuristicTile($s, \ell[s]$, ScalarVars[s], $\mathcal{A}$); ▷ Candidate tile for s
    Check conditions T1, T2* and T3* for CandTile[s], as described in Section 4.1;
    if (not timed out) AND (T1 or T3* fail) **then**
      Re-calculate CandTile[s] using different heuristics; **goto** 20;
    if (not timed out) AND (T2* or T3* fail) AND ($c_2 \neq$ End) **then**
      Re-calculate CandInv[c_2] using different heuristics; **goto** 20;
  else ▷ s not in any loop
    Check condition T2**, as described in Section 4.2;
    if (not timed out) AND (T2** fails) AND ($c_2 \neq$ End) **then**
      Re-calculate CandInv[c_2] using different heuristics; **goto** 26;
if timed out **then return** "Time out! Inconclusive answer!"
return "Post-condition verified!"

In the second phase, we generate candidate invariants at each cut-point c by considering every segment s that ends at c. For each such segment s, we identify the loop counter $\ell[s]$ corresponding to the innermost loop in which s appears, and the set of loop counters $\mathsf{OuterLoopCtrs}[s]$ corresponding to other loops that contain (or nest) s. Note that when the program fragment in the segment s executes, the *active* loop counter that increments from one execution of s to the next is $\ell[s]$. The loop counters in $\mathsf{OuterLoopCtrs}[s]$ can be treated similar to other scalar variables in $\mathcal{V}$ when analyzing segment s. We would like the candidate invariants identified at different cut-points to be of the form $\forall I\ (\Phi(I) \implies \Psi(\mathcal{A}, \mathcal{V}, I))$, whenever possible. We assume access to a routine findHeuristicCandidateInvariants for this purpose. Note that the candidate invariants obtained from this routine may not actually hold at c_2. In the next phase, we check using tiling whether a candidate invariant indeed holds at a cut-point, and use only those candidates that we are able to prove.

Algorithm 2. FINDHEURISTICTILE(s : segment, ℓ: loop counter, ScalarVars: set of scalars, $\mathcal{A}$: set of arrays)

Let c_1 be the starting cut-point (or Start node) of s;
for each array A updated in s **do**
  $\mathsf{UpdIndexExprs}^{\mathsf{A}}[s] := \emptyset$;
  for each update of the form $\mathsf{A}[e] := e'$ at location c in s **do** ▷ e and e' are arith expns
    $\widehat{e} := e$ in terms of ℓ, ScalarVars, $\mathcal{A}$ at c_1 ▷ Obtained by backward traversal from c to c_1
    $\mathsf{UpdIndexExprs}^{\mathsf{A}}[s] := \mathsf{UpdIndexExprs}^{\mathsf{A}}[s] \cup \{\widehat{e}\}$
  $\mathsf{InitTile}^{\mathsf{A}}(\ell, j) := \mathsf{Simplify}\big(\bigvee_{e \in \mathsf{UpdIndexExprs}^{\mathsf{A}}[s]} (j = e)\big)$; ▷ Initial estimate of tile
  for each $e \in \mathsf{UpdIndexExprs}^{\mathsf{A}}[s]$ **do**
    if $\big(\mathsf{InitTile}^{\mathsf{A}}(\ell, e) \wedge \mathsf{InitTile}^{\mathsf{A}}(\ell + k, e) \wedge (0 \leq \ell < \ell + k < \mathcal{E}_\ell)\big)$ is satisfiable **then**
      Remove e from $\mathsf{UpdIndexExprs}^{\mathsf{A}}[s]$;
  $\mathsf{Tile}^{\mathsf{A}}(\ell, j) := \mathsf{Simplify}\big(\bigvee_{e \in \mathsf{UpdIndexExprs}^{\mathsf{A}}[s]} (j = e)\big)$; ▷ Refined tile
  return $\bigwedge_{\mathsf{A} \in \mathcal{A}} \mathsf{Tile}^{\mathsf{A}}(\ell, \cdot)$;

In the third phase, we iterate over every segment s between cut-point c_1 and c_2 again, and use heuristics to identify tiles. This is done by a routine findHeuristicTile. The working of our current tiling heuristic is shown in Algorithm 2. For every array update $\mathsf{A}[e] := e'$ in segment s, the heuristic traverses the control flow graph of s backward until it reaches the entry point of s, i.e. c_1, to determine the expression e in terms of values of $\ell[s]$, $\mathcal{V}$, $\mathsf{OuterLoopCtrs}[s]$ and $\mathcal{A}$ at c_1. Let $\mathsf{UpdIndexExprs}^{\mathsf{A}}[s]$ denote the set of such expressions for updates to A within s. We identify an initial tile for A in s as $\mathsf{InitTile}^{\mathsf{A}}(\ell[s], j) \equiv \bigvee_{e \in \mathsf{UpdIndexExprs}^{\mathsf{A}}[s]} (j = e)$. It may turn out that the same array index expression appears in two or more initial tiles after this step. For example, in Fig. 3, we obtain $\mathsf{InitTile}^{\mathsf{A}}(\ell, j) \equiv (\ell \leq j \leq \ell + 1)$, and hence $\mathsf{InitTile}^{\mathsf{A}}(\ell, \ell+1) \wedge \mathsf{InitTile}^{\mathsf{A}}(\ell+1, \ell+1)$ is satisfiable. While the conditions T1, T2 and T3 do not forbid overlapping tiles in general (non-interference is different from non-overlapping tiles), our current tiling heuristic avoids them by refining the initial tile estimates. For each expression e in $\mathsf{UpdIndexExprs}^{\mathsf{A}}[s]$, we check if $\mathsf{InitTile}^{\mathsf{A}}(\ell[s], e) \wedge \mathsf{InitTile}^{\mathsf{A}}(\ell[s] + k, e) \wedge (0 \leq \ell[s] < \ell[s] + k < \mathcal{E}_{\ell[s]})$ is satisfiable. If so, we drop e from the refined tiling predicate, denoted $\mathsf{Tile}^{\mathsf{A}}(\ell[s], \cdot)$ in

Algorithm 2. This ensures that an array index expression e belongs to the tile corresponding to the largest value of the loop counter $\ell[s]$ when it is updated. The procedure Simplify invoked in lines 7 and 11 of Algorithm 2 tries to obtain a closed form linear expression (or Boolean combination of a few linear expressions) for $\bigvee_{e \in \mathsf{UpdIndexExprs}^A[s]}(j = e)$, if possible. In the case of Fig. 3, this gives the tile $(j = \ell)$, which suffices for proving the quantified assertion in this example.

Sometimes, the heuristic choice of tiling or the choice of candidate invariants may not be good enough for the requisite checks (T1, T2*, T2**, T3) to go through. In such cases, Algorithm 1 allows different heuristics to be used to update the tiles and invariants. In our current implementation, we do not update the tiles, but update the set of candidate invariants by discarding candidates that cannot be proven using our tiling-based checks. It is possible that the tiles and candidate invariants obtained in this manner do not suffice to prove the assertion within a pre-defined time limit. In such cases, we time out and report an inconclusive answer.

6 Implementation and Experiments

Implementation: We have implemented the above technique in a tool called TILER. The tool is built on top of the LLVM/CLANG [13] compiler infrastructure. We ensure that input C programs are adapted, if needed, to satisfy the syntactic restrictions in Sect. 3. The current implementation is *fully automated* for programs with non-nested loops, and can handle programs with nested loops semi-automatically.

Generating candidate invariants: We use a template-based dynamic analysis tool, DAIKON [2], for generating *candidate* invariants. DAIKON supports linear invariant discovery among program variables and arrays, and reports invariants at the entry and exit points of functions. In order to learn candidate quantified invariants, we transform the input program as follows. The sizes of all arrays in the program are changed to a fixed small constant, and all arrays and program variables which are live are initialized with random values. We then insert a dummy function call at each cut-point. Our transformation collects all array indices that are accessed in various segments of the program and expresses them in terms of the corresponding loop counter(s). Finally, it passes the values of accessed array elements, the corresponding array index expressions and the loop counter(s) as arguments to the dummy call, to enable DAIKON to infer candidate invariants among them. The transformed program is executed multiple times to generate traces. DAIKON learns candidate linear invariants over the parameters passed to the dummy calls from these traces. Finally, we lift the candidate invariants thus identified to quantified invariants in the natural way.

As an example, consider the input program shown in Fig. 4(a). The transformed program is shown in Fig. 4(b). In the transformed program, arrays a and b are initialized to random values. The *dummy* function call in loop $L1$ has four arguments $a[i]$, $b[i]$, $acopy[i]$ and i. Based on concrete traces, DAIKON initially detects the candidate invariants $(a\_i = acopy\_i)$ and $(a\_i \neq b\_i)$ on the parameters

```
void copynswap() {
   int s, i, tmp;
   int a[s], b[s], acopy[s];
   for (i = 0; i < s; i++) { //L1
      acopy[i] = a[i];
   }
   for (i = 0; i < s; i++) { //L2
      tmp = a[i], a[i] = b[i]; b[i] = tmp;
   }
   for (i = 0; i < s; i++) {
      assert(b[i] == acopy[i]);
   }
}
```

(a)

```
void dummy(int a_i, int b_i, int acopy_i, int i) { }
void copynswap() {
   int s=10, i, tmp;
   int a[s], b[s], acopy[s];
   for (i = 0; i < s; i++) {
      a[i] = rand(); b[i] = rand();
   }
   for (i = 0; i < s; i++) { //L1
      acopy[i] = a[i];
      dummy(a[i], b[i], acopy[i], i);
   }
   for (i = 0; i < s; i++) { //L2
      tmp = a[i], a[i] = b[i]; b[i] = tmp;
   }
}
```

(b)

Fig. 4. (a) Input program (b) Transformed program

of the dummy function. We lift these to obtain the candidate quantified invariants $\forall i.(a[i] = acopy[i])$ and $\forall i.(a[i] \neq b[i])$. In the subsequent analysis, we detect that $\forall i, (a[i] \neq b[i])$ cannot be proven. This is therefore dropped from the candidate invariants (line 24 of Algorithm 1), and we proceed with $\forall i, (a[i] = acopy[i])$, which suffices to prove the post-condition.

Tile generation and checking: Tiles are generated as in Algorithm 2. Condition T1 is checked using Z3 [10], which has good support for quantifiers. We employ CBMC [5] for implementing the checks T2*, T2** and T3*.

Benchmarks. We evaluated our tool on 60 benchmarks from the test-suites of BOOSTER [3] and VAPHOR [4], as well as on programs from an industrial code base. The benchmarks from BOOSTER and VAPHOR test-suites (Table 1(a)) perform common array operations such as array initialization, reverse order initialization, incrementing array contents, finding largest and smallest elements, odd and even elements, array comparison, array copying, swapping arrays, swapping a reversed array, multiple swaps, and the like. Of the 135 benchmarks in this test suite, 66 benchmarks are minor variants of the benchmarks we report. For example, there are multiple versions of programs such as `copy`, `init`, `copyninit`, with different counts of sequentially composed loops. In such cases, the benchmark variant with the largest count is reported in the table. Besides these, there are 22 cases containing nested loops which can currently be handled only semi-automatically by our implementation, and 25 cases with post-conditions in a form that is different from what our tool accepts. Hence, these results are not reported here.

Benchmarks were also taken from the industrial code of a battery controller in a car (Table 1(b)). These benchmarks set a repetitive contiguous bunch of cells in a battery with different values based on the guard condition that gets satisfied. The size of such a contiguous bunch of cells varies in different models. The assertion checks if the cell values are consistent with the given specification.

All our benchmarks are within 100 lines of uncommented code. The programs have a variety of tiles such as $4i - 4 \leq j < 4i$, $2i - 2 \leq j < 2i$, $j = size - i - 1$,

Table 1. Results on selected benchmarks from (a) Booster & Vaphor test-suite and (b) industrial code. #L is the number loops (and sub-loops, if any) in the benchmark, T is Tiler, S+C is SMACK+Corral, B is Booster, and V is Vaphor. ✓ indicates assertion safety, ✗ indicates assertion violation, ? indicates unknown result, and ⋆ indicates unsupported construct. All the times are in seconds. TO is time-out. * indicates semi-automated experiments and the corresponding execution times are of the automated part. See text for explanation.

Benchmark	#L	T	S+C	B	V
init2ipc.c	1	✓0.5	†	✓0.01	✓1.0
initnincr.c	2	✓5.8	†	✓0.01	✓0.7
evenodd.c	1	✓0.4	†	✓0.01	✓0.04
revrefill.c	1	✓0.6	†	✓0.01	✓0.79
largest.c	1	✓0.4	†	✓0.01	✓0.02
smallest.c	1	✓0.4	†	✓0.01	✓0.02
cpy.c	1	✓0.6	†	✓0.01	✓2.0
cpynrev.c	2	✓3.8	†	✓3.1	✓5.4
cpynswp.c	2	✓4.2	†	✓12.4	✓1.38
cpynswp2.c	3	✓10.2	†	✓198	✓7.2*
01.c	1	✓0.44	†	✓0.05	✓0.38
02.c	1	✓0.65	†	✓0.02	✓2.3
06.c	2	✓8.15	†	✓0.04	✓0.35
27.c	1	✓0.41	†	✓0.01	✓0.12
43.c	1	✓0.45	†	✓0.03	✓0.05
maxinarr.c	1	✓0.51	†	✓0.01	✓0.11
mininarr.c	1	✓0.53	†	✓0.02	✓0.13
compare.c	1	✓0.44	†	✓0.04	✓0.62
palindrome.c	1	✓0.52	†	✓0.02	✓0.39
copy9.c	9	✓34.6	†	✓0.46	TO
init9.c	9	✓29.2	†	✓0.34	✓0.16
seqinit.c	1	✓0.45	†	✓0.03	✓0.43
nec40t.c	1	✓0.50	†	✓0.06	✓0.48
sumarr.c	1	✓0.55	†	✓0.56	✓4.2
vararg.c	1	✓0.42	†	✓0.03	✓0.12
find.c	1	✓0.52	†	✓0.02	✓0.14
running.c	1	✓0.62	†	✓0.04	✓0.12
revcpy.c	1	✓0.7	†	✓0.01	✓0.73
revcpyswp.c	2	✓6.3	†	✓0.02	TO
revcpyswp2.c	3	✓8.6	†	✓0.03	TO

(a)

Benchmark	#L	T	S+C	B	V
copy9u.c	9	✗0.16	✗4.48	✗0.44	✗30.8
init9u.c	9	✗0.15	✗3.77	✗0.32	✗0.14
revcpyswpu.c	2	✗0.18	✗3.11	✗0.01	TO
skippedu.c	1	✗0.81	✗2.94	✗0.02	TO
mclceu.c	1	? 0.37	✗2.5	⋆	⋆
poly1.c	1	TO	†	✓15.7	TO
poly2.c	2	? 6.44	†	? 19.5	TO
tcpy.c	1	? 0.65	†	TO	✓25.1
skipped.c	1	✓1.24	†	TO	TO
rew.c	1	✓0.48	†	✓0.01	TO
rewrev.c	1	✓0.39	†	TO	TO
rewnif.c	1	✓0.49	†	✓0.01	TO
rewnifrev.c	1	✓0.28	†	✓0.01	TO
rewnifrev2.c	1	✓0.47	†	✓0.01	TO
pr2.c	1	✓0.51	†	TO	TO
pr3.c	1	✓0.70	†	TO	TO
pr4.c	1	✓0.68	†	TO	TO
pr5.c	1	✓1.32	†	TO	TO
pnr2.c	1	✓0.55	†	TO	TO
pnr3.c	1	✓0.98	†	TO	TO
pnr4.c	1	✓0.86	†	TO	TO
pnr5.c	1	✓1.98	†	TO	TO
mbpr2.c	2	✓6.48	†	TO	TO
mbpr3.c	3	✓9.24	†	TO	TO
mbpr4.c	4	✓12.75	†	TO	TO
mbpr5.c	5	✓18.08	†	TO	TO
nr2.c	1-1	✓1.48*	†	TO	TO
nr3.c	1-1	✓2.02*	†	TO	TO
nr4.c	1-1	✓2.43*	†	TO	TO
nr5.c	1-1	✓2.90*	†	TO	TO

(b)

$j = i$ etc., with the last one being the most common tile, where i denotes the loop counter and j denotes the array index accessed.

Experiments. The experiments reported here were conducted on an Intel Core i5-3320M processor with 4 cores running at 2.6 GHz, with 4 GB of memory running Ubuntu 14.04 LTS. A time-out of 900 s was set for Tiler, SMACK+Corral [14], Booster [3] and Vaphor [4]. The memory limit was set to 1GB for all the tools. Spacer [15] was used as the SMT solver for the Horn formulas generated by Vaphor since this has been reported to perform well with Vaphor. In addition, C programs were manually converted to mini-Java, as required by Vaphor. Since SMACK+Corral is a bounded model checker, a meaningful comparison with Tiler can be made only in cases where the benchmark violates a quantified assertion. In such cases, the verifier option `svcomp` was used for CORRAL. In all other cases, we have shown a † in the column for SMACK+CORRAL in Table 1 to indicate that comparison is not meaningful.

TILER takes about two seconds for verifying all single loop programs that satisfy their assertions. For programs containing multiple loops, 10 random runs of the program were used to generate candidate invariants using DAIKON. The weak loop invariant Inv, mentioned in Sect. 4, was assumed to be **true**. TILER took a maximum of 35 s to output the correct result for each such benchmark. The execution time of TILER includes instrumentation for DAIKON, trace generation, execution of DAIKON on the traces for extracting candidate invariants, translating these to `assume` statements for use in CBMC, proving the reported candidate invariants and proving the final assertion. The execution of DAIKON and proving candidate invariants took about 95% of the total execution time.

To demonstrate the application of our technique on programs with nested loops, we applied it to the last four benchmarks in Table 1(b), each of which has a loop nested inside another. We used TILER to automatically generate tiles for these programs. We manually encoded the *sliced post-condition* queries and ran CBMC. We did not have time to automate trace generation for DAIKON and for making the above CBMC calls automatically for this class of programs. We are currently implementing this automation.

Analysis. BOOSTER and VAPHOR performed well on benchmarks from their respective repositories. Although VAPHOR could analyze the benchmark for reversing an array, as well as one for copying and swapping arrays, it could not analyze the benchmark for reverse copying and swapping. Since the arrays are reversed and then swapped, all array indices need to be tracked in this case, causing VAPHOR to fail. VAPHOR also could not verify most of the industrial benchmarks due to two key reasons that are not handled well by VAPHOR: (i) at least two distinguished array cells need to be tracked in these benchmarks, and (ii) updates to the arrays are made using non-sequential index values.

BOOSTER could analyze all the examples in which the assertion gets violated, except for a benchmark containing an unsupported construct (shift operator) indicated by $\star$. This is not surprising since finding a violating run is sometimes easier than proving an assertion. BOOSTER however could not prove several other industrial benchmarks because it could not accelerate the expressions for indices at which the array was being accessed. TILER, on the other hand, was able to generate interesting tiles for almost all these benchmarks.

In our experiments, SMACK+CORRAL successfully generated counter-examples for all benchmarks in which the assertion was violated. As expected, it was unable to produce any conclusive results for benchmarks with parametric array sizes where the quantified assertions were satisfied.

Limitations. There are several scenarios under which TILER may fail to produce a conclusive result. TILER uses CBMC with small loop unwinding bounds to find violating runs in programs with shallow counter-examples. Consequently, when there are no short counter-examples (e.g. in `mclceu.c`), TILER reports an inconclusive answer. TILER is also unable to report conclusively in cases where the tile generation heuristic is unable to generate the right tile (e.g. in `tcpy.c`), when DAIKON generates weak mid-conditions (e.g. in `poly2.c`) or when CBMC takes too long to prove conditions T2* or T3* (e.g. in `poly1.c`).

Our work is motivated by the need to prove quantified assertions in programs from industrial code bases, where we observed interesting patterns of array accesses. Our tile generation heuristic is strongly motivated by these patterns. There is clearly a need to develop more generic tile generation heuristics for larger classes of programs.

7 Related Work

The VAPHORtool [4] uses an abstraction to transform array manipulating programs to array-free Horn formulas, parameterized by the number of array cells that are to be tracked. The technique relies on Horn clause solvers such as Z3 [10], SPACER [15] and ELDARICA [16] to check the satisfiability of the generated array-free Horn formulas. VAPHOR does not automatically infer the number of array cells to be tracked to prove the assertion. It also fails if the updates to the array happen at non-sequential indices, as is the case in array reverse and swap, for example. In comparison, TILER requires no input on the number of cells to be tracked and is not limited by sequential accesses. The experiments in [4] show that Horn clause solvers are not always efficient on problems arising from program verification. To be efficient on a wide range of verification problems, the solvers need to have a mix of heuristics. Our work brings a novel heuristic in the mix, which may be adopted in these solvers.

BOOSTER [3] combines acceleration [17,18] and lazy abstraction with interpolants for arrays [19] for proving quantified assertions on arrays for a class of programs. Interpolation for universally quantified array properties is known to be hard [20,21]. Hence, BOOSTER fails for programs where simple interpolants are not easily computable. Fluid updates [22] uses bracketing constraints, which are over- and under-approximations of indices, to specify the concrete elements being updated in an array without explicit partitioning. This approach is not property-directed and their generalization assumes that a single index expression updates the array.

The analysis proposed in [23,24] partitions the array into symbolic slices and abstracts each slice with a numeric scalar variable. These techniques cannot easily analyze arrays with overlapping slices, and they do not handle updates to multiple indices in the array or to non-contiguous array partitions. In comparison, TILER uses state-of-the-art SMT solver Z3 [10] with quantifier support [25] for checking interference among tiles and can handle updates to multiple non-contiguous indices.

Abstract interpretation based techniques [9,26] propose an abstract domain which utilizes cell contents to split array cells into groups. In particular, the technique in [26] is useful when array cells with similar properties are non-contiguously present in the array. All the industrial benchmarks in our test-suite are such that this property holds. Template-based techniques [27] have been used to generate expressive invariants. However, this requires the user to supply the right templates, which may not be easy in general. In [28], a technique to scale bounded model-checking by transforming a program with arrays and possibly unbounded loops to an array-free and loop-free program is presented. This technique is not compositional, and is precise only for a restricted class of programs.

There are some close connections between the notion of tiles as used in this paper and similar ideas used in compilers. For example, tiling/patterns have been widely used in compilers for translating loops into SIMD instructions [8,29]. Similarly, the induction variable pass in LLVM can generate all accessed index expressions for an array in terms of the loop counters. Note, however, that not all such expressions may be part of a *tile* (recall the tiles in Fig. 3). Hence, automatically generating the right *tile* remains a challenging problem in general.

8 Conclusion

Programs manipulating arrays are known to be hard to reason about. The problem is further exacerbated when the programmer uses different patterns of array accesses in different loops. In this paper, we provided a theory of tiling that helps us decompose the reasoning about an array into reasoning about automatically identified tiles in the array, and then compose the results for each tile back to obtain the overall result. While generation of tiles is difficult in general, we have shown that simple heuristics are often quite effective in automatically generating tiles that work well in practice. Surprisingly, these simple heuristics allow us to analyze programs that several state-of-the-art tools choke on. Further work is needed to identify better and varied tiles for programs automatically.

References

1. Gupta, A., Rybalchenko, A.: InvGen: an efficient invariant generator. In: Bouajjani, A., Maler, O. (eds.) CAV 2009. LNCS, vol. 5643, pp. 634–640. Springer, Heidelberg (2009). doi:10.1007/978-3-642-02658-4_48
2. Ernst, M.D., Perkins, J.H., Guo, P.J., McCamant, S., Pacheco, C., Tschantz, M.S., Xiao, C.: The daikon system for dynamic detection of likely invariants. Sci. Comput. Program. **69**, 35–45 (2007)
3. Alberti, F., Ghilardi, S., Sharygina, N.: Booster: an acceleration-based verification framework for array programs. In: Cassez, F., Raskin, J.-F. (eds.) ATVA 2014. LNCS, vol. 8837, pp. 18–23. Springer, Cham (2014). doi:10.1007/978-3-319-11936-6_2
4. Monniaux, D., Gonnord, L.: Cell Morphing: from array programs to array-free horn clauses. In: Rival, X. (ed.) SAS 2016. LNCS, vol. 9837, pp. 361–382. Springer, Heidelberg (2016). doi:10.1007/978-3-662-53413-7_18
5. Clarke, E., Kroening, D., Lerda, F.: A tool for checking ANSI-C programs. In: Jensen, K., Podelski, A. (eds.) TACAS 2004. LNCS, vol. 2988, pp. 168–176. Springer, Heidelberg (2004). doi:10.1007/978-3-540-24730-2_15
6. Lal, A., Qadeer, S., Lahiri, S.K.: A solver for reachability modulo theories. In: Madhusudan, P., Seshia, S.A. (eds.) CAV 2012. LNCS, vol. 7358, pp. 427–443. Springer, Heidelberg (2012). doi:10.1007/978-3-642-31424-7_32

7. Sundararajah, K., Sakka, L., Kulkarni, M.: Locality transformations for nested recursive iteration spaces. In: Proceedings of ASPLOS, pp. 281–295 (2017)
8. Jo, Y., Kulkarni, M.: Enhancing locality for recursive traversals of recursive structures. In: Proceedings of OOPSLA, pp. 463–482 (2011)
9. Cousot, P., Cousot, R., Logozzo, F.: A parametric segmentation functor for fully automatic and scalable array content analysis. In: Proceedings of POPL, pp. 105–118 (2011)
10. Moura, L., Bjørner, N.: Z3: an efficient SMT solver. In: Ramakrishnan, C.R., Rehof, J. (eds.) TACAS 2008. LNCS, vol. 4963, pp. 337–340. Springer, Heidelberg (2008). doi:10.1007/978-3-540-78800-3_24
11. Hähnle, R., Bubel, R.: A hoare-style calculus with explicit state updates. In: Formal Methods in Computer Science Education, pp. 49–60 (2008)
12. Jacobs, B., Smans, J., Philippaerts, P., Vogels, F., Penninckx, W., Piessens, F.: VeriFast: a powerful, sound, predictable, fast verifier for C and Java. In: Bobaru, M., Havelund, K., Holzmann, G.J., Joshi, R. (eds.) NFM 2011. LNCS, vol. 6617, pp. 41–55. Springer, Heidelberg (2011). doi:10.1007/978-3-642-20398-5_4
13. Lattner, C.: LLVM and Clang: next generation compiler technology. In: The BSD Conference, pp. 1–2 (2008)
14. Haran, A., Carter, M., Emmi, M., Lal, A., Qadeer, S., Rakamarić, Z.: SMACK+Corral: a modular verifier. In: Baier, C., Tinelli, C. (eds.) TACAS 2015. LNCS, vol. 9035, pp. 451–454. Springer, Heidelberg (2015). doi:10.1007/978-3-662-46681-0_42
15. Komuravelli, A., Gurfinkel, A., Chaki, S.: SMT-based model checking for recursive programs. In: Biere, A., Bloem, R. (eds.) CAV 2014. LNCS, vol. 8559, pp. 17–34. Springer, Cham (2014). doi:10.1007/978-3-319-08867-9_2
16. Rümmer, P., Hojjat, H., Kuncak, V.: Disjunctive interpolants for Horn-clause verification. In: Sharygina, N., Veith, H. (eds.) CAV 2013. LNCS, vol. 8044, pp. 347–363. Springer, Heidelberg (2013). doi:10.1007/978-3-642-39799-8_24
17. Bozga, M., Iosif, R., Konečný, F.: Fast acceleration of ultimately periodic relations. In: Touili, T., Cook, B., Jackson, P. (eds.) CAV 2010. LNCS, vol. 6174, pp. 227–242. Springer, Heidelberg (2010). doi:10.1007/978-3-642-14295-6_23
18. Jeannet, B., Schrammel, P., Sankaranarayanan, S.: Abstract acceleration of general linear loops. In: Proceedings of POPL, pp. 529–540 (2014)
19. Alberti, F., Bruttomesso, R., Ghilardi, S., Ranise, S., Sharygina, N.: Lazy abstraction with interpolants for arrays. In: Bjørner, N., Voronkov, A. (eds.) LPAR 2012. LNCS, vol. 7180, pp. 46–61. Springer, Heidelberg (2012). doi:10.1007/978-3-642-28717-6_7
20. Jhala, R., McMillan, K.L.: Array abstractions from proofs. In: Damm, W., Hermanns, H. (eds.) CAV 2007. LNCS, vol. 4590, pp. 193–206. Springer, Heidelberg (2007). doi:10.1007/978-3-540-73368-3_23
21. Monniaux, D., Alberti, F.: A simple abstraction of arrays and maps by program translation. In: Blazy, S., Jensen, T. (eds.) SAS 2015. LNCS, vol. 9291, pp. 217–234. Springer, Heidelberg (2015). doi:10.1007/978-3-662-48288-9_13
22. Dillig, I., Dillig, T., Aiken, A.: Fluid updates: beyond strong vs. weak updates. In: Gordon, A.D. (ed.) ESOP 2010. LNCS, vol. 6012, pp. 246–266. Springer, Heidelberg (2010). doi:10.1007/978-3-642-11957-6_14
23. Gopan, D., Reps, T.W., Sagiv, S.: A framework for numeric analysis of array operations. In: Proceedings of POPL, pp. 338–350 (2005)
24. Halbwachs, N., Péron, M.: Discovering properties about arrays in simple programs. In: Proceedings of PLDI, pp. 339–348 (2008)

25. Bjørner, N., Janota, M.: Playing with quantified satisfaction. In: Proceedings of LPAR, pp. 15–27 (2015)
26. Liu, J., Rival, X.: Abstraction of arrays based on non contiguous partitions. In: D'Souza, D., Lal, A., Larsen, K.G. (eds.) VMCAI 2015. LNCS, vol. 8931, pp. 282–299. Springer, Heidelberg (2015). doi:10.1007/978-3-662-46081-8_16
27. Gulwani, S., McCloskey, B., Tiwari, A.: Lifting abstract interpreters to quantified logical domains. In: Proceedings of POPL, pp. 235–246 (2008)
28. Jana, A., Khedker, U.P., Datar, A., Venkatesh, R., Niyas, C.: Scaling bounded model checking by transforming programs with arrays. In: Proceedings of LOPSTR (2016)
29. Ren, B., Agrawal, G., Larus, J.R., Mytkowicz, T., Poutanen, T., Schulte, W.: SIMD parallelization of applications that traverse irregular data structures. In: Proceedings of CGO, pp. 20:1–20:10 (2013)

Incremental Analysis for Probabilistic Programs

Jieyuan Zhang[1(✉)], Yulei Sui[1], and Jingling Xue[1,2]

[1] School of Computer Science and Engineering, UNSW, Sydney, Australia
{jieyuan,ysui,jingling}@cse.unsw.edu.au
[2] Advanced Innovation Center for Imaging Technology, CNU, Beijing, China

Abstract. This paper presents ICPP, a new data-flow-based **InC**remental analysis for **P**robabilistic **P**rograms, to infer their posterior probability distributions in response to small yet frequent changes to probabilistic knowledge, i.e., prior probability distributions and observations. Unlike incremental analyses for usual programs, which emphasize code changes, such as statement additions and deletions, ICPP focuses on changes made to probabilistic knowledge, the key feature in probabilistic programming. The novelty of ICPP lies in capturing the correlation between prior and posterior probability distributions by reasoning about the probabilistic dependence of each data-flow fact, so that any posterior probability affected by newly changed probabilistic knowledge can be incrementally updated in a sparse manner without recomputing it from scratch, thereby allowing the previously computed results to be reused. We have evaluated ICPP with a set of probabilistic programs. Our results show that ICPP is an order of magnitude faster than the state-of-the-art data-flow-based inference in analyzing probabilistic programs under small yet frequent changes to probabilistic knowledge, with an average analysis overhead of around 0.1 s in response to a single change.

1 Introduction

Uncertainty is a common feature in many modern software systems, especially statistical applications (e.g., climate change prediction, spam email filtering and ranking the skills of game players). Probabilistic programming provides a powerful approach to quantifying and characterizing the effects of these uncertainties. A Probabilistic Programming Language (PPL) usually extends an imperative language (e.g., C and Java) by adding two types of language constructs, i.e., *probabilistic assignments* for generating random values based on prior probability distributions and *observe statements* for conditioning values of variables.

Unlike an imperative program, which is mainly written for the purposes of being executed, a probabilistic program is a specification that specifies implicitly posterior probability distributions to model uncertainty of the program. Probabilistic inference is the key to reasoning about a probabilistic program by extracting explicit distributions that are implicitly specified in the program.

Generally, there are two approaches to probabilistic inference: (1) *dynamic inference*, which runs a probabilistic program a finite number of times through sampling-based Monte Carlo methods [4,7,19,25,28] and then performs inference

F. Ranzato (Ed.): SAS 2017, LNCS 10422, pp. 450–472, 2017.
DOI: 10.1007/978-3-319-66706-5_22

to calculate the statistics based on the execution traces, and (2) *static inference*, which statically computes the probability distributions without repeatedly executing the program. A typical static method [2] is to abstract a loop-free program as a probabilistic model (e.g., a Bayesian network) and then resorts to existing inference algorithms, e.g., belief propagation [24] and variational inference [35]. A recent work, DFI [8], provides more precise inference results than sampling algorithms and Bayesian modeling methods by applying data-flow analysis to analyze probabilistic programs with and without loops.

Unlike the case for imperative programs, applying data-flow analysis to infinite-state probabilistic programs is generally more expensive. Data-flow facts of probabilistic programs are probability distributions, including the values of program variables and their corresponding probabilities. Given a probabilistic program, the number of its data-flow facts depends not only on its size parameters but also the prior distributions at its probabilistic assignments and the conditions at its observe statements. As a common practice in probabilistic programming, probabilistic knowledge, which is represented by prior probability distributions and observations, is often updated under different scenarios or settings [3,6,37]. To achieve precise modeling, probabilistic assignments and observe statements are often changed in order to obtain various posterior probability distributions when writing a probabilistic program [36]. However, such small yet frequent changes affect the performance of static inference as the previous inference results become invalid once the program has been modified. Repeatedly reanalyzing a probabilistic program that undergoes small changes makes static inference costly.

Incremental analysis aims to efficiently update existing analysis results without recomputing them from scratch, allowing the previously computed information to be reused. There are a few existing works that support incremental analysis, such as pointer analysis [18,31], IDE/IFDS analysis [1], data race detection [38], symbolic execution [26], and fixed-point analysis for logic programs [14]. However, these existing techniques cannot be directly applied to analyze probabilistic programs. For probabilistic programs, frequent changes in probabilistic knowledge pose a new challenge to incremental analysis. It is still an open question as to whether we can replicate the success of previous incremental analysis for usual programs in analyzing probabilistic programs.

In this paper, we present ICPP, a new **InC**remental analysis for analyzing **P**robabilistic **P**rograms, to infer its posterior probability distributions in response to small yet frequent changes to probabilistic knowledge, i.e., prior probability distributions and observations. Unlike previous incremental analyses for usual programs, which emphasize code changes, such as statement additions and deletions, ICPP focuses on changes made to probabilistic knowledge, which is the key feature in probabilistic programming.

As illustrated in Fig. 1, ICPP first performs data-flow-based pre-inference. Unlike DFI [8], which explicitly computes and maintains the probability of every program state, our pre-inference generates data-flow facts with each consisting of a program state and its corresponding *probabilistic dependence*, which is

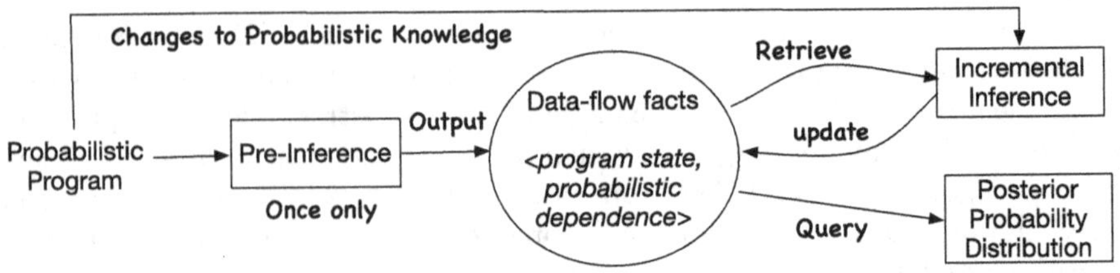

Fig. 1. Workflow of ICPP.

used to maintain the correlation between the posterior and prior probability distributions at probabilistic assignments. This probabilistic dependence is later retrieved to facilitate incremental inference once a change is made to a probabilistic assignment or an observe statement. Based on the dependence information, the data-flow facts are updated incrementally and propagated sparsely along the control flow to adapt to program changes, making ICPP an instantaneous incremental analysis for users to query posterior probability distributions, while achieving the same precision achieved when the program is re-analyzed entirely.

In summary, the contributions of this paper are as follows:

- We present ICPP, a new **InC**remental analysis for **P**robabilistic **P**rograms, in response to small yet frequent changes to probabilistic knowledge.
- We propose a new probabilistic dependence analysis to analyze the two distinct language constructs in probabilistic programs, probabilistic assignments and observe statements.
- We evaluate ICPP using a set of probabilistic programs from R2 [25] and DFI [8]. Our results show that ICPP is an order of magnitude faster than the state-of-the-art data-flow-based inference [8] in analyzing these programs under small yet frequent changes to probabilistic knowledge, with an average analysis overhead of around 0.1 s in response to a single change.

2 Background

In this section, we describe the preliminaries for our analysis, by focusing on the representation and inference of a probabilistic program.

2.1 Probabilistic Programs

Following [8,12], we represent a probabilistic program using a tiny language defined in Fig. 2. This is a single-function imperative language with two added constructs: (1) a *probabilistic assignment*, $x = \mathtt{Dist}(\overline{\theta})$, that assigns random values to variable x based on a probability distribution $\mathtt{Dist}(\overline{\theta})$, such as `Bernoulli`, `UniformInt` and `Gauss`, where $\overline{\theta}$ is a list of parameters according to a distribution model (with a continuous distribution being approximated by a discrete distribution over a finite set, following [8,21]), and (2) an *observe statement*, **observe**($\mathcal{E}$),

x, y, a, b	$\in$ Vars	program variables
θ	$\in \mathbb{R}$	real numbers
`Dist`	$\in$ `{UniformInt, Bernoulli, Gauss, ...}`	distributions
`uop`	$::= \{++, --, !\}$	unary operations
`bop`	$::= \{+, -, \times, /, \&\&, \|\|, ==, \neq, <, >, \leq, \geq\}$	binary operations
$\mathcal{E}$	$::=$	expressions
	$\mid$ x	variable
	$\mid$ c	constant
	$\mid \mathcal{E}_1$ **bop** $\mathcal{E}_2$	binary operation
	$\mid$ **uop** $\mathcal{E}$	unary operation
ℓ	$::=$	labeled statements
	$\mid x = \mathcal{E}$	deterministic assignment
	$\mid \ell_1; \ell_2$	sequential composition
	$\mid$ if $\mathcal{E}$ then ℓ_1 else ℓ_2	conditional composition
	$\mid$ while $\mathcal{E}$ do ℓ	loop
	$\mid$ skip	skip
	$\mid$ **x = Dist($\overline{\theta}$)**	**probabilistic assignment**
	$\mid$ **observe($\mathcal{E}$)**	**observe**
Prog	$::= \overline{\ell}$	program

Fig. 2. Syntax of a probabilistic program.

that conditions the expression $\mathcal{E}$ to be true. The effect of the observe statement is to block all program executions violating condition $\mathcal{E}$.

Figure 3 gives examples to illustrate the differences between an imperative program in Fig. 3(a) and its probabilistic counterparts in Figs. 3(b) and (c). Figure 3(b) replaces the deterministic assignment at line 2 in Fig. 3(a) with a probabilistic assignment, so that the variable b is assigned a random value based on the discrete uniform distribution `UniformInt(0, 1)`, which returns one of two integers 0 and 1 with equal probability, 1/2. Figure 3(c) gives another probabilistic program by adding further `observe`(b==1) after statement ℓ_4 in Fig. 3(b) to block any execution such that b is not equal to 1 at ℓ_5.

As shown in Fig. 3(d), executing the imperative program in Fig. 3(a) always produces the deterministic result ($a = 0$, $b = 1$). However, probabilistic programs are nondeterministic. Executing the one in Fig. 3(b) may produce one of the two different results: ($a = 1$, $b = 0$) and ($a = 0$, $b = 1$). Figure 3(e) shows a posterior distribution with equal probability 1/2 for each result. The imperative program in Fig. 3(a) can be seen as a special case of the probabilistic program in Fig. 3(b) with the probability of its unique deterministic result being 1.

Figure 3(f) demonstrates that the result ($a = 1$, $b = 0$) becomes infeasible with its possibility being 0 due to the condition at the observe statement. After normalization, the probability for the other result ($a = 0$, $b = 1$) becomes 1.

2.2 Probabilistic Inference

The key mechanism for reasoning about a probabilistic program is probabilistic inference, which explicitly calculates the posterior probability distributions implicitly specified in the program. There are two approaches: (1) *dynamic inference*, which executes programs a finite number of times through sampling-based methods [19], such as importance sampling [11], Gibbs sampling [28] and

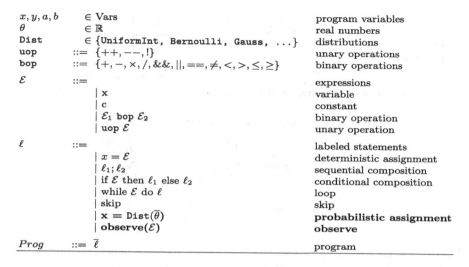

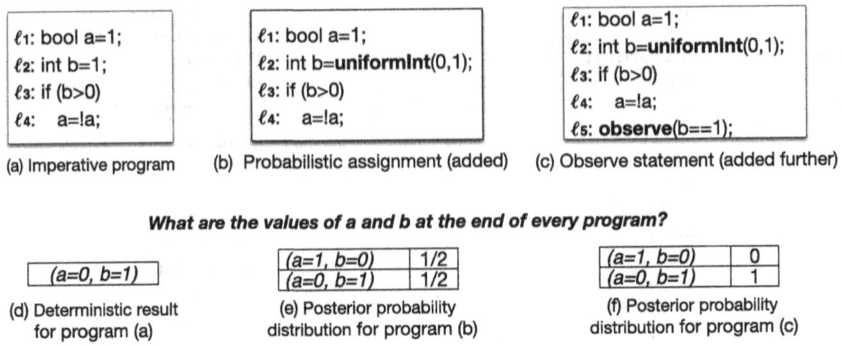
ℓ1: bool a=1;
ℓ2: int b=1;
ℓ3: if (b>0)
ℓ4: a=!a;
(a) Imperative program
ℓ1: bool a=1;
ℓ2: int b=uniformInt(0,1);
ℓ3: if (b>0)
ℓ4: a=!a;
(b) Probabilistic assignment (added)
ℓ1: bool a=1;
ℓ2: int b=uniformInt(0,1);
ℓ3: if (b>0)
ℓ4: a=!a;
ℓ5: observe(b==1);
(c) Observe statement (added further)
What are the values of a and b at the end of every program?
(a=0, b=1)
(d) Deterministic result for program (a)
(a=1, b=0) 1/2
(a=0, b=1) 1/2
(e) Posterior probability distribution for program (b)
(a=1, b=0) 0
(a=0, b=1) 1
(f) Posterior probability distribution for program (c)

Fig. 3. Imperative vs. probabilistic programs.

Metropolis-Hastings sampling [7], and (2) *static inference*, which computes the probability distributions statically without running the program.

A recent data-flow-based inference, DFI [8], applies the data-flow theory for probabilistic inference by treating probability distributions as data-flow facts. DFI is path-sensitive by analyzing control-flow branch conditions. The resulting inference provides better precision than many existing methods, e.g., Expectation Propagation [22], message passing algorithm [16] and MCMC sampling [13].

In DFI, the static inference is formulated as a forward data-flow problem $(D, \sqcap, F)$. Here, D represents all data-flow facts with each $\langle \sigma, \rho \rangle \in D$ consisting of a program state σ (a set of values) and its corresponding probability ρ when σ holds. $\sqcap$ is the meet operator. $F : D \to D$ represents the set of transfer functions with f_ℓ being associated with node (statement) at ℓ in the CFG of the program.

A path-sensitive analysis computes the data-flow facts (probability distributions) by considering every executable path. We write π to denote a path $[\ell_1, \ell_2 \ldots \ell_n]$ consisting of a sequence of n statements in a CFG. The transfer function for π is $f_\pi \in F$, which is the composition of transfer functions of the first $n-1$ statements on π, i.e., $f_\pi = f_{\ell_1} \circ f_{\ell_2} \cdots f_{\ell_{n-1}}$. Note that we speak of the path π by excluding the last statement at ℓ_n. Finally, the set of data-flow facts, $D_{\ell n}$, that reach the beginning of a statement ℓ_n is computed as follows:

$$D_{\ell n} = \bigsqcap_{\pi \in paths(\ell_n)} f_\pi(\top) \tag{1}$$

where $paths(\ell_n)$ denotes the set of paths from the program entry to statement ℓ_n and $\top \in D$ is the standard top element in the lattice used.

When analyzing a statement ℓ in DFI [8], its transfer function f_ℓ, which is defined based on the standard *Gen*/*Kill* sets, is distributive, so that $f_\ell(d_1) \cup f_\ell(d_2) = f_\ell(d_1 \cup d_2)$ holds, where $d_1, d_2 \in D$. Therefore, the meet operator $\sqcap$ is the set union ($\cup$), causing the data-flow facts at a joint point to be merged, in order to reduce the number of facts propagated without affecting the precision of the posterior probability distribution results. In particular, two data-flow facts $\langle \sigma_1, \rho_1 \rangle$ and $\langle \sigma_2, \rho_2 \rangle$ at a joint point are merged into $\langle \sigma_1, \rho_1 + \rho_2 \rangle$ if $\sigma_1 == \sigma_2$.

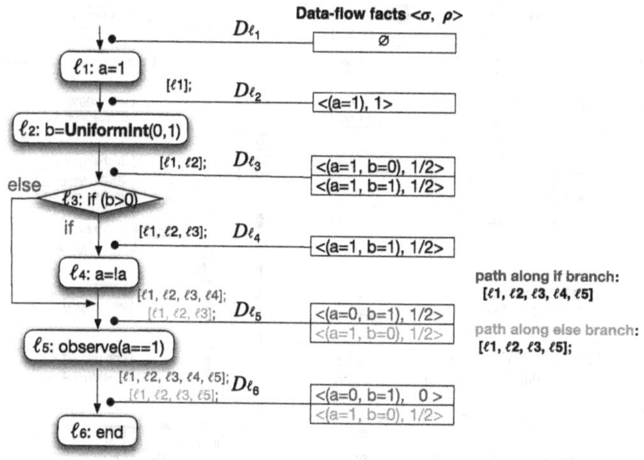

Fig. 4. Data-flow-based probabilistic inference.

Let us take a look at the data-flow-based inference in Fig. 4 by revisiting the example in Fig. 3(c). After analyzing the deterministic assignment ℓ_1, D_{ℓ_2} at the beginning of ℓ_2 is $\langle(a=1), 1\rangle$. After analyzing the probabilistic assignment ℓ_2, we obtain two data-flow facts representing the probability distributions for two possible states, $(a=1, b=0)$ and $(a=1, b=1)$, with their corresponding probabilities being $\rho_{(a=1,b=0)} = Pr(\ell_1\!:\!a\!=\!1) * Pr(\ell_2\!:\!b\!=\!0) = 1 * 1/2 = 1/2$ and $\rho_{(a=1,b=1)} = Pr(\ell_1\!:\!a\!=\!1) * Pr(\ell_2\!:\!b\!=\!1) = 1 * 1/2 = 1/2$, respectively.

D_{ℓ_5} contains the two data-flow facts reaching the beginning of ℓ_5, $\langle(a=0, b=1), 1/2\rangle$ and $\langle(a=1, b=0), 1/2\rangle$, which are computed and propagated from the `if` and `else` branches, respectively. Finally, after analyzing the observe statement ℓ_5, D_{ℓ_6} (without normalization) is the same as D_{ℓ_5} except that the probability of $(a\!=\!0, b\!=\!1)$ has been updated to from 1/2 to 0.

3 A Motivating Example

Figure 5 gives an example to illustrate the basic idea behind ICPP when the prior probability distribution at ℓ_2 is changed from `UniformInt`(0, 1) to `UniformInt`$(-1, 1)$. This change affects the probabilities of b's existing values and introduces a new value -1 to b. Note that observe statements are handled as a special case of probabilistic statements and will be discussed in Sect. 4.2.2.

Unlike DFI [8], which explicitly computes and maintains the probability ρ of every state σ reaching statement ℓ in terms of a data-flow fact $\langle\sigma, \rho\rangle \in D_\ell$, ICPP represents a data-flow fact in the form of $\langle\sigma, \gamma_\sigma\rangle \in D_\ell$, where γ_σ is σ's all-path probabilistic dependence (Definition 3), which implicitly represents σ's probability ρ_σ. We obtain γ_σ by merging σ's single-path dependences $\gamma_{\pi,\sigma}$ for all the paths π reaching ℓ (Definition 2), where $\gamma_{\pi,\sigma}$ collects the probability seeds generated from the relevant probabilistic assignments on π (Definition 1). When

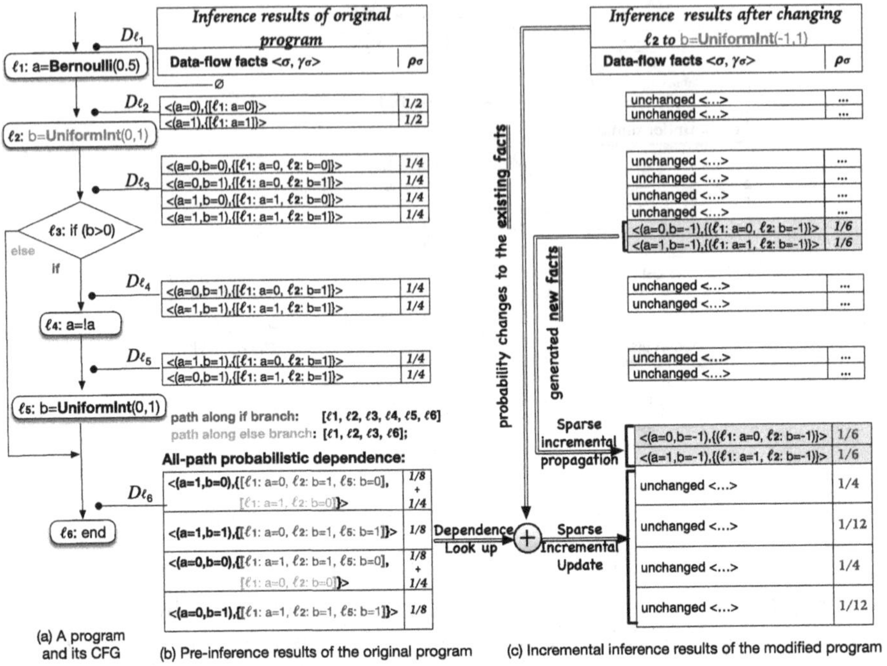

Fig. 5. A motivating example illustrating how ICPP works in response to the change at ℓ_2 from `UniformInt`(0, 1) to `UniformInt`$(-1, 1)$ (as highlighted in red). (Color figure online)

building a particular single-path dependence $\gamma_{\pi,\sigma}$, only one single seed is selected for a probabilistic assignment every time when it is analyzed. Therefore, a seed may appear multiple times in $\gamma_{\pi,\sigma}$ when π contains a loop, which is handled by approximating a KL-divergence [22] between two consecutive loop iterations.

Definition 1 (Probability Seed). *For a probabilistic assignment $\ell : x = \texttt{Dist}(\overline{\theta})$, we define a probability seed s at ℓ as $\ell : x = a$, where a is one of all the possible values returned by the prior distribution $\texttt{Dist}(\overline{\theta})$. One probabilistic assignment ℓ may induce multiple seeds $s \in Seeds(\ell)$ from the distribution.*

Definition 2 (Single-Path Probabilistic Dependence). *For a data-flow fact $\langle\sigma, \gamma_{\pi,\sigma}\rangle \in f_\pi(\top)$ associated with path $\pi = [\ell_1, \ldots, \ell_n]$, its single-path probabilistic dependence is $\gamma_{\pi,\sigma} = [s_1, \ldots, s_m]$, which consists of a sequence of probability seeds (Definition 1) based on all the probabilistic assignments on π $(m < n)$. The probability of σ for π is $\rho_{\pi,\sigma} = Pr(\gamma_{\pi,\sigma}) = Pr(s_1) * Pr(s_2) * \cdots * Pr(s_m)$.*

Definition 3 (All-Path Probabilistic Dependence). *For a data-flow fact $\langle\sigma, \gamma_\sigma\rangle \in D_\ell$ at the beginning of ℓ, its all-path probabilistic dependence $\gamma_\sigma = \{\gamma_{\pi,\sigma} \mid \pi \in paths(\ell)\}$ consists of the dependence information for every single path π reaching ℓ, with σ's probability being $\rho_\sigma = Pr(\gamma_\sigma) = \Sigma_{\pi \in paths(\ell)}\ \rho_{\pi,\sigma}$.*

Let us look at the example in Fig. 5 to illustrate how ICPP incrementally computes the posterior probability distributions at ℓ_6 once the prior probability distribution at a probabilistic assignment is changed. *Pre-inference* is first performed to generate the probabilistic dependences for all the data-flow facts during the on-the-fly data-flow analysis. Based on the dependence information, *sparse incremental update* is performed to recalculate the posterior probability distributions of the existing data-flow facts at ℓ_6 affected by the change made. Finally, we propagate the new data-flow facts introduced by the change across the entire program in a sparse manner via *sparse incremental propagation.*

Pre-inference. For the program given in Fig. 5(a), the data-flow facts obtained by pre-inference are listed in Fig. 5(b).

To start with, the probabilistic assignment ℓ_1 based on the Bernoulli distribution assigns a random value 0 or 1 to variable a with each value's probability being 1/2. As shown, D_{ℓ_2} therefore contains the two data-flow facts, where the probabilistic dependence of each state is its corresponding probability seed generated from ℓ_1 (e.g., $(a = 0)$ is annotated with its seed $[\ell_1 : a = 0]$).

The probabilistic assignment at ℓ_2 gives variable b a random value, 0 or 1, based on a discrete uniform distribution. By combining with the two values of variable a, we obtain the four data-flow facts in $D_{\ell 3}$ to represent the four possible states for a and b with the probability of each state being 1/4. The corresponding probabilistic dependence of each state (e.g., $(a = 0, b = 0)$) is a sequence of probability seeds (e.g., $[\ell_1 : a = 0, \ell_2 : b = 0]$), which are used to compute its corresponding probability (e.g., $\rho_{(a=0,b=0)} = Pr(\ell_1 : a = 0) * Pr(\ell_2 : b = 0) = 1/4$).

There are two branches at ℓ_3 when propagating D_{ℓ_3} forward. Only two data-flow facts whose states satisfy condition $b > 0$ are propagated to the `if` branch as illustrated in D_{ℓ_4} while the other two are propagated to the `else` branch. After analyzing ℓ_4, a's value in each data-flow fact of D_{ℓ_4} is flipped, while b's value stays the same. Note that the probabilistic dependence recorded in each data-flow fact remains unchanged, as indicated in D_{ℓ_5}, because ℓ_4 is a deterministic statement, which does not affect any probabilistic dependence in any way.

After analyzing ℓ_5, D_{ℓ_6} contains six data-flow facts at the join point before ℓ_6 (the end of the program). The four data-flow facts highlighted in green are generated after analyzing ℓ_5 in the `if` branch and the two data-flow facts in orange are propagated from the `else` branch. Let $\pi_{\text{if}} = [\ell_1, \ell_2, \ell_3, \ell_4, \ell_5, \ell_6]$ and $\pi_{\text{else}} = [\ell_1, \ell_2, \ell_3, \ell_6]$ as shown in Fig. 5(b). The data-flow facts whose states are the same are merged by computing their all-path probabilistic dependence (Definition 3). Therefore, $\langle (a = 0, b = 0), \gamma_{\pi_{\text{if}},(a=0,b=0)} \rangle$ from the `if` branch and $\langle (a = 0, b = 0), \gamma_{\pi_{\text{else}},(a=0,b=0)} \rangle$ from the `else` branch are merged into $\langle (a = 0, b = 0), \{\gamma_{\pi_{\text{if}},(a=0,b=0)}, \gamma_{\pi_{\text{else}},(a=0,b=0)}\} \rangle$, where

$$\begin{aligned} \gamma_{\pi_{\text{if}},(a=0,b=0)} &= [\ell_1 : a = 1, \ell_2 : b = 1, \ell_5 : b = 0] \\ \gamma_{\pi_{\text{else}},(a=0,b=0)} &= [\ell_1 : a = 0, \ell_2 : b = 0] \end{aligned} \tag{2}$$

Likewise, the two data-flow facts with the same state $(a = 1, b = 0)$ are also merged. Finally, we calculate the joint posterior probability ρ_σ for each data-flow fact reaching ℓ_6 based on its probabilistic dependence as shown in Fig. 5(b).

Sparse Incremental Update. Here, our incremental analysis is concerned with updating the posterior probabilities of the existing data-flow facts in D_{ℓ_6}, which are affected by the changes made to the prior probability distributions discovered by the computed probabilistic dependences. ICPP does not reanalyze the program to recompute any of the existing data-flow facts $\langle \sigma, \gamma_\sigma \rangle \in D_{\ell_6}$. Instead, it just recalculates its posterior probability ρ_σ. For example, the probabilistic assignment ℓ_2, changed from $b = \texttt{UniformInt}(0, 1)$ to $b = \texttt{UniformInt}(-1, 1)$, causes the prior probabilities of the two probability seeds to change from $Pr^{old}(\ell_2 : b = 0) = Pr^{old}(\ell_2 : b = 1) = 1/2$ to $Pr^{new}(\ell_2 : b = 0) = Pr^{new}(\ell_2 : b = 1) = 1/3$. In this motivating example, we are interested in the effects of the change on the posterior probabilities at ℓ_6. As shown in Fig. 5(b), D_{ℓ_6} contains four data-flow facts that are computed before the change is made. Therefore, their probabilities need to be updated. Consider first $\langle (a = 0, b = 0), \{\gamma_{\pi_{\text{if}},(a=0,b=0)}, \gamma_{\pi_{\text{else}},(a=0,b=0)}\}\rangle$, where $\gamma_{\pi_{\text{if}},(a=0,b=0)}$ and $\gamma_{\pi_{\text{else}},(a=0,b=0)}$ are given in (2). The following equation recalculates the posterior probability of its corresponding state $(a = 0, b = 0)$, whose probabilistic dependence contains the two probability seeds, $\ell_2 : b = 0$ and $\ell_2 : b = 1$:

$$\begin{aligned} \rho^{new}_{(a=0,b=0)} &= \frac{Pr^{old}(\gamma_{\pi_{\text{if}},(a=0,b=0)}) * Pr^{new}(\ell_2 : b = 1)}{Pr^{old}(\ell_2 : b = 1)} \\ &\quad + \frac{Pr^{old}(\gamma_{\pi_{\text{else}},(a=0,b=0)}) * Pr^{new}(\ell_2 : b = 0)}{Pr^{old}(\ell_2 : b = 0)} \\ &= \frac{1/8 * 1/3}{1/2} + \frac{1/4 * 1/3}{1/2} = 1/4 \end{aligned}$$

Likewise, the probabilities of the other three data-flow facts in D_{ℓ_6} are updated as $\rho^{new}_{(a=1,b=0)} = 1/4$, $\rho^{new}_{(a=1,b=1)} = 1/12$ and $\rho^{new}_{(a=0,b=1)} = 1/12$. These updated posterior probabilities are reflected in the bottom of Fig. 5(c).

Updating existing data-flow facts incrementally this way is lightweight. As we are interested in the effects of a change on ℓ_6 in our motivating example, the posterior probabilities for the data-flow facts in D_{ℓ_6} are recalculated directly. All the other data-flow facts from D_{ℓ_1} to D_{ℓ_5} remain untouched, without requiring any expensive data-flow analysis that computes and propagates data-flow facts (probabilistic dependences) along the program's control-flow.

Sparse Incremental Propagation. The change made to the prior probability distribution at ℓ_2 also introduces a new probability seed $[\ell_2 : b = -1]$ with its probability $Pr(\ell_2 : b = -1) = 1/3$, as illustrated in Fig. 5(c). During the sparse incremental propagation, the two new data-flow facts, $\langle (a = 0, b = -1), \{[\ell_1 : a = 0, \ell_2 : b = -1]\}\rangle$ and $\langle (a = 1, b = -1), \{[\ell_1 : a = 1, \ell_2 : b = -1]\}\rangle$, are generated and appended to D_{ℓ_3}. In general, the new data-flow facts generated this way are propagated sparsely along the control flow in the program, without causing the existing data-flow facts to be modified. Finally, we obtain the updated posterior joint distributions at ℓ_6 by combining the results of both existing and new data-flow facts incrementally computed for ℓ_6, as shown in Fig. 5(c).

4 ICPP: Incremental Analysis for Probabilistic Programs

In this section, we describe our pre-inference and incremental inference, which are conducted in response to changes made to probabilistic knowledge at probabilistic assignments and/or observe statements.

4.1 Pre-inference

The probabilistic dependence analysis during pre-inference forms the basis for ICPP. It takes a probabilistic program as input and produces as output the data-flow facts with a probabilistic dependence γ_σ over each state σ of the program. Figure 6 gives our algorithm, which introduces the transfer functions for analyzing each type of statements in Fig. 2 by computing the data-flow facts in a forward traversal of the CFG of the program being analyzed.

4.1.1 Notations. We adopt some notations from [8]. For a state σ, $\sigma(x)$ denotes the value of variable x in σ. Likewise, the notation $\sigma(\mathcal{E})$ evaluates the value of expression $\mathcal{E}$ in σ. $\sigma[x \leftarrow \sigma(x)]$ represents the state obtained by updating the value of x in σ, with the values of all the other variables in σ remaining unchanged. The function $ite(b, x, y)$ evaluates to x if $b = true$ and y if $b = false$.

Given a statement ℓ, Ω_ℓ is used to denote all the states recorded in the data-flow facts of D_ℓ. For the purposes of explaining our algorithm cleanly, D_ℓ is represented by a lambda function $\lambda_\sigma.expr$, where each state $\sigma \in \Omega_\ell$ is bounded in expression $expr$, which represents the all-path probabilistic dependence of σ. By default, we define $\top = \lambda_\sigma.\emptyset$. For $(\sigma, \gamma_\sigma) \in D_\ell$, we write $\gamma_\sigma \oplus s$ for seed collection by adding a probability seed s into every single-path dependence $\gamma_{\pi,\sigma} \in \gamma_\sigma$ (where $\pi \in paths(\ell)$ ranges from all the paths reaching ℓ by Definition 3).

4.1.2 Probabilistic Dependence Analysis. Given a program $\ell \in Prog$, we call PREIN$(\top, \ell)$ (Fig. 6) recursively to compute its data-flow facts.

Lines 2–3 handle a deterministic assignment $\ell : x := \mathcal{E}$, where multiple states $\sigma \in \Omega_\ell$ of the data-flow facts in D_ℓ may become (i.e., be merged into) the same new state σ' after the value of x is updated with a new value $\sigma(\mathcal{E})$. Consequently, the corresponding probabilistic dependences of these states $\sigma \in \Omega_\ell$ are merged together to obtain the all-path probabilistic dependence of σ'.

For each probability seed $[\ell : x = a]$ generated at a probabilistic assignment ℓ, lines 4–5 compute new data-flow facts for all states $\sigma \in \Omega_\ell$ similarly as the case when a deterministic statement is handled, except that the all-path dependence γ_σ of σ is updated by adding the new probability seed $[\ell : x = a]$ into γ_σ. The set of data-flow facts obtained at a probabilistic statement ℓ is the union of the sets of data-flow facts computed for all its probability seeds $s \in Seeds(\ell)$ at ℓ.

Lines 6–7 handle an observe statement `observe`$(\mathcal{E})$ by simply removing the dependence information γ_σ of any state $\sigma \in \Omega_\ell$ if $\sigma(\mathcal{E})$ evaluates to false. Lines 9–10 handle a sequence of two statements $\ell_1; \ell_2$ by first computing the data-flow facts for ℓ_1 and using the resulting facts as the input to analyze ℓ_2.

Algorithm PREIN(D_ℓ, ℓ)
`Input`: set of data-flow facts $\langle \sigma, \gamma_\sigma \rangle \in D_\ell$ over all the states
$\sigma \in \Omega_\ell$ before analyzing ℓ and a statement at ℓ
`Output`: set of data-flow facts $\langle \sigma', \gamma'_\sigma \rangle \in D'_\ell$ in the form of $\lambda_\sigma.expr$ after analyzing ℓ
1: **switch**(ℓ)
2: **case** $x := \mathcal{E}$:
3: **return** $\lambda\sigma'.\bigcup_{\{\sigma\in\Omega_\ell \mid \sigma[x\leftarrow\sigma(\mathcal{E})]=\sigma'\}} \gamma_\sigma$;
4: **case** $x :=$ `Dist`$(\overline{\theta})$:
5: **return** $\lambda\sigma'.\bigcup_{(\ell:x=a)\in Seeds(\ell)}((\bigcup_{\{\sigma\in\Omega_\ell \mid \sigma[x\leftarrow a]=\sigma'\}} \gamma_\sigma) \oplus (\ell : x = a))$;
6: **case** `observe`$(\mathcal{E})$:
7: **return** $\lambda\sigma.ite(\sigma(\mathcal{E}), \gamma_\sigma, \emptyset)$;
8: **case** *skip*:
9: **return** D_ℓ;
10: **case** ℓ_1; ℓ_2:
11: $D_{\ell_2} =$ PREIN(D_ℓ, ℓ_1);
12: **return** PREIN(D_{ℓ_2}, ℓ_2);
13: **case** if $\mathcal{E}$ then ℓ_1 else ℓ_2:
14: $D_{\ell_1} = \lambda\sigma.ite(\sigma(\mathcal{E}), \gamma_\sigma, \emptyset)$;
15: $D_{\ell_2} = \lambda\sigma.ite(\sigma(\mathcal{E}), \emptyset, \gamma_\sigma)$;
16: **return** $\lambda\sigma'.$(PREIN(D_{ℓ_1}, ℓ_1)(σ') $\bigcup$ PREIN(D_{ℓ_2}, ℓ_2)(σ'));
17: **case** while $\mathcal{E}$ do ℓ_1:
18: $D_{pre} = \bot$, $D_{cur} = D_\ell$;
19: **while** KL-divergence(D_{pre}, D_{cur}) $\neq$ *true* **do**
20: $D_{pre} = D_{cur}$;
21: $D_{cur} =$ PREIN(D_{pre}, **if** $\mathcal{E}$ **then** ℓ_1 **else** skip);
23: **end while**
24: **return** $\lambda\sigma'.ite(\sigma'(\mathcal{E}), \emptyset, D_{cur}(\sigma'))$;
25: **end switch**

Fig. 6. An algorithm for pre-inference.

Lines 13–16 handle an if statement. Our path-sensitive analysis first splits the set of data-flow facts reaching ℓ into two subsets, D_{ℓ_1} and D_{ℓ_2}, based on the Boolean predicate $\mathcal{E}$. Then the bodies of the `if` and `else` branches are recursively computed by applying PREIN. Finally, we return the results by merging the data-flow facts obtained from both the `if` and `else` branches.

Lines 17–24 handle a while loop by computing the results until a fixed-point is reached. We define D_{pre} and D_{cur} to represent the sets of previous and current data-flow facts across two consecutive iterations of the while loop. Initially, D_{pre} is set as $\bot$ and D_{cur} as D_ℓ obtained just before the while loop. PREIN is repeatedly applied to the data-flow facts in D_{pre} with the statement "**if** $\mathcal{E}$ **then** ℓ_1 **else** *skip*" until a fixed-point based on KL-divergence [17]. Due to the non-determinism of probabilistic programs [8,10,12] (e.g., a probabilistic assignment generates a probability seed randomly during each loop iteration), finding a loop iteration under which $D_{cur} = D_{pre}$ is potentially nonterminating. Thus, we use KL-divergence to enforce the termination of a while loop. In line 19, KL-divergence(D_{cur}, D_{pre}) is true if the following condition holds:

$$\mid \sum_{\sigma \in \Omega_{cur}} \rho_\sigma * \ln(\frac{\rho_\sigma}{\rho'_\sigma}) \mid \; < \; threshold \tag{3}$$

where ρ_σ is the probability of $\sigma \in \Omega_{cur}$ calculated based on $\langle \sigma, \gamma_\sigma \rangle \in D_{cur}$, ρ'_σ is the probability calculated based on $\langle \sigma, \gamma'_\sigma \rangle \in D_{pre}$, and *threshold* is a user-determined parameter (set to 0.01 in our experiments). Note that a probability seed s may appear multiple times in a single-path dependence when a fixed-point is reached. For example, $\gamma_{\pi,\sigma} = [s, s, \ldots, s]$ if the path π contains some loops.

```
ℓ1: b=0;
ℓ2: while(!b) do {
ℓ3:    b=Bernoulli(0.5)
ℓ4: }
```

Fig. 7. An OneCoin example.

Example 1. Let us use a simple OneCoin program in Fig. 7 to explain KL-divergence in a while loop. At the k-th iteration, there are two states, $(b = 0)$ and $(b = 1)$, with their all-path probabilistic dependences being $\gamma_{(b=0)} = \{[\ell_3 : b = 0, \ell_3 : b = 0; \cdots]\}$ and $\gamma_{(b=1)} = \{[\ell_3 : b = 1], [\ell_3 : b = 0, \ell_3 : b = 1], [\ell_3 : b = 0, \ell_3 : b = 0, \ell_3 : b = 1], \cdots\}$ immediately after ℓ_3. Their corresponding probabilities are $\rho_{(b=0)} = (0.5)^k$ and $\rho_{(b=1)} = 0.5 + ... + (0.5)^k$. Thus, the KL-divergence between iterations k and $k-1$ is computed as follows:

$$(0.5)^k \times \ln(\frac{(0.5)^k}{(0.5)^{k-1}}) + (0.5 + ... + (0.5)^k) \times \ln(\frac{0.5 + ... + (0.5)^k}{0.5 + ... + (0.5)^{k-1}})$$

□

Let us revisit the example in Fig. 5 to go through our pre-inference algorithm in Fig. 6. Given the program $\ell_1; \ell_2; \ell_3; \ell_6$ in Fig. 5(a), we see how calling PREIN($\top, \ell_1; \ell_2; \ell_3; \ell_6$) yields the data-flow facts obtained in Fig. 5(b).

Example 2. The sequence $\ell_1; \ell_2; \ell_3; \ell_6$ is analyzed in order, starting from $\ell_1 : a =$ `Bernoulli(0.5)` (lines 10–12). ℓ_1 generates two probability seeds, $\ell_1 : a = 0$ and $\ell_1 : a = 1$ (lines 4–5). Thus, we obtain two states, $(a = 0)$ and $(a = 1)$, which are recorded in Ω_{ℓ_2}. Their probability seeds are added to their probabilistic dependences, resulting in $\gamma_{(a=0)} = \{[\ell_1 : a = 0]\}$ and $\gamma_{(a=1)} = \{[\ell_1 : a = 1]\}$. As a result, D_{ℓ_2} contains the two data-flow facts, as shown in Fig. 5(b).

When analyzing $\ell_2 : b =$ `UniformInt(0, 1)` (lines 4–5), we obtain also two probability seeds, $\ell_2 : b = 0$ and $\ell_2 : b = 1$. By combining each seed with each of the two states in $\Omega_{\ell_2} = \{(a = 0), (a = 1)\}$, we obtain the four states in D_{ℓ_3}, as shown in Fig. 5(b), with the probabilistic dependence γ_σ of each state $\sigma \in \Omega_{\ell_3}$

containing an additional probability seed of either $\ell_2 : b = 0$ or $\ell_2 : b = 1$. As a result, D_{ℓ_3} contains the four data-flow facts, as shown in Fig. 5(b).

When analyzing ℓ_3 : **if** $(b > 0)$ **then** $\ell_4; \ell_5$ **else** *skip* (lines 13–16), we split D_{ℓ_3} into $D_{\ell_4;\ell_5}$ and D_{skip} according to the condition $b > 0$, where $D_{\ell_4;\ell_5}$ is propagated into the `if` branch and D_{skip} into the `else` branch. Then we continue to apply PreIn to compute the data-flow facts for $\ell_4; \ell_5$ (lines 10–12) and *skip* (lines 8–9). Finally, we merge the data-flow facts flowing out of the two branches at the beginning of ℓ_6 to obtain D_{ℓ_6} (line 16). □

4.2 Incremental Inference

Based on the computed probabilistic dependence information, our incremental analysis handles two type of changes made to a probabilistic program, i.e., prior distribution changes at a probabilistic assignment (Sect. 4.2.1) and condition changes at an observe statement (Sect. 4.2.2). ICPP aims to recalculate the posterior probability ρ_σ for each data-flow fact $\langle \sigma, \gamma_\sigma \rangle \in D_{\ell_{end}}$ at ℓ_{end} (the end of a program) according to the computed probabilistic dependence γ_σ, in response to the changes made to probabilistic knowledge in the program.

Without loss of generality, we restrict ourselves to a change made to one single statement at a time. Our incremental inference generalizes straightforwardly to the changes made simultaneously to multiple statements.

4.2.1 Handling Changes Made at Probabilistic Assignments. For a probabilistic assignment $x = \texttt{Dist}(\overline{\theta})$, ICPP focuses on a change made to the prior distribution $\texttt{Dist}(\overline{\theta})$, which is defined over a measurable sample space with a probability measure. Thus, a change can be a modification of the sample space or the probability measure. For example, if $x = \texttt{Bernoulli}(0.5)$ is modified to $x = \texttt{Bernoulli}(0.6)$, the sample space, $\{0, 1\}$, remains the same, but the probability measure is adjusted, with the probability of $x = 1$ changed from 0.5 to 0.6. However, modifying $x = \texttt{UniformInt}(0, 1)$ into $x = \texttt{UniformInt}(-1, 1)$ will change both its sample space and probability measure. Similarly, modifying a distribution model from `Dist` to `Dist'` also affects both.

Modifying a probability measure changes the posterior probabilities of existing data-flow facts computed by pre-inference. Modifying a sample space generates new probability seeds, and consequently, introduces new data-flow facts.

For a change made at a probabilistic assignment, the algorithm in Fig. 8 updates the posterior probabilities of the existing data-flow facts affected via IncUpdate and propagates the newly introduced data-flow facts via IncProp.

Sparse Incremental Update. According to our algorithm in Fig. 8, $S^{com} = Seeds(\ell_{old}) \cap Seeds(\ell_{new})$ is the set of probability seeds that exist in both the original and modified programs. $D_{\ell_{end}}$ is the set of data-flow facts that reach ℓ_{end} computed before the change. IncUpdate$(D_{\ell_{end}}, S^{com})$ can instantly recalculate the posterior probability distributions for the states in $D_{\ell_{end}}$ based on the all-path probabilistic dependence γ_σ computed by pre-inference for each data-flow fact in $D_{\ell_{end}}$, without a need for performing any data-flow analysis.

HANDLEPROBASSIGN(ℓ_{old} : x=Dist($\overline{\theta}$), ℓ_{new} : x=Dist'($\overline{\theta}'$))
$S^{com} = Seeds(\ell_{old}) \cap Seeds(\ell_{new})$;
Let $D_{\ell_{end}}$ be the set of existing data-flow facts before the end of the program;
Ψ_1=INCUPDATE($D_{\ell_{end}}, S^{com}$); // handling the existing data-flow facts
D^{Δ} = PREIN($D_{\ell_{old}}, \ell_{new}$) \ PREIN($D_{\ell_{old}}, \ell_{old}$);
Ψ_2=INCPROP(D^{Δ}); // handling the new data-flow facts
return $\Psi_1 \cup \Psi_2$;

Fig. 8. An algorithm for performing incremental analysis due to a change made from ℓ_{old}:x=Dist($\overline{\theta}$) to ℓ_{new}:x=Dist'($\overline{\theta}'$) at a probabilistic assignment. Ψ_1 and Ψ_2 are the posterior distributions obtained in analyzing the existing and new data-flow facts.

The new posterior probability distributions for $D_{\ell_{end}}$ are obtained directly:

$$\text{INCUPDATE}(D_{\ell_{end}}, S^{com}) = \{\langle \sigma, \rho_\sigma^{new} \rangle \mid \langle \sigma, \gamma_\sigma \rangle \in D_{\ell_{end}}\} \tag{4}$$

with the new posterior probability $\rho_\sigma^{new} = Cal(\gamma_\sigma, S^{com})$ being obtained as:

$$Cal(\gamma_\sigma, S^{com}) = \sum_{(\gamma_{\pi,\sigma}, S) \in \mathsf{Affected}_\sigma} Pr^{old}(\gamma_{\pi,\sigma}) \times \prod_{s \in S} \frac{Pr^{new}(s)}{Pr^{old}(s)} + \sum_{\gamma_{\pi,\sigma} \in \mathsf{NotAffected}_\sigma} Pr^{old}(\gamma_{\pi,\sigma}) \tag{5}$$

where $\mathsf{Affected}_\sigma = \{(\gamma_{\pi,\sigma}, S) \mid \gamma_{\pi,\sigma} \in \gamma_\sigma, S = \{s \mid s \in \gamma_{\pi,\sigma} \wedge s \in S^{com}\}\}$, which consists of a set of pairs with each $(\gamma_{\pi,\sigma}, S)$ representing the fact that the single-path dependence $\gamma_{\pi,\sigma} \in \gamma_\sigma$ is affected by some seeds in S whose probabilities are changed, on the path π containing ℓ_{old}. Note that S is a multiset as it may contain multiple instances of a seed s from $\gamma_{\pi,\sigma}$ due to loops on π.

We also define $\mathsf{NotAffected}_\sigma = \{\gamma_{\pi,\sigma} \in \gamma_\sigma \mid \forall\ s \in \gamma_{\pi,\sigma} : s \notin Seeds(\ell_{old})\}$. This contains the single-path dependences such that each $\gamma_{\pi,\sigma}$ is not affected by any seed in $Seeds(\ell_{old})$ generated by the old statement ℓ_{old}, i.e., ℓ_{old} is not on π.

The probability of $\gamma_{\pi,\sigma}$ is set to 0 if $\gamma_{\pi,\sigma}$ contains any seed $s \in (Seeds(\ell_{old}) \backslash Seeds_\ell^{com})$, which will be removed from the modified program.

Finally, $Pr^{old}(s)$ and $Pr^{new}(s)$ represent the probabilities of seed s in the original and modified programs, respectively.

Example 3. Let us revisit the example in Fig. 5(c) to explain our incremental update for an existing data-flow fact $\langle (a = 0, b = 0), \gamma_{(a=0,b=0)} \rangle \in D_{\ell_6}$. Recall that $\gamma_{(a=0,b=0)} = \{\gamma_{\pi_{\text{if}},(a=0,b=0)}, \gamma_{\pi_{\text{else}},(a=0,b=0)}\}$, where $\gamma_{\pi_{\text{if}},(a=0,b=0)}$ and $\gamma_{\pi_{\text{else}},(a=0,b=0)}$ are from (2). Given the change from $\ell_{old}:b$=UniformInt$(0,1)$ to $\ell_{new}:b$=UniformInt$(-1,1)$, we have $S^{com} = Seeds(\ell_{old}) = \{\ell_2 : b = 0, \ell_2 : b = 1\}$. Thus, $\mathsf{Affected}_{(a=0,b=0)} = \{(\gamma_{\pi_{\text{if}},(a=0,b=0)}, \{\ell_2 : b = 1\}), (\gamma_{\pi_{\text{else}},(a=0,b=0)}, \{\ell_2 : b{=}0\})\}$ and $\mathsf{NotAffected}_{(a=0,b=0)} = \emptyset$. Based on (5), we obtain:

$$\begin{aligned} Cal(\gamma_{(a=0,b=0)}, S_{com}) &= \frac{Pr^{old}(\gamma_{\pi_{\text{if}},(a=0,b=0)}) * Pr^{new}(\ell_2{:}b{=}1)}{Pr^{old}(\ell_2{:}b{=}1)} + \frac{Pr^{old}(\gamma_{\pi_{\text{else}},(a=0,b=0)}) * Pr^{new}(\ell_2{:}b{=}0)}{Pr^{old}(\ell_2{:}b{=}0)} \\ &= \frac{1/8 * 1/3}{1/2} + \frac{1/4 * 1/3}{1/2} = 1/4 \end{aligned}$$

□

Sparse Incremental Propagation. According to Fig. 8, we first collect D^{Δ}, the set of new data-flow facts introduced by comparing the data-flow facts obtained after analyzing ℓ_{new} and ℓ_{old}. Then we make use of $\textsc{IncProp}(D^{\Delta})$ to perform incremental propagation by calling $\textsc{PreIn}(D^{\Delta}, L)$, where L is the set of statements L reachable from ℓ_{old} on the CFG of the program being analyzed:

$$\textsc{IncProp}(D^{\Delta}) = \{\langle \sigma, Pr(\gamma_\sigma)\rangle \mid \langle \sigma, \gamma_\sigma\rangle \in D^{\Delta}_{\ell_{end}} = \textsc{PreIn}(D^{\Delta}, L)\} \tag{6}$$

Example 4. Let us still consider the example in Fig. 5(c). For the change made from $b = \texttt{UniformInt}(0,1)$ to $b = \texttt{UniformInt}(-1,1)$ at ℓ_2, we first collect the two new data-flow facts introduced by the change at ℓ_2: $D^{\Delta} = \{\langle(a = 0, b = -1), \{[\ell_1 : a = 0, \ell_2 : b = -1]\}\rangle, \langle(a = 1, b = -1), \{[\ell_1 : a = 1, \ell_2 : b = -1]\}\rangle\}$. In this case, $L = \{\ell_3, \ell_6\}$. Following (6), we then call $\textsc{PreIn}(D^{\Delta}, \{\ell_3, \ell_6\})$ to obtain the two new data-flow facts in $D^{\Delta}_{\ell_6}$ highlighted in red at the end of the program by incrementally propagating the two new data-flow facts in D^{Δ} across the CFG of the program without affecting any of the existing data-flow facts. □

4.2.2 Handling Changes Made at Observe Statements. In our data-flow analysis, an observe statement $\ell : \texttt{observe}(\mathcal{E})$ filters out any data-flow fact $\langle \sigma, \gamma_\sigma\rangle$, whose state σ violates the condition $\mathcal{E}$ by blocking the propagation of $\langle \sigma, \gamma_\sigma\rangle$ after analyzing ℓ. All the others satisfying $\mathcal{E}$ remain unchanged.

For a modification of a probabilistic assignment ℓ, we find any existing data-flow fact $\langle \sigma, \gamma_\sigma\rangle \in D_{\ell_{end}}$ affected by the change and update its probability based on the new seeds generated at ℓ. However, for a modification of an observe statement, we will need to find any $\langle \sigma, \gamma_\sigma\rangle \in D_{\ell_{end}}$ affected by the change based on the dependence information from one or more probabilistic assignments. This is because the value $\mathcal{E}$ in $\texttt{observe}(\mathcal{E})$ may be affected by multiple probabilistic assignments. For example, $\texttt{observe}(a||b)$ contains $a||b$, where a and b may be defined by two different Bernoulli assignments in the program.

Our algorithm given in Fig. 9 for handling an observe statement is the same as the one for handling a probabilistic assignment given in Fig. 8, except that $\textsc{IncUpdate}$ in Fig. 8 is replaced by $\textsc{IncUpdate}^{\sharp}$ in order to deal with existing

$\textsc{HandleObserve}(\ell_{old} : \texttt{observe}(\mathcal{E}),\ \ell_{new} : \texttt{observe}(\mathcal{E}'))$
$D^{diff} = \textsc{PreIn}(D_{\ell_{old}}, \ell_{old}) \setminus \textsc{PreIn}(D_{\ell_{old}}, \ell_{new})$;
$\Gamma^{diff} = \bigcup_{\langle \sigma, \gamma_\sigma\rangle \in D^{diff}} \gamma_\sigma$;
Let $D_{\ell_{end}}$ be the existing data-flow facts before the end of the program;
$\Psi_1 = \textsc{IncUpdate}^{\sharp}(D_{\ell_{end}}, \Gamma^{diff})$; // handling the existing data-flow facts
$D^{\Delta} = \textsc{PreIn}(D_{\ell_{old}}, \ell_{new}) \setminus \textsc{PreIn}(D_{\ell_{old}}, \ell_{old})$;
$\Psi_2 = \textsc{IncProp}(D^{\Delta})$; // handling the new data-flow facts
return $\Psi_1 \cup \Psi_2$;

Fig. 9. An algorithm for performing incremental analysis due to a change made from $\texttt{observe}(\mathcal{E})$ to $\texttt{observe}(\mathcal{E}')$. Ψ_1 and Ψ_2 are the posterior distributions obtained in analyzing the existing and new data-flow facts.

data-flow facts in $D_{\ell_{end}}$. Unlike INCUPDATE, which uses the seeds in S^{com} collected from only one probabilistic assignment ℓ (modified), INCUPDATE$^\sharp$ uses Γ^{diff}, which contains a set of single-path dependences possibly from multiple probabilistic assignments based on the data-flow facts in D^{diff} that exist in the original program but not the modified program (lines 1–2).

At line 6, INCPROP is reused based on (6) to propagate the new data-flow facts that were filtered out by the original observe statement but become valid after the change. At line 7, we obtain the new posterior probability distributions at ℓ_{end} by combining the results from incremental update and propagation.

To update the posterior probability distributions of the states in $D_{\ell_{end}}$, we first find a set of affected single-path probabilistic dependences: $\mathsf{Affected}_\sigma = \{\gamma_{\pi,\sigma} \in \gamma_\sigma \mid \exists\ \gamma \in \Gamma^{diff} : \gamma \subseteq \gamma_{\pi,\sigma}\}$ for each fact $\langle\sigma, \gamma_\sigma\rangle \in D_{\ell_{end}}$. These affected dependences are no longer existent in the modified program according to Γ^{diff} due to the change made at ℓ, Thus, they are excluded with their old probabilities set to 0. We only recalculate the posterior probabilities based on $\mathsf{NotAffected}_\sigma = \{\gamma_{\pi,\sigma} \mid \gamma_{\pi,\sigma} \in (\gamma_\sigma \backslash \mathsf{Affected}_\sigma)\}$, which contains the single-path dependences that are not affected by the change. Therefore, the new posterior distributions for the states in $D_{\ell_{end}}$ are computed as:

$$\text{INCUPDATE}^\sharp(D_{\ell_{end}}, \Gamma^{diff}) = \{\langle\sigma, \rho_\sigma^{new}\rangle | \langle\sigma, \gamma_\sigma\rangle \in D_{\ell_{end}}\} \tag{7}$$

with the new posterior probability $\rho_\sigma^{new} = Cal^\sharp(\gamma_\sigma, \Gamma^{diff})$ being obtained by:

$$Cal^\sharp(\gamma_\sigma, \Gamma^{diff}) = \sum_{\gamma_{\pi,\sigma} \in \mathsf{Affected}_\sigma} Pr^{old}(\gamma_{\pi,\sigma}) \times 0 + \sum_{\gamma_{\pi,\sigma} \in \mathsf{NotAffected}_\sigma} Pr^{old}(\gamma_{\pi,\sigma}) \tag{8}$$

Example 5. Figure 10 illustrates our incremental analysis for handing a change at an observe statement. In Fig. 10(a), its top part shows a small program containing an observe statement, `observe`$(a||b)$, at ℓ_3. In Fig. 10(b), its top part shows the same program with the observe statement changed to `observe`$(a||!b)$. Figure 10(c) gives the data-flow facts in D_{ℓ_3} obtained just before either observe statement. In Figs. 10(a) and (b), their bottom parts give the data-flow facts after analyzing their observe statements in terms of the data-flow facts in D_{ℓ_3}.

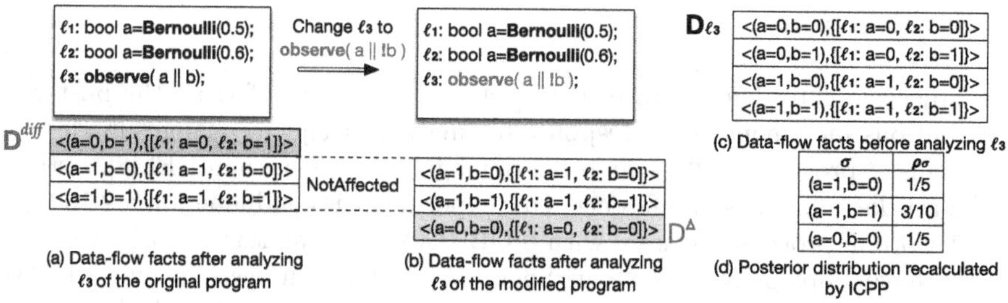

Fig. 10. An example for incremental analysis of an observe statement. (Color figure online)

We then obtain the single data-flow fact in D^{diff} blocked by the new observe statement as highlighted in green (Fig. 10(a)). Thus, we have $\Gamma^{diff} = \{[\ell_1 : a = 0, \ell_2 : b = 1]\}$, $\mathsf{Affected}_\sigma = \{[\ell_1 : a = 0, \ell_2 : b = 1]\}$, and $\mathsf{NotAffected}_\sigma = \{[\ell_1 : a = 1, \ell_2 : b = 0], [\ell_1 : a = 1, \ell_2 : b = 1]\}$. Based on (8), we recalculate the posterior probability of each state as $\rho^{new}_{(a=0,b=1)} = Pr([\ell_1 : a = 0, \ell_2 : b = 1]) \times 0 = 0$, $\rho^{new}_{(a=1,b=0)} = Pr([\ell_1 : a = 1, \ell_2 : b = 0]) = 1/5$, and $\rho^{new}_{(a=1,b=1)} = Pr([\ell_1 : a = 1, \ell_2 : b = 1]) = 3/10$.

The data-flow fact in D^{Δ} as highlighted in red in Fig. 10(b) is a new one introduced by the change. Finally, we combine the computed probabilities of the existing and new data-flow facts to obtain the posterior probability distributions given in Fig. 10(d). Note that $1/5 + 3/10 + 1/5 \neq 1$ due to the observe statement. Thus, after having computed the posterior probabilities as desired, we normalize these probabilities as $2/7, 3/7$ and $2/7$, respectively. □

4.3 Precision

Theorem 1. ICPP *achieves the same precision as DFI [8] (which analyzes a program from scratch) in terms of answering posterior probability distributions under the changes made to the probabilistic knowledge of a probabilistic program.*

Proof. *The pre-inference of* ICPP *(Fig. 6) captures the all-path dependence (Definition 3) of each data-flow fact in order to allow the posterior probability distributions to be updated during the incremental analysis. Every loop in the program is handled by approximating a KL-divergence between its two consecutive loop iterations. A continuous prior distribution is approximated by a discrete distribution over a finite set, following [8, 21].*

Based on the dependence information, our incremental sparse update recalculates the posterior probability of any existing data-flow fact affected by any change to a probabilistic assignment based on (4) or an observe statement based on (7) while keeping the probabilities of unaffected dependences unchanged. Our incremental sparse propagation computes and propagates any new data-flow fact introduced by the changes along the CFG based on (6). Following the algorithms in Figs. 8 and 9, we can obtain the same posterior probability distributions as the program is reanalyzed entirely by DFI (or our pre-inference). □

5 Evaluation

Our objective is to demonstrate that ICPP is effective in inferring the posterior distributions incrementally in response to small yet frequent changes made to a probabilistic program. ICPP is an order of magnitude faster than DFI [8], a state-of-the-art data-flow-based inference. Our experiment is conducted on a 2.70 GHz `Intel` Core i5 processor system with 8 GB RAM running `macOS.10.12.4`.

We have implemented ICPP in Soot [34], a Java analysis framework. We choose Figaro [27] as our probabilistic language, which is based on Scala and can be translated into the .class format for our analysis in Soot. Following DFI [8], we use the ADD library [30] to store our data-flow facts, i.e., probabilistic dependences over states, with each single-path dependence naturally represented by an ADD. Updating data-flow facts affected by changes to probabilistic assignments and observe statements is done by the graph operations in ADD.

To cover different change scenarios, we have selected a set of 6 probabilistic programs, with 3 using the `Bernoulli` distribution (`Grass`, `BurglarAlarm`, and `NoisyOR`) from the existing inference engine `R2` [25], 1 using a `UniformInt` (`MotWhile`) distribution by replacing `if` with `while` statement in our motivating example (Fig. 5), and 2 using the `Bernoulli` distribution (`Grade` and `Loopy`) from [15]. `Grass`, `BurglarAlarm`, `TwoCoins` and `NoisyOR` are loop-free, `Grade` contains an observe statement in its middle, and `Loopy` and `MotWhile` contain unbounded loops (similar to Fig. 5 with its `if` replaced by a `while` statement).

For each program, ten small changes are made to simulate the process of developing a probabilistic program with different versions and tuning new posterior probability distributions through each change. Note that we choose ten changes (a relatively small number) to demonstrate ICPP's effectiveness. Our incremental analysis becomes more effective than DFI [8] if more changes are added. These changes are selected to exercise as many scenarios as possible. For example, one worst-case scenario happens if a sample space is completely changed, e.g., from `UniformInt(-10,-1)` to `UniformInt (0,9)`, which requires computing all new data-flow facts without reusing any old ones. Our small modifications are made so that the probabilistic model underlying each program is not changed.

Table 1 compares ICPP with DFI [8] (which can be regarded as a special case of PREIN without recording probabilistic dependences but computing explicitly the probabilities for all the states). In Column 2, we compare the analysis times of DFI and ICPP's pre-inference in analyzing a program. Our pre-inference is slightly more costly as it must collect probabilistic dependences for all the states. In Columns 3 and 4, we compare DFI and ICPP in terms of the total analysis time spent for the 10 changes made in a program. ICPP is an order of magnitude faster than DFI. For each program, DFI must reanalyze it from scratch after each change. In contrast, ICPP performs incremental analysis for the program based on the probabilistic dependences computed during its pre-inference.

For the 5 programs with the `Bernoulli` distribution, which does not introduce new data-flow facts when prior probabilities are changed, their posterior distributions can be directly recomputed by INCUPDATE and INCUPDATE$^\sharp$, without using INCPROP. ICPP updates existing results instantaneously with negligible overheads. For `MotWhile` with a `uniform` distribution, ICPP also achieves a significant performance improvement over DFI by 13x.

Figure 11 shows that ICPP is much faster than DFI for three representative programs, `Grass`, `Loopy` and `MotWhile`. For `Grass` with the `Bernoulli` distribution, ICPP has negligible overheads for all the 10 changes made (Fig. 11(a)). For `Loopy` with a `Bernoulli` distribution containing an unbounded loop, ICPP spends relatively more time for the fourth and sixth changes (Fig. 11(b)) due to the modifications of a probabilistic assignment in its unbounded loop,

Table 1. Analysis times of DFI and ICPP (seconds).

Program	Analyzing original program	Analyzing 10 changes		Speedup
	DFI/PREIN$_{\text{ICPP}}$	DFI	ICPP	
`BurglarAlarm`	1.27/1.38	12.60	0.65	19
`NoisyOr`	1.85/2.22	19.01	1.70	11
`Grass`	1.91/2.31	21.85	1.71	13
`Grade`	1.31/1.57	12.78	0.93	13
`Loopy`	1.53/1.72	15.15	1.47	10
`MotWhile`	1.46/1.68	15.51	1.34	13

affecting the probability of a single-path dependence when the loop is analyzed until KL-divergence. For `MotWhile` with a `UniformInt` distribution, ICPP takes relatively more time in handling the fourth change (Fig. 11(c)), because the change is made to a probabilistic assignment with a `Uniform` distribution, causing new data-flow facts to be propagated repeatedly inside a loop.

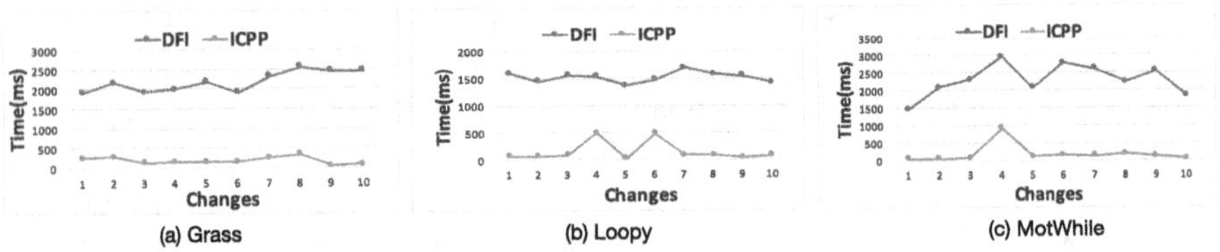

Fig. 11. Analysis times of ICPP and DFI over ten changes made in a program.

6 Related Work

In addition to the work already discussed in Sect. 1, we focus on the most relevant work on probabilistic inference and incremental static analysis.

Probabilistic inference for probabilistic programs. The existing approaches on probabilistic inference can be classified into static and dynamic ones. Dynamic inference methods usually execute a probabilistic program a finite number of times through sampling-based Monte Carlo methods [4,7,19,25,28] and then perform inference based on the execution traces. Static methods [5,8,20,23,29] statically infer the posterior probability distributions without running the program. Sankaranarayanan et al. [29] propose a static analysis to reason about infinite-state probabilistic programs by quantifying the solution space of linear constraints over bounded floating-point domains. DFI [8] performs data-flow-based static inference that explicitly computes and maintains distributions as data-flow facts at each program point following the program's control-flow on a CFG. DFI focuses on discrete distributions and makes approximations when computing data-flow facts over continuous distributions. Recently,

PSI [10] represents an exact symbolic inference for analyzing both discrete and continuous distributions for probabilistic programs with bounded loops. Based on DFI, our work enables (for the first time) efficient incremental Bayesian inference over discrete distributions with finite concrete states, in response to small yet frequent changes to probabilistic knowledge in a probabilistic program.

Incremental static analysis for usual programs. The goal of incremental static analysis is to efficiently update existing analysis results without recomputing them from scratch, allowing the previously computed information to be reused. Emu [18,31] represents an incremental analysis for performing demand-driven context-sensitive pointer analysis based on Context-Free Language (CFL) reachability, which precisely recomputes points-to sets affected by the program changes. Reviser [1] is an incremental analysis technique developed as an extension to the IDE-/IFDS- based framework for efficiently updating inter-procedural data-flow analysis results. Echo [38] is an incremental analysis for data-race detection based on program dependences computed by static happens-before analysis. DiSE [26] is an incremental symbolic execution technique that uses pre-computed results from a static analysis to direct symbolic execution for exploring only the parts of a program affected by the changes. Unlike previous incremental analysis techniques for imperative programs emphasizing on code changes, i.e., statement addition and deletion, ICPP focuses on changes made to probabilistic knowledge, the key feature in probabilistic programming.

7 Conclusion and Future Work

In this paper, we present ICPP, a new data-flow based incremental analysis for analyzing probabilistic programs. ICPP captures the correlation relation between prior and posterior probability distributions through a probabilistic dependence analysis. The resulting analysis significantly improves the efficiency of data-flow based inference by incrementally updating the posterior distributions with previous computed information being reused in response to small yet frequent changes made to probabilistic knowledge, i.e., prior distributions and observations.

This work has opened up some new research opportunities. We can extend our incremental analysis for probabilistic programs by combining it with traditional incremental analyses for usual programs via demand-driven [31,32] and/or partial program analysis [9,33] in order to also handle the changes made to usual statements. In addition, we can combine our incremental inference with symbolic analysis [10,29] to support incremental symbolic inference with hybrid discrete and continuous distributions being supported.

Acknowledgments. The authors wish to thank the anonymous reviewers for their valuable comments. The first author would like to thank Aleksandar Chakarov for some helpful email discussions. This work is supported by Australian Research Grants, DP150102109, DP170103956 and DE170101081.

References

1. Arzt, S., Bodden, E.: Reviser: efficiently updating IDE-/IFDS-based data-flow analyses in response to incremental program changes. In: Proceedings of the 36th International Conference on Software Engineering, pp. 288–298 (2014)
2. Borgström, J., Gordon, A.D., Greenberg, M., Margetson, J., Gael, J.: Measure transformer semantics for Bayesian machine learning. In: Barthe, G. (ed.) ESOP 2011. LNCS, vol. 6602, pp. 77–96. Springer, Heidelberg (2011). doi:10.1007/978-3-642-19718-5_5
3. Caticha, A., Giffin, A., Mohammad-Djafari, A.: Updating probabilities. In: 18th International Conference on Artificial Intelligence and Pattern Recognition, pp. 31–42 (2006)
4. Chaganty, A.T., Nori, A.V., Rajamani, S.K.: Efficiently sampling probabilistic programs via program analysis. In: 16th Artificial Intelligence and Statistics, pp. 153–160 (2013)
5. Chakarov, A., Sankaranarayanan, S.: Expectation invariants for probabilistic program loops as fixed points. In: Müller-Olm, M., Seidl, H. (eds.) SAS 2014. LNCS, vol. 8723, pp. 85–100. Springer, Cham (2014). doi:10.1007/978-3-319-10936-7_6
6. Chan, H., Darwiche, A.: On the revision of probabilistic beliefs using uncertain evidence. Artif. Intell. **163**(1), 67–90 (2005)
7. Chib, S., Greenberg, E.: Understanding the metropolis-hastings algorithm. Am. Stat. **49**(4), 327–335 (1995)
8. Claret, G., Rajamani, S.K., Nori, A.V., Gordon, A.D., Borgström, J.: Bayesian inference using data flow analysis. In: Proceedings of the 9th Joint Meeting on Foundations of Software Engineering, pp. 92–102 (2013)
9. Fan, X., Sui, Y., Liao, X., Xue, J.: Boosting the precision of virtual call integrity protection with partial pointer analysis for C++. In: 26th ACM SIGSOFT International Symposium on Software Testing and Analysis (2017)
10. Gehr, T., Misailovic, S., Vechev, M.: PSI: exact symbolic inference for probabilistic programs. In: 26th International Conference on Computer Aided Verification, pp. 62–83 (2016)
11. Glynn, P.W., Iglehart, D.L.: Importance sampling for stochastic simulations. Manag. Sci. **35**(11), 1367–1392 (1989)
12. Gordon, A.D., Henzinger, T.A., Nori, A.V., Rajamani, S.K.: Probabilistic programming. In: Proceedings of the on Future of Software Engineering, pp. 167–181 (2014)
13. Hastings, W.K.: Monte Carlo sampling methods using Markov chains and their applications. Biometrika **57**(1), 97–109 (1970)
14. Hermenegildo, M., Puebla, G., Marriott, K., Stuckey, P.J.: Incremental analysis of constraint logic programs. ACM Trans. Program. Lang. Syst. **22**(2), 187–223 (2000)
15. Hur, C.-K., Nori, A.V., Rajamani, S.K., Samuel, S.: Slicing probabilistic programs. In: Proceedings of the 35th ACM SIGPLAN Conference on Programming Language Design and Implementation, pp. 133–144 (2014)
16. Koller, D., Friedman, N.: Probabilistic Graphical Models: Principles and Techniques. The MIT Press, Cambridge (2009)
17. Kullback, S.: Information Theory and Statistics. Dover Publications, New York (1997)
18. Lu, Y., Shang, L., Xie, X., Xue, J.: An incremental points-to analysis with CFL-reachability. In: Jhala, R., Bosschere, K. (eds.) CC 2013. LNCS, vol. 7791, pp. 61–81. Springer, Heidelberg (2013). doi:10.1007/978-3-642-37051-9_4

19. MacKay, D.J.: Introduction to Monte Carlo methods. Learning in Graphical Models, vol. 89, pp. 175–204. Springer, Berlin (1998)
20. Mardziel, P., Magill, S., Hicks, M., Srivatsa, M.: Dynamic enforcement of knowledge-based security policies using probabilistic abstract interpretation. J. Comput. Secur. **21**(4), 463–532 (2013)
21. Miller, A.C., Rice, T.R.: Discrete approximations of probability distributions. Manag. Sci. **29**(3), 352–362 (1983)
22. Minka, T.P.: Expectation propagation for approximate Bayesian inference. In: Proceedings of the 17th Conference on Uncertainty in Artificial Intelligence, pp. 362–369 (2001)
23. Monniaux, D.: Abstract interpretation of probabilistic semantics. In: Palsberg, J. (ed.) SAS 2000. LNCS, vol. 1824, pp. 322–339. Springer, Heidelberg (2000). doi:10.1007/978-3-540-45099-3_17
24. Murphy, K.P., Weiss, Y., Jordan, M.I.: Loopy belief propagation for approximate inference: an empirical study. In: Proceedings of the 15th Conference on Uncertainty in Artificial Intelligence, pp. 467–475 (1999)
25. Nori, A.V., Hur, C.-K., Rajamani, S.K., Samuel, S.: R2: an efficient MCMC sampler for probabilistic programs. In: Proceedings of the 29th National Conference on Artificial Intelligence, pp. 2476–2482 (2014)
26. Person, S., Yang, G., Rungta, N., Khurshid, S.: Directed incremental symbolic execution. In: Proceedings of the 32nd ACM SIGPLAN Conference on Programming Language Design and Implementation, pp. 504–515 (2011)
27. Pfeffer, A.: Figaro: an object-oriented probabilistic programming language. Charles River Analytics Technical report 137:96 (2009)
28. Plummer, M., et al.: Jags: a program for analysis of Bayesian graphical models using Gibbs sampling. In: Proceedings of the 3rd International Workshop on Distributed Statistical Computing, p. 125 (2003)
29. Sankaranarayanan, S., Chakarov, A., Gulwani, S.: Static analysis for probabilistic programs: inferring whole program properties from finitely many paths. In: Proceedings of the 34th ACM SIGPLAN Conference on Programming Language Design and Implementation, pp. 447–458 (2013)
30. Sanner, S., McAllester, D.: Affine algebraic decision diagrams (AADDs) and their application to structured probabilistic inference. In: Proceedings of the 19th International Joint Conference on Artificial Intelligence, pp. 1384–1390 (2005)
31. Shang, L., Lu, Y., Xue, J.: Fast and precise points-to analysis with incremental CFL-reachability summarisation: preliminary experience. In: Proceedings of the 27th IEEE/ACM International Conference on Automated Software Engineering, pp. 270–273 (2012)
32. Sui, Y., Xue, J.: On-demand strong update analysis via value-flow refinement. In: Proceedings of the 24th ACM SIGSOFT International Symposium on Foundations of Software Engineering, pp. 460–473 (2016)
33. Sui, Y., Xue, J.: SVF: interprocedural static value-flow analysis in LLVM. In: Proceedings of the 25th International Conference on Compiler Construction, pp. 265–266 (2016)
34. Vallée-Rai, R., Co, P., Gagnon, E., Hendren, L., Lam, P., Sundaresan, V.: Soot - a Java bytecode optimization framework. In: Proceedings of the Conference of the Centre for Advanced Studies on Collaborative Research, p. 13 (1999)
35. Wainwright, M.J., Jordan, M.I., et al.: Graphical models, exponential families, and variational inference. Found. Trends® Mach. Learn. **1**(1–2), 1–305 (2008)
36. Wanke, C., Greenbaum, D.: Incremental, probabilistic decision making for en route traffic management. Air Traffic Cont. Q. **15**(4), 299–319 (2007)

37. Yue, A., Liu, W.: Revising imprecise probabilistic beliefs in the framework of probabilistic logic programming. In: Proceedings of the 23rd National Conference on Artificial Intelligence, pp. 590–596 (2008)
38. Zhan, S., Huang, J.: ECHO: instantaneous in situ race detection in the IDE. In: Proceedings of the 24th ACM SIGSOFT International Symposium on Foundations of Software Engineering, pp. 775–786 (2016)

Author Index

Printed in the United States
By Bookmasters